A History of Fascism, 1914–1945

Stanley G. Payne

A History of Fascism, 1914–1945

The University of Wisconsin Press

The University of Wisconsin Press
2537 Daniels Street
Madison, Wisconsin 53718

Copyright © 1995
The Board of Regents of the University of Wisconsin System
All rights reserved

8   7   6   5   4

Printed in the United States of America

Illustrations for this book are reproduced courtesy of the following sources:
Editori Laterza, Rome: pp. 97, 236
Editorial Planeta, Barcelona: pp. 109, 159, 166, 177, 193, 219, 283,
    301, 304, 307, 359, 366, 374
Historia 16, Madrid: pp. 257, 259, 265, 432, 433, 434
Museum of Contemporary History, Budapest: p. 418
Süddeutscher Verlag, Munich: pp. 241, 285, 303, 393, 408
State Historical Society of Wisconsin, Madison: p. 169; WHi(X3)49792;
    p. 171, WHi(X3)49796; p. 175, WHi(X3)49794; p. 183, WHi(X3)49795;
    p. 199, WHi(X3)49793

Library of Congress Cataloging-in-Publication Data
Payne, Stanley G.
    A history of fascism, 1914–1945 / Stanley G. Payne.
    628 p.   cm.
    Includes bibliographical references and index.
    ISBN 0-299-14870-X (alk. paper)
    ISBN 0-299-14874-2 (pbk.: alk. paper)
    1. Fascism.   2. Fascism—History.   I. Title.
JC481.P375   1995
320.5'33—dc20   95-16723

*This book is dedicated to
Juan J. Linz and George L. Mosse,
pathbreakers in fascist studies.*

Contents

PART II: INTERPRETATION

Illustrations

Tables

Preface

In 1980 I published a brief book, *Fascism: Comparison and Definition*, which sought to establish a working definition and a comparative taxonomy of historic European fascism. The work was well received, and I hope that it added some clarity and precision to the "fascism debate" of the two preceding decades. It remains in print in English and Spanish.

That book, however, did not narrate the history of fascism, and it often proved dense and baffling to undergraduates, unless it was extensively supplemented with basic descriptive literature. The present volume, therefore, does not constitute a revision of the earlier book but is a completely new study designed to provide a narrative of generic European fascism and to extend the framework of analysis and interpretation. The result is a book as long as the first was short, but one that is, I hope, more complete.

Any inquiry into fascism has to grapple with the fundamental problem which George L. Mosse once described as attempting to analyze the irrational through rational study. The goal is not to rationalize the irrational but to elucidate the historical problems and contradictions involved.

The bibliography pertaining to the history of fascism is now enormous. I make no claim to having read everything, for that would require several decades in itself. The citations and bibliography here are not intended to be comprehensive, but only to include those works which I found most useful. For the main body of literature, the reader should consult Philip Rees's *Fascism and Pre-Fascism in Europe, 1890–1945: A Bibliography of the Extreme Right* (1984).

Once more I wish to acknowledge and thank my chief mentors in fascist studies, first of all Juan J. Linz and George L. Mosse (to whom the book is dedicated), and in the key area of Italian fascism, Renzo De Felice, Emilio Gentile, and A. James Gregor. Gregory Kasza shared his own research prior to publication and provided invaluable help with the Japanese case. Special thanks are also due to Luca De Caprariis for his assistance in obtaining Italian materials, and to Daniel Kowalsky, who prepared the Bibliography. Angela Ray edited the manuscript with unusual care and skill, and Raphael Kadushin and Carol Olsen supervised production of the manuscript at the University of Wisconsin Press. Additional photos were provided by the State Historical Society of Wisconsin, Editori Laterza, Editorial Planeta, and the Süddeutscher Verlag. To all of them—and very many more unnamed—I offer my thanks and gratitude.

STANLEY G. PAYNE

A History of Fascism, 1914–1945

Introduction
Fascism: A Working Definition

At the end of the twentieth century *fascism* remains probably the vaguest of the major political terms. This may stem from the fact that the word itself contains no explicit political reference, however abstract, as do *democracy, liberalism, socialism,* and *communism.* To say that the Italian *fascio* (Latin *fasces,* French *faisceau,* Spanish *haz*) means "bundle" or "union" does not tell us much.[1] Moreover, the term has probably been used more by its opponents than by its proponents, the former having been responsible for the generalization of the adjective on an international level, as early as 1923. *Fascist* has been one of the most frequently invoked political pejoratives, normally intended to connote "violent," "brutal," "repressive," or "dictatorial." Yet if *fascism* means no more than that, then Communist regimes, for example, would probably have to be categorized as among the most fascist, depriving the word of any useful specificity.

Definition in fact bedeviled the original Italian Fascists from the beginning.[2] The problem is compounded by the fact that whereas nearly all Communist parties and regimes have preferred to call themselves Communist, most of the movements in interwar Europe commonly termed fascist did not in fact use

1. One of the first German works on Italian Fascism, by the Social Democrat Fritz Schott-höfer, aptly observed that "Fascism has a name that tells us nothing about the spirit and goals of the movement. A fascio is a union, a league; Fascists are unionists and Fascism a league-type organization [Bündlertum]." Schotthöfer, *Il Fascio. Sinn und Wirklichkeit des italenischen Fascismus* (Frankfurt, 1924), 64. For further discussion of the problem, see the chapter "Was ist Faschismus: politischer Kampfbegriff oder wissenschaftliche Theorie?" in W. Wippermann, *Faschismustheorien* (Darmstadt, 1989), 1–10.

2. In this study the names of the Italian Fascist Party and its immediate antecedents, members, and components will be capitalized, while the terms *fascism* and *fascist* used in a broader and more generic sense will not.

3

the name for themselves. The dilemmas of definition and categorization which arise are so severe that it is not surprising that some scholars prefer to call putative fascist movements by their individual names alone without applying the categorical adjective. Still others deny that any such general phenomenon as fascism—as distinct from Mussolini's own Italian movement—ever existed. Finally, the great majority of the hundreds of authors of works on fascism or individual fascist movements make little or no effort to define the term and simply assume that their readers will understand and presumably agree with the approach, whatever that may be.

This book argues that it is useful to treat fascism as a general type or generic phenomenon for heuristic and analytic purposes, just as other categories of political forces are so treated. As Arthur L. Stinchcombe has observed, "Whenever a large number of variables go together, so that specific values of one are always associated with specific values of another, the creation of typologies, or sets of type-concepts, such as the chemical elements, is scientifically useful."[3] Like all general types and concepts in political analysis, generic fascism is an abstraction which never existed in pure empirical form but constitutes a conceptual device which serves to clarify the analysis of individual political phenomena.

If fascism is to be studied as a generic and comparative phenomenon, it has first to be identified through some sort of working description. Such a definition must be derived from empirical study of the classic interwar European movements. It must be developed as a theoretical construct or an ideal type, for all general political concepts are broadly based abstractions. Thus no single movement of the group under observation would necessarily be found to have announced a program or self-description couched in the exact terms of this definition. Nor would such a hypothetical definition be intended to imply that the individual goals and characteristics identified were necessarily in every case unique to fascist movements, for most items might be found in one or more other species of political movements. The contention would be, rather, that *taken as a whole* the definition would describe what all fascist movements had in common without trying to describe the additional unique characteristics of each individual group. Finally, for reasons to be discussed later, the definition might refer only to interwar European fascist movements and not to a presumed category of fascist regimes or systems.

Any definition of common characteristics of fascist movements must be used with great care, for fascist movements differed from each other as significantly as they held notable new features in common. A general inventory of their distinctive characteristics is therefore useful, not as a full and complete definition of such movements in and of themselves, but only as an indication

---

3. A. L. Stinchcombe, *Constructing Social Theories* (New York, 1968), 43.

of the chief characteristics that they shared which distinguish them (in most respects, but not absolutely) from other kinds of political forces.

The problems involved in reaching an inductive set of characteristics may be illustrated by reference to the six-point "fascist minimum" postulated by Ernst Nolte, who helped to initiate the "fascism debate" of the 1960s and 1970s.[4] It consists of a set of negatives, a central organizational feature, a doctrine of leadership, and a basic structural goal, expressed as follows: anti-Marxism, antiliberalism, anticonservatism, the leadership principle, a party army, and the aim of totalitarianism. This typology is helpful as far as it goes and correctly states the fascist negations, yet it does not describe the positive content of fascist philosophy and values and makes no concrete reference to economic goals.

More recently, Roger Griffin has sought to achieve elegance, parsimony, and precision through the definition of fascism as "a genus of political ideology whose mythic core in its various permutations is a palingenetic form of populist ultra-nationalism."[5] This once more is accurate and useful, referring tersely to the cross-class populist appeal of fascist politics and its grounding in ultranationalism. Fascist ideology was certainly "palingenetic"; that is, it emphasized above all the rebirth of the national spirit, culture, and society. Yet leftist, moderate, conservative, and extreme right-wing nationalisms are also frequently "palingenetic," for the rebirth and re-creation of the nation are goals fundamental to many different forms of nationalism. Similarly, there have been nonfascist populist revolutionary forms of nationalism, such as that of the MNR in Bolivia in 1952, that were also palingenetic, so that the qualification of "populist" does not serve adequately to restrict and to specify. Finally, as we shall see, Griffin's definition—while admirably succinct—cannot describe certain of the central characteristics fundamental to a definition of fascism.

Indeed, the uniqueness and complexity of fascism cannot be adequately described without recourse to a relatively complex typology, however laudable the principle of parsimony may be. Thus in his authoritative article on *fascismo* for the new *Enciclopedia Italiana* (1992), Emilio Gentile presents the "constituent elements for an orientative definition of fascism" in a dense list of ten complex points.[6]

---

4. E. Nolte, *Die Krise des liberalen Systems und die faschistischen Bewegungen* (Munich, 1968), 385.

5. R. Griffin, *The Nature of Fascism* (London, 1991), 44. This is the best work on the comparative analysis of fascism to appear in the past decade.

6. Gentile defines *fascismo* as follows:

"1) a mass movement with multiclass membership in which prevail, among the leaders and militants, the middle sectors, in large part new to political activity, organized as a party militia, that bases its identity not on social hierarchy or class origin but on the sense of comradeship, believes itself invested with a mission of national regeneration, considers itself in a state of war against

The common characteristics of fascist movements were grounded in specific philosophical and moral beliefs, a new orientation in political culture and ideology, generally common political goals, a distinctive set of negations, common aspects of style, and somewhat novel modes of organization—always with notable differences in the specific character of these new forms and ideas among the various movements. To arrive at a criterial definition applicable to all the interwar fascist movements sensu stricto, it becomes necessary therefore to identify common points of ideology and goals, the fascist negations, and also special common features of style and organization.[7] The descriptive typology in table I.1 is suggested merely as an analytic device for purposes of comparative analysis and definition. It does not propose to establish a rigidly reified category but a wide-spectrum description that can identify a variety of differing

---

political adversaries and aims at conquering a monopoly of political power by using terror, parliamentary tactics, and deals with leading groups, to create a new regime that destroys parliamentary democracy;

"2) an 'anti-ideological' and pragmatic ideology that proclaims itself antimaterialist, antiindividualist, antiliberal, antidemocratic, anti-Marxist, is populist and anticapitalist in tendency, expresses itself aesthetically more than theoretically by means of a new political style and by myths, rites, and symbols as a lay religion designed to acculturate, socialize, and integrate the faith of the masses with the goal of creating a 'new man';

"3) a culture founded on mystical thought and the tragic and activist sense of life conceived as the manifestation of the will to power, on the myth of youth as artificer of history, and on the exaltation of the militarization of politics as the model of life and collective activity;

"4) a totalitarian conception of the primacy of politics, conceived as an integrating experience to carry out the fusion of the individual and the masses in the organic and mystical unity of the nation as an ethnic and moral community, adopting measures of discrimination and persecution against those considered to be outside this community either as enemies of the regime or members of races considered inferior or otherwise dangerous for the integrity of the nation;

"5) a civil ethic founded on total dedication to the national community, on discipline, virility, comradeship, and the warrior spirit;

"6) a single state party that has the task of providing for the armed defense of the regime, selecting its directing cadres, and organizing the masses within the state in a process of permanent mobilization of emotion and faith;

"7) a police apparatus that prevents, controls, and represses dissidence and opposition, even by using organized terror;

"8) a political system organized by a hierarchy of functions named from the top and crowned by the figure of the 'leader,' invested with a sacred charisma, who commands, directs, and coordinates the activities of the party and the regime;

"9) a corporative organization of the economy that suppresses trade union liberty, broadens the sphere of state intervention, and seeks to achieve, by principles of technocracy and solidarity, the collaboration of the 'productive sectors' under the control of the regime, to achieve its goals of power, yet preserving private property and class divisions;

"10) a foreign policy inspired by the myth of national power and greatness, with the goal of imperialist expansion." (Quoted with the kind permission of Professor Gentile.)

7. The idea of a tripartite definition was first suggested to me by Juan J. Linz at a conference in Bergen, Norway, in June 1974. The specific content is my own.

Table I.1. Typological Description of Fascism

A. Ideology and Goals:
    Espousal of an idealist, vitalist, and voluntaristic philosophy, normally involving the
    attempt to realize a new modern, self-determined, and secular culture
    Creation of a new nationalist authoritarian state not based on traditional principles
    or models
    Organization of a new highly regulated, multiclass, integrated national economic structure,
    whether called natiônâl corporatist, national socialist, or national syndicalist
    Positive evaluation and use of, or willingness to use, violence and war
    The goal of empire, expansion, or a radical change in the nation's relationship with
    other powers

B. The Fascist Negations:
    Antiliberalism
    Anticommunism
    Anticonservatism (though with the understanding that fascist groups were willing to under-
    take temporary alliances with other sectors, most commonly with the right)

C. Style and Organization:
    Attempted mass mobilization with militarization of political relationships and style and
    with the goal of a mass party militia
    Emphasis on aesthetic structure of meetings, symbols, and political liturgy, stressing emo-
    tional and mystical aspects
    Extreme stress on the masculine principle and male dominance, while espousing a strongly
    organic view of society
    Exaltation of youth above other phases of life, emphasizing the conflict of generations, at
    least in effecting the initial political transformation
    Specific tendency toward an authoritarian, charismatic, personal style of command,
    whether or not the command is to some degree initially elective

allegedly fascist movements while still setting them apart as a group from other kinds of revolutionary or nationalist movements. Individual movements might then be understood to have also possessed further doctrines, characteristics, and goals of major importance to them that did not necessarily contradict the common features but were added to them or went beyond them. Similarly, an individual movement might differ somewhat with regard to one or two individual criteria but nonetheless conform generally to the overall description or ideal type.

The term *fascist* is used not merely for the sake of convention but because the Italian movement was the first significant force to exhibit those characteristics as a new type and was for a long time the most influential. It constituted the type whose ideas and goals were the most readily generalized, particularly when contrasted with racial National Socialism.

It has often been held that fascism had no coherent doctrine or ideology, since there was no single canonical or seminal source and since major aspects of fascist ideas were contradictory and nonrationalist. Yet fascist movements did possess basic philosophies that were eclectic in character and in fact, as Roger Eatwell has pointed out, represented a kind of synthesis of concepts from varied sources.[8] Griffin reminds us that all ideology contains basic contradictions and nonrational or irrational elements, usually tending toward utopias that cannot ever be realized in practice. Fascist ideology was more eclectic and nonrational than some others, but these qualities did not prevent its birth and limited development.

The extreme nationalism of each fascist movement inevitably produced certain distinct or idiosyncratic features in each group, so that every fascist organization tended to differ more from its fellows in other countries than, for example, any given Communist party in comparison with other Communist groups. Different national emphases did not, however, blur a common physiognomy based on the common fascist beliefs and values.

Fascist ideology, unlike that of most of the right, was in most cases secular but, unlike the ideology of the left and to some extent of liberals, was based on vitalism and idealism and the rejection of economic determinism, whether of Manchester or Marx. The goal of metaphysical idealism and vitalism was the creation of a new man, a new style of culture that achieved both physical and artistic excellence and that prized courage, daring, and the overcoming of previously established limits in the growth of a superior new culture which engaged the whole man. Fascism was not, however, nihilistic, as many critics charged. Rather, it rejected many established values—whether of left, right, or center—and was willing to engage in acts of wholesale destruction, sometimes involving the most ghastly mass murder, as "creative destruction" to usher in a new utopia of its making, just as Communists murdered millions in the name of an egalitarian utopia.

Fascist ideas have often been said to stem from opposition to the Enlightenment or the "ideas of 1789," when in fact they were a direct by-product of aspects of the Enlightenment, derived specifically from the modern, secular, Promethean concepts of the eighteenth century. The essential divergence of fascist ideas from certain aspects of modern culture lay more precisely in the fascist rejection of rationalism, materialism, and egalitarianism—replaced by philosophical vitalism and idealism and the metaphysics of the will, all of which are also intrinsically modern. Fascists aspired to recover what they considered the true sense of the natural and of human nature (themselves originally eighteenth-century concepts) in opposition to the reductionist culture of modern materialism and prudential egotism.

Fascists strongly reflected the preoccupation with decadence in society

8. R. Eatwell, "Towards a New Model of Generic Fascism," *Journal of Theoretical Politics* 4:1 (April 1992): 1–68; idem, "Fascism," in *Contemporary Political Ideologies*, ed. R. Eatwell and A. Wright (London, 1993), 169–91.

and culture that had been growing since the mid–nineteenth century. They believed that decadence could only be overcome through a revolutionary new culture led by new elites, who would replace the old elites of liberalism and conservatism and of the left.

The free man of developed will and determination would be self-assertive like few before him, but he would also be able to transvalue and go beyond himself and would not hesitate to sacrifice himself for the sake of those ideals. Such modern formulations rejected nineteenth-century materialism but did not represent anything that could be called a reversion to the traditional moral and spiritual values of the Western world before the eighteenth century. They represented a specific effort to achieve a modern, normally atheistic or agnostic form of transcendance and not, in Nolte's words, any "resistance to transcendance." Griffin has aptly observed that fascist doctrine encouraged self-assertion and self-transcendance at the same time.

One key modality in which fascist movements seemed to parallel certain religious groups was the projection of a sense of messianic mission, typical of utopian revolutionary movements. Each had the goal of realizing a new status and mode of being for its nation, but the fascist ambitions typically paralleled those of other secular revolutionary movements in functioning within an immanent, this-worldly framework, rather than the otherworldly transcendance of religious groups.

Fundamental to fascism was the effort to create a new "civic religion" of the movement and of its structure as a state. This would build a system of all-encompassing myths that would incorporate both the fascist elite and their followers and would bind together the nation in a new common faith and loyalty. Such civic religion would displace preceding structures of belief and relegate supernatural religion to a secondary role, or to none at all.

This orientation has sometimes been called political religion, but, though there were specific examples of religious or would-be "Christian fascists," fascism basically presupposed a post-Christian, postreligious, secular, and immanent frame of reference. Its own myth of secular transcendance could earn adherents only in the absence or weakness of traditional concepts of spiritual and otherworldly transcendance, for fascism sought to re-create nonrationalist myth structures for those who had lost or rejected a traditional mythic framework. Ideologically and politically, fascism could be successful only to the extent that such a situation existed.

Fascists were even more vague about the shape of their ultimate utopia than were members of most other revolutionary groups, because their reliance on vitalism and dynamism produced a mode of "permanent revolution" that almost by definition could take no simple, clear final form. They sought nothing so seemingly clear-cut as the classless society of Marxists or the stateless society of anarchists but rather an expansive nationalism built of dynamic tension ever seeking new expression. This generated an inherent irrationality that was itself one of the greatest handicaps, if not the greatest, that fascist movements had to overcome.

Much of the confusion surrounding interpretation of the fascist movements stems from the fact that only in a very few instances did they succeed in passing to the stage of governmental participation and only in the case of Germany did a regime in power succeed in carrying out the broader implications of a fascist doctrine, and even then incompletely. It is thus difficult to generalize about fascist systems or the fascist doctrine of the state, since even the Italian variant was seriously compromised. All that can be established with clarity is that fascist aspirations concerning the state were not limited to traditional models such as monarchy, mere personal dictatorship, or even corporatism but posited a radical new secular system, authoritarian and normally republican. Yet to specify the full aim of totalitarianism, as has Nolte, seems unwarranted, for, unlike Leninism, fascist movements never projected a state doctrine with sufficient centralization and bureaucratization to make possible complete totalitarianism. In its original Italian meaning, the sense of the term was more circumscribed. This problem will be treated in greater detail in subsequent chapters.

Least clear within fascist ideology was the issue of economic structure and goals, but in fact all fascist movements generally agreed on a basic orientation toward economics. This subordinated economic issues to the state and to the greater well-being of the nation, while retaining the basic principle of private property, held inherent to the freedom and spontaneity of the individual personality, as well as certain natural instincts of competitiveness. Most fascist movements espoused corporatism, beginning with the Italian prototype, but the most radical and developed form of fascism, German National Socialism, explicitly rejected formal corporatism (in part because of the pluralism inherent in it). The frequent contention of Marxist writers that the aim of fascist movements was to prevent economic changes in class relationships is not borne out by the movements themselves, but since no fascist movement ever fully completed the elaboration of a fascist economic system, the point remains theoretical. What fascist movements had in common was the aim of a new functional relationship for the social and economic systems, eliminating the autonomy (or, in some proposals, the existence) of large-scale capitalism and major industry, altering the nature of social status, and creating a new communal or reciprocal productive relationship through new priorities, ideals, and extensive governmental control and regulation. The goal of accelerated economic modernization was often espoused, though in some movements this aspect was muted.

Equally if not more important was the positive evaluation of violence and struggle in fascist doctrine. All revolutionary mass movements have initiated and practiced violence to a greater or lesser degree, and it is probably impossible to carry violence to greater lengths than have some Leninist regimes, practitioners of, in the words of one Old Bolshevik, "infinite compulsion." The only unique feature of the fascist relationship to violence was the theoretical evaluation by many fascist movements that violence possessed a certain positive and therapeutic value in and of itself, that a certain amount of continuing violent struggle, along the lines of Sorelianism and extreme Social Darwinism, was necessary for the health of national society.

Fascism is usually said to have been expansionist and imperialist by definition, but this is not clear from a reading of diverse fascist programs. Most were indeed imperialist, but all types of political movements and systems have produced imperialist policies, while several fascist movements had little interest in or even rejected new imperial ambitions. Those which appeared in satisfied national or imperialist states were generally defensive rather than aggressive. All, however, sought a new order in foreign affairs, a new relationship or set of alliances with respect to contemporary states and forces, and a new status for their nations in Europe and the world. Some were frankly oriented toward war, while others merely prized military values but projected no plans for aggression abroad. The latter sometimes sought a place of cultural hegemony or other nonmilitary forms of leadership.

Though fascism generally represented the most extreme form of modern European nationalism, fascist ideology was not necessarily racist in the Nazi sense of mystical, intra-European Nordic racism, nor even necessarily anti-Semitic. Fascist nationalists were all racists only in the general sense of considering blacks or non-Europeans inferior, but they could not espouse Germanicism because most of the movements were not Germanic. Similarly, the Italian and most western European movements were not initially—or in some cases ever—particularly anti-Jewish. All fascist movements were nonetheless highly ethnicist as well as extremely nationalist, and thus they held the potential for espousing doctrines of inherent collective superiority for their nations that could form a functional parallel to categorical racism.

The nature of the fascist negations is clear enough. As "latecomers" (in Linz's phrase), the post–World War I radical nationalist movements that we call fascist had to open new political and ideological space for themselves, and they were unique in their hostility to all the main currents, left, right, and center. This was complicated, however, by the need to find allies in the drive for power. Since such movements emerged mostly in countries with established parliamentary systems and sometimes relied disproportionately on the middle classes, there was no question of their coming to power through coups d'état or revolutionary civil wars, as have Leninist regimes. Though Fascists in Italy established a short-lived tactical alliance with the right center and in Portugal with the anarchist left, their most common allies lay on the right, particularly on the radical authoritarian right, and Italian Fascism as a fully coherent entity became partly defined by its merger with one of the most radical of all right authoritarian movements in Europe, the Italian Nationalist Association (ANI). Such alliances sometimes necessitated tactical, structural, and programmatic concessions. The only two fascist leaders who actually rose to power, Hitler and Mussolini, began their governments as multiparty coalitions, and Mussolini, despite the subsequent creation of a one-party state, never fully escaped the pluralist compromise with which he had begun. Moreover, since the doctrines of the authoritarian right were usually more precise, clear, and articulate— and often more practical—than those of the fascists, the capacity of the former for ideological and programmatic influence was considerable. Nonetheless, the ideas and goals of fascists differed in fundamental respects from those of the new authoritarian right, and the intention to transcend right-wing conservatism was firmly held, though not always clearly realized in practice.

Most fascist movements did not achieve true mass mobilization, but it was nonetheless characteristic that such was their goal, for they always sought to transcend the elitist parliamentary cliquishness of poorly mobilized liberal groups or the sectarian exclusiveness and reliance on elite manipulation often found in the authoritarian right. Together with the drive for mass mobilization went one of the most characteristic features of fascism, its attempt to militarize politics to an unprecedented degree. This was done by making militia groups central to the movement's organization and by using military insignia and terminology in reenforcing the sense of nationalism and constant struggle. Party militia were not invented by fascists but by nineteenth-century liberals (in countries such as Spain and Portugal) and later by the extreme left and radical right (such as Action Française). In interwar Spain the predominant "shirt movements" practicing violence were those of the revolutionary left. The initial wave of central European fascism, however, was disproportionately based on World War I veterans and their military ethos. In general, the party militia played a greater role and were developed to a greater extent among fascists than among leftist groups or the radical right.

The novel atmosphere of fascist meetings struck many observers during the 1920s and 1930s. All mass movements employ symbols and various emotive effects, and it might be difficult to establish that the symbolic structure of fascist meetings was entirely different from that of other revolutionary groups. What seemed clearly distinct, however, was the great emphasis on meetings, marches, visual symbols, and ceremonial or liturgical rituals, given a centrality and function in fascist activity which went beyond that found in the left revolutionary movements. The goal was to envelop the participant in a mystique and community of ritual that appealed to the aesthetic and the spiritual sense as well as the political.

This has aptly been called theatrical politics, but it went beyond mere spectacle toward the creation of a normative aesthetics, a cult of artistic and political beauty that built upon the broad diffusion of aesthetic forms and concepts in much of nineteenth-century society to create a "politics of beauty" and a new visual framework for public life. More than any other new force of the early twentieth century, fascism responded to the contemporary era as above all a "visual age" to be dominated by a visual culture. This relied on stereotypes of form and beauty drawn from neoclassical concepts as well as key modern images of the nineteenth and early twentieth centuries. Standard motifs included the representation of male and female bodies as the epitome of the real and the natural, almost always in poses that emphasized the dynamic and muscular, even though normally balanced by a posture of discipline and self-control.[9]

Another fundamental characteristic was extreme insistence on what is now termed male chauvinism and the tendency to exaggerate the masculine principle in almost every aspect of activity. All political forces in the era of fascism were overwhelmingly led by and made up of men, and those that paid lip service to women's equality in fact seem to have had little interest in it. Only fascists, however, made a perpetual fetish of the virility of their movement and its program and style, stemming no doubt from the fascist militarization of politics and need for constant struggle. Like that of many rightist and also some leftist groups, the fascist notion of society was organic and always made a place for women, but in that relationship the rights of the male were to enjoy predominance.[10] Griffin has termed this fascist reality a "radical misogyny or flight from the feminine, manifesting itself in a pathological fear of being engulfed by anything in external reality associated with softness, with dissolution, or the uncontrollable." [11] No other kind of movement expressed such complete horror at the slightest suggestion of androgyny.

Nearly all revolutionary movements make a special appeal to young people and are disproportionately based on young activists. By the 1920s even moderate parliamentary parties had begun to form their own young people's sections. Fascist exaltation of youth was unique, however, in that it not only made a special appeal to them but also exalted youth over all other generations, without exception, and to a greater degree than any other force based itself on generational conflict. This no doubt stemmed in part from the lateness of fascism and the identification of the established forces, including much of

9. Here I am drawing particularly on George L. Mosse's unpublished paper "Fascist Aesthetics and Society: Some Considerations" (1993).

10. The term *organic* will be used in this study in a general sense to refer to concepts of society in which its various sectors are held to bear a structured relationship to each other that serves to define and delimit their roles and rights, taking precedence over the identities and rights of individuals.

11. Griffin, *Nature of Fascism* 198.

the left, with leaders and members from the older, prewar generation. It also stemmed in part from the organic concept of the nation and of youth as its new life force, and from the predominance of youth in struggle and militarization. The fascist cult of daring, action, and the will to a new ideal was inherently attuned to youth, who could respond in a way impossible for older, feebler, and more experienced and prudent, or more materialistic, audiences.

Finally, we can agree with Gaetano Mosca, Vilfredo Pareto, and Roberto Michels that nearly all parties and movements depend on elites and leadership but some recognize the fact more explicitly and carry it to greater lengths. The most unique feature of fascism in this regard was the way in which it combined populism and elitism. The appeal to the entire people and nation, together with the attempt to incorporate the masses in both structure and myth, was accompanied by a strong formal emphasis on the role and function of an elite, which was held to be both uniquely fascist and indispensable to any achievement.

Strong authoritarian leadership and the cult of the leader's personality are obviously in no way restricted to fascist movements. Most of them began on the basis of elective leadership—elected at least by the party elite—and this was true even of the National Socialists. There was nonetheless a general tendency to exalt leadership, hierarchy, and subordination, so that all fascist movements came to espouse variants of a *Führerprinzip,* deferring to the creative function of leadership more than to prior ideology or a bureaucratized party line.

If these fundamental characteristics are to be synthesized into a more succinct definition, fascism may be defined as "a form of revolutionary ultra-nationalism for national rebirth that is based on a primarily vitalist philosophy, is structured on extreme elitism, mass mobilization, and the *Führerprinzip,* positively values violence as end as well as means and tends to normatize war and/or the military virtues." [12]

THREE FACES OF AUTHORITARIAN NATIONALISM

Comparative analysis of fascist-type movements has been rendered more complex, and often more confused, by a common tendency to identify these movements with more conservative and rightist forms of authoritarian nationalism in the interwar period and after. The fascist movements represented the most extreme expression of modern European nationalism, yet they were not synonymous with all authoritarian nationalist groups. The latter were pluriform and highly diverse, and in their typology they extended well beyond or fell well short of fascism, diverging from it in fundamental ways.

The confusion between fascist movements in particular and authoritarian

12. A different but noncontradictory and partially parallel approach may be found in Eatwell's "Towards a New Model of Generic Fascism."

Table I.2. Three Faces of Authoritarian Nationalism

Country	Fascists	Radical Right	Conservative Right
Germany	NSDAP	Hugenburg, Papen, Stahlhelm	Hindenburg, Brüning, Schleicher
Italy	PNF	ANI	Sonnino, Salandra
Austria	NSDAP	Heimwehr	Christian Socials, Fatherland Front
Belgium	late Rex, Verdinaso, Légion Nationale		early Rex, VNV
Estonia		Veterans' League	Päts
France	Faisceau, Francistes, PPF, RNP	AF, Jeunesses Pat., Solidarité Française	Croix de Feu, Vichy
Hungary	Arrow Cross, National Socialists	"Right Radicals"	Horthy, National Union Party
Latvia	Thunder Cross		Ulmanis
Lithuania	Iron Wolf	Tautininkai	Smetona
Poland	Falanga, OZN	National Radicals	Pilsudski, BBWR
Portugal	National Syndicalists	Integralists	Salazar/UN
Romania	Iron Guard	National Christians	Carolists
South Africa	Greyshirts	Ossewabrandwag	National Union
Spain	Falange	Carlists, Renovación Española	CEDA
Yugoslavia	Ustasa	Zbor, Orjuna	Alexander, Stojadinovic

nationalist groups in general stems from the fact that the heyday of fascism coincided with a general era of political authoritarianism that on the eve of World War II had in one form or another seized control of the political institutions of most European countries. It would be grossly inaccurate to argue that this process proceeded independent of fascism, but neither was it merely synonymous with fascism.

It thus becomes crucial for purposes of comparative analysis to distinguish clearly between fascist movements per se and the nonfascist (or sometimes protofascist) authoritarian right. During the early twentieth century there emerged a cluster of new rightist and conservative authoritarian forces in European politics that rejected moderate nineteenth-century conservatism and simple old-fashioned reaction in favor of a more modern, technically proficient authoritarian system distinct from both leftist revolution and fascist radicalism. These forces of the new right may in turn be divided into elements of the radical right and the more conservative authoritarian right.[13] (For suggested examples, see table I.2.)

13. These analytic distinctions bear some analogy to Arno J. Mayer's differentiation of the counterrevolutionary, reactionary, and conservative in his *Dynamics of Counterrevolution in Europe, 1870–1956* (New York, 1971). Yet as will be seen below, my criterial definitions differ considerably in content from Mayer's.

The new right authoritarian groups combated many of the same things that fascists opposed (especially liberalism and Marxism) and did espouse some of the same goals. Moreover, there were numerous instances of tactical alliances—usually temporary and circumstantial—between fascists and right authoritarians, and sometimes even cases of outright fusion, especially between fascists and the radical right, who always stood rather closer to fascists than did the more moderate and conservative authoritarian right. Hence contemporaries tended to lump the phenomena together, and this has been reenforced by subsequent historians and commentators who tend to identify fascist groups with the category of the right or extreme right.[14] Yet to do so is correct only insofar as the intention is to separate all authoritarian forces opposed to both liberalism and Marxism and to assign them the arbitrary label of *fascism* while ignoring the basic differences between them. It is a little like identifying Stalinism and Rooseveltian democracy because both were opposed to Hitlerism, Japanese militarism, and western European colonialism.

Fascism, the radical right, and the conservative authoritarian right differed among themselves in a variety of ways. In philosophy, the conservative authoritarian right, and in many instances also the radical right, based themselves upon religion more than upon any new cultural mystique such as vitalism, nonrationalism, or secular neoidealism. Hence the "new man" of the authoritarian right was grounded on and to some extent limited by the precepts and values of traditional religion, or more specifically the conservative interpretations thereof. The Sorelianism and Nietzscheanism of core fascists were repudiated in favor of a more practical, rational, and schematic approach.

If fascists and conservative authoritarians often stood at nearly opposite poles culturally and philosophically, various elements of the radical right tended to span the entire spectrum. Some radical right groups, as in Spain, were just as conservative culturally and as formally religious as was the conservative authoritarian right. Others, primarily in central Europe, tended increasingly to embrace vitalist and biological doctrines not significantly different from those of core fascists. Still others, in France and elsewhere, adopted a rigidly rationalistic position quite different from the nonrationalism and vitalism of the fascists, while trying to adopt in a merely formalistic guise a political framework of religiosity.

The conservative authoritarian right was only anticonservative in the very limited sense of having partly broken with the parliamentary forms of moderate parliamentary conservatism. It wished, however, to avoid radical breaks in

---

14. For example, J. Weiss, *The Fascist Tradition* (New York, 1967). In a somewhat similar vein, Otto-Ernst Schüddekopf's *Fascism* (New York, 1973), which is distinguished primarily for being one of the best illustrated of the volumes attempting to provide a general treatment of fascism, also tends to lump various fascist and right authoritarian movements and regimes together.

legal continuity, if at all possible, and normally proposed only a partial transformation of the system in a more authoritarian direction. The radical right, by
contrast, wished to destroy the existing political system of liberalism root and
branch. Even the radical right, however, hesitated to embrace totally radical
and novel forms of authoritarianism and normally harkened back to a reorganized monarchism or an eclectic neo-Catholic corporatism or some combination thereof. Both the radical and the conservative authoritarian right tempered
their espousal of elitism and strong leadership by invoking traditional legitima-
cies to a considerable degree. The conservative authoritarian right preferred
to avoid novelty as much as possible in forming new elites, as in dictatorship,
while the radical right was willing to go further on both points, but not so far
as the fascists.

The conservative authoritarian right usually, though not always, drew a
clear distinction between itself and fascism, whereas the radical right sometimes chose deliberately to blur such differences. In the fascist vertigo that
afflicted so much of European nationalism in the 1930s, however, even some
sectors of the conservative authoritarian right adopted certain of the trappings
of fascism, though they neither desired nor would have been able to reproduce
all the characteristics of generic fascism.

Though the conservative authoritarian right was sometimes slow to grasp
the notion of mass politics, it sometimes managed to exceed the fascists in
mobilizing mass support, drawing on broad strata of rural and lower-middle-
class people. The radical right was normally the weakest of all three sectors
in popular appeal, for it could not compete with the fascists in a quasirevolu-
tionary cross-class mobilization campaign and could not hope for the backing
of the broad groups of more moderate elements who sometimes supported the
conservative authoritarian right. To an even greater degree than the latter, the
radical right had to rely on elite elements of established society and institutions
(no matter how much they wished to change political institutions), and their
tactics were aimed at manipulation of the power structure more than at political
conquest from outside that would draw on popular support.

Thus the radical right often made a special effort to use the military system
for political purposes, and if worst came to worst it was willing to accept outright praetorianism—rule by the military—though mostly in accordance with
radical right principles. The fascists were the weakest of these forces in generating support among the military, for the conservative authoritarian right might
in moments of crisis expect even more military assistance than could the radical right, since its legalism and populism could more easily invoke principles
of legal continuity, discipline, and popular approval. Consequently efforts by
both the conservative authoritarian right and the radical right to organize their
own militia usually stopped short of paramilitary competition with the armed
forces. By contrast, fascists sought only the neutrality or in some cases the

partial support of the military while rejecting genuine praetorianism, realizing full well that military rule per se precluded fascist rule and that fascist militarization generated a sort of revolutionary competition with the army. Hitler was able to make his power complete only after he had gained total dominance over the military. When, conversely, the new system was led by a general—Franco, Pétain, Antonescu—the fascist movements were relegated to a subordinate and eventually insignificant role. Mussolini, by contrast, developed a syncretic or polycratic system which recognized broad military autonomy while limiting that of the party.

Contrary to a common assertion, economic development was a major goal of groups in all three categories, though there were exceptions (perhaps most notably the early Portuguese Estado Novo). The fascists, as the most "modernizing" of these sectors, gave modern development greater priority (again with some exceptions), though depending on national variations, some radical right and conservative authoritarian groups also gave it major priority. Right radicals and conservative authoritarians almost without exception became corporatists in formal doctrines of political economy, but the fascists were less explicit and in general less schematic.

One of the major differences between fascists and the two rightist sectors concerned social policy. Though all three sectors advocated social unity and economic harmony, for most groups of the radical and conservative authoritarian right this tended to mean freezing much of the status quo. The question of fascism and revolution will be taken up later, but suffice it to say here that the fascists were in general more interested in changing class and status relationships in society and in using more radical forms of authoritarianism to achieve that goal. The rightist sectors were simply more rightist—that is, concerned to preserve more of the existing structure of society with as little alteration as possible, except for promoting limited new rightist elites and weakening the organized proletariat.

The conservative authoritarian right was in general less likely to advocate an aggressive form of imperialism, for that in turn would imply more drastic domestic policies and incur new risks of the kind that such movements were primarily designed to avoid. The same, however, could not necessarily be said of the radical right, whose radicalism and promilitaristic stance often embraced aggressive expansion. Indeed, elements of the radical right were frequently more imperialistic than the moderate or "leftist" (social revolutionary) elements within fascism.

As a broad generalization, then, the groups of the new conservative authoritarian right were simply more moderate and generally more conservative on every issue than were the fascists. Though it had taken over some of the public aesthetics, choreography, and external trappings of fascism by the mid-1930s, the conservative authoritarian right in its style emphasized direct conservative and legal continuity, and its symbolic overtones were more recognizably traditional.

The radical right, on the other hand, often differed from fascism, not by being more moderate, but simply by being more rightist. That is, it was tied more to the existing elites and structure for support, however demogogic its propaganda may have sounded, and was unwilling to accept fully the cross-class mass mobilization and implied social, economic, and cultural change demanded by fascism. It sought a radically distinct political regime with radically distinct content, but it sought to avoid major social changes and any cultural revolution (as distinct from radical cultural reform). In some respects, with regard to violence, militarism, and imperialism, however, the radical right was almost as extreme as were the fascists (and sometimes, with regard to individual aspects, even more so). Such differences will be more easily understood in the concrete examples to be discussed in the chapters that follow.

PART I
History

1
The Cultural Transformation of the Fin de siècle

The era of world wars from 1914 to 1945 constituted the most intense period of international strife and also of domestic social and political conflict in modern history. Many of the forces that helped to generate such conflict had undergone long gestation during the eighteenth and nineteenth centuries, as in the cases of nationalism, imperialism, socialism, communism, and anarchism. Only one major new force—fascism—was novel and seemingly original, a product of the great conflict generation itself. Yet no major force suddenly emerges without prior development; the roots of fascism lay in the innovations of the late nineteenth and early twentieth centuries, and particularly in the new doctrines and concepts produced by the cultural changes of the 1890s and the years that immediately followed.

Though the generation that preceded 1914 was soon remembered as a golden age of stability and prosperity, a veritable belle époque, it had in fact been the time of the most rapid change in all human history to that point, a time in which the physical terms of life were altered with unprecedented rapidity, while the cultural and spiritual foundations of the nineteenth century worldview were severely challenged and increasingly subverted. The late nineteenth century was the time of the "second industrial revolution," with the rapid expansion of heavy industry, accompanied by unprecedented technological innovation. It inaugurated the beginning of large-scale electrification and the modern revolution in communication and transportation, with the expansion of telegraph, telephone, and cable lines, of high-speed oceanic vessels, and with the introduction of the automobile, followed by the airplane. Speed of movement and demographic growth provoked an ever-greater transfer of popu-

23

lation, as increasing numbers crossed continents and oceans, with large-scale emigration becoming a feature of the period. New inventions and discoveries succeeded one another at a dizzying pace, with the discovery of X rays, radioactivity, and the electron taking place between 1895 and 1897. Major discoveries were also made in the fields of chemistry and physics. In social science this was the golden age of sociological theory, producing the seminal formulations of Tönnies, Durkheim, Simmel, Pareto, and others.

Changes in social structure were equally rapid and profound, due to an unprecedented increase in urbanization and the growth of the new working class, accompanied by expansion of sectors of the middle classes as well. Thus the fin de siècle became the first age of the masses, the emergence of a mass society being paralleled by commercial mass consumption and industrial mass production. This had major implications for the acceleration of a more modern form of politics and resulted in a new mass culture fed by mass media, featuring the introduction of the cinema and the dawning of a new "visual age." Important aspects were the growth of mass leisure for the first time in history and the beginning of large-scale spectator sports.[1] The French writer Charles Péguy declared in 1900 that the world had changed more in the preceding thirty years than in the entire two millennia since Christ. Such far-reaching and unprecedented change created a new sense of the acceleration of history and of the transformation of human society and culture.

The fin de siècle was a time of radical innovations in thought. Whereas the nineteenth century had been increasingly dominated by liberalism in politics and by materialism and science in culture, part of the generation of the 1880s and 1890s rejected such values, replacing them with a new orientation toward subjectivism, emotionalism, nonrationalism, and vitalism. This attempt to reverse dominant values produced what one historian has called "the intellectual crisis of the 1890s."[2] That concept is valid in drawing attention to the drastic innovations of new thinkers, writers, and artists, though it must be kept in mind that these new trends were not generally accepted at that time by most of intellectual and artistic society.

The most famous and influential harbinger of the new trends was the German philosopher Friedrich Nietzsche, who preached the "death of God" and categorically repudiated nineteenth-century materialism and rationalism. Nietzscheanism rejected what it called the "herd psychology" of modern democracy and collectivism. It espoused the "will to power" as the primordial

---

1. An account of the inventions and innovations of the period may be found in M. Teich and R. Porter, eds., *Fin de siècle and Its Legacy* (Cambridge, 1993).

2. The term was coined by Zeev Sternhell with regard to the intellectual background of fascist doctrines in his "Fascist Ideology," in *Fascism: A Reader's Guide*, ed. W. Laqueur (Berkeley, 1976), 315–76.

instinct and called for the "transvaluation of all values" and the dominance of healthy emotion and instinct over repression, with the goal of achieving the *Ubermensch*—the "overman"—a superior kind of human being who had achieved self-mastery and a higher morality that balanced creative thought and feelings.[3]

More broadly, during the late nineteenth century there was a movement away from rationalist and positivist philosophy among numerous thinkers, particularly in Germany, Italy, and France but also to a lesser degree in other countries. The most fashionable philosopher after the turn of the century was the French thinker Henri Bergson, whose *L'évolution creatrice* (1907) placed vital instinct, which he termed the *élan vital,* at the very origin of life and creativity, emphasizing free choice and denying ineluctable processes of materialism and determinism.

Though renewed efforts were made to refine and reaffirm rationalist and positivist thought in England and in some philosophical circles elsewhere, a growing "revolt against positivism" emphasized neoidealist approaches to life. Thus in some quarters theories of vitalism and *Lebensphilosophie* replaced rationalism, materialism, and pragmatism, emphasizing new values and the importance of a new morality, however variously defined. These tendencies even came to affect heterodox Marxists. By the turn of the century a number of Marxists began to embrace ethics (contrary to their master's teaching) and the importance of moral education in society.

The revolt against positivism was clearly marked in Italy, where the leader of neoidealist philosophy was Benedetto Croce. Croce rejected mere rationalism and required that truth to some extent be grounded on faith, since one could not know ahead of time how history would develop. Neoidealism required more than a little subjectivism as well as a marked voluntarist orientation.[4]

This orientation was to some extent paralleled by the new emphasis on vitalism and holism in biology and psychiatry, a trend particularly marked in Germany and Austria.

> From the neo-vitalistic biology of Hans Driesch, the "Umwelt" ethology of Jacob von Uexküll, the "personalistic" psychology of William Stern, . . . the probings of the zoologist Karl von Frisch into the inner world of bees and fish, the

3. Contrary to what was often claimed after the rise of Nazism, Nietzsche was not himself a fascist generally and certainly not a Nazi specifically, even though aspects of his thought did contribute to fascist doctrine. On his influence, see S. E. Aschheim, *The Nietzsche Legacy in Germany, 1890–1990* (Berkeley, 1992); R. H. Thomas, *Nietzsche in German Politics and Society, 1890–1918* (New York, 1986); and W. Howard, "Nietzsche and Fascism," *History of European Ideas* 11 (1989): 893–99.

4. See, among the many works on Croce, E. E. Jacobitti, *Revolutionary Humanism and Historicism in Modern Italy* (New Haven, 1981), and M. Abrate, *Benedetto Croce e la crisi della società italiana* (Turin, 1966).

existential psychiatry of Karl Jaspers, and—on a somewhat different level—the psychoanalysis of Sigmund Freud, the trend in the sciences of life and mind at this time was increasingly subjectivist and non-reductionist; increasingly towards a view "in which life, instead of being interpreted from beneath in terms of supposed physical and chemical processes of accretion and blind interaction, somehow sets the stage upon which physical and chemical realities can occur."[5]

This approach held that vitalist life forces created, encouraged, or otherwise strongly influenced the physical and chemical world. The new physiology tended toward "dynamic, systems-oriented models" rather than mechanical or atomistic concepts. Freudian psychiatry emphasized the analysis of motivation and vital instinct, stressing the importance of the emotive and the subconscious, in the long run effectively reversing the dominant concepts of mechanicism in psychiatry. The new biology was oriented toward holistic interpretation, and in Germany, particularly, this overflowed into broader cultural and social concepts of "wholeness" and "oneness."

Physical science was in the process of revolutionizing the older concepts of a rational and mechanical world. The discovery of the corpuscular theory of matter and of subatomic physics led to the "new physics" of the early twentieth century. The theory of relativity developed by Einstein was followed by quantum mechanics and wave theory, which concluded that flows of energy were continuous but made up of distinct and separate units. Later the "indeterminacy principle" posited a kind of anarchic behavior at the core of physical matter. Though the latter concept was not worked out until after World War I, the fundamental changes took place during the fin de siècle generation.

New trends in literature, music, and the arts also led away from the realism and harmonies of nineteenth-century culture. Neoromanticism became a major vogue at the end of the century, while in opera the grand works of Richard Wagner had already created a mystic world of the Germanic past that exalted instinctive forces and tragic heroism. After the beginning of the century, the new styles in painting would reject the representative realism of the preceding period, turning to expressionism and abstraction that sought to portray internal and emotive forces. In music the classic harmonic system was being dissolved by new compositions using exotic scales, fractional tones, and microtonality.

Social sciences such as anthropology and criminology also questioned standard assumptions. Cultural anthropologists who studied diverse societies in widely scattered parts of the world seemed to report great variation in concepts of ethics and morality, questioning the assumption of a universal moral code. Already during the preceding generation, the Italian criminologist Cesare Lombroso had sought to establish the definition of an innately criminal type of

5. Anne Harrington, in Teich and Porter, eds., *Fin de siècle* 261.

person, challenging the assumption of a constructive rationality in the mental and emotional constitution of nearly all human beings.

New students of social psychology, led by the Frenchman Gustave Le Bon, attempted to analyze the thinking and emotions of crowds. Le Bon concluded that crowds were essentially irrational in behavior and tended toward mass hysteria, and this notion in turn led him to theorize about the need for strong leadership in society.[6]

The role of leadership and the futility of standard political doctrine— whether liberal, democratic, or socialist—was emphasized by the new Italian school of elitist theory in political sociology, led by Gaetano Mosca, Vilfredo Pareto, and later Roberto Michels. They subjected existing parliamentary systems, particularly that of Italy, to scathing criticism and affirmed the necessary dominance of elites in all systems. Mosca held that the concept of the rights of man was totally unscientific. For Pareto, the most distinguished of the group, both democracy and socialism were mere myths, and politics ultimately rested on emotion, thus requiring an enlightened system of stronger authority.[7] Lesser-known writers and theorists supported roughly similar doctrines elsewhere. Even so sober and rationally analytic a sociologist as Max Weber could look to a new kind of charismatic leadership as the alternative to the stultification of government by bureaucratic mediocrity.

In social agitation and trade union organization, the revolutionary revision of Marxist doctrine provided new nonrational approaches which emphasized the significance of myth, symbols, emotive appeals, and, especially, violence. Before 1900 European Marxism had almost universally adopted the form of social democratic parties that were increasingly adjusted to liberal parliamentarianism and to a de facto evolutionary policy.[8] Soon after the turn of the century this consensus was challenged from several directions. In parts of central and eastern Europe the new generation of revolutionary leaders insisted that socialism be oriented toward revolutionary action, less evolutionary and "merely democratic," to prepare for the violent destruction and replacement of capitalism. Of these leaders, only Lenin completely rejected the social demo-

6. See particularly R. A. Nye, *The Origins of Crowd Psychology: Gustave Le Bon and the Crisis of Mass Democracy in the Third Republic* (London, 1975), and S. Barrows, *Distorting Mirrors: Visions of the Crowd in Late Nineteenth-Century France* (New Haven, 1981).

7. R. A. Nye, *The Anti-Democratic Sources of Elite Theory: Pareto, Mosca, Michels* (London, 1977); A. Patrucco, *Italian Critics of Parliament, 1890–1918* (New York, 1992); R. Bellamy, *Modern Italian Social Theory* (Stanford, 1987), 12–99; E. Ripepe, *Gli elitisti italiani* (Pisa, 1974); E. A. Albertoni, *Gaetano Mosca* (Milan, 1978); F. Vecchini, *La pensée politique de Gaetano Mosca et ses différentes adaptations au cours du XXme siècle* (Paris, 1968); and G. Busino, *Gli studi su Vilfredo Pareto oggi* (Rome, 1974).

8. Gary P. Steenson, in *After Marx, before Lenin: Marxism and Socialist Working-Class Parties in Europe, 1884–1914* (Pittsburgh, 1991), presents a useful survey.

cratic framework, and they all maintained in theory the universalist schema and the rationalist, materialist organization of Marxism.

The revolutionary revision of Marxism in France and Italy went much further. This was pioneered by the retired French engineer Georges Sorel, who, in a series of writings after 1901, proposed a fundamental alteration of socialism. He held that the "decadence" of current Marxism could be overcome by restructuring revolutionary socialism in three different dimensions: economically, the free market and free competition must be accepted and affirmed, for that would result in a more developed and modern economy and also in sharpened competition between the bourgeoisie and the proletariat, helping eventually to promote the emancipation of the latter; culturally, revolutionary socialism must espouse a new culture and psychology which recognized the importance of moral and emotional forces and the motivating power of idealism and myth; and politically, revolutionary socialism must totally reject the parliamentary trap of liberal democracy in favor of direct action.

In his seminal *Réflexions sur la violence* (1908), Sorel emphasized the "moral" character of violence, its importance in generating a sense of seriousness, commitment, purpose, solidarity, and common bonding. Sorel held that violence was not merely a necessary evil or an unfortunate means to a higher end, but a creative aspect of group conflict that in and of itself produced benefits provided by no other form of activity. Simplifying the point slightly, violence was a good in itself, creating something unavailable through any other experience. This was the first clear theoretical statement of a doctrine that, mutatis mutandis, would be fundamental—though not absolutely unique—to the development of subsequent fascist theory. Sorel held that Marx could not have foreseen the rise of the reformist bourgeoisie, which would make great concessions to maintain peace and the existing system. Hence a new revolutionary consciousness should be created through violence, and also materialism and rationalism should be rejected in the name of a heroic pessimism that would build heroism, sacrifice, and asceticism.[9] Sorel's doctrines had their greatest effect on revolutionary syndicalists in Italy, who increasingly espoused the importance of nonrational approaches to social organization, particularly the significance of myth, symbolism, and emotive appeals.

More broadly influential, however, than the ideas of new revolutionaries were doctrines publicized at the turn of the century by pseudoscientists, which

9. On Sorel, see J. J. Roth, *The Cult of Violence: Sorel and the Sorelians* (Berkeley, 1980); J. R. Jennings, *Georges Sorel* (London, 1985); and Z. Sternhell, M. Sznajder, and M. Asheri, *The Birth of Fascist Ideology* (Princeton, 1994), 1–176.

The principal anthologizer of the new doctrines of aggression, imperialism, and nonrationalism was Ernest Seillière [pseud.], who published *Der demokratische Imperialismus* (Berlin, 1907); *Introduction a la philosophie de l'imperialisme* (Paris, 1911); *Les Mystiques du néo-romanticisme* (Paris, 1911); and *Mysticisme et domination* (Paris, 1913).

bore the trappings of "scientism." Whereas nineteenth-century science had seemed to encourage liberalism, democracy, and egalitarianism, the new scientism (usually based on vulgarized and popularized writings that were merely pseudoscientific) encouraged concepts of race, elitism, hierarchy, and the glorification of war and violence. By the late nineteenth century Social Darwinism was in full vigor and had engendered a variety of new theories, especially involving pseudoscientific extrapolations from anthropology and zoology. Leading scientists who propagated Social Darwinist doctrines, such as the zoologist Ernst Haeckel in Germany and the psycho-physiologist Jules Soury in France, attracted many readers. Haeckel's *Welträtsel* (Riddle of the Universe, 1900) had enormous sales, and the German Monist League that he founded in 1904 enjoyed extensive membership and considerable influence. It stressed the need for a cultural, not a socioeconomic, revolution to develop the race through a strong authoritarian state.[10]

By the beginning of the new century a search for the unity of nature was attracting more and more followers. In the German-speaking world (and to a lesser degree in some other areas), this meant a quest to associate the ideal and the physical, the cultural and the material, the spiritual and the biological, and the natural and the social, so that the ultimate unity and hidden essence of "nature" might be revealed. Such tendencies strongly reenforced the conceptualization and appeal of nationalism, for they exalted biogroup identity and placed a new value on organic relations within societies and on nations as whole units. This reenforced a growing stress on order, authority, and discipline rather than individualism or self-indulgence, for only through stronger authority could organic relations be buttressed and biogroup identity more fully affirmed.

Such attitudes were accentuated by concern about social and racial decadence, a concern that had grown through the second half of the nineteenth century. A sense of decadence could hardly be considered novel, for it had been expressed by elements of the elite (and others) in established high cultures for at least three thousand years and was not altogether uncommon in the later eighteenth century. The nineteenth-century concept of decadence, however, seems first to have been voiced by members of the Parisian literary elite in the last phase of classic romanticism, during the 1830s and 1840s. Worry over decadence became generalized during the second half of the century, apparently intensified by mass urbanization and the growth in crime. Some criminologists,

10. D. Gasman, *The Scientific Origins of National Socialism: Social Darwinism in Ernst Haeckel and the German Monist League* (New York, 1971). Certain exaggerations in this work are corrected in A. Kelley, *The Descent of Darwin: The Popularization of Darwinism in Germany, 1860–1914* (Chapel Hill, 1981). Earlier French parallels are detailed in Z. Sternhell, *La droite révolutionnaire, 1885–1914: Les origines françaises du fascisme* (Paris, 1978), 146–76. More broadly, see H. W. Koch, *Sozialdàrwinismus* (Munich, 1973).

such as Lombroso, developed anthropological and virtually racial definitions of the criminal type, said to be rapidly increasing in numbers. The growth of racial doctrines produced fears of racial decay amid what were perceived as the expanding proportions of the déclassé and degraded sectors of society.

Wide acceptance of concepts about evolution sometimes also brought concern over the reversal of development through entropy—the inevitable decay of energy and vitality. Proponents of decadence theories often held that the very terms of modern life encouraged decadence, producing physical enfeeblement through urbanization and sedentary customs and the survival of the least fit. Such was often held to be the inevitable outcome of modern culture, with its tendencies toward individualistic anomie, self-indulgence, nonconformity, and egalitarianism. The main popularizing work was Max Nordau's *Entartung* (Degeneration, 1892), which was widely translated and sold all over Europe. Concern about decadence often accompanied or fueled nationalism, increasingly held to be the necessary antidote for decadence.[11]

New racial doctrines exerted wide appeal. Some racial analysts were serious, apolitical students of comparative physiology and anthropology who propounded the investigation of "scientific racism," which had adepts in France, England, Germany, the United States, and elsewhere. The noted German scientist Rudolf Virchow participated in these endeavors, as did other founders of the German Anthropology Society, one offshoot being the foundation of the *Journal for Racial and Social Biology* in Germany in 1904. Many other writers, however, presented the most vulgarized and nonsensical notions of racial differences and hierarchies passed off as demonstrated scientific fact.

Modern racial concepts originated amid the eighteenth-century Enlightenment, as geographers and anthropologists first made systematic attempts to categorize the diverse inhabitants of the earth. The first racial concepts were, however, relatively benign and accorded respect to all peoples, who were generally recognized as part of one human family.[12]

The father of modern discriminatory racism in Europe is generally acknowledged to have been the French aristocrat Comte Arthur de Gobineau, author of the seminal *Essai sur l'inégalite des races humaines* (1853).[13] Gobineau divided humanity into three basic races—white, yellow, and black—and

---

11. Amid the growing "decadence" literature, see K. W. Swart, *The Sense of Decadence in Nineteenth-Century France* (The Hague, 1964); R. A. Nye, *Madness and Politics in Modern France: The Medical Concept of National Decline* (Princeton, 1984); D. Pick, *Faces of Degeneration: A European Disorder, c. 1848–c. 1918* (Cambridge, 1989); and the special number on "Decadence" of the *Journal of Contemporary History* (hereinafter cited as *JCH*) 17:1 (Jan. 1982).

12. The best guide to the development of racial thought in Europe is G. L. Mosse, *Toward the Final Solution* (New York, 1978). See also L. L. Snyder, *The Idea of Racialism* (Princeton, 1962), and C. Guillaumin, *L'idéologie du racisme* (Paris, 1972).

13. On a French forerunner, see J. Boissel, *Victor Courtet (1813–1867) premier théoricien de la hiérarchie des races* (Paris, 1972).

found the white or "Aryan" race completely superior, the black race hopelessly inferior. Despite this clear-cut categorization, Gobineau's conclusions were thoroughly pessimistic, holding that no race could maintain its purity and integrity and was condemned to decay through racial mixing and degeneration. Thus the Jews, whom Gobineau found to have been initially one of the higher branches of the white race, had also fallen prey to miscegenation and undergone decay.

Other racial theorists rejected Gobineau's pessimism, employing it instead as a call to action for eugenic racial policy, discriminatory politics, and the defense of the allegedly higher races. This was the burden of another French aristocrat, Comte Georges Vacher de Lapouge, who extensively disseminated racial doctrines in France during the late nineteenth century. Vacher de Lapouge specifically demonized Jews, whom he believed were more dangerous than yellow or black people because of their internal roles within European society.

The adoption of racial thought for political purposes soon became most extensive in German-speaking central Europe. It went beyond the rather simple black-white dichotomies common to the English-speaking world and developed into doctrines of "mystical racism" that created sharp distinctions and categories among the various white peoples of Europe, to establish the absolute superiority of Aryan, "Nordic," or Germanic Europeans as distinct from Slavs, Latins, or Balkan peoples. The greatest popularizer of mystical racism in Germany was the Germanized Englishman Houston Stewart Chamberlain, whose *Die Grundlagen des XIX Jahrhunderts* (The Foundations of the Nineteenth Century, 1899) codified the new Germanistic doctrines of mystical racism as earlier developed by Wagner and others. Beyond the Aryan racial stereotype (tall, blond, blue-eyed), he affirmed the existence of a special "race soul" that created a more imaginative and profound spirit in Aryans and produced a "German religion," though the latter was still (in part) vaguely related to Christianity. The ultimate anti-Aryan and most bitter racial foe was the Jew. Chamberlain combined Social Darwinism with racism and thus emphasized an endless racial struggle on behalf of the purity of Aryanism and against Jews and lesser peoples, virtually creating a scenario for race war.[14]

Racism was accompanied by the rapid growth of new, more modern, and increasingly racial doctrines of anti-Semitism. Enmity toward Jews had at no time disappeared, though it was considerably muted during the eighteenth-century Enlightenment and amid the liberalism and romanticism of the first half of the nineteenth century. During the last four decades of the century, however, anti-Semitism revived; it accelerated during the 1890s and afterward. The

14. G. G. Field, *Evangelist of Race: The Germanic Vision of Houston Stewart Chamberlain* (New York, 1981). See L. Poliakov, *The Aryan Myth* (New York, 1971). One of the earliest definitions of history as racial struggle was L. Gumplowicz, *Der Rassenkampf* (Innsbruck, 1883).

most notorious document of the new anti-Semitism was the infamous *Protocols of the Elders of Zion*, forged by agents of the Russian secret police in Paris between 1894 and 1899 to constitute the alleged self-revelation of the Jewish "world conspiracy."[15]

The new anti-Semitism was increasingly racist, whereas traditional anti-Jewish feeling had been justified by religious arguments, but the connecting link between the old and the new was the continued definition of Jews as the alien and subversive, destructive of morality and culture. Whereas traditionally this had been imputed to the Jewish religion, such characteristics were now inherently imputed to Jews themselves ipso facto, as rootless cosmopolitans and quintessential materialists who allegedly reduced all aspects of life to monetary profit.[16] By the end of the nineteenth century Jews were even being defined as a unique race, a subversive antirace devoted to the destruction of the purity of other higher races.[17]

At certain extremities these nonrationalist and/or pseudoscientistic concepts merged directly into the remarkable rise of modern occult interests. The latter had grown throughout the nineteenth century, some of their first manifestations in Masonry and the Illuminati accompanying the early development of liberalism and leftist revolutionism. What might be called the hard-core occult grew rapidly from midcentury and by 1900 counted untold millions of devotees in hundreds of different cults and forms. Astrological activity multiplied with particular rapidity, and it has been calculated that by 1925 the German Astrologische Gesellschaft had a larger membership than any half dozen scientific societies.[18] Most believers in the occult, as in many other forms of nonrational belief, were probably politically harmless, but in central Europe they tended to be tied more and more to racialist groups.

Quite aside from any specific political proclivity, a concern for new approaches and new values—and possibly a new style of life—was heightened by the unique growth of boredom in industrial society and the rejection—particularly by portions of the middle classes—of what soon came to be perceived as the stifling new urban environment of the fin de siècle. A growing sense

15. N. Cohn, *Warrant for Genocide: The Myth of the Jewish World Conspiracy* (London, 1967). The notion of a grand Jewish conspiracy had apparently first been publicized by the French aristocrat Gougenot des Mousseaux in his *Le Juif, le judaïsme et la judaisation des peuples chrétiens* (Paris, 1869).

16. This common denominator is clearly defined in P. L. Rose, *Revolutionary Antisemitism in Germany from Kant to Wagner* (Princeton, 1990).

17. The major theoretical work on the notion of a Jewish race, however, was I. Zollschan, *Das Rassenproblem unter besonderer Berucksichtigung der theoretischen Grundlagen der jüdischen Rassenfrage* (The Racial Problem with Special Attention to the Theoretical Foundation of the Jewish Race, 1910), which, though Aryanist, was pro-Zionist and not categorically anti-Semitic.

18. W. F. Albright, *History, Archaelogy and Christian Humanism* (New York, 1964), 125–26.

of ennui had been a special feature of the nineteenth century. Boredom, of course, had been found among elites and aristocracies for millennia, but only in nineteenth-century Europe did leisure begin to extend so broadly, even among the greater middle classes, that boredom became a growing symptom of malaise in a broader minority of society. This in turn was increasingly identified with resentment against stuffiness and restrictive mores, varyingly interpreted and denounced as bourgeois piety, prudery, and philistinism, and always as hypocrisy.

Parallel to this phenomenon were the first major expressions of modern environmentalism. These views initially were espoused only by certain extremes of left and right, and by nonpolitical advocates, but would later be adopted, first by fascists, among mass movements. By the end of the century there was a new emphasis on fresh air and the outdoor life, if only because for the first time large sectors of the population had become urban and sedentary and also possessed the leisure to alter aspects of their lives.

Such trends encouraged the reaffirmation of the physical, a new emphasis on restoring contact with nature, the outdoors, and the countryside. The new physicality or corporeality brought with it a heightened concern for the body and the senses, relieved of the practical restrictions of urban life. This could lead simply to a healthier or more hedonistic lifestyle, or alternately to new forms of political expression, which would be exploited after World War I.

During these years one can also find the genesis of twentieth-century youth culture, as the expansion of economic well-being and leisure for the first time made it possible for youth to be set apart as a distinct and even privileged period of life for a significant part of society. The first modern youth movements date from the latter part of the nineteenth century. Youth movements, nature societies, the growth of weekend excursions, and the rapid expansion of organized sports all reflected common trends—mostly healthful and recreative—but also exhibited new styles and values that might later be mobilized in distinct ways for political purposes.

The later nineteenth century also witnessed the spread of a new cult of manliness and a more self-conscious emphasis on masculine expression, in reaction to the sedentary, egalitarian, and homogenizing tendencies of modern society. The new style of self-conscious virility, though in some sense first fashioned in private life, held clear implications for nationalism and militarism, with which it became increasingly associated politically.[19]

It would be a considerable exaggeration to claim that there was a cultural crisis for European society as a whole during the period 1890–1914, but changes of attitude among sectors of the cultural elite were striking, particularly in some

19. Cf. G. L. Mosse, *Nationalism and Sexuality* (New York, 1985).

of the larger continental countries and especially in central Europe, Italy, Russia, and, to some extent, France. A mood of rejection of some of the dominant values of preceding generations had set in. Faith in rationalism, the positivist approach, and the worship of materialism came increasingly under fire. Hostility toward bureaucracy, the parliamentary system, and the drive for "mere" equality often accompanied this spirit of rejection.

By the time of World War I, the shift in attitudes, ideas, and sensibilities created a different climate among much of the cultural elite, and among younger political and social activists, than had prevailed during most of the nineteenth century. The new cultural mood would not fully run its course until 1945, with the end of the era of world wars and intense internal conflict in Europe. In the meantime, it contributed to the proliferation and acceptance of radical new doctrines of varied hues.

2
Radical and Authoritarian Nationalism in Late Nineteenth-Century Europe

Though the nineteenth century was the time of the greatest expansion of civic and personal freedom in world history to that point, individualist liberalism was increasingly contested by two new forms of political collectivism—nationalism and socialism. Each emphasized the priority of group identity, competition, and conflict and might appeal to violence as political means. Though socialism seemed for a time to be moving in the direction of social democracy, nationalism had assumed more radical and drastic forms by the end of the century. Whereas earlier nationalism had often been liberal and fraternal, later nationalist groups were becoming aggressive, authoritarian, and intolerant.

Indeed, nationalism has exerted one of the two or three strongest kinds of political appeals known to modern times, and in some parts of the world it has been the strongest single political force. There is no general agreement among scholars concerning its cause, or even its definition.[1] Defensive patriotism is known to almost all societies, but modern nationalism is normally distinguished from traditional patriotism by several fundamental qualities. One is the definition of an individual nation of citizens who form part of a cultural and civic entity and thus share certain equivalent rights and characteristics—

---

1. A good brief introduction is P. Alter, *Nationalism* (London, 1989). On the evolution of modern nationalism, see C. J. H. Hayes, *The Historical Evolution of Modern Nationalism* (New York, 1931); idem, *Nationalism: A Religion* (New York, 1960); B. C. Shafer, *Nationalism* (Washington, D.C., 1963); A. D. Smith, *Nationalism in the Twentieth Century* (Oxford, 1979); and idem, *Theories of Nationalism* (London, 1983).

35

a modern political concept as distinct from a traditionalist identity. Another feature often—though not always—present is an active quality that seeks to carry out a new civic project and that often exhibits aggressive characteristics, seeking not merely to preserve and defend but also to unite, to change, and frequently to expand.

Liah Greenfeld, author of one of the most influential recent works on the origins of nationalism, has found that the first structure of modern nationality developed in sixteenth- and seventeenth-century England.[2] Whereas classic English nationality was individualistic and civic, emphasizing constitutionality and civic rights, the nationalism that developed in late eighteenth-century France was more collectivist in character, stressing central unity and collective purposes, though in the nineteenth century its civic qualities were reenforced and it became more liberal. The German nationalism that emerged during the Napoleonic wars was collectivist and ethnic, emphasizing a romantic Germanism often at the expense of liberal civic development.

Though historians of nationalism disagree on many things, there is general agreement that modern radical nationalism first achieved full expression during the Jacobin phase of the French Revolution. Though the rationalist and egalitarian aspects of that revolution would later be violently rejected by twentieth-century fascists, for our purposes it is also important to remember that certain key aspects of the fascist form of revolutionary nationalism were themselves pioneered in the French Revolution. These included nationalism itself as a radical new force whose claims superseded other political rights, the invocation of an authoritarian single or "general" will to achieve its ends, and the justification of extreme violence in its name. The French Revolution strove to achieve a new man, a new kind of citizen—an aim paralleled by all other revolutionary nationalists in the future. It exalted new civic festivals and rituals and formed its own cult of youth, together with that of patriotic death and martyrdom, values that would be equally dear to later nationalist revolutionaries.[3] For much of the nineteenth century nationalism would indeed be the dominant form of revolutionism in European affairs, superseded by social revolutionism only after 1870.[4]

If nationalism as project has in most cases focused initially on the task of national liberation, it has almost as often turned into imperialism as an individual nationalism sought to expand its power beyond the intrinsic ethnic boundaries of the nation. Indeed, as European powers carved up most of the outer world for their expanding empires, the projection of nationalism into

2. L. Greenfeld, *Nationalism: Five Roads to Modernity* (Cambridge, 1992).

3. The clearest discussion will be found in G. L. Mosse, "Fascism and the French Revolution," in his *Confronting the Nation* (Hanover, N.H., 1993), 70–90.

4. See especially J. S. Billington, *Fire in the Minds of Men: Origins of the Revolutionary Faith* (New York, 1980), 128–364.

imperialism became seemingly de rigueur. Such tendencies were further encouraged by the cultural changes of the fin de siècle, which stimulated group
identity, the projection of power, aggressiveness, and the propensity toward
violence. Within Europe itself, nationalism during the course of the century
moved increasingly toward the right and tended to take on ever more authoritarian form. This became so much the case that by the beginning of the new
century nationalism had generally become the main political vehicle of the new
forces of the authoritarian right. Though the authoritarian right did not appeal
to nationalism alone, it had become the most common denominator of a variety
of new forces which challenged both liberalism and socialism.

At first glance it might be assumed that the origins of the early twentieth-
century authoritarian right lay in the first reactions to the eruption of liberal and
leftist forces during the French Revolution and its aftermath. While there are
undeniable links between the new authoritarian right of the late nineteenth and
early twentieth centuries and certain forces of traditionalism, neolegitimism,
and reaction that preceded them by a hundred years, major differences also
exist. The reactionary movements of the early nineteenth century tended to
be simply and directly traditionalist and aimed at avoiding the development of
modern urban, industrial, and mass society rather than transforming it. By the
latter part of the century the new rightist groups had achieved much greater
sophistication, and they tried in their own way to come to terms with modern
social, cultural, and economic problems.

Emergence of the new forms of right authoritarianism was a long, often
slow and complex process, for liberal parliamentarianism seemed on its way
to an almost complete victory in formal institutions by the last decades of
the nineteenth century. Though certain major exceptions to liberalism might
be found in the constitutional structures of Russia and Germany, at first the
main challenges appeared to come from the socialist, anarchist, or populist
left rather than from new forms of rightism. So complete was the intellectual
and theoretical triumph of liberalism in the formal culture of many European
countries that its opponents on the right sometimes groped helplessly for new
concepts of a more authoritarian structure of government.

By the end of the century, nonetheless, at least six distinct forms of rightist and/or nationalist authoritarianism had emerged: a traditionalist monarchist
authoritarian right, programs for corporatist socioeconomic and political reorganization, neomonarchist authoritarianism as "integral nationalism," new
programs of moderate constitutional authoritarianism or authoritarian liberalism, a new modernizing nationalist and authoritarian right, and revolutionary
or semirevolutionary new doctrines of national socialism and national syndicalism.

The traditionalist monarchist authoritarian right. Unlike the situation in
northern Europe, the transition to liberal parliamentary systems in southwest-

ern Europe during the late eighteenth and early nineteenth centuries was carried out by violent and revolutionary or semirevolutionary means. These convulsions produced drastic revolution and temporary civil war in France, coups and countercoups leading to a brief civil war in Portugal, and no less than three civil wars in Spain (between 1821 and 1876).[5] In all three countries, the supporters of traditionalist monarchy continued to oppose the liberal system well into the nineteenth century, urging a return to traditional authority and traditional laws instead of modern liberal constitutions, administrative centralization, and near-absolute private property rights. The Portuguese movement, called Miguelism after the traditionalist pretender, Dom Miguel, had been completely defeated by 1834, but French "legitimism" remained a major force in French affairs through the 1870s.

Most tenacious of all the traditionalist monarchists were the Spanish Carlists. Traditionalists won the first modern Spanish civil war of 1821–23, though they lost the more decisive struggles of 1833–40 and 1869–76. After the last civil war, Carlists were reduced primarily to bastions of regional particularism in Navarre and the Basque country, but their movement did not completely disappear, and it would be revived once more during the 1930s.

Doctrines of corporatism. The organization of sectors of society into distinct "corporations," partly autonomous and partly state-regulated, dates from Roman times, and various partial systems of limited autonomy and self-regulation within a broader framework of civic authority and limited representation were a common feature of the Middle Ages, particularly in local city-states but also to some degree within larger kingdoms. The beginnings of modern corporatism stem from the early nineteenth century in reaction to the individualism, social atomization, and new forms of central state power arising from the French Revolution and modern liberalism. The first ultra-right corporatist ideas, prominent mainly in Germany and Austria (but also in France), proposed a partial return to the medieval estates system under a more authoritarian government.[6]

The best succinct working definition of what is usually meant by *corporatism* has been provided by Philippe Schmitter:

> Corporatism can be defined as a system of interest representation in which the constituent units [i.e., social and economic sectors] are organized into a limited number of singular, compulsory, noncompetitive, hierarchically ordered and

---

5. The first organized monarchist group in France may have been the Chevaliers de la Foi, formed around a cell structure in 1810. For an overview of doctrine, see C. T. Muret, *French Royalist Politics since the Revolution* (New York, 1933).

6. Not all German corporatist theories of the first half of the nineteenth century were authoritarian and/or reactionary. The "social federalist" corporatism of Karl Marlo in the 1840s sought equal and balanced representation. See R. H. Bowen, *German Theories of the Corporate State* (New York, 1947), 53–58.

functionally differentiated categories, recognized or licensed (if not created) by the state and granted a deliberate representational monopoly within their respective categories in exchange for observing certain controls.[7]

Theoretically reactionary or semireactionary corporatism should be distinguished from some of the doctrines of Catholic corporatism that were developed in the middle and later nineteenth century and were directed toward reducing the powers of government and providing for social group autonomy, with less concern for strictly political and economic issues. The difference here, at least in part, is that between what some corporatists called societal (socially autonomous) and state (government-induced and controlled) corporatism.

Yet another strand of corporatist thought developed toward the end of the century among moderate liberals in reaction to the atomistic and invertebrate, conflict-oriented character of purely individualist liberalism. One expression of this was the "solidarist" school of Léon Bourgeois in France, paralleled by minor theorists in other countries and to some extent by the "juridical" corporatist school of Anton Menger.

Some leftist groups also developed variants of corporatist theory by the first years of the twentieth century. These might have been found among some of the revolutionary syndicalists in France and Italy as well as the "guild socialists" of Great Britain.[8]

By the beginning of the twentieth century, however, there was growing convergence among rightist exponents of corporatism toward state rather than societal corporatism, even though abstract doctrines tended to disguise the degree of compulsion that would be required to implement them in practice. By that point most right authoritarian groups had espoused varying kinds and degrees of compulsory state corporatism for economic organization and controlled political representation.[9]

Neomonarchist authoritarianism as "integral nationalism." While corporatism took many different forms, and while surviving monarchist legitimists in southwestern Europe soon adopted corporatism as a doctrine, a new rightist movement in France made the monarchy itself the focus of corporative and authoritarian nationalism in a novel and aggressive new manner, unlike more moderate Catholic corporatists or moderate conservatives. Action Française, the new exemplar of French monarchism, was founded in 1899. Its uniqueness lay not in its legitimist monarchism nor in its corporatism, but in the creation

7. P. C. Schmitter, "Still the Century of Corporatism?" in *The New Corporatism*, ed. F. Pike and T. Stritch (South Bend, Ind., 1974), 85–131.

8. See C. Landauer, *Corporate State Ideologies* (Berkeley, 1983), 38–58.

9. In addition to the works cited above, see P. J. Williamson, *Varieties of Corporatism* (London, 1985); idem, *Corporatism in Perspective* (London, 1989); M. H. Elbow, *French Corporative Theory, 1789–1948* (New York, 1953); C. Vallaura, *Le radici del corporativismo* (Rome, 1971); and P. C. Mayer-Tasch, *Korporativismus und Autoritarismus* (Frankfurt, 1971).

of a new fin de siècle synthesis that converted legitimist monarchism from a dynastic principle and a purely reactionary ideal into a new political system of "integral nationalism." Charles Maurras, the principal leader, and other ideologues of the movement created a set of doctrines based not merely on monarchism but on an exclusive and ideologically sophisticated nationalism. The appeal to the entire nation, its cultural tradition, and its broader interests gave exclusivist "integral nationalism" a greater appeal than traditional legitimism could possibly have had. Since France had been a republic since 1871, monarchism could to some extent be made to seem drastically new and integrative.

Later, after Portugal became the second new European republic in 1910, a derivative movement of Integralismo Lusitano sought to create a complete Portuguese variant of Action Française, gaining considerable vogue on the right and among elite university youth. Action Française was later copied with some success in Spain and also had followers in Greece.

Moderate constitutional authoritarianism. Another divergence, though much more moderate, took place among some establishment conservatives and moderate liberals who feared that liberal parliamentarianism was becoming unmanageable and advocated or imposed more authoritarian limitations on government. The chief expressions of "authoritarian liberalism" were found in central Europe, and also in Spain and Portugal. One aspect might have first appeared in Germany, where the constitutional structure had never become fully liberal and responsible. Even so, in his last year as chancellor (1889–90), Bismarck began to consider seriously reducing the existing liberal prerogatives to limit the parliamentary franchise and certain other civil rights. As political systems become more quasidemocratic and in many cases conflictive, there were mounting calls for a moderately authoritarian alternative, even if no more than a temporary "Cincinnatian" dictatorship. In Austria, the Habsburg crown had on several occasions before 1914 to close the parliament and rule briefly by decree because of internal parliamentary obstructionism.

A broader step was taken during the decomposition of the Portuguese parliamentary monarchy, when João Franco was given power by the crown to rule temporarily by decree in 1907–8. As distinct from limited "decree powers" recognized by the Third Republic in France, for example, or the emergency authority of the Habsburg crown, Franco's dictatorship could not be legitimated by the Portuguese constitutional system but operated on the dubious responsibility of the monarchy alone. Franco personified one variant of the new "managerial" trend in conservative liberalism, his motto being *Pouca política, muita administração* (Little politics, much administration).

The new modernizing nationalist and authoritarian right. The most aggressive new fin de siècle nationalism was interested neither in traditionalism—as with many monarchists—nor in maintaining the status quo—as among the conservative right. Particularly in lesser developed southern Europe, new nationalist movements aimed not merely at national expansion and imperialism but also at the establishment of new authoritarian regimes which would not merely maintain unity but also promote economic development and modernization. The Italian Nationalist Association, founded in 1910, adopted the goal of the authoritarian corporate state to achieve an expanded empire and also a stronger industrialized economy. The militant Serbian Unification or Death society had somewhat the same goals, and beginning in 1919 two Spanish monarchist groups adopted a program of modernizing authoritarianism (though without an equivalent stress on expansionism). The significance of this new kind of movement lay in its projection of a modern new authoritarian nationalism and imperialism not tied to past norms and ideals but striving to create new twentieth-century forms of authoritarianism and a more modern society.

Revolutionary national socialism. More novel and radical than the modernizing nationalist right were the new national socialist groups that began to emerge from the 1880s on. They sought to recapture the earlier revolutionary potential of nationalism, which they associated with revolutionary or semirevolutionary social, cultural, and economic transformation. The national socialist groups in France, Germany, and Austria, together with the national syndicalists in Italy, eventually absorbed more of the new ideas and theories produced by the radical fin de siècle cultural changes than did any other kind of nationalist movement. They were the most immediate precursors of what after 1918 would become fascism.

FRANCE

New political tendencies have normally appeared earlier in France than almost anywhere else in the world. Of all continental European countries, France moved most rapidly through the early phases of democratization and political conflict. France pioneered not only the revolution of 1789 but also the novel form of empire under Napoleon that followed. Some have called Napoleon I the first modern dictator, building an essentially secular regime on military power that was not historically legitimated, resting on a hybrid ideology, and creating perhaps the first modern police state. French political development led the "convulsive" pattern of political modernization common to most of southern Europe, particularly the southwest. Thus the restored legitimist monarchy was followed in 1830 by a new liberal constitutional monarchy and then by a second republic in 1848–51.

The restored Napoleonic regime which then emerged, the Second Empire of Louis-Napoleon (1851–70), became even more clearly the first modern, syncretic, postliberal national authoritarian regime, preceding all others by half a century. Hence arose the concept found in some quarters of "Bonapartism" as the "first fascism," [10] an interpretation derived from Karl Marx's original analysis of Louis-Napoleon's regime as the product of a new phase of social conflict that produced an authoritarian system no longer primarily dependent on a single social class—that is, a dictatorship that was politically autonomous and self-perpetuating, however buttressed by the backing of wealthy elites and broader lower-middle-class sectors.[11]

The Second Empire was extraordinarily eclectic, a remarkable mixture of conservatism, clericalism, classic Bonapartist authoritarianism, and electoral neoliberalism, accompanied by mass propaganda and economic modernization. Though it anticipated certain individual features of twentieth-century dictatorships, the Second Empire was in fact a precocious syncretistic product of the mid–nineteenth century, lacking several of the most novel qualities of the more radical twentieth-century regimes. Its state structure was basically that of a traditional form of empire, unlike Nazi Germany or the Soviet Union. It never proposed a very novel, much less collectivist, economic system or an original regulatory framework, though several kinds of ideas were proposed. The Second Empire's political culture was almost as rationalist as that of most contemporaries, and it never attempted a party movement, much less a new political militia. Louis-Napoleon was about as squeamish as most of his contemporaries about the use of violence and, though a caesarean or praetorian figure, strove to legitimate himself as much as possible in traditional terms. His Bonapartism relied directly on the military while striving to accommodate conservative and traditionally religious forces. His regime for the most part preserved existing class relationships while seeking to promote economic modernization through largely orthodox means. Insofar as Bonapartism in France was the precursor of any particular state system, it seems more related to several of the right-wing, primarily nonfascist systems of the period between the world wars, which were sometimes similarly praetorian-led and proclerical, retained pseudoliberal formulae, and tried to promote economic modernization without mass mobilization or new state economic systems.[12]

The authoritarian interludes in modern French government occurred very early, probably because of the precocity of political and social mobilization and

10. The comparison was apparently first made by August Thalheimer in 1930. His essays have been partially reprinted in W. Abendroth et al., *Faschismus und Kapitalismus* (Frankfurt, 1967), 19–38, and in R. Kühnl, ed., *Texte zur Faschismusdiskussion I* (Reinbek, 1974), 14–29. The concept has been further elaborated by Gustav A. Rein, in his *Bonapartismus und Faschismus in der deutschen Geschichte* (Göttingen, 1960).

11. K. Marx, *The Eighteenth Brumaire of Louis Napoleon* (New York, 1970). See M. Rudel, *Karl Marx devant le Bonapartisme* (Paris, 1960).

12. The best brief critique of the fascism-Bonapartism thesis is J. Dülffer, "Bonapartism, Fascism and National Socialism," *JCH* 11:4 (Oct. 1976): 109–28. On the politics and structure of the Second Empire, see T. Zeldin, *The Political System of Napoleon III* (Oxford, 1958).

of modern social conflict in France. Their overthrow did not come as the result of domestic rebellion but, as in the case of nearly all institutionalized modern European authoritarian systems before 1975, of foreign military defeat. After 1870 France moved slowly and uncertainly into stable liberal democratic government and managed to institutionalize most of its attendant forms and values before the new collectivist, semirevolutionary nationalism could fully develop.

The Earliest Precursors of Fascism: The League of Patriots and Boulangism

Something at first glance analogous to a "prefascist" situation nonetheless developed in France in the aftermath of defeat in the Franco-Prussian War and the bloody repression of the revolutionary Paris Commune in 1870–71. One of the main motivations for a revolutionary nationalism—status deprivation—weighed upon France after 1871. The new nationalist movement which attempted to exploit this situation was Paul Déroulède's League of Patriots. In place of the Jacobin nationalism of the late eighteenth and early nineteenth centuries, which had touted universal progressive values and nominal democracy, the League preached a clearly authoritarian new form of nationalism. It stressed the need for unity behind a single leader who, though ratified by popular suffrage, would concentrate all executive power in his own hands. A central motif was national vengeance, based on a doctrine of militarism and a mystique of discipline and death rooted in the national soil and the culture of the people. Contemptuous of the new parliamentary democracy, the League nonetheless directed its appeal toward the masses, seeking to harmonize social interests with promises of new economic regulations that appealed especially to small shopkeepers and the lower middle classes.[13]

Founded in 1882, the League was able to join forces five years later with a sizable portion of the extreme left Blanquists, proponents of the coup d'état and the revolutionary Jacobin tradition. Together they formed part of the base of the Boulangist movement of 1886–89, the major new popular and radical force of the decade in France. It centered on the romantic figure of General Georges Boulanger, a colorful former minister of war who had a reputation as a reformer and something of a leftist, but above all as a militant anti-German nationalist and militarist, "Le Général Révanche" (General Revenge). By 1886 he had become a charismatic and caesarean figure who led an eclectic populist and nationalist movement without central organization, but one

13. The best discussion of Déroulède and the League will be found in Z. Sternhell, *La droite révolutionnaire, 1885–1914: Les origines françaises du fascisme* (Paris, 1978), 77–145. In the wake of France's defeat, the need for a more unified and dynamic approach to national affairs, involving even a degree of authoritarianism, was embraced by erstwhile leading liberal thinkers, such as the historians Ernest Renan and Hippolyte Taine. See C. Digeon, *La crise allemande de la pensée française, 1870–1914* (Paris, 1959).

which scored resounding electoral victories in 1888–89. It raised major contributions from wealthy monarchists and pioneered a new style of mass agitation and propaganda, in many ways a harbinger of mass politics. The Boulangist movement was based on popular nationalism and comprised supernationalist *révanchards*, radicals who favored plebiscitary direct government with strong presidential leadership, neo-Bonapartist peasants yearning for a strong leader, revolutionary Blanquists seeking direction and overthrow of the bourgeois republic, social nationalists of the patriotic left, and numerous royalists of the authoritarian extreme right. Boulangist victories occurred above all in conservative and royalist districts, but in January 1889 the movement made a dramatic breakthrough in the popular districts of Paris, home of the left, and talk of a coup d'état was in the air. The government took resolute action, temporarily suppressing the League of Patriots and prosecuting some of its leaders. Boulanger fled abroad, revealing himself to be a paper tiger, and his movement soon collapsed.[14]

Despite the military defeat of 1870 and the economic recession of the following decade, French society was not so broadly frustrated and unsuccessful. France had rebounded from military defeat to spectacular success in the new imperialism and now had the second largest new empire in the world. The economy was expanding, albeit rather slowly, and generally prosperous. French society was better balanced than that of either Germany or England, with a large, stable rural population, a broad middle class and wide diffusion of property, and a limited industrial proletariat. The democratic republic had thus become stabilized, was generally accepted, and, finally, took resolute, even somewhat harsh, action against its ultranationalist enemies. Though the League of Patriots and Boulangism incorporated some of the concepts of fascism, Boulangism was not a true fascist-type movement, and France was not suffering from a genuine "prefascist crisis" in the 1880s. It was too stable, prosperous, and successful to fall prey to such temptations. Nonetheless, the ideas to some extent pioneered by Déroulède and the Boulangists would not disappear in France, for Paris was more nearly the prime center of the fin de siècle crisis than any other city, save Vienna, and the new doctrines of antirationalism and antipositivism would continue to find enthusiastic expression.

A more serious crisis was touched off by the celebrated Dreyfus Affair of

14. Standard works are A. Dansette, *Le Boulangisme* (Paris, 1947), and F. H. Seager, *The Boulanger Affair* (Ithaca, 1969). William D. Irvine, in *The Boulanger Affair Reconsidered* (New York, 1989), emphasizes the crucial role of monarchist support and of monarchist and other conservative voters in the provinces. See also M. Burns, *Rural Society and French Politics: Boulangism and the Dreyfus Affair, 1866–1900* (Princeton, 1984), and P. H. Hutton, "Popular Boulangism and the Advent of Mass Politics in France, 1886–1890," *JCH* 11:1 (Jan. 1976): 85–106; on the League, see P. M. Rutkoff, *Revanche and Revisionism: The Ligue des Patriotes and the Origins of the Radical Right in France, 1882–1900* (Athens, Ga., 1981).

1898–1900, which polarized French political society between right and left, between nationalists and progressives, between anti-Semites and partisans of republican justice. The nominal issue—false prosecution and imprisonment for treason of a Jewish staff officer—became secondary to the broader dimensions of the crisis, which would determine whether France was to be democratic and egalitarian or chauvinist and elitist. The victory of the Dreyfusard liberals determined the course of French politics for the next decade and guaranteed much more thoroughly than the collapse of Boulanger the defeat of a more authoritarian nationalism.

The Dreyfus Affair also revealed a political anti-Semitism more active in France than almost anywhere else in Europe at that moment, led by Edouard Drumont, whose *La France juive* (Jewish France, 1886) sold a million copies and, along with many other publications, made him the most popular anti-Semitic writer in Europe. His Anti-Semitic League of France (1889–1902) gained ten thousand members and won local elections in Constantine and Algiers.[15] The winners in Algiers organized a veritable pogrom in 1897 that killed several Jews and wounded a hundred, though the French government soon removed its leader from office. The League returned four deputies from Algeria in the national elections of 1898, and in the following year Déroulède tried to incite a coup d'état, provoking his banishment from France.[16] The victory of the Dreyfusards and the liberalization of the republic decisively defeated these forces, sending them into irreversible decline.

Emergence of French National Socialism

The first active proponent of a national socialism in France was a quixotic adventurer, the Marquis de Morès, sometime ranch-owning neighbor of Theodore Roosevelt in the Dakota Territory of the 1880s. Returning to Paris, he founded a radical circle, which for want of a better title was called Morès et Ses Amis (Morès and His Friends). This group attempted to combine extreme nationalism with limited economic socialism, racism, and direct action. It also organized a strong-arm group for street battle, not being reluctant to engage in extreme violence and even killing. Morès also attempted to employ racist anti-Semitism as a means of popular mobilization but met little success. He was later killed on an expedition to the Sahara.[17]

Morès did not, however, employ the specific label of national socialism, a

15. M. Winock, *Edouard Drumont et Cie* (Paris, 1982); F. Busi, *The Pope of Antisemitism: The Career and Legacy of Edouard-Adolphe Drumont* (Lanham, Md., 1986).

16. See A. Chebel d'Appollonia, *L'extrême-droite en France de Maurras à Le Pen* (Brussels, 1988), 127–41.

17. D. J. Tweton, *The Marquis de Morès* (Fargo, N.Dak., 1972); R. F. Byrnes, "Morès, the First Nationalist Socialist," *Review of Politics* 12:3 (July 1950): 341–62.

concept introduced under the phrase "socialist nationalism" by Maurice Barrès in the electoral campaign of 1898. Barrès's own career provided a clear literary reflection of fin de siècle cultural crisis. Once an ivory-tower aesthete whose first novels were devoted to *le culte du moi* (the cult of myself), he soon sought to overcome the isolation and sterility of mere aestheticism and found his new identity in the national collectivity, creating a new series of *romans de l'énergie nationale* (novels of national energy). Barrès developed a mystique of *la terre et les morts* (the national soil and the dead) that was derived in considerable measure from Déroulède's doctrines, and he tried to combine the search for energy and a vital style of life with national rootedness and a sort of Darwinian racism. His national socialism stressed cross-class interests, while his political and cultural philosophy relied on intuition and emotion. Barrès vigorously espoused a racial anti-Semitism, whose mobilizing potential he grasped. He also propounded hero worship and charismatic leadership, and yet despite his effort to stimulate a new semirevolutionary kind of nationalism, Barrès never fully overcame a lingering conservatism. He later lapsed into cultural traditionalism and reconciled himself to parliamentary conservatism, but in his radical period he contributed significantly to the concepts of an integral and extremist nationalism and had been among the first to pay lip service to a kind of national socialism. Barrès had helped to win over a sector of the activist intelligentsia to nationalism and, though not a personal political success, had made important contributions to the nationalist revival in Paris in the generation before 1914.[18]

Somewhat more successful in establishing contact with workers was a parallel effort to create an ultranationalist trade union movement commonly known as Les Jaunes (The Yellows), from the color of paper placed in windows broken by their enemies soon after the start of the movement. Les Jaunes succeeded in establishing a national federation that at one point boasted nearly a hundred thousand members. Their chief leader, François Biétry, then initiated a French National Socialist Party in 1903, only five years after the first official national socialist party in Europe had been founded in Bohemia. Biétry's party was a mere flash in the pan, collapsing before the end of the year owing to lack of funds, though the Jaune trade union movement survived until 1910.[19]

18. There are three biographies: Z. Sternhell, *Maurice Barrès et le nationalisme français* (Paris, 1972); R. Soucy, *Fascism in France: The Case of Maurice Barrès* (Berkeley, 1972); and C. S. Doty, *From Cultural Rebellion to Counterrevolution: The Politics of Maurice Barrès* (Athens, Ohio, 1976). See also M. Curtis, *Three against the Third Republic: Sorel, Barrès, and Maurras* (Princeton, 1959).

On the *réveil national*, see E. Weber, *The Nationalist Revival in France, 1905–1914* (Berkeley, 1959), and R. Tombs, *Nationhood and Nationalism in France: From Boulangism to the Great War, 1889–1919* (New York, 1992).

19. Sternhell, *Droite révolutionnaire* 245–317; G. L. Mosse, "The French Right and the Working Classes: Les Jaunes," *JCH* 7:3–4 (July–Oct. 1972): 185–208; E. Weber, "National-

Action Française

The only one of the new authoritarian nationalist organizations in France to survive until World War I and beyond was the most right-wing, the neomonarchist
Action Française. Founded in 1899 and publishing a daily newspaper of the
same name as the group from 1908, Action Française became the most enduring organization of the extreme right. Though it never generated much popular
support, it established a secure elitist position because of the high literary
quality of its publications, coated in vitriol though they were. Its core principles
of legitimist monarchy and corporate representation under a neotraditionalist
state were not novelties, having formed part of the basis for traditionalism in
the past century.

The uniqueness of Action Française lay in its achieving a new synthesis of
all the nineteenth-century traditionalist ideas and combining them with a radical nationalism, thus converting monarchism from a dynastic principle into a
complete system of "integral nationalism," authoritarian, anti-Semitic, exclusivist, and intolerant. This rested not merely or even primarily on the traditional
patrimonial kingdom but on the nation as an organic whole, of which the monarchy was head. Charles Maurras and the other ideologues of the movement
thereby achieved a more sophisticated monarchist nationalism. Their culti-
vation of style and aesthetics, combined with a seemingly up-to-date, often
deftly rendered elitist propaganda of the most extreme new tones, made Action
Française—much more than any of the preceding groups—*the* nationalist party
of early twentieth-century France. Its band of street activists—Les Camelots
du Roi (Streethawkers or Vendors of the King)—sold publications and engaged
in violent demonstrations and brawls with liberals and leftists. This group followed in the footsteps of Morès and has been called the first prefascist "shirt
movement" of radical nationalism.

Ernst Nolte has even seen in Action Française the "beginning of fascism,"
though in fact it became the prototypical movement of the monarchist radical
right of the early twentieth century.[20] Action Française never aspired to develop a full "movement militia" in the later style of fascism and Nazism—
which were far removed from its literary and upper-class elitist style—just as
it never attempted to become a full-scale, organized political party. Political
gangs or militias were not unprecedented in southern Europe. Only after 1918

---

ism, Socialism and National-Socialism in France," *French Historical Studies* 2:3 (Spring 1962):
273–307.

20. According to Nolte, "the Action Française was the first political grouping of any influence or intellectual status to bear unmistakably fascist traits. . . . In spite of all its doctrinal rigidity,
the system of Maurras's ideas is of an extent, acuteness, and depth without parallel in Germany
and Italy of that time." E. Nolte, *Three Faces of Fascism* (New York, 1966), 25–26.

were they transformed into mass militias, and that process was not initiated by the ultra-right-wing Action Française.

So extreme a movement was rejected both by the pretender to the throne and later—despite the group's official support of Catholicism—by the papacy, which excommunicated Maurras in 1927. The movement's approach to religion was in fact utilitarian and theologically skeptical, yet another way in which Action Française differed from traditional monarchists. Though formally a rationalist, Maurras himself was more interested in spiritualism and magic than in Christian theology.

The economic program of Action Française was derived in large measure from the nineteenth-century corporatist doctrines of René de la Tour du Pin and was not worked out in detail until the 1920s. Action Française could never have been called a modernizing nationalist movement. Its chief historian, Eugen Weber, has judged that the function of Action Française was "to furnish the right with an ideology with which it could mask its lack of positive program or purpose in what was largely an obstinate—and often effective—holding action against change." [21] Though some effort was briefly made to consider cooperation with revolutionary syndicalists against the centralized republican state, [22] the rigid rightist confines of the movement eventually prompted many activist younger members to leave in search of more radical and modernizing doctrines being developed in imitation of Italian Fascism. Withal, Action Française had more than a little influence on early twentieth-century French culture and survived politically into World War II.

GERMANY AND AUSTRIA

Nationalism was slower to develop in Germany, emerging in reaction to the French Revolution and Napoleonic imperialism. Though early nineteenth-century German nationalism sometimes participated in the broader European trend of "liberal nationalism," the unification drive of the liberals was defeated in 1848–49, so that subsequently Germany was unified by Prussian diplomacy and military force. Moreover, throughout the history of German nationalism ran a strain that emphasized a "German revolution" of the nation that would achieve a profound cultural transformation whose revolutionary implications went beyond mere nationalism. Count Otto von Bismarck, the unifier who presided over German affairs from 1870 to 1890, distrusted nationalism and

21. E. Weber, *Action Française* (Stanford, 1962), 530. See also E. R. Tannenbaum, *Action Française* (New York, 1962); S. M. Osgood, *French Royalism since 1870* (The Hague, 1970); M. Sutton, *Nationalism, Positivism, and Catholicism: The Politics of Charles Maurras and French Catholics, 1890–1914* (New York, 1982); and B. Renouvin, *Charles Maurras, l'Action Française et la question sociale* (Paris, 1982).

22. P. Masgaj, *Action Française and Revolutionary Syndicalism* (Chapel Hill, 1979).

imperialism for both their liberal and their radical implications. Germany was a latecomer among major powers and only entered imperial competition in the late 1880s, failing to achieve an overseas empire equivalent to that of most western European states. This, together with Germany's partial diplomatic isolation, produced increasing resentment among the growing numbers of nationalists who looked for Germany's "place in the sun," or at least a place equivalent to that of Britain, France, and Russia.

During the 1880s and 1890s nationalism grew rapidly in German society, producing a plethora of new voluntary associations, such as the Pan-German League, the Army League, the Navy League, the German Union of the Eastern Marches, the Society for Germandom Abroad, and the German Colonial Society. Moreover German nationalism grew increasingly militant and potentially aggressive around the turn of the century, as the more extreme nationalist sectors championed authoritarian and racist policies.

Quick and decisive victory in the Franco-Prussian War of 1870 had established Germany as potentially the leading military power in the world. Conversely, political liberalism in Germany was somewhat weak, and under its unified political system the government remained partially autocratic, responsible on most issues to the Kaiser and not to the parliament. Liberalism itself seemed different in Germany, because moderate liberals and conservatives tended to think of liberal government not so much as a system for guaranteeing individual freedom and civil rights as in England and France, but for creating a *Rechtsstaat*—a modern, civilized, progressive "state of reason." In the concept of the *Rechtsstaat*, the rights of the collectivity and the state took precedence over the "mere" rights of liberals. The state, based on modern civilized principles, would use its authority to guide civil society and to provide opportunity for individual emancipation within its own framework of laws and entitlements. True freedom and emancipation would thus be found within an enlightened plan of responsibility, constraints, and obedience to the laws of the state.[23]

The Question of Germany's *Sonderweg* and the Development of "Pre-Nazism"

Owing to the relative weakness of German liberalism and the increasing prominence of nationalism and militarism in Germany even before World War I, the concept developed after 1945 that modern German history had followed a "special path" (*Sonderweg*), distinct from the course of development in the rest of liberal democratic northwestern Europe and the north Atlantic. Before then, anti-Nazi polemicists during World War II had argued that much of modern German history had followed a clear "pre-Nazi" routing even before Hitler.

23. L. Krieger, *The German Idea of Freedom* (Chicago, 1957), 252–61.

In support of the latter contention, at least ten developments might be cited: the statist tradition of Prussia, carried over into unified Germany;[24] the strength of Prussian-German militarism; the aforementioned limitations of German liberalism; the school of statist "German economics"; nineteenth-century German doctrines of "revolutionary nationalism"; the expansion of nationalism and the nationalist leagues in the late nineteenth century; the vogue of *völkisch* culture; the growth of racial thinking in the late nineteenth century; the relative rise of racial anti-Semitism before World War I; and the general influence of romantic, mystical, and idealist thought in modern Germany, followed by the effects of the cultural crisis of the fin de siècle.

This is a weighty bill of particulars, yet specialists in German history both at home and abroad have tended to question the decisiveness of the German *Sonderweg*. It is an obvious truism that all national histories are unique. Liberal England differed profoundly from generally liberal France, and the Sweden that became social democratic was quite distinct from both. Thus in a general sense there is no question that a German *Sonderweg* existed, just as different kinds of "special paths" existed for France, Spain, Russia, and all other countries.

The question rather is whether or not modern Germany can be considered to have been *primarily* different from most western European countries, and here the more recent tendency has been to respond in the negative.[25] The general course of modern German history before 1933 followed all the classic modern Western trends: capitalism, industrialism, urbanization, science and technology, modern art and culture, expanding education, a growing middle class, and also increasing liberalism and democracy. Moreover, critiques of German exceptionalism have tended to assume that there was a "standard path" toward modernization and democracy, although the courses of England and France differed profoundly from each other, with France having originated nearly all the modern antidemocratic ideas and forms. Thus we may conclude

24. For a relatively sober description of the authoritarian aspects, see B. Chapman, *Police State* (London, 1970).

25. The classic critique of the *Sonderweg* thesis is D. Blackbourn and G. Eley, *The Peculiarities of German History* (Oxford, 1984). See also R. J. Evans, *Rethinking German History: Nineteenth Century Germany and the Origins of the Third Reich* (London, 1987), and, for balanced summaries, R. G. Moeller, "The Kaiserreich Recast? Continuity and Change in Modern German History," *Journal of Social History* 17 (1984): 442–50, and J. Kocka, "German History before Hitler: The Debate about the German *Sonderweg*," *JCH* 23:1 (Jan. 1988): 3–16. Slightly different perspectives may be found in Kocka's edited volumes *Bürgertum im 19. Jahrhundert: Deutschland im europäischen Vergleich*, 3 vols. (Munich, 1990), and the brief volume 4 of his *Bildungsbürgertum im 19. Jahrhundert* (Stuttgart, 1990), dealing with the politics of the "cultural bourgeoisie."

For historic French perceptions of modern Germany, see J.-M. Carré, *Les écrivains français et le mirage allemand (1800–1940)* (Paris, 1947); Digeon, *Crise allemande;* and Jörg von Uthman, *Le diable est-il Allemand? Deux-cent ans de préjugés franco-allemands* (Paris, 1984).

that absolute insistence on German exceptionalism will create a distorted focus, and that the comparison between German history and that of the northwestern European countries is extremely complex and requires careful nuance. It is a mistake to read German history teleologically backward from 1933, for in fact it revealed broad potential for any one of several courses of development or outcomes.

With this understanding, we may proceed with a brief survey of certain extreme nationalist tendencies in late nineteenth-century Germany. This should be accompanied by the recognition that some of these forces were no stronger or weaker than in a few other countries, and even collectively they lacked the power absolutely to determine the future course of German development in the twentieth century.

The German Philosophy of Revolution and Nationalism

Beginning in the late eighteenth century, some of the leading thinkers and philosophers in Germany conceived of a special modern mission for German culture—and usually for German institutions and the German nation— to transform modern life and culture, creating new dimensions of liberation, freedom, and achievement. This tendency began with intellectuals such as Kant and Humboldt even before the French Revolution, then took a sharply nationalist turn with Fichte after 1800. The philosopher Hegel continued one variant, while the Young Hegelians, led ultimately by Karl Marx, moved it sharply to the left, in the direction of class revolution and socialism, though still with a major role to be played by Germany, in this case in a world socialist revolution.[26] The emphasis on a special German revolution was sustained and intensified during the second half of the nineteenth century by many cultural spokesmen and writers, though the concept increasingly narrowed, focusing more exclusively on German nationalism. Liberation and freedom in the German philosophy increasingly rarely meant individualism and civil liberties in the English or French senses, while doctrines of nationalism moved toward the right and toward authoritarian politics. German philosophy had always been mildly anti-Jewish, but by the later nineteenth century it often embraced mystical concepts of Nordic racism and virulent anti-Semitism, though most of German society did not politically endorse such ideas as late as 1900 or 1910.[27]

26. For a recent discussion of the orientation of German thought toward a romantic messianism, see Greenfeld, *Nationalism* 322–95.

27. The development of anti-Semitism in German doctrines of revolution and nationalism is treated in P. L. Rose, *Revolutionary Antisemitism in Germany from Kant to Wagner* (Princeton, 1990).

The Pervasiveness of German *Völkisch* Thought and Culture

It is generally agreed that the culture of romanticism and of philosophical idealism had a deeper, longer-lasting effect in Germany than elsewhere. Romanticism by definition discouraged rationalism and analysis in favor of emotion and idealism. It sought hidden and underlying meanings and often emphasized association with tradition and the culture of the past. In Germany romantic attitudes and nationalist feeling soon intersected to create a school of popular Germanist thought and art, developing what was called *völkisch* culture. The term *völkisch* is derived from *das Volk* (the people) and in the simplest sense refers to cultural and philosophical populism. Populist thinking and tendencies are widespread in the modern world, found in such distinct locales as eastern Europe and North and South America. In eastern Europe, however, populism was almost exclusively oriented toward the traditional peasantry, while in the Western Hemisphere the term is associated with cross-class politics, often progressive or democratic in hue. German *völkisch* culture was distinct from either of these kinds and probably is best defined as "ethnic-nationalist culture."

Romantic nationalism originally held that each true language-nation possessed an immortal and distinctive culture of deep significance, inimitable elsewhere. German nationalist romantics derived from this orientation the concept of a distinct Germanic culture and life totally unique and set apart from all other cultures, which bore unique truths and values for German people and which, if properly developed, would raise Germany to eminence among the nations.

Völkisch thought was mystical in tone, embracing at best a kind of highly abstract rationalism divorced from analytic thinking. It was ontologically grounded in a concept of nature which flowed from a "higher reality" of the cosmos to man, becoming crystallized in the landscape, environment, and life of the people. Such an attitude rejected Christianity in favor of a pantheistic sense of the cosmos and of nature, credited with creating special conditions and unique human potential. The very landscape of Germany supposedly elicited superior cultural characteristics. The *Volk* thus became the intermediary and expression of a transcendental essence and was the basis of all that was good in Germany or any higher good that might be developed. For Germans to be truly free and capable of superior achievement, life and thought had to be thoroughly grounded in the *Volk* and purged of extraneous and corrupting influences. The latter category included most of the effects of modernization, such as urbanization, industrialization, materialism, mere scientism, class differentiation and conflict, and hedonistic individualism. Germany could be truly liberated and capable of realizing its greater mission only by overcoming these pernicious effects and by returning as much as possible to the soil. *Völkisch* culture thus preached a kind of withdrawal into nature, cultural purification, and social unity. The *völkisch* goal became the creation of an "organic" society, as harmoniously interrelated as pure nature was thought to be. The true German "producing" middle class and above all farmers, rooted in the soil, were idealized, just as urbanization and cosmopolitanism were abhorred.

Völkisch ideas were propagated by scores of writers and artists. They were reflected in the work of leading historians such as Heinrich von Treitschke and Heinrich von Sybel, especially in the latter's *Die Deutschen bei ihrem Eintritt in die Geschichte* (The Germans at Their Entry into History, 1863). The full definition of *völkisch* ideology was then completed by the *völkisch* philosophers Paul de Lagarde and Julius Langbehn, writing in the final quarter of the century.

Thus a culture that was at most only "vaguely relevant" to modern problems became one of the most pervasive influences in middle-class society, and Germany, home of the most dynamic science and industry in Europe, proved to be deeply divided and ambivalent in much of its thought and feeling.[28] Notions somewhat similar to *völkisch* attitudes might be found in varying degrees or formulations in nearly all countries undergoing the changes associated with modernization, but only in Germany did *völkisch* culture achieve a broad following both among part of the intelligentsia and the middle classes. By 1900 *völkisch* concepts had become a relatively formalized ideology, spread by publishing houses, numerous writers and artists, many professors, and thousands of schoolteachers. It seems to have become predominant among teachers and was preached in the classroom, and it also permeated the quasirebels of the organized youth movement that had sixty thousand members—often the elite of middle- and upper-middle-class youth—by 1914.[29] Though *völkisch* culture was not crystallized in any major political party or movement, it had become probably the principal cultural base of German nationalism and drew broad allegiance among the middle classes in particular.

The Racist and Authoritarian Radical Right

During the 1870s, the first decade of united Germany, the leading nationalist group and the largest political party generally was the National Liberals,

---

28. G. L. Mosse, *The Crisis of German Ideology: Intellectual Origins of the Third Reich* (New York, 1964), 9. This is the best introduction to *völkisch* culture in Germany. See also F. Stern, *The Politics of Cultural Despair* (Berkeley, 1961), and W. D. Smith, *Politics and the Sciences of Culture in Germany, 1840–1920* (Oxford, 1991).

Even the high German cultural concept of *Bildung* (formation or education) was based on the goal of developing the internal form already inherent in the individual. This was different from, for example, the liberal arts educational theories elsewhere.

29. W. Laqueur, *Young Germany* (New York, 1962).

indicating the tenor of most German nationalism during those years. Conservatives, by comparison, were more lukewarm in their nationalism, and extreme conservatives were often very skeptical of the new order in Germany.

The new Germany seemed little different from most other western European countries, with its largest parliamentary group a liberal party, with a rapidly expanding educational and industrial system, with a rapidly shrinking conservative rural base and a growing urban population, with a rapid expansion of blue-collar workers and also of the middle classes. Beginning in the 1890s, however, and increasingly to 1914, the political party structure began to fragment and to shift to the left. The established parties were unsuccessful in capturing many votes of workers, so that the only political party which grew rapidly after 1890 was the Socialist Party. By 1912 the Socialists had won a third of the popular vote and more than a quarter of all seats in the Reichstag (Parliament). The only other party to grow at all was that of the middle-class left liberals, who reorganized as the Progressive Party in 1910. By contrast, the conservative groups declined greatly, as did the National Liberals. Among the moderate and conservative parties, only the Catholic Center Party and the small groups representing the national ethnic minorities maintained steady support.

In this society in rapid change—being transformed at a more rapid pace than any other large society in Europe—one sector of the conservatives moved to a position on the radical right from the 1890s on. The Bund der Landwirte (Landowners' League), particularly, a bastion of social and political conservatism, adopted a program of authoritarian nationalism which promoted militarism and imperialism as well. It advocated a corporative system of representation, made attempts at demagogic mass mobilization, and espoused political racism and anti-Semitism. Part of the regular Conservative Party supported these doctrines, as did much of the militant Pan-German League, and some of these attitudes could also be found in the other *nationale Verbände* (nationalist leagues). Interest in corporative systems of representation grew steadily among conservatives.[30]

Nonetheless, in the years before 1914 the authoritarian nationalist radical right was unable to develop a major organized force. The radical right dominated only a minority of conservatives and rightists, while the rightists even in general held less than 20 percent of all seats in the Reichstag—scarcely more than the left. The leftist superiority in the popular vote was even greater. Liberal and moderately liberal groups still held nearly 40 percent of the par-

---

30. The principal treatment of the agrarian radical right will be found in the works of Hans-Jürgen Puhle: *Agrarische Interessenpolitik und preussischer Konservatismus im wilhelmischen Reich, 1893–1914* (Bonn, 1975); *Von der Agrarkrise zum Präfaschismus* (Wiesbaden, 1972); and "Radikalisierung und Wandel des deutschen Konservatismus vor dem ersten Weltkrieg," in *Deutsche Parteien vor 1918*, ed. G. Ritter (Cologne, 1973), 165–86.

liamentary seats. Though the German government itself was not as liberal and representative as other systems in northern and western Europe—since the government was responsible to the Kaiser rather than to the Reichstag, and suffrage for local elections was generally unequal and undemocratic—German civic life remained predominantly liberal. Despite the divisions between moderate liberals and the left, the two sectors together garnered more than 80 percent of the votes and four of every five seats in the Reichstag.[31]

The German School of Economics

A relatively unique feature of German thought was the existence of a distinct "German school" of economics, sometimes also called the historical, romantic, or statist school. It stressed the need for an organic, partially authoritarian state system to intervene directly in economics, promoting development and regulating malfunctions, in opposition to the prevailing nineteenth-century western Europe doctrines of laissez-faire individualism. This was originated by the philosopher J. G. Fichte, often considered the father of German nationalism, in his *Der geschlossene Handelstaat* (The Closed Mercantile State, 1800). He was followed by other theorists, such as the right-wing romantic Adam Müller and most notably Friedrich List, whose *Das nationale System der politischen Okonomie* (The National System of Political Economics, 1841) became the leading theoretical statement, yoking national economics to a new concept of a "pan-continental economy" led by Germany.

List was followed by the "historical school" proper, active for the remainder of the nineteenth century. Theorists of the historical school emphasized the uniqueness and the historical facts of German development, insisting that economic policy not follow universal doctrines but be tailored specifically to German needs. They developed an organic concept of *Volkswirtschaft* (a people's or national economy). Adolf Wagner, a leading later practitioner of this school, defined the term *state socialism* for comprehensive state intervention in and regulation of the economy.

From the unification of Germany in 1871, state policy was never so fully liberal as in England, France, or the west of western Europe. The government quickly nationalized the rail system and municipalized utilities and services at the local level, while expanding to a much lesser degree into mining and in-

31. G. Eley, *Reshaping the German Right* (New Haven, 1980), is the most important study of the German right as a whole in this period. See also Eley's *From Unification to Nazism* (Boston, 1986), and J. N. Retallack, *Notables of the Right: The Conservative Party and Political Mobilization in Germany, 1876–1914* (Boston, 1988). F. Coetzee and M. Shevin Coetzee, in "Rethinking the Radical Right in Germany and Britain before 1914," *JCH* 21:4 (Oct. 1986): 515–38, stress the latter's relative weakness. For German imperialist doctrine in this period, see W. D. Smith, *The Intellectual Origins of Nazi Imperialism* (New York, 1986).

dustry. Thus the leading economic historian Gustav Stolper would describe the German economy as "an economic system very different from the so-called classical liberal system. . . . Even in its resplendent time German capitalism showed a generous admixture of state and association control of business."[32] No pure model of laissez-faire ever existed, and the French government more than the British took measures to encourage and regulate economic activity,[33] but the degree of direct ownership and intervention of the government in Germany always set the German model somewhat apart from more liberal western Europe, buttressed further by a long line of nationalist theorists going back to 1800.

Origins of German and Austrian National Socialism

A number of small groups emerged in imperial Germany and Austria that attempted to combine nationalism with semicollectivism, corporatist or statist economics, and broad social appeals to workers, though none achieved any electoral or political success for more than a fleeting moment. The first of these was the Christian Social Workers Party, founded in Berlin in 1878 by a Protestant minister, Adolf Stöcker. It sought a "Christian state" that would more strongly regulate the economy, and it soon adopted the banner of anti-Semitism, a term apparently coined by the anti-Jewish writer Wilhelm Marr in the 1860s.

As we have seen, a certain anti-Jewish strain was present in German nationalist thought from the beginning, but this was comparatively muted in the more liberal nationalism of the early and mid–nineteenth century. In 1871 the Jewish minority in Germany amounted to 1.25 percent of the total population. This figure had dropped to 0.95 percent by 1910 because of a low birthrate. The figures for Berlin were 5.1 percent in 1895 and 4.4 percent in 1910. In some parts of the Austro-Hungarian Empire the Jewish minority was larger: the Jewish population of Vienna amounted to 12.0 percent in 1890 and to 8.6 percent in 1910.[34] The Jewish population in German-speaking areas was overwhelmingly middle class, concentrated in such businesses as finance and commerce (though not industry), the professions, and later in the arts and entertainment. In all these areas, the percentage of Jewish businessmen and professionals was much higher than that of the small Jewish minority of the total population.

Increasing animus was directed against Jews by the more extreme nation-

<hr />

32. G. Stolper, *The German Economy, 1870–1940* (New York, 1940), 92. The best succinct summary of the German school will be found in A. Barkai, *Nazi Economics* (New Haven, 1990), 71–105.

33. S. B. Clough, *France: A History of National Economics* (New York, 1964).

34. These statistics are from P. Pulzer, *The Rise of Political Anti-Semitism in Germany and Austria* (Cambridge, 1988), 8–12.

alists because of their distinct religious identity (though German and Austrian Jewish society was strongly secular and often not religiously observant) and even more because they were the only ethnic group in Germany that had both a distinct identity and elite status in finance, commerce, the professions, and culture. Traditional religious anti-Jewishness identified the Jews as uniquely perverse and iniquitous because they rejected Christianity. The new anti-Semitism of the nineteenth century stigmatized Jews in modern secular terms as uniquely perverse and iniquitous because of their supposed extreme materialism and supposed refusal to merge completely with the *Volk,* as well as their alleged rejection of fraternity and "love." Such supposed differences were increasingly defined in racial terms, so that by the close of the century most anti-Semitism in the German-speaking world was racial in doctrine.

Despite the failure of Stöcker's group, by the early 1890s three more small anti-Semitic national socialist parties had been formed, the Anti-Semitic German Social Party, the Anti-Semitic People's Party, and the Peasant League in Hesse. It was at this point that such doctrines began to draw support from the Bund der Landwirte, and in the Reichstag elections of 1893 official anti-Semitic candidates momentarily won nearly 3 percent of the vote and with allies briefly formed a bloc of eleven deputies. The Peasant League was able to organize a number of cooperatives under a national socialist banner but virtually went bankrupt in 1894. The main sector of racial national socialist anti-Semites came together that year to form a small new German Social Reform Party but was unable to repeat the modest success of 1893. Their doctrines were overwhelmingly rejected by workers and did not appeal to middle-class propriety. The only success of racial anti-Semitism, such as it was, was to gain a growing acceptance among certain sectors of the Conservative Party.[35]

In Austria liberalism was considerably weaker than in Germany. Restricted primarily to Vienna and a few of the other larger cities, it was supported especially by the civil service and the wealthier middle classes (and especially by Jewish business and professional men). Austria remained proportionately more agrarian than Germany and thus socially more conservative, leaving the basis of liberalism inevitably weaker.

With the rise of nationalist movements throughout the multinational Austro-Hungarian Empire, it was almost inevitable that the German-speaking population of Austria would respond in kind. This took the form not of an Austrian German–speaking nationalism for Austrians only, but of pan-Germanism, founded by the aristocratic Georg von Schönerer, formerly a liberal, who organized a tiny pan-German Nationalist Party in 1879, superseded by an

---

35. On the failure of the radical anti-Semite parties, see, in addition to Pulzer's *Rise of Political Antisemitism,* R. S. Levy, *The Downfall of the Anti-Semitic Political Parties in Imperial Germany* (New Haven, 1975), and R. Manning, *Rehearsal for Destruction* (New York, 1967).

equally small German Nationalist League. Schönerer's movement was important not because of any political success but because of the ideological precedents which it created. It preached a radical pan-German nationalism that was militaristic and imperialistic, anti-Slavic and anti-Jewish. It differed from other rightist groups in its vigorous espousal of German social egalitarianism, equal voting rights, and extensive social reforms. The impact of Schönerer's "Linz Program" of 1882 on the subsequent politics of both radical nationalism and social progressivism was considerable. Thus, despite the failure of his initial movement, Schönerer is counted among the fathers of central European national socialism. At that time, however, his shrill, radical, and secular tone was unattractive to Austrian society, and his organization was dissolved in 1889.[36]

The main political expression of anti-Semitism would be found in Austria not in a national socialist group but in the populist and reformist Catholic Christian Social Party, which originated in 1889.[37] Within less than a decade it became the most popular force in Vienna under its charismatic leader, Karl Lueger. Catholic and culturally conservative, the Christian Socials advocated practical economic reforms and drew strong support from the lower middle and lower classes. Their platform was not strictly racist but was strongly anti-Jewish, demanding a restriction of Jewish immigration and activities in Austria. Lueger's demagogy was calculated above all for electoral purposes; he seems to have felt little personal animus toward Jews.[38]

Aside from the electoral dominance of the Christian Social Party in Vienna, none of the anti-Semitic organizations enjoyed much electoral success. Yet though the extremist groups almost without exception failed—and indeed provoked something of a backlash, particularly in Germany, against anti-Semitism—anti-Semitic ideas became more widely disseminated after 1890 than ever before. Though extreme anti-Semitism was almost universally rejected, moderate anti-Semitic notions were in some respects becoming more acceptable. One of the more influential currents of racist anti-Semitism was that propagated in Vienna after 1900 by Guido von List and the defrocked monk Jörg Lanz von Liebenfels, who developed the occult doctrine of "Ariosophy," the supposed secret Arian racial wisdom that had once guaranteed strength, purity, and racial superiority in ancient times but had been lost and/

---

36. A. G. Whiteside, *The Socialism of Fools* (Berkeley, 1975). W. J. McGrath, in *Dionysian Art and Populist Politics in Austria* (New Haven, 1974), emphasizes the attempt to use art, music, and theatrical forms in politics to influence mass psychology and emotions.

37. J. W. Boyer, *Political Radicalism in Late Imperial Vienna: Origins of the Christian Social Movement, 1848–1897* (Chicago, 1981).

38. R. S. Geehr, *Karl Lueger* (Detroit, 1990). More broadly, for the entire historical spectrum of anti-Semitism in Austria, see B. F. Pauley, *From Prejudice to Persecution: A History of Austrian Anti-Semitism* (Chapel Hill, 1992).

or contaminated by a conspiracy of racial inferiors and egalitarians. The rule of a race of ethnically pure Aryan supermen could be achieved on the basis of occult and mystical racial Aryan doctrines and secret knowledge and practices, termed Ariosophy, with occult symbols and rituals and hidden lore.[39] This formed the foundation of the shrill Ostara Society, which preached extreme Nordic racism, anti-Semitism, and cultural revolution, buttressed by sun worship and forms of the occult. Before 1913 the young Adolf Hitler in Vienna was apparently an assiduous reader of the Ostara Society's publications.[40]

The only Germanic national socialist party to survive into and beyond World War I was the German Workers Party (DAP) founded among German workers in Austrian Bohemia (now the Czech Republic) in 1904. Germans constituted only a sizable minority among the Czech population of greater Bohemia, and the DAP was designed to appeal on both nationalist and social lines to German workers, who sometimes faced ethnic discrimination. Though strongly nationalist, it was not at first racist, imperialist, or militaristic, and it advocated that standing armies be replaced with national militias. It called for the democratization of political and social institutions, and its national socialism sought the nationalization of big business enterprises. It differed from Marxist socialism in advocating a common economic policy to benefit all the working and producing sectors of national society, whether farmer, worker, lower-middle, or middle-middle class, pressing for a mixed socialism within the existing framework of German-speaking society.[41]

The original German-Bohemian national socialism "was in essence a radical democratic movement."[42] By 1913, though, the DAP had become seriously infected with pan-German racialism and imperialism. It adopted anti-Semitism and became increasingly shrill and bellicose. By the end of World War I it expanded into a German National Socialist Workers Party (DNSAP) for German-speaking workers in both Bohemia and Austria proper, anticipating with but a slight transposition of words the name of the Nazi Party (NSDAP) organized in Munich two years later. The DNSAP retained its cross-class orientation and program of partial socialism as a "labor association of all producers" (*Gewerk-*

---

39. The best introduction is N. Goodrick-Clarke, *The Occult Roots of Nazism: Secret Aryan Cults and Their Influence on Nazi Ideology. The Ariosophists of Austria and Germany, 1890–1935* (London, 1985).

40. W. Dahm, *Der Mann der Hitler die Ideen gab* (Munich, 1958).

41. Even earlier, a Czech National Socialist Party had been formed in 1898 as a democratic, radically reformist, and socially progressive party for Czech-speaking workers. The German and Czech parties largely ignored each other, a main goal of the former being the transformation of Austria into a *völkisch* democratic German state. The Czech movement also survived World War I and later played a not unimportant role in the political system of the new democratic state of Czechoslovakia.

42. The principal study asserts this: A. G. Whiteside, *Austrian National Socialism before 1918* (The Hague, 1962), 112.

schaft aller Schaffenden). It soon cooperated with the nascent Nazi movement across the German frontier, and part of the DNSAP became the nucleus of the subsequent Austrian Nazi Party.

ITALY

Like Germany, Japan, Hungary, and Romania, Italy was one of the new nations of the 1860s and 1870s. The "Meiji restoration" created a modern state in Japan after 1867, the *Ausgleich* that restored the kingdom of Hungary occurred in the same year, Germany was unified in 1871, and the full independence and sovereignty of Romania was recognized in 1878. Though most of Italy was unified under the constitutional monarchy of the Piedmontese dynasty in 1860, the situation of the united Italy differed considerably from that of Germany. Whereas Germany soon developed the second strongest industrial and scientific complex on the globe, Italy had an underdeveloped southern European agrarian economy with a largely illiterate population. Whereas Germany was immediately recognized as the strongest military power in the world, unified all the smaller German principalities, and incorporated Alsace-Lorraine from France, Italy had a weak army, lost any independent military initiatives that it undertook, depended on the military strength and diplomatic assistance of others, and even after incorporating Rome in 1870 was still frustrated by the continued domination of Italian-inhabited *terra irredenta* (unredeemed land) by Austria-Hungary.

The unification of Italy had been inspired by the movement Risorgimento (Resurgence or Renewal) that inspired much of the Italian elite during the middle years of the century. The goals of Risorgimento were not merely to eliminate foreign rule and unify the Italian-speaking lands but also to create a modern and progressive society. After 1860 most of the former goal had been accomplished, but to many patriots the economically pinched, elitist, and oligarchic new Italian system seemed a pathetic failure or a betrayal of the second aspiration.

The new Italian system was led by a middle- and upper-class elite from the north. Under constitutional monarchy, it narrowly restricted suffrage, emphasized law and order, dominated the poverty-stricken south (for which some northerners felt a kind of racial aversion), and maintained one of the highest tax levels in Europe, despite the weakness of the economy. Though a slow liberalization of the political system began after 1876 and modern industrial development accelerated by the 1890s, Italy remained predominantly agrarian and backward compared with northern Europe. Universal male suffrage was not approved until the eve of World War I.

If Italy was too weak to reclaim its own *terra irredenta*, it seemed too weak also to develop its own empire. Tunisia lay just across the Mediterranean from Sicily, but in 1881 it was snapped up by France. The Italian government did establish small colonies in Eritrea and Somaliland, on either side of the horn of East Africa, but an effort to advance into Ethiopia in 1896 ended in complete defeat at Adowa, marking the only occasion during the nineteenth century in which a sizable European force had been so decisively defeated by a black African army that colonial expansion had to be completely renounced. At this rate Italy could never become the "sixth great power" of Europe, but at best only a larger Spain, Greece, or Portugal.

La rivoluzione mancata

Among nationalists, this situation gave rise to the myth of the *rivoluzione mancata*—the missing or frustrated revolution—within the new Italy. The need to combine national self-affirmation with internal political, social, and economic development had been recognized by many leaders of the Risorgimento. Giuseppe Mazzini, one of the key founders of Italian nationalism, had also endorsed a kind of moderate socialism for internal development, while Count Carlo Pisacane, one of the leaders of early Italian socialism, died as a martyr to nationalism and the goal of unification. Thus the problematic relationship between nationalism and internal development had been recognized since the origins of modern Italian nationalism.

By the 1880s the country's most popular poet, Giosuè Carducci, would call for a new nationalism and a new policy of national greatness.[43] Pasquale Turiello, in his *Governo e governati in Italia* (1882), proclaimed the need for an "organic state" that must be led by great men, asserting that the army was Italy's most useful existing institution. In later years other major literary figures and political writers would echo these themes.

By the turn of the century Italy's modernization slowly accelerated, urbanization increased, and social differentiation grew. With the expansion of an industrial labor force in the urban north, a socialist movement crystallized, increasing demands on the system. Pressure for political liberalization was growing year by year, every decade or so the suffrage was widened, and under the leadership of Giovanni Giolitti after 1900 the government encouraged accelerated modernization while prosecuting pragmatic reform.

The Alternative of Restricted or Authoritarian Liberalism

To extreme conservatives or even to some worried moderates, internal tensions threatened to get out of hand. The natural dynamic of modern liberal systems,

---

43. The nationalism of Carducci and other literary figures is discussed in R. Drake, *Byzantium for Rome: The Politics of Nostalgia in Umbertian Italy, 1878–1900* (Chapel Hill, 1980).

even under limited and restrictive nineteenth-century liberalism, tended toward greater liberalism, more reform, and even incipient democratization. This had been clear to most elitist or conservative liberals since the early nineteenth century, and several proposals had been made in France and Spain to reduce civic participation, to freeze a restrictive liberalism in order to keep it from decaying.

By the 1880s conservative liberals such as Ruggiero Bonghi and Giorgio Arcoleo were proposing such restrictions in Italy, Bonghi advocating a limitation though corporatism and Arcoleo praising German concepts of the *Rechtsstaat*. The new leader of conservative liberalism in the following decade was the austere Sydney Sonnino, who published a notorious article in 1897 entitled "Torniamo allo Statuto," urging the Italian state to "go back" to the original strict terms of the constitutional statute of 1849, repealing subsequent liberalization. Neither the crown nor most political opinion would agree, but the alternative of a more authoritarian liberalism remained alive as a political option in the thinking of many conservatives and moderate liberals for the next thirty years.[44]

The Nationalism of the Avant-Garde: Futurism and the Cultural Elite

An important shift occurred immediately after 1900, when much of the cultural elite moved to a militant and violent nationalism. The cultural crisis of the fin de siècle had greater impact in Italy than in most other lands. Italian philosophers vied with those of Germany in leading the antipositivist revolt on behalf of neoidealism, while Italian social scientists and theorists such as Mosca, Pareto, and Scipio Sighele were international leaders of the new elitist and antiparliamentary doctrines. Nowhere in the world were there more vehement opponents of bourgeois culture, liberalism, humanitarianism, and pacifism. The corollary of aggressive nationalism was held to be strong elite leadership and imperialism.

The most prominent spokesmen for the new trend were the leaders of the Florentine avant-garde, Giovanni Papini and Giuseppe Prezzolini, together with the radical new nationalist writer Enrico Corradini and Italy's most popular poet, the sensuous neoromantic Gabriele D'Annunzio, whose achievement is sometimes said to have been to make violence seem erotic. Papini and Prezzolini initiated the new modernist journal *Leonardo* in Florence, which hailed national genius and expansion, but their most important vehicle was the magazine *La Voce,* founded in 1908. Their Florentine modernism called for spiritual

44. These and other rightist and nationalist currents are ably examined by John Thayer, in *Italy and the Great War: Politics and Culture, 1870–1915* (Madison, 1964), 3–142.

and cultural regeneration, proclaiming the need for a kind of secular religion. They preached elitism, war, the "imperial ideal," and the importance of regenerative violence. Prezzolini advocated the need "to love war," since "violence is . . . a moral cure." [45] The literary nationalists condemned humanitarianism and the nineteenth-century liberal fear of shedding blood, as well as the belief that "mere life" is sacred. The outbreak of the Russo-Japanese War in 1904–5 thrilled some of them. D'Annunzio would say that "never had the world been so ferocious." [46] What was needed was a grand national enterprise; even the sober Pareto lamented in 1904 that Italy, unlike Germany or France, had no real theory of authoritarianism or the police state. Mosca also supported war and imperialism, while Papini claimed that these were the only means of uniting Italy internally. In October 1913 he shrilled in the Futurist journal *Lacerba:* "The future needs blood. It needs human victims, butchery. Internal war, and foreign war, revolution and conquest: that is history. . . . Blood is the wine of strong peoples, and blood is the oil for the wheels of this great machine which flies from the past to the future." [47]

Equally vehement were the voices of Italy's principal new contribution to the early twentieth-century artistic avant-garde, the Futurist movement developed by Filippo Marinetti. Futurism was absolutely neophiliac; it reflected the new mechanical and industrial Italy springing up in the north and rejected all past artistic canons, hailing novelty, speed, machines, and all the dramatic changes of the twentieth century. Futurists presented both new content and a new style. Their theatrical productions were provocative happenings, their paintings full of factories, machines, dynamic moving parts, and symbols of the new acceleration of life. The Futurists were, in a sense, metaphysical motorcycle riders.

Unlike the artistic avant-garde in some other countries, Italian Futurists were not mere individualists but ardent nationalists. To them, Italy was historically the land of genius, and the great new "third Italy" (after Rome and the Renaissance) should be led by a new elite of "young geniuses" (like, they thought, themselves) who would carry it to war, empire, and new national greatness.

The Futurists were more given to radical and provocative manifestos than any other avant-garde group, "and indeed most historians of Italian futurism agree that the series of fifty-odd manifestos published between 1909 and

45. Quoted in W. L. Adamson, *Avant-Garde Florence: From Modernism to Fascism* (Cambridge, Mass., 1993), 88.

46. Quoted in Thayer, *Italy and the Great War* 193.

47. Ibid., 259. There is a lengthy bibliography on the new nationalism of the cultural elite. See particularly E. Gentile, *"La Voce" e l'età giolittiana* (Milan, 1972), and F. Cereja, *Intellettuali e politica dall'epoca giolittiana all'affermazione del fascismo* (Turin, 1973).

Italy's entrance into the war in 1915 were the movement's literary form par excellence."[48] Their rhetoric was even more bloodthirsty than that of other nationalists. The original Futurist manifesto of 1909 declared:

> 1. We want to sing the love of danger, the habit of energy and rashness.
> 2. The essential elements of our poetry will be courage, audacity and revolt.
> 3. . . . We want to exalt movements of aggression, feverish sleeplessness, the forced march, the perilous leap, the slap and the blow with the fist. . . .
> 9. We want to glorify war—the only cure for the world—and militarism, patriotism, the destructive gesture of the anarchists, the beautiful ideas which kill, and contempt for women.
> 10. We want to demolish museums and libraries, fight morality, feminism, and all opportunist and utilitarian cowardice.[49]

Much of what became Italian Fascism in 1919 could already be found in the Futurist manifesto ten years earlier.

The Italian Nationalist Association

The Italian Nationalist Association (ANI), Italy's first nationalist political party, was founded in 1910, but the way had been prepared for it by the literary, cultural, and political agitation of the past decade. Nationalism's most persistent publicist was the prolific novelist and writer Enrico Corradini, who not only helped to establish the doctrinal base and justification but also provided a broader rationale for a popular movement. Drawing on the suggestions of some of the revolutionary syndicalists, he termed Italy a "proletarian nation," that is, systematically exploited by the international power structure and division of labor, condemned to inferior status, discriminated against in trade. From this perspective the main Italian problem was not that of poor peasants or low-paid industrial workers, but the proletarian status of its entire society on the international level. Nationalism had the responsibility to unite all Italians to build a strong, modern, and prosperous country in which all could thrive. The national revolution should take precedence over class revolution and would benefit all classes. Corradini even occasionally used the term *national socialism*.[50]

The ANI was at first a conflicting assemblage of diverse kinds of national-

48. M. Perloff, *The Futurist Moment* (Chicago, 1986), 90.

49. Quoted in A. Lyttelton, ed., *Italian Fascism from Pareto to Gentile* (London, 1973), 211–12. See G. L. Mosse, "The Political Culture of Italian Futurism: A General Perspective," *JCH* 25:2–3 (May–June 1990): 229–52, and, for a survey of the movement, R. T. Clough, *Futurism* (New York, 1961). Andrew Hewitt, in *Fascist Modernism* (Stanford, 1993), presents an esoteric theoretical analysis of Marinetti as aesthetic avant-gardist.

50. M. de Taeye-Hedren, *Le nationalisme d'Enrico Corradini et les origines du fascisme dans la revue florentine "Il Regno" (1903–1906)* (Paris, 1973); R. S. Cunsolo, *Italian Nationalism* (Melbourne, Fla., 1990).

ists—democratic, moderate, and authoritarian. At its second congress in 1912, a split developed between democrats and rightists, with the authoritarians gaining control. By 1914 the association achieved relative unity by accepting the doctrine of the authoritarian corporate state developed by the law professor Alfredo Rocco. Unlike Catholic corporatists, who theoretically strove to minimize the role of the state, Rocco held statism to be the only logical, consistent, and scientific approach to modern political organization. He claimed to derive much of his theory from German doctrines of the juridical state, which defined human rights as not inherent but resulting from the self-limitation of sovereign state power.

The divisiveness of party politics and the social strife and underdevelopment besetting Italy were all to be overcome by an authoritarian corporate state. This would replace the parliament with a corporate assembly representing economic interest groups and regulated by a state with predominant power. Its functions would be to achieve social harmony, promote economic modernization, and make Italy a strong imperial country. Though his enemies often termed Rocco's corporate state reactionary, he distinguished it from that of Catholic conservatives as not being based on archaic blueprints of medieval estates but rather being planned to promote modern industrial coordination and expansion to build a new, modern society. Yet though the ANI's goals were modernizing, they were not revolutionary, for the existing sovereignty of the Italian crown and the general class structure were to be preserved through authoritarian means while the technology and industrial potential of the society as a whole were being transformed.

Perhaps the most radical aspect of the ANI's program lay in its ultimate goal, which was to strengthen Italy for modern war and imperial expansion. These the Nationalists held to be necessary and, indeed, from a kind of Social Darwinist viewpoint, inevitable. They were the first new political group in Italy to organize on their own to meet the revolutionary left in violent confrontation, and it was the Nationalist militia—the Sempre Pronti (Always Ready)—that first responded to leftist violence with physical assault in Bologna in July 1919, before the minuscule new Fascist movement was ready or willing to do so.

Despite Corradini's concept of "proletarian nationalism," the ANI was a rightist and elitist movement, becoming by the time of World War I probably the most sophisticated and clear-minded right authoritarian movement in Europe (with the possible exception of Action Française). Its most effective ties were with sectors of the upper classes and with economic and institutional leaders. It would never become a mass movement, but it was soon able to wield influence disproportionate to its somewhat limited membership.[51]

51. The broadest studies are F. Perfetti, *Il nazionalismo italiano dalle origini alla fusione col fascismo* (Bologna, 1977), and A. J. De Grand, *The Italian Nationalist Association and the Rise*

The Nationalization of Revolutionary Syndicalism

The nucleus that eventually founded Fascism in Italy did not, however, stem either from the cultural elite or from the right-wing nationalists, but from the transformation of part of the revolutionary left, particularly the sector known as revolutionary syndicalists. Revolutionary syndicalism originated in France early in the 1890s, as a reaction against the weakness and moderation of socialism and the trade union movement. It sought to overcome such limitations through "direct action" or what its proponents termed *la manière force* (the tactics of force), with the goal of achieving revolution through a grand general strike that would make it possible to restructure society around the syndicates (trade unions). Revolutionary syndicalists detested reformism, compromise, and parliamentary government, or what they called "the superstitious belief in majorities." They were more influenced than most socialists by the cultural crisis of the fin de siècle, particularly by Social Darwinism, the importance of group conflict, and Sorelian ideas about the moral value of violence. In France their apogee occurred in 1902–6, after which their influence quickly waned.[52]

Revolutionary syndicalism began to grow in Italy after 1900, based particularly on the Camere del Lavoro, regional labor exchanges in northern Italy designed to remedy the numerical weakness of the regular trade unions. Though the revolutionary syndicalists called themselves Marxists, their doctrines and tactics were unorthodox, and they had left the Italian Socialist Party by 1907. During 1907–8 they led a radical strike wave and by 1909 had mostly withdrawn from the predominantly Socialist trade union federation, the CGL, three years later organizing a smaller Unione Sindacale Italiana (USI) with no more than a hundred thousand members.

In the process, the ideas of the revolutionary syndicalist leaders became increasingly radical and heterodox. Arturo Labriola, one of their main theorists, had briefly emigrated abroad and had observed discrimination against Italian workers. He developed his own concept of the "proletarian nation"— that Italians as a nationality, rather than merely as a class, were the objects of exploitation by the international division of labor, and that revolutionary transformation must therefore be concerned not merely with one class but with the

---

of Fascism in Italy (Lincoln, 1978). Other works include F. Leoni, *Origini del nazionalismo italiano* (Naples, 1965); idem, *La stampa nazionalista* (Rome, 1965); F. Gaeta, *Nazionalismo italiano* (Naples, 1965); R. Molinelli, *Per una storia del nazionalismo italiano* (Urbino, 1966); and W. Alff, "Die Associazione Nazionalista Italiana von 1910," in his *Der Begriff Faschismus und andere Aufsätze* (Frankfurt, 1971), 51–95. Paolo Ungari, in *Alfredo Rocco e l'ideologia giuridica del fascismo* (Brescia, 1963), discusses Rocco's ideas, and some links with big business are scrutinized in R. A. Webster, *Industrial Imperialism in Italy, 1908–1915* (Berkeley, 1975).

52. F. F. Ridley, *Revolutionary Syndicalism in France* (Cambridge, 1970); P. Stearns, *Revolutionary Syndicalism and French Labor* (New Brunswick, N.J., 1971).

entire society. Increasingly, revolutionary syndicalists held that, as Marxists, they must encourage the full development and maturation of Italian capitalism, since without a fully developed capitalism there could be no successful revolutionary collectivism. Moreover, in Italy the revolutionary movement could never achieve success on the basis of the working class alone. To triumph it must become a cross-class movement, drawing the support of farmers, farmworkers, and as much as possible of the productive middle classes as well. Nor was it a mistake to support "proletarian nationalism" in national war and colonial expansion, for Marx and Engels had themselves consistently endorsed British and French imperialism, together with the American conquest of Texas, as bringing progress to benighted regions. By 1910, therefore, a process was under way by which many revolutionary syndicalists would become nationalist syndicalists.[53]

The intellectual leaders of revolutionary syndicalism were able to devote considerable time to the elaboration of theory because of their movement's lack of practical opportunities. Seeing the futility of mere insurrection, they emphasized the importance of structure and organization. While rejecting the irrationality and mere lust for violence of the Futurists, Sergio Panunzio and other theorists stressed the necessity and indeed the vital role of violence.[54] Syndicalists argued for lucidity as distinct from mere emotionalism but strove for a new approach that would mobilize the vital instincts of workers. Roberto Michels—the most distinguished of their intellectuals—elaborated on the need for new elites, the role of leadership and voluntarism, the psychology of mass groups, and the problems of mass mobilization.[55] Equally important in syndicalist theory was the emphasis on new ideals and symbols, as well as the creation of a more positive morality in place of Marxist materialism to motivate and guide workers.[56]

By 1910 Arturo Labriola and Enrico Leone had developed new economic doctrines which emphasized the need to develop a society of producers based

53. For detailed discussion, see D. D. Roberts, *The Syndicalist Tradition and Italian Fascism* (Chapel Hill, 1979), and Z. Sternhell, M. Sznajder, and M. Asheri, *The Birth of Fascist Ideology* (Princeton, 1994).

54. Largely unknown outside Italy, Panunzio would become arguably the most prolific and coherent theorist of fascism, from the years of the transformation of revolutionary syndicalism until the collapse of the regime. See A. J. Gregor, *Sergio Panunzio: Il sindacalismo ed il fondamento razionale del fascismo* (Rome, 1978), and F. Perfetti, *Sergio Panunzio: Il fondamento giuridico del fascismo* (Rome, 1987).

55. F. Pfetsch, *Die Entwicklung zum faschistischen Führerstaat in der politischen Philosophie von Robert Michels* (Karlsruhe, 1964); W. Röhrich, *Robert Michels von sozialistischsyndikalistischen zum faschistischen Credo* (Berlin, 1972).

56. Z. Sternhell, "The 'Anti-Materialist' Revision of Marxism as an Aspect of the Rise of Fascist Ideology," *JCH* 22:3 (July 1987): 379–400; M. Sznajder, "I miti del sindacalismo rivoluzionario," *Storia Contemporanea* (hereinafter cited as *SC*) 24:1 (Feb. 1993): 21–57.

on "realistic" economics, recognizing the role of marginality and the hedonistic psychology of the consumer. In these concepts a free market would be the most effective force in eliminating surplus value and achieving modern development, a necessary basis for a true revolution of collectivism. Thus a pluralist syndicalist-corporatist system within a limited state would provide the surest path to socialism.[57]

Italy's main opportunity for colonial expansion occurred in 1911, when the government fought a limited war against the Ottoman Empire to conquer the territory of Libya, just across the Mediterranean. This was supported by a number of the revolutionary syndicalists and by nearly all the nationalists, though it was opposed by many of the former and also at first by the cultural nationalists of *La Voce* as being still too reactionary in concept and goal. In the war's aftermath, most of the revolutionary syndicalist leaders began to take the position that the chief problem in Italy was not the bourgeoisie—which did not really rule—but the oligarchic and, from their viewpoint, reactionary political system. From that point there was talk about the need for a "preliminary" political revolution, which would open up the political and economic system to more progressive forces. As an alternative, syndicalist corporatism might provide intermediate political leadership until full development and true socialism could be achieved.

Thus by 1914 the revolutionary syndicalists had drastically revised Marxist theory and replaced it with new doctrines for the achievement of a "positive" revolution. These included emphasis on the importance of ethics, ideas, and symbols and attention to social psychology; the importance of voluntarism rather than economic determinism; the key role of the elite in providing leadership for a revolutionary vanguard; the importance of cross-class mobilization; the importance of stimulating economic production and development rather than distribution; the identification of the political establishment rather than capitalism and industrialists as the chief immediate enemy; the concept of the proletarian nation as a key to revolution; and the need for direct action, violence, and heroic deeds, first in revolutionary strikes and later in national political and military action. Some of their leaders had already become nationalists, and after Italy entered World War I most of their spokesmen would support the "national revolutionary war," in the process of moving from revolutionary syndicalism to national syndicalism. In this guise they would provide the most coherent support for the founding of the Fascist movement in 1919.

57. M. Sznajder, "Economic Marginalism and Socialism: Italian Revolutionary Syndicalism and the Revision of Marx," *Praxis International* 11:1 (April 1991): 114–27.

EASTERN EUROPE

Eastern Europe had become the area of some of the most intense nationalist movements by the end of the nineteenth century, yet most of the area was still dominated by the multinational empires of tsarist Russia, Austria-Hungary, and Ottoman Turkey. Much of eastern European nationalism consisted of liberation movements organized among nationalities that did not enjoy independence. All the nationalities that had gained independence during the course of the century (in Greece, Serbia, Romania, and Bulgaria) formed states as liberal constitutional monarchies, and this was true of the tiny region of Montenegro as well. In these kingdoms, most political expression conformed to the liberal model, and nearly all the liberation movements espoused no contrasting ideals. There were nonetheless several expressions of a new kind of authoritarian nationalism.

The Union of the Russian People

The Union of the Russian People, organized in response to the left liberal revolution of 1905 in Russia, was the first attempt at a new mass-mobilized rightist nationalism there. The URP combined authoritarian monarchism and a vague corporatism with some effort at mass mobilization and nominal social reform, basing itself especially on an appeal to traditional religiosity of an obscurantist sort. It emphasized strong-arm units (the Black Hundreds) more than any of the new central or western European groups and was extreme in its semiracial anti-Semitism and support of the new style of Russian nationalist imperialism.[58] By 1907 there were some three thousand local branches, strong among certain sectors of the lower middle classes and urban workers, enrolling "in some places up to 15 or 20 percent of the people."[59] A short-lived response to a profound political crisis, the URP functioned in a predemocratic environment and failed to sustain its early mobilization. Russia before 1914 was too underdeveloped to harbor all the stimuli and forces which would soon bring fascism to life in central Europe. "Though it was moving in the direction of fascism, [the URP] was as yet very far from reaching this indistinct goal."[60]

58. H. Rogger, "Was There a Russian Fascism? The Union of Russian People," *Journal of Modern History* (hereinafter cited as *JMH*) 36:4 (Dec. 1964): 398–415; idem, "Russia," in *The European Right* ed. H. Rogger and E. Weber (Berkeley, 1965), 443–500. Further data may be found in J. J. Brock Jr., "The Theory and Practice of the Union of the Russian People, 1905–07," Ph.D. diss., University of Michigan, 1972, and D. C. Rawson, "The Union of the Russian People, 1905–07," Ph.D. diss., University of Washington, 1971.

59. W. Laqueur, *Black Hundred: The Rise of the Extreme Right in Russia* (New York, 1993), 26–27.

60. Ibid., 28.

The Serbian Unification or Death

Conflictive nationalism was more frequent and intense in eastern than in western Europe, and it was not uncommon for eastern European nationalist movements to advocate tactics of violence or war, though most of them normally espoused a parliamentary system of national politics.[61] A notable exception was the pan-Serb secret society Ujedinenje ili Smrt (Unification or Death). This group, led in large measure by the Serbian army officers who had carried out the gruesome assassination of King Alexander in 1903 that restored the Karageorgević family to the Serbian throne, advocated an expansionist foreign policy that would unify all the Serb lands and bring neighboring southern Slav territories under Serbian rule. It preached a policy of militarism and the replacement of the parliamentary system by an authoritarian form of government to concentrate national energies and develop the nation. Also known as the Crna Ruka (Black Hand), it endorsed the economic claims of workers and peasants but insisted that they must be subordinated to national expansion, irredentism, and common goals. The title of its journalistic organ, *Pijemont* (Piedmont), underscored the special role that it believed the kingdom of Serbia shared in southern Slav expansion, similar to the view of the kingdom of Piedmont held by the Italian Risorgimento. Unification or Death also strongly urged the development of Serbian Orthodoxy to foster common links and provide spiritual leadership. It facilitated the activities of the allied Young Bosnia conspirators in carrying out the assassination of Archduke Franz Ferdinand in 1914, which precipitated World War I. The society was broken up during World War I, and its leader, chief of Serbian military intelligence Colonel Dragutin Dimitrijević, was executed in 1917.[62]

61. For example, "it is interesting that the Montenegrin youth organized a secret society in Belgrade in 1909 for the purpose of assassinating all persons in Montenegro who were against the major goals of the Montenegro People's Party." V. Dedijer, *The Road to Sarajevo* (London, 1967), 291–92. Such extreme goals were for the most part not realized.

62. D. MacKenzie, *Apis: The Congenial Conspirator* (Boulder, 1989). See also A. Dragnich, *Serbia, Nikola Pasic, and Yugoslavia* (New Brunswick, N.J., 1974), and M. B. Petrovich, *A History of Modern Serbia, 1804–1918* (New York, 1976), 2:608–11.

3
The Impact of World War I

.

The continuity of government, culture, and institutions in much of Europe was shattered by the impact of World War I, which ended the century-long peace that, with a few exceptions, had existed since the close of the Napoleonic wars in 1815. Its destructiveness not only cost ten million military lives but also swept away all the principal governments and dynasties of central and eastern Europe, opening the twentieth-century era of mass political violence and revolution. The basic habits of politics were altered, as the secular trend toward liberal democracy and greater representative government was challenged and in some areas reversed. The consequence was a brutalization of political life which made the recourse to political violence seem natural and even normal. The impact on culture and social psychology was equally profound, as the trend toward optimism and faith in progress characteristic of the preceding century and a half was increasingly questioned and often rejected.

The war had a major emancipatory effect as well. Though all the modern movements toward emancipation—whether national, social, cultural, or sexual—had begun to take shape well before the war, the change and destruction wrought by the conflict gave them all greater impulse and momentum.

The war was initially greeted with enthusiasm, at least in some of the larger cities of the main belligerents, and it was welcomed at least as much by intellectuals as among ordinary citizens.[1] Nowhere was this so much the case as in Germany. There the war was hailed as revolution and as liberation, a rebellion against stultifying conditions and the domination of Western culture by France and Britain, providing the chance for the full affirmation of Germany and German culture for the first time. This is not to say that the German

1. The best brief survey of this phenomenon and its connections with the fin de siècle cultural crisis is R. N. Stromberg, *Redemption by War: The Intellectuals and 1914* (Lincoln, 1982).

government was any more responsible for the conflict than its counterparts in Austria, Russia, or Serbia, but simply to underscore the more expectant attitude unleashed in Germany.

Many historians have dwelt on the paradox of early twentieth-century Germany, which in many ways had become not merely the newest but also the most modern and successful power in Europe. During the past two generations Germany had led in such diverse areas as education, university achievement, industry, science, technology, and urban landscape and architectural development. To fearful French commentators Germany had stood as the epitome of the modern and of "practical reason," for centuries the special domain of the West. At the same time, spokesmen for German interests in politics and in culture often expressed a sense of frustration and lack of fulfillment, a need to achieve a decisive new breakthrough.

Modris Eksteins has developed the argument that "Germany, more extensively than any other country, represented the aspirations of a national avant-garde."[2] For Germans more than any of the other principal belligerents, nationalism took the form of a mystic sense of revolt against and liberation from the existing order; it did not inspire a social revolution but gave rise to military hegemony and new cultural forms. Thus it is probably not an exaggeration to say that increasingly the old German cultural emphasis on *Innerlichkeit* (inwardness, or depth) gave way to a subjective nationalist fantasy, a special mission against philistine bourgeois Western culture as well as against its imperialist dominance. It may well be that, as Eksteins says, this had the effect of broadening the fixation on narcissism and fantasy—before the war primarily the province of the avant-garde—to embrace nationalist culture itself. The war could thus be a liberation and a creation, and a means through death of achieving a higher life based on a superior German culture.

All the powers followed militarist policies, and all broke various rules of conduct and committed atrocities, but from the beginning the key initiatives in the war came from Germany. The escalations of weaponry and tactics—poison gas, flamethrowers, aerial bombing of cities, unrestricted submarine warfare—were German enterprises. Relatively harsher occupation policies were also carried out, the more noticeable in German policy since only Germany conquered foreign territories in the first two years of the war.[3] All these things elicited the greater shock because of the apparent success achieved during the nineteenth century in establishing more civilized regulations for international disputes and, supposedly, for war. Finally, though the German government

---

2. M. Eksteins, *Rites of Spring: The Great War and the Birth of the Modern Age* (New York, 1989), 49.

3. Cf. J. Horne and A. Kramer, "German 'Atrocities' and Franco-German Opinion, 1914: The Evidence of German Soldiers' Diaries," *JMH* 66 (March 1994): 1–33.

itself was conservative and authoritarian, it acted as the prime international agent in encouraging and subsidizing sociopolitical revolution among its foes, as in Barcelona, in Poland, and, above all, in Russia in 1917.[4]

A case can be made, then, that German policy—both political and military—was both more novel and original on the one hand and rather more radical on the other. German nationalism became more extreme culturally and ideologically than was the case with any of the other great powers (though probably no more so than that of Serbia), and Germany was willing to go to greater lengths than any of the other major belligerents. Whether this was more a question of degree than principle depends on one's point of view. Despite the great radicalizing impact of the war, German policy and politics did not absolutely pass beyond the general European categories and norms of that generation, but they strained the bounds of those norms more than any other.

The Trench Experience

Conduct of war on the western and Italian fronts produced a kind of experience never before known to such large numbers of men for such prolonged periods of time.[5] The virtually static trench fronts tied down millions for months on end, creating a new collective consciousness of a separate society, a warrior group partially isolated from the rest of the nation and from normal experiences, bonded by a prolonged camaraderie and a new sense of collective identity, a consciousness made more deep and lasting by common suffering and self-sacrifice. This sense of collective identity and mission would survive the war and help to create a new sense of nationalist identity, mission, and purpose among many veterans. It produced the sense of a perceived new "civilian military class" that would play a special role of militance and leadership in postwar nationalism, and in the political endeavors of the 1920s and 1930s. It made concepts of "blood socialism" and "trenchocracy" valid in the thinking of hundreds of thousands of veterans.

Destructive Impact of the War on Constitutional Government

The war placed considerable strain on the political systems of all participants. Whereas the stable western European democratic systems were able to respond

4. The principal historiographic controversy during the past two generations over German aggressiveness in World War I has dealt with war aims, though all the belligerents had major expansionist goals. Concerning the "Fischer controversy" over German war aims, see F. Fischer, *From Kaiserreich to Third Reich* (New York, 1986), and J. A. Moses, *The Politics of Illusion: The Fischer Controversy in German History* (London, 1975).

5. On the basic war experience, see E. J. Leed, *No Man's Land: Combat and Identity in World War I* (New York, 1979).

with various forms of coalition "national union" governments, the situation deteriorated further in central, southern, and eastern Europe. The tsarist regime in Russia, whose state was the most backward and arbitrary of the powers, was ultimately torn apart by the new pressures. It totally collapsed in 1917, leading to revolution, Communist dictatorship, and civil war.

In Germany the real power was in effect usurped by the military command in 1916, halfway through the conflict. A new organization of authoritarian nationalism, the Fatherland Party, was organized in 1917–18 by Admiral von Tirpitz and Wolfgang Kapp. Its promoters hoped to develop a broad patriotic association uniting all classes behind a militarist and imperialist program under strong leadership, while carefully avoiding any alteration of domestic social relations.[6] A wartime phenomenon, this was the first authoritarian nationalist association to gain mass support, though it collapsed with German defeat.

In neutral Spain and Portugal tensions resulting from the war soon destabilized the governments, helping to revive the praetorian tradition of military intervention in politics. In Portugal, where a new liberal republic had been introduced in 1910, conflict over domestic issues and the question of intervention in the war briefly led to a short-term military government under General Pimenta de Castro in January 1915, before an armed revolt restored constitutional rule. In Spain, multiple conflicts were generated by regionalist and democratic reformists, new syndicates of army officers, and the revolutionary labor movements, producing three different kinds of revolt in Spain during 1917, though none of them overturned the system.[7]

After Portugal entered the war on the side of the Allies, a broad revolt by conservatives overthrew the regular Republican administration in a coup of December 1917, in which at least 350 were killed. Its leader, Sidonio Pais, a former army officer and conservative Republican politican, had recently served as ambassador in Berlin, where he had been impressed by the authoritarian tendencies of the German government at war. During the year that followed he endeavored to replace the parliamentary system with a presidentialist republic, a semiauthoritarian system of charismatic and populist personal leadership that was nominally ratified by a popular plebiscite. By trying to create new institutional and political mechanisms to structure strong presidentialist rule, Pais anticipated the new postwar dictators and even the later Gaullist system in France, but his rule was cut short by assassination in December 1918.[8]

6. G. E. Etue Jr., "The German Fatherland Party," Ph.D. diss., University of California, Berkeley, 1959, and K. Wortmann, *Geschichte der Deutschen Vaterlandspartei, 1917–1918* (Halle, 1926).

7. G. Meaker, "A War of Words: The Ideological Impact of the First World War on Spain, 1914–18," in *Neutral Europe between War and Revolution, 1917–23*, ed. H. Schmitt (Charlottesville, 1988), 1–65, and J. A. Lacomba, *La crisis española de 1917* (Madrid, 1970).

8. J. Brandão, *Sidonio* (Lisbon, 1983), and A. J. Telo, *O sidonismo e o movimento operario português* (Lisbon, 1977).

Even the process of entering the war might strain or overturn the existing systems. In Italy the parliament was partly bypassed by new forms of popular mobilization to pressure entry into the war in 1915, and in Greece both the government and the king were overthrown. There the Entente intervened directly in a civil war between conservative neutralists (rather favorable to the Central Powers) and pro-Entente Liberals, which the Liberals had initiated late in 1916. Entente military intervention brought victory to the Liberals in the following year and Greece's entrance on the side of the Entente, while forcing King Constantine into exile.[9]

The Genocide of the Armenians by the Turks

A war that had been produced in part by extremist nationalism had the effect of greatly exacerbating that same nationalism. In Turkey the traditional regime had been overthrown in 1908 by Young Turk nationalist revolutionaries, who eventually joined the Central Powers during the war. Their ultimate aim was a "Greater Turkey" stretching from Anatolia to central Asia, but internally their principal animus was directed against the Armenian Christian minority, who constituted the only significant non-Muslim group in Turkish society. Possibly as many as a hundred thousand Armenians had already been slaughtered in Turkish orgies during 1894–96. Though Armenian troops fought valiantly as soldiers in the Turkish army during the first phase of World War I, Armenians also sought freedom and autonomy and allegedly favored the Entente. In 1915 the Turkish government turned on the Armenians as the chief source of internal dissidence and "sabotage." It began to round up the Armenians in all of Turkey save Istanbul and the Aegean cities; they were driven from their homes en masse and herded toward the southeastern frontier, which many failed to reach. The Armenians were attacked and murdered in innumerable incidents, shot, stabbed, beaten to death or drowned, robbed of their possessions, the women frequently raped or carried off as slaves. When such atrocities finally concluded in 1923, approximately a million Armenians (or nearly half their total population in prewar Turkey) had been killed.[10]

The slaughter of the Armenians was the first great genocide of the twentieth century. Though other governments protested, there was no intervention and no concerted international effort to punish the Turkish authorities afterward. Though the main leaders had to flee abroad, they had "gotten away with it." This fact was fully registered by Hitler, who was reported to have ob-

9. G. B. Leontaritis, *Greece and the First World War, 1917–1918* (New York, 1990).

10. There is an extensive literature on the massacre of the Armenians. See R. G. Hovannisian, ed., *The Armenian Genocide in Perspective* (New Brunswick, N.J. 1987), and idem, ed., *The Armenian Holocaust: A Bibliography Relating to the Deportations, Massacres, and Dispersion of the Armenian People, 1915–1923* (Cambridge, Mass., 1978).

served on the eve of war in 1939, "Who now remembers the massacre of the Armenians?" [11]

There were a few proposals elsewhere to emulate the Turks and even to systematize their work. After the occupation of Macedonia by Bulgarian forces, Bulgarian extremists proposed the employment of mobile gas chambers—a sort of precocious anticipation of both the Nazi Final Solution and later Balkan "ethnic cleansing"—to liquidate alien sectors of the population. So grisly a proposal was rejected by Bulgarian authorities, but its very conception was a further indication of how much the war had altered the political and mental landscape.

The Russian Revolution

One of the most profound consequences of the war was the Russian Revolution, resulting in the Communist dictatorship imposed in October 1917. The revolution was the product not merely of the war itself but equally of conditions unique to Russia. The Communist coup was in fact a counterrevolution to the democratic revolution of February 1917, and initially it had little impact outside the lands of the old Russian Empire.

11. *Nazi Conspiracy and Aggression* (Washington, D.C., 1948), 7:753.
There seems little doubt that the slaughter of the Armenians can properly be termed a genocide, that is, the mass destruction of nearly all, or as many as possible, of a targeted ethnic, religious, or social group. Since World War II the term has been invoked increasingly to the point of debasement; any killing of a number of people of the same identifiable group has been loosely termed a genocide. Thus the word has become trivialized approximately as much as the term *fascism*.
At the opposite pole stands what might be termed the "Jewish exclusivist school," whose proponents seem to want to protect the uniqueness of the Hitlerian Final Solution, or Holocaust, to the extent of virtually denying legitimate use of the term to any other mass murder, however extensive. This reaches such extremes as to imply that if the Final Solution had succeeded in killing only three million Jews, rather than nearly six million, the resulting Holocaust would not have qualified as a genocide because over half of Europe's Jews would have escaped.
Robert Melson, in *Revolution and Genocide: On the Origins of the Armenian Genocide and the Holocaust* (Chicago, 1992), provides the only book-length comparative study of these two major genocides. He carefully points out differences as well as similarities, concluding that probably a little more than half the Armenians escaped. Their persecutors were revolutionary nationalists, but not millenarian racists like the Nazis. Conversely, much of the killing was done by hand publicly, inside Turkey itself, and often within view of ordinary Turks. A common denominator was revolutionary nationalism, exacerbated by wartime conditions. Indeed, the common denominators of all the great political mass slaughters of the century have been revolution and/or nationalism, whether the revolution is motivated by social class or ethno-racial considerations. For other comparative studies, see S. T. Katz, *The Holocaust in Historical Context*, vol. 1, *The Holocaust and Mass Death before the Modern Age* (New York, 1994); H. Fein, *Genocide: A Sociological Perspective* (London, 1993); L. Kuper, *Genocide: Its Political Use in the Twentieth Century* (New Haven, 1982); and R. J. Rummel, *Death by Government: Genocide and Mass Murder since 1900* (New Brunswick, N.J. 1994).

Lenin nonetheless created a new political model of complete one-party dictatorship and of totalitarian state control of all institutions, though the effort at total control had to be relaxed by 1921. By the close of the war, the new Communist regime had begun to exert an increasingly strong appeal on the more extreme sectors of the European left, and it served as a sharp provocation to the European right, though no other government was willing to intervene decisively in Russian affairs to overthrow the Communists.

Lenin assayed a series of successful new experiments for authoritarian political movements: the massive manipulation of crowds and opinion in the most extreme and irresponsible demagogy, often based on sweeping false-hoods; the technique of the coup d'état, seizing power directly through armed force; the one-party dictatorship; the effort at total control of all institutions; the successful cult of personality and charismatic dictatorship, initiated after the nearly successful attempt on Lenin's life in September 1918; dictatorship based on total opportunism, willing to add or drop major new programmatic features or policies from time to time as needed; the introduction of systematic mass terror and mass murder, with institutionalized permanent concentration camps for political prisoners, featuring large-scale forced labor combined with liquidationist policies;[12] the systematic brutalization of political life and be-havior, oriented toward mass violence; the militarization of political rhetoric, symbolism, and organization; the liquidation or elimination of entire classes and categories of people.[13]

Lenin did not create the political doctrines of fascism, but his Commu-nist totalitarianism based on systematic mass violence initiated most of the new practices and institutions of fascist-type regimes. The effect of all this on political extremists soon became pronounced.[14]

The Communist regime expected social revolution to spread through-out Europe. In Germany during the first months after the war a situation of dual power existed, with a broad-based *Räte* movement (the German term for "councils" or soviets) organized in the larger cities and industrial areas, even though not dominated by Russian-style Communists. There was intermittent violence, followed by a crackdown on the revolutionaries in Berlin (the mis-

12. The extreme violence of the Bolsheviks had been preceded a decade earlier by an ex-traordinary wave of terrorism by the revolutionary left, which claimed nearly seventeen thousand victims between 1905 and 1910, nearly half of them fatalities. This mass terrorism escalated only after, not before, the tsarist regime had begun to liberalize. See A. Geifman, *Thou Shalt Kill: Revolutionary Terrorism in Russia, 1894–1917* (Princeton, 1993).

13. The best introduction to the Leninist regime will be found in the major studies by Richard Pipes: *The Russian Revolution* (New York, 1990) and *Russia under the New Regime: Lenin and the Birth of the Totalitarian State* (New York, 1994).

14. Thus Hitler wrote in the *Völkischer Beobachter* on March 13, 1921: "One prevents the Jewish corruption of our people, if necessary, by confining its instigators to concentration camps." At that moment, the only existing model lay in the new Communist system.

leading named "Spartacist Uprising" of late January 1919). This was followed by the temporary establishment of a *Räterepublik* in Munich, soon suppressed with armed force in March 1919. Only in Hungary did a Communist party seize power briefly under the Bela Kun regime of 1919. Other efforts to establish Bolshevik-style regimes in the Baltic were soon crushed by civil wars in which the anti-Communists won.

The Communist regime organized its own revolutionary Third International of Communist parties, to be formed throughout Europe and the world. Though none of these was an immediate danger, the International created a persistent challenge and menace from the extreme revolutionary left that had never existed before, adding a new polarization and tension to political life in many European countries. Politics by systematic violence was now a latent possibility in most of the continent. The response was not simply more rigorous and repressive policies by many governments, but the formation of new rightist anti-Communist groups ready to practice violence in turn, helping to produce the unprecedented brutalization of political life which soon developed in much of Europe.

A Summary of the Consequences

To summarize, the First World War was the most destructive in history to that date. Its major consequences included the following:

1. The destruction of the long peace of the nineteenth century, together with its accompanying ethos of increasing moral restraint and humanitarianism.
2. The destabilization of the liberal cultural synthesis of the nineteenth century and the discrediting of the leadership associated with it, already increasingly questioned before the war and henceforth to be rejected by larger and larger sectors of European political actors.
3. The growth of state power, sharply accelerating a trend toward stronger and more dominant government, with curtailment of civil liberties and increasing state control over the economy.
4. The increasing prominence of organized mass political propaganda, employing all the modern mass media.
5. The experience of mass mobilization of much of society for the first time, together with the concept of total war.[15]
6. The destruction of the monarchies and empires of Austria-Hungary, Russia, Germany, and Ottoman Turkey.
7. The exacerbation of the very militarism and nationalism that had helped to provoke the war.

15. On the impact on Germany, see J. Kocka, *Facing Total War: German Society, 1914–1918* (Cambridge, Mass., 1985).

8. The Balkanization or fragmentation of much of eastern Europe, opening the way for new domestic and international conflicts.

9. The brutalization of political life in many parts of Europe, accompanied by a new acceptance of violence.

10. The opportunity for the creation of totalitarian socialism by Lenin, which provided a new model of one-party dictatorship; totalitarian control of institutions; systematic mass murder and permanent mass concentration camps for political opponents; the mobilization of mass propaganda and wholesale distortion of facts; the charismatic cult of the dictatorial personality; the new technique of violent coup d'état; the subordination of political programs to the most extreme opportunism; the militarization of political style, structure, and action; and the goal of liquidating entire classes of people.

11. The first major example of large-scale genocide in the Turkish massacre of the Armenians.

12. Chaotic social and economic conditions in central and eastern Europe in the immediate aftermath, producing hyperinflation and social crisis that encouraged extreme solutions.

The profoundly altered political and cultural landscape which resulted made it impossible to regain the relative peace and stability of the prewar era and would encourage greater evils and more widespread destruction in the future. These consequences were in turn exacerbated by an inadequate peace settlement that failed to resolve all the issues of the war, producing only an armed truce that would lead to an even more destructive war twenty years later.

The First World War did not, however, simply "cause" fascism, for most of the concepts that would create fascism already existed, and there was no process of teleological determinism which ipso facto would make it inevitable that fascism would dominate a significant part of Europe. Such a development would be the consequence of postwar politics, not simply of the war itself. The war nonetheless introduced a new brutalization of public life, a routinization of violence and authoritarianism, and a heightening of nationalist conflict and ambition without which fascism could not have triumphed in key countries during the generation that followed.

4
The Rise of Italian Fascism, 1919–1929

Italy, like the other new nations of the 1860s—Germany, Japan, Hungary, and Romania—was a latecomer to international competition and, like all the other new nations save Germany, faced daunting problems of internal development and modernization. After its most serious effort at imperial expansion had ended in humiliating defeat at Adowa in 1896, for a number of years the Italian government prudently avoided major new international involvement. The economic growth of the first years of the new century was, however, accompanied by an increase in nationalist and imperialist sentiment, primarily among sectors of the middle classes and the intelligentsia. The ruling liberal government of Giovanni Giolitti decided to accommodate this pressure by invading Libya, a territory of the Turkish Empire directly across the Mediterranean, on the specious grounds that vital interests of Italy had been violated there. Libya was therefore invaded and the main Mediterranean districts occupied in 1911–12, together with the Dodecanese islands in the south Aegean. Turkey was forced to cede these territories officially to Italy in 1912. Yet this did not appease extreme nationalists, whose appetite was only whetted. They coveted other territory in East Africa and the Balkans, and especially the Italian *terra irredenta* (unredeemed Italian-inhabited territory) of Trieste and the Trentino within Habsburg Austria.

Social differentiation increased steadily after 1900, with the expansion of the urban middle classes and the rapid growth of an industrial working class. The new Italian Socialist Party emerged as a major force, though it was increasingly divided between reformists and revolutionaries, the latter vociferously pacifist and internationalist. Led by the young journalist Benito Mussolini and

80

others, the revolutionaries seized control of the party in 1912 and, two years later, in June 1914, helped to lead it into the abortive general strike and partial insurrection of the Settimana Rossa (Red Week), which was effectively repressed and ended in complete failure.

After the general European war began six weeks later, each of the opposing alliances sought to draw Italy in on its side. Though Italy had a defensive alliance with Germany and Austria-Hungary, its terms did not apply to the situation in 1914. Italian government leaders found that the anti-German Entente had more to offer, and the eventual secret Treaty of London of April 1915 pledged Italy to enter the conflict on the side of the Entente in return for Trieste, all the greater Trentino area, and further territory in the east Adriatic, in Turkey, and in Africa. Implementing this drastic new policy seemed initially more complicated, however, for most Italian opinion exhibited little enthusiasm for war, and the majority liberal bloc in the parliament was tepid.

Italian "Left Interventionism"

While right-wing nationalists were eager for Italian intervention, support for the war also suddenly appeared among an enthusiastic and heterogeneous group of leftists who would be subsequently referred to as left interventionists. Some of these were comparatively moderate leftists from the ranks of the middle-class Radicals and Republicans. More vociferous backers of intervention, however, came from the revolutionary left. A minority of the leaders and writers of revolutionary syndicalism had supported the war of 1911 against Turkey. The syndicalist labor confederation, the Unione Sindacale Italiana, quickly adopted a resolution supporting neutrality in August 1914, but this was rejected by some syndicalist leaders, particularly by such spokesmen as the young Alceste de Ambris, who brought the Unione Sindacale Milanese (USM)—the syndicalist organization in Italy's largest industrial center—to call for intervention on the side of the Entente. By October various syndicalist leaders and several key local groups formed a new ad hoc organization, the Fascio Rivoluzionario d'Azione Internazionalista.

Forming a *fascio*—the term means band, union, or league—had been standard practice among various sectors of Italian radicalism since the 1870s.[1] *Fasci* (the plural form) had been organized by trade unions, middle-class radicals, or reformist peasants, the most famous being the Fasci Siciliani, the broad federation of peasants and others in Sicily during 1895–96 that had brought much of the island out in revolt against the existing political and economic

---

1. *Fascio* is derived from the Latin *fasces*, which originally referred to the bundle of lictors (rods with protruding axeheads) carried by the judges of ancient Rome, symbolizing justice, unity, and the sovereignty of the Roman Republic.

structure. Thus the nomenclature adopted by the new Fascio Rivoluzionario was standard practice among the Italian left.

Its leaders held that to participate in the war was not to abandon social revolution, for the war itself would be the most direct route toward revolution. Class-based revolts such as the Parma general strike of 1908 or the Red Week only two months before the war had failed to mobilize broad support or engage all the forces of society. Entry into the war could supposedly expedite such a course because it would mobilize all Italy for the first time, generating massive commitment that could catalyze the entire society. The cause of the Entente was becoming synonymous with progress and ultimate revolution, they insisted, because German-Austrian militarism and imperialism were the main obstacles to decisive revolutionary change in Europe. Thus entry into the war would be the gateway to revolution, and if the liberal parliament would not support the war, the Italian people should revolt against the parliament.

Most European socialist parties adopted somewhat analogous rationales and supported their own countries' war efforts, though in some cases only as "defensists" against erstwhile foreign aggression. A number of French revolutionary syndicalists committed themselves enthusiastically to the French cause from the beginning, a dramatic step epitomized by the change in title of Gustave Hervé's revolutionary organ from *La Guerre Sociale* (Social War) to *La Victoire* (Victory).

The Italian Socialist Party (PSI), however—like the Bolsheviks in Russia—refused to support the war effort, rejecting the arguments of left interventionists. Its abstention reflected the deep social division and lack of national integration in Italy, the strongly elitist character of government, and the great gap between the north and the south. Nationalism was primarily a passion of sectors of the urban middle classes in a still primarily rural and agricultural society.

Benito Mussolini

The most important new member of the Fascio Rivoluzionario was the former Socialist leader Benito Mussolini who abandoned his neutralist party to join the left interventionists in December 1914.[2] Mussolini had been born in 1883

---

2. Of the numerous biographies of Mussolini, by far the best and most thorough is the eight-volume work by Renzo De Felice, the first volume of which appeared in 1965 and the last in 1990. In English there are D. M. Smith, *Mussolini* (New York, 1982); I. Kirkpatrick, *Mussolini: A Study in Power* (New York, 1964); C. Hibbert, *Benito Mussolini* (London, 1962); and R. Collier, *Duce!* (New York, 1971). See also A. Brissaud, *Mussolini*, 3 vols. (Paris, 1983), and G. Giudice, *Mussolini* (Turin, 1971). Luigi Preti, in *Mussolini giovane* (Milan, 1982), treats his early years. The most extensive treatment by admirers is G. Pini and D. Susmel, *Mussolini: L'Uomo e l'opera*, 4 vols. (Florence, 1953–55). Mussolini was the author of *My Autobiography* (London, 1928) and

in a village of the Romagna in northeastern Italy, in a disrict known for re-belliousness and left-wing politics. His mother was a schoolteacher, and his father, a Socialist and a blacksmith who had named him for the Mexican lib-eral Benito Juárez. Though his education in local schools was occasionally marred by his violent assaults on fellow students, Mussolini earned an elemen-tary school teacher's certificate at the age of nineteen. During a brief sojourn in Switzerland he became a Socialist, then returned to Italy to complete mili-tary service and for a short time taught school. Mussolini soon displayed talent as a journalist, and in 1908 he briefly became editor of an Italian Socialist paper in Austrian Trieste but was expelled for revolutionary agitation. From that point he rose rapidly in Socialist Party ranks as an outspoken champion of violent revolution, and he helped lead the revolutionaries to control of the party apparatus in 1912. Mussolini was made editor of *Avanti* (Forward), the official Socialist newspaper, emerging as one of the party's top leaders at the age of twenty-nine.[3]

Despite his ardent revolutionism, Mussolini, like many Italian Socialists, had never been an orthodox Marxist. He was deeply influenced by the theoreti-cal critique of Marxism of the revolutionary syndicalists and of Sorel, and by the Pareto theory of elites. For the young Mussolini this meant that revolution required violent action and leadership by elites and that the masses could only be moved by sentiments, emotions, and myths. Mussolini spoke of himself as an "authoritarian" and "aristocratic" Socialist; he was elitist and antipar-liamentarian, and he believed in regenerative violence. Like the revolutionary syndicalists (and, in a different manner, Lenin), Mussolini believed that only a special revolutionary vanguard could create a new revolutionary society.

Lenin hailed the victory of Mussolini and the other revolutionary leaders of Italian socialism in 1912. A. James Gregor observes,

> Lenin's endorsement is interesting particularly in retrospect. Many have commented on the views shared by the young Mussolini and Lenin, since it is evi-dent that their Marxism did in fact have substantial similarities. Both insisted on intransigent opposition to bourgeois parliamentarianism, reformist policies, and compromissary political strategies. Both considered the Party a hierarchically organized agency for the effective furtherance of socialist objectives. Both envi-sioned a leadership composed of a minority of professional revolutionaries, who would serve as a catalyst in mobilizing mass revolutionary sentiment. Neither had any faith in the spontaneous organization of the working classes. Both ar-

Memoirs, 1942–1943 (London, 1949), the latter edited by R. Klibansky. His various writings are collected as *Opera omnia di Benito Mussolini*, 36 vols. (Florence, 1951–63).

3. The fullest account of Mussolini as a Socialist will be found in R. De Felice, *Mussolini il rivoluzionario, 1883–1920* (Turin, 1965), 1–220. See also L. Dalla Tana, *Mussolini massima-lista* (Salsomaggiore, 1964); G. Bozzetti, *Mussolini direttore dell' "Avanti"* (Milan, 1979); and E. Gentile, *Mussolini e "La Voce"* (Florence, 1976).

gued that the preoccupation with immediate economic interests condemned exclusively economic organizations to a bourgeois mentality of calculation for personal profit and well-being. Both argued that only organized violence could be the final arbiter in a contest between classes. And both agreed that revolutionary consciousness could only be brought to the masses from without, through a tutelary, revolutionary, and self-selected elite.[4]

Like other revolutionary Socialists, Mussolini condemned the Libyan war of 1911, arguing that such an enterprise under a bourgeois government left the national flag a "rag" to be "planted on a dunghill." Yet in Trieste he had supported irredentism to emancipate Italian workers, and he was also associated with some of the more progressive and radical of the new nationalists, primarily on cultural issues.

Under the aegis of the revolutionaries, the PSI nearly doubled its membership in two years, and at the party congress of Ancona in April 1914 Mussolini emerged as the dominant figure in the party. Yet he continued to stress the role of minorities both in leadership and in action and the importance of emotion and moral concepts to the regeneration of Marxism. In his earlier attacks on the reformist leaders, he had published a series of biting articles under the pseudonym "L'homme qui cherche" (The man who is seeking). This restlessness and search for new definitions and new opportunities would remain characteristic of his entire political career. The failure of Red Week in June 1914 only sharpened his concern for an alternative to the Socialist strategy, all the more as it became clear that the moderates and trade unionists remained strong within the movement.

As a revolutionary, Mussolini supported certain patriotic interests and the defense of the nation, though not aggressive war. After the First World War began, it became clear that the sympathies of Italian Socialists lay with the Entente and opposed "oppressive, militaristic" Germany and Austria-Hungary. Yet they officially stood for neutrality, holding that the latter could be defeated without Italian or Socialist participation. As the weeks passed, Mussolini became increasingly dissatisfied with this position, for the failure of Red Week had shown the severe limitations of the present narrow class socialism. Italy was an only partially industrialized country which had not fully developed a modern bourgeoisie, much less a modern proletariat, and was, he argued, menaced by the powerful central European empires. Before a modern social revolution could take place, the country's interests must be defended and its structures modernized. Participation in the war on the side of the Entente would further these goals, strengthening the modern forces of the country, weaken-

4. A. J. Gregor, *Young Mussolini and the Intellectual Origins of Fascism* (Berkeley, 1979), 133. This is the best study of Mussolini's early intellectual development. For further comparison with Bolshevism, see D. Settembrini, *Il Fascismo controrivoluzione imperfetta* (Florence, 1978), 21–29.

ing moderates and conservatives who wanted to preserve the status quo on the basis of neutralism. On October 18, 1914, Mussolini publicly came out against the official Socialist position, and two days later he resigned as editor of *Avanti*. In mid-November he began publication of a new paper, pointedly called *Il Popolo d'Italia* (The People of Italy), rather than merely "The Workers of Italy," financed by prointerventionist business interests. The goal now was revolutionary war.

After joining the Fascio Rivoluzionario in December, Mussolini soon became its most prominent spokesman. His associates were heterogeneous, consisting of revolutionary syndicalists, new "national syndicalists," such as Sergio Panunzio, who had left revolutionary syndicalism behind them, a handful of other prowar revolutionary Socialists, prowar reformist Socialists, progressive nationalists from *La Voce,* and radical republicans. The emphasis was on mobilization of the masses, incorporating them for the first time into a great national enterprise, which would subsequently become a great revolution. On January 6, 1915, *Il Popolo d'Italia* announced reorganization of the Fascio as the Fasci d'Azione Rivoluzionaria and referred to it as the "fascist movement." Meanwhile Marinetti's avant-garde Futurists, who held the most bloody-minded prowar doctrines of any group, organized their own Fasci Politici Futuristi to promote Italian participation in the conflict.

By May Italy stood on the brink of war. It was an open secret that negotiations had been conducted with the Entente but that the moderate liberal majority in the parliament was reluctant to vote for entry. Thus interventionists of all political hues descended on Rome in mass demonstrations for five days in mid-May, creating the spectacle and subsequent myth of a Maggio Radioso (Radiant May) by which nationalist activists took command of the public sphere and pressured the deputies into voting for war. At that point, in fact, the deputies had little choice; foreign policy decisions by law and custom were largely reserved by the monarchy, and the main liberal leaders had no desire to take responsibility for thwarting the recent negotiations or blocking irredentist goals.[5] The Fasci d'Azione Rivoluzionaria hailed the "victory over the parliament" as the beginning of what would ultimately be an antiparliamentary revolution.

Italy in World War I

The conservative liberal prime minister, Antonio Salandra, had conceived of Italian participation as a means not merely of gaining irredentist territory and expanding the empire but also of strengthening the monarchy and government

5. A. Repaci, *Da Sarajevo al "maggio radioso"* (Milan, 1985); A. Staderini, "Mobilitazione borghese e partecipazione politica a Roma alla vigilia della prima guerra mondiale," *SC* 18:3 (June 1987): 507–48.

enough to roll back recent democratizing reforms.[6] His goal was a system of authoritarian or reactionary liberalism, and his ministry calculated on a relatively short war in which Italian intervention would tip the scales on behalf of the Entente. In fact, they had initiated a massive mobilization far exceeding anything in the history of modern Italy, which would continue at an increasing pace for three and a half years and take more than six hundred thousand lives. No sector of society was quite so conspicuous in volunteering as the younger leaders of revolutionary and national syndicalism. Of some fifty who presented themselves, thirty-six were accepted; within six months, six of these had been killed and another nine wounded.

The great majority of Italians did their duty, military service falling disproportionately on the poor and downtrodden southern peasantry, never otherwise integrated into national life. The war almost immediately settled into a stalemate in difficult mountain terrain not far beyond the original Italo-Austrian border. Successive Italian offensives largely failed, with increasing loss of life. The Salandra government, which had entered the war championing Italy's *sacro egoismo* (sacred egoism), fell from office within a year, and broader coalitions were subsequently organized to keep Italy in the war. The national debt eventually increased some 500 percent, and inflation grew well over 300 percent by war's end. Military service seemed hopeless to semiilliterate peasants; tens of thousands of soldiers had to be court-martialed for desertion, though only about 750 were executed. Through all this ordeal, the Italian forces managed at least to hold their front, tying down a large portion of the Austro-Hungarian army and thus contributing to the Entente victory in November 1918.[7]

The war experience had the effect of pushing many patriots further to the right. As the ordeal became increasingly traumatic, a series of new leagues and *fasci* were formed by nationalists to support present governmental policies and keep Italy in the war.[8] The main victims of this trend were the two leading left interventionist groups, the Fasci d'Azione Rivoluzionaria and the republicans. Some of the more leftist of the left interventionists became uneasy and by late

6. B. Vigezzi, *L'Italia dalla neutralità all'intervento nella prima guerra mondiale* (Milan, 1965); E. Rosen, "Italiens Kriegseintritt im jahre 1915 als innen politisches Problem der Giolitti-Ara," *Historische Zeitschrift* 187:2 (April 1959): 289–363.

7. P. Melograni, *Storia politica della grande guerra* (Bari, 1971); and the collective *Il trauma dell'intervento, 1914–1919* (Florence, 1968).

8. Thus there were formed such wartime ad hoc groups as the Fascio Nazionale Italiano, Fascio Romano per la Difesa Nazionale, Federazioni dei Fasci di Resistenza, Lega Nazionale Italiana, Lega Antitedesca, Comitato d'Azione per la Resistenza Interna, Comitato d'Azione Patriottica, and Comitato d'Azione del Fronte Interno. At the end of 1917 the most nationalistic deputies in the parliament formed their own Fascio Parlamentario. There was considerable overlapping membership between these groups, and the thinking in some of them became increasingly frenzied, with discussion of the kidnapping or assassination of liberals or pacifists, possible street violence, or the formation of a wartime dictatorship.

1916 criticized Mussolini's *Il Popolo d'Italia* for being too rigid and authoritarian. Others, like the national syndicalist Panunzio, tried to reconcile military aggressiveness and international justice, as in his work of 1917, *Il concetto della guerra giusta* (The Concept of the Just War). The contradictions became too great, and the Fasci d'Azione Rivoluzionaria eventually dissolved.

Mussolini served in the army seventeen months, eight of them on the front lines. He was severely injured when a mortar exploded in a training accident in February 1917, terminating his military service. During the war his commitment to nationalism became complete and extreme, and his goal became combining nationalism and some form of socialism that would come to terms with all classes. The new Communist dictatorship in Russia he judged a contradictory product of peculiarly Russian conditions engaging in mass violence and compulsion, an attempt to overcome Russia's backwardness with a ruthless policy of "primitive accumulation" not likely to last long. The war had given many Italians a new sense of national identity and pride and of achievement. Mussolini and some of his colleagues sought now to project this spirit of discipline, self-sacrifice, and fraternity onto Italy as a whole through a revolutionary and social nationalism.

Meanwhile the Italian Socialist Party had remained, with the Bolsheviks of Lenin, one of the two major neutralist socialist parties in Europe. It had adopted the slogan *Ne aderire, ne sabotare* (Neither support nor sabotage), and many thousands of Socialist industrial workers enjoyed draft deferments to maintain production. The *combattenti* (army combat veterans) came increasingly to resent those denounced as *imboscati,* or shirkers, on the home front.

The Postwar Crisis

The years immediately after the war did not produce the triumphant and unified Italy promised by wartime patriots but rather a major political and social crisis, compounded by short-term economic depression. Though the peace settlement awarded Italy all the Trentino–Alto Adige district up to the Brenner Pass (territory that included two hundred thousand German-speaking Austrians), as well as the city of Trieste and a border with the newly created state of Yugoslavia that left half a million Slovenes on Italian land, it denied all further Italian claims in the east Adriatic, Turkey, and Africa. It also excluded any right to the largely Italian-inhabited city of Fiume on the Adriatic coast of Yugoslavia.[9] Thus nationalists denounced the governmental leaders who accepted

9. In a practical sense, the peace settlement might be considered advantageous, for it incorporated all genuinely irredentist claims (save for Fiume) and gave Italy a compact new territory on the northeast that offered a strong and defensible strategic position, while avoiding further imperial costs overseas.

these terms as *rinunciatari* (renouncers) and labeled the outcome a *vittoria mutilata* (mutilated or truncated victory) which had failed to justify the costs and sacrifices of the war.[10]

If patriotic opinion in some respects felt frustrated and even outraged, social opinion in much of Italy was even more resentful. The war had indeed mobilized most of the population for the first time, as the left interentionists had correctly foreseen. In Italy, as in other belligerent countries, many promises had been made concerning social and economic improvements once victory had been achieved, but improved wartime wages normally did not compensate for inflation, and amid the postwar reconversion slump hundreds of thousands were out of work.[11] The result was an attitude of social resentment and explosiveness without precedent in the modern history of Italy, for northern city workers, poor southern peasants, and farm laborers in diverse regions felt exploited and betrayed, leading to a massive new wave of strikes in the north and land seizures in the south.

These conditions produced drastic political changes, thanks also to further reform in the electoral law, which added to the universal male suffrage introduced in 1912 a new system of proportionate representation and large multimember constituencies for the first postwar elections, of September 1919. This arrangement sought to eliminate much of the corruption in Italian elections but also favored mass parties and large bloc coalitions. The old prewar parliamentary system had been based on small single-member constituencies manipulated by a narrow political elite, now outflanked in much of the country by newer mass parties.

The big winner in the elections of September 1919 was the Socialists, who gained 156 seats, nearly one-third of all those in the 508-member parliament. They were followed by a new outsider mass party, the Italian People's Party (PPI), a large Christian democratic group formed only a few months earlier, which won 100 seats. The Popolari, as they were called, were split between progressivists and conservatives, and they refused to cooperate with the atheistic and anticlerical Socialists, who in turn took a similar attitude toward them. Thus though the two new mass parties had won a bare majority, they would not cooperate to form a new reform ministry.

Government still remained largely—though no longer exclusively—in the hands of the old middle-class liberals, who for fifty years had maintained a kind of minority rule based on *trasformismo* (transformism), which referred to

10. See H. J. Burgwyn, *The Legend of the Mutilated Victory: Italy, the Great War, and the Paris Peace Conference, 1915–1919* (Westport, Conn. 1993).

11. The postwar economic crisis is treated in D. J. Forsyth, *The Crisis of Liberal Italy* (New York, 1993), and F. Catalano, *Potere economico e fascismo: La crisi del dopoguerra (1919–1921)* (Lerici, 1964).

the systematic co-optation of new reformist elements. The old liberals were still the largest single force in the parliament but could not command a majority and thus could not govern without allies. They had lost their secure political base and also much of their self-confidence, for the new mass parties would not cooperate in *trasformismo* as had reformist predecessors.

Revolutionary Socialists, known as *massimalisti* (maximalists), dominated the party congress of October 1919. They introduced a new party statute stipulating that "the violent conquest of political power on behalf of the workers will signify the passing of power from the bourgeois class to the proletarian class, thus establishing the transitory regime of the dictatorship of all the proletariat." [12] They also declared adherence to Lenin's new Communist International. [13] Their affiliated trade union confederation, the CGL, swelled from 250,000 members at war's end to approximately 2 million by mid-1920. During 1919 there were 1,663 industrial strikes, involving more than a million workers, and 208 agrarian strikes, involving half a million farmworkers. In the year following there were 1,881 industrial strikes, again involving more than a million workers, and 189 agrarian strikes, this time involving more than a million farmworkers. Between September and November 1919 a wave of land seizures occurred in provinces of the south and center as dwarfholders and laborers seized patches of uncultivated or marginally cultivated land. Socialists now routinely proclaimed that it was only a matter of time until a revolution equivalent to Russia's broke out in Italy; not without reason did 1919–20 soon become known as the *bienio rosso* (red biennium).

To all this the government had little answer. Finally in June 1920 the liberals turned in desperation to Giovanni Giolitti, prewar leader of Italian politics, who was a reformer and progressivist (though also an adept of the old minority system and electoral corruption). Now seventy-eight years of age, Giolitti himself, however, symbolized a system that seemed in inevitable decline. [14]

Founding of the *Fasci Italiani di Combattimento*

Both nationalists and Socialists had expected the end of the war to produce great things, and the resultant mood of expectation and activism gave rise to the broader rubric of *diciannovismo* (1919-ism). Thus a typical, though at first quite

12. Quoted in E. Gentile, *Storia del Partito Fascista, 1919–1922* (Bari, 1989), 63.

13. See G. Petracchi, *La Russia revoluzionaria nella politica italiana: Le relazioni italiano-sovietiche, 1917–1925* (Rome, 1982).

14. The lengthiest study of the postwar crisis is R. Vivarelli, *Storia delle origini del fascismo: L'Italia dalla grande guerra alla marcia su Roma* (Bologna, 1967, 1991), in two rather disparate volumes a quarter century apart. In addition, see C. Giovannini, *L'Italia da Vittorio Veneto all'Aventino* (Bologna, 1972).

unimportant, *diciannovista* phenomenon was the gathering of about two hundred left interventionists and ardent nationalists, including at least six women, in a rented hall of the Piazza San Sepolcro in Milan on March 23, 1919, to form a revolutionary new nationalist movement called the Fasci Italiani di Combattimento. The participants came almost exclusively from four backgrounds: they comprised revolutionary syndicalists turned national syndicalists, a few former Socialists who had made the journey to extreme nationalism with Mussolini, Marinetti and some of his Futurists (who were relinquishing efforts begun shortly before to found a Partito Politico Futurista),[15] and above all some former members of the Italian army commandos known as *arditi* (who had worn black uniforms during the war to symbolize the color of death).[16] Of 85 identifiable participants, there were 21 writers and journalists, 20 white-collar employees, 12 workers, 5 manufacturers, and 4 teachers. Of 104 identifiable by age, the majority were between twenty and forty, with only 18 over forty, while 14 were under twenty.[17]

15. On Futurist politics, see E. Gentile, "Il futurismo e la politica," in *Futurismo, cultura e politica*, ed. R. De Felice (Turin, 1988), 105–57; N. Zapponi, "La politica come espediente e come utopia: Marinetti e il Partito Politico Futurista," in *F. T. Marinetti Futurista* (Naples, 1977), 220–39; and E. Santarelli, *Fascismo e neofascismo* (Rome, 1974), 3–50.

Futurist avant-gardism had become slightly eroded by the end of the war with the emergence of the "new tendencies" and "new reality" trends. Umberto Boccioni, the best of the Futurist painters, had died in the military in 1916. Marinetti nonetheless sustained the original doctrines and emphases of the movement.

While Italian Futurism helped to found Fascism, the other leading group of artistic Futurists, in Russia, eagerly embraced communism in 1917–18. Russian Futurism lacked the nationalist-constructionist characteristics of the Italian movement and was motivated by an if anything even more extreme hatred of the status quo, whose destruction would be replaced by some sort of highly abstract utopia. Russian Communists and Futurists retained a high opinion of Marinetti, whom the Soviet commissar for culture Anatoly Lunacharsky called in 1920 "the one intellectual revolutionary in Italy." They considered the Italian Futurists more in the nature of mistaken heterodoxists like Russian Mensheviks rather than counterrevolutionaries or enemies. In these early years "both Lenin and Gramsci hurled abuse not so much at the Fascists as at the Socialists, Mensheviks, Social-Democrats and other 'liberals.' " I. Golomstock, *Totalitarian Art* (New York, 1990), 11, 12.

16. G. Rochat, *Gli arditi della grande guerra* (Milan, 1981); F. Cordova, *Arditi e legionari dannunziani* (Padua, 1969). Giovanni Sabbatucci, in *I combattenti nel primo dopoguerra* (Rome, 1974), treats the politics of veterans in general.

17. Gentile, *Storia del Partito Fascista* 35. This is the best history of the Fascist movement in its early years. Other accounts of this period include P. Alatri, *Le origini del fascismo* (Rome, 1956); F. Catalano, *La nascita del fascismo (1918–1922)* (Milan, 1976); G. Dorso, *Mussolini alla conquista del potere* (Turin, 1949); A. D'Orsi, *La rivoluzione antibolscevica* (Milan, 1985); and E. Santarelli, *Origini del fascismo (1911–1919)* (Urbino, 1963). The best participant account is M. Rocco, *Come il fascismo divenne una dittatura* (Milan, 1952). Robert Vivarelli, in "Interpretations of the Origins of Fascism," *JMH* 63:1 (March 1991): 29–43, presents a lucid discussion of the principal interpretations.

The best general account of the first decade of Italian Fascism is A. Lyttelton, *The Seizure*

The principal leader was Mussolini, flanked by an executive commission of nine, in which he would function as the first among equals. He announced the new movement as an "antiparty," rejecting the standard structure of political parties as rigid and sterile. What was needed was a new nationalist elite to mobilize the masses for an "Italian revolution." Yet the goal was to attract a broad young following on both the left and the center, so that Mussolini described the minimal program published on March 30 in *Il Popolo d'Italia* as not new "and not even revolutionary" but designed to achieve democracy and renovate the nation. It called for universal suffrage for both men and women at age twenty-one, abolition of the elitist Senate, democratic election of a new national assembly to decide on the form of the state, the eight-hour day, worker participation in industrial management, election of national technical councils in all branches of the economy and public services, and strong anticlerical policies. Subsequent "postulates" published on May 13 were rather more detailed and more radical.[18] On other occasions the Fasci leaders spoke of the need for decentralization of the executive and an elective, independent magistracy, the confiscation of unproductive capital and of land on large estates for redistribution to the peasantry, the abolition of secret diplomacy, and a new foreign policy based on the independence and solidarity of all peoples within a general federation of nations. This basically leftist, sometimes revolutionary, program is not what people normally mean when they refer to fascism. Mussolini did not, apparently, believe that he was actually founding a new movement in March 1919 as much as creating some sort of front to rally left interventionists in the immediate postwar era. The only act of violence came three weeks later, on April 15, in Milan, when a group of former *arditi*, together with Fasci members (more the former than the latter), attacked a provocative Socialist

---

of Power: Fascism in Italy, 1919–1929 (New York, 1973). Other leading accounts include E. Santarelli, *Storia del movimento e del regime fascista* 3 vols. (Rome, 1967); A. J. De Grand, *Italian Fascism* (Lincoln, 1982); E. R. Tannenbaum, *The Fascist Experience: Italian Society and Culture, 1922–1945* (New York, 1972); and P. Milza and S. Berstein, *Le fascisme italien, 1919–1945* (Paris, 1980).

The first major pro-Fascist account was G. Volpe, *L'Italia in cammino: L'ultimo cinquantennio* (Milan, 1927), and the lengthiest G. A. Chiurco, *Storia della rivoluzione fascista, 1919–1922*, 5 vols. (Florence, 1929). The principal neofascist history is P. Rauti and R. Sermonti, *Storia del Fascismo*, 6 vols. (Rome, 1976–78).

The best Italian bibliography is R. De Felice, ed., *Bibliografia orientativa del fascismo* (Rome, 1991), while P. V. Cannistraro, ed., *Historical Dictionary of Fascist Italy* (Westport, Conn., 1982), is very useful.

18. The "postulates" of May 13 included abolishing the Senate, lowering the voting age to sixteen for both sexes, establishing the eight-hour day, worker participation in technical management, a national technical council for labor, old age and sickness insurance for all, confiscation of uncultivated land, development of a full secular school system, progressive taxation with a capital levy, an 85 percent tax on war profits, confiscation of the property of religious institutions, and declaration of the principle of the "nation in arms."

demonstration, killing three of the demonstrators and later burning the offices of *Avanti,* the Socialist daily.[19] This was not planned, however, and was not a formal Fasci action.

The main radical nationalist initiative in 1919 was not taken by the Fasci di Combattimento but by the war hero Gabriele D'Annunzio, Italy's most popular poet, who rallied a small expeditionary force to seize the east Adriatic city of Fiume for Italy in September. D'Annunzio governed Fiume as a separate city-state for fifteen months, to the grave embarrassment of the Italian government, which hesitated to move against the irredentists, even though their ranks included troops who had deserted the regular army. Even more important, D'Annunzio succeeded in creating a new style of political liturgy made up of elaborate uniforms, special ceremonies, and chants, with speeches from the balcony of city hall to massed audiences in the form of a dialogue with the leader. In other key contributions to what soon became "Fascist style," D'Annunzio and his followers adopted the *arditi*'s black shirts as uniform, employed the Roman salute of raising the right arm, developed mass rallies, brought out the hymn *Giovinezza* (Youth), organized their armed militia precisely into units, and developed a series of special chants and symbols. By August 1920 the national syndicalists Alceste de Ambris and A. O. Olivetti had completed the Carta del Carnaro (Carnaro Charter), Europe's first corporatist constitution, which featured the civic equality of citizens of both sexes, decentralization, and a relatively democratic structure of corporatism. A treaty of November 1920 between Yugoslavia and Italy eventually recognized Fiume as a "free city" but territorially affiliated with Italy, and the following month an Italian military force finally drove D'Annunzio's band from the city. The Fiume episode, however, demonstrated the weakness of the government and the explosive force of nationalism and also resulted in the creation of what would later become Fascist style.[20]

For Mussolini the effort was an embarrassment, for he doubted its success and yet as a radical nationalist had to support it, even though he was always careful not to become seriously involved. He was well aware that D'Annunzio

19. See the account in De Felice, *Mussolini il rivoluzionario* 520–21.

20. The lengthiest narrative is F. Gerra, *L'impresa di Fiume,* 2 vols. (Milan, 1974). See also P. Alatri, *Nitti, D'Annunzio e la questione adriatica* (Milan, 1959); idem, *Gabriele D'Annunzio* (Turin, 1983); M. A. Ledeen, *The First Duce* (Baltimore, 1977); R. De Felice, *D'Annunzio politico, 1918–1938* (Bari, 1978); P.Chiara, *Vita di Gabriele D'Annunzio* (Milan, 1978); A. Spinosa, *D'Annunzio* (Milan, 1987); G. Host-Venturi, *L'impresa fiumana* (Rome, 1976); and Cordova, *Arditi e legionari dannunziani.* Paolo Valesio, in *Gabriele D'Annunzio: The Dark Flame* (New Haven, 1992), presents a positive reevaluation of the poet's literary work.

On de Ambris and the Carta del Carnaro, there are three works by Renzo De Felice: *La Carta del Canaro nei testi di Alceste de Ambris e di Gabriele D'Annunzio* (Bologna, 1973); *Sindacalismo rivoluzionario e fiumanesimo nel carteggio De Ambris-D'Annunzio* (Brescia, 1966); and *Intellettuali di fronte al fascismo* (Rome, 1985), 259–76.

enjoyed much more popularity than he did, and after 1920 he had to face another radical nationalist alternative to the Fasci in the symbol of D'Annunzio and *fiumanesimo* (the idea of the Fiume enterprise)—corporatist, nationalist, and nominally democratic.

For the Fasci, it made little difference. Though eighteen of its nineteen candidates had been *combattenti,* all but one met defeat in the general elections of November 1919. In industrial Milan, the center of the Fasci, they drew only 5,000 of 275,000 votes and elected no one, the only successful deputy being elected in Genoa. The Fasci were in fact neither fish nor fowl, nationalist but leftist, and they drew from neither side. After the elections Milan Socialists paraded past Mussolini's apartment carrying a coffin that bore his name. By the end of the year the Fasci retained only thirty-one local groups with members totaling a mere 870. Only small sections in Milan, Turin, Cremona, Venice, and Trieste remained.

During the following year, at first a dreary one, the chief strategist of the Fasci was the former revolutionary syndicalist Cesare Rossi, who edited the official weekly *Il Fascio.* Rossi was a member of the central committee, and from June 1920 he served as vice-secretary-general. The tactic which he and Mussolini devised was based first on an effort to win over the moderate left and to transform the movement into one of "national socialism" in the form of a kind of "labor party." [21] This was designed as a cross-class movement of producers, welcoming all producers to a national syndicalist system that would minimize the role of the state.

The Fasci recovered very slightly in the spring of 1920, relying still on "the contributions of members and donations collected from sympathizers." [22] Ceremonies were being developed for meetings involving flags, uniforms, and the wearing of daggers, and at the second national congress of May 24–25, 1920, sixty-five local *fasci* totaling 2,375 dues-paying members were represented.[23] It was agreed that the program should be moderated to appeal to the middle classes, and in the following month the Futurist Marinetti, who strongly favored the original revolutionism, abandoned the movement.

Mid-1920 was meanwhile the high-water mark of the Socialist offensive. The strike wave reached its peak, accompanied by demonstrations and occasional acts of violence. There were even several mutinies among military units. In September occurred the "occupation of the factories," as organized Socialist labor, faced with a sudden lockout, took physical possession of factories in the main northern industrial areas. This seemed to be the equivalent of the

21. Early in 1920 the Futurist and sometime Fascist Gastone Gorrieri had organized a tiny Partito del Lavoro (Labor Party) in Florence.

22. Gentile, *Storia del Partito Fascista* 40.

23. Ibid., 115.

revolutionary general strike; if labor could operate an industrial economy on its own, then it could take over Italy. The Giolitti government wisely refrained from intervention; after two weeks the Socialists realized that they could not operate an industrial economy on their own and relinquished control of the factories in return for improved contracts and the legalization of councils of factory workers.

The autumn of 1920 marked the Socialist high tide in the countryside, particularly in the Po Valley of the north. The Socialists won most of the agrarian strikes and endeavored to set up the rural equivalent of the closed shop in the northern countryside, establishing exclusive contracts and placing themselves in a position to dominate the agrarian economy. Moreover, in October the government legalized the tenure of farmworkers and sharecroppers who had seized parcels of private land in many different provinces. Despite the partial setback in the occupation of the factories, socialism appeared to be still on the march, and the government not only did little to stop it but seemed to be encouraging it.

The Rise of *Fascismo*, 1920–1921

The appearance of Italy as a country in the process of social revolution was partially genuine, but also deceptive. Italy was no backward unindustrialized peasant-and-worker country like Russia in 1917, for in fact during the past generation it had experienced one of the highest economic growth rates in the world, and its middle classes were expanding rapidly in numbers. According to one study, in 1881 all the middle classes (including holders of very small farms) amounted to 46 percent of the active population, and farmworkers and urban workers composed about 52 percent, whereas by 1921 the middle classes had increased to more than 53 percent, and the workers had declined to 45 percent.[24] This shift was caused especially by the acquisition of title to farmland by landless families in the decade 1911–21, during which period the number of landholders doubled from about 1.1 million to nearly 2.3 million—a revolution of sorts, but one much more capitalist than socialist in nature. These new small farm owners—including some of those who had just gained title through direct action—often became increasingly conservative and resentful of the drive by rural trade unions to control the agrarian economy. Moreover, while organized labor was able to maintain or in some cases improve its standard of living, the real income of government and white-collar employees was declining. These general conditions encouraged an increasingly broad consen-

---

24. P. S. Labini, *Saggio sulle classe sociali* (Bari, 1975). Between 1911 and 1921 the proportion of Italy's total rural population composed of landless laborers declined from 55 to 44 percent, according to V. Zamagni, *The Economic History of Italy, 1860–1990* (Oxford, 1993), 264.

sus within the middle classes on the need for energetic defense of their interests against revolutionary socialism.

With the weak and divided government apparently either unable or unwilling to contain the Socialists, a series of diverse middle-class defense leagues were formed during 1919–20, including one called the Fascio d'Azione Popolare. The most important militant anti-Socialist organization was the Italian Nationalist Association (ANI), which possessed a clear program of authoritarian corporatism and imperialism. Its members had organized the first significant nationalist militia, the blue-shirted Sempre Pronti (Always Ready), and they had carried out the first planned assault on the left in their attack on the Bologna Camera del Lavoro as early as July 15, 1919. The Nationalists were nonetheless clearly right-wing and oriented toward a middle- and upper-class elite, with no potential to spearhead a mass movement.

Violence in Italy generally increased after World War I, and several hundred deaths resulted from political disorders during 1919 and the first half of 1920, most of these the result of activities by Socialists or the army and police. Members of the Fasci di Combattimento had engaged in comparatively few such acts during the first year of their organization's existence, if for no other reason than numerical weakness. By the spring of 1920 the Fasci were organizing a political militia of *squadre* (squads) in various parts of the north, the strongest at the newly incorporated city of Trieste, an Italian island in a Slovene hinterland. Using the excuse of the murder of two Italian naval officers at Split on the Yugoslav coast, the Trieste *squadre* seized the offensive on July 20, carrying out the first in a series of assaults against both Socialists and Slovene organizations in the city and in the surrounding countryside. They soon dominated the streets and had the Socialists on the run, with local Italian military authorities watching complacently and even providing equipment. On July 3 *Il Popolo d'Italia* declared that the Fasci were neither "legalitarian at any price, nor a priori antilegalitarian," and said that "they do not preach violence for the sake of violence, but reply to all violence by passing to the counterattack," and so would use "means adapted to the circumstances."

In the autumn of 1920 the focus of Fasci action shifted for the first time from the cities to the countryside, where new opportunities beckoned. The Socialist offensive reached its zenith in the northern rural areas that autumn, as a massive strike wave followed a series of Socialist victories in local municipal elections. The Socialists announced that control of local government would provide the initial basis for revolution, while farmworker strikes and organizational campaigns tried to coerce smallholders as well as laborers into Socialist unions. Black-shirted Fasci *squadristi* began to launch assaults on Socialists in the countryside, for here they could count on newfound support among virtually all sectors of the middle and upper classes, and even among some laborers. For the first time Fasci membership grew rapidly, increasing nearly tenfold during the last seven months of the year. Mussolini had at first supported the Socialist occupation of the factories strictly as a means of improving labor conditions, but he soon declared war on the Socialist organizations, not, he said, so much because of their economic program per se but because of their internal subversion of Italian unity and their internationalism. Against the revolution of class internationalism, the Fasci declared the Italian national revolution (increasingly vague in socioeconomic content) and launched numerous "punitive expeditions" of *squadre* into the countryside to sack Socialist headquarters and break up trade unions. *Il Fascio* declared on October 16, "If it is to be civil war, so be it!" [25] The *squadre* were organized in groups of thirty to fifty members, often led by former army officers and partly composed of military veterans. They soon proved much more efficient and aggressive in the use of violence than any of the leftist groups. Following a bloody combat with Socialists at Bologna on November 20, violence spread rapidly in northern Italy.[26]

Though the term had occasionally been used ever since 1914 (and possibly even earlier), it was not until the autumn of 1920 that a new "ism" became prominent in Italian usage: *Fascism* was used to indicate the now increasingly violent movement of the Fasci di Combattimento, whose members were called Fascists tout court. Thus the use of organized political violence—much more organized, concerted, and aggressive than the limited violence of the Italian left—proved integral to the sudden rise of Fascism in the autumn and winter of 1920–21. The notion, however, that the Fascists had somehow invented modern political violence is lamentably superficial. Some sort of military or paramilitary militia was more or less inherent in the Jacobin tradition and was characteristic of the left and even of liberals in countries like Spain and Portugal during the nineteenth century. The inventor of the "shirt movement" was indeed an Italian, but he was Giuseppe Garibaldi of the democratic republicans in the 1860s, not Mussolini. By the close of the nineteenth century, organization of paramilitary militia was more and more commonly discussed among a variety of organizations. Systematic deployment of a political militia was nonetheless an innovation of Lenin's Bolsheviks in Russia, who quickly raised political violence to unprecedented heights. In Italy, however, Socialist violence was never more than sporadic, while the Fascists began to make its systematic employment their basic mode of activity. Fascism soon became a political force that rested on a military organization, something unknown outside of Russia.

As leader of a nationalist "war against Bolshevism," the Fasci grew from 20,000 dues-paying members at the end of 1920 to nearly 100,000 by the end of

---

25. Quoted in Gentile, *Storia del Partito Fascista* 149.
26. See M. Cancogni, *Storia del squadrismo* (Milan, 1959), and idem, *Gli squadristi* (Milan, 1980).

Italo Balbo leads a "punitive expedition" in Parma

April 1921, and then nearly doubled during the following month to 187,588.[27] They had become a mass movement, indeed the largest political organization in Italy, since Socialist members were organized primarily through trade unions. New members came disproportionately from the lower middle classes, and in some cases local farmer groups in northern Italy moved directly from the Socialist CGL or other organizations to the Fasci. Political postulates were now in flux. Mussolini and other spokesmen made a clear distinction between what they called the productive and the parasitic bourgeoisie, declaring the Fasci a movement for all productive Italians. There was increasing talk about the need for a strong "new state," even a nationalist dictatorship, but one that would follow a more liberal economic policy to reduce or eliminate many state economic powers and permit an autonomous and decentralized national syndicalism to free Italy's productive forces. Some local Fascist leaders nonetheless proclaimed "land to those who work it," and in February the first Fascist trade union was organized, an initiative soon expanded into a national trade union organization.

In the process,

> between the end of 1920 and the first months of 1921, the Fasci completely changed physiognomy, character, social structure, key centers, ideology, and even members. Of their leaders only Mussolini and a very few others completely followed this change in all its phases. Many original members fell by the wayside, and a number even passed over to the opposite side, but the majority almost inadvertently found themselves at a certain point different from what they had been in the beginning, supplanted in the leadership of the movement by new elements, of diverse origin and development, tied to quite different realities.[28]

The Fascism of San Sepolcro was tiny and urban, while the mass Fascism of 1921 was predominantly rural, directed by new *ras,* or local leaders, in key northern districts, such as Italo Balbo in Ferrara, Dino Grandi in Bologna, and Roberto Farinacci in Cremona. The new mass Fascism had not been created by Mussolini so much as it had sprung up around him in the rural areas of the north. It was more middle-class, more economically moderate, and more categorically violent and anti-Socialist.[29] It also eased the movement's financial problems by providing wealthier contributors, particularly in the countryside.

27. Gentile, *Storia del Partito Fascista* 163.
28. De Felice, *Mussolini il rivoluzionario* 460–61.
29. A lengthy literature on the rise of Fascism in the various provinces and regions has developed since the appearance of S. Sechi, *Dopoguerra e fascismo in Sardegna* (Turin, 1969), and S. Colarizzi, *Dopoguerra e fascismo in Puglia* (Bari, 1971). Some of the more noteworthy works are R. Cavandoli, *Le origini del fascismo a Reggio Emilia* (Rome, 1972); P. Corner, *Fascism in Ferrara* (Oxford, 1974); A. Roveri, *Le origini del fascismo a Ferrara, 1918–1921* (Milan, 1974); F. J. Demers, *Le origini del fascismo a Cremona* (Bari, 1979); L. Nieddu, *Dal combattentismo al fascismo in Sardegna* (Milan, 1979); L. Casali, ed., *Bologna, 1920: Le origini del fascismo*

In the national elections of May 1921 the elderly prime minister Giolitti decided to try to tame the Fascists by applying to them the time-honored liberal tactic of *trasformismo,* including them in the governmental electoral coalition. In this contest the Fascists presented seventy-four candidates, who ran on a relatively moderate program, though claiming a virtual monopoly on true patriotism. The government slate won nearly 48 percent of the vote; this enabled thirty-eight Fascists, including Mussolini, to gain seats in the parliament, where they formed a minority of slightly more than 7 percent.[30] The elections were also a personal triumph for Mussolini, who drew nearly two hundred thousand votes in Milan. The Socialist vote dropped from 32.4 percent of the national total to 24.7 percent, while the new Communist party attracted only 2.8 percent.

Violence continued through the electoral period. According to one record, during the first four and a half months of 1921 there were at least 207 political killings, with distinctly more Socialist than Fascist victims, while another ten Socialists were killed on the day after elections.[31] Army and government employees were generally (though not universally) sympathetic to the Fascist offensive and in some areas helped the *squadristi* to obtain arms, though on April 20 the prime minister had issued strong orders to end such complicity. Not all violence was initiated by Fascists; on March 23 a bomb placed by anarchists in a Milan theater killed twenty-one people and injured perhaps as many as two hundred.

The expansion of Fascism into a mass organization and its success, however modest, in the new elections raised the question of its future. Despite the influx of middle-class people who in some cases were relatively conservative, Mussolini did not want to lose his position on the left. He was still thinking of the possibility that the movement would crystallize in a possible "Fascist Labor Party" or "National Labor Party." On May 22 he announced that the republicanism of the Fasci must be accentuated and raised the possibility of

---

(Bologna, 1982); A. L. Cardoza, *Agrarian Elites and Italian Fascism: The Province of Bologna, 1901–1926* (Princeton, 1983); P. Alberghi, *Il fascismo in Emilia Romagna* (Modena, 1989); F. Snowden, *The Fascist Revolution in Tuscany, 1919–22* (Cambridge, 1989); and L. Ganapini, ed., *La storiografia sul fascismo locale nell'Italia nordorientale* (Udine, 1990).

30. See J. Petersen, "Elettorato e base sociali del fascismo italiano negli anni venti," *Studi Storici* 16 (1975): 627–29. William Brustein has produced data to demonstrate that the Fascists succeeded in winning some votes away from the Socialists, particularly among the rural upwardly mobile lower middle class. See Brustein, "The 'Red Menace' and the Rise of Italian Fascism," *American Sociological Review* 56 (Oct. 1991): 652–64.

31. Data from the archive of the undersecretary of the interior in G. De Rosa, *Giolitti e il fascismo in alcune sue lettere inedite* (Rome, 1957), 78, cited in De Felice, *Mussolini il rivoluzionario* 607–8. Interior Ministry documentation indicated that during the first four months of 1921 the police had arrested 396 Fascists and 1,421 Socialists. R. De Felice, *Mussolini il fascista* (Turin, 1966), 1:35–39.

a new agreement with the Socialists—assuming they would shed their internationalism and class revolutionism—and the democratic Catholic Popolari to form a sort of nationalist-leftist coalition government. This brought howls of protest both from the more conservative neo-Fascists and also from the governing liberals, who felt betrayed after having included the Fascists in the electoral bloc.

Mussolini in fact felt considerable pressure to curtail the anti-Socialist violence and still could not imagine taking a categorically antileftist position. Any real danger from a revolutionary leftist offensive was now over, for, as Mussolini declared in *Il Popolo d'Italia* on July 2, 1921: "To maintain *that the Bolshevist danger still* exists in Italy is to mistake fear for reality." One goal might be to detach the CGL, the trade union confederation, from its close association with the Socialists. Meanwhile, in July Mussolini began negotiations with the Socialist leaders for an interim "pact of pacification"—also desired by the Socialists—that would bring the violence under control.

Just at this point, however, the violence threatened to get entirely out of hand. An expedition of some five hundred *squadristi* to Sarzana, a town near Genoa, on July 21 was blocked by police, who uncharacteristically fired on the Fascists. Local Socialists then joined in a counterattack; eighteen Blackshirts were killed, and a great cry arose for vendetta vengeance. Fascist reprisals mounted in the weeks that followed; at the town of Grosseto nine people were murdered. Such deeds were magnified by blackshirt hardliners to sabotage negotiations with the Socialists.

Mussolini responded on July 22 by establishing the Fasci's first membership purge commission to weed out uncontrollables and criminals, and *Il Popolo d'Italia* admitted that in some areas *squadristi* were out of control. A Pact of Pacification was then officially signed by leaders of the Fasci and the Socialist Party in Rome on August 2.

Two weeks later an independent meeting of the *ras* for most of the northern provinces met in Bologna to denounce the pact. Fascist cadres and provincial leaders saw the Socialists as the enemies of the nation who must be destroyed. Though some local Fasci accepted the pact, the main provincial leaders sharply criticized Mussolini, declaring that he had not created the movement, which could get along without him. They strongly rejected the notion of any "parliamentary solution" to Italian problems, and on August 18 Mussolini resigned as head of the Fasci's national executive commission, though the resignation was not accepted.[32]

During September party leaders held two secret anti-Mussolini meetings. The doctrines of the Fasci required strong leadership, but resentment against

---

32. Conversely, the resignation of the moderate and leftist Cesare Rossi as vice-secretary-general was accepted on August 20. He publicly denounced Fascist violence and realized that his goal of a Fascist Labor Party was becoming impossible.

Mussolini's lingering leftist loyalties and tendency to compromise was strong. One alternative leader was D'Annunzio. Since being evicted from Fiume he had created his own extreme nationalist organization, though with progressivist overtones, the Federazione Nazionale dei Legionari Fiumani (FNLF). For the most part, however, he had withdrawn once more into literary work, whence he played both ends against the middle, alternately presenting himself as a supporter of Fascism and as an alternative to Fascism.[33] Similarly, some hoped that the revolutionary syndicalist Unione Italiana del Lavoro (UIL) might endorse Fascism and help create a more nationalistic worker base than the Socialist CGL, but the congresses of both the UIL and the FNLF in September adopted strong anti-Fascist positions.[34]

The Pact of Pacification became a virtual dead letter as soon as it was signed, generally ignored by the more active *squadristi*. They argued that official founding of the Italian Communist Party earlier in the year, followed by formation of the militant left-wing Arditi del Popolo, merely created new violence and subversion. September featured a large-scale Fascist "march on Ravenna"; altogether, in the sixty days following the signing of the pact, twenty-one Fascists (mainly *squadristi*) and an undetermined number of leftists were killed.[35] In October a new Socialist congress was once more dominated by the revolutionary "maximalists." This situation only played into the hands of hardline Fascists, who were determined to continue to foment civil war against the left as their own springboard to power.

Organization of the Partito Nazionale Fascista

Finding the Pact of Pacification a dead letter, Mussolini soon grasped that he could achieve more to organize and discipline the Fasci by accepting the continued violence in return for agreement on calling a national congress that would convert the movement into an organized party. Such a congress met at Rome from November 7 to 10, 1921, amid the relative indifference of the local population—demonstrating that despite Fascism's success at mobilizing support in the north, it was not a completely national movement and grew weaker the farther south on the peninsula one went.

The great majority of delegates supported transformation of the Fasci into

33. F. Perfetti, *Fiumanesimo, sindacalismo e fascismo* (Rome, 1988), 1–115. On D'Annunzio's subsequent relations with Fascism, see N. Valeri, *D'Annunzio davanti al fascismo* (Florence, 1963), and G. Rizzo, *D'Annunzio e Mussolini* (Rome, 1960). D'Annunzio enjoyed considerable support among the members of the Arditi del Popolo, while the Fiume Carta del Carnaro was in vogue among the more leftist Fascists.

34. The UIL had been founded initially at the end of 1914 by the revolutionary syndicalists who had been expelled from the Unione Sindacale Italiana for supporting nationalism and entry into the war.

35. Gentile, *Storia del Partito Fascista* 357.

a regular Partito Nazionale Fascista (PNF), led by a central committee of nine-teen members representing the various regions and an executive committee of eleven headed by Mussolini, whose leadership was generally accepted once more. He was now becoming known increasingly as Duce (Leader), one of the Roman neologisms ever more popular in the movement, derived from the Latin *dux*. His chief lieutenants, however, were now mostly different people from those with whom he had founded the movement two years earlier.[36]

The new party was defined as "a revolutionary militia placed at the ser-vice of the nation. It follows a policy based on three principles: order, disci-pline, hierarchy."[37] The congress called for a strong Italian state supported by national technical councils and—unlike the original Fasci of 1919—endorsed Italian imperialism. Economically the party stood for productivism and "eco-nomic liberalism" as opposed to classism and collectivism, but the congress's program differentiated this from nineteenth-century liberalism by assigning stronger leadership and coordination to the state. The party would comprise three units: cadres of members, the *squadre*, and Fascist trade unions. Each local *fascio* was expected to organize its own *squadra d'azione*, which would elect its own leader, while the party would also create *gruppi di competenza* (lit., "competence groups") to provide advice and leadership in all important technical areas of national life.

In a major speech in parliament on December 1, Mussolini declared that "the Fascist program is not a theory of dogmas about which no discussion is tolerated. Our program is in process of continual elaboration and tranfor-mation."[38] This pragmatism, opportunism, and open-endedness were already giving rise to the criticism that Fascists had no real doctrine save brute force. Emphasis on action and dynamism, and the precept that action preceded ide-ology, had the effect of exaggerating the Fascists' philosophical vitalism and nonrationalism. Economically the party wanted to reduce state expenditures, improve the tax structure, eliminate most state subsidies, guarantee free trade, and encourage capital formation, as well as support the eight-hour day and pro-gressive social legislation. The formerly republican movement now declared itself "agnostic" on the issue of republic versus monarchy.

By this time a number of dissident Fascist groups had drawn off and cre-

---

36. There are various biographies of Mussolini's chief lieutenants: G. B. Guerri, *Giuseppe Bottai, un fascista critico* (Milan, 1976); idem, *Italo Balbo* (Milan, 1984); E. Misefari, *Il quadrum-viro col frustino: Michele Bianchi* (Cosenza, 1977); G. Rochat, *Italo Balbo* (Turin, 1986); P. Nello, *Dino Grandi* (Bologna, 1987); M. Canali, *Cesare Rossi* (Bologna, 1991); and H. Fornari, *Musso-lini's Gadfly: Roberto Farinacci* (Nashville, 1971). The best of all books on Balbo is C. G. Segrè, *Italo Balbo: A Fascist Life* (Berkeley, 1987). See also F. Cordova, ed., *Uomini e volti del fascismo* (Rome, 1980), and N. Caracciolo, *Tutti gli uomini del Duce* (Milan, 1982).

37. Gentile, *Storia del Partito Fascista* 398.

38. Ibid., 400.

Table 4.1. Social or Professional Background of PNF Members, November 1921

Background	Percent of PNF Members
Farmworkers	24.3
Urban workers	15.4
Students	13.8
Farmers and landowners	12.0
Private employees	9.8
Salesmen and artisans	9.2
Members of free professions	6.6
State employees	4.8
Manufacturers	2.8
Teachers	1.1
Seamen	1.0

Source: R. De Felice, *Mussolini il fascista* (Turin, 1966), 1:6.
Note: The percentages do not sum to 100.0 due to rounding.

ated "autonomous" and opposition circles in such widely scattered cities as Florence, Ferrara, Bari, and Taranto.[39] Mussolini, however, had been successful in pulling the bulk of the movement back together under his leadership. The antagonistic provincial bosses rallied to him almost without exception, led by the most important of his critics, Dino Grandi, the twenty-six-year-old *ras* of Bologna.

The congress reported party membership of approximately 220,000, which is roughly corroborated by a subsequent police report. More than half the members—135,349—were concentrated in the north, with 42,576 in the south, 26,846 in central Italy (proportionately the weakest membership), and 13,682 in the islands.[40] Of 151,644 members for which data are available, more than half—87,182—were army veterans, and nearly 25 percent were under voting age. Data were collected on the social or professional background of a large portion of the membership, and the members proved to be rather less heavily middle class than had seemed to be the case (see table 4.1). During 1922 membership would increase further, to approximately 250,000. (Meanwhile membership in the Socialist Party would decline to 70,000, and that of the CGL would drop from 2 million to only 400,000.) By 1922 the party was publishing five daily newspapers, two magazines, and more than eighty other local publications. Mussolini now referred to the party members as the

39. R. Cantagalli, *Storia del fascismo fiorentino, 1919–1925* (Florence, 1972), 283–301; S. Versari, *Una pagina di storia del fascismo fiorentino: Il fascismo autonomo* (Rocco S. Casciano, 1938).

40. De Felice, *Mussolini il fascista* 1:7. See also W. Schieder, "Der Strukturwandel der Faschistischen Partei Italiens in der Phase der Herrschaftsstabilisierung," in *Faschismus als soziale Bewegung*, ed. W. Schieder (Hamburg, 1976), 69–96.

new elite of Italy, a special new class that had arisen "from the people," and especially from the countryside, to provide leadership for the revitalization and expansion of the nation.

If the data on the membership were accurate, then at this time the PNF came close to representing the overall social structure of Italy. Urban and rural workers constituted 41.4 percent of the active population and made up 39.7 percent of the party membership. The only sector significantly overrepresented was students in higher education, who contributed 13.8 percent of the membership. The leadership, on the other hand, was heavily middle class, with at least 80 percent of its members coming from the middle sectors. Of the 127 highest-ranking leaders, 77 percent belonged to the middle class but only 4 percent to the wealthy bourgeoisie. Of this total group, about 35 percent were lawyers, while writers and journalists amounted to 22 percent and teachers constituted 6 percent. Of the 14 highest-ranking leaders, including Mussolini, the political origins of 7 lay with the revolutionary left and the republicans. But of 136 federal secretaries to serve in the first year of the party's existence, only 37 came from the left, while 22 were Freemasons (a group later to be proscribed by the Mussolini regime).[41]

Auxiliary organizations were being expanded. Special Fascist student groups had existed since mid-1920 and were originally the most radical sector of the party. At the party congress they were reorganized into the Avanguardia Giovanile Fascista for secondary students and the Federazione Nazionale Universitaria Fascista for university students.[42] The first *fasci femminili* sections for women members had also been formed in 1920, and the new party statutes created a separate hierarchy for these groups, with membership open to women aged sixteen years and older.[43] The trade unions, first organized in several cities early in 1921, were restructured in February 1922 as the Confederazione Nazionale delle Corporazioni Sindacali (CNCS). This organization soon claimed to have half a million members, though the autonomous ambitions of its leaders were already being dashed.[44] During the first half of 1922, 40 percent of the party's income came from dues and private contributions; most of the rest was provided by banks and certain major industrialists.[45]

By the end of 1921 Fascist liturgy and style, built especially from the precedents introduced by D'Annunzio at Fiume, had been fully developed.

41. Gentile, *Storia del Partito Fascista* 557.
42. On the former, see P. Nello, *L'avanguardismo giovanile alle origini del fascismo* (Bari, 1979).
43. D. Detragiache, "Il fascismo femminile da San Sepolcro all'affare Matteotti (1919–1925)," *SC* 14:2 (April 1983): 211–51.
44. F. Cordova, *Le origini dei sindacati fascisti* (Bari, 1974); F. Perfetti, *Il sindacalismo fascista* (Rome, 1988).
45. Gentile, *Storia del Partito Fascista* 436–40.

Elaborate ceremonies were now conducted, decorated by innumerable flags and special new visual symbols, accompanied by mass chants. Frequent and large-scale public marches were a common feature. Especially impressive were the opulent funeral services for the fallen, which had become a centerpiece of Fascist ritual, uniting the living and the dead in a tribute to courage and the overcoming of mere mortality. The massed response of "Presente!" to the calling of the slain comrade's name expressed the new Fascist cult of transcendence through violence and death.

Though *squadrismo* was given relatively free rein, at the beginning of 1922 Mussolini made an effort to build a more organized superstructure, creating a national command for the *squadre*, now placed under four regional inspector generals, with a set of national regulations finally issued on October 3, 1922. Conversely, being unable (and partly unwilling) to compete in mass violence, top Socialist leaders were now giving orders to their own followers not to fight back. This passivity was also revealed in the decline in strikes during 1921, when the number of agrarian work stoppages fell precipitately (by more than 90 percent), and the total number of strikers dropped by half.

There is no adequate study of political violence in Italy for these years. Before the war, southern Italy had a very high homicide rate, and northern Italy, a low one. Adrian Lyttelton writes, "The homicide rate for Italy as a whole jumped from 8.62 in 1919 (still below pre-war levels) to 13.95 in 1920 and reached a maximum of 16.88 in 1922." [46] Political violence was concentrated in the otherwise relatively nonviolent north, and during 1919 and 1920 it scarcely amounted to as much as the increase in the number of homicides in Sicily during those two years (390). The two years of maximal political violence were 1921 and 1922, when the Fascist offensive was at its height. The Fascists also suffered numerous fatalities and sometimes referred to "thousands" of their member slain by "subversives," but the nearest thing to a detailed Fascist report indicates that a total of 463 Fascists were slain during 1919–22.[47] A later Fascist government report indicated that only 428 members were slain through the end of 1923. The number of leftists, mainly Socialists, killed by Fascists was probably at least twice as high. Gaetano Salvemini later calculated roughly that approximately 900 Socialists had been killed by the end of 1922, and that figure may be close to the mark.[48] Not all the latter were slain

46. A. Lyttelton, "Fascism and Violence in Post-War Italy," in *Social Protest, Violence and Terror in Nineteenth- and Twentieth-Century Europe*, ed. W. Mommsen and G. Hirschfeld (New York, 1982), 262.

47. This detailed 4 Fascists killed in 1919, 36 in 1920, 231 in 1921, and 192 in 1922, indicating that they suffered casualties in approximate proportion to their own aggressiveness. J. Petersen, "Violence in Italian Fascism, 1919–25," in Mommsen and Hirschfeld, eds., *Social Protest* 275–99.

48. G. Salvemini, *Le origini del fascismo in Italia* (Milan, 1979), 321.

by Fascists, for official statistics reported 92 people killed by the police and army during 1920 and 115 the following year. The total number of deaths from political violence in Italy for the four years 1919–22 may have amounted to nearly 2,000. On December 21, 1921, Prime Minister Ivanoe Bonomi ordered prefects throughout Italy to disarm all political militias, but little effort was made to carry this instruction out on the local level. Similarly, national authorities commanded that justice be administered firmly and fairly to all, but local government, judicial authority, and the police more often than not continued to favor the Fascists.

The March on Rome

By 1922 two major new myths had emerged in Fascist thinking: the myth of ancient Rome emerging in a new Rome, ever dear to Italian nationalists, and the idea of the "Stato Nuovo," the new Rome to be crystallized in a new kind of nationalist state that would play the central role in the revitalization of the nation.[49] In keeping with the burgeoning cult of Rome, the Blackshirt militia was being reorganized into units based on the ancient Roman designations of legions, cohorts, and centuries, with Roman emblems and Roman titles for the commanders.

This was accompanied by frank calls for a Fascist dictatorship. Mussolini announced early in 1922 that "il mondo va a destra" (the world is turning politically toward the right) and against democracy and socialism, and that the twentieth century would be an "aristocratic" century of new elites, which in Italy would carry out a spiritual and moral revolution. A cult of youth and of direct action had become fully developed, and Fascist spokesmen were even less defensive about the use of violence than before. It was now embraced simply as a "style of life." Violent action served to maintain the spirit of the patriotic war through the "communion" of the *squadre* and would ultimately lead to national justice in Italy.[50]

The goal now was political power, and the tactic was concerted direct action. In May 1922 a new offensive was launched in which Fascists simply took over local government in more and more districts of the north. During the summer the eastern Po Valley was almost completely occupied politically, though in July the escalation of violence was so great that even Fascist leaders grew concerned that it might escape their control. Moderates expressed so little opposition that the government often felt itself forced to remove any pre-

49. The principal study of the development of this concept is E. Gentile, *Il mito dello Stato Nuovo* (Bari, 1982).

50. The chief theoretical statements in this phase were Sergio Panunzio's essay *Diritto, forza e violenza: Lineamenti di una teoria della violenza* (Bologna, 1921), which developed Sorelian ideas with a degree of originality, and his subsequent *Lo stato di diritto* (1922).

fect overtly hostile to Fascism, and by October the only northern cities where Socialist strength remained intact were Turin and Parma.

Bonomi was replaced as prime minister in February 1922 by the moderate liberal Luigi Facta, who formed another center-right coalition.[51] Economic conditions were now clearly improving, but the political crisis showed no sign of abating. There were two main weaknesses: the left—especially Socialists and Catholic Popolari—would not unite effectively with the minority liberal center, and genuine centrist liberals and the more conservative liberals would not agree resolutely to resist the Fascists. For most of the more conservative elements, Fascism was simply too useful as a force to quell the worker left.

In February 1922 the Alleanza del Lavoro (Labor Alliance) was formed by nearly all the non-Catholic left—the Socialists, the CGL, the remaining independent revolutionary syndicalists, anarchists, and republicans—to resist Fascism. Even so, the Socialists still refused to engage in a frank democratic coalition with bourgeois liberals, and they grew weaker with each passing month. Socialist leaders therefore attempted a protest that ended in disaster. The tactic was what was termed a *sciopero legalitario,* a defensive "legalitarian strike," not to press for new labor demands but simply to protest the need for return to the law and order spurned by Socialists two years earlier. It turned out to be completely counterproductive, for just as moderates had begun to take alarm at the relentless spread of Fascist aggressiveness in the north, the protest strike suddenly reawakened fear of the "Red menace." The strike lasted three days, August 1–3, during which at least twelve were killed. Five days of Fascist reprisals followed.

The Facta government was divided between three sectors: Facta himself and two other liberals who wanted to bring Fascists into the government; three liberals ready to resist that with force; and the two Popolari and one other liberal who wanted to resist but avoid the use of force. Meanwhile, a new congress on October 8 to found an official Liberal Party was dominated by the conservative liberals of Antonio Salandra, who was happy to be called an "honorary Fascist."

Within the royal family, the queen mother was known to be quite sympathetic to the Fascists, as was the king's cousin, the duca d'Aosta. On October 7 two senior generals informed Victor Emmanuel III that the army was generally well disposed toward Fascism.[52] Italy's leading liberal intellectual, Benedetto Croce, declared that Fascism was ultimately compatible with liberalism.[53] The

---

51. D. Veneruso, *La vigilia del fascismo: Il primo ministero Facta nella crisi dello stato liberale in Italia* (Bari, 1968).

52. The role of the army is analyzed in G. Rochat, *L'esercito italiano da Vittorio Veneto a Mussolini* (Bari, 1967).

53. Cf. U. Benedetti, *Benedetto Croce e il fascismo* (Rome, 1967), and S. Zeppi, *Il pensiero politico dell'idealismo italiano e il nazionalfascismo* (Florence, 1973).

new pope, Pius XI, elected in February 1922, adopted a similarly benevolent attitude, while the archbishop of Milan flew Fascist banners from his cathedral.

After the Socialist strike, Mussolini realized that the Fascists would probably never again have so favorable an opportunity, and he feared that Giolitti might soon be recalled to form a broad coalition which would effectively bar the path to a Fascist-led government. The *squadristi* were actively expanding what was now being referred to as the Fascist state in the north, taking over the entire regional administration of the Alto Adige, while in some of the largest northern cities the party had the support of the elected municipal councillors and of the appointed provincial prefects. During the middle of October Mussolini met with D'Annunzio, who had continued to play a double game, and managed to neutralize him, while also gaining the support of one small sector of the dissident left (Captain Giuseppe Giulietti and his seamen's union).

Final decisions for the March on Rome were taken between October 16 and 24. While some party radicals urged an outright coup d'état, moderate and conservative Fascists (now led by Grandi) opposed the new strategy to force the creation of a Mussolini-led coalition government, but they were overruled. Action began on October 27 with direct Fascist takeovers, most without violence, of many police headquarters, community centers, and even arsenals in north and north central Italy. The plan was to concentrate about twenty-five thousand *squadristi* in Rome as a display of force, without any intention of attempting a coup (even though twenty-five small Fascist *arditi* squads were being organized for minor terrorist acts, if further pressure was needed).

There was not the slightest danger of a violent Fascist coup against the government itself. Not only had no plan for this been developed, but the army and police forces outnumbered the Fascists to be concentrated in Rome, and the district commander, General Pugliese, was prepared to execute any order given by the crown. Leaders of the Italian Nationalist Association also assured King Victor Emmanuel that their own Sempre Pronti militia was ready to fight the Blackshirts, if requested. As far as economic interests were concerned, leaders of the Confindustria (the industrialists' association) would have preferred a strong government led by Giolitti, though they liked the current Fascist economic program and would accept a new coalition government with some Fascist participation.

Resolution of the crisis depended ultimately on the king. The diminutive Victor Emmanuel (scarcely five feet tall) was not lacking in intelligence but tended toward pessimism and cynicism. He feared civil war among the non-Socialist forces and wanted to avoid any outcome that might revive the left. On October 28 Blackshirts began slowly to move toward Rome by rail, truck, and foot; eventually some twenty-six thousand assembled on the outskirts of the city in the rain, mostly armed only with *manganelli*, the clubs which were their favorite (usually nonlethal) weapons. When Victor Emmanuel refused

The fascist leaders Bianchi, De Bono, De Vecchi, Mussolini, and Balbo head a demonstration immediately after the March on Rome, October 1922

to grant a decree of martial law, the Facta government resigned. The king then sought to resolve the crisis by asking the conservative pro-Fascist liberal Antonio Salandra to form a coalition that would include Mussolini and a few other Fascist ministers. Mussolini, remaining in the north near Milan, was intransigent on the issue of becoming prime minister himself, however, and by the morning of the twenty-ninth Salandra gave up further efforts to organize a new government. The Fascist contingency plan was to form an alternative revolutionary government in the north if denied power in Rome, but on the night of October 29 Victor Emmanuel invited Mussolini to come to Rome to lead a new parliamentary coalition. The Fascist leader arrived in the capital the next morning. The Blackshirts waited outside the city for two more days, then entered Rome in a victory parade on the thirty-first. Thirteen people died in the violence that ensued.[54]

Mussolini as Semiconstitutional Prime Minister, 1922–1925

The March on Rome had been a sort of *pronunciamiento*, or political imposition, but not a violent coup d'état. The Blackshirts did not seize Rome; Mussolini came to power legally, heading a normal multiparty parliamentary coalition. He was prime minister and also held the portfolio of foreign affairs, but only three of the other thirteen cabinet members were Fascists. There were two senior military commanders for army and navy, two Catholic Popolari, two democratic liberals, one conservative liberal, one social democrat, and one minister from the Nationalist Association, while Italy's leading academic philosopher, the pro-Fascist Giovanni Gentile, was minister of education. At thirty-nine, Mussolini was the youngest prime minister in Italian history, but otherwise this seemed a normal government. One of the leading liberal critics, Gaetano Salvemini, opined that this government would be no different from its predecessors, for all Italian administrations had been elitist and authoritarian.

In his opening address to the parliament, Mussolini sneered that he could have eliminated the assembly, and then asked for and easily received constitutional authorization by parliamentary vote to rule by decree for a year—a legal procedure, once properly voted upon. The initial priority was economic policy. Alberto de Stefani, the new Fascist minister of finance, was an economic liberal. He balanced the budget by severe cutting and initiated a sharp reduction in the size of the civil service. This scarcely looked like a leviathan on the march. The only overt police measures at first were taken against

54. A. Repaci, *La marcia su Roma* (Milan, 1972); idem, *Sessant'anni dopo: 28 ottobre 1922, il giorno che stravolse Italia* (Milan, 1982); A. Casanova, *Il '22: Cronaca dell'anno piu nero* (Milan, 1972); G. F. Venè, *Il golpe fascista del 1922* (Milan, 1975); E. Lussu, *Marcia su Roma e dintorni* (Rome, 1945).

Communists and a few Dannunzian rebels. The economy had already begun to recover and continued to improve. Labor proved remarkably quiet. In the twelve months before Mussolini became prime minister, there had been 680 strikes, 522,354 strikers, and well over seven million lost workdays. During his first twelve months in office, this declined sharply to only a quarter of a million workdays lost.[55]

One of Mussolini's main concerns was to take the Fascist Party itself more firmly in hand. In December 1922 he created a new organ, the Fascist Grand Council, to provide a governing executive under his own leadership, but he himself would control its agenda. Since Blackshirt disorders continued, a decree law of January 1923 reconstituted the party militia as the Milizia Volontaria per la Sicurezza Nazionale (Voluntary Militia for State Security, MVSN), now an institution of the state, with regular army officers to be named as senior commanders. A party circular in June stressed that henceforth the regular state prefects would be the supreme state and political authority in each province, even over the party. In February 1923 the Nationalist Association, with its Sempre Pronti militia, had officially joined the Fascist Party en masse.

Paradoxically, the successful outcome of the March on Rome led during 1923–24 to a new crisis of Fascism, in this phase a crisis over goals, policies, and identity. Membership increased steadily, tripling by the end of 1923 to 782,979, but the bulk of these adherents were opportunists eager to be on the winning side. Mussolini busied himself with affairs of state, attending to governmental detail, and gave the party itself little attention. Veteran Blackshirts grew ever more restive, for Mussolini was operating a seminormal constitutional government. Militants demanded the beginning of the "Fascist revolution," but this was nowhere in sight. Restiveness and resentment led in turn to occasional renewed *squadristi* outbursts that incurred the Duce's mounting displeasure.

In the rambling discussion that developed concerning the future of Fascism, at least four positions can be defined: the moderate revisionists, the national syndicalists, the right wing of Nationalists and hardliners, and diverse minor currents. The so-called revisionists comprised a core group of leaders, headed by Massimo Rocca and also by such figures as Grandi and Giuseppe Bottai, who was making a name for himself as one of the most rational and critical of the younger *gerarchi* ("hierarchs," or leaders). They sought to moderate Fascism in order to effect a new synthesis with the established system, in which Fascism would provide leadership and inspiration in such key areas as nationalism, culture, and labor organizations. Rocca pressed the development of the *gruppi di competenza* as a way to promote new elites and more modern

55. On economic policy in this phase, see F. Catalano, *Fascismo e piccola borghesia* (Milan, 1979), 7–86.

leadership. For the revisionists, the Fascist revolution would be a cultural and political revolution but not a rigid dictatorship.[56]

The national syndicalists, led by Sergio Panunzio, A. O. Olivetti, and Edmondo Rossoni (head of the CNCS) formed the most coherent "Fascist left." They advocated a new system based on national syndicalism to replace parliamentary liberalism. A syndicalist-based structure would supposedly advance the interests of workers and the ordinary population, provide a more authentically nationalist and representative government than a parliament dominated by political parties, and also carry out a true revolution by modernizing the economy.[57]

The "Fascist right" or hardliners comprised two distinct sectors. The first stemmed from the most intransigent *squadristi* and their leaders, who sought to extend Fascist violence into a complete dictatorship. The other was made up of most members of the former Italian Nationalist Association, led ideologically by Alfredo Rocco, who stood for a fully articulated and authoritarian corporate state to replace the entire liberal system. Such a government would build a united and culturally renewed Italy and would actively promote Italian imperialism. Right-wing former Nationalists and veteran *squadristi* nonetheless differed considerably, for the former wanted no extended "Fascist revolution" but simply a revamped authoritarian corporate state that would coalesce with the existing elite.[58]

In addition, there were a variety of minor currents, such as the "Catholic Fascists" or *clerico-fascisti*, members who had joined only since 1921 and who sought to harmonize an originally anti-Catholic movement with Catholicism, which Mussolini had courted for some time.[59] Farther right yet was a small coterie of "monarchist Fascists," whose goal was to use the strength of Fascism not for a Fascist revolution but to establish the more traditional dictatorship of an absolute monarchy under Victor Emmanuel.[60] Then there were the cultural or idealist Fascists, most notably the philosopher Giovanni Gentile, who aspired to the leadership of a cultural revolution. There was the populist extreme left, whose main spokesman was the journalist Curzio Malaparte, who

---

56. The best discussion of these ideological currents will be found in E. Gentile, *Le origini dell'ideologia fascista* (Bari, 1975). See also L. Mangoni, *L'interventismo della cultura* (Bari, 1974).

57. In addition to the works on Panunzio previously cited, see J. J. Tinghino, *Edmondo Rossoni* (New York, 1991).

58. Some of the more moderate former ANI militants, such as Luigi Federzoni, were more akin to right-wing revisionists than devotees of Rocco's full authoritarian corporate state ideology. Cf. L. Federzoni, *Italia di ieri per la storia di domani* (Verona, 1967).

59. J. F. Pollard, "Conservative Catholics and Italian Fascism: The Clerico-Fascists," in *Fascists and Conservatives*, ed. M. Blinkhorn (London, 1990), 31–49.

60. The history of this small sector is recounted in F. Perfetti, *Fascismo monarchico* (Rome, 1988).

wanted to see Fascism make a "revolution of the people" that would reflect what the populist left considered true Italian popular culture, both intellectually and socially.[61] There were small sectors of a dissident extreme left or "free Fascism" that promoted a progressivist and leftist revolution of "liberty" under the Fascist banner.[62] Arguably the most bizarre was a small group of neopagan elitists who sought to re-create the aristocratic culture of ancient Rome, propounding extreme elitism, revived Roman imperialism, and a mystical ethos that borrowed from the pagan occult.[63]

Mussolini found no solution for the dilemma of the party, but more important, he found it very difficult to define the future course of his government as well. He groped for some formula that would enable him to retain power, almost as much as ever *l'homme qui cherche*. Ultimately, his government would still depend on a parliamentary majority, and he cast about for means of creating a more genuinely Fascist or pro-Fascist parliament. This finally took the form of the Acerbo Law (named after a young Fascist deputy), passed by the parliament with many abstentions, which would give the list of candidates with the highest plurality in the new elections two-thirds of the seats in parliament, provided that the plurality amounted to 25 percent of all votes cast.

New elections were then held in April 1924 amid considerable violence and intimidation. The Fascist-led *listone* (major coalition of Fascists, moderates, and conservatives) was announced as having won 66 percent of the vote, giving it 403 seats (most of them belonging to Fascist deputies) and an absolute majority in the parliament. Thirty-six percent of the Fascist deputies who were elected were inexperienced young men still in their twenties. Despite this commanding new position, Mussolini was still uncertain how to proceed, and he even went back to considering a political deal with moderate Socialists and/or the CGL. Fascist hardliners made it clear, however, that any sort of compromise would not be acceptable: they expected an authoritarian Fascist regime.

61. Malaparte. who was in fact the best of all the Fascist journalists and went on to a somewhat distinguished career in literature, tried to articulate a kind of pseudo-anthropological cultural Fascism, based on the notion of Italian identity with Mediterranean Catholic "southern" and "Oriental" culture, opposed to the German Protestant "West." M. Ostenc, *Intellectuels italiens et fascisme (1915–1929)* (Paris, 1983), 68–75, 159–68, 276–95.

62. P. Lombardi, *Per le patrie libertà: La dissidenza fascista tra "mussolinismo" e Aventino (1923–1925)* (Milan, 1990).

63. The leading theorist of this current was Julius Evola, who published *Saggi sull'idealismo magico* (Rome, 1925) and *Teoria dell'individuo assoluto* (Turin, 1927). His elitist solipsism and extreme misogyny produced the article "La donna come cosa" (Woman as Thing) in 1925. The pagan-elitist current was strongly discouraged after the sharper turn toward modus vivendi with the Church in 1925. M. Rosi, "L'interventismo politico-culturale delle reviste tradizionaliste negli anni venti: Atanor (1924) e Ignis (1925)," *SC* 18:3 (June 1987): 457–504. Evola would later become Italy's leading "racial philosopher," and later yet the chief ideologue of the country's terrorist radical right in the period after World War II. (See the Epilogue.)

Within two months the government was rocked by the Matteotti Affair, the most serious crisis Mussolini would experience before World War II. On June 10 the moderate Socialist Giacomo Matteotti, leading parliamentary spokesman for the opposition, was kidnapped outside his home. It would later develop that those who sequestered and murdered him were members of a special *squadra* under the orders of one of Mussolini's personal aides. Though the corpse would not be discovered for more than two months, the approximate truth was suspected almost immediately, creating a great scandal. The stock market went into a tailspin, while some of the more moderate Fascists stopped attending party meetings and even mailed in their membership cards in protest. There has never been direct evidence that Mussolini personally ordered the murder—some have even conjectured that it was carried out by hardliners to prevent a new compromise—but Mussolini was certainly guilty of continuing to tolerate the *squadre* and their persistent violence. Though he fired the aide involved and several top officials, the crisis only became more acute.[64]

The leftist minority in the parliament, together with some of the remaining liberals, abandoned the chamber in protest. They moved to an auditorium on the Aventine Hill, where they became known as the Aventine Secession and adopted the slogan *Non mollare!* (Don't give in). Yet the withdrawal was a blunder, for in so doing they lost their most direct opportunity to challenge the government in parliament.[65]

The crisis lasted for six months, with the opposition unable to force a change and Mussolini unable to find a solution. He may well have suffered much of his life from a bipolar (manic-depressive) emotional disorder; at any rate, he was paralyzed by depression for much of the summer and autumn of 1924. Again, as in 1922, the arbiter of the situation was King Victor Emmanuel. He had the constitutional authority to withdraw confidence in Mussolini as prime minister, but he feared the alternative of a potentially weak, divided, non-Fascist government. Moreover, Mussolini technically had a large, newly elected parliamentary majority, so the king did nothing. Fascist leaders grew increasingly impatient, and thirty of the top party bosses appeared in Mussolini's office on the final day of 1924 to demand action. They feared that

64. L. Battistrada and F. Vancini, *Il delitto Matteotti* (Bologna, 1973); C. Carini, *Giacomo Matteotti* (N.p., 1984).

65. G. Salvemini et al., *Non mollare (1925)* (Florence, 1955); F. Rizzo, *Giovanni Amendola e la crisis della democrazia* (Rome, n.d.); L. Zani, *Italia Libera: Il primo movimento antifascista clandestino (1923–1925)* (Bari, 1975).

For broad treatment of the anti-Fascist opposition, see C. F. Delzell, *Mussolini's Enemies* (Princeton, 1961); F. Rosengarten, *The Italian Anti-Fascist Press (1919–1945)* (Cleveland, 1968); S. Fedele, *Storia della concentrazione antifascista (1927–1934)* (Milan, 1976); and M. Chiodo, ed., *Geografia e forme del dissenso sociale in Italian durante il fascismo (1928–1934)* (Cosenza, 1990). On Italian and European antifascism, see L. Valiani et al., *L'altra Europa, 1922–1945* (Turin, 1967), and J. Droz, *Histoire de l'antifascisme en Europe, 1923–1939* (Paris, 1985).

he might even jettison his own party in a deal with moderates from other groups so that he could remain in power. Conversely, Mussolini feared that even the relatively pro-Fascist conservative liberals might soon join the opposition, and he promised finally to take decisive action.

Construction of the Fascist Dictatorship, 1925–1929

Despite the eventual proliferation of dictatorships, it was not easy in the 1920s to find a formula or structure for a new authoritarian regime. A sharp break with nineteenth-century liberalism was required, yet its norms had been so broadly accepted that it was difficult to take the plunge into a completely alternative regime. Mussolini hesitated many times between October 1922 and January 1925. Finally, the need to overcome the Matteotti crisis, combined with the apparent impotence of a weak and divided opposition, brought him to decisive action.

He appeared before a parliament dominated by Fascist deputies on January 3, 1925, to take personal responsibility for what had happened. He insisted that he had done nothing wrong and that Italy had no alternative leadership. "I declare that I, and I alone, assume the political, moral, and historical responsibility for all that has happened. . . . If Fascism has been a criminal association, . . . responsibility for this is mine." [66] He announced that he would assume full executive responsibility for government and dismissed the parliament. The police were given orders for the first time to break up subversive opposition organizations, and 111 people were arrested in the next forty hours. Twenty-six months after the March on Rome, the dictatorship was begun.

Other parties were not at first outlawed, but the deputies of the opposition were not allowed to return to the chamber. Henceforth the only function of the parliament would be to rubber-stamp decree laws issued by the government. Censorship was introduced, and the Masonic lodges were closed, even though a number of Masons had been among the founders of Fascism. The Palazzo Vidoni agreement of October 1925 guaranteed exclusive recognition of the Fascist trade unions by the industrial confederation (Confindustria); all other trade unions were frozen out. A decree of December 1925 made Mussolini responsible only to the king.

Changes were gradual, but they accelerated during 1926, the "Napoleonic year" of Fascism. The minister in charge of drafting new *leggi fascistissime* (ultra-Fascist laws) was Alfredo Rocco, the law professor who had been the chief ideologue of the ANI and of the corporate state. Mussolini made him minister of justice; he would become known as the *guardasigillo* (keeper of the seals) of the new institutionalization. In September the first pillar of the

66. Quoted in Lyttelton, *Seizure of Power* 265.

corporate state was introduced, when a structure of national syndicalism was created for the economy. Twelve national syndicates were set up for the various branches of economic production, plus a thirteenth for professionals and artists. Employers and workers would be organized in separate branches of each national syndicate.[67] These were not yet integrated corporations, but a ministry of corporations was created to develop them. Eventually, in 1934, the national syndicates were replaced by twenty-two national corporations, structured much the same way. In 1927 an official Labor Charter was created, theoretically guaranteeing rights of Italian labor.

Establishment of the political dictatorship was marked by several attempts on Mussolini's life (not all of them very serious) in 1925–26. After the fourth, late in 1926, all other political parties were officially banned, and special legal measures were taken to deal with subversion. A further step in creating the corporate state took place in 1928, when the directly elected parliament was replaced by a corporative chamber in which four hundred nominal representatives would be indirectly selected by various public and private groups, agencies, and professions. This was supposed to achieve "organic unity" through the representation of genuine social, economic, and professional interests, instead of the divisive special interests of individual voters and political parties. By 1938 the parliament would be further reorganized into an official Chamber of Fasces and Corporations.[68]

In September 1928 the Fascist Party Grand Council was officially made "the supreme organ that coordinates all activities of the regime," with the power to approve all deputies for the chamber and all statutes and policies of the party, as well as the right to be consulted on all constitutional issues. This was virtually the only *legge fascistissima* that directly violated the Italian constitution, creating a new overarching institution that infringed on the powers of the monarchy. Yet the Grand Council itself had no power to initiate anything; its utility was to give Mussolini more complete authority over his own party, now a state institution whose leaders were appointed by the Duce.[69]

The new system was a personal political dictatorship under Mussolini, yet legally still under the monarchy. King Victor Emmanuel was still head of the Italian state, while the political dictator was Capo del Governo (Head of Government). Italy's appointive Senate remained in place but had virtually no authority. The government ruled by decree and repealed laws on the accountability of cabinet ministers. Local elections were eliminated; all mayors were now appointed by decree.

67. See B. Uva, *La nascita dello Stato corporativo e sindacale fascista* (Assisi, 1974).

68. G. Lowell Field, in *The Syndical and Corporative Institutions of Italian Fascism* (New York, 1938), presents a formal description.

69. On the structure and functioning of the new state, see A. Acquarone, *L'Organizzazione dello Stato Totalitario* (Turin, 1965), and A. Acquarone and M. Vernassa, eds., *Il regime fascista* (Bologna, 1974).

Yet the basic legal and administrative apparatus of the Italian government remained intact. There was no "Fascist revolution," save at the top. Mussolini became minister of war in April 1925 and took over the Ministries of the Navy and Air Force a few months later. At one point he was nominally in charge of eight different ministries. In fact, he personally administered almost none, leaving them to be run by senior officials. State administration changed comparatively little; the provinces were still administered by state prefects, not by the Fascist *ras,* and on the local level, affairs were still dominated more often than not by local notables and conservatives.

Purging of civil servants was minimal, and there was little interference with the courts. A Special Tribunal for the Defense of the State was introduced with powers of martial law in 1926 to deal with political subversives, but its modus operandi was less than draconian.[70] From January 1, 1927, to January 31, 1929, the Special Tribunal decided 4,805 cases. Of these, the great majority (3,904) resulted in absolution—the opposite of a Soviet or Nazi court. Of 901 convictions, only one resulted in execution, while the majority (679) produced sentences of less than three years. A special political police, the OVRA, was created in 1930, but this was neither a Gestapo nor an NKVD, only the elaboration of a long-standing secret branch of the Ministry of the Interior.[71] During the entire history of the regime, about 5,000 people were given prison sentences for political reasons, though twice as many were sent into *confino* (internal exile). Down to 1940 there were only 9 political executions (mostly of Slovenian terrorists), followed by 17 more during the war years, 1940 to 1943. In Italy the Mussolini regime was brutal and repressive, but not murderous and bloodthirsty.[72]

During the 1920s economic policy changed comparatively little, for the new national syndicates did not dominate affairs. Industrialists and owners remained largely autonomous, even though less free than before; the main function of the syndicates was to control workers. (After his fall in 1943, Mussolini would lament that "the greatest tragedy of my life" had been his inability to resist "false corporatists" who were really "agents of capitalism.") Mussolini did insist on several points of prestige, carrying through the Quota Novanta (Quota Ninety) in 1926 that revalued the lira from 140 to 90 against the British pound, even though this handicapped Italian exporters.[73]

70. C. Rossi, *Il Tribunale Speciale* (Milan, 1952).

71. On the police under Fascism, see F. Fucci, *Le polizie di Mussolini* (Milan, 1985).

72. It should be noted that Amerigo Dumini, the Blackshirt in charge of the *squadra* that murdered Matteotti, was eventually sentenced to two years' imprisonment—a very minor penalty, but still different from the absolutely lawless terror of many other regimes.

73. R. Sarti, *Fascism and the Industrial Leadership in Italy, 1919–1940* (Berkeley, 1971); P. Melograni, *Gli industriali e Mussolini* (Milan, 1972); G. Gualerni, *La politica industriale fascista, 1922–1935* (Milan, 1956); idem, *Industria e fascismo* (Milan, 1976); S. La Francesca, *La politica economica del fascismo* (Bari, 1972).

One of the most striking features of the regime was that the political dictatorship also became a dictatorship over the party rather than of the party, for the power of the PNF was comparatively limited, to the chagrin of many affiliates. Membership in the PNF soared under the new regime, as hundreds of thousands of ordinary middle-class people poured in, swelling party ranks to 937,997 by the end of 1926, at which point it had become—proportionate to the country's population—the largest political party in the world. The Duce seemed perfectly willing to have it fill up with opportunists and timeservers, so that the eventual joke would be that the initials PNF really stood for "Per Necessità Familiare" (For Family Need). At the same time, he was determined to discipline his unruly forces; to that end, Roberto Farinacci, one of the most hardline *ras*, became party secretary in February 1925.[74] Farinacci did not entirely accomplish that mission. After an unusually lethal outburst by Blackshirts in Florence in October 1925, in which eight liberals and Masons were publicly murdered, Mussolini intervened personally to conduct a purge of the Florence *fascio*.[75] A new decree officially stated that henceforth all positions in the party would be appointed from the top down. Mussolini now ordered the final demobilization of the *squadre*, and a purge was subsequently carried out under Augusto Turati (appointed secretary in March 1926).[76] Turati was probably the most honest and efficient secretary the PNF ever had; during 1926–27 he purged some sixty thousand of the most criminal, violent, and undisciplined, and after the close of 1926 new recruitment was temporarily ended.

New membership data for 1927 revealed that 75 percent of the membership now came from the lower middle and middle classes, only 15 percent from the working class, and nearly 10 percent from the elite.[77] This revealed a considerable change from 1921. The more Mussolini relied on former Italian Nationalist Association leaders like Alfredo Rocco and Luigi Federzoni (his minister of the interior), the less he needed the original *ras*. Party veterans now complained of the *imborghesimento* (middle-class character) and "Nationalization" of the party, referring to the prominence of the ANI leaders and Rocco's corporate state ideology.

The function of the party was thus to mobilize political support and help indoctrinate the young, but not to administer the state. The last party congress

---

74. U. Grimaldi and G. Bozzetti, *Farinacci, il piu fascista* (Milan, 1972); Fornari, *Mussolini's Gadfly.*

75. One set of data for political brawls during 1925 shows thirty-five Fascists and only twenty-seven opponents killed. De Felice, *Mussolini il fascista* 2:126.

76. For his background, see P. Corsini, *Il feudo di Augusto Turati: Fascismo e lotta politica a Brescia, 1922–1926* (Milan, 1988).

77. Schieder, "Der Strukturwandel," and J. Petersen, "Wählerverhalten und sozialer Basis des Faschismus in Italien zwischen 1919 und 1928," both in Schieder, ed., *Faschismus* 69–96, 119–56.

met in 1925; the following year the party was given a new hierarchical constitution by its Duce. Even the Grand Council, as an organ of the state, played little role. Its members were appointed by Mussolini, and it rarely met. Edmondo Rossoni, the head of the Fascist trade unions, still hoped that the national syndicates might play the hegemonic role originally envisioned for them by left-wing Fascists, but in 1928 Mussolini ordered the *sbloccamento* (unlinking) of all the federations of worker syndicates, so that worker sections in the seven national syndicates formed thus far would have no broader organization than that at the provincial level, further weakening them. Rossoni was soon forced to resign. Moreover, unlike the subsequent situation in Nazi Germany, worker syndicates had been denied the appointment of local shop stewards since 1925.

The regime's official position was that Fascist Party members would not necessarily take over governmental and bureaucratic positions but that the spirit and policy of the government, and its existing bureaucrats, would simply be *fascistizzato* (Fascistized) in accord with the doctrines of the party. Beginning in 1926 there was some movement of Fascist members into lower-level governmental posts, and this became more noticeable with the *ventottisti* (twenty-eighters) who entered in larger numbers in 1928. Fascist Party members would be found in the Foreign and Interior Ministries and, particularly, in aspects of local administration, but there were few in the judicial system or universities. In 1928 only 2 percent of all professors were regular Fascists, and into 1929 only about 30 percent of the new prefects appointed were party members. As late as 1936 all the top posts in the Ministry of Corporations were held by neo-Fascists who had joined the party after 1922. From 1922 to 1929 only twenty of eighty-six new appointments of prefects were made politically outside the regular state prefectoral corps, nor did this change greatly during the 1930s.

The new system was not a revolution but an authoritarian compromise. The monarchy, the Church, the armed forces, the economic interests, and even to some extent the judiciary all remained in place. Moreover, the party never had developed major technical cadres to provide trained personnel, and there were so many opportunistic new elements in the party that after 1925 the appointment of a Fascist had limited significance. When Bottai's journal *Critica Fascista* initiated a debate on the situation of the party in the autumn of 1927, it was quickly slapped down.

For Mussolini, the final achievement in the creation of a political structure was to sign a concordat with the Church, which would in effect bring the blessing of Italy's most influential institution. Overt, often intense, hostility between church and state had existed since unification in 1860, but as early as 1922 the Vatican had indicated it would not oppose a Mussolini government and appreciated Fascism's role in the defeat of the left. Signature of the three Lateran Pacts in 1929 completed the system. One granted the papacy full independent state sovereignty over an area around St. Peter's Cathedral now designated Vatican City, ending the Vatican's long period as a territorial "prisoner" of the Italian state. A second agreed to terms of financial compensation for the seizure of Church lands by the liberal state in the nineteenth century, while the third created a concordat in which the Italian state granted official status to the Catholic religion, promised freedom for all nonpolitical activities of the large laymen's association, Catholic Action, and other Catholic groups, and provided for Catholicism to be taught in all state primary and secondary schools. For the Church it was an agreement that restored the status of religion and would promote the re-Christianization of Italy; for Mussolini it was a useful compromise that raised his government to a plateau of acceptance it had never enjoyed before.[78]

By this time Mussolini had given up seven of his eight nominal ministries and had even considered the possibility of recognizing a moderate leftist opposition party as a tolerated counterpoint, but found moderate Socialists unwilling to cooperate. A so-called plebiscite on March 24, 1929, was then held on the new law for a corporate parliament as well as the first list of four hundred candidates approved by the Grand Council, and the nominal vote was registered overwhelmingly in favor.

The Fascist regime proclaimed a "revolution" and a "new era," beginning the practice of renumbering years according to the age of Mussolini's government. The cult of Rome—replete with all manner of Roman symbols—reigned, with the *fasces* of Rome the official symbol of the regime, reproduced everywhere (though in 1928 Mussolini did order that it be removed from Italian garbage carts).

Over this presided the individual cult of the Duce, which developed particularly in the late 1920s, with slogans such as *Il Duce ha sempre ragione* (The Duce is always right). Mussolini was seen as the universal genius leading Italy into a new era of unity, development, and expansion.[79] He was constantly photographed—in cars and airplanes, skiing, riding horseback, even working bare-chested in the harvest. In fact, the universal genius and strongman suffered from a severe digestive disorder and gastric ulcer that had immobilized

78. R. A. Webster, *The Cross and the Fasces* (Stanford, 1960); P. C. Kent, *The Pope and the Duce* (London, 1981); S. Rogari, *Santa Sede e fascismo* (Bari, 1977); P. Scoppola and F. Traniello, eds., *I cattolici tra fascismo e democrazia* (Bologna, 1975); F. M. Broglio, *Italia e Santa Sede dalla Grande Guerra alla Conciliazione* (Bari, 1966); P. Scoppola, *La Chiesa e il fascismo durante il pontificato di Pio XI* (Bologna, 1966).

79. P. Melograni, "The Cult of the Duce in Mussolini's Italy," *JCH* 11:4 (Oct. 1976): 221–37, presents a good brief treatment. The primary authorized biography was Margherita Sarfatti's *The Life of Benito Mussolini* (Rome, 1925), which was used in schools, was translated into eighteen languages, and sold three hundred thousand copies, as far away as Japan. Sarfatti, a talented Italian writer and art critic of Jewish background, was Mussolini's principal mistress during the twenties and played a role in his rise to power. See P. V. Cannistraro and B. Sullivan, *Il Duce's Other Woman* (New York, 1993).

him during part of the Matteotti crisis and kept him on a diet largely restricted to milk and vegetarian items for the rest of his life.

The Totalitarian State

In 1925, with the imposition of the dictatorship, Mussolini and his education minister, the philosopher Giovanni Gentile, began to use the term *totalitario* to refer to the structure and goals of the new state. Aspiring to an organic unity of government, economic activity, and society, the new state was to achieve total representation of the nation, incorporating the broad masses for the first time in Italian history, and was to exercise total guidance of national goals. Thus was born the original concept of totalitarianism.

The paradox is that serious analysts of totalitarian government now recognize that Fascist Italy never became structurally totalitarian. In the decade following establishment of Mussolini's system, the Leninist dictatorship in the Soviet Union was ruthlessly expanded by Stalin into a complete state socialist system of almost total de facto control over the economy and all formal institutions, achieving almost complete atomization of society under the state— something not even remotely comparable with Fascist Italy. A few years later, the Hitler regime in Germany, with its efficient police, military power, concentration camp system, and eventual extermination policies in conquered territories, appeared to create a non-Communist National Socialist equivalent of Stalinist dictatorship. These two regimes have provided the dominant models of what political analysts, particularly between 1940 and 1960, tended to call totalitarianism. Mussolini's Italy bore little resemblance to either one.

It is important to understand what was really implied by the initial concept of the totalitarian state used by Mussolini, Gentile, and also Alfredo Rocco. The terminology had first been developed by the liberal anti-Fascist leader Giovanni Amendola as a pejorative to describe the extremes of dictatorship toward which he thought Mussolini's government would lead. It was taken over in Fascist parlance and combined, in Gentile's usage, with his own theory of the "ethical state" (also elaborated by the national syndicalist ideologue Panunzio). This doctrine posited a tutorial state with greater authority than the old liberal regime to develop the higher ("ethical") aspirations of the nation, an ambition derived from aspects of the thought of Rousseau and Hegel that has become increasingly common in the twentieth century.[80] Though the cruder Mussolinian formulation seemed to hold that nothing was to be developed beyond the scope of a superstate that would in one sense or another (it was never

---

80. G. Gentile, *Origini e dottrina del fascismo* (Rome, 1927); idem, *Fascismo e cultura* (Milan, 1928). For the broader scope of Gentile's thought, see H. S. Harris, *The Social Philosophy of Giovanni Gentile* (Urbana, 1960), and G. Giraldi, *Giovanni Gentile* (Rome, 1968).

structurally defined) be all inclusive, there was never the slightest proposal, nor so far as we know the slightest practical intention, to develop a complete police system with direct control over all institutions. Rocco, as minister of justice, did speak of the overriding authority of the new state over other institutions, but he seemed to be referring primarily to spheres of conflict rather than to any bureaucratic structure for applying governmental intervention to all aspects of Italian life on a daily basis. In practice, Fascist "totalitarianism" referred to the preeminent authority of the state in areas of conflict, not to total— or in most cases even approximate—day-to-day institutional control. Nevertheless, though there can be little debate that this was the concept and actual nature of the Mussolinian state, it is also true that the "totalitarian" doctrine of the preeminent state and its "ethical" demands did provide a theory of much broader state power that might become greatly expanded in practice. The hypothetical possibility always remained—a concern for leftists and conservatives alike—that the Mussolini dictatorship might eventually become more radical and expansive.

In practice, it can be described as a primarily political dictatorship that presided over a semipluralist institutional system. Victor Emmanuel III, not the Duce, remained the constitutional head of state. The Fascist Party itself had become almost completely bureaucratized and subservient to, not dominant over, the state itself. Big business, industry, and finance retained extensive autonomy, particularly in the early years. The armed forces also enjoyed considerable autonomy and to a considerable degree—though never entirely— were left to their own devices. The Fascist militia was placed under military control, though it in turn enjoyed a semiautonomous existence when made part of the regular military institutions.[81] The judicial system was left largely intact and relatively autonomous as well. The police continued to be directed by state officials and were not taken over by party leaders, as in the Soviet Union and Nazi Germany, nor was a major new police elite created as in the other two systems. There was never any question of bringing the Church under overall subservience, as in Germany, much less the near-total control that often existed in the Soviet Union. Sizable sectors of Italian cultural life retained extensive autonomy, and no major state propaganda-and-culture ministry existed until the German example was belatedly taken up in 1937. Political prisoners were usually numbered in the hundreds—the total never amounted to more than a few thousand—rather than in the tens and hundreds of thousands as in Nazi Germany or the millions as in Stalin's Russia. As major twentieth-century dictatorships go, the Mussolini regime was neither especially sanguinary nor particularly repressive. "Totalitarianism" remained a possible threat for the

81. See A. Acquarone, "La milizia volontaria nello stato fascista," and G. Rochat, "Mussolini e le forze armate," both in Acquarone and Vernassa, eds., *Il regime fascista* 85–111, 112–32.

future, but in practice the term had a limited meaning. Mussolini came to power on the basis of a tacit compromise with established institutions, and he was never able fully to escape the constraints of that compromise.

At the same time, his was the first organized and institutionalized non-Marxist authoritarian regime to remain in power for a lengthy period, and after 1925 it would become increasingly common to label as a "Fascist regime" any organized non-Communist dictatorship, just as the word *totalitarian* would be increasingly and vaguely used to refer to any authoritarian system.[82]

The First Interpretations of Fascism

Formation of the first Mussolini government brought Fascism to international attention, leading to several attempts at direct imitation, particularly in southern and eastern Europe, during the next two years. In general, Fascism was criticized by liberals,[83] but it sometimes drew mild approbation from moderates and conservatives as constructive of order and progress.[84] It was often attractive to radical nationalists and right-wing authoritarians elsewhere, though from the beginning there was great uncertainty and disagreement as to just what Fascism was or exactly what was happening in Italy. Since there was no official codification, the specific character or doctrine of Fascism was a matter of some debate and uncertainty (not least among Fascists themselves).[85]

The first serious analysis, not surprisingly, took place in Italy, particularly in the writings of left liberal intellectuals and journalists. The radical Mario Missiroli and the Socialist Giovanni Zibordi both drew attention during 1921–22 to the fact that Fascism was a product of the revolutionary situation created by World War I—a revolutionary situation in which the left itself could not readily triumph. This was being taken advantage of by newly emerging lower-middle-class people, whose numbers had grown even though they had been placed in increasingly difficult economic circumstances by the crisis which developed after the end of the war. For them, Fascism became a new political vehicle for their own social and political aggrandizement.[86] This line of analy-

---

82. This is pointed out in H. Buchheim, *Totalitarian Rule* (Middletown, Conn., 1968), 28–29.

83. For a good example from a leading liberal German newspaper, see M. Funk, "Das faschistische Italien im Urteil der 'Frankfurter Zeitung' (1920–1933)," *Quellen und Forschungen aus Italienischen Archiven und Bibliotheken* 69 (1989): 255–311.

84. J. P. Diggins, *Mussolini and Fascism: The View from America* (Princeton, 1972); A. Berselli, *L'opinione pubblica inglese e l'avvento del fascismo (1919–1925)* (Milan, 1971).

85. Two of the more detailed early accounts were F. Schotthöfer, *Il Fascio: Sinn und Wirklichkeit des italienischen Fascismus* [sic] (Frankfurt, 1924), and J. W. Mannhardt, *Der Faschismus* (Munich, 1925).

86. For the analyses of Missiroli and Zibordi, see R. De Felice, *Il fascismo: Le interpretazioni dei contemporanei e degli storici* (Rome, 1970), 8–10, 23–53.

sis climaxed in 1923 with the publication of the book *Nazional fascismo* by the liberal democrat Luigi Salvatorelli, which declaimed, "Fascism represents the 'class struggle' of the petite bourgeoisie."

For Communist commentators, the matter was simpler. They saw in Fascism a unique new phenomenon—a violent multiclass anti-Marxist movement, made the more formidable because it employed some of communism's own weapons. This was most easily explained by defining Fascism as primarily a tool of the bourgeoisie to destroy the working class. In *Der Faschismus in Italien* (1923), the Hungarian Communist Gyula Šaš ("Giulio Aquila") elaborated this "agent" interpretation in detail, adding an ideological feature to the effect that some Fascist leaders and workers apparently did believe in the cross-class Fascist nationalist ideology. Within the Soviet Union, German Sandomirsky's *Fashizm* (1923) employed a similar "agent" theory, though emphasizing that Fascism was also a product of aggressive extreme nationalism and of the interventionist movement in the war. He nonetheless saw Fascism becoming internationalized as counterrevolution, with the most important imitators likely to be various rightist and patriotic groups in France and the United States, while he distinguished the German radical right from Fascism by the former's allegedly defensive goals vis-à-vis French expansionism, thus illustrating the quandary which faced comparative taxonomists from the very beginning. For Sandomirsky, Fascism nonetheless was ultimately a matter of the bourgeoisie "throwing off the mask." The Hungarian Communist Matyas Rakosi published his *Italianski fashizm* two years later in the Soviet Union, writing along somewhat the same lines, though reaching a less extreme conclusion. For Rakosi, the Fascists were petit bourgeois nationalists who had first served the bourgeoisie by helping to get Italy into the war and then by enabling the bourgeoisie to defeat the organized working class. Rakosi claimed to find, however, that Fascist rule was already beginning to weaken. Individual Communist writers would later also emphasize such aspects as imperialism and the petit bourgeois origins of Fascism or, in the case of the Hungarian Georg Lukács, interpret fascism generally as an "irrational" movement of capitalist cultural crisis.[87]

In general, both non-Communist and Communist critics tended toward simplistic, sweeping generalizations. While some among the liberals and the moderate left came to think that Fascism simply represented an inherent national Italian disorder—a sort of illness of national culture—the Communist Party of Italy often came in practice, and occasionally in theory, to present Fascism as a natural result of "bourgeois" parliamentary democracy. The shorthand equation became "Democracy equals Fascism."[88]

---

87. The commentary of German Communists, intellectually among the more active, is treated in K.-E. Lönne, *Faschismus als Herausforderung: Die Auseinandersetzung der "Roten Fahne" und des "Vorwärts" mit dem italienischen Faschismus, 1920–1933* (Cologne, 1981).

88. Cf. P. G. Zunino, *Interpretazione e memoria del fascismo* (Bari, 1991), 81–96.

The only Communist theorists to adopt a more complex perspective were the Italian leaders Antonio Gramsci and Palmiro Togliatti, who authored a number of articles and essays, climaxing in the writings of Togliatti in *L'Internationale Communiste* in 1928. Togliatti criticized the tendency to label all forms of "reaction" as "fascist," observing that while this might be useful for political agitation, it confused political analysis. He asserted that the Communist decision in 1921 to label the Fascist Party as "capitalist" pure and simple ignored its internal contradictions and made it impossible to appeal to dissident sectors, while the labeling of the French right as "fascist" in 1924 had simply confused the understanding of French politics. For Togliatti, it was necessary to look at the weaknesses in Italian economic structure after the war to understand why Fascism could become strong, and to grasp the role of large sectors of the urban and rural petite bourgeoisie. This in turn would indicate that the countries where fascism might pose the greatest danger in the future would be those of eastern Europe, which struggled against somewhat similar social and economic problems, the latter supposedly being the key to Fascism. At the same time he also pointed out that it was a mistake to think that Fascism did not have an ideology, for in fact it did, based on extreme nationalism and the state; it was opportunistic, lacking in internal homogeneity, and subject to increasing contradictions as economic conditions worsened. Gramsci and Togliatti emphasized that Fascism was a genuine mass movement, in some ways more a consequence than a cause of the defeat of the revolutionary left. They also pointed out the difference between the social bases of the movement and those of the regime, highlighting what were perceived as the internal contradictions in the regime.[89]

The only other Marxist theories to emerge by the end of the decade were the "Bonapartist" theories of August Thalheimer and later Otto Bauer. Thalheimer, a dissident Communist, developed in 1928 an explanation of Fascism as an updated version of "Bonapartism" as in the Second Empire of Louis-Napoleon. He held that the principal features, mutatis mutandis, were essentially the same and had already appeared in 1849–52 during an earlier crisis of capitalism in France. Thalheimer's account was relatively simplistic and in some particulars demonstrably false; moreover, it was simply a variant of the standard Marxist "agent" theory, for he defined Fascism ultimately as "the open but indirect dictatorship of capital."[90]

More sophisticated was the interpretation developed soon afterward by Otto Bauer, one of the chief theorists of Austro-Marxism. He held that the

89. Some of their writings are reprinted in De Felice, *Il fascismo* 106–35, and in D. Beetham, ed., *Marxists in Face of Fascism* (Totowa, N.J., 1984). They are analyzed in Beetham's own discussion of their analysis (1–14). Some of Togliatti's analyses were later collected in his *Lezioni sul fascismo* (Rome, 1970).

90. Thalheimer's chief writings of 1928–29 are anthologized in the works edited by Beetham and De Felice, cited in the previous note.

growth of capitalism, together with other changes in society, shifted the weight of various classes considerably, and that the Italian crisis resulted from a new situation of class equilibrium that provided an opportunity for a new political force to establish its dictatorship with an initial degree of autonomy.[91] Though inadequate as a complete interpretation of Fascism, it was more penetrating than any of the preceding Marxist analyses save that of Togliatti.

In practice, the Communist attitude toward Fascism was more ambivalent than the theories of individual Communist writers might have suggested. On the one hand, Communists seem to have been the first to grasp the potential which lay in the pejorative and polemical use of the term *fascist,* so that even before Mussolini came to power, Communist writers and propagandists had occasionally extended the term to cover other nationalist and authoritarian groups. On the other hand, the initial press commentary in Moscow on the formation of the first Mussolini government was not overwhelmingly anti-Fascist, despite the Duce's talk of a "revolutionary rivalry" with Lenin. Fascism was sometimes perceived not inaccurately as more of a heresy from, rather than a mortal challenge to, revolutionary Marxism.[92] Mussolini's government was one of the first in western Europe to recognize the Soviet Union officially in 1924. Moreover, in the case of Germany, extreme German nationalism even of the early Nazi variety was seen as useful to the USSR, and at the Twelfth Party Congress in Moscow in 1923 Nikolai Bukharin stressed that the Nazi Party had "inherited Bolshevik political culture exactly as Italian Fascism had done."[93] On June 20, 1923, Karl Radek gave a speech before the Comintern Executive Committee proposing a common front with the Nazis in Germany. That summer several Nazis addressed Communist meetings and vice versa, as the German Communist Party took a strong stand for "national liberation" against the Treaty of Versailles and inveighed against "Jewish capitalists." It is said that a few of the more radical Nazis even told German Communists that if the latter got rid of their Jewish leaders, the Nazis would support them.[94] Yet the two radicalisms ultimately proved exclusive, and each went ahead with separate, equally unsuccessful, efforts at insurrection in Germany.

91. See G. Botz, "Austro-Marxist Interpretations of Fascism," *JCH* 11:4 (Oct. 1976): 129–56; the critique in the same issue by Jost Dülffer, "Bonapartism, Fascism and National Socialism," 109–28; and J. M. Cammett, "Communist Theories of Fascism, 1920–1935," *Science and Society* 31:1 (Winter 1967): 149–63.

92. See M. Agursky, *The Third Rome: National Bolshevism in the USSR* (Boulder, 1987), 300, and, more broadly, L. Luks, *Entstehung der kommunistischen Faschismustheorie* (Stuttgart, 1985).

93. Agursky, *Third Rome* 301.

94. O.-E. Schüddekopf, *Linke Leute von Rechts* (Stuttgart, 1960), 445–46; R. Abramovitch, *The Soviet Revolution* (New York, 1962), 259; E. von Reventlow, *Völkisch-kommunistische Einigung?* (Leipzig, 1924); K. Radek, *Der Kampf der Kommunistische Internationale gegen Versaille und gegen die Offensive des Kapitals* (Hamburg, 1923), 117, as cited in Agursky, *Third Rome* 378.

All this notwithstanding, the Fourth Comintern Congress in November 1922 had declared that Italian Fascism had become the tool (in this rendering) of the large landowners and was not just a local phenomenon but a danger that might reappear throughout greater central Europe. By the time of the Fifth Comintern Congress in June–July 1924, this idea had been expanded (or simplified) to interpreting Fascism as the tool of capitalism in general. The Comintern line at this point held that Fascism represented the right wing of capitalism, while the non-Communist Socialist parties represented its left wing. The aim was to establish the equivalency of both the latter movements, leading to the notorious official labeling of social democracy as "social fascism." [95] Comintern definitions of fascism henceforth grew increasingly narrow and reductionist, climaxing in the famous maxim coined by Georgi Dimitrov at the 1935 congress that fascism constituted "the open terrorist dictatorship of the most reactionary, most chauvinist and most imperialist elements of finance capital." [96] None of this prevented official Soviet relations with Fascist Italy from remaining relatively friendly until 1935.

A number of writers, including some Fascists, early commented on similarities between these two violent and authoritarian revolutionary movements and the two dictatorships to which they gave rise. Obviously all violent revolutionary movements and all full-scale dictatorships have some things in common,[97] though in the cases of Italian Fascism and Bolshevism the differences were at least equally important. After the death of Lenin in 1924 and Stalin's subsequent articulation of "Socialism in One Country," there was increasing speculation about the Russian nationalization of Bolshevism and the emergence of a Russian "national communism." The concept of "Red fascism" and general common totalitarianism would later spread further, particularly during the first phase of World War II in Europe and the first decade or so of the subsequent Cold War.

As dictatorships were established in a number of southern and eastern European countries during the middle and later 1920s, some observers began

95. See Luks, *Entstehung,* and also L. Ceplair, *Under the Shadow of War: Fascism, Anti-Fascism and Marxists, 1918–1939* (New York, 1987), 46–50. Stalin wrote in 1924 that "Social Democracy objectively represents the moderate wing of fascism."

96. Quoted in Beetham, ed., *Marxists* 22, and many others. The fullest study of Comintern doctrines and policies will be found in T. Pirker, ed., *Komintern und Faschismus 1920 bis 1940* (Stuttgart, 1965).

97. In addition to such obvious features as authoritarianism and violence, their social philosophies also converged at certain points such as opposition to hedonism and mere consumerism, and the common ascetic Sorelianism which held that harshness, both in policy and in general style of life, was inherently good for people. Cf. the remarks of Alexander S. Tsipko, in his *Is Stalinism Really Dead?* (New York, 1990), 142–49.

Togliatti simply observed that whereas Lenin called the Communist Party the new type of proletarian Marxist party, one could call Fascism the new type of bourgeois party, rejecting any congruence.

to speak of the broader phenomenon of contemporary dictatorship, rather than the specific political form of fascism, for it was clear that all the other new dictatorships had no organized political force equivalent to the Fascist Party in Italy. It appeared that dictatorship was more likely to occur in underdeveloped countries, and this became a prime variable in some analyses,[98] just as others distinguished between a party-based regime and a military-led regime or noted the relative absence of ideology and political mobilization in the latter.[99]

There nonetheless early developed a tendency, primarily but not exclusively among Communists, to label as fascist any new nationalist or rightist movement or regime that was both authoritarian and antileftist, and to call nonleftist dictatorships (that is, all save the Soviet Union) fascist regimes. This was conceptually coherent, at least with regard to anti-Communist dictatorships, though as Togliatti said, such broad usage was more useful for agitation than for analysis. Descending from the regime level, there developed a tendency, again especially but by no means exclusively among Communists, to label as fascist any nonleftist or non-Communist group with which the analyst disagreed, which totally confused serious analysis and had practical consequences ranging from the mischievous to the disastrous. The problem would be compounded by the fact that whereas nearly all Communist parties and subsequent Communist regimes (with some exceptions) preferred to call themselves Communist, most of the political movements commonly termed fascist by others did not use that name for themselves and sometimes vehemently denied any such identity.

98. In Spain, for example, those of the non-Marxist Francesco Cambó, *Las dictaduras* (Barcelona, 1929), and the Marxist-Leninist Andrés Nin, *Las dictaduras de nuestro tiempo* (Madrid, 1930).

99. For example, W. Scholz, *Die Lage des spanischen Staates vor der Revolution (unter Berucksichtigung ihres Verhältnisses zum italienischen Fascismus)* [*sic*] (Dresden, 1932).

5
The Growth of Nonfascist Authoritarianism in Southern and Eastern Europe, 1919–1929

Though liberal and democratic principles largely prevailed in the peacemaking of 1919 and in the formation of the new regimes of central and eastern Europe, this triumph was temporary. During the generation that followed, liberal democracy survived primarily in the advanced societies of northern and northwestern Europe, where deep foundations had been laid well before 1919. The only new states that managed to preserve democratic and constitutional systems were Finland, Ireland, and Czechoslovakia. In all other societies of central, southern, and eastern Europe, parliamentary government succumbed to varying forms of authoritarianism during the 1920s and 1930s.

The most important factors in sustaining a democratic and constitutional system seem to have been the level of economic development and modernization; the length of historic experience as a participatory liberal and constitutional regime; resolution prior to World War I of basic problems of religion, regional integration, and most other internal middle-class issues; the existence of a primarily social democratic rather than revolutionary left; and the status of either victor or neutral in World War I. Not one or even two of these factors were enough to preserve constitutional government in interwar systems, but taken as a whole they seem to account for the major differences.[1] The poten-

1. Germany was technologically and economically highly modern and yet failed to maintain democracy; the new Irish Republic rested on a largely rural and underdeveloped economy, yet

tially independent variable in any historical circumstance is that of political contingency, particularly the factor of leadership.[2]

One of the most important variables was simply that of having developed broad political participation relatively early in the era of modern politics. For those societies in which universal male suffrage arrived only in 1919, it would turn out to have come too late, at least for the interwar generation. Equally important would be the issue of sociopolitical alliances. In the surviving parliamentary regimes, alliances of liberals and moderate social democratic labor forces were established before or soon after World War I. By contrast, isolated labor movements were usually unable or unwilling to reenforce democracy, particularly when they organized broad fronts of rural as well as urban workers, as in Italy and Spain.[3] Democratic political outcomes took the form in northern and northwestern Europe either of broad middle-class center–right center alliances (as in Britain), or social democratic left-center alliances of moderate urban workers and middle-class farmers, as in Scandinavia.

The generation following World War I produced the most extreme political conflict in all European history, as political society in many countries both fragmented and at the same time often tended to polarize between right and left. That this was such an era of extreme conflict was caused not merely by the traumatic effects of the war but also by fundamental new changes, for this was also the first generation to experience the full impact of the broad processes of both modernization and democratization. Urbanization increased, educational opportunities were extended, and the lower and middle classes were much more broadly organized and politically conscious than before the war. But for most of Europe, the war had ended and even reversed the trend toward expanding economic production and greater well-being, so that there was much keener competition after the war for larger shares of a smaller pie. The destruction of the old order and the weakening of prewar institutions greatly increased the strength of the left in most countries, but these same experiences also encouraged the rapid expansion of new nationalist groups that were generally more radical and more broadly based than those before the war, creating conditions for heightened conflict. By 1939, when the next war began, authoritarian regimes of diverse stripes would outnumber representative constitutional systems by sixteen to twelve. Whether or not this amounted to a true

---

preserved it. Similarly, workers in a number of the countries where democracy broke down were primarily social democratic.

2. The best brief discussion of the reasons for success or failure in interwar democracies is J. J. Linz, "La crisis de las democracias," in *Europa en crisis, 1919–1939*, ed. M. Cabrera et al. (Madrid, 1992), 231–80.

3. Gregory M. Luebbert, in *Liberalism, Fascism or Social Democracy* (New York, 1991), has presented the most original new analysis of interwar sociopolitical alliances and emphasizes this point (303–5 and throughout).

"fascist era" will be discussed below, but it was clearly an era of dictators and authoritarianism.[4]

THE MILITARY-LED REACTION IN SOUTHERN AND EASTERN EUROPE

The parliamentary regimes established or continued after World War I soon encountered major difficulties in nearly all the less-developed countries, located primarily in southern and eastern Europe. In a modern, industrial society such as that of Germany, the parliamentary parties initially had the strength to overcome daunting problems and to maintain constitutional government, but this was not the case in the poorer countries. Alternative leadership was provided not by new fascist-type movements—though there were several efforts to establish these—but by sections of the military, who had often led in introducing new political changes in the more underdeveloped states of southern Europe and Latin America during the nineteenth century.

Hungary

The first military-led reaction took place in Hungary, where the democratic parliamentary regime established during the final days of the war collapsed in March 1919, to be replaced by a revolutionary Marxist dictatorship led by the Socialists and the new Hungarian Communist Party. This "dictatorship of the proletariat," the only one established outside Russia, is known somewhat inaccurately as the Bela Kun regime, from the leader of the Communists. Its opportunity had arisen from the destruction of the old Hungarian empire at the hands of the victorious allies, which created a temporary vacuum filled by the revolutionary parties. Their brand of revolutionary socialism, though, was no more successful in preventing the total dismemberment of the old kingdom, and it itself collapsed after five months under the combined assaults of the Romanian, Czechoslovak, and Yugoslav armies.

The rightist opposition formed in the southern Hungarian town of Szeged, led by the senior Hungarian commander in the old Austro-Hungarian armed forces, Admiral Miklos Horthy, former chief of the Austro-Hungarian navy. His forces were able to occupy Budapest after the overthrow of the Socialist-Communist dictatorship, and they endeavored as far as possible to restore the old order in the territory remaining to the Hungarian state.

The resulting "Horthy regime," which governed Hungary until 1944, was

4. Brief overviews of the rise of authoritarianism include S. E. Lee, *The European Dictatorships, 1918–1945* (London, 1987); H.-E. Volkmann, *Die Krise des Parlamentarismus in Ostmitteleuropa zwischen den beiden Weltkriegen* (Marburg, 1967); and Akademiya Nauk SSSR, *Fashizm i antidemokraticheskie rezhimy v Evrope. Nachalo 20-x godov—1945 g.* (Moscow, 1981).

that rarity among twentieth-century systems, a truly reactionary state which endeavored to maintain as much as possible of the nineteenth-century order. Since return of the Habsburg monarchy was barred by international treaty, Horthy became regent for life and chief of state. The elitist liberal parliamentary system of the late nineteenth century was restored, based on limited male suffrage. Horthy was not, strictly speaking, a dictator but governed under the laws of the old Hungarian constitution, with power to appoint a prime minister who led the normal functions of government. In this system Hungary returned to the leadership of the middle and upper classes.[5] The lower classes were not totally deprived of representation, for the Socialist Party, which now repudiated the Communist alliance and proletarian dictatorship, enjoyed legal status, and urban workers were permitted to elect opposition Socialist delegates to each parliament, while the Smallholders Party also enjoyed not insignificant representation. The dominant political party was the conservative National Union, sponsored by the government. This system preempted any need in Hungary for a rigorous nationalist dictatorship, and amid the relative stability of the 1920s efforts to create a Hungarian fascist-type movement enjoyed little success.

To the right of the ruling conservatives were minorities, at first fairly small, of what in Hungary were called right radicals. These people were mainly responsible for the creation of the astonishing total of 101 semisecret nationalist societies by 1920.[6] The right radicals may be divided into two categories, the more conservative right radicals and the more revolutionary, who soon tried to approximate the fascist movements that had emerged in Italy and Germany. The key group of more extreme right radicals was associated with the Association of Hungarian National Defense (known from its acronym in Hungarian as MOVE), formed by army officers in Szeged in 1919 who were subsequently known as Szeged fascists. Its leader, an officer named Gyula Gömbös, called himself a national socialist as early as 1919 and propounded drastic changes in property ownership. He and other MOVE leaders admired Mussolini and also established relations with Hitler and Erich Ludendorff in Germany. Their "national socialism" championed radical land reform and "Christian capital," as opposed to an exploitative Jewish bourgeoisie, and they preached a revanchist foreign policy. Though on good personal terms with Horthy, Gömbös found the regime much too conservative. By 1923 he abandoned the government party altogether, spoke of a "march on Budapest," and founded the Hungarian National Independence Party (also known as the Party of Racial Defense). Though at first this party managed to place seven deputies in the

5. See W. M. Batkay, *Authoritarian Politics in a Transitional State: Istvan Bethlen and the Unified Party in Hungary, 1919–1926* (New York, 1982), and A. C. Janos, *The Politics of Backwardness in Hungary, 1825–1945* (Princeton, 1982), 201–37.

6. According to the principal political history of Hungary in this period, C. A. Macartney's *October Fifteenth: A History of Modern Hungary, 1929–1945* (Edinburgh, 1957), 1:30.

parliament, the election of 1926 eliminated all save the seat of Gömbös himself. Amid the stabilization of the 1920s, hopes for a Hungarian fascism faded, and in 1929 Gömbös temporarily espoused more moderate positions and was co-opted by the government as minister of war.[7]

Bulgaria

Smallest of the defeated powers, Bulgaria also underwent political democratization. Indeed, nominal democratic suffrage had come earlier to the Balkans than to any other part of southern Europe, for universal male suffrage had existed in Greece since 1864, in Bulgaria since 1879, and in Serbia since 1889. However, this was only generally effective in Serbia after 1903, for in Greece and Bulgaria electoral outcomes were controlled by patronage and corruption. Bulgarian affairs had been dominated by the crown, the urban elite, and the military. The Bulgarian state had followed a militant and expansionist policy that earned it the nickname "Prussia of the Balkans" but ended in complete military defeat in 1913 and even more decisively five years later. Conversely, Bulgaria's chief socioeconomic strength lay in having the most equitable land distribution in the Balkans, even though the government before 1919 had not directly reflected peasant interests.

The main new popular force was the Agrarian Union, a broad peasant movement led by Alexander Stamboliski, that won postwar elections and led the government from 1919 to 1923. Stamboliski's was by far the most progressive government that Bulgaria had ever had or would have until nearly the end of the century. It promoted economic development and the interests of the peasantry—who constituted nearly 80 percent of the population—and reversed traditional Bulgarian foreign policy, encouraging peace and cooperation. The Agrarian Union also formed its own peasant militia, known as the Orange Shirts from their attire, and tended to ride roughshod over political opposition.

Stamboliski's government drew the ire of all the former established elites. Conservatives formed their own White Guards, while urban politicians organized a loose new group early in 1922 called the National Alliance, which professed great admiration for Italian Fascism. More violent was the terrorist IMRO (Internal Macedonian Revolutionary Organization) that had been formed in 1897 to win Macedonia for Bulgaria. It had sparked armed insurrections in old Turkish Macedonia and threatened the same in the new Bulgaria, while actively engaging in political assassination.[8]

---

7. On the early history of the Szeged fascists, see N. M. Nagy-Talavera, *The Green Shirts and the Others* (Stanford, 1970), 49–122.

8. D. M. Perry, *The Politics of Terror: The Macedonian Revolutionary Movements, 1893–1903* (Durham, N.H., 1988); J. Swire, *Bulgarian Conspiracy* (London, 1939).

The most decisive group was the Military League, an association of army officers, who had come to form a virtual caste. Some sixty-five hundred Bulgarian officers had been permanently demobilized after the war, but army activists hoped to regain a dominant position, subdue reformers, and reassert an expansionist policy. A conspiracy of Military League activists and IMRO terrorists carried out a coup d'état in June 1923, overthrowing Stamboliski, who was tortured and summarily executed.[9] The Agrarian Union was subdued and subsequently split. Though Bulgaria retained the form of a parliamentary state, its affairs were now dominated by King Boris, the military, and the successors of the old minority urban parties. As in Hungary, the government in Bulgaria was taken over by conservatives and patterned on prewar politics.

Since the right was strong enough to subdue the left, there was little room or support for imitators of Italian Fascism during the 1920s. Early in 1923 a former army general organized the Rodna Zashtita (Home Defense), an illegal militia group that adopted the black shirt and Roman salute, but it remained very small and failed to develop all the characteristics of a fascist enterprise. More directly imitative was Dr. Alexander Staliski's National League of Fascists, but it failed to attract followers.

Romania

Totally overrun by German and Austro-Hungarian forces after it entered the war on the side of the Entente in 1916, Romania emerged, along with Serbia, as one of the big winners from the war among existing states. Its territory was approximately doubled, as Transylvania in the northwest, Bukovina in the north, Bessarabia in the northeast, and southern Dobrudja to the southeast were annexed. Yet Romanian society was one of the poorest and most underdeveloped in eastern Europe, with nearly 50 percent illiteracy. Its political system had been dominated by two elitist parties (the Liberals and Conservatives). Its elections had been manipulated, and its politics and government were perhaps the most corrupt in Europe. Extreme suffering among the vast peasant majority helped to spark the great Romanian peasant revolt of 1907, the greatest social revolt in prewar Europe save for the first Russian Revolution of 1905. To extreme social and economic tensions were added internal ethnic problems, for Romania had become in 1919 a multinational state, with a large Hungarian minority in the northwest and small Ukrainian and Turkish minorities in the east. Moreover, the native Romanian middle class was small and weak, and it had been partially supplemented by a rapid influx of Jews from the tsarist empire and Austria-Hungary in the nineteenth century, who did much of the

9. The key study is J. D. Bell, *Peasants in Power: Alexander Stamboliski and the Bulgarian Agrarian Union, 1899–1923* (Princeton, 1977).

work of a Romanian middle class. Anti-Jewish feeling was common, with a strong strain of domestic anti-Semitism added to Romanian nationalism even before the war. An anti-Semitic National Democratic Party, founded by A. C. Cuza and other university professors in 1905, sought to cater to this sentiment but at first drew little support.

Postwar Romania lacked the resources to assimilate readily its new territory and population, while the grievances of millions of peasants remained unresolved. The National Peasant Party became a mass organization and prevented the urban Liberals from winning a majority in the first elections held under universal male suffrage. This provided a brief opportunity for the new People's Party of General Alexandru Averescu, a national war hero hailed as the "Romanian Mackensen." The People's Party was an attempt to create a more populist kind of ultranationalist organization, and when Averescu was named prime minister in 1920, it won new elections. Averescu formed a coalition government with the old elites and crushed an attempted general strike by the Socialists. His only positive achievement was to carry out a partial land reform the following year, but redistributing more land in tiny parcels to an impoverished peasantry was not enough to overcome the lack of education, roads, credit, or new techniques. Averescu's elite allies soon turned on him. He was forced to resign in December 1921, though his party remained in existence as an ever-diminishing, increasingly right-wing organization.[10]

A new democratic constitution of 1923 extended civil rights to all Romanians for the first time, enabling the country to enjoy a decade of at least partially representative government. Romania's natural majority force, the Peasant Party, won the elections of 1928 and formed the first—almost the only—democratic and representative government in the country's history.[11]

As was common throughout central and eastern Europe, the border hostilities and social tensions in Romania during the immediate aftermath of World War I had produced several new right-wing nationalist and militia groups. One that tried to carve out a new ideological position was the so-called National-Christian Socialist Party, but its only support seems to have been a few fringe members of the intelligentsia. Contact with the Italian Fascist Party was later stimulated by Elena Bacaloglu, a young Romanian journalist married to an Italian. This led to formation of a derivative National Fascist Party in 1925, which attracted few and was soon closed by police. Somewhat more successful was the Fascia Nationala Romana (Romanian National Fascio), organized by

10. Averescu led another government in 1926 that conducted unusually fraudulent elections. On the general, see F. Duprat, "Naissance, développement et echec d'un fascisme roumain," in *Etudes sur le fascisme,* by M. Bardèche et al. (Paris, 1974), 113–64.

11. The best general guide to interwar Romanian affairs in many ways is still H. L. Roberts, *Rumania: Political Problems of an Agrarian State* (New Haven, 1951).

dissidents from the former organization who may have gained fifteen hundred members. The National Fascio's program defined it as a "national socialist" movement aiming at a corporative system that would develop a higher standard of living. It championed further land reform, agrarian cooperatives, and the eight-hour day, but not industrialization, which was said to lead to unrest. There was little evidence here of the Fascist concept of cultural revolution, but much opposition to large landowners and ethnic minorities.[12]

More important was the new rightist and anti-Semitic nationalist party revived by Professor A. C. Cuza and others in 1922, which in the following year took the name League for National Christian Defense (LANC). It appealed to university students (whose numbers increased nearly fivefold in Romania during the 1920s) and by the close of 1925 incorporated the other three radical nationalist organizations.

The eventual leader of revolutionary nationalism in Romania, Corneliu Zelea Codreanu, emerged from the ranks of LANC, of which his father was a cofounder. Tall, handsome, and prone to a kind of religious mysticism, Codreanu came from a family in the northern fringe of Romania that was partly German and Slavic in ancestry but highly nationalistic (his rabidly anti-Semitic father having changed the family name from Zilinsky to the Romanian form, Codreanu). He had been a militia volunteer in 1919 and believed devoutly in redemptive violence. This conviction led to his murder in 1924 of the corrupt, "unpatriotic" police chief of Iaşi (the university city where Cuza taught and Codreanu had been a student), for which he was absolved and drew much favorable nationalist publicity.

During 1925–27 Codreanu studied in Germany and further developed his extremist ideas, deciding that LANC—which won only 5 percent of the vote in the 1926 elections—was too rightist and compromising to regenerate Romania. In 1927 he founded a new movement, the Legion of the Archangel Michael (named for the patron saint of Romania's wars of liberation against the Turks), with fifteen associates. This group would develop the Romanian variant of fascism, becoming arguably the most unique of the entire genus, except for the German Nazis. The Legion affirmed its full identity with the religion of the Romanian Orthodox Church, declaring it consubstantial with the national community. Its goal was to regenerate Romania and to save the souls of all Romanians, living or dead. Codreanu held that the true goal of all life was warfare, physical and spiritual.

The Legion was centered in Iaşi, whose university was a focus of ultra-nationalism. Organized in local cells called *cuiburi*, or nests, it had created fifty

12. A small Romanian Action organization was also founded in Cluj in imitation of Action Française. On these early organizations, see A. Heinen, *Die Legion "Erzengel Michael" in Rumänien* (Munich, 1986), 102–19.

Corneliu Zelea Codreanu

by 1929, with about a thousand members. By the following year Codreanu had formed a Legionnaire senate, appointed by himself, to help lead the movement. It employed the Roman salute (first placing the right hand over the heart), and members wore green shirts to symbolize the life and rebirth of the fatherland. Legionnaire leaders had a strong sense of affinity with (as well as differences from) the Italian and German movements and occasionally used the term *fascist* to refer to themselves. They would not develop significant strength, however, until the middle of the following decade.[13]

The Primo de Rivera Dictatorship in Spain, 1923–1930

Within Europe, Spain was considered the classic land of praetorianism, though there had been no successful military intervention in politics since 1874. Spain prospered as a neutral during World War I and survived the three diverse revolts of 1917, but in the aftermath of the war the country was as troubled politically and socially as any other land in eastern or southern Europe. The Spanish army suffered a short-term disaster in 1921 as it attempted to quell the revolt of the native Riffi kabyles in the Spanish protectorate of northern Morocco, while its main industrial center, Barcelona, was wracked by labor strife, terrorism, and counterterrorism. More seriously yet, the nineteenth-century political system of elitist liberalism, which had maintained institutional stability since 1874, was unable to adjust to mass politics and electoral democracy, a common failing in all of southern and eastern Europe.

With the political system stalemated and the future of the Moroccan campaign uncertain, the captain-general of Barcelona, Miguel Primo de Rivera, carried out a *pronunciamiento* in September 1923. The pusillanimous Liberal government in Madrid resigned, and King Alfonso XIII appointed Primo de Rivera as prime minister with full decree powers. He thus became a quasilegal military dictator and appointed a Military Directory of generals to run the government, all the while claiming he was taking power for only ninety days to solve a severe crisis. The ninety days stretched into years, and the Military Directory was replaced in 1926 by civilian ministers. With French cooperation, the rebellion in Morocco was finally put down, while the economic prosperity of the 1920s provided a surplus for ambitious new public works.

Though Primo de Rivera had been encouraged by the success of the March on Rome and cultivated good relations with the Italian state, he lacked any clear political doctrine of his own.[14] A state labor arbitration system was developed

13. Ibid., 119–50; R. Ioanid, *The Sword of the Archangel* (New York, 1990), 1–23.

14. The Primo de Rivera dictatorship's lack of ideology compared with Italian Fascists was emphasized in the contemporary study W. Scholz, *Die Lage des spanischen Staates vor der Revolution (unter Berucksichtigung ihres Verhältnisses zum italienischen Fascismus)* [sic] (Dresden, 1932).

partially in imitation of Fascist corporatism, but it relied on the independent cooperation of the Spanish Socialists and was never completed. A new corporative assembly was convened in 1928 to consider a new constitution, but its proposal for a more authoritarian form of parliamentary monarchy embarrassed even the king and so was withdrawn. As the depression struck Spain's economy, Primo de Rivera's health also declined, and the army turned against him. Alfonso XIII obtained his resignation on January 30, 1930, bringing to an end a dictatorship that had offered no real alternative but would bear with it the doom of the Spanish monarchy as well.[15]

Though Primo de Rivera had no direct connection with Italian Fascism and had failed to develop any kind of political movement, his downfall was something of a blow to Mussolini. Even though the Spanish regime had not been fascist, it had been a friendly southern European dictatorship in a comparatively large country that resembled Italy more than any other, and one that was of some importance for Italian foreign policy. Its irremediable collapse deprived the Italian regime of what might have been its most direct international support.[16] According to Renzo De Felice, the conclusions which Mussolini drew from this were that the leading right-wing institutions—monarchy, army, and church—merited little confidence and that the future would depend on some sort of accentuation of Fascist authoritarianism.[17]

The Authoritarian Coups of 1926: Greece, Poland, Lithuania, and Portugal

In 1926 a series of military coups established authoritarian regimes in four other southern and eastern European countries, two of which would endure considerably longer than the Spanish dictatorship. The first successful coup took place in Greece, even though its influence was brief. Greece had the most disturbed political history of any country in Europe during the early twentieth century,

---

15. The best study is S. Ben-Ami, *Fascism from Above: The Dictatorship of Primo de Rivera in Spain, 1923–1930* (Oxford, 1983), a work which, despite its title, admits that the Spanish regime was not fascist. See also J. Tusell, *Radiografía de un golpe de Estado: El ascenso al poder del general Primo de Rivera* (Madrid, 1987); J. L. Gómez Navarro, *El régimen de Primo de Rivera* (Madrid, 1991); and C. Navajas Zubeldía, *Ejército, Estado y sociedad en España (1923–1930)* (Logrono, 1991).

16. This is not to imply that Primo de Rivera and Mussolini were ever close allies. The Spanish dictator's only state visit was made to Rome at the close of 1923, and a treaty of friendship and trade was signed between the two regimes in 1926, but Primo de Rivera was well aware of the Duce's desire to play a dominant role in the western Mediterranean and increasingly kept his distance. See G. Palomares Lerma, *Mussolini y Primo de Rivera: Política exterior de dos dictaduras mediterráneas* (Madrid, 1989); J. Tusell and I. Saz, "Mussolini y Primo de Rivera: Las relaciones diplomáticas de dos dictaduras mediterráneas," *Boletín de la Real Academia de la Historia* 179:3 (1982): 413–83; and S. Sueiro Seoane, *España en el Mediterráneo* (Madrid, 1993).

17. R. De Felice, *Mussolini il Duce*, vol. 1, *Gli anni del consenso, 1929–1936* (Turin, 1974), 129–231.

particularly with regard to abrupt regime changes. Democratization had been advanced by a liberal military revolt of 1909 and the subsequent victory in democratic elections of Eleutherios Venizelos and his Liberal Party. These events, however, quickly produced polarization in Greece, where society was broadly divided between Liberals and conservative Populists. The latter reacted by the time of World War I with a project for a new rightist regime that would rely on the monarchy and the state, structured around the army and bureaucracy. This rightist concept of a semiauthoritarian "new state," together with the split in opinion over the opposing sides in the war, resulted in a Greek civil war of 1916–17 that was decided by the military intervention of the Entente on behalf of the Liberals. Venizelos then led Greece into the war on the side of the Entente,[18] and in 1919 he invaded Turkey, to complete the long-standing ambition of the "Megali Idea"—the concept of a greater Greece that would include not merely the sizable Greek minority remaining within Turkey but most of western Anatolia as well. The conservative Populists then won the first postwar elections of 1920 but continued to support a hopelessly ambitious military campaign, which was thoroughly crushed by a Turkish counteroffensive in 1922.

At this point the military reentered Greek politics, some of the more liberal and pro-Venizelos senior officers overthrowing the conservative government and subsequently forcing King Constantine to abdicate. The Liberals then returned to power, but the military remained the true arbiter of Greek affairs.

In June 1925 the nominally Liberal general Theodoros Pangalos intervened to overthrow one ministry, and in January 1926 he took over the government himself as a temporary military dictator. In many respects Pangalos was a fairly typical southern European caudillo. He derived some inspiration from Mussolini but not to the extent of wishing to imitate Italian Fascism in any systematic way. He considered himself, in fact, still a liberal and claimed not to oppose democracy, advancing no particular doctrine or ideology of his own. A strong anti-Communist, he hoped to unite Liberals and Populists, and "in this, he may have achieved a measure of success as indicated during his tours around the country and when he was 'elected' president of the Republic in an uncontested but probably not entirely falsified vote." [19] Pangalos claimed to be saving Greece from the politicians and serving as a guarantor of peace and economic prosperity. The former already existed, and the latter he could not provide. He became known chiefly for his effort to enforce puritanical dress codes, but he failed in both foreign and economic affairs. He was finally overthrown by his own Republican Guard after only seven months (in August 1926). Following this, Greece returned to parliamentary government. "Pangalos's main achieve-

18. G. B. Leontaritis, *Greece and the First World War, 1917–1918* (New York, 1990).
19. G. T. Mavrogordatos, *Stillborn Republic* (Berkeley, 1983), 34.

ment, after a brief flirtation with corporatist schemes, was to disillusion the middle classes with the idea of extra-parliamentary rule." [20]

In Poland the leaders of the new independent state, headed by Josef Pilsudski, had tried to restore a "great Poland" in 1919–20 and had partly succeeded. The 1923 census registered a population of twenty-eight million, of whom eight million were members of non-Polish minorities (13–14 percent Ukrainian, 10 percent Jewish, 5 percent White Russians, and a small number of Germans). The first regular president of this multiethnic state was assassinated, and by 1926 there were, according to one count, twenty-six Polish political parties and thirty-three among the minorities.

Pilsudski, the former socialist who had led the restoration of independence in 1919–20, tried to overcome political division and stalemate through a military coup d'état in May 1926 that was supported by a number of dissident groups (including the Communists). Pilsudski was neither an anti-Semite nor a particular admirer of Mussolini. He relied on nationalist sectors of the military and former volunteers and did not lead a mere "march on Warsaw" but had to wage three days of stiff fighting to gain control, as the left urged him to set up a "worker-peasant government." [21]

The resulting Pilsudskiite or "Colonels" regime that governed Poland until the German invasion in 1939 was a moderate military regime that did not seek to introduce a one-party state or to eliminate parliamentary elections altogether. It should be classified as a moderate pluralist authoritarian regime that remained in power because of the prestige and charisma of Pilsudski, the strength of the military, and the force of nationalism, as well as an interventionist economic policy. Pildsudski was normally not president or prime minister but minister of defense in charge of the army. His government did organize a state political front, the BBWR (Nonpartisan Bloc for Cooperation with the Government), which won a moderate majority in the 1928 elections. During the difficult years of the depression it became increasingly restrictive and, just before Pilsudski's death in 1935, introduced a more authoritarian constitution. Even so, opposition forces were never entirely banned.[22]

Neighboring Lithuania was one of the new Baltic republics created by the defeat of the old Russian Empire and the peace settlement of 1919. The new state carried out a major land reform that eliminated large properties, but political stability in a backward agrarian land was more difficult to achieve. The chief

20. M. Mazower, *Greece and the Inter-War Economic Crisis* (Oxford, 1991), 22.

21. J. Rothschild, *Pilsudski's Coup d'Etat* (New York, 1966).

22. A. Polonsky, *Politics in Independent Poland, 1921–1939* (Oxford, 1972); J. Rothschild, *Eastern Europe between Two World Wars* (Seattle, 1974), 27–64.

nationalist party, Tautininkai, was a moderate right authoritarian and Catholic movement which reacted angrily to the government's 1926 nonaggression treaty with the USSR. In December 1926, some seven months after Pilsudski's coup, a group of army officers took over the Lithuanian parliament and appointed a general as temporary dictator. A state of emergency was declared, followed by creation of a new minority government made up of the Tautininkai and the Christian democrats. Antanas Smetona became president. From the close of 1926 Lithuania functioned as a limited, partially authoritarian parliamentary system, though never a ruthless one-party dictatorship. The Christian democrats, who at that point held thirty-five of the eighty-five seats in the parliament, left the government early in 1927, whereupon Smetona simply dissolved parliament. His subsequent constitution of 1928 greatly increased the powers of the presidency, giving Lithuania a semiauthoritarian presidential state in place of a parliamentary government. This was a moderate rightist authoritarian regime that made no effort to introduce direct fascist-style politics.[23]

Portugal was the fourth country in which a successful military coup seized power in 1926, about three weeks after Pilsudski's takeover in Warsaw. Portugal had one of the oldest traditions of liberal constitutional government in continental Europe, yet, as in Spain and a variety of other countries, its historic liberalism had been elitist and oligarchic, restrictive and never democratic. Moreover, Portugal had the least-developed economy in western Europe coupled with the highest illiteracy rate. From the late nineteenth century liberals as well as radicals and conservatives increasingly called for an "iron surgeon" who could reform and/or modernize the country. Similarly, elitist liberals by the 1890s practiced "authoritarian" or "reactionary" liberalism, governing without the parliament in temporary dictatorships. The Republican movement that ousted the monarchy in 1910 had also been marked by a pronounced strain of militia violence and middle-class elitist authoritarianism, though nominally governing under a parliamentary structure of limited suffrage. Praetorianism, or military intervention in politics, had never been as pronounced in Portugal as in Spain, yet it reemerged in 1915 as a threat to Republican liberalism. Finally, a new form of authoritarian presidentialist republic, the República Nova of Sidonio Pais, had held power in 1917–18, before Republican liberals once more regained control of the government.

During and after World War I, new forms of rightist authoritarianism emerged in Portugal. There first appeared the elitist intellectual movement Integralismo Lusitano, a neomonarchist organization of the radical right patterned directly on Action Française.[24] More pragmatic was the right radical Cruzada

23. G. von Rauch, *The Baltic States: The Years of Independence, 1917–1940* (Berkeley, 1974), 146–64.

24. C. Ferrão, *O Integralismo e a República*, 3 vols. (Lisbon, 1964–65).

Nun'Alvares Pereira, formed after World War I, which sought to establish a nationalist authoritarian regime and called for a powerful leader. In 1921 a small group of army officers formed a National Republican Presidential Party to restore the authoritarian presidentialist system that had existed briefly in 1917–18, but failed in an abortive coup d'état attempted in conjunction with the monarchist Integralists. More moderate was the Academic Center of Christian Democracy (CADC), a Catholic corporatist circle founded at Coimbra University in 1901, expanded into the Portuguese Catholic Center in 1917.[25] None of these, however, were regular organized political parties, and their followings were very limited. This was even more the case with Nacionalismo Lusitano, a tiny protofascist movement formed in Lisbon in 1923 in imitation of Italian Fascism. All the while the Republican parliamentary regime tottered, registering the greatest cabinet instability of any state in Europe, accompanied by high inflation, a massive public debt, and only minimal economic growth.[26]

As in the other cases discussed in this section, the reaction in Portugal against a weak and divisive parliamentary system in an underdeveloped society was led by the military, who seized power at the end of May 1926, almost without violence.[27] The previous regime was so discredited that at first the new military government was praised by the most diverse opinion from right to left. It rested particularly on the support of right authoritarian elements, though these were considerably divided among themselves. A new right radical movement, the Liga Nacional 28 de Maio, was formed in 1928 to try to guarantee the permanent rule of authoritarian nationalism.[28] The military, however, proved no more successful than parliamentary liberals in solving financial and political problems.[29] Leadership would eventually be provided not by a general but by a university professor, Antonio de Oliveira Salazar, who began to develop a new authoritarian corporatist republic in 1930.

The King Alexander Dictatorship in Yugoslavia, 1929–1934

The last of the southern and eastern European dictatorships of the 1920s was the one imposed by King Alexander of Yugoslavia in 1929. Yugoslavia had never been a true democracy since its founding as a multiethnic state in 1919, yet it had a nominally parliamentary government, dominated largely by Serb parties and the Serbian—since 1919 Yugoslav—King Alexander. Political con-

25. M. Braga da Cruz, *As origens da democracia cristã e o salazarismo* (Lisbon, 1980), 15–351.

26. On this highly unstable party system in its final years, see A. J. Telo, *Decadencia e queda da I República portuguesa*, 2 vols. (Lisbon, 1980–84).

27. A. Madureira, *O 28 de maio* (Lisbon, 1978).

28. A. Costa Pinto, "The Radical Right and the Military Dictatorship in Portugal: The National May 28 League (1928–33)," *Luso-Brazilian Review* 23:1 (Summer 1986): 1–16.

29. D. Wheeler, *A ditadura militar portuguesa (1926–1933)* (Lisbon, 1986).

flict was rife in so complex and divided a polity, and the Serbian establishment had increasing difficulty in dominating the system, leading Alexander to institute dictatorship under the monarchy in January 1929. The official title of the state was soon changed from Kingdom of the Serbs, Croats, and Slovenes to Kingdom of Jugoslavia in recognition of the newly imposed unity. Alexander appointed a regular cabinet to conduct government while searching for a doctrine and new political forms. An effort to create a broader political organization met very limited success, and finally in desperation the king promulgated a new semiliberal constitution that in fact retained considerable power for himself. Fascism was one of several sources of inspiration, but Alexander completely failed to develop an ideology or political organization equivalent to those of Mussolini.[30] Assassination of the king in 1934 only encouraged a milder line, and by 1939 the Yugoslav regime had virtually returned to a kind of parliamentary pluralism.

A variety of nationalist groups, several of them quite extreme, appeared among the peoples of Yugoslavia. The most notable were the Ustashi (Insurgents) in Croatia and the Zbor movement of Ljotic in Serbia. Later, during World War II, the Ustashi would quickly develop into one of the most gruesome of the fascist-type movements, but for twelve years after its founding in 1929 it would remain small, weak, and partially undefined. The Zbor was a more conservative and elitist right radical party, even though in foreign affairs it would later look to Hitler and be subsidized by him.

Turkey

In Turkey, the "other" Balkan country, the military-led regime of Kemal Atatürk ("father of the Turks") would remain dominant throughout the interwar period. It became a prototype of the modernizing and westernizing developmental dictatorship in a non-Western country. The six principles of the Kemalist regime were nationalism, republicanism, statism, populism, laicism, and the revolutionary spirit, but the latter was not conceived in a fascist sense. The government nationalized railroads and part of the banking system, together with some foreign enterprises, but no effort was made to create any broader structure of nationalization or socialism. The "national bourgeoisie" was encouraged, and though considerable reform in landownership was carried out, much of the larger landowning structure remained intact.

The Turkish regime relied on the army rather than a political party and developed no political militia. It was neither militarist nor imperialist, and eventually it guided an electoral process into the desired outcomes, apparently

---

30. The best discussion is J. J. Sadkovich, "Il Regime di Alessandro in Iugoslavia, 1929–1934: Un'interpretazione," *SC* 15:1 (Feb. 1984): 5–37.

enjoying considerable popular support. After a generation it would evolve into an increasingly representative parliamentary system, and altogether it constituted probably the most positive example of a developmental dictatorship in the process of creating a sort of "guided democracy."

The Nonfascist Character of Most Authoritarian Movements in Southern and Eastern Europe

The spread of authoritarianism in southern and eastern Europe during the 1920s made evident the fact that this was a new phenomenon characteristic particularly of backward and underdeveloped countries of the European periphery. Such a conclusion also formed part of the standard Communist interpretation of fascism and was pointed out by many other observers.[31] Thus some Marxists would hold later (in 1932–33) that Hitler could not establish a successful Nazi dictatorship in Germany because it was not an underdeveloped country.

Equally evident was the fact that though the success of the March on Rome and of Mussolini's dictatorship was a source of inspiration, none of these regimes and few of the new authoritarian movements were categorically of the fascist type. They were generally more conservative and more tied to traditional elites, and they lacked the distinctive new doctrines of Italian Fascism. The dictatorships of Primo de Rivera in Spain and later those in Greece, Poland, Lithuania, and Portugal were all imposed by the military and that of Yugoslavia by the crown, though civilian-led systems later emerged in Portugal and Lithuania. The Hungarian regime was essentially one of reactionary liberalism, while that of Greece (quickly) and later (more slowly) those of Spain, Poland, and Yugoslavia all reverted, at least partially or temporarily, to liberalism.

The only generically fascist-type parties founded were mostly ephemeral grouplets such as the Romanian National Fascist Party and Nacionalismo Lusitano, quickly doomed to extinction. The exceptions would be Codreanu's Legion of the Archangel Michael and Gömbös's Szeged fascists, yet these also found it hard to expand amid the relative stability of the 1920s.

The Italy in which Mussolini rose to power had, by contrast, reached a kind of intermediate situation between development and underdevelopment. Alternately, it may be considered the most backward of the more advanced and developed countries, or the most advanced of all the nonindustrialized societies of southern and eastern Europe. The latter is probably the more accurate perspective. As in some other countries, universal male suffrage and mass mobilization only arrived in Italy in 1919, yet Italy was more developed at

31. For example, see the works of the moderate liberal Catalan politician Francesc Cambó: *En torn del feixisme italià* (Barcelona, 1925) and *Las dictaduras* (Barcelona, 1929).

that point than Spain, Portugal, or the eastern lands, and the Italian crisis became more acute and difficult to control. A more sophisticated political and ideological culture had already emerged, and the intermediate social strata were both more numerous proportionately and more active politically. Only in Italy was there a persistent challenge from an internationalist and protorevolutionary left. Italy became the center of convergence of a greater variety of political, cultural, social, economic, and international pressures than any of the other polities just entering democracy, and it was this process of multiple convergence that helped to produce a more radical and organized authoritarian outcome in Italy than elsewhere in southern and eastern Europe. For all these reasons, fascism was possible at that time only in Italy. To triumph, it required both protracted crisis and the opening of at least a partial vacuum politically. In the less sophisticated societies of other southern and eastern European countries, such a novel and revolutionary force as fascism was as yet not possible, and crises that threatened breakdown were more quickly resolved by simple military intervention.

6
German National Socialism

Many who use the term *fascism* are referring not to the Italian movement led by Mussolini but to German National Socialism, or the "Nazis" (as their foes soon termed them, from the pronunciation of the first two syllables of *national* in German). Most theories and interpretations of fascism refer primarily to Germany, not to Italy or other countries. After 1933 the Nazi regime quickly seized primacy as the most dynamic new force in Europe, promoted an enormous and terrible war, conquered much of the continent and dominated most of the rest, and became arguably the most destructive single regime in modern history, before undergoing total defeat and destruction in 1945. Adolf Hitler and Nazism have haunted the historical imagination ever since, even among those who are not generally interested in history.

An enormous scholarly and nonscholarly literature now exists which has explored many different aspects of Hitler, National Socialism, and the history of modern Germany. Much of this literature seeks to explain what made possible "the German catastrophe," as a leading German historian entitled a book published in 1946. During the Second World War, a determinist and Manichaean literature developed among Germany's foes, attempting to trace the roots of National Socialism far back into German history, making it the natural outcome of powerful influences in German development.[1] After more sober research following the war, it became evident that matters were not so simple. Modern Germany has been in fact a highly complex and often contradictory country, subject to the most diverse influences, most of which were not nec-

---

1. Much later, in his widely acclaimed book *The Germans* (New York, 1984), Gordon Craig, the dean of American Germanists (and himself no determinist), indicted the modern German intellectual tradition of romanticism as responsible for a general intellectual climate of nonempiricism and antiliberalism.

essarily related to National Socialism. It can readily be argued, of course, that from Prussia and from the Second Reich of 1871 Germany inherited a tradition of militarism, authority, and discipline, that German national government did not become fully democratic until 1919, and that by the late nineteenth century nationalism was assuming great intensity in a variety of different organizations. All of these are essentially correct. It is equally correct that Germany became one of the world's most dynamic centers of modern capitalism, technology, and culture, that its middle classes were large and not lacking in political organization, that its cultural and artistic avant-garde was among the most advanced in the world, that its social democratic movement was proportionately the largest in the world, and that the more racist and anti-Semitic of its political groupings were doomed to political defeat and ever-declining influence in the years before World War I, while its more liberal political parties were gaining strength. Thus, although there existed certain strong influences of ultranationalism, ethnocentrism, and authoritarianism, the general movement of most of German political, social, and cultural life took an opposite direction during the two generations before 1914.

The keys to understanding the German catastrophe do not lie in grasping any innate or inevitable tendencies in German life or in defining deterministic political and cultural influences, but in understanding the interplay of destructive ultranationalist tendencies with the unique chain of crises and traumas which afflicted German society in the two decades between 1914 and 1933. This "concatenation of crises" involved a sequence of traumas unparalleled in the history of other European countries during that generation. The onset of a massive war in 1914 was followed by great human losses and suffering, a sort of wartime dictatorship, and some remarkable military victories followed by sudden and inexplicable collapse, albeit in the face of great odds. After military defeat came a harsh and humiliating peace, accompanied by convulsive political change following the collapse of the imperial government, together with the threat (and partial reality) of social revolution accompanied by an unprecedented brutalization of public life and mass violence. This occurred within a framework of great loss of national wealth, unemployment, and decline of living standards. Temporary political stabilization was followed within a year by new efforts at violent political rebellion from the right and left, and three years later by a partial foreign military invasion that led to unimaginable hyperinflation, temporary economic collapse, and the destruction of savings, with further attempted armed revolts from right and left. Even the five years of democratic stabilization (1924–29) were a period of considerable social and economic uncertainty, as sizable unemployment persisted, the country became almost totally dependent on foreign credit, and middle-class interests continued to be threatened economically and fragmented politically. This shaky recovery was soon followed by the Great Depression, leading to truly massive unemployment, total political fragmentation, and major political and social crisis. By mid-1930 the democratic system had already stalemated, and the government was directed by nonparliamentary administrations which ruled by decree but lacked majority support and were completely unsuccessful in ending the political or economic crises. Though National Socialism was not merely the product of this succession of unprecedented traumas, it would have been impossible without them.

The Postwar Crisis, 1919–1923

For most Germans, the causes of total collapse in November 1918, after so much toil and sacrifice and so many victories, were incomprehensible. As recently as the previous summer German forces, having totally dominated Russia in the east, were surging forward on the western front. But by August American troops were arriving in ever-increasing numbers, while German reserves were exhausted. Unable to continue the long contest of attrition, the military command sought to obtain easier peace terms by placing the government in the hands of civilian liberals, while Kaiser Wilhelm II was forced to flee into exile in Holland. The liberals were quickly outflanked by a surge of revolutionary enthusiasm in the larger cities, which fed a broad movement of worker radicalism and placed a Socialist government in power in Berlin. The German Social Democratic Party, however, was led by reformists who channeled revolutionary activism into democratic and constitutional channels. Thus early in 1919 a newly elected democratic parliament met in Weimar to prepare the constitution for a democratic federal republic which would be known, from the site of this first assembly, as the Weimar Republic. This produced a model constitution and the first fully democratic regime in German history, yet the republic would be distrusted by many from the start as the product of national defeat, as an effort to mimic Anglo-American and French liberalism.

The terms of the peace diktat, imposed by the victorious allies, were as traumatic as the loss of the war. According to the treaty signed at Versailles, Germany was forced to return Alsace-Lorraine to France and cede large amounts of eastern land to Poland. Altogether, it lost 13 percent of its territory and 12 percent of its population, including 14.3 percent of all arable land and 15 percent of the nation's productive capacity. The key industrial Saar basin was temporarily detached, and western Germany was to be placed under partial military occupation for fifteen years. Germany's army would be limited to one hundred thousand men, its navy to twenty-five thousand, and its air force would be abolished. All large weapons were prohibited, and all western Germany to a line fifty kilometers east of the Rhine was made a demilitarized zone without any fortifications. Germany lost all its colonies, its fleet, and its foreign patents, and the country was reduced to a status of international debtor.

Finally, Article 231, the "war guilt clause," required the German government to recognize full responsibility for having started the war, and a huge economic reparations bill was imposed, its exact terms to be determined later.

During the first months of 1919 Germany was in turmoil.[2] "Free corps" of right-wing nationalist volunteers supplanted the police and army on Germany's eastern frontier and also did battle with the workers' militia of the revolutionary left. Some two thousand were killed in the repression of the "Spartacist" rebellion of socialist revolutionaries in Berlin, and a local *Räterepublik* (worker council or "soviet" republic) in Munich was also drowned in blood. In 1920 right-wing monarchists attempted a coup in Berlin that was thwarted by a general strike. With the economy sluggish, the new democratic government subsequently requested a delay in reparations payments. To enforce the terms, the French and Belgian armies invaded the vital Ruhr industrial zone in January 1923. The German government responded with noncompliance and passive resistance, meeting all obligations by printing ever more paper money. Inflation, which had accelerated ever since the start of the war, now shot out of sight, so that by the autumn of 1923 the mark had become worthless, scarcely worth the paper it was printed on.[3] The German Communists meanwhile developed the largest Communist party outside the Soviet Union and attempted two different insurrections, while radical nationalists plotted on their own.[4]

Adolf Hitler and the Founding of the National Socialist German Workers Party

In the first years after Germany's defeat, dozens of radical new nationalist groups were formed to combat the left and revive German nationalism. These were mostly obscure and unimportant and soon expired.[5] The only decisive one began its life in equally insignificant form as the German Workers Party in Munich at the beginning of 1919.

It was descended from the last new proponent of racist anti-Semitism to have emerged in Germany before World War I, the milling engineer Theodor Fritsch. Much influenced by the occult "Ariosophist" doctrines of the Austrians Guido von List and Jörg Lanz von Liebenfels, Fritsch early recognized that

2. The most recent study is H. Friedlander, *The German Revolution of 1918* (New York, 1992).

3. G. D. Feldman, *The Great Disorder: Politics, Economics, and Society in the German Inflation, 1914–1924* (New York, 1993), is a massive study of the entire process.

4. Richard Bessel, in *Germany after the First World War* (New York, 1993), presents a broad discussion of German problems.

5. The most important of the new groups during the first years is studied in U. Lohalm, *Völkischer Radikalismus: Die Geschichte des Deutschvölkischen Schutz- und Trutzbundes, 1919–1923* (Hamburg, 1970).

organized political anti-Semitism was doomed to failure in the relatively liberal climate of early twentieth-century Germany. He therefore concentrated on organizing a series of tiny local groups linked together as the Reichshammerbund (named after his biweekly *Hammer*), an initiative aimed at being "above parties" and at transcending capitalism to define a new German way of life. These groups had only a few hundred members. In 1911 Fritsch also organized the semisecret Germanenorden (German Order) devoted especially to occult Ariosophist symbols, which adopted the swastika emblem but had even fewer members. The Germanenorden, however, survived into the postwar period and helped to organize violent right radical activities in 1920–21.[6]

The Bavarian branch of the Germanenorden was expanded by a bizarre international adventurer, Rudolf von Sebottendorff, in 1917–18. The organization reached possibly fifteen hundred members and took the cover name of the Thule Society. Sebottendorff also formed a militia group that played an active role in the political violence in Bavaria during 1919, while also endeavoring to develop a parallel nationalist workers' circle. The most active figure in the latter was the railway mechanic Anton Drexler, who was less influenced by occult Ariosophy than by *völkisch* nationalism and the ambition to develop a nationalist workers' movement. He took the initiative in founding a new German Workers Party (DAP) in Munich in January 1919, which was partly inspired by the tradition of prewar Germanic national socialism in Bohemia.[7] Its initial party "guidelines" declared, "The DAP seeks the ennoblement of the German worker. Educated and resident workers have the right to be part of the middle class. A sharp dividing line should be drawn between proletarians and workers."[8] It denounced all income not directly earned by work—particularly usury and financial exploitation—and demanded the confiscation of war profits but defended capital properly expended in the national interest. The DAP declared that its workerism opposed only the unproductive and nonnational sectors of the bourgeoisie, above all the Jews. Party members at first called each other "comrade," just as did leftists, and in the initial months most party flags and posters were predominantly colored red. Yet scarcely anyone paid attention to the tiny DAP, which had only fifty-four members when one of its modest meetings in a small Munich beer hall was attended by a thirty-year-old army veteran named Adolf Hitler.

6. Though it is clear that occult doctrines played a significant role in the background of the Nazi movement and in the thinking of certain leaders, an extensive literature on this topic somewhat exaggerates its significance. See, inter alia, J.-M. Angebert, *The Occult and the Third Reich* (New York, 1974); J. H. Brennan, *The Occult Reich* (New York, 1974); and J. Webb, *The Occult Establishment* (London, 1976).

7. A few months later certain members of the Thule Society also founded a German Socialist Party, which merged with the Nazis in 1922.

8. Quoted in E. Nolte, *Die faschistischen Bewegungen* (Munich, 1966), 35.

Hitler was born in the Austrian border town of Braunau-am-Inn on April 20, 1889, the son of a customs officer in the Austrian civil service. He was an intelligent but willful child and an increasingly poor student, due to lack of concentration. His father died in 1903, and Hitler dropped out of secondary school two years later. Young Hitler had no occupation but spent much of his time drawing and painting, and he conceived the ambition to become an architectural artist. At the age of eighteen he went to Vienna but was denied admission to the Austrian Academy of Fine Arts. His mother, apparently the only person to whom he felt close, died in December 1907. The attending physician was the family's Jewish doctor (for whom, in fact, Hitler seems to have had great respect).[9]

He returned to Vienna, where he spent the next five and a half years, a period Hitler later described as "the saddest of my life." Contrary to legend, he did not endure great poverty, receiving an orphan's pension from the civil service for several years and subsequently a small family inheritance. He spent his time in museums and libraries, in drawing architectural and other sketches, sometimes in painting watercolors, and in attending the opera when he could afford it. Hitler's financial resources eventually dried up, however, and then he was reduced to living in cheap boardinghouses and public shelters and occasionally trying to sell sketches for money.[10]

The importance of these Vienna years was their role in forming his general political and philosophical outlook. The most influential factors were the pan-German nationalism and anti-Semitism of Georg von Schönerer, the highly successful electoral anti-Semitism of the popular mayor of Vienna, Karl Lueger, and the occult racist anti-Semitism of Jörg Lanz von Liebenfels. These pan-German, Aryan racial and intensely anti-Jewish attitudes formed the core of Hitler's adult Weltanschauung.

Lonely, isolated, and down-and-out, Hitler fled Vienna in 1913 to avoid service in the multiethnic Austro-Hungarian army, moving across the German

9. There are numerous biographies of Hitler. Among the more recommendable are A. Bullock, *Hitler: A Study in Tyranny* (New York, 1964); W. Maser, *Adolf Hitler* (New York, 1973); J. Fest, *Hitler* (New York, 1974); J. Toland, *Adolf Hitler* (New York, 1976); R. G. L. Waite, *The Psychopathic God* (New York, 1977); W. Carr, *Hitler: A Study in Personality and Politics* (New York, 1979); and M. Steinert, *Hitler* (Paris, 1991). Also useful are S. Hafner, *Anmerkungen zu Hitler* (Munich, 1978); E. Jaeckel, *Hitler in History* (Hanover, N.H., 1984); and M. Hauner, *Hitler: A Chronology of His Life and Times* (New York, 1983). Gerhard Schreiber, in *Hitler: Interpretationen, 1923–1983* (Darmstadt, 1984), presents sixty years of interpretations. Among the best accounts by friends and acquaintances are O. Strasser, *Hitler and I* (Boston, 1940); H. Hoffmann, *Hitler Was My Friend* (London, 1955); E. Hanfstaengel, *Hitler: The Missing Years* (London, 1957); and H. A. Turner Jr., ed., *Hitler—Memoirs of a Confidant* (New Haven, 1985).

10. On these early years, see F. Jetzinger, *Hitler's Youth* (London, 1958); W. Jenks, *Vienna and the Young Hitler* (New York, 1960); and B. Smith, *Adolf Hitler: His Family, Childhood and Youth* (Stanford, 1967).

border to Munich. Later apprehended by the authorities, the sedentary youth was then rejected by the Austro-Hungarian army as physically unfit for service. In Munich he led the same idle, aimless life until World War I broke out, when he was immediately swept up in the tidal wave of German nationalist war enthusiasm, which accorded so well with his racist, Nordicist beliefs. The recent Austrian draft dodger was quickly accepted as a volunteer in the German army, in which he served throughout the long war. For the first time Hitler had a purpose in life, and he compiled an excellent record, spending many months on the front lines, part of them in the dangerous role of dispatch runner. Yet, though a committed and courageous soldier, Hitler remained in some respects a loner who did not fully fit in. He was never promoted beyond the rank of corporal.

At the moment of Germany's defeat he lay in a military hospital, temporarily blinded after a poison gas attack. All that he and millions had fought for seemed to be lost. Convinced as he was of the inherent superiority of Germans, he agreed with many others that their war effort had been subverted by sinister forces, "stabbed in the back" by Jews and other traitors. The army was the only institution that had given any meaning to his life, and he clung to a place in the shrunken Reichswehr of 1919, being kept on as a special "political observer" assigned to report on meetings of the new nationalist groups. In this capacity he attended a routine meeting of the DAP in September 1919 and immediately responded to its ideas, which seemed to explain how his radical anti-Semitic notions might be combined with a popular socioeconomic doctrine to create a broad nationalist movement. Hitler immediately joined the DAP as party member number fifty-five. Within a month he made his first political speech at another small meeting, proving surprisingly effective in the role of speaker. Soon he became the party's leading orator and chief source of fund-raising, and small admission charges were levied for the public to listen to his impassioned rhetoric. Hitler had a rather powerful though delusionary mind which concentrated on basic ideas to the point of infantilism, rigidly dividing his thinking into clear dualities. His remarkable near-photographic memory was particularly effective in giving many the impression that he possessed superior intellect. Hitler thus became a minor "happening" in Munich, and in February 1920 he was the focus of the DAP's first mass meeting, attracting an audience of two thousand.

This meeting also presented the party's new "Twenty-five Points," composed by Drexler and Hitler (though considerably influenced by the DAP's chief social ideologue, Gottfried Feder, and the Thule Society's principal theorist, Dietrich Eckhart). The Twenty-five Points proclaimed a German "national socialism" derived from the prewar Austro-Bohemian German National Socialists and other groups, based on extreme nationalism and the union of all true Germans, whose superior racial identity allegedly set them apart from others. National socialism would not mean general economic collectivism, for private property and individual initiative represented German values, but did mean opposition to the idle rich and to capitalist exploitation. Small businesses would be protected, but 51 percent of large corporations should be nationalized to guarantee they would be administered in the common interest. Similarly, there should be a partial nationalization of banking and credit, while large landholdings should be divided into family farms. The Twenty-five Points also called for confiscation of war profits, prosecution of usurers, profit sharing, a broader pension system, an end to child labor, and education for all. They denounced Jews, Communists, and the Treaty of Versailles. Jews were termed cosmopolitan, rootless exploiters who belonged to a distinct race: "No Jew can be a member of the nation." The Treaty of Versailles must be overturned and German power and well-being restored.

To give the party a more attractive and descriptive name, its title was changed to National Socialist German Workers Party (NSDAP). In April 1920 Hitler retired from the army to devote himself completely to the party, becoming director of propaganda. By July 1921 he had taken over uncontested leadership and thus was known as its *Führer* (Leader).[11] Though small, it grew steadily, gaining more than three thousand members at that time. Hitler grasped the importance of mass propaganda and tried to convert each major meeting into a grand ceremonial event. His keen visual sense emphasized symbols, solemn rituals, and the orchestration of public mass enthusiasm. The wearing of uniforms, the use of special party badges and emblems, and the employment of flags and party banners became standard. The swastika—an ancient occult device already used by various *völkisch* and racial groups as a symbol of the sun—was adopted as the key symbol. The party greetings of "Heil" (Hale) and "Sieg Heil" (Hale victory), apparently borrowed from earlier national socialists and militant youth groups, were also introduced. During 1921 a brown-shirted party militia, christened the Sturmabteilung (Storm Division, SA), was created.[12]

By 1923 the NSDAP had grown to fifty-five thousand members, with fifteen thousand in the SA. At this point some 36 percent of the members were workers (who otherwise amounted to about half of German society as a whole). Though unskilled workers constituted only 12 percent of members and were thus drastically underrepresented compared with general society, skilled

11. On Hitler's early leadership of the party, see A. Tyrell, *Vom "Trommler" zum "Führer"* (Munich, 1975), and E. Davidson, *The Making of Adolf Hitler* (New York, 1977).

12. The principal history of the party is D. Orlow, *The History of the Nazi Party, 1919–1945*, 2 vols. (Pittsburgh, 1969). James Rhodes, in *The Hitler Movement: A Modern Millenarian Revolution* (Stanford, 1980), treats it as the development of a modern millenarian movement. On the first years, see G. Franz-Willing, *Die Hitler-Bewegung, 1919–1922* (Hamburg, 1962), and W. Maser, *Die Frühgeschichte der NSDAP* (Frankfurt, 1965). N. F. Hayward and D. J. Morris, *The First Nazi Town* (New York, 1988), describes the first popular election of a Nazi official.

workers amounted to 24 percent and were thus overrepresented. Members were most numerous from the lower middle classes, totaling 52 percent—only slightly more than their percentage in society as a whole—and of these white-collar employees and lower civil servants accounted for 18 percent together, and farmers about 11 percent (roughly equivalent to the proportion of farmers in German society). The upper middle class and other elite sectors of society were overrepresented, totaling about 12 percent of party members (as compared with 3 percent of German society). Despite the latter characteristic, the NSDAP had largely succeeded in becoming a genuine cross-class and populist movement, even though not primarily a movement of blue-collar workers, with a broader social composition than any other political group save perhaps the Catholic Center Party.[13]

The opportunity for Hitler's first bid for power was created in 1923 by France's occupation of the Ruhr, the German campaign of passive resistance, and the accompanying social crisis of hyperinflation. As German Communists carried out two different insurrections, nationalists from several groups planned coups of their own. During the summer there were mass demonstrations and paramilitary rallies in Munich, as Hitler formed his own Kampfbund (Combat League), a loose umbrella organization of various small extremist nationalist groups.

As it turned out, the nationalist conspirators waited too long. An effective German government under Gustav Stresemann was formed in September; when the right-wing government in Bavaria declared its own state of emergency, the national administration countered with martial law throughout Germany, crushing Communist insurrections in Saxony and Thuringia in October. Finally, sensing that time was running out, Hitler decided to strike with his Kampfbund. Seizing control of a rightist rally in one of Munich's largest beer halls, he tried to convince the regional government to join him. General Erich Ludendorff and two thousand followers began a march through the streets. They were stopped by a police barricade, and after one fusillade all but Ludendorff turned and fled. Hitler threw himself to the ground, dislocating one shoulder. The leaders were arrested, and the NSDAP outlawed. At the subsequent trial in March 1924, sympathetic judges sentenced Hitler to the lightest term allowed—five years with the possibility of early probation. The "Beer Hall Putsch" had been a total failure—the very opposite of the March on Rome— and the movement lay in disarray.[14]

13. The best study of party membership is M. H. Kater, *The Nazi Party: A Social Profile of Members and Leaders, 1919–1945* (Cambridge, Mass., 1983), 17–31, 242–43. See also P. Manstein, *Die Mitglieder und Wähler der NSDAP, 1919–1933* (Frankfurt, 1988), and D. Mühlberger, *Hitler's Followers* (London, 1991).

14. See H. J. Gordon Jr., *Hitler and the Beer Hall Putsch* (Princeton, 1972); J. Dornberg, *Munich, 1923* (New York, 1982); and G. Franz-Willing, *Krisenjahre der Hitlerbewegung: 1923* (Preussich Oldendorf, 1975).

Temporary Stabilization of the Weimar Republic, 1923–1930

The concatenation of crises in the early history of the Weimar Republic finally ended with the ignominious failure of the Beer Hall Putsch. The new government under Gustav Stresemann provided strong leadership and quickly restored a stable currency. The economy recovered well during 1924–25, and social tensions eased. All the major national political parties save the Communists proved willing to collaborate in coalition government, and there was no serious crisis for the remainder of the decade. Reparations payments were successively scaled down, and so much money was provided in foreign loans that for every mark paid in reparations for the balance of the decade Germany received three marks from abroad.

Altogether, the Weimar Republic constituted the first fully democratic political system in Germany and one of the most progressive states in the world. Politically, it was a model democratic parliamentary regime that featured women's voting rights and mass mobilization. In social policy, it was the most advanced larger state in the world, with broad coverage of insurance and certain aspects of welfare, so that with little exaggeration it can be called the first democratic proto–welfare state in a large country. In culture, it was a focus of modernism in the arts and a world center for new art forms, while pioneering the mass media and mass culture, together with a new emphasis on youth culture. Economically Germany constituted a fully modern industrial society, though with severe problems of heavy taxation, lack of capital, and alternating inflation and stagflation. Demographically the republic presided during a time of major change, with a rapid decline in the birthrate and a shift in the roles of women. Because of the remarkable convergence of all these modern trends, one historian has labeled the underlying crisis of Weimar a "crisis of classical modernity." [15]

Yet even amid the partial prosperity and relative stability of 1924–29, the political equilibrium remained fragile, and the society faced manifold economic problems. There was a sharp temporary recession in 1925. Unemployment was always considerable, and domestic capital remained in short supply. Rapid economic and technological changes threatened both blue-collar jobs and established middle-class interests, as millions of people had to face declining opportunities or the search for new employment.

Even during the mid-1920s middle-class political and economic interests continued to fragment, and voting support for middle-class liberal parties, particularly among Protestants, declined noticeably. The three middle-class liberal parties garnered only 33.7 percent of the vote in 1924, and this dropped further to 28.7 percent in 1928, with only the Catholic Center Party holding its ground.

15. D. Peukert, *The Weimar Republic: The Crisis of Classical Modernity* (New York, 1992).

Equally troublesome was the rise of the special interest splinter parties, as various middle-class economic sectors formed separate single-issue parties under the conviction that the prevailing system failed to protect their interests. These splinter parties garnered 14 percent of the vote in 1928, half as much as the liberal democratic parties.[16]

The democratic government was generally cooperative in the international affairs of Europe during the middle and later 1920s, yet even the relatively liberal Stresemann actively maintained a hidden agenda of expansion on Germany's eastern and southern borders. Thus even the Weimar cabinets did not fully accept Germany's existing frontiers under the Versailles treaty, an underlying national tendency later exploited by the Nazis. In time, both domestic and foreign problems might have been peacefully resolved. What proved fatal was the continued overloading of the system with further traumas when the world depression began to affect Germany dramatically in 1930. This set the stage for the next sequence of crises, following those of the decade 1914–23, which would end with the collapse of the democratic system in 1933.[17]

Mein Kampf and the Reorganization of National Socialism, 1924–1928

Hitler was required to serve only one year of his five-year sentence for the Munich rebellion, and after an initial bout of despondency he used the time to prepare his political autobiography, *Mein Kampf* (My Struggle), which outlined the goals of the National Socialist movement. Here he reelaborated the extreme racist and Social Darwinist ideas he had ingested in earlier years, revolving around the two key concepts of race and space. All history was declared a history of racial struggle, the fundamental unit of human society being the race. Hitler's philosophy was purportedly founded on the natural order, nature itself having divided human society into distinct races, whose differing qualities determined all else.[18] The races formed a kind of pyramid, with the Aryan or Nordic race at the top, superior in cultural creation and all other higher attributes. (Thus, in the technical sense, Hitler was not, strictly speaking, a mere German nationalist, for the concept of the Nordic race, as he privately admitted, extended to certain other peoples—or sectors of certain other peoples—in central and northern Europe.)

The superior race should become dominant, but to achieve dominance

16. The key study is L. E. Jones, *German Liberalism and the Dissolution of the Weimar Party System, 1918–1933* (Chapel Hill, 1988).

17. For an overall survey of the travails of the republic, see E. Eyck, *A History of the Weimar Republic*, 2 vols. (Cambridge, Mass., 1962–64). Briefer treatments include A. J. Nicholls, *Weimar and the Rise of Hitler* (New York, 1991); E. Kolb, *The Weimar Republic* (London, 1988); and I. Kershaw, ed., *Weimar: Why Did German Democracy Fail?* (New York, 1990).

18. R. A. Pois, *National Socialism and the Religion of Nature* (New York, 1986).

would require space, or *Lebensraum*, which Hitler indicated should be achieved in the east, primarily at the expense of the Soviet Union. Contrary to what has often been said, Hitler did not outline all his revolutionary goals in *Mein Kampf*—for that would have frightened most Germans—but he did set forth his main racial concepts and some of his ambitions for expansion abroad, as well as his extreme anti-Semitism. Hitler preached that the most dangerous foe of Aryans was not inferior races or Communists but the Jews, defined as a demonic antirace devoted to destroying the purity of all other races. This extreme Jewish danger would have to be eliminated, though Hitler did not explain exactly what he meant by that. His doctrine of demonic racial anti-Semitism was not new, having been advanced in varying degrees by diverse French, Russian, German, and Austrian ideologues in the late nineteenth century, but he gave it a new virulence and a special centrality.[19] Motivated by remarkable hatreds, Hitler divided problems into simple dualities and revealed an intuitive approach to propaganda and mass psychology. He stressed the importance of lies and exaggerations in propagating ideas and also emphasized that the masses were impressed by extremism and wished to see a certain amount of violence in action.[20]

The NSDAP was officially refounded on February 17, 1925.[21] It soon had to face a major challenge from its own left wing in the northern cities, which had formed a National Socialist Workers Association, led by the brothers Gregor and Otto Strasser and Paul Joseph Goebbels, an unsuccessful writer. In two dramatic meetings early in 1926, Hitler won over the dissidents, who

19. For an overview of the development of Nazi racial doctrine, see R. Breitling, *Die nationalsozialistische Rassenlehre* (Meisenheim am Glan, 1971), and also R. Ceicel, *The Myth of the Master Race: Alfred Rosenberg and Nazi Ideology* (London, 1972). The contribution of the émigré Russian radical right is explained in W. Laqueur, *Russia and Germany* (New York, 1963).

20. Somewhat contrasting expositions of Hitler's ideas will be found in E. Jaeckel, *Hitler's Weltanschauung* (Middletown, Conn., 1972), and R. Zitelmann, *Hitler: Selbstverständnis eines Revolutionärs* (Hamburg, 1987). The ideological background is treated in G. L. Mosse, *The Crisis of German Ideology: Intellectual Origins of the Third Reich* (New York, 1964), and H. Glaser, *The Cultural Roots of National Socialism* (Austin, 1978). The best Soviet treatment is A. A. Galkin, "Fashistskii ideinyi sindrom: Genesis germanskogo varianta," *Voprosy Filosofii* 11 (1988): 124–34.

21. While outlawed during 1924, the NSDAP nonetheless indirectly participated in national elections for the first time through the device of the Völkisch-Sozialer Block, an alliance with General Ludendorff's Deutschvölkische Freiheitspartei (German Ethnic Freedom Party, DVFP), the right radical group nearest the Nazis. Unlike certain of the prewar anti-Semitic groups that had been semidemocratic, the DVFP campaigned for an authoritarian regime, declaring itself on the "far right" on nationalist issues and on the "far left" on socioeconomic questions, calling for the closing of stock exchanges and the nationalization of banks. The DVFP vote reached 6.5 percent in the elections of May 1924 but fell to 3 percent in the second general election that year, in December. Much of the DVFP would later merge with the Nazis.

Josef Goebbels addressing a street rally in Berlin, 1926

fell under the spell of his charisma.[22] He projected a messianic image to his followers and, together with his remarkable oratorical ability, had also by this point developed great skill in striking carefully calculated poses, adjusted according to the audience. The command of the party became fully centralized, the official proclamation of the *Führerprinzip* (leadership principle) canceling the original system of internal election and giving all authority to Hitler.[23] The brown-shirted militia of the SA was refounded in 1926, and a broad range of subsidiary organizations were formed. These included the Hitler Youth, the National Socialist Women's League, and other leagues for lawyers, doctors, teachers, and students.[24] In 1928 the NSBO (the Nazi shop-floor labor organization) was created, and the party even set up its own internal court system.[25] Though overall growth in these years was rather slow, it was also steady. NSDAP membership reached 75,000 in 1927 and grew to 108,000 two years later.[26]

Until 1928 the party followed an urban strategy designed to attract blue-collar workers, but it enjoyed very limited success, gaining only 2.6 percent of the vote in the national elections of 1928. It did poorly in worker districts but quite well in a number of rural areas, and this prompted Hitler to a change in strategy. Ever since the failure of 1923 he had given up Communist-style insurrectionary tactics and had committed the party to a legalistic course, recognizing that in Germany power could only be achieved by legal means. In

22. On this sector of the party, see R. Kühnl, *Die nationalsozialistische Linke 1925 bis 1930* (Meisenheim am Glan, 1966), and also M. Kele, *Nazis and Workers* (Chapel Hill, 1972). On Gregor Strasser, see U. Kissenkoetter, *Gregor Strasser und die NSDAP* (Stuttgart, 1978), and P. D. Stachura, *Gregor Strasser and the Rise of Nazism* (London, 1983). The latest of several biographies of Goebbels is R. G. Reuth, *Goebbels* (New York, 1993).

23. I. Kershaw, *The "Hitler Myth"* (Oxford, 1987); W. Horn, *Führerideologie und Partei-organisation in der NSDAP, 1919–1933* (Düsseldorf, 1975); J. Nyomarkay, *Charisma and Factionalism in the Nazi Party* (Minneapolis, 1967); F. Nova, *The National Socialist Fuehrerprinzip and Its Background in German Thought* (Philadelphia, 1943).

24. By 1933, of all sectors of German society, the one most disproportionately attracted to Nazism was the students, and the literature about them is extensive: see P. D. Stachura, *Nazi Youth in the Weimar Republic* (Santa Barbara, 1975); M. H. Kater, *Studentenschaft und Rechtsradikalismus in Deutschland, 1918–1933* (Hamburg, 1975); A. Faust, *Der Nationalsozialistische Deutsche Studentenbund*, 2 vols. (Düsseldorf, 1976); M. P. Steinberg, *Sabers and Brownshirts: The German Students' Path to National Socialism, 1918–1935* (Chicago, 1977); and G. Giles, *Students and National Socialism in Germany* (Princeton, 1985).

25. D. M. McKale, *The Nazi Party Courts* (Lawrence, Kans., 1974).

26. Growth naturally varied by region and district. Among the best of a number of local and regional studies are R. Koshar, *Social Life, Local Politics and Nazism: Marburg, 1880–1935* (Chapel Hill, 1986); G. Pridham, *Hitler's Rise to Power: The History of the NSDAP in Bavaria, 1923–1933* (London, 1973); and J. Noakes, *The Nazi Party in Lower Saxony, 1921–1933* (London, 1971). For a bibliography and appraisal, see J. H. Grill, "Local and Regional Studies of National Socialism: A Review," *JCH* 21:2 (April 1986): 253–94.

1928 Hitler made a second fundamental change in strategy: the NSDAP would become a more explicitly cross-class movement, aiming at nearly all major sectors in society. In industrial areas, it would still target the worker vote, but elsewhere it would appeal equally to the various sectors of the middle classes and to farmers, who seemed to be particularly susceptible.

The new strategy soon began to pay dividends. In 1929 the party gained greatly increased publicity by joining with rightist elements in an attack on reparations, enjoying greater access to national media. By the end of the year membership had climbed to 178,000, and the vote in local elections rose sharply.

Other Organizations and Interest Groups of Authoritarian Nationalism

Despite the temporary success of democratic forces in stabilizing the Weimar Republic, a nationalist and authoritarian counterculture was expressed in many forms quite apart from the NSDAP. In some respects this effort had been enhanced by the immediate postwar experience. The political and cultural groups involved were numerous and diverse. In almost every case they were more moderate—often much more moderate—than the Nazis, and in no other case were they generically fascist, yet in toto they contributed to an atmosphere in which authoritarian nationalist alternatives were increasingly publicized and encouraged. The principal organizations and interest groups are treated in the following paragraphs.

The Freikorps. National militia groups were organized in most countries of central and eastern Europe to defend borders and guard against subversion in the immediate aftermath of World War I. The German variant of these forces was called the Freikorps and flourished during 1919–20, helping to defend the eastern frontier and repress the revolutionary left. Subsequently disbanded, the group created a precedent for the militarization of nationalist politics and the use of violence.[27]

The Stahlhelm. Dozens of rightist and radical nationalist groups, mostly ephemeral, were formed in the years immediately after the war. The largest of all the right-wing nationalist organizations was the Stahlhelm (Steel Helmet), the main German veterans organization. Ultranationalist and essentially authoritarian, it was the German organization most favored with financial support by Mussolini. The Stahlhelm, however, was not a political party and did not contest elections, though it influenced the political thinking of many.[28]

---

27. R. G. L. Waite, *Vanguard of Nazism* (Cambridge, Mass., 1954); J. M. Diehl, *Paramilitary Politics in Weimar Germany* (Bloomington, 1978); H. W. Koch, *Der deutsche Bürgerkrieg: Eine Geschichte der deutschen und österreichischen Freikorps, 1918–1923* (Berlin, 1978).

28. V. R. Berghahn, *Der Stahlhelm* (Düsseldorf, 1966).

The conservative revolution. Diverse intellectuals, writers, and publicists of the right preached what many of them called a conservative revolution, which would reject the novelties and seeming radicalism of Weimar to restore true German values under strong authority and leadership. They rejected foreign materialist and "American" influences in the name of a higher German culture. The conservative revolution was led by the journal *Die Tat* (Action) and such figures as the hieratic poet Stefan George, one of the two leading German poets of the early twentieth century; the historian Oswald Spengler, the first volume of whose influential *Decline of the West* had appeared in 1918; and the publicist Arthur Moeller van den Bruck, whose *Das dritte Reich* (The Third Reich) was published in 1923. The diverse proponents of the conservative revolution, who formed no common political organization, preached that the world of modernism and materialism was doomed and that Europe and Germany were facing a major turning point, which would require the restoration of higher spiritual and cultural values in the name of Germanism, unity, and national self-affirmation.[29]

The expansion of völkisch *culture.* The *völkisch* or ethnicist culture that had developed during the nineteenth century expanded further during the 1920s, particularly in the form of novels and popular art. Such works publicized Germanic attitudes and values and rejected the new elite cosmopolitan cultural influence of the larger cities. They proclaimed that peace, harmony, and true development could only be found within ethnicist culture, which required German unity and—by implication—firmer and more authoritarian leadership.

Völkisch culture particularly affirmed a myth dear to all nationalist opinion—the mystique of the *Kriegserlebnis*, or "myth of the war experience." This insisted on the sacred union of the war, the mutual relationship and common responsibility engendered by national struggle and sacrifice, and the higher values and transvaluation of life made possible by German unity in militant patriotic causes.[30]

Bündisch *youth and the youth culture.* The modern youth movement, as we saw in chapter 1, had taken form in Germany in the years before World

---

29. A. Mohler, *Die konservative Revolution in Deutschland, 1918–1933* (Darmstadt, 1972); K. Sontheimer, *Antidemokratisches Denken in der Weimarer Republik* (Munich, 1962); J. P. Faye, *Langages totalitaires* (Paris, 1972); K. von Klemperer, *Germany's New Conservatism* (Princeton, 1957); H. Lebovics, *Social Conservatism and the Middle Classes in Germany, 1914–1933* (Princeton, 1969); D. Barnouw, *Weimar Intellectuals and the Threat of Modernity* (Bloomington, 1978); H. J. Schwierskott, *Arthur Moeller van den Bruck und der revolutionäre Nationalismus in der Weimarer Republik* (Göttingen, 1962). On the chief political theorist within this sector, see J. Bendersky, *Carl Schmitt: Theorist for the Reich* (Princeton, 1983).

30. G. L. Mosse, *Fallen Soldiers* (New York, 1990). On the expansion of *völkisch* culture in these years, see Mosse, *Crisis of German Ideology* 237–317.

War I. During the 1920s this tendency spread; nearly all major political forces had youth groups as well. Among the most militant were the nationalist and *völkisch*-minded youth, organized into various formations sometimes independent of political parties. *Bündisch* (nationalist-bonded) youth groups were eager for patriotic unity and strong leadership in a higher cause that would transcend normal life. Moreover, youth were particularly important at this time because of the high birthrate before 1914 and the mortality of the older generation in the war. By 1925 there were more young men in the fifteen-to-twenty age group than ever before in German history, heavily outnumbering more mature men in their thirties. This large and often alienated youth generation was prone to radicalization, while its greater numbers gave apparent credence to the propaganda of Nazis and other ultranationalists that Germans were a *Volk ohne Raum* (a people without adequate living space).

National Bolsheviks. The most socially radical of the ultranationalists was a tiny group led by Ernst Niekisch whose members called themselves National Bolsheviks and claimed to espouse much of the Leninist social revolution, along with German political and cultural principles. This attempt to combine two utter extremes condemned them to narrow isolation.[31]

The German National People's Party (DNVP). The chief political party of the ultranationalist right was the DNVP, which sometimes played a significant role in parliament. For most of the 1920s, it was a party of the conservative and legalistic (if protoauthoritarian) right, largely accepting the rules of the political game and sometimes participating in coalition government. In 1928, however, leadership was taken by Alfred Hugenburg, a press and film baron, together with other figures of the radical right. They moved the party into direct opposition to the democratic system. Thus from 1928 the DNVP became a classic right radical authoritarian party, but its narrow social and economic policies and ultrarightism limited popular appeal. After 1930 it could not compete with Nazism.[32]

The cryptoauthoritarian right in the moderate parties. The right wing of the moderate liberal parties, especially the Catholic Center and the conservative liberal German People's Party (DVP), tended toward a moderate authoritarianism, sometimes with monarchist overtones.[33] These elements, plus some of those in the middle-class splinter parties, were thus potentially willing to collaborate in a moderate authoritarianism with other sectors.

31. O.-E. Schüddekopf, *Nationalbolschewismus in Deutschland, 1918–1933* (Frankfurt, 1973); L. Dupeux, *"Nationalbolschewismus" in Deutschland, 1919–1933* (Munich, 1985).

32. On the later period of the DNVP, see J. A. Leopold, *Alfred Hugenburg* (New Haven, 1978); F. H. von Cärtringen, "Die Deutschnationale Volkspartei," in *Das Ende der Parteien: 1933,* ed. E. Mathias and R. Morsey (Düsseldorf, 1960), 543–652; and A. Chanady, "The Disintegration of the German National Peoples' Party, 1924–1930," *JMH* 39:1 (1967): 65–91.

33. W. H. Kaufmann, *Monarchism in the Weimar Republic* (New York, 1953).

Hindenburg and the rightist presidential clique. When Friedrich Ebert, the first president of the republic (and a Socialist) died in 1925, rightists encouraged the candidacy of the seventy-eight-year-old Marshal Paul von Hindenburg, wartime head of the army high command. A national hero, he was neither a democrat nor a republican, and he won by only a small margin over the moderate liberal candidate. Though Hindenburg's election to the presidency had no immediate consequences, it was a fateful event, for the elderly man, who would later verge on senility, had no interest in maintaining the integrity of parliamentary government. Moreover, he was surrounded by rightist advisers and military contacts such as General Kurt von Schleicher, head of the political office of the small postwar German army, who favored turning the republic into a more authoritarian presidential system. Hindenburg's advisers in turn maintained contacts with conservative authoritarian personalities on the right wings of the parliamentary parties of the center and right. Before the end of the 1920s Hindenburg began to interfere more and more with the work of the parliament and the government's coalition process. With such leadership at the top, the fate of the democratic republic could not but be uncertain.[34]

Ultimately all these groups lost ground to the Nazis, and in most cases they disappeared as autonomous forces by the middle of 1933. They failed as organizations and political tendencies for lack of leadership and internal unity, efficient administration, and a broader, cross-class appeal, remaining generally narrow and rightist both in image and in practice.

The Depression Crisis and the Rise of Nazism, 1930–1933

Onset of the Great Depression suddenly added a new crisis to the long concatenation of national traumas suffered by German society since 1914. The only years since the war that had been generally prosperous had been 1920–21, 1924, and 1926–28. A sharp recession had jolted much of the population in 1925,[35] and unemployment had never been eliminated even in the best years. The German economy was persistently short of capital, and industrial production overall expanded only a little beyond the 1913 level. Foreign loans were always necessary to balance state budgets, so that Germany became more dependent on the international economy than any other industrial country.[36] Once the depression struck, unemployment mounted rapidly. The number of unemployed, 1.3 million at the close of 1929, mounted to 3 million a year later

34. A. Dorpalen, *Hindenburg and the Weimar Republic* (Princeton, 1964).
35. D. Hertz-Eichenrode, *Wirtschaftskrise und Arbeitbeschaffung: Konjunkturpolitik 1925/26 und die Grundlagen der Krisenpolitik Brünings* (Frankfurt, 1982).
36. W. C. McNeil, *American Money and the Weimar Republic* (New York, 1985).

and 6 million by the end of 1932.[37] Fear and resentment grew on every hand. Unemployed workers turned more and more to the Communist Party (KPD), while middle-class people, who suffered less direct unemployment, became increasingly anxious and sought new alternatives. The moderate parties had been losing votes since 1924, so that the liberal center was already seriously weakened even before the depression struck. The latest calamity only increased the tendency of the moderate parties to fragment and subdivide further.

The depression quickly destroyed the "Weimar coalition" of middle-class parties and Social Democrats that had governed for the past decade. In a sense, it produced the first modern crisis of the welfare state, for the German republic had nearly doubled the share of national income spent by the state, to more than 30 percent. Employers were already accustomed to speaking of oppression by a "trade union state" that exacted high taxes and imposed compulsory labor arbitration. The previous level of funding could not be maintained, but the Social Democrats insisted on retaining as much as possible, and the coalition parties could find no compromise.[38]

A new coalition would have been difficult to construct, but President Hindenburg scarcely even tried. He was a monarchist at heart with little faith in parliamentary government, and he appointed as chancellor Heinrich Brüning, from the right wing of the Catholic Center Party. The new chancellor had no parliamentary majority but was given authority by the president to govern by decree under the emergency powers of Article 48 of the constitution. Though these powers were only temporary, they made it unnecessary to rely on parliamentary votes, so that representative government on the national level was interrupted in mid-1930, not to be restored until after World War II. President Hindenburg and Chancellor Brüning calculated that strong government would enjoy practical success and public approbation, leading to a more authoritarian system and possibly to restoration of the monarchy.[39]

The decision to test the new currents by Reichstag elections in September 1930 turned out to be a fundamental miscalculation. As the economic crisis deepened, the propaganda appeal of the Nazis as economic saviors offering something to all was dramatically demonstrated by an 800 percent increase in the Nazi vote: the Nazis obtained 18.3 percent of the national total and 107

37. H. James, *The German Slump* (New York, 1986); P. D. Stachura, ed., *Unemployment and the Great Depression in Weimar Germany* (New York, 1986).

38. For a sympathetic critique of the Socialist position, see D. Abraham, *The Collapse of the Weimar Republic: Political Economy and Crisis* (Princeton, 1981). The policies of the Social Democrats throughout the crisis are treated in D. Harsch, *German Social Democracy and the Rise of Nazism* (Chapel Hill, 1993), and H. A. Winkler, *Der Weg in die Katastrophe: Arbeiter und Arbeiterbewegung in der Weimarer Republik 1930 bis 1933* (Berlin, 1987).

39. Cf. H. Brüning, *Memoiren* (Frankfurt, 1975).

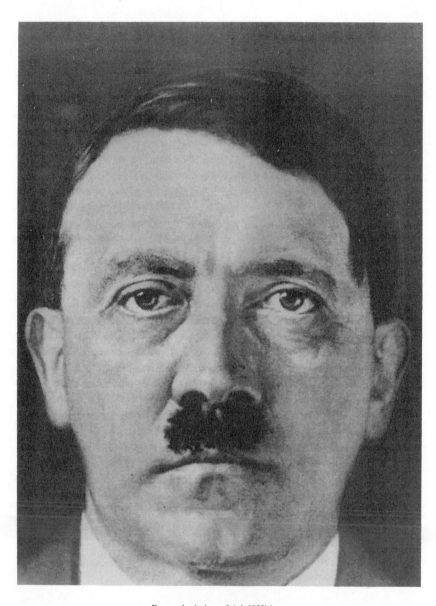

Poster depiction of Adolf Hitler

seats, and suddenly Hitler's group was the second largest in the parliament, exceeded only by the Social Democrats. The Communists also registered a sharp increase, while the moderate middle-class parties declined further. More than half of the new Nazi votes were drawn from the latter, at least a fifth came from voters who had previously abstained, and a smaller share came from former Socialist voters.

By 1930 the success of the party reorganization and the realignment of its strategy became fully apparent. The NSDAP enjoyed solid and centralized administration and had a hard-working membership, with a party apparatus that now proved remarkably adept at mass propaganda. All forms of the media were exploited, from posters and billboards to leaflets, newspaper, radio, movies, and innumerable mass meetings.

Two aspects of the Nazi strategy made it especially effective. On the one hand, National Socialist propaganda appealed to each major segment of society in its own terms, promising solutions to economic problems. On the other, the Nazis proclaimed themselves the only true all-German movement which stood above party, class, and faction. Thus they alleged that Hitler was the only true national leader with a program for the entire society, able to save the Fatherland from disaster. Hitler was emerging as the master political rhetorician of the century, whose impassioned oratorical techniques—though they might have seemed ludicrous in a different society at a calmer time—were able to sway millions and give them new hope and joy.[40]

As National Socialist propaganda reached a mass audience, the more extreme aspects of Hitlerian doctrine were toned down. Anti-Semitism played a role, but only in moderation, as Nazis were increasingly careful not to frighten ordinary people by preaching dire tactics against Jews.[41] Similarly, the goal of war to achieve *Lebensraum* while destroying the Soviet Union was normally not mentioned. Instead, party propaganda repeated over and over that only Hitler could give Germany a government strong enough to maintain security, emphasizing the slogan *National Socialism means peace.* The main themes were nationalism, economic salvation, and anticommunism. Thus the Nazis proved fully the equal of the Communists in the big lie, and they enjoyed greater acceptance among the populace at large.

Like Mussolini during 1921–22, Hitler worked during 1931–32 to establish ties with influential sectors of society, cooperating part of the time with the

40. Perhaps the fullest account of the rise of Hitler is G. Schulz, *Aufstieg des Nationalsozialismus* (Berlin, 1975).

41. S. Gordon, *Hitler, Germans and the Jewish Question* (Princeton, 1984). Hitler had already toned down anti-Semitism so much in the propaganda campaigns of 1928–29 that Ludendorff denounced him as a traitor to anti-Semitism. E. Ludendorff, *Weltkrieg droht auf deutschen Boden* (Munich, 1930), 19–20, cited in M. Michaelis, *Mussolini and the Jews* (Oxford, 1978), 49.

right and trying to reassure businessmen that they had no reason to be apprehensive of Nazi "socialism." Yet despite massive leftist propaganda that Hitler was the paid agent of capitalism, Hitler garnered only limited financial support from big business.[42] While there was considerable support for Hitler among small industrialists, most sectors of big business consistently advised against permitting him to form a government.[43] The Nazi Party was primarily financed by its own members.

When Hindenburg's presidential term expired in 1932, Hitler decided to challenge his reelection, knowing that Hindenburg was reluctant to appoint him chancellor. Though Hindenburg failed by a narrow margin to gain an absolute majority in a three-way race with Hitler and the Communist candidate, in a runoff he easily bested Hitler by 53 to 37 percent. Hindenburg's right-wing advisers then convinced him to appoint as chancellor another right-wing Center Party figure, the aristocrat Franz von Papen. This he did in mid-July. Papen's goal was much the same as Brüning's: to convert the German government into a more authoritarian and rightist presidential system. Seeing the Nazis as his main rival, he obtained permission to hold new elections, but in the balloting of July 31 the Nazi vote zoomed to 37 percent, giving the party 230 Reichstag seats and making it the largest single party in Germany. Papen could not possibly dominate such a parliament with only a minority of votes behind him. Soon after the parliament convened in September, he called yet another election, hoping this time to break the Nazis' momentum. In this he was partially successful; for the first time the National Socialist vote fell, but only to 33 percent and 196 Reichstag seats.

During the electoral campaigns of 1932, the Nazis claimed that only they could save Germany from civil war. They promised security from Marxism but campaigned vigorously against "reaction" in the form of Papen's right-wing "cabinet of barons," promising also to rescue Germany from "the American system, or high capitalism." By the end of the year party membership reached 450,000, more than any other political party, with 400,000 men in the SA and about the same number of workers in the Nazi worker groups. Nearly 8 percent of party members were women. Twenty-five percent were blue-collar workers,

42. More scholarly presentations of the "agent" theory may be found in E. Czichon, *Wer verhalf Hitler zur Macht?* (Cologne, 1967); D. Stegmann, "Kapitalismus und Faschismus in Deutschland, 1929–1934," *Beiträge zur Marxschen Theorie* 6 (1976): 19–91; and U. Horster-Philipps, "Grosskapital, Weimarer Republik und Faschismus," in *Die Zerstörung der Weimarer Republik,* ed. G. Hardach and R. Kühnl (Cologne, 1977), 38–141.

43. H. A. Turner Jr., *German Big Business and the Rise of Hitler* (New York, 1985); idem, "Hitlers Einstellung zu Wirtschaft und Gesellschaft vor 1933," *Geschichte und Gesellschaft* 2 (1976): 89–117. See also J. Pool and S. Pool, *Who Financed Hitler?* (New York, 1978), and R. Neebe, *Grossindustrie, Staat und NSDAP, 1930–1933* (Göttingen, 1981).

An SA parade in Munich

with nearly three-quarters coming from various sectors of the middle classes.[44] The most blue-collar Nazis were the stormtroopers of the SA, at least 50 to 55 percent of whose members were working class.[45] In July 1932 Nazi voting support increased among virtually all social sectors, but most noticeably in Protestant small towns and rural areas. The Nazis also did very well in elite districts and among self-employed members of the "old middle class," and among civil servants and workers in small shop and handicraft industries. Though most of the vote came from the middle classes, a third or more came from blue-collar workers. Conversely, the Nazis did poorly among Catholics and among most industrial workers, and not particularly well among white-collar employees. Their support was generally weaker among women voters than among men.[46]

44. Kater, *Nazi Party* 51–71.

45. According to Kater (*Nazi Party*), approximately 55 percent were workers; Mühlberger (*Hitler's Followers* 159–80) arrives at a cross-regional average of 49 percent. Conan Fischer, in *Stormtroopers* (London, 1983), concludes that workers constituted a clear majority of SA members, though Mathilde Jamin points out, in *Zwischen den Klassen: Zur Sozialstruktur der SA-Führerschaft* (Wuppertal, 1984), 116–69, that her research indicates that workers provided only 12 percent of SA leaders.

46. R. F. Hamilton, *Who Voted for Hitler?* (Princeton, 1982); T. Childers, *The Nazi Voter* (Chapel Hill, 1983); idem, ed., *The Formation of the Nazi Constituency, 1919–1933* (Totowa,

A notable feature of the 1932 elections was the drastic decline of all the liberal and moderate middle-class parties except for the Catholic Center, with support for the right radical DNVP dropping less than that for the liberal Protestant parties. The middle-class parties denounced the Nazis' "socialism" and their "preaching of revolution," declaring them essentially leftists who were "arm in arm" with the Communists, but this had less and less effect.[47] Simultaneously, all the middle-class parties save the Catholic Center fractured. New splinter groups were formed, and without exception they moved further toward the right.

The only party to increase its vote significantly, except the Nazis', was the Communists'. The Communists always saw the Social Democrats as their chief enemies, and sometimes they collaborated with the Nazis against the existing democratic system. At the same time, since they were aware that the Nazis were gaining support among some workers, the Communists also employed some of the same nationalist demagogy. The Socialist daily *Vorwärts* (Forward) complained that the Communists had become "more National Socialist than the Nazis," as the Communists adopted the tactic of the "united front from below" by trying to win over pro-Nazi workers through a limited number of joint actions with the Nazis.[48] These, however, produced no real benefit for the Communists.[49]

Political violence grew steadily from 1928 to 1933, expanding noticeably in the mass mobilization of 1930 and continuing to rise rapidly thereafter. These mainly involved *zusammenstösse,* or gang fights, between Nazis and Communists, though the Nazis also sometimes attacked Socialists, who were much more reluctant to engage in violence than the Communists. This did not involve general terrorism or the calculated assassination of leading figures, but simply an increasing number of brawls, beatings, and killings on the streets of the larger cities and also sometimes in political meetings and taverns. Normally the goal was not necessarily to kill the enemy, and many frays resulted in only comparatively minor injuries. German Communists had never been reluctant to commit violent acts, and though they did engage in a few joint strike actions and political initiatives with the Nazis, more frequent were their independent aggressive gestures that sometimes involved seizing the initiative in violence.

N.J., 1986). See also H. A. Winkler, *Mittelstand, Demokratie und Nationalsozialismus* (Cologne, 1970); R. J. Evans, "Women and the Triumphs of Hitler," *JMH* 48:1 (March 1976): 73–91; and R. I. McKibbin, "The Myth of the Unemployed: Who Did Vote for Hitler?" *Australian Journal of Politics and History* 15:2 (Aug. 1969): 25–69.

47. Childers, *Nazi Voter* 207.
48. Ibid., 182.
49. C. Fischer, *The German Communists and the Rise of Nazism* (New York, 1991).

Hitler reviewing an SA parade in Munich

There has never been any precise census of political violence under the Weimar Republic. Considerably more than 2,000 people were killed in the strikes, revolutionary outbreaks, and repression of 1919–23.[50] German Communists claimed that "fascists" killed 92 workers between the end of 1923 and the beginning of 1930, while the Nazis in turn alleged that 30 of their members had been killed by political enemies during approximately the same period. During 1930 the Nazis claimed to have suffered 17 fatalities in political combat, the Communists 44. These figures increased the following year to 42 for the Nazis and 52 for the Communists. For 1932 the respective claims were 84 Nazis and 75 Communists killed, exceeded in each year by more than a hundred times that number of injured (2,500 injured Nazis in 1930, 9,715 in 1932).[51]

50. E. J. Gumbel, *Vier Jahre Politischer Mord* (Berlin, 1923). In addition, there were allegedly more than three hundred political murders during these years, overwhelmingly committed by the right against the left.

51. E. Rosenhaft, *Beating the Fascists? The German Communists and Political Violence, 1929–1933* (Cambridge, 1983), 6–7. Richard Bessel, in *Political Violence and the Rise of Nazism: The Storm Troopers in Eastern Germany, 1925–1934* (New Haven, 1974), 74–75, presents lower figures, with 24 Nazis killed from 1924 to 1929, 15 in 1930, 42 in 1931, and 70 in 1932, the majority of whom in the last three years were SA members. For further material on Nazi violence, see Fischer's *Stormtroopers* and two works by Peter H. Merkl: *Political Violence under the Swastika: 581 Early Nazis* (Princeton, 1975) and *The Making of a Stormtrooper* (Princeton, 1980).

The electoral decline of nearly 10 percent in November 1932 had nonetheless been a serious blow for the Nazis, their first reverse after more than three years of uninterrupted success. Papen hoped to take advantage of this situation to domesticate the Nazis in the same way that Italian conservatives had once hoped to domesticate the Fascists, offering Hitler the subordinate post of vice-chancellor in the Papen government. This Hitler refused, insisting on taking power legally as chancellor on the calculation—no doubt correct—that any lesser position would seriously compromise his chances.

Papen thus did not have the choice of constructing a legal majority coalition, for the Reichstag was now hopelessly splintered. His only hope would be a kind of presidential coup by Hindenburg to convert the German government into a more authoritarian, right-wing presidentialist system. Hindenburg was uncertain, and his chief military adviser, Schleicher, convinced him that Papen's alternative would never work but would end in leftist insurrection and civil war. Instead, Schleicher pledged that if appointed chancellor he would create a legal majority by courting Gregor Strasser (number two leader in the party and head of its bureaucracy) and the Nazi "left" to split the party, while reflating the economy through public works and other government spending. Schleicher thus replaced Papen as chancellor on December 2, 1932. He energetically set to work with his new economic program, which soon showed some signs of success.[52] The vice-chancellorship was offered to Strasser, in the hope that a significant proportion of Nazis would desert Hitler and rally to the government. Hitler vetoed Strasser's participation, and though the latter then resigned from the NSDAP, scarcely anyone followed his example.

The end of 1932 was nonetheless a time of crisis for Hitler, for there was a distinct possibility that the Nazi tide, already ebbing slightly, would recede much more. Since the summer of 1932 the decline in the German economy had bottomed out, and unemployment ceased to rise. Output of producers' goods increased during the second quarter of 1932, and that of consumer durables rose in the third quarter. Costs were falling, profits were rising, and the stock market was also starting to grow. A few weeks after Schleicher became chancellor, a new international treaty ended the Versailles arms restrictions on Germany. Reparations had in effect come to an end more than a year earlier. The two principal "shackles of Versailles" had been broken with no assistance from the Nazis. The *Frankfurter Zeitung* confidently announced on January 1, 1933,

52. On Schleicher, see F.-K. von Plehwe, *Reichskanzler Kurt von Schleicher: Weimars Letzte Chance gegen Hitler* (Esslingen, 1983); K. Caro and W. Oehme, *Schleichers Aufstieg* (Berlin, 1933); and H. Marcon, *Arbeitsbeschaffungspolitik der Regierung Papen und Schleicher* (Frankfurt, 1974). On the role of the military during Weimar, see T. Vogelsang, *Reichswehr, Staat und NSDAP* (Munich, 1962); F. L. Carsten, *The Reichswehr and German Politics, 1918–1933* (New York, 1966); and R. J. O'Neill, *The German Army and the Nazi Party* (London, 1964).

that "the mighty National Socialist assault on the democratic state has been repulsed."

Moreover, the Nazis made the mistake of supporting a Communist-inspired wildcat transportation strike in Berlin, which paralyzed the city for five days at the beginning of 1933. This revived conservatives' fear of Nazi "socialism," and *Vorwärts* declared that Hitler had lost any credit with high finance and big business. The Nazi Führer was at first extremely depressed and talked momentarily of ending it all with a pistol. Schleicher calculated that another round of elections would end the Nazis' chances for good.

The chancellor's weakness was that he was only an army general governing with decree powers under Article 48, exclusively at the pleasure of the president. Graver yet was the fact that his search for political alternatives produced no real benefits while arousing suspicions on all sides. Having failed to split the Nazis, he tried next to approach the Socialists, with the result that, as a leading German historian of this period, Karl D. Bracher, has written, Schleicher "courted everyone and aroused the mistrust of everyone." [53] Particularly distressing for Hindenburg was the chancellor's proposal to settle landless and unemployed farmworkers on bankrupt aristocratic estates in the president's own beloved east Prussia.

Schleicher's brief two-month government was an economic success but a political failure. He tried finally to break the continuing political impasse by proposing to Hindenburg that the government act unilaterally to outlaw both the Communists and the Nazis, dissolve the parliament (at least temporarily), and impose a more authoritarian presidential system by decree. Since this was precisely the policy which had been recommended by Papen and criticized by Schleicher as leading to insurrection and civil war, Hindenburg was not impressed. It was, however, the only practical alternative that remained in Germany at the beginning of 1933.

Papen had been plotting revenge against Schleicher ever since his ouster as chancellor. He now proposed to the aged and uncertain president his own variation on Schleicher's first plan: a parliamentary coalition government with a working majority that would have to be led by Hitler but would theoretically be dominated by Papen as vice-chancellor. Most cabinet members would not be Nazis, so Hitler would be "bound hand and foot," yet a working majority in the Reichstag would make an effective government possible for the first time since 1930. Papen was only one of many rivals and opponents of the Nazi Führer who seriously underestimated his ruthlessness and ability. Hindenburg accepted the plan, giving Hitler the opportunity for which he had worked and waited.

53. K. D. Bracher, *Die Auflösung der Weimarer Republik* (Villingen, 1964), 680.

The Seizure of Power

Hitler thus became chancellor of the German government on January 30, 1933, as the leader of a normal, legal parliamentary coalition. Of the eleven cabinet positions, only two others went to Nazis. What neither Hindenburg nor Papen could grasp was that by awarding the leadership of the government to Hitler, he was given the tools of power to create a personal dictatorship.[54] The Nazi Party had gained new impetus by victory in several local and regional elections in January, but in the first weeks Hitler had to preserve nominal legality. For Hitler, as for Mussolini ten years earlier, it was important to gain a complete parliamentary majority to create a facade of legitimacy for the transition to dictatorship. Thus on February 4 he obtained Hindenburg's approval for yet another dissolution of the Reichstag, with new elections to be held a month later. The president also agreed to issue an immediate decree curtailing some aspects of press freedom and banning "subversive" political meetings.

Within a matter of only a few weeks Hitler began to establish Nazi control over most regional governments. A standard tactic was for the SA to foment public disorder, followed by Nazi demands that Wilhelm Frick, the new Nazi minister of the interior, intervene to restore order. Using a decree of February 28 which gave the central government power to take over administration of provincial governments, Frick would then appoint a Nazi as police chief of the region in question. Nazi pressure would force the provincial government leaders to resign, and they would be replaced by a largely Nazi administration. In addition, fifty thousand auxiliary police were installed, four-fifths of them members of the SA, the rest coming from the right-wing Stahlhelm.

There was only limited deception in the Nazis' all-out campaign for the elections of March 5, 1933. These were announced as the "last elections for a hundred years," a slogan accepted by the Nazis' right-wing allies of the DNVP and other sectors who still thought that they, rather than revolutionary Nazis, would ultimately control a new authoritarian regime. Whereas the right had provided only limited funding to the Nazis in the past, money now poured in from big business. The mysterious burning of the Reichstag on February 27 was used as nominal justification for a decree the following day that suspended certain civil liberties. This event marked the real beginning of the Nazi police state, as the police began to arrest Communist leaders and activists. There was considerable Nazi violence during the electoral campaign, primarily directed against Communists and Socialists. In a less than fully free election, the balloting gave the Nazis a plurality of 43.9 percent and 288 Reichstag seats, while their chief allies of Hugenburg's DNVP gained 52 seats. With the Communists banned, Hitler now had a strong parliamentary majority.

54. Cf. L. E. Jones, " 'The Greatest Stupidity of My Life': Alfred Hugenburg and the Formation of the Hitler Cabinet, January 1933," *JCH* 27:1 (Jan. 1992): 63–87.

Hitler at a Nazi rally

After the Reichstag reopened, the presence of this majority made possible the *Ermächtigungsgesetz*, or enabling act, of March 23 (technically the "Law to Relieve the Distress of the People and Reich"), which gave Hitler power to govern by decree for four years. The passage of this law required a two-thirds majority because it involved a change in the constitution: the act passed overwhelmingly, 444 to 94, with even the Catholic Center supporting it. Much was made of how relatively bloodless the transfer of power had been in Germany.[55]

55. The classic work is K. D. Bracher, W. Sauer, and G. Schulz, *Die nationalsozialistische Machtergreifung*, 3 vols. (Frankfurt, 1979). See also M. Broszat, *Die Machtergreifung* (Munich, 1984); W. Michalka, ed., *Die nationalsozialistische Machtergreifung* (Paderborn, 1984); and P. D. Stachura, ed., *The Nazi Machtergreifung* (London, 1983). A classic study at the local level is W. S. Allen, *The Nazi Seizure of Power: The Experience of a Single German Town* (New York, 1984).

The *Gleichschaltung:* Nazi Coordination of Institutions

The second phase of the seizure of power consisted of taking control of and reorganizing basic institutions. Laws of March 31 and April 7 authorized the government to appoint special Reich governors for provincial administration who would have power to issue laws without approval of provincial legislatures. A parallel law for "restoration of the civil service" began the removal of Jews and leftists from the German bureaucracy and educational system.

May Day, the traditional festival of organized labor, was declared the Day of National Labor, and on the morrow the police occupied all trade union offices. On May 10 the government announced creation of the German Labor Front (DAF), the new Nazi organization for all workers. Similarly, farmers were soon organized into the new Reich Food Estate.

The Communist Party had been outlawed at the beginning of March, followed by the Socialists on June 22. Hitler's rightist associates had now abandoned their illusions about having him "bound hand and foot." Alfred Hugenburg, the nearest thing to a political party rival in the cabinet, was ousted on June 26, and his DNVP was dissolved the following day. On July 14 the NSDAP was declared the sole political party of Germany. In a continuing purge of the left and of Jews, approximately a hundred thousand people (mainly leftists) were arrested between February and September, with about five hundred killed, and all opposition now lay both crushed and fragmented.

After a year in power, Hitler's only immediate problem (rather like that of Mussolini earlier) concerned the extremists in his own party. The brownshirted SA, which had numbered 450,000 when Hitler became chancellor, had swelled to 2.9 million by the spring of 1934. The SA was the most blue-collar of all party organizations, and its leaders talked of the "second revolution" in which Nazis would replace all other elites, with the mass membership of the SA forming the basis of a new revolutionary Nazi "People's Army."

This constituted a threat to the German army itself, the only conservative institution in Germany that might still be able to overthrow Hitler. Papen and other avatars of a right-wing, non-Nazi authoritarianism hoped that the need to take action against the SA might serve as the catalyst for a military intervention that would end by ousting Hitler himself. On June 17, 1934, the vice-chancellor gave a public speech denouncing any Nazi "second revolution" and, by implication, any full Nazification of institutions.

Aware that authoritarian rightists still hoped to outflank him through the use of the army and/or restoration of the monarchy as soon as the increasingly feeble Hindenburg died, Hitler acted decisively to throttle potential rivals on both the Nazi left and the non-Nazi authoritarian right. In the "Blood Purge" of June 30, 1934, elite SS squads murdered approximately one hundred politi-

Hitler greets Hindenburg, March 21, 1933

cal figures, ranging from Ernst Roehm, head of the SA, and several other top SA leaders to Gregor Strasser and several figures of the authoritarian right, such as General Schleicher. Papen was placed under house arrest. This action not only reasserted Hitler's complete control but also somewhat reassured army commanders and conservatives in general who had been apprehensive of SA radicals.[56]

Hindenburg died on August 2. The cabinet then rubber-stamped Hitler's decision to combine the offices of president and chancellor. He would now become the Führer of the German people. All military and government personnel were then required to take a public oath of loyalty to Hitler himself. Following a plebiscite, the government announced that 85 percent of German voters had approved. Hitler was now officially head of state and complete dictator.

56. On the Nazi leader's difficult relations with the SA, see H. Bennecke, *Hitler und die SA* (Vienna, 1962).

Why Did Nazism Triumph?

Authoritarianism in one form or another was the standard experience for countries defeated in World War I, for most of the new states created after the war, and for all the more underdeveloped lands of southern and eastern Europe. Nonetheless, the victory of so extreme a movement as National Socialism in a country with so high a level of education, technology, and culture as Germany was absolutely without parallel.

German (and other) commentators have pointed out that the ideas of Hitler were by no means exclusively German but were in part derived from more general trends of racist, ultranationalist, and authoritarian ideas in diverse parts of Europe. While that is correct, nowhere else did these ideas coalesce in such extreme and destructive form. Moreover, since the nineteenth-century, general concepts of nationalist and *völkisch* opposition to common Western liberal norms had taken manifold and diverse form in Germany, influencing larger sectors of the intelligentsia and politically literate society than in any other industrial country. The ideas of National Socialism might in various forms have been found all over Europe, but their victory was made possible by a specifically German background that was like no other.

The Weimar Republic was itself democratic and progressive—the first major modern quasi–welfare state—and not without elements of strength. That Weimar succumbed was due to profound internal divisions which made parliamentary government virtually impossible, and also to the specific convergence of major problems—a period of partial stagnation in economic development which made the resolution of sociopolitical controversies most difficult, a unique sequence of national crises and traumas which eventually overburdened political society, the peculiar status of Germany in international relations (no longer defeated or truly exploited but still somewhat unequal—a theme easily exploited by hypernationalists), and finally the international political and economic conjuncture, which toppled parliamentary governments all over the world.

Unemployment is frequently suggested as the key to Nazi success, and indeed without the massive unemployment the Nazis might not have triumphed. Yet as table 6.1 indicates, unemployment was no worse in Germany than in a stable democracy such as Norway; it was only a little worse than in the United States, Austria, Belgium, Holland, Denmark, and Sweden. Thus it cannot have had the determinative role assigned to it by earlier interpretations.

If specific circumstances made it impossible for the liberal and democratic forces to win, it was nonetheless not inevitable that the final outcome would become the worst possible. That end was, however, encouraged by deliberate decisions made by the two other political extremes, the authoritarian right and the Communist left. The authoritarian right helped Hitler to power, while

Table 6.1. Unemployment, 1931–1936

	1931	1932	1933	1934	1935	1936
Germany	23.3	30.1	26.3	14.9	11.6	8.3
Austria	15.4	21.7	26.0	25.5	24.1	24.1
Norway	22.3	30.8	33.4	30.7	25.3	18.8
Denmark	17.9	31.7	28.8	22.1	19.7	19.3
Sweden	17.8	22.8	23.7	18.9	16.1	13.6
Holland	14.8	25.3	26.7	28.0	31.7	32.7
Belgium	14.5	23.5	20.4	23.4	22.9	16.8
France	6.5	15.4	16.1	13.8	14.5	10.4
United Kingdom	16.4	17.0	15.4	12.9	12.0	10.2
United States	15.9	23.6	24.9	21.7	20.1	16.9

Source: J. J. Linz, "La crisis de las democracias," in Europa en crisis, 1919–1939, ed. M. Cabrera et al. (Madrid, 1992), 231–80.

Comintern strategy in Germany was aimed not at preventing a Nazi triumph but at weakening the Socialists and other democratic forces, a strategy in which the Communists were completely successful. In the typically distorted Marxist-Leninist reading of European politics, fascism in whatever form was not a primary danger, for fascism was simply a destructive form of capitalist radicalism in which the bourgeois order turned on itself. Hence fascism's nominal victory might even be desirable, for a fascist or Nazi government would soon destroy itself, hastening the victory of communism. This totally fallacious strategy was only altered (and even then not completely) in 1935.

In situations roughly analogous to that of Germany in 1933, sectors of the authoritarian right in various European countries and in other parts of the world intervened to establish comparatively more moderate authoritarian governments to stabilize the situation and try to deal with pressing problems. This was basically the goal of Hindenburg, Brüning, Papen, and Schleicher in Germany, yet they totally failed to agree among themselves (partly due to the semisenility of the octogenarian president). Mutual conflicts led some of them to settle for a Hitler-led coalition. While Nazis and others argued that Germany was too advanced a country for a merely right-wing dictatorship, something like a continuation of the Schleicher government may have been the only possible short-term solution in 1933. Certainly the mutual divisions, jealous rivalries, and ineptitude of the right destroyed the final opportunity for such an alternative.

THE NATIONAL SOCIALIST STATE AND SYSTEM, 1933–1939

Hitler had much clearer goals when he seized power than had Mussolini. The one-party state and political dictatorship were achieved in five and a half months instead of three years. His new regime was sometimes called a "total state" and a "Führer state," but the Italian-derived term *totalitarian* was rarely used.[57]

Hitler's concept of National Socialism was unremittingly revolutionary, but he sought revolution of a unique kind—a racial revolution. In the process, he had absolute contempt for the aristocracy, the business leaders, and all the old elites, who were to be replaced by new racial elites from the pure German *Volk*. This would also require a *revolution der Gesinnung* (a revolution of feeling), in which Germans would develop not merely a purified race but also a new mind and spirit. In Hitler's words, "Those who see in National Socialism nothing more than a political movement know scarcely anything of it. It is more even than a religion; it is the will to create a new man."

There was no question of any immediate totalitarian social and economic revolution, as in the Soviet Union, for this was not Hitler's primary goal. National Socialism had come to power in an advanced society undergoing political decomposition, but one in which other institutions and structures were both sophisticated and intact. Their transformation would have to await the completion of Hitler's primary agenda, which required him to invert the Leninist-Stalinist priority of internal revolution. In the preceding decade the limitations on Soviet power abroad had required Stalin to concentrate on internal "socialist revolution in one country." Conversely, Hitler could only realize his ultimate goal of complete racial revolution by foreign conquest, and he believed that he enjoyed only a brief window of opportunity—scarcely more than a decade—to achieve external ascendancy in Europe and to conquer the *Lebensraum* needed for this racial revolution.[58] Hitler therefore sought to develop rapidly a functional dictatorship that would enable him to concentrate on military expansion in less than a decade. This required the thorough subordination of all other elites to such a system, but, for the time being, not their complete elimination.

There was no question of totally revolutionizing the structure of the state either, for Hitler would rely on the relatively efficient state bureaucracy, together with Germany's highly professional army officer corps, to develop the strength for military expansion. Consequently the Nazi Party could not simply take over the state, as in the Soviet Union, but at the same time Hitler would not settle for the limited pluralist dictatorship of Mussolini, where the party in effect was subordinate to the state.

There developed instead in Germany a kind of "dual state," in which the regular state system largely continued to function within its own specialized

---

57. Jane Caplan, in "National Socialism and the Theory of the State," in *Reevaluating the Third Reich*, ed. T. Childers and J. Caplan (New York, 1993), 54–69, finds little evidence of any formal Nazi theory of the state itself.

58. Cf. M. Hauner, "A German Racial Revolution?" *JCH* 19:4 (Oct. 1984): 669–88.

structure but was increasingly paralleled by the ever-expanding bureaucracy and functions of the National Socialist Party. The product was a dual system which featured an ever-increasing number of new Reich "boards," eventually amounting to some sixty special state commissions, bureaus, and agencies. This produced such an administrative maze that it would be almost impossible to diagram the state structure accurately—a multiform "administrative chaos" presided over by Hitler alone. It has been suggested that Hitler in fact preferred the confusion and competition in such a system because it enhanced his personal domination. He alone held superior authority over it, and no one else could amass equivalent power. All other administrators had to look to him to resolve disputes.[59]

In 1935 two more Nazis were placed in charge of government ministries, but they still held only five of twelve cabinet positions. On the regional level, the regional state minister-presidents retained nominal authority, though real power was exercised more and more by the local Reich governors, positions usually held by district party Gauleiters, who had responsibility for enforcing governmental decrees. After several years, about 60 percent of local city and town mayorships were also held by party leaders.

The National Socialist Party under the Third Reich

Party membership at first grew rapidly. During the first two years of Hitler's regime 1.6 million new members joined, until the opportunists amounted to approximately two-thirds of the entire affiliation. At that point a moratorium was declared, and the party rolls were not reopened until 1937. At that point Hitler indicated that he expected that party membership, which passed the 5 million mark two years later, would constitute an elite of about 10 percent of the total German population.

Rudolf Hess, arguably Hitler's most trusted subordinate, was made special deputy of the Führer for party affairs, in charge of internal supervision. In July 1933 the previously obscure party bureaucrat Martin Bormann was made secretary of the party chancellery, and he used this position to amass more and more administrative power within the Nazi organization. By 1936

59. The leading one-volume history of the National Socialist regime is K. D. Bracher, *The German Dictatorship* (New York, 1970). There are numerous analyses of the Nazi state: E. Fraenkel, *The Dual State* (New York, 1941); M. Broszat, *The Hitler State* (London, 1981); G. Hirschfeld and L. Kettenacker, eds., *Der "Führerstaat"* (Stuttgart, 1981); P. D. Stachura, ed., *The Shaping of the Nazi State* (London, 1978); E. Jaeckel, *Hitlers Herrschaft* (Stuttgart, 1986); J. Caplan, *Government without Administration* (Oxford, 1988); H. Mommsen, *Beamtentum im Dritten Reich* (Stuttgart, 1966); O. C. Mitchell, *Hitler's Nazi State* (New York, 1989); P. Diehl-Thiele, *Partei und Staat im Dritten Reich* (Munich, 1969). See also H. A. Turner Jr., ed., *Nazism and the Third Reich* (New York, 1972), and C. S. Maier et al., *The Rise of the Nazi Regime* (Boulder, 1985).

Bormann also began to play a role in government, as Hitler relied on him as a kind of personal government secretary to coordinate matters with cabinet ministers and pass on instructions. This role later made Bormann increasingly influential in ordinary governmental affairs as well.[60] Dozens of party leaders were eventually made heads of special boards, agencies, and commissions of the government, expanding their administrative functions within the ever more confusing structure of the dual state. As the years passed, Nazi influence in the state increased further, until by its final year in 1944 the regime had indeed almost become a true party-state, though never so fully totalitarian as in the Soviet Union.

An elaborate national party organization existed down to the level of *Ortsgruppe* (local groups). One was organized for every small town or district with at least 1,500 households. Party cells were organized for smaller sectors of the population ranging from 160 to 480 households, and local block units were organized for each microneighborhood of 40 to 60 households, creating a more detailed and elaborate organization than in Italy or the Soviet Union.

The majority of members continued to come from the middle classes, which remained overrepresented in the party. Civil servants hurried to affiliate in 1933, and the proportion of white-collar employees also increased, until by 1937 they also were overrepresented in the party membership. Physicians were a particularly overrepresented sector, with nearly three times as many proportionately in the party as in the population as a whole.

Above all, the membership continued to consist of young males, so that one might call the NSDAP a party of young men from all classes, though more the middle classes than the workers. One historian writes, "Acceptance of the fact that irrational political behavior is not the prerogative of any particular class, but of sections of all class groupings, is an essential step to the ultimate understanding of the very complex social response on which Nazism was based."[61] Workers had constituted about a third of all members when Hitler took power, but their proportion among all new members reached 40 percent by 1939 and 43 percent by 1942–44. If master craftsmen were included in the category of workers, the percentages would be distinctly higher. Workers also composed an equal or higher proportion of the membership of the Hitler Youth. For women, a recruitment quota of 5 percent of total party membership was set in 1933, but the proportion enrolled had reached 16.5 percent by 1939. The number of student members, conversely, dropped off, and within a few years the changes introduced in the universities had the effect of reducing the proportion of members and sympathizers there. The social elites were overrepresented in party membership, but this sector of society was the one that most extensively turned its back on Nazism after the war began. Middle- and

60. See J. von Lang, *The Secretary Martin Bormann* (New York, 1989).
61. Mühlberger, *Hitler's Followers* 209.

Rudolf Hess and Heinrich Himmler

upper-middle-rank party leaders, such as district Gauleiters, tended to come from the lower middle classes, while as of the end of 1934 only 11 percent of lower-level leaders were workers.[62]

The separate women's affiliate, the Nationalsozialistische Frauenschaft,

62. Kater, *Nazi Party* 190–212, 252–74. See also P. Baldwin, "Social Interpretations of Nazism: Renewing a Tradition," *JCH* 25:1 (Jan. 1990): 5–37, and P. Hüttenberger, *Die Gauleiter* (Stuttgart, 1969).

headed by Gertrud Scholtz-Klink, was designed to create a cadre of Nazi women to function as the leaders of German women and to supervise their political indoctrination and training. The NS Frauenschaft reached 2 million members by 1938 (at that point it was equal to more than 40 percent of the party membership), but in the process this large organization lost much of its erstwhile elite status.

The SS

The black-uniformed SS (*Schütz Staffeln*, or Defense Squads) became the most important of all Nazi organizations, a group that had no exact equivalent in any other modern dictatorship—though perhaps the Soviet Cheka-OGPU-NKVD was the nearest equivalent. Defense squadrons were first formed in 1925 to protect Hitler and other top leaders and constituted a special part of the broader SA. Almost from the beginning SS members wore black caps bearing the death's-head insignia of a skull and crossbones. Later they would also be known for their belt-buckle inscription *Meine Ehre heisst Treue* (My honor is loyalty).[63]

Heinrich Himmler became Reichsführer-SS in 1929, and from that point the organization grew rapidly. Himmler had been born in 1900 of middle-class background.[64] He was a fanatical believer in Nazi racial ideology and soon conceived of the SS as the movement's racial elite, the spearhead of its racial revolution. He modeled the organization as a special "order," to some extent along the lines of the medieval Teutonic Knights, and steadily gained greater autonomy for it. In 1931 a special Security Service (SD) was set up within the SS as an elite political intelligence operation. Its leader was the brilliant young former naval officer Reinhard Heydrich, the only top Nazi leader to fit the racial stereotype of being tall (six feet three), blond, and blue-eyed. Heydrich was very different from the fanatical Himmler, since he was basically a cynical psychopath, but he also possessed intelligence and a remarkable array of personal talents.[65]

Himmler took control of special party police functions and in April 1934

63. The best overall history is H. Höhne, *The Order of the Death's Head* (London, 1969), while R. L. Koehl, *The Black Corps: The Structure and Power Struggles of the Nazi SS* (Madison, 1983), presents the organizational history.

64. B. Smith, *Heinrich Himmler: A Nazi in the Making, 1900–1926* (Stanford, 1971); R. Manvell and H. Fraenkel, *Heinrich Himmler* (London, 1965); P. Padfield, *Himmler: Reichsführer-SS* (New York, 1990); J. Ackermann, *Heinrich Himmler als Ideologe* (Göttingen, 1970); J. Fest, *The Faces of the Third Reich* (New York, 1970); L. L. Snyder, *Hitler's Elite* (New York, 1989).

65. G. Deschner, *Reinhard Heydrich* (New York, 1981); S. Aronson, *Reinhard Heydrich und die Frühgeschichte von Gestapo und SD* (Stuttgart, 1971); G. C. Browder, *Foundations of the Nazi Police State: The Formation of Sipo and SD* (Lexington, Ky., 1990).

was given command of the new government political police Gestapo (an acronym for Secret State Police). Hitler then made use of special SS units for his Blood Purge of June 30, 1934, and three weeks later the SS became a completely independent organization, answerable only to Hitler. In 1936 Himmler became head of all German police, a position he held concurrently with that of Reichsführer-SS, in effect independent of the government's minister of the interior. The Gestapo, conversely, was mostly made up of regular policemen, but it also stood over and above the regular court system and could do virtually whatever it wanted.[66]

SS members became a caste unto themselves, not answerable to the courts, and the SD was made a special parastate intelligence agency. Unlike party or general SA members, SS men had to meet special racial criteria, being taller and blonder than the Nazi rank and file. Before the seizure of power, 44 percent of them came from the working class, a proportion that rose to 55 percent afterward. SS membership thus eventually drew workers into its ranks in almost the exact same percentage as in the general structure of society. Although the SS was nominally an elite, the class background of its members generally mirrored the overall structure of German society more than those of any other large Nazi organization. As its status increased, by 1934 it attracted more members from the upper class, even though "this proved to be the necessary precondition for depriving traditional social elites of their power, while exploiting their professional skills." [67] Though members from the working class did not reach the highest leadership levels in the same proportions as those from the upper and middle classes, one-fourth of the SS leadership was of worker background.[68]

Concentration camps, which arose in the spring of 1933, were staffed by both the SA and the SS, but by the middle of the following year they came exclusively under SS administration. By 1937 there were three major camps in Germany, now policed by the special SS *Totenkopfverbände* (Death's-head units). In 1938 the SS began to organize its own *Verfügungstruppe* ("ready" or action troops). At first these troops numbered two hundred thousand, and they were later transformed into the Waffen-SS (Armed or Military SS), which became the equivalent of regular army divisions.[69] The SS operated institutions

66. R. Gellately, *The Gestapo and German Society* (Oxford, 1990).

67. B. Wegner, *The Waffen-SS* (Oxford, 1990), 286.

68. H. F. Ziegler, *Nazi Germany's New Aristocracy: The SS Leadership, 1925–1939* (Princeton, 1989), 103; R. B. Birn, *Die Höhern SS- und Polizeiführer: Himmlers Vertreter im Reich und in den besetzen Gebieten* (Düsseldorf, 1986).

69. On the Waffen-SS, see Wegner, *Waffen-SS*, and G. H. Stein, *The Waffen-SS* (Ithaca, 1966). The extensive literature on this organization is treated in B. Wegner, "Die garde des 'Führers' und die 'Feuerwehr' der Ostfront: Zur neueren Literatur über die Waffen-SS," *Militärgeschichtliche Mitteilungen* 23 (1978): 210–36.

to encourage racial breeding[70] and administered Nazi racial science and "research."[71] It also published the nearest thing to a Nazi theoretical journal, *Das Schwarze Corps* (The Black Corps).[72]

The SS thus became a sort of "state within a state," a special "order" devoted to the antithesis of the basic Christian virtues of charity, mercy, and humility.[73] Its death's-head insignia symbolized the constant willingness to kill, as well as to be killed. By the close of 1938 SS membership had reached 238,159.[74] At its maximum during the war, membership in all SS organizations would stand at approximately 1 million.

The System of Justice

The Hitler regime maintained the existing German court structure and system of justice but passed many new laws to target political enemies and Jews. It also increased the rigor with which the system operated. In March 1933, however, a new system of special courts with Nazi judges was inaugurated to prosecute all political crimes save high treason. For the latter, the regime instituted new people's courts in 1934, which eventually condemned more than twelve thousand civilians to death.[75]

Hitler's Economic Policy

The character of the "socialism" in National Socialism was always a question in the rise of the movement. Early on, and particularly from the late 1920s, party spokesmen had made it clear that they were not opposed to private property or capitalism as such, but only to its excesses and "foreign" capitalist domination. The left or Strasserite wing had championed extensive state inter-

---

70. The Lebensborn (Life Source) organization operated homes for prospective mothers of racially superior children, whether married or unmarried.

71. M. H. Kater, *Das "Ahnenerbe" der SS, 1933–1945* (Stuttgart, 1974).

72. W. L. Combs, *The Voice of the SS: A History of the SS Journal "Das Schwarze Corps"* (New York, 1986).

73. H. Buchheim, "Die SS in der Verfassung des Dritten Reiches," *Vierteljahrhefte für Zeitgeschichte* 3 (1955): 127–57.

74. The SA, severely curtailed after the Blood Purge, fell from 2.9 million members in June 1934 to 1.2 million by 1938.

75. I. Müller, *Hitler's Justice: The Courts of the Third Reich* (Cambridge, Mass., 1991); H. W. Koch, *In the Name of the Volk: Political Justice in Hitler's Germany* (New York, 1989); M. Hirsch et al., eds., *Recht, Verwaltung und Justiz im Nationalsozialismus* (Cologne, 1989); L. Gruchmann, *Justiz im Dritten Reich, 1933–1940* (Munich, 1988); B. Rüthers, *Die unbegrenzte Auslegung: Zum Wandel der Privatrechtsordung im Nationalsozialismus* (Frankfurt, 1973); D. Kirschenmann, *"Gesetz" im Staatsrecht und in der Staatslehre des Nationalsozialismus* (Berlin, 1970).

vention, though not full socialism.[76] *Völkisch* conservatives, particularly as represented by O. W. Wagener, sometime head of the political economy section of the party organization, promoted a program of conservative corporatism, and indeed Nazi spokesmen had sometimes invoked a system of *Ständesozialismus* (corporative socialism). The economic right wing within Nazism was represented by Walther Funk, who hoped to avoid any genuine corporatism, believing it to be too restrictive for big business, and instead encouraged authoritarian *Planwirtschaft* (a limited planned economy) as the best solution for industrial expansion.[77]

There were frequent complaints both before and after the seizure of power that the Nazis had no coherent economic theory or program, but in fact they had a well-established general approach in the long German tradition of authoritarian statist economics, which dated well back into the nineteenth century.[78] Hitler had no interest in collectivism per se and used the term *socialist*— an "unfortunate term," as he once put it—essentially in a political or demagogic sense. He believed that competition was necessary for high achievement, though he had no intrinsic regard for the financial and industrial elite, whom ultimately he would wish to be rid of.[79]

Hitler quickly quashed any expectations of a conservative corporatism of the Wagener or Catholic varieties. There would be no new "system" but a pragmatic imposition of numerous forms of state regulation and intervention. The liberal economics of the first phase of the Brüning administration had already been discarded by Papen and Schleicher; the Nazi state would employ a reflationist policy that did not, however, rely primarily on monetary strategy alone. Only one billion *Reichsmark* (RM) could be spent on rearmament in 1933, but about three times that sum was expended on public works and on subsidies for new housing construction and jobs creation in private industry, accompanied by a wage freeze to hold costs down. Some taxes were reduced for business, but in general taxes were raised somewhat to augment state spending. The government organized a huge "Let's get back to work" campaign which, combined with practical policies and a pronounced restoration of confidence, within eleven months had reduced the number of unemployed from 6 million to 4.5 million. The number then fell to only 2.6 million by the end of 1934. Harold

76. The Strasserite sector was not very consistent in its economic radicalism, and Strasser himself had taken a more conservative tack by 1932. See P. D. Stachura, " 'Der Fall Strasser,' " in Stachura, ed., *Shaping of the Nazi State* 88–130, and Stachura, *Gregor Strasser*.

77. See the analysis by Dirk Stegmann, "Kapitalismus und Faschismus in Deutschland, 1929–1934," *Beiträge zur Marxschen Theorie* 6 (1976): 19–91.

78. See the references in chapter 2, and especially A. Barkai, *Nazi Economics* (New Haven, 1990).

79. This is argued most extensively in Zitelmann, *Hitler: Selbstverständnis*.

James writes, "The most plausible view of the early stages of recovery—the first two years, 1933 and 1934—would be as a relatively spontaneous cyclical recovery." [80] In practical terms, unemployment was eliminated by 1938. Consumer production returned to the per capita level of 1928 by 1936, and by 1939 stood 8 percent above that, before sinking to the 1936 level by 1942, once the pressures of wartime had taken effect.

The first notable increase in arms expenditures took place in 1934, but only to 3.4 billion RM (about as much as had been spent on public works the preceding year). This, combined with generally increased economic activity and accelerated imports of raw materials, led to a crisis in foreign exchange by August 1934. At that point Hjalmar Schacht, the minister of economics, unveiled a new plan to establish strict import quotas, accompanied by new bilateral trade agreements. By 1938 arrangements with twenty-five different countries (especially in the Balkans and Latin America) made it possible to raise the average price of German exports by 10 to 15 percent. Moreover, in 1935 the volume of exports increased 19 percent, somewhat reducing the pressure on exchange.

In fact, no completely coherent model of political economy was ever introduced in Nazi Germany. Hitler's basic stance was that National Socialism meant the subordination of the economy to the national interest: *Gemeinnutz geht vor Eigennutz* (The common good before the individual good), according to one of the most widely publicized Nazi slogans. Hitler sometimes boasted that he had no need to nationalize the economy, since he had nationalized the entire population.

From 1936, especially, the tendency was firmly toward ever more state regulation and control, a network of government *Zwangswirtschaft* (a forced or compulsion economy). This did not take the form of direct state ownership but instead the systematic subordination of all sectors of the economy through controls, regulation, strict taxation, contracts, and allocation. During the first phase of the regime national pressure group associations of business and industry were broken up, to be replaced by territorial and functional administrative groups regulated by the state. The accelerated cartelization that ensued was also conducted in conformity with governmental guidelines. Because of widespread governmental intervention to rescue banks that were failing during 1931–32, a large part of German bank capital was already owned by the

---

80. H. James, "Innovation and Conservatism in the Economic Recovery: The Alleged 'Nazi Recovery' of the 1930s," in Childers and Caplan, eds., *Reevaluating the Third Reich* 124. Dan P. Silverman, in "Fantasy and Reality in Nazi Work-Creation Programs, 1933–1936," *JMH* 65:1 (March 1993): 113–51, concludes that the jobs creation projects were rather like those of Franklin Roosevelt's in the United States and did not work much better. See also W. Fischer, *Die Wirtschaftspolitik des Nationalsozialismus* (Hanover, 1961).

state. The war accentuated such tendencies, which might as well be termed "military socialism" as anything else. In many respects it was a continuation of World War I controls and long-standing concepts of *Planwirtschaft*. Nazi propaganda sometimes presented this amalgam as "the most modern socialist state in the world."

Large-scale rearmament did not begin until mid-1936. Hitler declared in August of that year that the German army must be "operational" within four years. That autumn a "Four Year Plan" was instituted under the leadership of Hermann Göring, now the number two figure in the party.[81] This was the first initiative to build new state-owned industry—the huge Hermann Göring Reichswerke—to supplement private industry in arms production, and it was geared especially toward synthetics. The first huge jump in military expenditures occurred that year, nearly trebling, to 9.3 billion RM. The 1937 level was only slightly more, but 1938 registered 13.6 billion, and another huge increase to 30 billion in 1939 seemed to threaten an economic crisis. Most of this increase was financed by a parallel program of state bonds that did not require repayment for five years, while the role of private banks was greatly reduced. Under frantically accelerated rearmament, private ownership and private profit were preserved. Profit ratios, in fact, increased substantially, though the regime increasingly restricted and channeled the use of private profit.[82]

Later, during the war, more extreme Nazis—including some SS leaders— speculated about a partially state-owned socialist economy under a completed Nazi revolution once victory had been achieved, but one can cite quotations from Hitler on both sides of the issue.[83] During the last phase of the war he tried specifically to reassure industrialists that a triumphant National Socialism would *not* nationalize most German industry.[84] What would in fact have come in the event of a Nazi victory is a matter of speculation.

81. See R. J. Overy, *Göring, the Iron Man* (London, 1984); D. Irving, *Göring* (London, 1989); L. Mosley, *The Reich Marshal* (London, 1974); H. Mommsen, "Reflections on the Position of Hitler and Göring in the Third Reich," in Childers and Caplan, eds., *Reevaluating the Third Reich* 86–97; and especially A. Kube, *Pour le mérite und Hakenkreuz: Hermann Göring im Dritten Reich* (Munich, 1986).

82. On rearmament and German industry before 1939, see R. J. Overy, *The Nazi Economic Recovery, 1932–1938* (London, 1982); B. A. Carroll, *Design for Total War: Arms and Economics in the Third Reich* (The Hague, 1968); B. Klein, *Germany's Economic Preparations for War* (Cambridge, Mass., 1959); P. Hayes, *Industry and Ideology: IG Farben in the Nazi Era* (Cambridge, 1987); J. Gillingham, *Industry and Politics in the Third Reich* (New York, 1985); G. Meinck, *Hitler und die deutsche Aufrüstung, 1933–1939* (Wiesbaden, 1959); and W. Deist, *The Wehrmacht and German Rearmament* (Toronto, 1981).

83. Rainer Zitelmann, in *Hitler: Selbstverständnis*, argues that Hitler ultimately intended to develop a broadly state socialist system.

84. Toland, *Adolf Hitler* 789.

Much was made by Marxist commentators, during the 1930s and for nearly half a century afterward, about the alleged capitalist domination of the German economy under National Socialism, when the truth of the matter was more nearly the opposite. It is important "to distinguish between contingent benefits that capitalists enjoyed because of Nazi rule and the actual identity of interests between industry and the Nazi regime."[85] Alan Milward, perhaps the most systematic student of comparative fascist economics, has judged that "the new [fascist] governments did not . . . 'preserve the capitalist system.' They changed the rules of the game so that a new system was emerging."[86] He adds: "It is this final insistence on revolution at all costs, the utter refusal to compromise, the fact that Hitler in his Final Testament laid most emphasis on the extermination of Jews, that makes historians wonder whether there was not a fundamental incompatibility between the fascist outlook and the aspirations of big business."[87]

Thus it is doubtful that a final triumph by Hitler would have "saved German capitalism" in the conventional sense of such a phrase. German capitalism enjoyed much more autonomy under liberal democracy both before and after Hitler. What ultimately "saved German capitalism" was the defeat of National Socialism in the West by the Anglo-American capitalist powers and the incorporation of West Germany into the Western sphere during the Cold War.

85. J. Colby et al., *Between Two Wars* (Celtic Court, Bucks., 1990), 169.

86. A. Milward, "Fascism and the Economy," in *Fascism: A Reader's Guide*, ed. W. Laqueur (Berkeley, 1976), 399.

87. Quoted in Hauner, "German Racial Revolution?" 683.

On the political economy of Hitlerism, see the clear statement by T. W. Mason, "The Primacy of Politics," in *European Fascism*, ed. S. J. Woolf (London, 1969), 165–95. For a discussion of economic policy as it related to Hitler's broader goals, see N. Rich, *Hitler's War Aims*, 2 vols. (New York, 1973–74), and K. Hildebrand, "Le forze motrici di politica interna agenti sulla politica estera nazionalsocialista," *SC* 5:2 (June 1974): 201–22. Hildebrand tends to agree with A. Kuhn, who terms National Socialism "an absolute contrast with capitalism" in his *Das faschistische Herrschaftssystem und die moderne Gesellschaft* (Hamburg, 1973), 31. Thilo Vogelsang has concluded that "the economy, whose fundamentally capitalist structure was maintained, had become, for utopian objectives and even more for the imperial goals of the regime, a prisoner of the National Socialist state." Vogelsang, *Die nationalsozialistische Zeit: Deutschland 1933 bis 1939* (Frankfurt, 1967), 75, quoted in Hildebrand, "Le forze motrici" 206.

The Marxist Social Democrat Rudolf Hilferding saw little difference between Russian totalitarian state ownership and National Socialist strict state regulation and control. "The controversy as to whether the economic system of the Soviet Union is 'capitalist' or 'socialist' seems to me rather pointless. It is neither. It represents a *totalitarian state economy*, i.e., a system to which the economies of Germany and Italy are drawing closer and closer." Hilferding, "State Capitalism or Totalitarian State Economy," *Modern Review* 19:2 (June 1947): 266–71, reprinted in R. V. Daniels, ed., *The Stalin Revolution* (Boston, 1965), 94–97.

The *Gleichschaltung* of Social Institutions

The "coordination" of social institutions under the Third Reich required the destruction of most existing social and economic associations, to be replaced by new institutions dominated by the state. This was done with all the important economic interest associations, from the national industrialists' federation on down the line. The leadership principle was progressively introduced into social institutions and into the economy, factory owners now becoming factory "fuehrers" and so forth. Special organizations were set up for all the major professions.

One of the most important new social organizations was the German Labor Front (DAF). Under its director, Robert Ley, the DAF quickly swelled to more than 6 million members and by 1938 maintained a larger budget than the Nazi Party. The Law for the Ordering of German Labor of January 1934 created a structure of leaders and their "retinues" (workers) in each factory, with Courts of Social Honor for both. Though under strict hierarchical control, the DAF did not ignore worker interests and often acted to improve conditions. Unlike the situation in Fascist Italy, shop stewards did operate under the DAF, though the first elections to "councils of trust" in factories produced so few positive votes they were never tried again. Like his counterparts in the Soviet Union, Fascist Italy, and Franco's Spain, Ley hoped to build the Labor Front into a major autonomous force, even conceiving the ambition of having it replace the party as the basis of National Socialism, though such aims were soon quashed.[88]

After the first years of recovery, the introduction of more modern and efficient methods was generally encouraged to boost productivity. Group wage incentives were increasingly emphasized, together with concepts such as the *Leistungsgemeinschaft* (performance community) and *Kameradschafts- und Gemeinschaftsstärkung* (strengthening of comradeship and community) to make faster and more efficient new processes acceptable. Wages were increasingly tied to productivity, and by 1939 a 5 to 10 percent decline in real wages had developed, though this was partly offset by new fringe benefits. The more skilled sectors and those responsible for war goods received rising pay differentials. Such tendencies increased after the war began, with growing attention to automation and tighter flow-production processes, promoting industrial modernization.[89]

Two major fringe benefits were the Kraft durch Freude (Strength through Joy) and Schönheit der Arbeit (Beauty of Labor) programs. Strength through Joy (initially called "Nach der Arbeit," in imitation of the Italian Dopolavoro)

88. R. M. Smelser, *Robert Ley, Hitler's Labor Front Leader* (Oxford, 1988).
89. R. Hachtmann, *Industriearbeit im "Dritten Reich"* (Göttingen, 1989).

developed an enormous leisure and vacation program for workers' free time that enjoyed mass participation and by 1939 had increased to twelve days the number of annual paid holidays per worker. The Beauty of Labor endeavored to improve aesthetic amenities and working conditions in a considerable number of large factories.[90] Another major fringe benefit involved the huge worker subscription campaign begun in 1938 to produce the new Volkswagen, a small economical private car for the ordinary *Volk*, the workers themselves, but then the entire project had to be diverted to the war effort.

Generally effective, the DAF was still not able totally to control German labor. Down to 1942 it had to continue to rely to some extent on the free market principle of contract. Strikes and slowdowns did occasionally occur but were always prevented from expanding.[91]

For farm owners, Hitler quickly lived up to his campaign promises by promulgating the *Erbhofgesetz* (hereditary farm law) of 1933, which guaranteed family farm holdings of less than three hundred acres as individual property in perpetuity. Restrictions included transmission to a single heir and prohibition of use as collateral for loans. Since such properties were in effect withdrawn from the market, their value fell, while that of larger unprotected properties rose. Yet with their credit reduced, family farmers could rarely afford to buy any of the available land. There was in fact something of a flight from the land under National Socialism—the very opposite of what was intended—and the number of those employed in agriculture had dropped by five hundred thousand (mainly farmworkers) by 1939. Efforts to increase food production achieved only limited results.[92]

Mobilization and indoctrination of youth were major goals. The Hitler Youth proper organized fourteen-to-eighteen year olds, including 82 percent of all males in that age group by 1939, and about 90 percent in the early war years.[93] The Jungvolk for younger males was less extensive, while the Bund Deutscher Mädel (League of German Girls) had three million members by 1937.

Fundamental changes were introduced into the educational curriculum,

90. A. G. Rabinbach, "The Aesthetics of Production in the Third Reich," *JCH* 11:4 (Oct. 1976): 43–64.

91. T. W. Mason, *Arbeiterklasse und Volksgemeinschaft* (Opladen, 1975); idem, *Social Policy in the Third Reich* (Providence, 1993).

92. J. Farquharson, *The Plough and the Swastika, 1928–1945* (London, 1976); T. Tilton, *Nazism, Neonazism and the Peasantry* (Bloomington, 1975); A. Branwell, *Blood and Soil: Richard Walther Darré and Hitler's "Green Party"* (Bourne End, Bucks., 1985); G. Corni, *Hitler and the Peasants, 1930–1939* (New York, 1990).

93. L. Walker, *Hitler Youth and Catholic Youth, 1933–1936* (Washington, D.C., 1970); H. W. Koch, *The Hitler Youth* (New York, 1976); G. Rempel, *Hitler's Children: The Hitler Youth and the SS* (Chapel Hill, 1989); J. von Lang, *Der Hitler-Junge: Baldur von Schirach* (Hamburg, 1988).

Hitler youth poster

and by 1937 the National Socialist Teachers Association enrolled 97 percent of all teachers. Soon 15 percent of all school time was being devoted to physical education, with boxing required for boys in secondary schools. Students who could not pass physical education courses were denied graduation certificates. The quality of education declined as the student-teacher ratio worsened and more time was devoted to extracurricular activities. In the universities about 15 percent of the faculty was initially dismissed, and the curriculum changes weakened the teaching of physics and certain other sciences.[94] In 1931 about 60 percent of all university undergraduates had voted for the Nazi Student League, and under Hitler the Nazi Students Association monopolized student affairs. Apathy and even antagonism later developed, however, and the total university student population dropped from 128,000 in 1933 to only 58,000 by 1939.[95]

The Nazi *Volksgemeinschaft*

National Socialism, like most German nationalist groups before it, proclaimed for German society a *Volksgemeinschaft,* or "people's community," that would unite all true Germans and transcend old social divisions. The goal was not absolute social equality but a system of organized unity in which different sectors of society cooperated in harmony to meet the needs of all. This would also permit unprecedented social mobility and a relatively greater equality of access to new opportunities. With the *Führerprinzip* to be subinfeudated at all levels, Nazi Germany was to become a "nation of leaders." The most tangible aspects would be, first, full employment and, second, a kind of psychological revolution of status, not income, in which all Germans became common members of a new racial elite. The standard slogan *Common need before individual need* appealed to idealism and self-sacrifice—some of the highest qualities of German religion and culture—while reenforcing discipline and solidarity. Ultimately this was to help produce the Germanic and racial "new man," with a new consciousness and a new self-image.

In practice, National Socialism no more achieved a truly organic society and full status revolution than the Soviet Union achieved a classless society. Leaders remained leaders, workers remained workers, and the wealthy largely remained wealthy. Yet no class or sector any longer retained class autonomy; all were reduced to dependence on the state. Old social and economic ties were replaced by new ones to the Führer, *Volk,* army, or race, and this did have some effect in reducing old class barriers. George L. Mosse has observed that

---

94. More than 25 percent of physicists in universities were dismissed. See A. D. Beyerchen, *Scientists under Hitler: Politics and the Physics Community in the Third Reich* (New Haven, 1977), and K. Macrakis, *Surviving the Swastika: Scientific Research in Nazi Germany* (New York, 1993).

95. G. W. Blackburn, *Education in the Third Reich* (Albany, 1985); R. G. S. Weber, *The German Student Corps in the Third Reich* (New York, 1986).

for many, National Socialism "felt" more democratic than Weimar because of common participation in collective ceremonials and grand national projects. The new emphasis lay on a hierarchy of function rather than of status. This was not a true social revolution, but the old German class system would never again be restored according to the pre-1933 structure. In that sense National Socialism did mark something of a dividing line.[96]

Women enjoyed a nominally protected but thoroughly subordinate status as the present or future mothers of the race. A major goal was to increase the birthrate, and live births did grow from 971,000 in 1933 to 1.4 million in 1939, but this may largely have reflected improved economic conditions. A variety of economic incentives and marriage loans were provided to make parenthood more attractive.

In fact, economic recovery and expanded arms production stimulated both urbanization and industrialization, contrary to long-term Nazi goals of a more healthy and rural population. These trends also increased employment of women from 11.5 million in 1933 to 12.7 million by 1939. Though a slight decline took place in the number of girls in secondary school, the proportion of women in the universities increased by nearly 50 percent as male enrollment dropped. The percentage of women teachers rose slightly, and the number of women doctors went up from 5.6 percent in 1930 to 7.6 percent by 1939.[97]

National Socialist policy was generally successful in gaining broad conformity and even broad complicity, though there were also exceptions and variations, both in local districts and across social and professional groups. One marked expression of disfunctionality within the nominal people's community was the sharp rise in juvenile delinquency from 1937 on.

The Racial State

The ultimate Hitlerian goal of *Volksgemeinschaft* was designed not merely for a community of Germans as they currently existed but for a rigorously purified racial community that could only be achieved by a biological racial revolution at some undetermined point in the future. This would require extensive purification of the existing German gene pool, a concept so radical that it normally was not even mentioned to the ordinary population.

For the time being, racial purification began with the segregation of the

---

96. One interpretation is presented in D. Schoenbaum, *Hitler's Social Revolution* (New York, 1966), which may be compared with M. Prinz, *Vom neuen Mittelstand zum Volksgenossen* (Munich, 1986), and R. Grunberger, *A Social History of the Third Reich* (London, 1971).

97. J. McIntyre, "Women and the Professions in Germany, 1930–1940," in *German Democracy and the Triumph of Hitler*, ed. A. Nicholls and E. Matthias (London, 1971), 175–213. Standard treatments are J. Stephenson, *Women in Nazi Society* (London, 1975), and C. Koontz, *Mothers in the Fatherland* (New York, 1987).

Jews and later continued with the beginning of the elimination of the physically and mentally unfit. Exclusionary measures against the Jewish minority began immediately after the seizure of power, though physical violence in the early phases was more random than systematic. Regulations became increasingly restrictive, and by the time the war began, more than half the Jewish population had fled Germany. Hitler at first deliberately limited the scope of persecution. "Quarter Jews" who professed some other creed could escape the exclusionary legislation, as could any Jew before the end of 1938 who chose to be baptized. Though aware that Nazi persecution would provoke criticism in some quarters abroad, Hitler nonetheless believed that he would draw support from anti-Semites all over Europe. The ultimate extent of his ambitions for liquidating the "Jewish problem" nonetheless remained hidden.[98]

The German population was targeted for a sweeping campaign of eugenics, designed ultimately to help breed a new master race. At first, however, only negative measures could be introduced, beginning with a sterilization campaign for those categorized as the most disordered or physically degenerate. Some two hundred thousand people so labeled had been sterilized by 1937. A second step was a euthanasia campaign to dispatch the hopelessly ill and handicapped. During the spring of 1939 about five thousand mentally defective and severely handicapped children were put to death, while a second phase in the autumn liquidated about a hundred thousand of the "incurably sick." In a sort of trial run for the Final Solution, six special euthanasia installations, complete with poison gas "shower rooms," were constructed, and some of the same personnel manning them would later be used to kill Jews. The euthanasia program soon became public knowledge, however, and after increasing protests (particularly from religious leaders), Hitler nominally cancelled the operation in the interest of wartime unity.[99] Killings continued in secret on a smaller scale.

Culture and Propaganda

Possibly even more than leaders in the Soviet Union, the rulers of Fascist Italy and Nazi Germany sought to persuade and mobilize their peoples through

98. M. Burleigh and W. Wippermann, *The Racial State: Germany, 1933–1945* (New York, 1991), is the fullest treatment. Fundamental studies include K. A. Schleunes, *The Twisted Road to Auschwitz* (Urbana, 1970); S. Gordon, *Hitler, Germans and the Jewish Question* (Princeton, 1984); D. Bankier, *The Germans and the Final Solution* (Oxford, 1992); and H. Graml, *Anti-Semitism and Its Origins in the Third Reich* (London, 1992).

99. K. Nowak, *Euthanasie und Sterilisierung im "Dritten Reich"* (Göttingen, 1980); G. Bock, *Zwangssterilisation im Nationalsozialismus* (Opladen, 1986); R. W. Proctor, *Racial Hygiene: Medicine under the Nazis* (Cambridge, Mass., 1988); M. H. Kater, *Doctors under Hitler* (Chapel Hill, 1989); S. Kuhl, *The Nazi Connection: Eugenics, American Racism, and German National Socialism* (New York, 1993).

elaborate public ceremony and visual arts of all kind. One German historian has recently concluded that "to a great extent National Socialism—perhaps more than any other system of domination in modern times—tried to define and legitimate itself by its art and its mass culture. It was not the economic achievements, but the 'great cultural innovations,' among which were counted new technological conquests, that in the thinking of the leaders and of large parts of the population represented the real 'performances of art and community.' " [100] Exploitation of the mass media was one of the most striking features of Nazi cultural mobilization, and in the process Dr. Paul Joseph Goebbels became the most famous propaganda minister of the century.[101] Direct propaganda, whether printed or spoken, was only one aspect of a broad assault on the mind and senses to create a new psychology, and ultimately a "new man." [102] Public culture, art, and propaganda were equally designed to conceal as well as to persuade, and though they did not convince everyone, their effects were nonetheless impressive.

Whereas Soviet artistic policy was directed more toward literature, Nazi policy especially prized the visual arts, reflecting the personal priorities of Hitler, who is quoted as having said that "art is the only truly enduring investment of human labor." The Third Reich thus moved quickly to canonize its own style of racial art, though it was never given an official new title comparable to the Soviet "Socialist Realism." [103] Nazi art tended to create romanticized versions of realism, accompanied by frequent neoclassical motifs in architecture.[104] Whereas the Soviet style tended toward the sentimental and heroic, the Nazi style was romantic and heroic, with a strong penchant for a certain brutality of expression. It expressed the usual themes of "totalitarian art": leaders, heroes, battles, historic themes, labor as struggle and joy, and the common *Volk* (especially farmers). Nazi art also emphasized nudes as revealing of race (something strongly de-emphasized by Soviet art, since the absence of clothing obscured class origins). Nazi and Soviet art faced each other directly in two grand buildings at the 1937 Paris International Exhibition, and later, after the Nazi-Soviet Pact, Stalin himself developed a passing interest in Nazi art, arranging a private exhibition for himself in Moscow.[105]

100. P. Reichel, *Der schöne Schein des Dritten Reiches* (Munich, 1991), 349.

101. E. K. Bramsted, *Goebbels and National Socialist Propaganda, 1925–1945* (London, 1965); H. Heiber, *Goebbels* (New York, 1972).

102. The work by Reichel summarizes the diverse modes of public ceremony, sport, art, and propaganda that constituted the visual appeal of the Third Reich. Propaganda is treated in Z. A. B. Zeman, *Nazi Propaganda* (London, 1972); W. Rutherford, *Hitler's Propaganda Machine* (New York, 1978); and H. Burden, *The Nuremberg Party Rallies, 1923–39* (New York, 1967).

103. At one point Goebbels suggested the theme of "Steely Romanticism."

104. A functionalist kind of modern architecture was retained, however, using flat roofs and wide expanses of glass.

105. The best comparative introduction is I. Golomstock, *Totalitarian Art* (New York,

In September 1933 Goebbels, the information minister, was also made head of the new Reich Chamber of Culture, organized into the seven divisions of the press, radio, literature, music, theater, visual arts, and film.[106] Though most German intellectuals and artists—including major figures—nominally supported the regime, approximately twenty-five hundred writers fled the country.[107] The press was ruthlessly consolidated under strict censorship, and over the next decade most German newspapers simply went out of existence.[108]

Goebbels himself was especially interested in cinema, but he did not try to turn the entire movie industry into a direct propaganda machine. From 1933 to 1944 about eleven hundred films were produced in Germany, about half of them love stories or comedies. Only ninety-six were made by direct order of the minister of propaganda, though most of these were lavish productions. It is generally agreed that the highest-quality Nazi films were the documentaries by Leni Riefenstahl, *Triumph des Willens* (1934) and *Olympiad* (1936).[109]

Great attention was given to physical culture and sport, as evidenced by the reordering of the school curriculum. Huge sport ceremonies in turn became part of the public spectacles and the civil liturgy of the regime.

Nazi art and culture were also appealing because they exalted the fundamental values dear to German life: hard work, discipline, cleanliness, family integrity. This was to reflect a new synthesis of individual and community, though the meaning of such values took a very different turn in the aggressive racial polity of National Socialism.[110]

1990). Useful for Nazi art and culture are G. L. Mosse, *Nazi Culture* (New York, 1966); L. Richard, *Le Nazisme et la culture* (Paris, 1978); H. Brenner, *Die Kunstpolitik des Nationalsozialismus* (Reinbek, 1963); R. Schnell, ed., *Kunst und Kultur im deutschen Faschismus* (Stuttgart, 1978); B. Hinz, *Art in the Third Reich* (New York, 1979); B. M. Lane, *Architecture and Politics in Germany, 1918–1945* (Cambridge, Mass., 1968); R. Merker, *Die bildenden Künste im Nationalsozialismus* (Cologne, 1983); and K. Backes, *Hitler und die bildenden Künste* (Cologne, 1988).

106. The Reich Chambers of Music, Theater, and the Visual Arts are treated in A. E. Steinweis, *Art, Ideology, and Economics in Nazi Germany* (Chapel Hill, 1993).

107. On literature, see J. M. Rotchie, *German Literature under National Socialism* (Totowa, N.J., 1983), and H. Denkler and K. Prümm, eds., *Die deutsche Literatur im Dritten Reich* (Stuttgart, 1976).

108. O. J. Hale, *The Captive Press in the Third Reich* (Princeton, 1984).

109. D. S. Hull, *Film in the Third Reich* (Berkeley, 1969); D. Welch, *Propaganda and the German Cinema* (New York, 1985).

110. Because of the conventionality of most moral values expressed in Nazi culture, George L. Mosse has observed that "the new German was the ideal bourgeois." Mosse, *Nazism: A History and Comparative Analysis of National Socialism* (New Brunswick, N.J., 1978), 43.

Golomstock points out that "this would indeed have been so but for the fact that under totalitarianism these universal values had acquired a new meaning: devotion meant blind faith in the Führer, optimism meant a thoughtless, uncritical attitude to the present, a readiness to make sacrifices meant murder or betrayal, love meant hatred, honor meant informing. The exceptional

Nazi party rally in Nuremberg, 1934

199

Nazism and Christianity

Theologically, National Socialism may be termed a purely pagan movement that has also sometimes been called a political religion. There is no question that Hitler intended the Aryan racial ideology to fulfill a kind of religious function; the liturgical character of Nazi public rituals was pronounced.[111] Hitler himself observed in private, "I am a religious man although not in the usual sense of the word."[112] As National Socialism expanded into a mass movement, Nazis were normally (though not always) careful to speak of Christianity and the churches with respect, decrying the "antireligious" character of Marxism. It is also clear that this was sheer opportunism aimed at the winning and consolidation of power. Indications are that Hitler intended to destroy central European Christianity after the war as part of the consolidation of the Nordic racial revolution. As Nazi Party secretary Martin Bormann declared, "The National Socialist and Christian conceptions are incompatible." Despite the partial origin of Nazi ideology in Ariosophic occultism, Hitler and most Nazi leaders believed that Nazi doctrine was modern, objective, and grounded in fact. Bormann later observed: "The Christian churches are based on human ignorance and the attempt to keep a vast part of humanity in ignorance, since this is the only way for the Christian churches to retain their power. National Socialism, on the other hand, is based on a scientific foundation. . . . National Socialism . . . must always be guided by the most recent data of scientific researches."[113]

A special group of Nazi "German Christians" had been organized in 1932. Soon after taking power, Hitler negotiated an official concordat with the Vatican, but for German Protestants a new Nazi "Reich Church of German Christians" was formed. By April 1934 this produced a formal revolt by a minority of anti-Nazi German Protestant pastors, who formed an independent Confessional Church with the support of four thousand of Germany's seventeen thousand Protestant ministers. Such resistance at an early stage in the

---

was put forward as the normal and typical. The 'new man' thus had many faces and was omnipresent. . . . If one is to say that he was the 'ideal bourgeois,' then one must add 'of the new type' " (*Totalitarian Art* 214–15).

111. H.-J. Gamm, *Der braune Kult: Das Dritte Reich und seine Ersatzreligion* (Hamburg, 1962).

112. Quoted in Golomstock, *Totalitarian Art* 291.

113. Ibid., 292, quoted. Bormann added: "When we National Socialists speak of a belief in God, by God we do not understand, as do naive Christians and their clerical beneficiaries, a manlike being who is sitting around in some corner of the spheres. . . . The force which moves all these bodies in the universe, in accordance with natural law, is what we call the Almighty or God. . . . The more thoroughly we know and attend to the laws of nature and life, the more we adhere to them, the more do we correspond to the will of the Almighty. The deeper our insight into the will of the Almighty, the greater will be our success."

development of the dictatorship caused Hitler to draw off, so that no further "German Christian" bishops were appointed to Protestant bishoprics.

Pressure soon increased, however, as spokesmen of the Confessional Church protested various state policies. Moreover, the papacy's encyclical *Mit brennender Sorge* (With Burning Concern), denouncing Nazi racism and persecution, was read in Catholic churches in April 1937. The government's offensive against opposition clergy had begun, in fact, well before that. During 1936–37 approximately seven hundred pastors and priests were sentenced to the Buchenwald concentration camp, though only about fifty received long sentences. Many Catholic clergy (including nuns) were arrested on trumped-up morals charges. Though 94.5 percent of the adult German population wsa registered in 1939 as nominally belonging to a church, by that point most of the Christian population was pretty well cowed.[114] Subsequently, after the war began, religious persecution was eased in the name of patriotic unity, and in 1941 the Christian campaign against euthanasia brought nominal cancellation of that policy.[115]

The Political Opposition

Political opposition continued to exist until the end of the regime, but it was thoroughly and effectively repressed. Destruction of the Communist and Socialist Parties was a Nazi priority, and both were driven deep underground. Neither the worker parties nor liberals could function overtly as opposition forces. Socialists and Communists did maintain a clandestine resistance, and though their acts of sabotage achieved little, the latter did develop an effective espionage system. In the long run, the small right-wing opposition, which increased from 1938, was potentially in a position to do the most damage, because of elite positions held by its members and their contacts abroad. It was the right-wing opposition that developed nearly all the active conspiracies against Hitler, as well as the abortive assassination attempts of 1943–44.[116]

114. Of the remainder, 3.5 percent were listed as *gottgläubig* (believers) and only 1.5 percent as atheists.

115. The literature on the churches under Nazism is extensive: G. Lewy, *The Catholic Church and Nazi Germany* (New York, 1964); J. S. Conway, *The Nazi Persecution of the Churches, 1933–1945* (New York, 1968); E. C. Helmreich, *The German Churches under Hitler* (Detroit, 1979); K. Scholder, *The Churches and the Third Reich,* 2 vols. (London, 1988); V. Barnett, *For the Soul of the People: Protestant Protest against Hitler* (New York, 1993). M. Broszat, ed., *Bayern in der NS-Zeit,* 6 vols. (Munich, 1977–83), provides much material on the experience of Catholics. For the earlier bibliography, see V. Conzemius, "Eglises chrétiennes et totalitarisme national-socialiste: Un bilan bibliographique," *Revue d'Histoire Eclesiastique* 63 (1968): 437–503.

116. P. Hoffman, *The History of the German Resistance, 1933–1945* (Cambridge, Mass., 1977); idem, *German Resistance to Hitler* (Cambridge, Mass., 1988); E. N. Peterson, *The Limits of Hitler's Power* (Princeton, 1969); I. Kershaw, *Popular Opinion and Political Dissent in the Third*

Nazism and Modernity

The Hitler regime was so bewildering in its methods and goals that interpretation has frequently given up altogether and fallen back on sheer negatives—such as the "revolution of nihilism" or the overriding motivation of "antimodernism." Certainly the Nazi attitude toward modernization was ambivalent. Nazi racism was strongly environmentalist, opposed to the toxic and psychopathic effects of large cities.[117] The regime held out the goal of a cleaner environment based on more outdoor life and spoke of retaining as much as possible of the population in small towns and on farms.

At the same time, National Socialism exhibited immense pride in modern German achievements and boasted of national technology, identified with the Faustian spirit, the overcoming of limits, and even new norms of beauty.[118] Hitler was obsessed with speed and the setting of new mechanical records. Above all, there was a strong identification with aviation and air power.[119] Nazi leaders eagerly employed virtually all the latest techniques at hand, ranging from the mass media to public opinion surveys and industrial policies. Urban planning constituted a special interest, with preliminary designs for major modernized "garden cities" of the future, full of abundant green space.[120] Historians more recently have thus come to stress the continuity, rather than the hiatus, in modernization under National Socialism.

However extreme, Hitler was in fact a symptomatic product of the modern world. However repellent, he and his coterie were not nihilists but held tenaciously to firm and evil values. Nihilism is more nearly what came after Hitler (unless sheer hedonism is considered a value rather than the absence of values). Hitler's ideas were partly rooted in the modern scientism of German biological and zoological ideas of the late nineteenth century, and the Nazi leaders' keen interest in the occult was not directed toward traditional folk superstition so

---

Reich: Bavaria, 1933–1945 (New York, 1983); F. R. Nicosia and L. D. Stokes, *Germans against Nazism* (New York, 1991); D. C. Large, ed., *Contending with Hitler* (New York, 1992). A different approach toward dissent has been provided by the "everyday life" school of research. For this, see D. Peukert, *Inside Nazi Germany: Conformity, Opposition, and Racism in Everyday Life* (New Haven, 1987); D. Peukert and J. Reulecke, eds., *Die Reihen fast Geschlossen: Beiträge zur Geschichte des Alltags unterm Nationalsozialismus* (Wuppertal, 1981); and the colloquium *Alltagsgeschichte der NS-Zeit: Neue Perspektive oder Trivialisierung?* (Munich, 1984).

117. For the background of such attitudes, see K. Bergmann, *Agrarromantik und Grossstadtfeindlichkeit* (Meisenheim am Glan, 1970).

118. This syndrome in the German radical right has been studied by Jeffrey Herf in his *Reactionary Modernism* (New York, 1984).

119. See P. Fritzsche, *A Nation of Flyers* (Cambridge, Mass., 1992), and idem, "Machine Dreams: Airmindedness and the Reinvention of Germany," *American Historical Review* 98:3 (June 1993): 685–709.

120. Nazi urban plans were used in the rebuilding of Hanover in 1949.

much as toward new modern and racial myths of the supernatural.[121] Hitler in fact rejected nearly all the formal ideas of European culture of the medieval era, above all historical Christianity, and sternly derided premodern "superstition." Nazi racism was conceivable only in the twentieth century and at no previous time in human history. The animalistic, naturalistic, human anthropology of the Nazis was strictly a modern concept without any premodern parallels.

All of Hitler's political ideas had their origin in the Enlightenment.[122] These included the concept of the nation as a higher historical force, the notion of superior political sovereignty derived from the general will of the people, and the idea of the inherent racial differences in human culture.[123] These were distinct derivations from Enlightenment anthropology which rejected premodern theology and the common roots and transcendent interests of mankind. The cult of the will is the basis of modern culture, and Hitler merely carried it to an extreme. The very concept of National Socialism as the "will to create a new man" was possible only in the twentieth-century context as a typically modern, antitraditional idea. The same may be said of the Nazi search for extreme autonomy, a radical freedom for the German people. Hitler carried the modern goal of breaking the limits and setting new records to an unprecedented point. For no other movement did the modern doctrine of man as the measure of all things rule to such an extent.[124] Thus Daniel Bell has judged that all self-centered, subjective modern culture stresses the "triumph of the will"—one of the most common Nazi concepts—and that Hitler is another typical product of modernity.[125]

This also holds with regard to social and economic programs. No ruler in modern times has gone to such lengths as Hitler to acquire, among other things, the natural resources necessary for a modern economy. Nazi *Gleichschaltung* and the effort at status revolution tended to unite German society and overcome class distinctions for the first time in German history. Though Nazi

121. D. Sklar, *Gods and Beasts: The Nazis and the Occult* (New York, 1978).

122. This is largely the thesis of Marcel Déat, in *Révolution française et révolution allemande* (Paris, 1943).

123. It is conveniently forgotten that the *Führerprinzip* is eminently Rousseauian. "In Rousseau's conception, only a leader of divine genius is able to found the state in which men are free, albeit by compulsion, and to determine what the general will is." L. J. Halle, *The Ideological Imagination* (London, 1971), 36.

George L. Mosse formulates this in terms of the "new politics" of the nationalistic masses, stemming from eighteenth-century doctrines of popular sovereignty in which the people worship themselves as a national group or race and are ultimately directed not by laws or parliaments but by secular national religion. Mosse, *The Nationalization of the Masses* (New York, 1975), 1–20.

124. A trenchant and provocative interpretation of the problem was made by Steven E. Aschheim in a seminar paper, "Modernity and the Metapolitics of Nazism," University of Wisconsin, 1975.

125. D. Bell, *The Cultural Contradictions of Capitalism* (New York, 1976), 50–52.

antiurbanism is said to have been inherently reactionary, radical antiurbanism has become a major trend of the late twentieth century. In fact, though the German war economy promoted de facto urbanization and greater industrialization, rather than the reverse, an ultimate Nazi economic goal was to balance farm and industry. When sought by liberals, this is frequently deemed the height of enlightenment and sophistication. Finally, Hitler was well in advance of his times in his concern about ecology, environmental reform, and pollution.

Truly large-scale genocide or mass murder is a prototypical development of the twentieth century, from Turkey and Russia to Germany, Cambodia, and countries of Africa. The unique Nazi tactic was to modernize the process, to accomplish the mass murder more efficiently and surgically than other great liquidators in Turkey, Russia, or Cambodia have done. Nor was Hitler's genocidal program any more or less "rational," since the goal of mass murder is always political, ideological, or religious and not a matter of practical economic ends, pace Stalin or Mao Tse-tung.

National Socialism in fact constituted a unique and radical kind of modern revolutionism. This again is one of the most controverted interpretations of Hitlerism, for since many commentators hold National Socialism to have been antimodern (normally merely meaning antiliberal), they argue that it must necessarily have been "reactionary," not revolutionary. Such an approach is held all the more tenaciously by leftist commentators because of their a priori assumption that the concept of revolution must refer ipso facto to good revolution, revolution that is positive or creative. But of course revolutions are frequently destructive.

This problem has been approached most directly by Karl D. Bracher, who has identified the following revolutionary qualities of National Socialism:

1. A supreme new leadership cult of the Führer as the "artist genius."
2. The effort to develop a new Social Darwinist structure of government and society.
3. The replacement of traditional nationalism by racial revolution.
4. Development of the first new system of state-regulated national socialism in economics.
5. Implementation of the organic status revolution for a new national *Volksgemeinschaft*.
6. The goal of a completely new kind of racial imperialism on a world scale.
7. Stress on new forms of advanced technology in the use of mass media and mass mobilization, a cult of new technological efficiency, new military tactics and technology, and emphasis on aerial and automotive technology.[126]

126. K. D. Bracher, *Zeitgeschichtliche Kontroversen um Faschismus Totalitarismus Demokratie* (Munich, 1976), 60–78. The list presented constitutes my own reformulation, not an exact transcription of Bracher's.

This list might be refined and made even more detailed, but as a general formulation it covers the main points. For devotees of colonial and minority-population "national liberation" revolution, it should be pointed out that during World War II the promotion of national liberation movements among colonial and minority peoples around the world was almost exclusively the work of the Axis powers.[127] During his twelve years in power, Hitler had a more profound impact on the world than any other revolutionary of the twentieth century, and all the more because, as Eugen Weber and others have pointed out, wars constitute the primary revolutionary processes of this century.[128]

Jacques Ellul insists,

> Informed observers of the period between the wars are convinced that National Socialism was an important and authentic revolution. De Rougemont points out how the Hitler and the Jacobin regimes were identical at every level. R. Labrousse, an authority on the French revolution, confirms that, to cite only two opinions. . . .
>
> The practice of "classifying," and thus dismissing, Nazism should stop, for it represents a real Freudian repression on the part of intellectuals who refuse to recognize what it was. Others lump together Nazism, dictatorship, massacres, concentration camps, racism, and Hitler's folly. That about covers the subject. Nazism was a great revolution: against the bureaucracy, against senility, in behalf of youth; against the entrenched hierarchies, against capitalism, against the petit-bourgeois mentality, against comfort and security, against the consumer society, against traditional morality; for the liberation of instinct, desire, passions, hatred of cops (yes, indeed!), the will to power and the creation of a higher order of freedom.[129]

Interpreting the Nazi State

The Nazi system was in many ways unique and fortunately never reached full development; not surprisingly, it has been subject to diverse interpretations. A common early approach was the "dual state" concept, referring to the parallelism resulting from Hitler's continuation of much of the traditional German state and civil service apparatus together with the growth of the Nazi Party,

127. This is not to overlook Franklin Roosevelt's vigorous opposition to western European imperialism while acquiescing in Soviet imperialism. See W. R. Louis, *Imperialism at Bay* (New York, 1978). American support for decolonization was, however, expressed at the diplomatic, not the military, level.

128. E. Weber, "Revolution? Counterrevolution? What Revolution?" *JCH* 9:2 (April 1974): 3–47, reprinted in Laqueur, ed., *Fascism* 435–67.

129. J. Ellul, *Autopsy of Revolution* (New York, 1971), 288. In *The Phenomenon of Revolution* (New York, 1974), Mark Hagopian concluded that "the question about the revolutionary nature of fascism is not easy to answer," but "the twelve years of the Third Reich represent a definite revolutionary thrust" (363, 358).

its territorial organization, and its paragovernmental and governmental functions.[130] The Romanian Mihail Manoilescu, probably Europe's leading theorist of corporatism in the 1930s, liked to distinguish between the Soviet, Italian, and German systems—the former a state run by a party, the second a state to which the party was subordinate, and the third a dual system with powers divided between party and state.

For much of the first generation after the war, the concept of totalitarianism held vogue, likening Nazi Germany to the Soviet Union, however, much more than to Italy. The definition of *totalitarianism* has always been rather vague, and during the 1970s and 1980s it became fashionable to deny that such a thing had ever existed. Since theorists of totalitarianism rarely get beyond rudimentary concepts such as the single party, the use of terror, and mass mobilization, it is easy to argue either that many different kinds of regimes are totalitarian or conversely that none were perfectly total.

Yet the concept of totalitarianism is both valid and useful if defined in the precise and literal sense of a state system that attempts to exercise direct control over all significant aspects of all major national institutions, from the economy and the armed forces to the judicial system, the churches, and culture. It has been seen that in this sense the Mussolini regime was not totalitarian at all and that the Hitlerian system also failed to achieve full totalitarianism, though in its final phase it drew nearer and nearer. Here Hannah Arendt agrees, noting that full Nazi totalitarianism equivalent to the Soviet model could have developed only after victory in the war, given Hitler's reversal of Leninist-Stalinist revolutionary priorities. For that matter, only a socialist or Communist system can achieve full totalitarianism, since total control requires total institutional revolution that can only be effected by state socialism. Socialism need not be totalitarian, but totalitarianism must be socialist, and National Socialism, with its mixed approach, could never establish the complete model, even had it desired to do so, before 1945.

There are, broadly speaking, two schools of interpretation concerning the Third Reich: the intentionalists and the structuralists. The intentionalists hold that Hitler had clear and decisive goals from the start and was firmly in charge of all major decisions. This is roughly the interpretation that emerged from the war years themselves and dominated the generation immediately after the war.

From the 1960s, revisionist historiography, mainly but not exclusively among West German scholars, developed structuralist interpretations which contended that the understanding of the Nazi system and of Hitler's leadership had been overdetermined by earlier analysts who stressed intentionalism. These scholars asserted that the course of events and the major decisions were influenced much more by the structure of institutions, the pressure of cumu-

---

130. A classic formulation is Fraenkel, *Dual State*.

lative events or economic factors, and the changing international situation. Structuralist revisionism focused on new interpretations of the Nazi state and the responsibility for major decisions. New analyses emphasize the feudal characteristics of the Hitler regime and the numerous apparent contradictions and limited autonomies within it,[131] as reflected by the proliferation and mutual competition of a sometimes bewildering variety of state agencies and boards.[132] These factors were interpreted as an indication that the system was in fact a "polyocracy."[133] The system, some said, placed significant limits on Hitler's power.[134] Other analysts even wrote that Hitler could be considered a "weak dictator," out of touch with or lacking control over regime affairs.[135] Thus extreme structuralists would contend that the war in 1939 was determined by Germany's economic weakness, which was thought to require a war of conquest, or that Hitler never reached a concrete decision to liquidate physically all European Jewry, the major outcomes being the complex result simply of "cumulative radicalization." We will explore some of these issues further in chapter 11.

Though revisionist interpretation has helped to clarify important problems and has stimulated useful debate, it is doubtful that any of the new concepts is sufficiently accurate or comprehensive in its more extreme form to achieve a central place in the understanding of National Socialism.[136] Such interpretation tends toward reductionism, as does any extreme presentation of intentionalist theories. The "polyocracy" concept has usually been carried to excess, and it tends to overlook certain achievements in coordinating the state resulting from the *Rechtssreform* of 1934–36.[137] It may also underestimate the actual

131. R. Koehl, "Feudal Aspects of National Socialism," *American Political Science Review* 54:4 (Dec. 1960): 921–33.

132. As early as *Behemoth: The Structure and Practice of National Socialism, 1933–1944* (New York, 1944), Franz Neumann took the position that the Nazi system had neither a real political theory nor a coherent state structure.

133. P. Hüttenberger, "Nationalsozialistische Polykratie," *Geschichte und Gesellschaft* 2:4 (1976): 417–42.

134. Peterson, *Limits of Hitler's Power*.

135. This analytic gem has been polished particularly by Hans Mommsen in both "National Socialism: Continuity and Change," in Laqueur, ed., *Fascism* 179–210, and "Hitlers Stellung im nationalsozialistischen Herrschaftssystem," in Hirschfeld and Kettenacker, eds., *Der "Führerstaat"* 43–72. Rejoinders can be found in K. Hildebrand, "Monokratie oder Polykratie? Hitlers Herrschaft und das Dritte Reich," in Hirschfeld and Kettenacker, eds., *Der Führerstaat* 242–63, and K. D. Bracher, "The Role of Hitler: Perspectives of Interpretation," in Laqueur, ed., *Fascism* 211–25.

136. Lucid summaries and analyses of the historiographic wars over the Third Reich will be found in J. Hiden and J. Farquharson, *Explaining Hitler's Germany: Historians and the Third Reich* (Totowa, N.J., 1983), and I. Kershaw, *The Nazi Dictatorship: Problems and Perspectives of Interpretation* (London, 1985).

137. J. Caplan, "Bureaucracy, Politics, and the National Socialist State," in Stachura, ed., *Shaping of the Nazi State* 234–56.

role of the NSDAP in German administration. Hitler purposefully avoided a completely centralized and rationalized bureaucratic system—something quite alien to his own modus operandi—but the autonomies that he permitted within the Nazi system either by design, oversight, or necessity scarcely diminished his remarkable powers of personal dictatorship to implement his own priorities.

German Nazism and Italian Fascism

It was quickly apparent to observers that National Socialism and Italian Fascism had much in common: extreme nationalism, violence, a party militia and one-party dictatorship, a vitalist and nonrationalist culture, pretensions to achieve a revolutionary new man, and an ultimate propensity to militarism. They shared similar political negations, while possessing roughly similar styles crowned by the leadership principle. There were similar emphases on youth, the organic society, and a new nationalist economic program. Seen from afar, they appeared much the same. As movements, and to some degree also as regimes, they shared the basic "fascist minimum" outlined in the Introduction.

Yet sharp differences were also noticeable from the start, differences so profound that the two regimes can be grouped together only at a very general level of abstraction. When viewed closely, the differences were frequently more striking than the similarities, particularly in five areas:

1. The Hitlerian ideology was founded on mystical Nordic racism, something not merely unknown to Italian Fascists but for which Italians in general could not qualify. Hitlerian ideology tended toward revolutionary exclusivity, while that of Fascism was more sophisticated and syncretic and readily avowed its relationship to broader aspects of the Western tradition.[138] Mussolini insisted that Fascism incorporated aspects of liberalism, conservatism, and socialism into a higher synthesis; Hitler required revolutionary rejection of rival doctrines. All would-be revolutionaries aim at a "new man." The new man of National Socialism would be a new biological product as well as a new cultural one; Mussolini conversely relied on training, experience, and education.

2. In 1934 Hitler became unchallenged chief of state and complete dictator, a position never held by Mussolini. The Italian regime remained in large

138. This was stated by Mussolini and Giovanni Gentile in their article on "Fascismo" for the 1932 *Enciclopedia Italiana:* "The Fascist negation of socialism, democracy, and liberalism should not, however, be interpreted as implying a desire to move the world back to positions held prior to 1789. Fascism employs in its construction whatever elements in the liberal, socialist, or democratic doctrines still have a living value. No doctrine has ever been born completely new, completely defined, and owing nothing to the past; no doctrine can boast of complete originality; it must always be derived, if only historically, from the doctrines that have preceded it and develop into further doctrines which will follow."

measure a juridical state of semipluralism and formal law. Though it invented the term *totalitarian*, it did not seek to control all institutions. Italian writers and artists were largely free to produce what they pleased, so long as they did not challenge Fascism politically. Mussolini also had to respect greater religious autonomy for Italians as well. Police action was more restrained in every respect, and no true concentration camp system existed in Italy. Widespread terror as violent coercion, in Germany a rather pale imitation of Soviet practice, did not exist to an equivalent degree in Italy. This of course placed a considerable limitation on the revolutionary potential of the Mussolini system and eventually made it possible for the Duce's adversaries within the state to overthrow him.

By contrast, the National Socialist system was clearly totalitarian in intent, even though it formulated no elaborate theory using that term. The Hitlerian *Führerstaat* was a much more extensive dictatorship of one-man rule, creating agencies and institutions to regulate all sectors of economic, professional, and cultural society, with the partial exception of the churches. Economic corporatism of the Italian kind was rejected by Hitler because it implied at least a degree of genuine autonomy for some of the constituent parts. Hitler preferred an elaborate structure of direct state controls and regulations.

3. The NSDAP played a much more important role than did the PNF. Though the Hitler regime was not turned into a formal party-state run by the party, as in Communist regimes, a duality of party and state powers developed, and Hitler tended to shift more and more power toward the party or sectors thereof. The PNF, by comparison, enjoyed only a very limited autonomy and was largely transformed into a subordinate bureaucracy. Nevertheless, the semipluralist and juridical structure of the Mussolini regime did preserve a certain degree of formal autonomy for the Fascist Grand Council, which the council would finally use to depose Mussolini.

4. Anti-Semitism of the most extreme form was central to National Socialism. By contrast, Italian Fascism during its first two decades was not normally anti-Semitic and even welcomed Italian Jews into its ranks, to the extent that the percentage of Jews in the Fascist Party was higher than in Italian society as a whole. In that sense Italian Fascism for most of its history was not merely not anti-Jewish itself, but it had a disproportionately Jewish membership.

5. Hitler's foreign policy transcended traditional German expansionist and imperialist aims, attempting a revolutionary racial restructuring of Europe. Mussolini's aspirations, though considerable, remained to a large extent within the orbit of traditional Italian nationalist-imperialist policy, aiming at colonial expansion and the exploitation of limited conflict within the Mediterranean area.

These differences in one form or another were keenly felt by Fascists and Nazis themselves and in varying ways were expressed by the movements from beginning to end.[139]

National Socialism and Communism

The Mussolini regime's inability to overcome its rightist compromises, together with its doctrines and origins dissimilar from those of the Nazis, precluded any full convergence between the Mussolini and Hitler regimes. In turn the Hitler regime, in its rejection of Marxism and materialism and the formal principle of bureaucratic totalitarianism, did not take the same form as Russian communism, in spite of theories by critics about a supposed common totalitarianism. Nonetheless, in some specific ways National Socialism paralleled Russian communism to a much greater degree than Italian Fascism was capable of doing. Some of the similarities and parallels include

1. Frequent recognition by Hitler and various Nazi leaders (and also Mussolini) that their only revolutionary and ideological counterparts were to be found in Soviet Russia.
2. The founding of both National Socialism and Russian national communism on a revolutionary action theory, which held that success in practice validated ideological innovation, as the Soviet Union progressively relinquished main aspects of classic Marxist theory.
3. Revolutionary doctrines of "constant struggle."
4. Rigid elitism and the leadership principle: a National Socialist was someone who followed Hitler; a Bolshevik was not necessarily a Marxist but someone who followed Lenin.[140]
5. Espousal of the have-not, proletarian-nation theory, which Lenin adopted only after it had been introduced in Italy.
6. Construction of a one-party dictatorship independent of any particular class.
7. Major stress, not merely on a political militia (which was increasingly common in the late nineteenth and early twentieth centuries), but upon a party-army, with a regular army to be controlled by the party: by 1943

139. Thus Himmler would reiterate to the SS in 1943: "Fascism and National Socialism are two fundamentally different things. . . . There is absolutely no comparison between Fascism and National Socialism as spiritual, ideological movements." E. Kohn-Branstedt, *Dictatorship and Political Police* (London, 1945), quoted in H. Arendt, *The Origins of Totalitarianism* (New York, 1951), 7. Goebbels concluded that "Mussolini is not a revolutionary like the Führer or Stalin."

140. A curious parallel of elitist biological thinking found in communism was the "brain institute" set up by Stalin around 1935 to retain and study the brains of Lenin and other top Soviet leaders (including Stalin) to research the nature of their "genius."

Hitler had begun to introduce "National Socialist guidance officers" in the regular army as the equivalent of commissars.[141]

8. Emphasis on autarchy and major (not merely partial) militarization, though the absence of a totalitarian state bureaucratic system and economy in Germany made this proportionately somewhat less thoroughgoing than in Russia; and promotion of revolutionary war whenever possible as an alternative to complete and balanced internal development.

9. A New Economic Policy phase of partial pluralism on the road to more complete dictatorship (common, of course, to most dictatorial systems, though more abbreviated in countries such as China and Cuba).

10. International projection of a new ideological myth as an alternative to prevailing orthodoxies, capable of eliciting a not insignificant international response: variants of Fascist and Nazi ideologies constituted the last notable ideological innovations in the modern world after Marxism.

This tentative list is not presented to propound a theory of "Red fascism" or the notion that communism and Nazism were essentially the same thing. There were some fundamental differences, as previously noted, between the Russian and German systems. Nonetheless, Hitlerian National Socialism more nearly paralleled Russian communism than has any other non-Communist system.[142]

141. R. L. Quinnett, "The German Army Confronts the NSFO," *JCH* 13:1 (Jan. 1978): 53–64.

142. For further discussion, see J.-J. Walter, *Les machines totalitaires* (Paris, 1982); A. L. Unger, *The Totalitarian Party* (London, 1974); G. Hermet, P. Hassner, and J. Rupnik, *Totalitarismes* (Paris, 1984); E. Nolte, *Der europäische Bürgerkrieg, 1917–1945: Nationalsozialismus und Bolschewismus* (Hamburg, 1987); and J. Landkammer, "Nazionalsocialismo e bolscevismo tra universalismo e particolarismo," *SC* 21:3 (1990): 511–39.

7
The Transformation of Italian Fascism, 1929–1939

The Fascist regime passed through several relatively distinct phases during its history of more than two decades. The first phase of Mussolini's government, from the March on Rome to the beginning of 1925, had been a nominal continuation of the parliamentary regime, though under legally authorized executive dictatorship. The second phase was that of the construction of the Fascist dictatorship proper from 1925 to 1929. There followed a third phase of somewhat diminished activism from 1929 to 1934, which gave way to a fourth phase from 1934 to 1940 that featured an activist foreign policy, military campaigns abroad, and growing economic autarchy, climaxed by semi-Nazification. This was succeeded by the war (1940–43) and finally by the anticlimax of the puppet Italian Social Republic (1943–45).

The third phase of the dictatorship, from 1929 to 1934, has been termed in a well-known if somewhat controversial interpretation "the years of consensus."[1] Certainly there was very little active political opposition during this period, and though there were also no free elections, a passive acceptance broadly characterized most of Italian society, while all major interests participated in varying degrees in a general consensus of support.[2]

Mussolini still worked hard during the early 1930s and was actively involved in manifold problems of government. He continued to read fairly

---

1. R. De Felice, *Mussolini il Duce*, vol. 1, *Gli anni del consenso, 1929–1936* (Turin, 1974).

2. Even some of the leaders of the postwar democratic republic had been initially compromised or co-opted in varying ways during the 1920s and early 1930s, as demonstrated in the correspondence published by "Anonimo Nero," *Camerata dove sei? Rapporti con Mussolini ed il Fascismo degli antifascisti della prima Repubblica* (Rome, 1976).

broadly and also followed the foreign press, while his family generally lived with some degree of modesty. He regularized governmental administration in March 1929 by promoting to ministerial rank seven of the eight undersecretaries in the ministries which he nominally supervised. Mussolini retained in his own hands only the Ministry of the Interior in addition to his main position of Capo del Governo (Head of Government), his dictatorial title in lieu of Prime Minister.

By this time the process of the bureaucratization of the Fascist Party had been under way for several years. Augusto Turati, who served as party secretary until October 1930, had broken most of the autonomous power of the provincial *ras* (bosses). He was succeeded by the moderate and less effective Giovanni Giuriati until the end of 1931, at which point the Duce handed the secretaryship to the sycophantic Achille Starace, a formalist showman who would hold the position for most of the remainder of the decade. There was no further general purge, though two smaller ones took place between 1931 and 1933, partly to eliminate some of the most ultra-Catholic members. New laws of 1933–35 made all civil servants, including schoolteachers, members of the PNF, swelling the total eventually to 2.7 million. Though this was a smaller proportionate membership than in Germany, it was much larger than the proportion in the Soviet Union and accelerated the process of mass bureaucratization, while greatly diluting zeal for a revolutionary Fascism. The sections abroad, or Fasci all'Estero, claimed 101,500 members by 1929, but the real membership was only about 65,000 (of whom 10 percent were women), or less than 1 percent of the approximately 8 million Italians living abroad.[3]

During these years an effort was made to give greater importance to the corporative structure. In March 1930 the National Council of Corporations was reorganized into a three-tiered system: the base was composed of the national syndicates, above which was formed a general corporative assembly of the syndicates' nominal representatives (meeting together with officials of the party and the state bureaucracy), crowned by the Central Corporative Committee composed of government ministers, the presidents of the syndical confederations, and appointees from the government administration and the party. Giuseppe Bottai, minister of corporations from 1929 to 1932, hoped to give the components of the structure greater freedom and room for creative action, but in fact only the employer sections had any degree of autonomy. In February 1934 the national syndicates were officially replaced by twenty-two national corporations for diverse branches of the economy, each with its

---

3. In general, the membership of the Fasci all'Estero seems to have been rather more blue-collar than that of the PNF by this point. The statistics provided by Enzo Santarelli, in *Ricerche sul fascismo* (Urbino, 1971), 103–32, are corrected in L. De Caprariis, "Fascism and Italian Diplomacy, 1925–1928," Ph.D. diss., University of Wisconsin, Madison, 1995.

national chamber to regulate wages and working conditions.[4] In general, however, the corporative structure continued to have comparatively little direct economic power. Its main function was to regulate labor,[5] and even a Fascist innovation such as the new labor courts was downgraded because the activity of these bodies created some friction.[6] A new labor code for the economy went into effect in 1931, followed later by a new civil code for the system of justice. Both these legal codes survived the fall of Fascism because their structure was comparatively rational and efficient and did not contain any notable injection of Fascist radicalism.

There was a further attempt to define Fascist doctrine during the early 1930s. Giovanni Gentile, who had been the leading theoretical spokesman in recent years, rallied many intellectuals for collaboration in the publication of the multivolume *Enciclopedia Italiana* between 1929 and 1938. The key article on *fascismo*, which appeared in 1932, was written in large part by Gentile but signed by Mussolini. It hailed "the century of authority, of the 'right,' " "a Fascist century" that was also "the 'collective' century and hence of the state." But Fascism was of neither the right nor the left. "The Fascist negations of socialism, democracy, and liberalism should not lead to the conclusion that Fascism wants to return to the world before 1789. . . . One does not go back. Fascism has not chosen De Maistre as its prophet." "That a doctrine may utilize those elements of other doctrines which are still vital is perfectly logical." Gentile continued to insist that Fascism represented both a new form of community and an authoritarian "ethical state." Yet despite the earlier founding of the Istituto di Cultura Fascista, a clear and precise definition of Fascist ideology, above all an official one, was still not to be found. The concept of pragmatic relativism, as publicized by Adriano Tilgher in earlier years, provided a theoretical argument against it, while Mussolini found practical political utility on both the domestic and international levels in playing different sectors and ideas of Fascism off against each other. His overall position was that Fascism would provide the means to solve the problems of both liberalism and socialism in a new synthesis that would resolve the spiritual crisis of Europe, as well as the economic split between capitalism and socialism.[7]

4. On the overall development of the corporative system, see B. Uva, *La nascita dello Stato corporativo e sindacale fascista* (Assisi, 1974); G. Sapelli, *Fascismo, grande industria e sindacato: Il caso di Torino, 1929/1935* (Milan, 1975); S. Cassese, *La formazione dello Stato amministrativo* (Milan, 1974); and L. Franck, *Il corporativismo e l'economia dell'Italia fascista* (Turin, 1990). Franck's work comprises various writings first published in French between 1934 and 1939.

5. G. Parlato, *Il sindacalismo fascista*, vol. 2, *Dalla "grande crisi" alla caduta del regime (1930–1943)* (Rome, 1989).

6. G. C. Jocteau, *La magistratura e i conflitti di lavoro durante il fascismo* (Milan, 1978).

7. Among the more notable efforts of these years were A. Bertele, *Aspetti ideologici del fascismo* (Turin, 1930), and M. Palmieri, *The Philosophy of Fascism* (Chicago, 1936). The best theoretical reconstruction of Fascist doctrine ex post facto is A. J. Gregor, *The Ideology of Fas-*

With each year, increasing attention was paid to what historians have called *il culto del littorio* (the cult of the lictors), the elaborate public and cere- monial process which sought to convert Fascism into a civic cult, a kind of civil religion.[8] The "Fascist revolution" was declared to be an ongoing process, a "continuing revolution" which had, like the French Revolution, inaugurated a new calendar of the Fascist regime, with 1922 dating as Year 1. "Faith" was announced as the basis of the Fascist epistemology, and this was to be enhanced by public cult and cermony and the elaboration of Fascist art, architecture, and symbols. Such an epistemology emphasized both myth and mysticism, for myth enshrined the truths and goals of the regime, producing both politi- cal myths and, as Emilio Gentile says, a politics of mythmaking. The Fascist new man was defined by a new mystique, indeed a psychology of mysticism as distinct from the old bourgeois materialism. The official Scuola di Mistica Fascista (School of Fascist Mysticism) was inaugurated in 1930. Myth was held to be true not as existing empirical fact but as the metareality of the past and the absolute goal which would be realized in the future. During the brief leadership of Giuriati in 1931 the party introduced the most well-known of Fascist slogans: *Credere Obbedire Combattere* (Believe, obey, fight).

The regime openly sought a sacralization of politics and the state, for as Mussolini declared in the 1932 *Dottrina del Fascismo,* "Fascism is a religious conception of life," and Fascists formed "a spiritual community." Three years earlier one of the first scholarly accounts published abroad observed that Fas- cism "has the rudiments of a new religion," [9] while a secondary party leader had announced that "the idea of Fascism, like the Christian idea, is a dogma of perpetual becoming." [10] Theoretically Fascism was not in conflict or competi- tion with Roman Catholicism, for Mussolini had declared soon after becoming dictator that Fascism did not have a theology but a morality. He always empha- sized the importance of avoiding direct theological or purely religious conflict with Catholicism, in which he thought Fascism would only be diminished. In 1934 he declared to *Le Figaro,* "In the Fascist concept of the totalitarian state, religion is absolutely free and, in its own sphere, independent. The crazy idea of founding a new religion of the state or of subordinating to the state the religion professed by all Italians has never entered our minds." [11]

Fascism, however, sought to create an "ethical state" based on its own precepts, and Giovanni Gentile had always held that Fascism could contra- dict Catholicism whenever the two overlapped. Mussolini added in the 1934

cism (New York, 1969). See also P. G. Zunino, *L'ideologia del fascismo* (Bologna, 1985), and E. Santarelli, "Uno schema del fascismo italiano," in his *Ricerche sul fascismo* 181–91.

8. The best treatment is E. Gentile, *Il culto del Littorio* (Bari, 1993).
9. H. W. Schneider and S. B. Clough, *Making Fascists* (Chicago, 1929), 73.
10. Gentile *Il culto* 117.
11. Ibid., 138.

interview that "the Fascist state could . . . intervene in religious affairs . . . only when the latter touch the political and moral order of the state." Since Fascism also proclaimed a total philosophy of life, this might occur with increasing frequency. The cult of the fallen, for example, was central to Fascist liturgy. Fascism created its own cult of martyrs and its own immortality for the fallen through public ritual and an attitude of collective transcendence. Indeed, there was an increasing tendency for Fascist leaders to argue that Catholicism deserved respect not because it was sacred or true but simply because it was Italian, a church not so much instituted by God as developed by the history and culture of the Italian people. Mussolini in fact argued that Christianity only became a universal religion when it became Roman, the Roman part being superior to the Catholic creed. The goal clearly was to incorporate Catholicism within and under Fascism as part of a general "religion of Italy," in which Fascism would predominate.[12]

The honeymoon with the Roman Catholic Church only lasted two years beyond the signing of the Lateran Pact. By mid-1931 the regime began to crack down on the central laymen's association, Catholic Action, for being too ambitious in social and cultural activities. Later that year the papal encyclical *Non abbiamo bisogno* denounced Fascism's "pagan idolatry of the state" and "a revolution that seduces the young from the Church and from Jesus Christ and teaches them hatred, violence, and irreverence." It declared that Catholics could only take the formal oath to obey Mussolini's regime with mental reservations. This document provoked new restrictions: during 1932 ultra-Catholic Fascists were purged from the party, new pressures were imposed, and more and more schoolchildren were forced to enroll in Fascist organizations.[13] Catholic leaders were also angered by new religious toleration laws of 1931–32 that gave Protestants and Jews greater freedom than they had enjoyed under liberalism (or would later have under Christian Democrats in the late 1940s and the 1950s). More serious, though, were physical assaults on Catholic youth groups and worker sections. An understanding was eventually reached in 1932 in which the Catholic Action youth groups (more than one million strong) would be dissolved as separate units while all other Catholic organizations would enjoy continued freedom, though restricted primarily to religious activities.[14]

12. M. Cagnetta, *Anticristi e impero fascista* (Bari, 1979); L. Canfora, *Matrici culturali del fascismo* (Turin, 1980); E. Gentile, "Fascism as Political Religion," *JCH* 25:2–3 (May–June 1980): 229–51; idem, *Il culto* 130–46.

13. On the ultra-Catholic Fascists, see P. Ranfagni, *I clerico-fascisti* (Florence, 1975).

14. J. F. Pollard, *The Vatican and Italian Fascism, 1929–1932* (Cambridge, 1985); R. A. Webster, *The Cross and the Fasces* (Stanford, 1960); R. J. Wolff, *Between Pope and Duce: Catholic Students in Fascist Italy* (New York, 1990); P. C. Kent, *The Pope and the Duce* (London, 1981); P. Scoppola, *La Chiesa e il fascismo* (Bari, 1971).

This was a compromise, with both sides claiming victory. Catholic Action youth groups would still exist in semicovert form, but the Church concentrated on "Christian reconquest" in religious terms and on training both leaders and youth for the next generation, as well as on expanding the numbers of the clergy. Even though a book on Mussolini's philosophy published in Rome in 1934 pointed out quite correctly that Fascism was based on "fundamentally pagan principles," [15] the Church hierarchy would soon give the regime strong support in its expansion in Ethiopia and in its military contribution to the defeat of the revolutionary anticlerical left in the Spanish Civil War.

Central to the Fascist "religion of Italy" was the cult of Romanità—"eternal Rome," of which Fascism constituted "modern Rome"—which reached its peak during the 1930s. This had been in gestation since about 1920, providing the origin of the term *Duce*, the Fascist salute, and Fascism as universality. Scholarship and archaeology played roles as well: the journal *Roma* was founded the day after the March on Rome, and the Istituto di Studi Romani was created in 1925. Fascism was declared the revolutionary continuation of the original "Roman revolution" of the first century B.C., with the imperial Roman state considered the predecessor of the totalitarian Fascist state. One result was the rebuilding of part of the center of Rome to better display Roman ruins.[16] These ideas provided a myth for the expansive role of Fascism as well; if Piedmont had been the basis of Italian unification, then Italy would in turn become the "Piedmont of Europe" as the Fascist source of a *nuova civiltà*, a revolutionary reformulation of Western Catholic civilization. The future was then sometimes defined as a choice or clash between two competing modern universalisms: Rome or Moscow.[17] The cult of Romanità reached its height in 1937–38 with the celebration of the bimillennium of Caesar Augustus and the great Mostra Augustea della Romanità (Augustinian Exhibit of Romanism), in turn tied to a major new exhibit of the Fascist revolution.[18]

The ultimate Fascist cult was that of the Duce himself. The 1930s found Mussolini at the pinnacle of his prestige and now a figure much larger than life, even as he began to grow personally more remote and isolated, particularly after the death of his brother Arnaldo (editor of *Il Popolo d'Italia*) in 1931, and as his personal life grew more disordered.[19] The official slogan was *Il Duce ha*

---

15. A. Carlini, *Filosofia e religione nel pensiero di Mussolini* (Rome, 1974), 9, cited in Gentile, *Il culto* 137.

16. A. Cederna, *Mussolini urbanista: Lo sventramento di Roma negli anni del consenso* (Bari, 1981).

17. This generated an extensive literature, such as L. Pareti, *I due imperi di Roma* (Catania, 1938).

18. D. Cofrancesco, "Appunti per un analisi del mito romano nell'ideologia fascista," *SC* 11:3 (June 1980): 383–411; R. Visser, "Fascist Doctrine and the Cult of the *Romanità*," *JCH* 27:1 (Jan. 1992): 5–22; Gentile, *Il culto* 146–54.

19. The most important and influential of his love affairs, with the strong-minded and

sempre ragione (The Duce is always right), and respect for *ducismo* had probably more support than that for *fascismo*. In 1933 Winston Churchill hailed
Mussolini as "the greatest living legislator." [20] The relative moderation and success of his regime had many believing by the early 1930s that there would be
a new round of revisionism and greater liberalization. Political opposition was
divided and impotent, the Communists finding in their clandestine surveys that
a not insignificant portion of blue-collar workers had been won over. Opposition activists saw so little hope that their most famous deed of the early 1930s
was a suicide propaganda flight over Rome.[21] By 1933–34 even some of the
Socialists wanted to make a deal with Mussolini, while the popular Broadway
composer Cole Porter reflected the Duce's international image in his new hit
tune "You're the Top":

> You're the top!
> You're the great Houdini!
> You're the top!
> You are Mussolini! [22]

By the early 1930s Mussolini was entering a phase of megalomania, accentuated by his distrust and rejection of major government ministers and other
Fascist leaders. By July 1932 he had eliminated from government nearly all the
strong personalities from the "Ministry of All the Talents" that he had formed
in 1929.[23] Leading personalities such as Alfredo Rocco, Luigi Federzoni, and
Edmondo Rossoni had been removed from power earlier, the able party secretary Augusto Turati was fired in 1930, and Giuseppe Bottai, Dino Grandi, and
others were dismissed in 1932. Of these, only Bottai ever returned to cabinet
rank. Mussolini did not trust the top *fascisti* and preferred to replace them with
often second-rate new *mussoliniani*. As Adrian Lyttelton has observed, "The
development of the regime during 1929–33 showed Mussolini's determination
not to allow any stable governing elite to crystallize." [24] He would dominate all

---

capable Jewish art critic Margherita Sarfatti, came to an end in 1932. See P. V. Cannistraro and
B. Sullivan, *Il Duce's Other Woman* (New York, 1993).

20. Quoted in P. Melograni, "The Cult of the Duce in Mussolini's Italy," *JCH* 11:4 (Oct.
1976): 221–37. See R. De Felice and L. Goglia, *Mussolini: Il mito* (Bari, 1983); A. Sominini, *Il
linguaggio di Mussolini* (Milan, 1978); and, for the images and biographies, L. Passerini, *Mussolini
immaginario* (Bari, 1991).

21. This was the melancholy feat of Lauro de Bosis, who wrote "The Story of My Life"
and then flew from Corsica over Rome to drop opposition leaflets, without the fuel to complete the
return flight. F. Fucci, *Ali contro Mussolini: I raid aerei antifascisti degli anni trenta* (Milan, 1978).

22. These words from the 1934 original were later altered.

23. This also involved removing one of the most honest and effective party administrators,
Leandro Arpinati, from his post as undersecretary of the interior. He was later sentenced to five
years in jail on a morals charge. A. Iraci, *Arpinati l'oppositore di Mussolini* (Rome, 1970).

24. A. Lyttelton, *The Seizure of Power: Fascism in Italy, 1919–1929* (New York, 1973),
430.

Mussolini depicted as idealized worker among the people, 1934

major issues. Mussolini temporarily reassumed the powers of foreign minister himself in 1933, taking command of the three military ministries as well.

A minority of activists in the party and the Fascist youth organization remained restive, talking of the *seconda ondata* (second wave) of the Fascist revolution that would begin a true transformation. *Novismo* (lit., "newism") became a popular doctrine among Fascist youth, while a few revolutionary left Fascists, whose leading spokesman was Ugo Spirito, urged "social corporatism," the use of the corporations for a process of economic nationalization.[25]

Mussolini recognized privately that a true Fascist revolution had not yet occurred and that the imagined "new Italians" had not yet been created. His response was essentially propagandistic and pedagogical: he believed that through years of Fascist education, indoctrination, and ceremony a new generation would eventually be developed in the mystique of Fascism. As Macgregor Knox has suggested, his basic goals were threefold: to continue the regime, to build a Fascist culture in Italy that would create a new kind of Italian, and to lead Italy in a military expansion that would build a great Italian neo-Roman empire.

To this end the organization of youth continued to expand, all sections being grouped under the umbrella Gioventù del Littorio (GIL) in 1937. Membership did not become mandatory, however, until 1939 and even then was not fully enforced. At its maximum three years later, the GIL nominally enrolled 8.83 million, including 90 percent of adolescent and teenage boys but never more than about 30 percent of girls. Some critical discussion was always permitted in the Fascist youth groups, and around 1937–38 this would become increasingly negative, even to the point that some youth circulated a little subversive material.[26]

The Fascist regime increased spending more than a little in education: the proportion of the budget in that category grew from 4.2 percent in 1922 to 7.6 percent in 1926, and it remained at that level until the Ethiopian campaign. The original educational reform of Gentile in 1923 was elitist and authoritarian, restricting accessibility; it was generally judged a failure, unpopular even among Fascists. A serious effort at Fascistizing the schools did not begin until 1929, and this accompanied rising enrollments generally. The number of students increased at all levels.[27] In public schools a new *libro unico*, or standard text,

25. F. Perfetti, "Ugo Spirito e la concezione della 'Corporazione Proprietaria' al Convegno di Studi Sindacali e Corporativi di Ferrara del 1932," *Critica Storica* 25:2 (1988): 202–43. See also L. L. Rimbotti, *Il fascismo di sinistra* (Rome, 1989), 90–137; F. Leoni, *Il dissenso nel fascismo dal 1924 al 1939* (Naples, 1983), 50–89; and the classic autobiographical account of Ruggero Zangrandi, *Il lungo viaggio attraverso il fascismo* (Milan, 1962).

26. The broadest study is T. H. Koon, *Believe, Obey, Fight: Political Socialization of Youth in Fascist Italy, 1922–1943* (Chapel Hill, 1985). See also C. Betti, *L'Opera Nazionale Balilla e l'educazione fascista* (Florence, 1984).

27. M. Barbagli, *Disoccupazione e sistema scolastico in Italia* (Bologna, 1974), 173–75.

was introduced at most levels, and by 1935 administration had been central-ized, with some political indoctrination provided to all but the youngest. One scholar has judged that "Fascistization was most successful in the elementary schools. . . . Teachers at the elementary schools responded with the greatest enthusiasm . . . [and] were controlled more strictly by the government than teachers in the upper schools," so that "the Fascist regime did manage for a time to produce a broad, albeit superficial, consensus among many Italian young people."[28] Above all, this support came from the middle classes.[29]

It has been calculated that by 1939 half of the forty-four million Italian citizens were members of a Fascist political, economic, youth, or other orga-nization. Though the Dopolavoro recreation program was not as extensive as that of the Nazi Kraft durch Freude, it involved some five million people. Women members were always subordinated, yet were present in lesser num-bers in all these associations.[30] Though the reality would prove to be much more superficial, Italian society gave the appearance of general Fascistization.

The regime made distinctive use of the mass media and of popular culture, though it did not set up a full-scale propaganda ministry until 1935, creating the MinCulPop (Ministry of Popular Culture) two years later.[31] Particularly noticeable was the broad diffusion of sports, as both a participant and a spec-tator activity, to a greater extent perhaps than in Nazi Germany. New stadiums were built in many locales, while the Italian soccer team won the World Cup in 1934 and 1938 and the Olympic gold medal in 1936. The Dopolavoro was especially active, creating 11,159 sports sections, compared with 1,227 local theaters, 771 cinemas, 2,130 orchestras, and 6,427 libraries.[32] Censorship was largely limited to politics,[33] and the great majority of intellectuals and writers

28. Koon, *Believe* xix, 86–87. Another commentator goes further: "If one thinks of a young Italian in the 1930s, being educated by Fascist teachers on the basis of Fascist textbooks, joining the youth organization for out-of-school activities, beginning work as a member of a Fascist trade union with his or her spare time organized by the Dopolavoro, totalitarianism does not seem such a fanciful concept." J. Colby et al., *Between Two Wars* (Celtic Court, Bucks., 1990), 136.

29. On education, see M. Ostenc, *La scuola italiana durante il fascismo* (Bari, 1981); L. M. Paluello, *Education in Fascist Italy* (London, 1946); T. M. Mazzatosta, *Il regime fascista tra edu-cazione e propaganda (1935–1943)* (Bologna, 1978); M. Saracinelli and N. Totti, *L'Italia del Duce: L'informazione, la scuola e il costume* (Rimini, 1983); A. J. De Grand, *Bottai e la cultura fascista* (Bari, 1978); G. Bottai, *Vent'anni e un giorno* (Naviglio, 1949); and E. R. Tannenbaum, *The Fascist Experience: Italian Society and Culture, 1922–1945* (New York, 1972), 117–77.

30. V. de Grazia, *How Fascism Ruled Women: Italy, 1922–1945* (Berkeley, 1991); M. Mac-ciocchi, *La donna nera* (Milan, 1976). Even the Massaie Rurali, a Fascist organization of farm-wives begun in 1935, nominally enrolled more than a million and a half women.

31. P. V. Cannistraro, *La fabbrica del consenso: Fascismo e mass media* (Bari, 1975); M. Isnenghi, *L'educazione dell'italiano: Il fascismo e l'organizzazione della cultura* (Bologna, 1979); A. Monticone, *Il fascismo al microfono* (Rome, 1978).

32. V. de Grazia, *The Culture of Consent: Mass Organization of Leisure in Fascist Italy* (Cambridge, 1981).

33. M. Cesari, *La censura del periodo fascista* (Naples, 1978).

at least superficially conformed.[34] This situation permitted a highly diversified culture.[35] A great deal was invested in films, producing the large film complex outside Rome, Cinecittà, Italy's answer to Hollywood.[36]

In artistic criteria, as in many other ways, Fascism differed profoundly from National Socialism, particularly in its ambivalent relationship with avantgarde and modern art. Futurism had played an important role in the early development of Fascism, but in fact most Futurists had soon left Fascism and also soon left Futurism.[37] By 1930 only Giacomo Balla remained faithful to the old norms.[38] In 1922 a group of artists in Milan started a new movement which became Novecento Italiano, devoted to the thesis that art must be popular, national-ethnic, purged of foreign influences, and scornful of American industrialism. Novecento emphasized clear form and three-dimensionality; though eclectic in style, it tried to evoke a Mediterranean calm and repose. Since this was partly based on classical principles, the new movement was sometimes called neoclassicist. The first major Novecento exhibit took place in Milan in 1926. Novecento developed no rigid doctrine but portrayed stylized figures, nudes, heroic portraits, and calm allegories of virtue, with landscapes echoing Roman and Renaissance vistas.[39]

After the full consolidation of the regime, some called for a true Fascist art that would reflect Fascist reality. Novecento was advanced for such a role but was vigorously criticized by some sectors of the party for excessive aestheticism and lack of real *italianità*. An official Fascist art style never developed, and most forms of modern art continued to be practiced in Italy. Monumentality was prized, as in all major dictatorships, and there the Italian national and classical traditions could be utilized. Igor Golomstock has written that "the

34. G. Turi, *Il fascismo e il consenso degli intellettuali* (Bologna, 1980); ′A. L. de Castris, *Egemonia e fascismo: Il problema degli intellettuali negli anni trenta* (Bologna, 1981).

35. See M. Sechi, *Il mito della cultura fascista* (Bari, 1984); the collective *La cultura italiana negli anni trenta '30–'45*, 2 vols. (New York, 1984); G. Luti, *La letteratura nel ventennio fascista* (Florence, 1972); and Tannenbaum, *Fascist Experience* 211–302. On the most distinguished foreign writer to take up permanent residence in Fascist Italy, see T. Redman, *Ezra Pound and Italian Fascism* (New York, 1990).

36. E. Mancini, *The Struggle of the Italian Film Industry during Fascism, 1930–1935* (Ann Arbor, 1985); M. Landy, *Fascism in Film* (Princeton, 1986); J. Hay, *Popular Film Culture in Fascist Italy* (Bloomington, 1987). On the theater, see A. C. Alberi, *Il teatro nel fascismo* (Rome, 1974); E. Scarpellini, *Organizzazione teatrale e politica del teatro nell'Italia fascista* (Florence, 1989); and M. Berezin, "The Organization of Political Ideology: Culture, State, and Theater in Fascist Italy," *American Sociological Review* 56:5 (1991): 639–51.

37. Marinetti's relation with Fascism became ambivalent. By 1929 he had developed a "Second Futurism" that tried to reproduce the "optimal and psychic sensations of flight" through "aeropainting" and "aerosculpture." E. Crispoli, *Il secondo futurismo* (Turin, 1962).

38. Giorgio De Chirico and Carlo Carrà had begun looking for new styles as early as 1916, and in 1919 the former published a new manifesto, *Back to Craft*.

39. A. Pica, *Mario Siroli* (Milan, 1955), treats the most important Novecento painter.

most important form of official Fascist art was mural painting."[40] This genre was led by the work of Achille Funi.[41] Themes of labor, sport, struggle, and motherhood were common, emphasizing qualities of strength, courage, and physical perfection. The motif of youth was also repeated perhaps more than in any other dictatorship. In architecture, Mussolini was eventually led to endorse "rationalism," the Italian variant of modern abstract architecture.[42] In general, however, art, like other forms of high culture in Italy, was fragmented. All major artists continued to present purely individual exhibits, and the most prominent hardly ever did official Fascist "agitprop" art.

Relatively close relations were maintained with Soviet art.[43] Not only was Italy the first Western country to recognize the Soviet Union in 1924, but the new Soviet art first appeared in the West that year at the Venice Biennale, Italy's premiere art show. This was followed by large Soviet exhibits every year, to the extent that by 1932 some Fascist commentators would lament that there was much more of an official Soviet art than there was a Fascist art, while Goebbels sneered that Fascism was not "revolutionary" like National Socialism. Mussolini obtained from Stalin the directions for May Day ceremonies in Moscow to enhance the public liturgy of Fascism, and Fascist posters, with their industrial and military themes, resembled in style their Soviet counterparts more than did any other genre of Fascist art.

The greatest of all Fascist art extravaganzas was the huge Mostra della Rivoluzione Fascista (Exhibit of the Fascist Revolution), prepared for the tenth anniversary of the March on Rome, which was viewed by several million visitors between 1932 and 1934. This show combined several styles but was based on modernist and rationalist art, typically modern in form. One of the most widely viewed exhibits in history to that time, it marked a distinct contrast to National Socialist art.[44]

Mussolini remained ambivalent about artistic style and never made any grand categorical statement. He insisted that Italy was "the pioneer nation in the van of contemporary culture" which would create a new civilization, and in 1934 he defended modernist architecture from its Soviet and Nazi crit-

40. Golomstock, *Totalitarian Art* 45.

41. See P. Vergani, *Achille Funi* (Milan, 1949).

42. G. Ciucci, *Gli architetti e il fascismo* (Turin, 1989); R. A. Etlin, *Modernism in Italian Architecture, 1890–1940* (Cambridge, Mass., 1991); D. Ghirardo, *Building New Communities: New Deal America and Fascist Italy* (Princeton, 1989).

43. If Golomstock is correct that "it is the artistic avant-garde of the 1910s and 1920s who first elaborated a totalitarian theory of culture" (*Totalitarian Art* 21), this would be much more true of Russia than of Italy.

44. M. Stone, "Staging Fascism: The Exhibition of the Fascist Revolution," *JCH* 28:2 (April 1993): 215–43; Partito Nazionale Fascista, *Mostra della Rivoluzione Fascista* (Rome, 1990); Gentile, *Il culto* 214–35; J. T. Schnapp, "Epic Demonstrations," in *Fascism, Aesthetics, and Culture*, ed. R. Golsan (Hanover, N.H., 1992), 1–37.

ics because modernism was "rational and functional."[45] Yet like the Fascist revolution itself, the new art and culture, Mussolini held, could not be fully developed until after the full Fascist empire had been created. At the same time he also worried that Italians were too "arty," with an aestheticist orientation which contradicted Fascism's preferred tone of austerity and "virile pessimism." By the mid-1930s Mussolini was increasingly given to saying that Italians must prepare for continuing struggle and learn to eat and to sleep less, to "learn to hate more and rejoice in being hated." Art would have to become much more utilitarian to bolster the increasingly warlike orientation which he gave Fascist policy from 1935 on.

ECONOMIC POLICY AND PERFORMANCE

The two pillars of Fascism's economic policy had been national syndicalism and productionism. Both were implemented, but the latter was rather the more important aspect. As mentioned in chapter 4, the economic policy of the 1920s was comparatively orthodox. The tax base was widened, but rates were lowered, and the deficit, which in 1922 had amounted to 12 percent of Gross Domestic Product, was brought completely under control in fiscal 1924–25. As production increased, the percentage of GDP spent by the state dropped from 27.6 in 1922 to 16.5 in 1926, only regaining the 1922 level in 1932 under the stress of the depression.

During the first decade of Mussolini's government, the two most Fascist or nationalist aspects of economic policy were the revaluation of the lira in 1926 and the determination to make Italy self-sufficient in cereals. The comparatively rapid economic expansion of the 1920s was accompanied by considerable inflation, leading to a marked decline in the exchange value of the lira. Mussolini imposed the Quota Novanta (Quota Ninety) to regulate the lira at ninety to the pound in 1926 and also put Italy back on the gold standard. This stopped inflation but handicapped exports. The "Battle of the Grain" was nominally successful but actually harmful to the economy. Increased grain production at abnormally high costs raised prices for consumers and discouraged more rational and specialized food production.

The Italian economy's overall performance under Fascism was approximately average for an industrializing European economy during this period. Industrial production increased rapidly during the 1920s, with metallurgical

45. Golomstock, *Totalitarian Art* 29. It was this penchant which led Ernst Nolte to write of Mussolini: "Of all the outstanding totalitarian personalities of the era, Mussolini was not the man with the deepest thoughts, but he was probably the one with the most thoughts; he was not the most outstanding, but he was the most human; he was not the most single-minded, but he was the most many-sided. Thus to a certain extent he was the most liberal." Nolte, *Three Faces of Fascism* (New York, 1966), 231.

output nearly doubling between 1922 and 1929. This growth was checked by the depression, which brought a decline of nearly 20 percent in industrial production by 1932, while unemployment rose from three hundred thousand in 1929 to one million by 1933 (again, not so far from the European norm).

The regime's response to the depression was not to allow the national syndicates to take charge but to increase the direct role of the state. Public works were considerably expanded, while rationalization, reorganization, and cartelization were encouraged in industry. The first major instrument of state intervention was the creation of the Istituto Mobiliare Italiano (Italian Assets Institute, IMI) in 1931 as a state corporation to buy up shares of failing banks, beginning a process by which the state would directly or indirectly control most Italian banking assets. In 1933 the government established the Istituto per la Ricostruzione Industriale (IRI), a state corporation to buy shares of and infuse capital into failing industrial enterprises. This became a permanent institution, by 1939 acquiring 21.5 percent of the capital in all joint-stock companies in Italy, gaining control of a number of the major sectors of industry, and giving the Italian government ownership of a greater portion of the national economy than in any other nation-state west of the Soviet Union. The growth of other state agencies and regulations continued apace.

More than in Germany, full recovery from the depression in Italy would result from greatly expanded arms production for the Ethiopian war in 1935, when the index of industrial production rebounded almost to the level of 1929. By 1937 output clearly exceeded the predepression level, and it rose nearly 20 percent higher by 1939.

The banking system was broadly reorganized, and the dominant investment role of the old mixed banks ended. The state now dominated the financial system. The Bank of Italy was nationalized in 1936. A new commercial code paralleled the new civil and penal codes, and all survived long into postwar Italy. The lira only went off the gold standard in 1936, and from that time forward taxes were considerably increased, together with controls on prices. A general sales tax (IGE) was introduced in January 1940, on the eve of Italy's entry into World War II; this would be a centerpiece of postwar taxation. The state's expenditure proportionate to GDP surpassed the pre-Fascist level for the first time in 1934, reaching 28.6 percent compared with 27.6 percent in 1922, and continued to rise on the eve of the war.

Compared with the pre–World War I norm of 1913, total production in Italy had risen by 1938 to 153.8, compared with 149.9 in Germany and 109.4 in France. The aggregate index for output per worker in 1939, compared with the same 1913 base, stood at 145.2 for Italy, 136.5 for France, 122.4 for Germany, 143.6 for Britain, and 136.0 for the United States.[46] Even though Italy's

46. A. Maddison, *Economic Growth in the West* (New York, 1965), appendices A, E, H, I.

average rate of annual industrial growth in the depression years of 1.7 percent was less than Germany's and considerably less than Sweden's, it was only slightly below the western European norm and stood well above the figure of −2.8 for France.[47] Between 1922 and 1939 the economy grew more than twice as fast as the population, and 3.9 percent annually in manufacturing, the value of industrial production exceeding that of agriculture for the first time in 1937.

Economic policy under Fascism did not chart an absolutely clear course. On the one hand it sought greater production and modernization through semi-orthodox means, and on the other it sought to create a less materialist and more militant, ascetic society that would both reflect ecological *ridimensiona-mento* (redimensioning) and preparation for war. The former goal was partially achieved, though not at any spectacular rate.[48] The second set of goals were hardly achieved at all. There was little *ridimensionamento* beyond a major expansion of land reclamation and reforestation; in general, the urbanization of Italy increased pari passu with the growth of industry and services. There was much new urban construction, and the Fascist state was active in urban planning. Fascism in fact tended to neglect the countryside, though it was successful in dramatically reducing the proportion of landless laborers in the agricultural workforce from 44 percent in 1921 to 27 percent in 1936. Very few of those who left the laborers' ranks became landowners, the majority becoming tenant farmers and sharecroppers, the rest moving to the cities. Italian per capita consumption increased by only 7 percent between 1922 and 1939, and factory wages declined by twice that amount, though fringe benefits for urban workers increased considerably. In 1933 the government set up the Istituto Nazionale Fascista della Previdenza Sociale (Fascist National Institute of Social Security, INFPS) but in fact lacked the resources to create a complete system. Army statistics do reveal overall increases in height and weight of recruits during this period. By 1939 welfare expenditures amounted to 21 percent of the state budget, but no fully integrated system of welfare or social security was achieved.[49]

47. D. Lomax, *The Inter-War Economy of Britain, 1919–1939* (London, 1970); P. Ciocca, "L'economia nel contesto internazionale," in *L'economia italiana nel periodo fascista*, ed. P. Ciocca and G. Toniolo (Bologna, 1976), 36.

48. The principal study of Fascist modernization is A. J. Gregor, *Italian Fascism and Developmental Dictatorship* (Princeton, 1979). See also L. Garruccio [pseud.], *L'industrializzazione tra nazionalismo e rivoluzione* (Bologna, 1969); E. R. Tannenbaum, "The Goals of Italian Fascism," *American Historical Review* 74:4 (April 1969): 1183–204; R. Sarti, "Fascist Modernization in Italy: Traditional or Revolutionary?" *American Historical Review* 75:4 (April 1970): 1029–45; idem, *Fascism and the Industrial Leadership in Italy, 1919–1940* (Berkeley, 1971); P. Melograni, *Gli industriali e Mussolini* (Milan, 1972); S. La Francesca, *La politica economica del fascismo* (Bari, 1972); and A. Hughes and M. Kolinsky, " 'Paradigmatic Fascism' and Modernization: A Critique," *Political Studies* 24:4 (Dec. 1976): 371–96.

49. On the general performance of the economy under Fascism, see G. Toniolo, *L'economia*

FOREIGN POLICY AND EXPANSION

Unlike Hitler, Mussolini had no specific grand design in foreign policy other than to increase Italy's prestige and build a larger empire, a "modern Rome," probably outside Europe proper. During the 1920s there had been no remarkable Fascistization either of foreign policy or of the diplomatic corps. Though more party members were admitted to the latter in 1928, Mussolini conducted foreign affairs through the normal system of career diplomats and did not create separate party agencies for foreign relations, as did Hitler. During the years of regime consolidation, he understood that he was in no position to challenge seriously the status quo in Europe.[50]

By comparison with Hitler, Mussolini was thus only a "limited intentionalist," though his general policy was to support moderate "revisionism" (i.e., changes in the postwar settlement of 1919) in Europe, against the advice of conservatives in the Foreign Ministry. During the 1920s, revisionism was generally considered a relatively left liberal position, being strongly supported by the Comintern and the Soviet Union. Mussolini employed revisionism as a kind of pressure tactic that sought to leverage minor advantages for Italian diplomacy. His revisionist position vis-à-vis the Balkans and east central Europe soon resulted in an adversarial relationship with the new state of Yugoslavia, which was deemed inimical to Italy's interests in the Adriatic, while agreements with Albania in 1925–26 virtually turned that land into an Italian protectorate. A ten-year treaty of friendship with Hungary in 1927 began a special relationship with Europe's most aggrieved state, and this was combined with closer ties with Austria,[51] as well as a partially adversarial position vis-à-vis France, due to competition over Tunisia.[52] In February 1924 Italy was the first of the victor states to recognize the Soviet Union officially, signing a commercial accord.[53] Subsequently Italy developed a larger consular network in the Soviet

---

dell'Italia fascista (Bari, 1980), and V. Zamagni, The Economic History of Italy, 1860–1990 (Oxford, 1993), 243–317.

50. General works include L. Villari, Italian Foreign Policy under Mussolini (New York, 1956), and A. Arisi Rota, La diplomazia del ventennio (Milan, 1990). The early phases are treated in A. Cassels, Mussolini's Early Diplomacy (Princeton, 1970); G. Rumi, Alle origini della politica estera fascista, 1918–1923 (Bari, 1968); and G. Carocci, La politica estera dell'Italia fascista (1925–1928) (Bari, 1968). James Barros, in The Corfu Incident of 1923 (Princeton, 1965), recounts Mussolini's first vigorous initiative, and Giovanni Zambroni, in Mussolinis Expansionspolitik auf dem Balkan (Hamburg, 1970), describes his designs in the Balkans. The lengthy debate over the interpretation of Mussolini's foreign policy is analyzed in S. C. Azzi, "The Historiography of Fascist Foreign Policy," Historical Journal 36:1 (1993): 187–203.

51. See D. I. Rusinow, Italy's Austrian Heritage, 1919–1946 (Oxford, 1969).

52. J. Bessis, La Méditerranée fasciste (Paris, 1981); W. I. Shorrock, From Ally to Enemy: The Enigma of Fascist Italy in French Diplomacy (Kent, Ohio, 1988).

53. G. Petracchi, La Russia rivoluzionaria nella politica italiana: Le relazioni italiano-sovietiche, 1917–1925 (Rome, 1982).

Union than did any other country. Beginning in 1926, Italy, Germany, and the Soviet Union cooperated in several revisionist initiatives, but Mussolini was still careful not to be involved in any major direct challenges to the status quo.

The leading Fascist journal *Gerarchia* (Hierarchy) declared in February 1925 that "possibly before long a large part of Europe will become more or less fascist." Later that year the head of the Fasci all'Estero reported that it was possible to identify at least forty movements in Europe and further abroad "that call themselves Fascist or are declared to be such." [54] The party's Grand Council discussed the possibility of forming a sort of Fascist International, but Mussolini discouraged the notion. In 1928 he made a widely quoted declaration that "Fascism is not goods for export," and from 1929 to 1932 his foreign minister was the Fascist moderate Dino Grandi, who followed a policy of cooperation with the League of Nations. [55] Thus Fascist Italy was often viewed in the Western democracies as a relatively benign regime. [56]

The beginning of a change of policy took place in 1932, when Mussolini dismissed his most able ministers and personally took over the Foreign Ministry. It has been argued that by this point Mussolini's approach was conditioned above all by three factors: the imperialist character of Fascist ideology, the conviction that geographic and strategic circumstances required competition with Britain and France, and the growing determination to use foreign policy as a tool of domestic policy, enhancing the dominance of the Duce and of Fascism while eliminating the influence of the old elites. [57] Mussolini had become convinced that the depression crisis would produce at least some degree of power realignment, generating new circumstances which Italy would be able to exploit. The motivation was also ideological, for Mussolini had concluded that a Fascist revolution could not be completed inside Italy until a greater neo-Roman empire had been conquered abroad. In that sense the more activist policy was also a response to domestic frustrations of a political, institutional, and cultural character, but not simply to the economic problems of the depression, as has been alleged. The economic situation, in fact, would have discouraged accepting the greater expense of such a policy, but for Mussolini politics and ideology had become decisive. To that end he first ordered planning in November 1932 for a possible attack on Ethiopia. [58]

54. De Caprariis, "Fascism and Italian Diplomacy" 234.

55. Cf. J. A. Bongiorno, *Fascist Italy and the Disarmament Question, 1928–1934* (New York, 1992).

56. J. P. Diggins, *Mussolini and Fascism: The View from America* (Princeton, 1972); D. F. Schmitz, *The United States and Fascist Italy, 1922–1940* (Chapel Hill, 1988); P. Milza, *L'Italie fasciste devant l'opinion française* (Paris, 1967).

57. M. Knox, "Il fascismo e la politica estera italiana," in *La politica estera italiana, 1860–1985*, ed. R. Bosworth and S. Romano (Bologna, 1991), 287–330.

58. Aspects of this phase are treated in F. D'Amoja, *Declino e prima crisi dell'Europa di Versailles: Studio sulla diplomazia italiana ed Europa (1931–1933)* (Milan, 1967).

This was accompanied by an effort to expand the ideological and political influence of Fascism within Europe, an initiative dating initially from 1930, when limited support began to be provided for a number of fascist or profascist movements in other lands. It expanded a few years later, in accord with Mussolini's more aggressive foreign policy orientation of 1932, with the appearance of such new propaganda vehicles as the journal *Ottobre* (October; it became a daily paper in 1934), devoted to propounding the universal mission of Fascism; the Centro di Studi Internazionali sul Fascismo in Milan; and a variety of books and other publications.[59]

To coordinate such activity, in 1933 Mussolini created the Comitati d'Azione per l'Universalità di Roma (CAUR) under Eugenio Coselschi. The CAUR sponsored several meetings in Switzerland during the next two years, the most important of which was the Fascist international conference at Montreux in December 1934. One of the main problems concerned the criteria by which to identify fascist-type movements in other countries. There were many strongly nationalist groups, but which were "fascist"? No complete and official codification of Italian Fascist doctrine existed to serve as touchstone, so the proponents of the new international trend of "universal Fascism" made up their own, however vaguely, and by April 1934 had identified "fascist" movements in thirty-nine countries (including every European country except Yugoslavia, as well as the United States, Canada, South Africa, Australia, five countries in Asia, and six in Latin America).[60] Even so moderate an association as General Eoin O'Duffy's Blue Shirts in Ireland was declared to be fascist. All manner of problems then ensued, as many different groups tried to cadge subsidies and extreme disagreements appeared on issues such as racism, anti-Semitism, corporatism, and state structure. The effort to create a kind of international grouping of extreme nationalist movements was quickly doomed to frustration.

All this did not preclude even closer relations between Italy and Soviet Union. Contacts had generally been friendly, and Mussolini had an interest in patronizing Russia to promote revisionism in European affairs, though at the same time he was wary of the Comintern as a revolutionary rival of Fascism. While *fascism* had long been a term of abuse in Comintern propaganda, the Soviet government did not see Italy as a threat, and trade between the two powers increased during 1930–32. After the rise of Hitler, Stalin hoped to use Italy as a lever against Germany. A new economic accord was signed in May 1933, followed four months later by an Italo-Soviet Pact of Friendship, Neu-

59. For example, G. S. Spinetti, *Fascismo universale* (Rome, 1933), and O. Fantini, *L'universalità del Fascismo* (Naples, 1933), which had been preceded by J. S. Barnes, *The Universal Aspects of Fascism* (London, 1928). For further references and discussion, the key study is M. A. Ledeen, *Universal Fascism* (New York, 1972), 1–103.

60. The full report is in De Felice, *Mussolini il Duce* 1:872–919.

trality, and Nonaggression (this followed a similar treaty between France and the Soviet Union the year before).[61]

As Mussolini's policy became more expansive, there was talk in Rome of the "revolutionary affinity" between the two regimes and of Soviet "convergence" with Fascism, even though all the better Italian ideologues understood the basic differences between them.[62] Italian shipyards constructed a number of vessels for the Soviet fleet in 1933–34, before the Italian invasion of Ethiopia created a new gulf between the regimes. As late as 1938 Mussolini called Stalin a "cryptofascist," [63] and the following year the leading Fascist ideologue, Sergio Panunzio, declared that the Soviet Union had taken on more and more Fascist features: "Moscow bows before the light radiating from Rome. The Communist International no longer speaks to the spirit; it is dead." [64]

Mussolini was particularly attentive to the appearance of the two major figures who took power abroad early in 1933: Franklin Roosevelt and Adolf Hitler. His initial attitude was in fact more positive toward the American administration, and the Duce and Roosevelt established personal contact even before Roosevelt was inaugurated. Mussolini looked to the American economy to provide the strength to overcome the depression in Europe, and within a matter of months he was sure that the New Deal was copying Fascist economic policies—just as Roosevelt's critics in the United States alleged.[65] Particularly during his first year in office, Roosevelt in turn looked toward Mussolini as a particular friend of the United States and an important ally in keeping the peace in Europe.[66] The attitude of Fascists toward the United States in general was quite ambivalent. Though many made the standard criticisms of American materialism, hedonism, and lack of culture, there was also much praise even

61. J. C. Clarke III, *Russia and Italy against Hitler: The Bolshevik-Fascist Rapprochement of the 1930s* (Westport, Conn., 1991).

62. Mussolini later favorably reviewed Renzo Bertoni's *Il trionfo del fascismo nell' URSS* (Milan, 1937), which held that though the two regimes had originally followed different policies, Soviet strategies had destroyed the economy and family life and the Soviet Union would now be forced to adopt Fascist policies.

63. B. Mussolini, *Opera omnia di Benito Mussolini,* ed. E. and D. Susmel, 36 vols. (Florence, 1951–63), 29:63.

64. S. Panunzio, *Teoria generale dello Stato fascista* (Padua, 1939), 9–10, cited in Clarke, *Russia and Italy* 90–91.

65. What Fascist corporatism and the New Deal had in common was a certain amount of state intervention in the economy. Beyond that, the only figure who seemed to look on Fascist corporatism as a kind of model was Hugh Johnson, head of the National Recovery Administration. F. Perkins, *The Roosevelt I Knew* (New York, 1946), 206.

66. "The first two years of the Roosevelt administration saw Mussolini's stock continue to rise in Washington, and the viewpoint that Mussolini held a moderating influence on Hitler took hold." Schmitz, *United States* 141. See also G. G. Migone, *Gli Stati Uniti e il fascismo* (Milan, 1980); B. R. Sullivan, "Roosevelt, Mussolini e la guerra d'Etiopia," *SC* 19:1 (Feb. 1988): 85–106; and Cannistraro and Sullivan, *Other Woman* 395–417.

in the Fascist press of American dynamism and modernity.[67] Mussolini would not take a categorically negative position vis-à-vis the United States until 1937, after major points of friction had developed.

His attitude toward German Nationalism Socialism was even more complex. Mussolini was zealous to retain Fascism's role as the senior movement—this was part of the motivation behind the "universal Fascism" campaign—and sometimes privately termed National Socialism a "parody of Fascism." Though he had maintained unofficial contacts with Hitler for several years,[68] the political group he had most subsidized in Germany had been the right-wing Stahlhelm.[69] The Fascist press at first hailed Hitler's triumph in 1933, and Mussolini declared that it would be beneficial for the Italian regime.[70] He supported German rearmament and saw the Hitler regime as a potentially useful counterweight against Britain and France in his long-range campaign to alter the European power balance. Thus Mussolini's first major initiative after taking over the Foreign Ministry was to call in March 1933 for a "Four Power Pact" between Britain, France, Italy, and Germany that would officially permit eventual arms parity for Germany and would arrange for mutual cooperation among all the signatories on major European and colonial problems. This was more a ploy designed to raise Italy to equal great-power status than anything else. France vehemently opposed the whole idea, and even Hitler approved of it only tepidly; his withdrawal from the League of Nations before the end of 1933 and his independent arms policy robbed it of substance. The pact was only signed after its provisions were gutted of any significance.[71]

Hitler's attitude toward Mussolini was completely positive and unambiguous, for ever since the writing of *Mein Kampf* he had looked upon the Fascist regime as his natural ally. Though he offered to Mussolini an alliance "to impose Fascism on the world," as the German emissary put it, the Duce was much more cool. Their first meeting, during Hitler's visit to Italy in the spring of 1934, did not go well. Hitler lectured Mussolini about all Mediterranean peoples being tainted with Negro blood, as well as other topics from his extensive repertoire. Soon after came the abortive coup of Austrian Nazis to take over the Austrian government in July. Mussolini had for several years sought

67. E. Gentile, "Impending Modernity: Fascism and the Ambivalent Image of the United States," *JCH* 28:1 (Jan. 1993): 7–29.

68. R. De Felice, *Hitler e Mussolini: I rapporti segreti (1922–1933)* (Florence, 1983).

69. This, together with Nazi and German rightist attitudes toward fascism, is treated in K.-P. Hoepke, *Die deutsche Rechte und der italienische Faschismus* (Düsseldorf, 1968).

70. The earliest comparative accounts, whether eulogistic or critical, saw numerous parallels between Fascism and National Socialism, accompanied by significant differences: G. Bortolotto, *Fascismo e nazionalsocialismo* (Bologna, 1933); E. Schrewe, *Faschismus und Nationalsozialismus* (Hamburg, 1934); and M. T. Florinsky, *Fascism and National Socialism* (New York, 1936).

71. K. H. Jarausch, *The Four Power Pact* (Madison, 1965).

to cultivate Austria as a client state and deemed it an important buffer against Germany. He responded immediately, sending six divisions to the Brenner Pass and taking a firm stand on behalf of Austrian independence. Once again Mussolini appeared to be acting as a good European citizen, maintaining the peaceful status quo.[72]

There had always been some criticism of Nazism in Fascist publications, and after July 1934 this became much stronger. Italian publicists stressed Fascism's respect for individual rights, in sharp contrast to National Socialism. Fascists accused Nazis of being too socialistic, too anti-individualistic, and too anti-Catholic. Copies of Nazi publications denouncing Italian Jews who were in some cases officers of the Fascist Party circulated in Italy, and there were no Nazis at the Fascist international conference at Montreux, none probably having been invited. Even extremist ultra-Fascists such as Roberto Farinacci and Giovanni Preziosi wrote that Nazism, with its parochial and exclusivist racism, was offensive to the conscience of mankind and would push Europe into communism. Mussolini derided the Nazi concept of race, claiming that Germans did not constitute any race at all but were a blend of at least six different peoples, while in some parts of Bavaria 7 percent of the population were feeble-minded.[73] An article that appeared in *Gerarchia* in May 1934 (probably written by Mussolini) declared that Nazi racism was opposed "yesterday to Christian civilization, today to Latin civilization, and tomorrow to the civilization of the entire world." At the last recorded meeting of the commission created at the Montreux conference, in April 1935, the formal declaration "rejected any materialistic concept which exalts the exclusive domination of one race above others."[74] Some Fascist publications referred to Hitler as "anti-Christ," while others (in reference to the Blood Purge of June 1934 which eliminated Ernst Roehm and several other notoriously homosexual leaders of the Nazi SA) derided National Socialism as "a political movement of pederasts." By July 1935 *Gerarchia* said that the real differences between Fascism and Nazism were now "profound and unambiguous."[75]

72. The best general treatment of Italian policy in the 1930s is R. Quartararo, *Roma tra Londra e Berlino: La politica estera fascista dal 1930 al 1940* (Rome, 1980). See also R. De Felice, ed., *L'Italia fra tedeschi e alleati: La politica estera fascista e la seconda guerra mondiale* (Bologna, 1973).

73. In December 1927, when he had called for better relations with France and "a vast Latin bloc" of France, Italy, Spain, and Portugal, Mussolini had stressed that the latter should be based on "civilization and culture," not "race." The latter was "too vague an entity in view of the many mixtures during the course of centuries." Quoted in R. Rainero, *La rivendicazione fascista sulla Tunisia* (Milan, 1978), 151, 163.

74. Ledeen, *Universal Fascism* 123–24.

75. These quotations are drawn from D. M. Smith, *Mussolini's Roman Empire* (New York, 1976), 44–58. Cf. also Mussolini's remarks about Hitler as quoted by his would-be Austrian counterpart, E. R. von Starhemberg, in *Between Hitler and Mussolini* (London, 1942), 164–68.

What Hitler did offer Mussolini was the beginning of profound destabilization of the European balance of power and the opportunity for a more militant policy. Though he still preferred to work with rather than against that European balance, Mussolini was determined to expand Italy's empire. The most fundamental reference in his political discourse was to the need for struggle.[76] He increasingly spoke of the need to prepare for war. By 1935 Mussolini was dominated by the psychology of *ducismo,* convinced that he was the only fully reliable and capable leader produced by Fascism and that he must first lead it to greater empire before the movement would ever be strong enough to create the true Fascist revolution and the new Italian man. Only this would make it possible to transform "a gesticulating, chattering, superficial, and carnivalesque country," as he once put it, into a new nation of warriors, of real Fascists.[77] This was the only path to completing the Fascist revolution.

Mussolini's ambitions were directed toward expansion in Africa, both because it was safer and because Ethiopia, which had humiliated Italy in 1896, remained independent—and thus potentially open for conquest. The most ruthless face of Fascism was shown much more openly abroad than in affairs at home. Italy's main colonial possession, Libya, had finally been pacified, but only at the cost of a ruthless military policy directed against the civilian population that between 1928 and 1932 may have taken the lives of as many as 60,000 of the 225,000 inhabitants of the Cyrenaica region.[78] Mussolini believed that the road to Addis Ababa had been partly cleared by old agreements of 1906 with Britain and France that had vaguely promised Italy the lion's share of any future partition. Given French interest in mobilizing Italian support against Germany, a Franco-Italian agreement of January 1935 agreed to support the status quo in Austria and the Balkans while making minor border concessions to Italy in Libya and Eritrea. Mussolini also agreed to progressive elimination of special Italian minority rights in Tunisia. He would also claim, even though it was not specified in the agreement, that he had received assurances from French foreign minister Pierre Laval that France would accept an expansive Italian policy in Ethiopia.

The casus belli for what became the invasion of Ethiopia was the Wal-Wal incident concerning disputed territory between Ethiopia and Italian Somaliland in December 1934. Italian preparations were developing slowly, and Mussolini still hoped to receive the approval of the two major western European powers.

76. E. J. Nelson, "To Ethiopia and Beyond: The Primacy of Struggle in Mussolini's Public Discourse," Ph.D. diss., University of Iowa, 1988.

77. Quoted in De Felice, *Mussolini il Duce* 1:48.

78. These figures are taken from G. Rochat, *Il colonialismo italiano* (Turin, 1974), 101, and J. L. Miège, *L'imperialismo coloniale italiano dal 1870 ai nostri giorni* (Milan, 1976), 189. On Italian policy and activities in Libya, see C. G. Segrè, *Fourth Shore: The Italian Colonization of Libya* (Chicago, 1974).

Meanwhile the three powers briefly formed the "Stresa Front" of May 1935, at a conference which announced their general agreement on maintaining the status quo in Europe. From the British and French point of view, this obtained Italian support for containing Hitler; from Mussolini's, it was a statement of European concord that left the door open for expansion in East Africa, though nothing specific was said about the latter. Britain then went ahead to negotiate its own separate naval agreement with Hitler and, when it appeared that Mussolini might indeed march into Ethiopia, offered the tasteless and absurd bribe of a very small piece of British Somaliland.[79]

Convinced that the time had come to strike, probably with impunity, the Duce refused all mediation, invading Ethiopia on October 3, 1935. This action involved nearly six hundred thousand troops and was publicized as the "greatest colonial war of all time." It was also the first aggressive act by any European state in more than a decade (with the partial exception of the Soviet incursion into Iran in 1929) and immediately provoked a major outcry. On October 7 the League of Nations branded Italy an aggressor and several days later voted economic sanctions. The earlier repression in Cyrenaica had generated little criticism, but now foreign opinion was aghast to see poison mustard gas repeatedly used from the air by Italian forces. The British and French governments made a more serious effort to reach agreement with Mussolini in December, offering a secret deal that would give Italy much of Ethiopia yet leave a rump Ethiopian state independent. Mussolini initially accepted it, but news about the agreement soon began to leak out, and adverse reaction from the Italian public helped to kill it—a unique case of Mussolini's being partly pushed by sectors of Italian opinion to go even further than he thought best. The Ethiopian forces, however, soon made the mistake of meeting the Italians head-on in direct large-scale battle. Modern military technology quickly won out, and the conquest of the main part of Ethiopia—though far from the whole country—was completed in May 1936. Only about one thousand Italian troops had died in combat.[80]

The war generated tremendous enthusiasm, as Italian troops shipped out bearing tiny vials of Italian earth to the massed applause of the general public. A huge propaganda effort paid off, Italian opinion generally seeing the Duce as having succeeded where his liberal successors tended to fail: Italy had

79. On the diplomatic background, see G. Baer, *The Coming of the Italo-Ethiopian War* (Cambridge, Mass., 1967); Shorrock, *From Ally to Enemy* 99–169; E. M. Robertson, *Mussolini as Empire-Builder: Europe and Africa, 1932–1936* (New York, 1977); and L. Noel, *Les illusions de Stresa: L'Italie abandonnée a Hitler* (Paris, 1975).

80. A. Mockler, *Haile Selassie's War: The Italian-Ethiopian Campaign, 1935–1941* (New York, 1985); A. Del Boca, *La guerra d'Abissinia, 1935–1941* (Milan, 1966); G. Rochat, *Militari e politici nella preparazione della campagna d'Etiopia, 1932–1936* (Milan, 1971); F. Catalano, *L'impresa etiopica e altri saggi* (Milan, 1965), 143–221.

won a sizable campaign on its own, and Mussolini had defied the League of Nations and the great powers, in the process gaining new status. By 1936 even clandestine Communist reports declared that the themes of nationalism and "proletarian war" employed by Fascism had moved the ordinary population, among whom there was "a vast mass of workers influenced by Fascism."[81] Communist leaders concluded that they must be careful not to offend patriotic sentiment, even to the point of accepting a certain amount of nationalism and being prepared to cooperate with pro-Fascist workers. Mussolini was elated with the outcome of his aggression and believed that it showed that Fascism had changed the character of Italians.

The Ethiopian war was thus more than the last European colonial campaign of conquest. It also marked a turning point in the history of Fascism, as Mussolini introduced a new domestic radicalization inside Italy. "Foreign adventure was also internal forward policy, not the mere 'social-imperialist' defense of order at home characteristic of more staid [right-wing] authoritarian regimes."[82] In 1936 Mussolini endeavored to make the state more authoritarian in practice by expanding its powers, believing that a more powerful state would accelerate the creation of a more Fascist nation.[83] Mussolini now thought increasingly of government by personal decision and central administration; seventy-two cabinet meetings had taken place in 1933, but only four occurred in 1936. He also seems to have given serious consideration to eliminating the monarchy and making himself chief of state, though for the time being he decided to await the death of the nearly seventy-year-old Victor Emmanuel.[84] Early in 1938, to the king's outrage, Mussolini named himself "First Marshal" of the empire, with rank in military affairs equal to or even greater than that of the king. He also began to interfere more overtly in the judicial system, though he did not carry this tendency too far.[85]

Though the power of the Fascist Party was not greatly expanded, the party was to become even more active in propaganda and pedagogy. The PNF secretary was raised to cabinet rank in February 1937, and later that year the regime introduced a new Ministry of Popular Culture (MinCulPop), partly in imitation

81. P. Spriano, *Storia del Partito Comunista Italiano* (Rome, 1979), 3:58, quoted in De Felice, *Mussolini il Duce* 1:71. See also P. G. Zunino, *Interpretazione e memoria del fascismo* (Bari, 1991), 97–100.

82. M. Knox, "Conquest, Foreign and Domestic, in Fascist Italy and Nazi Germany," *JMH* 56:1 (March 1984): 44.

83. In his *Analisi del totalitarismo* (Messina, 1976), Domenico Fisichella argues that "Fascism had a doctrine of the total state but not an ideology of a totalitarian regime" (210).

84. On relations between Duce and king, see D. M. Smith, *Italy and Its Monarchy* (New Haven, 1989), 244–305, and L. Argenteri, "Victor Emmanuel III: The Fusion of Monarchy with Fascism. Dyarchy or Deception?" Ph.D. diss., UCLA, 1989.

85. The best survey of Mussolini's new policies in 1936–38 can be found in De Felice, *Mussolini il Duce* vol. 2, *Lo Stato totalitario, 1936–1940* (Turin, 1981), 3–300.

Fascist *gerarchi* demonstrate their vigor by "running" to their assignments for the camera

of its Nazi counterpart. From that point censorship was tightened, though it still remained much lighter than in Germany. Most of the films of political propaganda were in fact produced in the years 1936–40, and youth propaganda was expanded.[86] Giuseppe Bottai returned to the cabinet as education minister and introduced a new Fascist Carta della Scuola (School Charter), the third and final Fascist educational reform. This one was intended to make Italian education more active and functional and to introduce new methods of instruction, but in fact it largely remained a dead letter because of the outbreak of broader war. The Fascist parliament was then reorganized for the last time in 1938, becoming the Chamber of Fasces and Corporations to demonstrate that it was

86. Cf. M. A. Saba, *Gioventù Italiana del Littorio: La stampa dei giovani nella guerra fascista* (Milan, 1973).

founded not merely on corporative institutions but on the Fascist Party itself.[87] The goal was to eliminate any residue of the old parliamentary system and to further strengthen the state. The concept of *Duce del fascismo* was thereby theoretically given a new power.

In economics Mussolini introduced the term *autarchy* in March 1936, meaning that the Italian economy was now to become as self-reliant as possible under the growing tutelage of the state. International sanctions due to the Ethiopian war in fact ended three months later, but autarchy became permanent policy. Market forces and foreign competition would be reduced, resulting in growing inflation and higher taxes, as the state increasingly intervened to promote the arms industry and related sectors and dominated more and more of the economy. Felice Guarneri, the bureaucrat who controlled raw material imports for the state, was made minister of foreign exchange in 1937. This new ministry extended further the network of regulation and control.[88] Mussolini even threatened momentarily in a speech of 1936 to have the corporations begin the nationalization of part of industry. What happened instead was that the IRI extended its powers further, dominating industrial finance and encouraging concentration and cartels. Though military spending actually declined slightly in 1937–38, total state spending increased, with large amounts invested in creating a new infrastructure in Ethiopia.[89]

The positive aspect was a rapid increase in industrial production, as its total value now clearly exceeded that of agriculture. The stimuli and concentration of resources in engineering, metallurgy, and chemistry created a much stronger industrial base, so that "the changes witnessed during the second half of the 1930s were undeniably responsible for the formation of that technical, geographical, and social order which was to enable the performance of the so-called 'economic miracle' and the definitive transformation of Italy into an industrialized country" after World War II.[90]

Nevertheless, the complex of policies that made up autarchy won much less than complete approval from Italy's economic and industrial elite, for it had brought increasing state control, Fascistization, and a foreign policy oriented toward military activism. As Renzo De Felice has written, the economic elite became increasingly alarmed because of "a) the Fascist state's tendency to interfere and expand its own control over economic activity; b) the Fascist elite's tendency to transform itself into an autonomous ruling class and gradu-

87. F. Perfetti, *La Camara dei Fasci e delle Corporazioni* (Rome, 1991).

88. L. Zani, *Fascismo, autarchia, comercio estero: Felice Guarneri, tecnocrata al servizio dello "Stato Nuovo"* (Bari, 1988).

89. A. Sbacchi, *La colonizzazione italiana in Etiopia, 1936–1940* (Bologna, 1980).

90. R. Petri, "Acqua contro carbone," *Italia contemporanea* 168 (1987): 63, quoted in Zamagni, *Economic History* 321.

ally to alter the balance of compromise to its advantage; c) Mussolini's foreign policy which became increasingly aggressive and therefore correspondingly less attuned to the true interests both of Italy and of the upper bourgeoisie itself." [91]

Moreover, autarchy produced a new emphasis on "worker Fascism," with an expansion in the role and activism of the worker syndicates.[92] There was an increase in worker fringe benefits (though not much increase in wages), and in 1939 the huge Dopolavoro recreation program was transferred from the party to the syndicates themselves. Several new forms of nominal representation were created, including in 1939 for the first time individual local *fiduciari di fabbrica* (a kind of limited shop steward). More and more graduates of the Fascist Youth were entering the syndicates, and the younger workers seemed more pro-Fascist than the older generation. A parallel innovation by Mussolini was the attempt to impose the informal *voi* rather than the more formal *Lei* for "you," announced as a means of bringing all Italians closer together and further weakening the old bourgeois mentality.

Autarchy also coincided with the finding of a nominal successor in the form of Mussolini's son-in-law Galeazzo Ciano, the husband of Edda, the Duce's favorite offspring. Son of a leading Fascist *gerarca* ("hierarch"), Ciano was a diplomat by profession and succeeded his father-in-law as foreign minister in 1936, soon occupying a more important place in Mussolini's counsels than any previous figure.[93]

The Ethiopian war had been over less than two months when a major revolutionary-counterrevolutionary civil war broke out in Spain on July 18, 1936, between the authoritarian right and the revolutionary left. Within a week Mussolini had decided to intervene on behalf of the right, for a leftist republic in Spain would present a major challenge to the Fascist scheme of *mare nostrum* (our sea) in the Mediterranean. Of all the dictators (Hitler, Stalin, Salazar) who intervened in the Spanish conflict, Mussolini became the most committed. At one brief point as many as seventy thousand Italian troops served in Spain, including a small Italian air corps and an artillery corps. Moreover, more of the matériel for Franco's victorious Nationalist army came from Italy than from any other source. Though Franco's slow, unimaginative strategy was often the despair of the Italian leaders, Mussolini backed him all the way, even engaging Italy's submarine fleet against Spanish Republican and Soviet shipping in

91. R. De Felice, *Le interpretazioni del fascismo*, rev. ed. (Bari, 1971), 268–69.
92. Sergio Panunzio, ever the most prolific national syndicalist theorist, now pressed the concept of new autonomous "parasyndical" entities in the economy. P. Pastori, "Sergio Panunzio fra cesura rivoluzionaria e riordinamento dei poteri del regime fascista," *Archivio Storico Italiano* 146:2 (1988): 281–309.
93. G. B. Guerri, *Galeazzo Ciano* (Milan, 1979).

the summer of 1937 to guarantee the turn of the tide in favor of Franco.[94] The Italian leader was rewarded with a complete rightist victory and a Nationalist regime under Franco that largely identified itself with a Fascist new order in European affairs.

It was the Spanish Civil War that first brought Mussolini and Hitler together. Germany had been the only European state to discreetly support Italy during the Ethiopian war, and on July 25–26 Hitler and Mussolini independently but simultaneously decided to intervene on the same side in Spain. This in turn led to a formal meeting between Hitler and Foreign Minister Ciano in October 1936, after which the formation of a "Rome-Berlin Axis" was announced. The Axis, however, was not an alliance but merely a joint understanding between the two governments to coordinate their policies in Spain and vis-à-vis the League of Nations.[95]

A second turning point occurred at the time of Mussolini's first visit to Germany, in November 1937. He was enormously impressed by the new German Wehrmacht, and his attitudes toward Hitler reflected an unstable combination of envy and fear. The Italian government signed an Anti-Comintern Pact with Germany, and Mussolini announced that the Mediterranean was the center of Italian policy. One month later, in December, he followed Hitler's lead in withdrawing from the League of Nations.

Mussolini had reached the conclusion that Germany was about to become the dominant power in Europe and hence that it was better for Italy to be aligned with it than opposed to it. This meant not merely further aggressive measures abroad but also a limited program of semi-Nazification at home, to establish greater symmetry between the two regimes and give Italy a more privileged place vis-à-vis Nazi racism. Early in 1938 the Prussian goose step was declared to have been the *passo romano* (Roman step) and was instituted for Italian parade drill, while the regime began to prepare a new doctrine of "Italian racism" and to institute discriminatory measures against Jews.

The latter was unprecedented, for three reasons. First, Italian nationalism had normally been more liberal in orientation than that of Germany. Italian Jewry was very small in numbers—about 47,000 people, or scarcely more than one-tenth of 1 percent of the population—and was thoroughly integrated in society, with one of the highest rates of mixed marriages of any Jewish group in the world. The Jewish minority was thoroughly identified with Italian

94. J. F. Coverdale, *Italian Intervention in the Spanish Civil War* (Princeton, 1975); I. Saz, *Mussolini contra la II República* (Valencia, 1986); *Italia y la guerra civil española* (Madrid, 1986); R. Quartararo, *Politica fascista nelle Baleari (1936–1939)* (Rome, 1977); W. Schieder and C. Dipper, eds., *Der spanische Bürgerkrieg in der internationalen Politik (1936–1939)* (Munich, 1976).

95. J. Petersen, *Hitler-Mussolini: Die Entstehung der Achse Berlin-Rom, 1933–1936* (Tübingen, 1973).

patriotism and had a remarkably distinguished military record in World War I.[96] Second, Mussolini himself had always derided Nazi mystical racism.[97] Third, the Fascist movement was itself disproportionately Jewish—that is, Jews made up a greater proportion of the party at all stages of its history than of the Italian population as a whole. Five of the 191 *sansepolcristi* who had founded the movement in 1919 had been Jewish, 230 Jewish Fascists had participated in the March on Rome, and by 1938 the party had 10,215 adult Jewish members.[98] Mussolini had had several Jewish collaborators, including his favorite and most influential mistress, Margherita Sarfatti. He had been officially blessed by the chief rabbi of Rome and had assisted in the early development of a Zionist navy as a maneuver against British imperialism. Costanzo Ciano, high Fascist *gerarca* and father-in-law of Mussolini's daughter, had even made a speech in 1929 saying that Italy needed more Jews. There were very few overt anti-Semites in the country, limited to a few publicists in the radical sector of the Fascist Party.

The first racial regulations under Fascism had been drawn up in 1936 with regard to Ethiopia; this was standard black-white racism, not the Nazi variety.[99] Mussolini in the past had not been known to say anything more against Jews than an occasional passing verbal slur (of the kind indeed that he made against virtually all groups), but he became convinced that widespread international disapproval of Italy's conquest of Ethiopia was at least partly due to the opposition of "international Jewry." Moreover, if there was a disproportionate number of Jews in the Fascist Party, he was also increasingly annoyed by the very active and prominent roles played by a number of Italian Jews in the political opposition. Thus he became convinced by the beginning of 1938 that an Italian racial policy would make Italy the equal of Germany and would form an important part of a totalitarian and more revolutionary policy against the bourgeoisie, fundamental to the creation of the Italian "new man."

In July 1938 the new Ministry of Popular Culture published a Manifesto of Italian Racism, and a law in September removed Jewish teachers and students from the school system (though all Jewish converts to Catholicism were

96. "Out of a community of only 40,000 (according to the 1911 census), over 1,000 received decorations; eleven rose to become generals. Of Italy's three university professors who fell in battle, two were Jewish and the third was a 'half-Jew.' " F. Eberstadt, "Reading Primo Levi," *Commentary* 80:4 (Oct. 1985): 41.

97. The key study of Mussolini's attitudes toward mystical racism and anti-Semitism is M. Michaelis, *Mussolini and the Jews* (Oxford, 1978).

98. See particularly R. De Felice, *Storia degli ebrei italiani sotto il fascismo* (Turin, 1988). "Adolf Dresler, the first Nazi biographer of Mussolini, . . . roundly denounced Fascism as a 'Jewish' movement, utterly dissimilar to anti-Jewish Hitlerism." Michaelis, *Mussolini* 37.

99. L. Preti, *Impero fascista, africani ed ebrei* (Milan, 1968); L. Goglia, "Note sul razzismo coloniale fascista," *SC* 19:6 (1988): 1223–66.

Hitler greeted by Mussolini on his arrival in Italy, May 5, 1938

241

exempted), with separate Jewish schools to be established. The Fascist Grand Council expelled Jews from the party the following month and outlawed mixed marriages for party members. A purge then removed Jews from all major institutions, while the government decreed that they could no longer own land or businesses with more than one hundred employees. A subsequent Law for the Defense of the Race forbade all mixed marriages in Italy, though there were various exclusions from these rulings for Jewish war veterans, founding members of the party, and children from mixed marriages who did not themselves practice Judaism.

Since Mussolini's regime never approached the incredible extremes of Hitler's anti-Jewish policies, it has sometimes been supposed that its own anti-Jewish legislation was largely a halfhearted self-defensive measure to protect Fascists from Nazis and to win a higher place in the European new order. Such motivations doubtless existed, but Mussolini had become personally committed to an Italian Fascist racism, insisting correctly that he had been using the term *race* (albeit vaguely) since 1921. Thus the Manifesto of Italian Racism emphasized that all races had a biological foundation, though it differed from Nazi pronouncements in defining the Italian race as a product of several earlier ethnic and biological groups, the result of many centuries of history, culture, and environment. Thus the manifesto posited a kind of "bioenvironmental racism." [100] Elaborate criteria were set forth in the Italian legislation to determine who was and was not a Jew, but in contrast to Nazi Germany, in Italy only two ultimate categories were created. Thus under certain circumstances citizens with only one Jewish parent might qualify as "non-Jews," though in a few subcategories the definition of "Jew" was even more restrictive than in Germany.[101] Yet perhaps even more important was the fact that the anti-Semitic policies were badly received by Italian citizens and even within the Fascist Party, for the sudden propaganda campaign against Jews had comparatively little effect, and even some party leaders considered it servile kowtowing to Nazi practice.

By 1938 Mussolini was becoming increasingly isolated, victim of his own *ducismo*. His son-in-law Ciano had now become a second center of power, particularly in key aspects of foreign policy, as with Spain. Mussolini had cast his fortunes with a more aggressive policy both at home and abroad, yet he had no desire to participate in a major war, for which Italy was too weak. Thus he took the final key initiative in arranging the Munich conference at the close of September 1938 that kept the peace in Europe. This momentarily restored

---

100. The best account is in Gregor, *Ideology of Fascism* 241–82.

101. Michele Sarfatti, *Mussolini contro gli ebrei* (Milan, 1994), is an important revisionist study which emphasizes the seriousness of Mussolini's intentions and the relative rigor of the new policy.

his personal popularity with Italian public opinion, which had been slipping in recent months.

Public opinion and political support, however, no longer had the same importance in Mussolini's thinking as they did during the first decade of the regime. He seems to have failed to notice the lack of response to more militant Fascist propaganda and the new emphasis on war, that the birthrate—despite Fascist policy—continued to decline, or that Italians were not responding to the campaign to use *voi*. Younger Fascists grew more restive with anti-Semitism and pseudo-Nazification. The increasing military activism was disconcerting and indeed frightening to millions of Italians, while conservatives had become increasingly skeptical. Huge amounts of money were being diverted to the development of Ethiopia, but by 1940 only 305,000 Italians lived in Africa, compared with 500,000 in the city of New York. Another conflict with Catholic Action took place in 1938, settled by another compromise, demonstrating once more that the state—though constantly growing in power and intervention—had not become truly totalitarian. There was no particular increase in political opposition; the Special Tribunal convicted only 310 people of political offenses in 1938 and 365 in 1939, down from the level, for example, of 519 in 1931.[102] What was developing instead was a growing uneasiness and a kind of internal psychological distancing from the radicalization of Fascism. If the regime were to enjoy continued success in foreign and military affairs and in economic growth, this psychological malaise might well be overcome; if not, it would continue to grow.[103]

By 1939 Mussolini's main concern, paradoxically, was Hitler. The Duce had acquiesced in the German annexation of Austria the preceding year but was outraged by Hitler's abrupt dismemberment and seizure of Czechoslovakia without consultation or compensation for Italy, grumbling, "Every time Hitler occupies a country, he sends me a telegram." The Italian response, particularly as conceived by Ciano, was the formal occupation of Albania (for years a quasiprotectorate) the following month. Mussolini was tempted to revert to his old anti-Nazi stance but convinced himself that to renounce an aggressive policy now, along lines parallel with Hitler's, would be equivalent to turning his back on the whole revolutionary project of Fascism and the totalitarian state, the same as giving in to the hated peace-loving Italian bourgeoisie. Thus when he and Hitler met in May 1939, Mussolini insisted on going beyond Hitler's suggestion of a formal diplomatic alliance, asking instead for a complete military alliance that could be called the "Pact of Blood." This was more

102. De Felice, *Mussolini il Duce* 2:45–46.

103. See the discussion in A. J. De Grand, "Cracks in the Façade: The Failure of Fascist Totalitarianism in Italy, 1935–9," *European History Quarterly* 21:4 (Oct. 1991): 515–35, and L. Passerini, *Fascism in Popular Memory* (Cambridge, 1987).

than Hitler had asked for, since technically it bound Italy to go to war whenever Germany did, and he changed the name to the less melodramatic "Pact
of Steel." Bernardo Attolico, the Italian ambassador in Berlin, was thoroughly
disgusted with Mussolini's performance and privately likened it to a man who,
when asked to throw himself out a window, insists on rushing to the top of
the building and throwing himself off the roof. Mussolini was motivated above
all by the concern to make Italy the complete equal of Germany and also to
have his regime recognized as a reliable ally, not the semiturncoat that liberal
Italy had been in 1914–15. Moreover, the German officials assured their Italian
counterparts that the full development of the German armed forces would not
be completed for four more years (which was technically correct), and Mussolini also calculated that as full ally he would better be able to restrain Hitler
from premature adventurism.[104] At any rate, the die now was cast.

104. M. Toscano, *The Origins of the Pact of Steel* (Baltimore, 1967).

8

Four Major Variants of Fascism

Before World War II, only two fascist-type movements were able to come to power, and these two were the only ones to create historically significant fascist regimes. Though the radicalizing impact of the depression, combined with the influence of Nazi Germany, gave major impetus to fascist movements in a number of countries, only a few managed to attract significant support, and even in these cases none were capable of taking power independently. Nonetheless, the cases of Austria, Spain, Hungary, and Romania merit special attention, for these were the only other countries in which fascist-type movements came to play an important role, however briefly.

AUSTRIA

Austria presented perhaps the clearest case in Europe of the three faces of authoritarian nationalism: two moderate right authoritarian sectors (the large Christian Social Party and the smaller pan-German groups); a more radical, more overtly authoritarian, and violent rightist sector, led by the Heimwehr; and revolutionary fascist-type nationalists in the form of the Austrian Nazis.

The first fifteen years of the Austrian Republic were dominated by the political Catholicism of the Christian Social Party and by its principal adversary, the Socialists or Social Democrats. Both originally stood for the unification of Austria with Germany, but this was forbidden by the peace treaty, and during the first years they collaborated uneasily in constructing a new parliamentary regime in what remained of Austrian territory, beset by manifold problems of economic adjustment. The Socialists retained the support of the bulk of Austrian labor and blocked the path of communism, but their commitment to democracy was less than complete. They looked to the triumph

245

of socialism and the supersession of the present system, through a process which a few of the more radical still referred to as a dictatorship of the proletariat. Similarly, the Christian Socials—who before the war had been led by the popular anti-Semitic demagogue Karl Lueger—were also less than fully committed to democracy. Led by Dr. Ignaz Seipel (a priest and theology professor), they governed in coalition with other small parties for most of the 1920s but talked of "true democracy" as distinct from the present parliamentary system and tended to lean toward its replacement by a corporative regime, should circumstances permit.[1]

The most significant group espousing authoritarian activism was the Heimwehr—the "home guard" that was the largest of several paramilitary civilian forces created in 1919–20 to protect Austria's frontiers in a moment of great flux and secondarily to protect conservative interests from Marxism. The Heimwehr was to some extent the counterpart of the German Freikorps, and like the latter, it was committed to nationalism, paramilitary activism, and opposition to the left.[2] The Heimwehr never achieved tight organizational unity or a very specific ideology. Like the Austrian right in general, the Heimwehr had its social basis mainly in the small towns and countryside.

Conflict between the right and the Socialists first peaked in 1927, enabling the Heimwehr to gain recruits as an alternative to the party system. Its members enjoyed support from the Hugenburg sector of the DNVP and the Stahlhelm in Germany and, more important, financial assistance from Mussolini (channeled at first through the conservative Hungarian government, another patron).

At the same time, generic fascism was developing in the form of Austrian Nazism, hardly surprising in view of the fact that German-speaking national socialism had originated in greater Austria in 1903–4. Though the main support of the original German Workers Party (DAP) came from the Sudetenland in Bohemia-Moravia (after 1918 the new state of Czechoslovakia), there were also smaller sections in the territory of the postwar Austrian Republic. In 1918, shortly before the end of the war, the DAP in Austria changed its name to DNSAP (German National Socialist Workers Party), presaging the ultimate title of Hitler's party and also preceding it in the creation of a swastika flag and in coining the slogan *Gemeinnutz geht vor Eigennutz* (The common good before the individual good). Initially most of the DNSAP's membership lay in Czechoslovakia, and it won only 0.79 percent of the vote in the first Austrian

1. Klemens von Klemperer's biography *Ignaz Seipel* (Princeton, 1972) is reasonably favorable to Seipel. For the broader political context, see W. B. Simon, *Oesterreich, 1918–1938: Ideologien und Politik* (Vienna, 1984).

2. H. G. W. Nusser, *Konservative Wehrverbände in Bayern, Preussen und Oesterreich, 1918–1933* (Munich, 1973), is the principal comparative study. F. L. Carsten, in *Fascist Movements in Austria from Schönerer to Hitler* (London, 1977), presents an overview of all the right radical and national socialist groups in Austria.

elections of 1919. A series of conferences of the German-speaking national socialists from Austria, Germany, Czechoslovakia, and Polish Silesia began that same year, occasionally attended by Hitler himself. The DNSAP, however, combined its anti-Semitism with a semidemocratic political orientation (like the original DAP) and a more directly socialist approach to economic issues, including demands for the nationalization of larger properties. After a few years, therefore, the international conferences were discontinued, and by 1926 a split developed within the Austrian DNSAP between the older, more socialist and worker-oriented members and the radical youth, who were attracted by Hitler's violence and extremism in Germany. The latter seceded, setting up their own Austrian section of the German NSDAP, while the leaders of the Austrian party denounced German Nazis as "not really true national socialists at all, but reactionary fascists using national Bolshevik methods." [3] Down to its demise in 1935, the DNSAP never became a fascist organization, rejecting Italian Fascism, for example, as reactionary, authoritarian, and capitalistic. It retained a genuine worker orientation together with a degree of intraparty democracy but remained nothing more than a marginal little group.

In Austria as in Germany, the first opportunity for the regular Nazis came with the depression, but in the Austrian elections of 1930 the right radical Heimwehr more than doubled the 3 percent vote registered by the Nazis. By this point an effort was being made to give the Heimwehr some organizational coherence and an ideology. The doctrines of Othmar Spann, the chief Austrian ideologist of corporatism, were propagated, and on May 18, 1930, the main Heimwehr leaders took the so-called Korneuburg Oath to transform Austria's government into an authoritarian corporative system.[4] Even this was not clear-cut fascism, and it led to a new split in the movement between protofascist radicals and more moderate Catholics, papered over by the selection of a new national leader, E. R. von Starhemberg, who had been dealing directly with Mussolini but soon became lukewarm about the Korneuburg Oath. During 1931 the Heimwehr entered a process of partial disintegration. One radical section attempted an abortive putsch.[5] Some units began to go over to the Nazis, but most clung to a steadily amorphous if authoritarian conservatism.[6]

3. B. F. Pauley, *Hitler and the Forgotten Nazis: A History of Austrian National Socialism* (Chapel Hill, 1981), 169.

4. On Spann, see M. Schneller, *Zwischen Romantik und Faschismus: Der Beitrag Othmar Spanns zum Konservatismus der Weimarer Republik* (Stuttgart, 1970), and J. J. Haag, "Othmar Spann and the Politics of Totality," Ph.D. diss., Rice University, 1969.

5. Josef Hoffmann, *Der Pfrimer-Putsch* (Vienna, 1965).

6. On the Heimwehr, see W. Wiltschegg, *Die Heimwehr* (Munich, 1985), which also provides a brief summary of the other rightist paramilitary units; C. E. Edmondson, *The Heimwehr and Austrian Politics, 1918–1936* (Athens, Ga., 1978); and Carsten, *Fascist Movements*. For a brief discussion of the Heimwehr's failure to approximate the full characteristics of a fascist movement,

Individual leaders or publicists did sometimes use the term *fascist* to refer to their movement, but one small breakaway group that formed a little "Party of Austrian Fascists" soon disappeared.

By this time there were as many different kinds of political militias in Austria (especially in proportion to population) as anywhere in Europe. In addition to the Nazis, the Heimwehr, and various other rightist groups, the Socialists (like their counterparts elsewhere in central and southern Europe) had long had their own, and in 1931 the Christian Socials began to form their own *Sturmscharen* (stormtrooper) militia.

The Austrian Nazis made their first impressive showing in partial municipal and regional elections in the spring of 1932, gaining 16.4 percent of the votes cast (compared with 18.3 percent for the German Nazis in the German national elections of 1930) and drawing support away from all the major sectors, but particularly from the right. Austrian Nazism gained votes especially from sectors of the urban middle and lower middle class, but in a country where 90 percent of the electorate already voted, there was no reserve of unmobilized voters to organize as in Germany.[7]

At this juncture a government was formed in May 1932 by the new Christian Social leader Engelbert Dollfuss. At thirty-nine years of age and four feet eleven inches in height, he was both the youngest and the shortest head of government in Europe, a self-made man of modest origins who provided determined direction in a period of crisis. Neither of the two major parties commanded an absolute majority, but the Christian Socials were normally able to form a coalition with the small Pan-German Party. The latter, however, refused to join the new government because Dollfuss had negotiated a vital foreign loan on the basis of renouncing *Anschluss,* or union, with Germany for another ten years. The Socialists, as usual, refused to join with the Christian Socials, and Dollfuss was therefore able to achieve the barest majority only by bringing the Heimwehr into his government.

During the year that followed, political fragmentation only increased. After a temporary crisis brought the resignation of the chief officers of the Austrian parliament in March 1933, Dollfuss assumed full power, setting up a de facto dictatorship based on the Christian Socials and the Heimwehr. Two

see Wiltschegg 267–70. R. Griffin, in *The Nature of Fascism* (London, 1991), 125, observes, "That the bulk of the Heimwehr stopped short of full-blown fascism was clear." The most profascist sector, which eventually allied firmly with the Nazis, is treated in B. F. Pauley, *Hahnenschwanz und Hakenkreuz: Steirischer Heimatschutz und österreichischer Nationalsozialismus, 1918–1934* (Vienna, 1972). Jill Lewis, in *Fascism and the Working Class in Austria, 1918–1934* (New York, 1991), studies, inter alia, the numerous workers in Styria attracted to the Heimwehr.

7. G. Botz, "The Changing Patterns of Social Support for Austrian National Socialism (1918–1945)," in *Who Were the Fascists?: Social Roots of European Fascism,* ed. S. U. Larsen, B. Hagtvet, and J. P. Myklebust (Bergen, 1980), 202–25.

months later he announced formation of a Fatherland Front, a new government-based political group inspired by the state political organizations that had been formed from the top downward by the mild Spanish and Polish authoritarian governments of the mid-1920s (Primo de Rivera and Pilsudski). Mussolini was willing to serve as the regime's protector, both because at that time he wanted to preserve Austria as a bulwark against German expansion and because he hoped to encourage its conversion into a kind of satellite fascist state. Both the Nazi and the Socialist Parties, the main internal enemies of the new regime, were outlawed. The Socialists eventually responded with an abortive revolt in February 1934 that was easily crushed, leaving Dollfuss in full control.

Though both Dollfuss and the Heimwehr leader Starhemberg had promised Mussolini late in 1933 that they would move toward "fascism," the Austrian regime developed a different profile. A new constitution introduced on May 1, 1934, was the second corporatist constitution to appear in Europe (following the new Portuguese charter of the year before). It replaced the parliament with an elaborate system of four advisory councils (the Council of State, a Provincial Council, a Cultural Council, and an Economic Council composed of seven different economic corporations—all to be chosen by corporative procedures, rather than by direct suffrage), and these in turn would select a federal diet of fifty-nine members with the right to approve (but not initiate) legislation. This represented among other things an attempt to realize the Catholic ideals of the recent papal encyclical *Quadragesimo Anno* (1931), which endorsed corporative forms of organization and representation for Catholic society. The only recognized political association was the Fatherland Front, which was supposed to support the state but not be a state party in either the German or the Italian sense. It eventually reached a nominal membership of three million. Moreover, Dollfuss renounced any interest in *Anschluss* with Germany so long as Hitler remained in power, and he sought to create a positive sense of independent Austrian identity. He strongly emphasized the Catholic and Western values of his government as distinct from pagan and racist Nazi Germany, declaring that the true repository of German culture had now become Austria.[8]

After the defeat of the Socialists, the regime's chief antagonists were the Austrian Nazis, who launched a campaign of terrorism designed to cripple the economy and the tourist trade. The conflict reached its climax in an attempted coup by the Austrian Nazis on July 25, 1934, which produced sporadic fighting and the murder of Dollfuss. It ended with the total suppression of the rebels, the

8. The main biography is Gordon Brooke-Shepherd's *Dollfuss* (London, 1961), which is favorable to Dollfuss, as is G.-K. Kindermann, *Hitler's Defeat in Austria, 1933–1934: Europe's First Containment of Nazi Expansionism* (Boulder, 1988). On his regime's relation with the Catholic Church, see L. S. Gelott, *The Catholic Church and the Authoritarian Regime in Austria, 1933–1938* (New York, 1990).

death by combat or execution of 153 Austrian Nazis, and the flight to Germany of many leaders and activists.[9]

Thus in Austria, unlike in Germany, the nonfascist forces of the right were able to organize a preemptive authoritarian government of their own, barring the Nazis' path to power, due above all to the broad (though not majoritarian) support for the Christian Socials and the determined leadership of the martyred Dollfuss. Similar situations were also developing in parts of southern and eastern Europe, where right-wing regimes would also block the path of fascist movements.

Dollfuss was succeeded by his chief lieutenant, the university professor Kurt von Schuschnigg. Starhemberg, head of the Heimwehr, served as vice-chancellor during 1933–34 but grew increasingly critical of Schuschnigg's moderation and antifascism. In 1936 he was forced out of the Austrian government altogether, and the Heimwehr was dissolved by government order. Most of the leaders of the Austrian regime were comparatively sincere Catholics who rejected religious persecution, racism, and active anti-Semitism. The new constitution guaranteed the civic equality of all citizens, though denying them the right to form independent political parties. Although unofficial discrimination against Jews continued, many Austrian Jews (most notably, Sigmund Freud) supported the Dollfuss-Schuschnigg regime as a civilized bulwark against Nazism.[10]

The system did undergo a limited process of external fascistization, acquiring some of the outer trappings of fascism common to most other dictatorships in the 1930s. The Fatherland Front created a Frontmiliz in 1936 to replace the Heimwehr and other rightist paramilitary groups. In mid-1937 a special elite body, the Sturmkorps, was organized (adopting much the same name as the Assault Guards police force formed by the democratic new Spanish Republic in 1931). Members of the Sturmkorps wore dark blue uniforms and adopted the motto *Unser Wille werde Gesetz* (Our will becomes law), obvi-

---

9. Before 1934 there had been less political violence in Austria than in Germany, with the sole exception of the flare-up in 1927 mentioned above. With the rise of Austrian Nazism in 1932, political violence increased. This claimed a total of 104 victims in 1932 (of whom 42 percent were Nazis and 22 percent were Socialists) and 69 in 1933 (of whom 38 percent were from the Heimwehr or other rightist groups and 32 percent were Nazis), but few of these were actually killed. In the abortive Socialist revolt of February 12, 1934, and the attempted Nazi coup which followed in July, a total of 567 people were killed. Of these, 35 percent were Socialists, and 25 percent were Nazis. See G. Botz, *Gewalt in der Politik: Attentate, Zusammenstösse, Putschversuche, Unruhen in Österreich, 1918–1934* (Munich, 1976), and idem, "Political Violence in the First Austrian Republic," in *Social Protest, Violence and Terror in Nineteenth- and Twentieth-Century Europe*, ed. W. Mommsen and G. Hirschfeld (New York, 1982), 300–329.

10. Cf. B. F. Pauley, *From Prejudice to Persecution: A History of Austrian Anti-Semitism* (Chapel Hill, 1992), 260–73.

ously in an effort to provide a sort of alternative to the SS. In the style of all the new dictatorships, a youth movement and a variety of national social organizations were formed, but the regime consciously sought to achieve the style and structure of the conservative Catholic corporative authoritarian system— like that of Portugal—rather than the German or Italian systems. The distinct doctrines and goals of fascism were eschewed, for there was no intention of forming a revolutionary "new man" distinct from the patriotic Catholic Austrian, and gratuitous violence, militarism, and any aggressive foreign policy were categorically rejected.[11]

At the time of the abortive Austro-Nazi coup in 1934, Mussolini had rushed six Italian divisions to the Brenner Pass to guarantee Austrian independence, but the formation of the Rome-Berlin Axis in 1936 removed that protection. Hitler had renounced any claim to the German-speaking minority in northeastern Italy, and in turn Mussolini withdrew his objection to German incorporation of Austria. A new agreement between Vienna and Berlin in 1936 restored normal relations between Germany and Austria and withdrew the legal ban on the Austrian Nazis.

Austrian Nazism had developed more slowly than its German counterpart, probably due to the more conservative and Catholic character of Austrian society outside Vienna. The best indication is that if parliamentary elections had continued to be held, the Nazis would have drawn the support of about 25 percent of the electorate in 1934. This was less than the German party before Hitler's takeover but would still have made the Austrian movement the second most popular of its type (with more support, for example, than the Italian Fascists obtained in the elections of 1921). Austrian Nazism developed on the basis of much the same social support as its counterpart in Germany, with nearly as high a percentage of blue-collar support.[12] After the dissolution of the Socialist Party early in 1934, many members of the Socialist militia passed over to the Nazis, and even more from the Heimwahr joined the Nazis after its dissolution two years later. Perhaps the most unique feature of Austrian Nazism was the existence of a small cadre of "National Catholic" intellectuals such as Arthur

11. U. Kluge, *Der oesterreichische Ständestaat, 1934–1938* (Munich, 1984), treats the state system.

12. According to one sample, the proportion of unskilled workers in the Austrian NSDAP (27 percent) in 1934 was higher than the membership in either the Socialist (19.8 percent) or Communist (22.5 percent) Parties. P. H. Merkl, "Comparing Fascist Movements," in Larsen, Hagtvet, and Myklebust, eds., *Who Were the Fascists?* 767. Total membership of the Austrian Nazi Party on the eve of *Anschluss* was 147,000 (proportionately even greater than that of the German party when Hitler took power). G. Botz, "The Changing Patterns of Social Support for Austrian National Socialism (1918–1945)," in Larsen, Hagtvet, and Myklebust 210–15. Merkl raises this figure even higher, to 177,000.

Seyss-Inquart, who tried to reconcile Catholicism and an autonomous Austrian identity with Nazism. After 1938 they were largely brushed aside.[13]

Despite their growing strength, the Austrian Nazis (like the German Nazis before them in 1923) demonstrated once more that European fascist movements lacked the ability to carry out coups d'état, much less to launch civil wars, against institutionalized political systems, as certain Communist movements would later do amid more disturbed conditions elsewhere. Paradoxically, fascist movements required political freedom to have a chance to win power. Once this was barred by a preemptive nonfascist authoritarian regime, as in Austria and various countries of eastern and southern Europe, they could only come to power (like Communists in eastern Europe after 1945) through outside military intervention. In Austria this occurred with Hitler's sudden invasion in March 1938. Under those circumstances, however, Austria was directly incorporated into the greater Third Reich, and the Austrian National Socialists—though proportionately one of the largest fascist-type movements in Europe—became little more than a provincial branch of German Nazism.[14]

SPAIN

Spain retained a reputation for fascist politics longer than probably any other country in the world, yet categoric fascism was slow to develop there and for some years remained very weak. Spain may in many ways be usefully compared with Italy, the two countries having shown more similarity during the modern period than any other two large European countries. At the same time, there were important differences. Economic development accelerated more rapidly in Italy from the 1890s on, so that after World War I Italy was a full generation ahead of Spain. Second, both political nationalism generally and the structure and power of the state were stronger in Italy as well. Finally, the process of democratization and dictatorship in Spain developed in two distinct phases, unlike the situation in Italy.

For most of the modern period, nationalism has been weaker in Spain than in any other large European country. Among the principal factors responsible, the following may be considered:

13. W. Rosar, *Deutsche Gemeinschaft: Seyss-Inquart und der Anschluss* (Vienna, 1971). Most of the "National Catholics" apparently did not join the party, at least before 1938. On the Austrian Nazi underground, see H. Walser, *Die illegale NSDAP in Tirol und Vorarlberg, 1933–1938* (Vienna, 1983).

14. G. Botz, *Nationalsozialismus in Wien: Machtübernahme und Herrschaftssicherung, 1938/39* (Obermayer, 1988). Radomir Luza, however, argues that under the Reich Austrian Nazis at least enjoyed a degree of recognition and autonomy at the Austrian provincial level. Luza, *Austro-German Relations in the Anschluss Era* (Princeton, 1975), 319–20.

1. Spain has been independent since approximately the eleventh century, and it achieved the first true world empire in human history, long maintaining the status of an established power.
2. The traditional Spanish monarchy was confederal in structure and never created fully centralized institutions (with partial exceptions in the eighteenth century).
3. Culture and tradition in Spain were identified with religion more exclusively than in many other lands, creating a climate of national Catholicism that would long resist modern secularization.
4. No genuine foreign threat to Spanish security emerged after the defeat of Napoleon.
5. Similarly, because of its geographic location and limited external ambitions, the country avoided involvement in the major wars of the twentieth century.
6. Classical liberalism dominated Spanish political life for most of the nineteenth and early twentieth centuries, discouraging military and aggressive ambitions.
7. Before the First World War, the pace of economic and social modernization was slow. This made it possible to sustain an early nineteenth-century model of elitist liberalism without serious pressure from below until the 1930s. Similarly, cultural life was dominated by the values and attitudes either of nineteenth-century liberalism or of traditional Catholicism, discouraging the introduction or diffusion of new doctrines or philosophies except in the working-class subculture. Thus in Spain expressions of both the early twentieth-century nationalist new right and of generic fascism were at first weaker than elsewhere in southern and eastern Europe.

Thus in early twentieth-century Spain, *nationalism* did not refer to Spanish nationalism so much as to the "peripheral nationalisms" of the Catalans and Basques. The senior of these movements was Catalan nationalism, which had become the dominant force in industrial Catalonia before World War I. Catalan nationalism was not, however, merely centrifugal but sought in its originally conservative and bourgeois form to cooperate in a kind of "federal imperialism" for a modern "Great Spain." Conservative Catalanism pursued such a project from 1916 to 1930 and only relinquished the goal after Catalanism itself had fragmented, with predominance after 1930 passing to the Catalanist left.[15]

In the early twentieth century, Barcelona, not Madrid, was the center of cultural modernism and technological modernization in Spain. The first marginal efforts to form authoritarian nationalist and profascist groups, sometimes

15. This may be followed in part through the career of the great leader of moderate Catalanism, Francesc Cambó. See J. Pabón, *Cambó*, 3 vols. (Barcelona, 1952–69).

in imitation of Mussolini, therefore took place in the Catalan capital.[16] Similarly, the cultural avant-garde of Barcelona was the first to applaud Italian Futurist avant-garde Fascism, just as the first expression of avant-garde cultural fascism in Madrid after 1926 was also partially oriented toward Catalonia.[17]

In Spain as a whole, political change and democratization proceeded in two phases, the first coinciding with the shift to the left occurring in most countries by World War I and lasting from 1917 to 1923. It produced fragmentation and paralysis, being unable to break the grip of the established oligarchy, and was terminated by the seven-year dictatorship of General Miguel Primo de Rivera from 1923 to 1930. The first Spanish dictatorship failed completely, however, for lack of clear doctrines and the failure to introduce any new institutions. Its collapse soon brought down the Spanish monarchy as well, leading to the inauguration of Spain's Second Republic in April 1931.

The Spanish Republic was the only new regime in Europe to move against the tide of authoritarian and fascist politics during the 1930s. Its leaders were well aware of this fact and hoped to establish their own countertrend in Spain. The republic was governed at first by an alliance of middle-class Republicans and reformist Socialists, and it introduced a series of major institutional and socioeconomic reforms between 1931 and 1933, some well conceived and effective, others—like the separation of church and state that soon turned into an effort to persecute the Catholic Church—counterproductive. The reaction to this took the form of a new authoritarian right and victory for the center and right in the second republican elections of 1933. A large sector of the Socialists, disillusioned with the pace of democratic reformism, turned to revolutionary "Bolshevization," as they termed it, and an abortive revolutionary insurrection took place in October 1934 in which more than a thousand people were killed. The right then proceeded to reverse some of the earlier reforms, but in the elections of February 1936 a "Popular Front" of the more left-wing Republicans and most of the worker parties won a clear victory. From that point Spain entered what many historians have called a prerevolutionary situation, with increasing disorder, street violence, strikes, and destruction or occupation of property. This was the background to the civil war that began in July 1936.[18]

16. This refers to such ephemeral groups as the Liga Patriótica Española (1919), La Traza (1923), La Peña Ibérica, and the first expression of the Albiñana organization, which later became the tiny Spanish Nationalist Party in 1930. J. del Castillo and S. Alvarez, *Barcelona, objetivo cubierto* (Barcelona, 1958); C. M. Winston, *Workers and the Right in Spain, 1900–1936* (Princeton, 1985).

17. E. Ucelay da Cal, "Vanguardia, fascismo y la interacción entre nacionalismo español y catalán," in *Los nacionalismos en la España de la II República*, ed. J. Beramendi and R. Maíz (Madrid, 1991), 39–95.

18. See my study *Spain's First Democracy: The Second Republic, 1931–1936* (Madison, 1993).

Under the Second Republic all three variants of authoritarian nationalism—conservative, right radical, and fascist—took clear form. Moderate, technically legalistic, corporative authoritarianism in Spain emerged as mass political Catholicism in the CEDA (Spanish Confederation of Autonomous Rightist Groups), which flourished briefly as the country's largest single political party between 1933 and 1936, before being totally eclipsed by the Civil War. The ultimate goals of the CEDA were always vague. Though it was committed to legal, nonviolent parliamentary tactics in practice, the CEDA's cherished aim of constitutional revision seemed to point toward a more authoritarian and corporative Catholic republic. Like all but the most moderate and liberal groups in Spain, the CEDA organized its own youth movement and shirt formation. After 1933 the latter (JAP) underwent a certain vertigo of fascistization, like so many other right nationalist groups elsewhere, but the ambivalence of the JAP and the entire CEDA was symbolized by the half-fascist salute that was officially adopted—raising the right arm only halfway and bending it at the elbow back across the chest.[19]

The radical right in Spain comprised two different sectors: the neotraditionalists of a revitalized Carlism (the Traditionalist Communion, CT) and the more modernist Alfonsine monarchists (supporters of the former king). By the early 1930s Carlist doctrine, influenced by Catholic corporatist theories, presented a program of corporatist neotraditionalist monarchism that eschewed extreme statism and tried to clearly differentiate Carlism from fascist radicalism and dictatorship.[20] The outbreak of Republican and leftist anticlericalism provoked a sudden upsurge of Carlist support, and yet neotraditionalism could never directly rally more than 3 or 4 percent of Spain's population.

The neoauthoritarian *alfonsino* monarchists were in part an offshoot of the activist right wing of the old monarchist Conservative Party, their evolution being similar to that of part of the historic Destra of conservative liberalism in Italy. Only after the triumph of Republican radicalism did the Spanish monarchists turn to overt authoritarianism, under the twin influences of Action Française and the right (Rocco/Nationalist) wing of Italian Fascism. For several years their journal, *Acción Española*, patterned after *Action Française*,

19. The chief general account of the Spanish right under the republic is R. A. H. Robinson, *The Origins of Franco's Spain* (London, 1970); and of the CEDA, J. L. Montero, *La CEDA*, 2 vols. (Madrid, 1977). See also the shorter studies in J. Tusell et al., eds., *Estudios sobre la derecha española contemporánea* (Madrid, 1993), 395–447. There is an important memoir by the top CEDA leader, J. M. Gil Robles, *No fue posible la paz* (Barcelona, 1968). The ideas of the leading Spanish Catholic theorist of corporatism may be found in J. Azpiazu, S.J., *The Corporate State* (St. Louis, 1951).

20. There is an excellent study by Martin Blinkhorn, *Carlism and Crisis in Spain, 1931–1939* (Cambridge, Mass., 1975). See especially the chapter "Carlism and Fascism" 163–82.

elaborated an intellectual and theoretical basis for authoritarian neomonarchist government.[21]

The main spokesman of Spain's radical right was José Calvo Sotelo, a former Conservative and former finance minister under Primo de Rivera, who was not converted to clear-cut authoritarianism until his Parisian exile during 1931–32. Winning a seat in parliament in the 1933 elections enabled him to return to Spain, where he became the key leader of the small monarchist Spanish Renovation Party and organized a broader right nationalist grouping, the National Bloc, in 1934–35. During the final weeks before the Civil War he became the main spokesman for the rightist opposition in parliament, and his murder by leftist police agents became the signal for the start of the war.

In Spain as in Italy, the underlying doctrine and structure for institutionalized authoritarian government stemmed not from radical fascism but from the more right-wing authoritarianism. Calvo Sotelo proposed not the restoration but the "installation" (*instauración*) of an authoritarian new monarchy, whose reign would have to be preceded by an indeterminate period of dictatorship. He understood clearly that this was unlikely to come about through political mobilization but would probably require forcible intervention by the military. Parliament would have to be replaced by an indirect corporate chamber representing social and economic interests, and a strong government would then be in a position to stimulate the economy through state regulation and reflationary policies.

Calvo Sotelo admired Italian Fascism, attempted to join the Falange in Madrid in 1934, and did not object if critics referred to his goals as fascist. But his project was much nearer to Alfredo Rocco or Charles Maurras than to Mussolini, Panunzio, or the Spanish Falangists. He had no interest in promoting a revolutionary mass party or demagogic national syndicalism, and he preferred to rely on traditional elites rather than a new nationalist militia. Though he had been liquidated by the time the Civil War began, the somewhat vague blueprint outlined by Calvo Sotelo and the *Acción Española* ideologues more nearly approximated the structure and policies of the subsequent Franco regime than the revolutionary "national syndicalist state" posited by the fascistic Falangists.[22]

More categorically fascist politics were introduced in Spain in several stages, all unsuccessful, before the outbreak of the Civil War in 1936. The initial champion of the fascist idea was the avant-garde aesthete Ernesto Giménez Caballero ("the Spanish D'Annunzio"), who publicly announced his fascism in 1929 and was soon almost completely ostracized by the predominantly liberal

---

21. R. Morodo, *Orígenes ideológicas del franquismo: Acción Española* (Madrid, 1985), is a thorough ideological study.

22. J. Gil Pecharromán, *Conservadores subversivos: La derecha autoritaria alfonsina (1913–1936)* (Madrid, 1994), provides an excellent account of the evolution of the new monarchist radical right.

Ramiro Ledesma Ramos

Spanish cultural establishment, becoming what he himself called "a literary Robinson Crusoe." Giménez Caballero's fascism was derived directly from Rome (his wife was Italian) and was unusual in being avowedly international in scope and structure. He predicated fascism on Latin Catholic culture and saw it as the main hope for cultural renewal of the heartlands of historic Latin Christendom. By the same token, Giménez Caballero's fascism was opposed to the Protestant north and to Nazism (at one point he saw war between fascism and Nazism as inevitable).[23]

Giménez Caballero was not a political organizer, however, and the first fascist political grouping in Spain was created by Ramiro Ledesma Ramos, an underemployed university graduate who had specialized in mathematics and philosophy. Here again the inspiration was primarily Italian, his little band being named Juntas de Ofensiva Nacional-Sindicalista (rather equivalent to Fasci Italiani di Combattimento) and its weekly publication *La Conquista del Estado* (The Conquest of the State, also the title of a sometime publication directed by the leading Italian Fascist writer, Curzio Malaparte). Yet though Ledesma drew his inspiration from Italy (and also partly from Germany: he temporarily affected a Hitlerian hairstyle), he soon became keenly aware of the need to avoid, or at least to avoid the appearance of, imitating Italian Fascism or other foreign movements. The official program of the JONS, aiming at a "national syndicalist state," might be read as a carbon copy of the ideas and goals of Italian Fascism, yet Ledesma preferred not to use the label, realizing that it was counterproductive in the generally left liberal Spanish atmosphere.[24]

The JONS remained totally isolated at the small-sect level. Relying mainly on university and secondary students, the group was a typical product of radical intelligentsia politics. During its two and a half years of independent existence (1931–34), the JONS failed to have the slightest impact on Spanish affairs.

A more vigorous, better-financed attempt at a Spanish fascism was essayed by sectors of the right in 1933.[25] The triumph of Hitler stimulated interest in

23. D. W. Foard, *The Revolt of the Aesthetes: Ernesto Giménez Caballero and the Origins of Spanish Fascism* (New York, 1989).

24. As the organizational—and to a large degree ideological—founder of Spanish fascism, Ledesma has been the subject of two full-length biographies, both entitled *Ramiro Ledesma Ramos*. The first, by Tomás Borrás (Madrid, 1972), is descriptive, superficial, and hagiograhic. The second, by José M. Sánchez Diana (Madrid, 1975), has somewhat greater analytic depth.

25. For taxonomic purposes, it might be pointed out that a tiny right radical Spanish Nationalist Party had been organized by a physician named Albiñana in 1930. Albiñana early adopted more than a few of the trappings of fascism, stressing imperial expansion on the one hand and a broad, economically reformist state syndicalism on the other. He organized his own minuscule "Legion" for street battle and at one point apparently hoped to develop a mass movement. After 1933 he dropped his most fascistic overtones in favor of a more orthodox and conservative right radicalism. The only pertinent study is in M. Pastor, *Los orígenes del fascismo en España* (Madrid, 1975), 38–61.

José Antonio Primo de Rivera

Spain also, not so much among potential fascists—of whom there seemed to be few in the peninsula—but among right radicals or potential right radicals, who were distinctly more numerous. Basque financiers went shopping during the summer of 1933 for the leader of a potential counterrevolutionary, demagogic Spanish fascism. Though they provided a trickle of support to Ledesma and the JONS, the latter were deemed to be both too radical and too unimportant to merit major support.

The main leader of a would-be Spanish fascism who came to the fore in the summer and autumn of 1933 was José Antonio Primo de Rivera, eldest son of the late dictator. He first evolved from conservative authoritarian monarchism to a more radical brand of nationalist authoritarianism that was not entirely unlike Calvo Sotelo's new ideas. By 1933 the younger Primo de Rivera—soon to be known generally as José Antonio—had become interested in something rather like fascism (Italian style) as the vehicle for giving form and ideological content to the national authoritarian regime attempted so uncertainly and un- successfully by his father. Unlike Ledesma, who had greater initial experience

Funeral of a slain Falangist law student in Madrid, February 1934

and insight in such matters, José Antonio was not averse to using the label *fascist,* though the new movement that he founded with a group of colleagues in October 1933 was eventually called by the more original title of Falange Española (Spanish Phalanx).

The Falange began with much more financial support from big business prone to the radical right than had the JONS, prompting the JONS to merge with it in early 1934 (the resulting organization was called Falange Española de las JONS). During the next two years, and indeed all the way down to the beginning of the Civil War, the Falange was distinguished primarily by its insignificance. Like the Romanian Iron Guard, it relied at first on its student clientele, but unlike the Romanian movement, it completely failed to generate any broader lower- or middle-class support.

This period in the wilderness did, however, give the movement's leaders some time to reflect on what they were about. After a year or so, José Antonio Primo de Rivera began to move "left," as the national syndicalism of the Falangists took on more socially radical overtones. There was a somewhat belated reaction to the danger of mimesis, and before the close of 1934 most Falangists were denying that they were fascists. By 1935 the criticism of Italian corporatism as too conservative and capitalistic, a criticism fairly common among the more radical types of fascists and Nazis abroad, was being echoed by some Falangist leaders, including Primo de Rivera.

It was all somewhat bewildering to Italian Fascists. During the "universal fascism" phase of the mid-1930s, the Italian taxonomists somewhat inconclusively decided that Falangists were indeed fascists because of their belief in "authority, hierarchy, order" and their antimaterialist Falangist "mysticism."[26] José Antonio, for his part, recognized that all the "nationalist renewal" movements opposing Marxism, liberalism, and the old conservatism had some things in common but also exhibited pronounced national differences. The Spanish right having ceased to support a more radical fascism, the Falange figured on the foreign payroll of the Italian regime for approximately nine months in 1935–36.[27]

Unlike many other fascist movements, the Falange did develop an official program, the Twenty-seven Points, before the close of 1934. These exhibited all the main points of fascist doctrine and in the economic sphere called for the development of a complete national syndicalist state. Though most property was to remain in private hands, banking and credit facilities were to be nationalized, and large landed estates expropriated and divided. Despite Falangist criticism of the inadequacies of Italian corporatism, however, no detailed blueprint of the "national syndicalist state" was ever developed.[28]

That Falangism exhibited certain distinct characteristics of its own is undeniable, but these did not prevent it from sharing nearly all the general qualities and characteristics that would compose an inventory of generic fascism. As hypernationalists, all fascist groups by definition revealed certain distinct national traits. In the Spanish case, Falangism differed somewhat from Italian Fascism in its basic Catholic religious (if politically anticlerical) identity, for this was central to Falangism and only marginal to Fascism (even if it was stressed during the Fascist–National Socialist polemics of 1933–34). The Falangists' concept of the "new man" thus incorporated nearly all the qualities of the traditional Catholic hero, while fusing them with twentieth-century components. Yet this distinction still seems relative rather than absolute. One

26. M. A. Ledeen, *Universal Fascism* (New York, 1972), 100, 110–11.

27. J. F. Coverdale, *Italian Intervention in the Spanish Civil War* (Princeton, 1975), 50–64.

28. The most lengthy attempt to elaborate this program was José Luis de Arrese's *La revolucíon social del nacionalsindicalismo* (Madrid, 1940), which was either suppressed or confiscated by police in 1936 and appeared only in 1940 after the Civil War. The "social revolution" of national syndicalism consisted of an assortment of limited proposals, such as for profit sharing, vague workers' councils in factories, a family wage, restoration of municipal patrimonies for communal support, and the aforementioned nationalization of banking and credit. In general this did not go as far toward "semisocialism" as the original proposals of German National Socialists and Italian national syndicalists.

Falangist leaders José Antonio Primo de Rivera, Julio Ruiz de Alda, and Ramiro Ledesma Ramos leading a demonstration in the center of Madrid against the leftist revolutionary insurrection of October 1934

other presumably fascist movement, the Romanian Iron Guard, was considerably more thoroughgoing and fanatical in its religious identity, and Boleslaw Piasecki's Polish Falanga, whose name was derivative, was also more extreme and pronounced in its Catholicism.[29]

José Antonio Primo de Rivera remained a highly ambivalent figure, perhaps the most ambiguous of all European national fascist leaders. Major personal characteristics—such as a fastidious aestheticism combined with a genuine if sometimes contradictory sense of moral scruple, a cultivated intellectual sense of distance and irony, and, for a Spanish politician, a remarkably limited spirit of sectarianism and group rivalry—may have disqualified him for successful leadership. There is abundant testimony that he considered abandoning

29. The principal studies of Falangist doctrine are J. Jiménez Campos, *El fascismo en la crisis de la Segunda República española* (Madrid, 1979), and B. Nellessen, *Die verbotene Revolution* (Hamburg, 1963).

the project at several points but could not escape the commitment imposed by the deaths and sacrifices of other members of the movement.

Of all national fascist leaders, he was probably the most repelled by the brutality and violence associated with the fascist enterprise. He stopped using the term *fascist* before the end of 1934 and the term *totalitarian* before the end of 1935. He would occasionally refer to rightist conspirators as "fascist windbags" (*fascistas llenos de viento*). Yet however diffident and differential his approach may have been, he never renounced the fascist goals in politics. In the postfascist era his admirers have made much of José Antonio's "humanism," his opposition to total dictatorship, his stress on the individual personality and "man as the bearer of eternal values," and his Catholicism.[30] Yet in the Joseantonian formulation these do not necessarily contradict fascism; fairly similar formulations might be found by some nominally leading members of the PNF.

Large sectors of the Spanish right were becoming "fascistized," as Ledesma aptly put it, in one or more superficial senses, but the erstwhile fascist movement itself was worse than anemic. Antifascism had been strong among the left from 1932 on, but it was precisely the leftists who registered, as Ledesma commented ironically, the only truly "fascist" activity in Spain in violence and direct action. Malaparte's *Technique of the Coup d'Etat* exerted its main influence during 1931–33 on the direct-action proponents of Spanish anarchism (FAI), who engaged in various abortive insurrections.[31] In its first phases, Falangism seemed so fastidious, rhetorical, and averse to direct action that rightist critics labeled it "franciscanism" rather than fascism. After Ledesma broke with Primo de Rivera and the Falange, the question mark that he placed in the title of his memoir *Fascismo en España?* seemed fully appropriate. In the final elections of 1936 the Falange registered only forty-four thousand votes in all Spain, about 0.7 percent of all ballots cast, revealing fascism as weaker in Spain than in any other large continental European country.

The profound debility of fascism, so long as the regular Spanish political system existed, had several causes. The absence of any strong sense of Spanish nationalism deprived fascism of that key rallying point. In Spain mobilized nationalism was inverted: it was expressed through the intense "peripheral nationalism" of Catalans and Basques, directed against the unified Spanish nation-state. Another key factor was the limited secularization of rural and provincial society in much of Spain, particularly in the north. There, as in Slovakia and Austria, the most obvious and attractive cross-class alternative

30. The most systematic study of the Falangist leader's political thought is N. Meuser, "Nation, Staat und Politik bei José Antonio Primo de Rivera," Ph.D. diss., University of Mainz, 1993. In Spanish, see A. Muñoz Alonso, *Un pensador para un pueblo* (Madrid, 1969). Cf. C. de Miguel Medina, *La personalidad religiosa de José Antonio* (Madrid, 1975).

31. Cf. F. Miró, *Cataluña, los trabajadores y el problema de las nacionalidades* (Mexico City, 1967), 54–55.

to liberal or leftist politics was political Catholicism. Moreover, the nominal electoral success of the CEDA from 1933 down to early 1936 gave this tactic the appearance of victory. Fascism enjoyed much less cultural reinforcement in Spain than in central Europe, for the cultural and intellectual revolution of the 1890s had achieved less resonance in the peninsula. There was a rightist Catholic culture of considerable force, but not a secular-vitalist-Darwinist cultural environment of any vigor. Finally, as far as political revolutionism was concerned, the left seemed able to enforce a monopoly of its several brands; it enjoyed greater political success and support in Spain than in any other country in the world during the 1930s. There remained less of an outlet for fascism as the consummation of a frustrated, deviant revolution there than in central Europe.

The fascist movement in Spain could not immediately profit from the breakdown of the Spanish polity, because one of the last effective legal measures taken by the Republican government in the spring of 1936 was the suppression of the Falange. Though disillusioned rightists—primarily the young —began to flock to the clandestine, partially disarticulated movement, the collapse of political order erased the very concept of political victory in the Italian or German senses, and even Falangists had never seen that as a practical possibility.

Civil war produced a polarized revolutionary-counterrevolutionary conflict in which leadership passed completely into the hands of the insurgent Nationalist military who created the Franco regime. Growth of Falangist membership to several hundred thousand during the first year of the Civil War was not in itself decisive, for death in battle and execution had decapitated the movement, while military dictatorship in the Nationalist zone totally subordinated it.

The subsequent decision by Franco to take over the movement in April 1937 and create a syncretic, heterogeneous state party on the basis of Falangism was fully logical and practical. From the moment that he became dictator on October 1, 1936, he was concerned to avoid what he termed the "Primo de Rivera error," that is, the failure to transcend a Latin American–style personal military dictatorship without doctrine or structure. By that time most continental European states were in the process of converting themselves into syncretic national authoritarian systems, some of them following the Italian example of creating a state party and introducing corporative economic regulations.

The entity that Franco elevated into *partido único* in April 1937 was not, however, integral Falangism but a union of Falangists, Carlists, and all other members of various rightist and other groups who were willing to join. Though the Falangist program—now the Twenty-six Points—was raised to official state doctrine, Franco specifically announced that this was to be understood merely

Franco addressing a large political audience in Madrid soon after the Civil War

as a point of departure and would be modified or elaborated depending upon future requirements.[32]

For the next decade and more the Franquist state was normally taken, outside Spain, to be a "fascist regime." It is doubtful, however, than one can speak of a fascist regime unless it is dominated and constructed by generic or categorical fascists, and this was hardly the case with Franquism. Core Falangists, the *camisas viejas* (lit., "old shirts"), played only a small role in the new state and held only a small minority of positions in the new system. They did not even control all of the administration of the new state party, the Falange Española Tradicionalista. Addition of the last adjective, reflecting the nominal fusion with the Carlists, underscored the major right-wing limitations to the fascism of the new regime. That early Franquism contained a major component of fascism is undeniable, but it was so restricted within a right-wing, praetorian, Catholic, and semipluralist structure that the category of "semifascist" would probably be more accurate.[33]

Of course, the same adjective might be applied not inaccurately to Mussolini's Italy, and the similarities between that regime and early Franquism are greater than is sometimes thought. Both used subordinated state fascist parties that were merged with and subsequently incorporated unindoctrinated nonfascist elements. Both permitted limited pluralism in national society and institutions under executive dictatorship. In neither case was the institutionalization of the regime developed primarily by revolutionary fascist ideologues, but more commonly by monarchist theoreticians of the radical right, together with fascistic moderates. Though Franco enjoyed much more complete executive authority than did Mussolini, he eventually converted the juridical form of his regime into that of monarchy, retaining the powers of regent for life. In both cases the challenge of militant fascist national syndicalism was soon faced and thoroughly subordinated (the *sbloccamento* of Rossoni's national syndicates in 1928; the suppression of Salvador Merino's attempt at a more integral and autonomous national syndicalism in 1940).

The sequences of development of the two regimes were also somewhat parallel, finally diverging radically at the level of foreign policy. In both cases, an early coalition phase without official institutional structure (Italy, 1922–25; Spain, 1936–37) was followed by an institutionalization phase (Italy, 1925–29; Spain, 1937–45) succeeded by a period of equilibrium. That is of course a fairly common pattern for new systems. Foreign policy and international con-

32. J. Tusell, *Franco en la guerra civil* (Madrid, 1992); P. Preston, *Franco* (London, 1993), 248–74.

33. Mihaly Vajda concluded that the Franco regime could not be considered fascist "since it did not come to power as a mass movement applying pseudo-revolutionary tactics but as an open adversary of revolutionary power, a counter-revolution." Vajda, *Fascism as a Mass Movement* (London, 1976), 14.

text marked the sharpest points of divergence, for the ultimate structu
Franco regime was largely dependent on world affairs. Whereas Musso
to play a major independent role from 1933 on, Franco had no illusions that he
need not wait on events. Had Hitler won the war, there seems little doubt that
Franquism would have become less conservative and rightist and more radical
and overtly fascist in form. Acceptance of the term *fascist* was fairly common
though never official during the first year of the Civil War, and Franco employed the term *totalitarian* in several of his early speeches. All the trappings of
"Franco! Franco! Franco!" in the early years were simply imitations of Italian
Fascism (or occasionally National Socialism), as were numerous agencies and
institutions of the party and regime, such as the Directorate of Popular Culture
(MinCulPop) or the Auxilio de Invierno (Winterhilfe).

Nonetheless, there was always strong antifascist opinion among various
rightist and Catholic sectors of the regime. As a result of this, but above all
as a result of international events, the regime began to move in the opposite
direction, starting as early as 1942. The doctrine of *caudillaje,* the Spanish
equivalent of *ducismo* and the *Führerprinzip,* had always been more restrained
than its counterparts in Italy or Germany. Even before the tide turned in Russia,
a major theoretical article by a Falangist leader distinguishing the Spanish state
from the totalitarian regimes had gone to press. By 1943 this notion became
a general trend, so that when World War II ended, Spain was well into the
process of transition from a partially mobilized, semifascist state to a Catholic,
corporative, and increasingly demobilized authoritarian regime.

HUNGARY

Of all states in interwar Europe, Hungary probably took the prize for the largest
assortment per capita of fascist-type, semifascist, or right radical movements.
As explained in chapter 5, Hungary was probably the most nationally aggrieved
state in all Europe because of its territorial and demographic losses following
World War I. Second, it had been the second country to be governed briefly by
a revolutionary Communist dictatorship, the Bela Kun regime of 1919. Third,
compared with the limited development of its social structure, it had a large
unemployed or underemployed national bureaucratic middle class, heavily recruited for such politics. Amputation of so much Hungarian territory resulted
in a large influx of educated middle class and lower gentry from the lost provinces. Partly to accommodate them, rump Hungary retained the same size civil
service as the prewar empire, but with much less money, generating miser-
able salaries and great discontent. Fourth, Hungarian culture participated in
many of the same intellectual and literary processes that emphasized radical
nationalism and *völkisch* culture in the German-speaking world.

Fifth, after 1918 anti-Semitism emerged as a significant political force for the first time in modern Hungary. The first anti-Semitic political party had been organized in 1883 but had enjoyed even less electoral support than its abortive German counterparts. The shrinkage of Hungarian territory had the effect of increasing the proportionate size of the Jewish population of 473,000 by approximately one percentage point, to about 5.9 percent of the total population, making Hungary's Jews the second largest Jewish minority in the world. More significant than general numbers, however, was the success of Jewish men in the professions. This led to great resentment, particularly in the middle classes, and the rise of a new concept of "Christian nationalism." As early as 1920 a *numerus clausus* was introduced to restrict the number of Jews in higher education and the bureaucracy: whereas up to this time about 50 percent of the physicians in Hungary were Jewish, during the next generation new Jewish physicians would number only 13 percent.[34] The comparatively large number of Jewish Communist and Socialist leaders in the 1919 revolution provided further fuel for anti-Semitic propaganda.

Finally, government and politics were dominated by the "reactionary liberalism" or moderate rightist authoritarianism of the Horthy regime, as established by the counterrevolution of 1919. This system permitted limited pluralism and representation but generally repressed the left, creating a situation that in turn opened the field to more radical social agitation by national socialists and other right radicals, who enjoyed a greater degree of tolerance. Though the first efforts by the military-based "Szeged fascists" and others failed during the 1920s, the depression decade would open new opportunities, encouraged both by foreign example and the deepening frustrations of Hungarian society.

Thus by the 1930s four different sectors of antiliberal nationalism might be found: the old conservatives of the National Union or Government Party, led by Count Istvan Bethlen, who were based socially in the upper class and believed in the existing elitist parliamentary system, led by their own hegemonic but not dictatorial party; the new right radicals, led by Major Gyula Gömbös and later by Bela Imredy, who espoused some of the trappings of fascism but in fact sought a right radical authoritarian system based on the bureaucracy and army, with a single state party; the more socially radical and fully fascistic imitators of German National Socialism, who formed more than half a dozen

---

34. See R. Fischer, *Entwicksstufen des Antisemitismus in Ungarn, 1867–1939* (Munich, 1988); and I. Deak, "The Peculiarities of Hungarian Fascism," in *The Holocaust in Hungary*, ed. R. L. Braham and B. Vago (New York, 1985), 43–51.

On right radical politics in the Hungarian professions, see the work of Maria Kovacs: *The Politics of the Legal Profession in Interwar Hungary* (New York, 1987); "Luttes professionelles et antisemitisme: Chronique de la montée du fascisme dans le corps medical hongrois, 1920–1944," *Actes de la Recherche en Sciences Sociales* 56 (March 1985): 31–44; and "The Ideology of Illiberalism in the Professions: Leftist and Rightist Radicalism among Hungarian Doctors, Lawyers and Engineers, 1918–1945," *European History Quarterly* 21:2 (April 1991): 185–208.

small national socialist parties; and the main Hungarian expression of fascism, Ferenc Szalasi's Hungarist or Arrow Cross movement, momentarily the most popular force in the country by 1939.[35]

The right radicals first flourished between 1919 and 1922, then declined. The more extreme right radicals were influenced by Italian Fascism and by Nazism as well and became known as Szeged fascists, from the city where the counterrevolution had been organized in 1919. Their leader was an army staff officer, Gyula Gömbös, but amid the stability of the later 1920s he seemed to moderate his views and, when Admiral Horthy offered him the Defense Ministry in a new cabinet in 1929, Gömbös dissolved the Party of Racial Defense, the main political organization of the Szeged fascists.

The impact of the depression on Hungary was severe, eventually causing Horthy to look beyond the moderate conservatism of the past decade and seek a stronger leader. He therefore gave Gömbös the premiership in October 1932 but required him to renounce anti-Semitism publicly, which Gömbös did in order to gain power. In his opening radio speech, he announced that he sought "to transform the soul of the whole nation." [36] Then he immediately made an official visit to Italy, establishing a pro-Italian tilt for the remainder of his administration. Gömbös also took control of the main Government Party, changing its name to Party of National Unity and extending its organizational structure throughout the country. He also created a youth organization and a new cadre of Advance Guards, a sort of political militia with sixty thousand members. Gömbös placed some twenty-five top appointees in the main army commands and also made many new high-level appointments in the other ministries. He was moving the Unity Party and the state administration in the direction of right radicalism and even Szeged fascism, and he won the usual governmental victory in the elections of the spring of 1935. Social reform was a major plank, the government establishing the eight-hour day and the forty-eight-hour workweek in industry, though its land reform legislation proved to be modest.

After Hitler came to power in 1933, Nazi influence quickly increased. Gömbös traveled to Berlin within a month, apparently hoping to develop a friendly revisionist network of Rome, Budapest, Vienna, and Berlin. Hitler responded that Austria would soon disappear, as would Czechoslovakia, but that Hungary might be permitted to reacquire Slovakia. Subsequent economic agreements tied Hungary closely to Germany, making it possible to expand

35. This typology modifies but does not contradict the one presented in M. Szöllösi-Janze, *Die Pfeilkreuzlerbewegung in Ungarn* (Munich, 1989), 101. This is the key study of the Arrow Cross and also provides the most up-to-date bibliography on Hungarian fascism (9–16).

36. Quoted in C. A. Macartney, *October Fifteenth: A History of Modern Hungary, 1929–1945* (Edinburgh, 1957), 1:116. This is the principal political history of Hungary in the 1930s in a Western language.

economic activity once more, but further increasing German influence. During 1934 Gömbös apparently began to plan the introduction of a corporative system in Hungary, and in the following year he told Göring that within three years Hungary would be reorganized into a national socialist state, though just how fascist his goals were is not clear. Gömbös had built a position of some strength for himself politically, but it all came to naught when he died of a sudden illness before the close of 1936.

During the depression new fascist-type political organizations, often bearing the name "national socialist," proliferated in Hungary. One tiny National Socialist Party had already been organized during the 1920s. In 1931 Zoltan Böszörmeny founded a National Socialist Party of Work, known as the Scythe Cross, from its emblem. It sought to introduce the original Nazi social program into Hungary but made a special appeal to landless farmworkers, who were numerous in some areas. During 1933 three new national socialist parties were organized. Zoltan Mesko (formerly of the Smallholders Party) set up the Hungarian National Socialist Agricultural Laborers and Workers Party, which, despite its name, seems to have drawn most of its support from the rural middle classes. Within months it fused with the original National Socialist Party that had been founded in the previous decade and adopted its emblems of the green shirt and arrow cross. Meanwhile, Count Sandor Festetics created a Hungarian National Socialist People's Party, which took over most of the original Nazi Twenty-five Points, and before the end of the year another aristocrat, Count Fidel Palffy, formed yet another National Socialist Party, which adopted both the swastika and the program of the NSDAP and endeavored to create a miniature SA and SS. Both of these sections were immediately banned by the government, but Palffy's group seemed to rouse a certain amount of support in western Hungary. At the beginning of 1934 Mesko, Palffy, and Festetics formed a joint "directorium" of national socialists, with a general agreement to adopt the green shirt and arrow cross as common emblems. By June, however, Mesko and Palffy expelled Festetics for allegedly being soft on Jews. The latter then joined yet another Hungarian National Socialist Party organized in Debrecen by I. Balogh. Festetics and Balogh both got themselves elected to the parliament in 1935, though later Festetics found himself expelled the second time by his erstwhile partners. Assimilated German-Hungarians, or "Swabians," were prominent in most of these groups, and the general Nazi influence was obvious.

The two most socially radical leaders were Böszörmeny and Mesko, and Mesko was the only one to make an effort to distance himself from Nazism. Mesko and Palffy reorganized their groups as a single National Socialist Party of Hungary, but in September 1935 Palffy (having earlier expelled Festetics) now managed to expel Mesko and take over the organization for himself. Mesko then reestablished his old Hungarian National Socialist Agricultural Laborers and Workers Party. The only one of these little organizations to make any particular move on the national scene was Böszörmeny's Scythe Cross, which, with its erstwhile farm laborers orientation, selected May Day of 1936 for an attempted insurrection. This immediately fizzled. The leader fled abroad, and eighty-seven of his followers were subsequently convicted and sentenced to jail.

The only significant Hungarian fascist movement was not one of the above, but rather the Arrow Cross or Hungarist organization founded by Ferenc Szalasi. The first major study of the Arrow Cross in a Western language argued, to some extent convincingly, that Szalasi's movement and program could not be merely assimilated to any preexisting foreign model.[37] Szalasi was born in 1897, descended from an Armenian named Salosian who had immigrated into Hungarian Transylvania in the eighteenth century. His father, born of an Austro-German mother, had in turn married a Slovak-Hungarian woman, so that Szalasi, like Codreanu in neighboring Romania and numerous other extreme nationalists, was far from a full-blooded offspring of the group he championed. Compared with Hitler, Mussolini, or a number of other fascist leaders, Szalasi was a man of limited talents, skilled neither as an orator nor as a journalist. He was, rather, a virtual sleepwalker and intense ideologue for whom a rather mystical ideology was at least as important as it was for Hitler. A general staff officer in the Hungarian military, Szalasi seems to have developed his concept of "Hungarism" about 1931. This aimed at the creation of a Carpathian-Danubian Great Fatherland, which in turn would be divided into Magyar-land (that of Hungarians proper), Slovak-land, Ruthene-land, Croat-land, Slovene-land, and the Western March (Austrian Burgenland). This quasifederal state would be ruled by Hungarians, who were of a distinct race and enjoyed superior leadership and governing abilities, with Magyar as the official language, but there was to be no oppression or coercion. Except in areas of mixed population, the other peoples would enjoy autonomy in districts where a single ethnic group constituted 80–90 percent of the population. This scheme of "unity in diversity" he termed "conationalism" (*konnacionalizmus* in Magyar). It was to serve as a "compression model" for all peoples, in contrast to the typical imperial expansion model. Szalasi liked to distinguish between nationalism and chauvinism, declaring that Hungarism was nationalist but never chauvinist.

Such a design of cooperative hegemony would require a great leader to carry it out, and from this stemmed his mystical conviction that he was the chosen leader for Hungary and that Hungary was in turn the chosen leader for all of southeastern (and eastern) Europe, destined indeed to show the way to the future for the entire world. His ideal might require a great war to realize—hence the importance of rearmament and cultivating all the martial values—but

---

37. N. M. Nagy-Talavera, *The Green Shirts and the Others* (Stanford, 1970).

such a war would be a utopian cataclysm, a true war to end all wars because it would introduce the new millenarian world order to be led by Hungarism. Conversely, if Hungarism failed, an even worse and more destructive war would be inevitable, and its victors—most likely Communists—would impose their own unjust and amoral peace.

The Carpathian-Danubian Great Fatherland could thus become one of the three leaders of the new Europe and the world, along with Nazi Germany and Fascist Italy. While a classical expansion-model empire was approved for Italy, operating on the southern fringes of Europe and in Africa, this would not be acceptable for Germany. Szalasi was firm in insisting that Germans must renounce excessive ambition and accept their national zone in central Europe, though it was typical of Szalasi that he provided no indication of just how Hitler was to be persuaded of this. The unique vocation of "Turanian" (Turkic) Hungary was its capacity for mediating and uniting both east and west, Europe and Asia, the Christian Balkans and the Muslim Middle East, and from this stemmed its ultimate vocation to lead the world order through culture and example, a task that neither Italy nor Germany was prepared to accomplish. Contacts were later established with the Romanian Legion of the Archangel Michael, and Szalasi explicitly accepted an independent Romania on the border of the Great Fatherland, with Transylvania to be an autonomous region within the latter (something that his Romanian counterparts would never have accepted).

In his subsequent book *Ut es cel* (The Path and the Goal), Szalasi explained that the three great positive ideologies of the twentieth century were Christianity, Marxism, and Hungarism. The first was the highest spiritual religion but not a political creed, while the second ended in materialist reductionism; Hungarism would combine the best of both Christianity and socialism in an enlightened national socialism that could be applied to political and social affairs. Szalasi was himself a practicing Catholic and wavered between a religious and a racial basis for Hungarism. Hungarism aspired, he said, to "true Christianity," and all citizens of the Carpathian-Danubian Great Fatherland would be required to be a member of one of the three "received" churches (Catholic, Protestant, or Orthodox). Szalasi proclaimed himself not anti-Semitic but "a-Semitic"; Jews simply had no place in such a society. They would not be persecuted but would be required to emigrate.[38] Szalasi believed in the existence of a genuine Turanian-Hungarian race (to the extent that his followers went about collecting skull measurements) that was crucial for Hungarism.[39] Still, he rejected Nazi racial ideas as excessively "Jewish"—

38. Szalasi held that the Jews should be encouraged to set up their own prosperous, democratic state somewhere outside of Europe. Since Palestine seemed to be inhabited by Arabs, he thought that the interior of South America might be an appropriate site.
39. It was indeed argued in Szalasi's movement that Turanians constituted a pure and dis-

too much grounded in the idea of an exclusive chosen people or race and the creation of a special God or biological force to serve their own purposes. Given his critique of Nazism, it is not clear how he could ever expect Nazism and Hungarism to cooperate in leading the new Europe.

In economic policy, Hungarism stood for a national socialism to be organized through corporative institutions. It was partly based on the agrarian ideal, with the goal of dividing large estates among the landless laborers, though it was later decided that some large production units should be retained for efficiency of scale. Industrial development would also be required for a strong fatherland, in which workers were to enjoy a special place. Though the state should nationalize all credit, insurance, large cartels, war industry, and energy production, a national socialist economy was to be based on private property and a landowning peasantry and would be oriented more toward small private industrial firms, which Szalasi considered more creative, efficient, and humane.[40]

Szalasi's political writings soon caused trouble for him on the general staff, where by 1934 he was left without assignment. In the following year he organized a Party of the National Will just in time for the parliamentary elections, but only one candidate was successful. His was the first new national socialist party to concentrate primarily on urban areas, but Szalasi quickly became dissatisfied with it and distanced himself from his own creation.

Following the death of Gömbös in 1936, the new prime minister was Kalman Daranyi, who had also reflected right radical leanings but drew the line at any revolutionary fascism. Though he inherited most of the late Gömbös's support, when Berlin inquired if his predecessor's recent pledge to Göring to create a fascist system within two more years still held, Daranyi replied in the negative. Szalasi meanwhile visited Berlin in October 1936, and by the beginning of the following year national socialist activity became even more visible in Hungary. Szalasi's followers and others began to organize militia groups, stepping up propaganda as sympathetic junior officers in the military muttered about a move against the government. The government therefore carried out a minor purge among the military and jailed Szalasi for a few days in March 1937, but this gave him greater publicity than ever before and a new hero status among national socialists. The government dissolved his Party of National Will, but Szalasi simply reconstituted a new Hungarist movement. During the summer of 1937 he was joined by Balogh's Hungarian National Socialist Party and the new Race-Protecting Socialist Party, led by Laszlo Endre. Within a few

---

tinctive race, and even that Jesus Christ had been a Turanian. On earlier doctrines of Hungarian racism, see J. A. Kessler, "Turanism and Pan-Turanism in Hungary, 1890–1945," Ph.D. diss., University of California, Berkeley, 1967.

40. The best account of the Hungarist ideology will be found in Szöllösi-Janze, *Pfeilkreuzlerbewegung* 200–250.

months, seven other tiny national socialist groups decided to merge with them, forming by October a general Hungarian National Socialist Party.[41]

Szalasi had clearly become the most prominent leader, and much propaganda was distributed bearing the motif "1938—Szalasi." The government now saw national socialism as a distinct threat and in February 1938 briefly arrested Szalasi and seventy-two other activists. The months that followed were ones of increasing agitation and also a growing number of street clashes in Budapest. Yet another minuscule national socialist group was formed in June (the Christian National Socialist Front), but on the first of August the small party of Festetics joined the general Hungarian National Socialist Party–Hungarist Movement, now commonly known as the Arrow Cross.

The Hungarian government meanwhile sought to protect itself by strengthening its powers. New legislation in 1937 eliminated the right of the parliament to impeach the regent, Horthy, while also giving him the power to veto new legislation after two successive votes and even to dissolve parliament in favor of new elections before having to approve any bills of which he disapproved. Horthy now became regent for life, and the regime was clearly evolving away from conservative elitist liberalism in the direction of a moderate rightist authoritarian system. At the same time, important new social legislation was passed to benefit urban labor (the preferred propaganda targets of both the Socialists and the Arrow Cross), while an electoral reform introduced the secret ballot for men aged twenty-six and over and women thirty and over, for the first time. This was particularly effective in enfranchising urban workers and would be potentially of great benefit for any popular new movement. During 1937 the economy in Hungary improved, as in much of Europe, but this did not dissuade Prime Minister Daranyi from continuing to move in a right radical direction. On the one hand, a new progressive income tax was introduced; on the other, the government took advantage of the financial improvement to increase military spending considerably—now a common European trend—and also to introduce new measures to restrict Jewish rights for the first time in more than fifteen years, limiting the number of Jews in various professions. This was but a pale reflection of Arrow Cross demands; Daranyi was painfully aware of the rapid growth of popular support for Szalasi, leading him finally to undertake secret negotiations in order to co-opt the national socialist leader.

This infuriated Horthy, who refused any concessions to the Arrow Cross, and he fired Daranyi in May 1938, naming the economics minister, Bela Imredy, as his successor. Imredy planned a Schleicher-type strategy, intending to go further than Daranyi in a right radical direction so as to outflank the Arrow Cross without having to deal with it. After one Arrow Cross pamphlet insinu-

41. At this point apparently the only national socialist groups not joining in the unification process were those of Festetics and Palffy and a new National Front created by Janos Sallo.

ated that Horthy's wife was part Jewish, Imredy had Szalasi arrested in August, and for the first time he was sentenced to a prison term (three years). Before the close of the year Imredy passed a second round of anti-Jewish legislation (now using racial-hereditary criteria rather than religious affiliation), and at the beginning of 1939 he organized a new political front, the Movement of Hungarian Life (MEM). This was one of the typical ploys of rightist regimes in southern and eastern Europe, to create a new political party from the top down that would employ some of the trappings of fascism to rally support but would in fact be controlled by the state from above. As was usually the case in such enterprises, the maneuver was so artificial that it drew little support. Moreover, the regent's patience with the right radical maneuvers of Daranyi and Imredy had worn thin. Complaining that Imredy (who was now disclosed to be himself partly of Jewish ancestry) had been too extreme in both his anti-Jewish and his land reform legislation, Horthy decided to move back toward the center early in 1939, appointing the conservative but constitutionalist Pal Teleki as prime minister. Teleki neutralized Imredy's fledgling right radical MEM by incorporating it into the existing Government Party, where it was swamped by more conservative elements. Then he scheduled new elections for May 1939.

The Arrow Cross was officially dissolved once more in February, but though 348 activists accused of disorders had been arrested in December and more were arrested in February, the movement was permitted to continue in thinly veiled disguise. The elections of 1939 were the nearest thing to a democratic contest in Hungarian history, the number of voters enfranchised in the recent election having increased the electorate nearly 50 percent. The Arrow Cross and the other national socialists formed a coalition ticket. Even though men under twenty-six and women under thirty (the age sector most attracted to national socialism) were still excluded from the balloting and more than a little government interference occurred, the national socialist coalition was officially credited with nearly 25 percent of the popular vote. It did particularly well in the worker districts in cities and in areas with large numbers of farmworkers, and to some extent in neighborhoods of the old middle class. Though only 49 national socialists were declared elected, compared with 179 candidates of the Government Party, in a fair and completely democratic election the totals might have been approximately equal. The national socialists had become the largest independent political force in Hungary, and the Arrow Cross the largest single independent party.[42] This was the more impressive since the Arrow Cross had been able to field candidates in only half the electoral districts, partly due

42. Of the forty-nine national socialist deputies, thirty-one represented the Arrow Cross, eleven came from the United Hungarian National Socialist Party of Laszlo Baky (the largest new group), three were from Mesko's party, two hailed from the Christian National Socialist Front, and two came from still smaller groups.

to its own malorganization and lack of experience and partly due to government pressure. German funding had assisted in the campaign, as Nazi influence increased among most of the national socialist groups during 1938–39.

At this point the Arrow Cross claimed more than a quarter million members and may indeed have had two hundred thousand or more in a country of scarcely seven million. Certainly it was, in membership as well as in votes, the largest independent party in Hungary. Leadership was predominantly middle class, with strong support among the military (much of which was Swabian German in ethnic background) and with a broad following among workers and in many rural areas.[43] Arrow Cross national socialism promised revolutionary economic changes attractive to workers, farm laborers, and small farmers. The Hungarian Socialist Party was barely tolerated by the government and had a kind of gentleman's agreement to restrict its activity to skilled workers. By contrast, the unskilled and semiskilled workers were younger in age and also the recipients of certain social initiatives mounted by the Arrow Cross in the larger cities, which produced a situation that made many workers more susceptible to Arrow Cross demagogy. Hungarian students, on the other hand, were less drawn to national socialism than their counterparts in some countries and tended to be attracted by the more elitist right radicals.

The elections nonetheless produced a stalemate for the Arrow Cross. The government remained fully in control, and Teleki was a prime minister undisposed to experiment with the right radical ploys of Daranyi and Imredy. Governmental power was fully entrenched in most rural areas and small towns as well, while the upper-class Hungarian senate was now given more voice by the government to counter the presence of the national socialists in the lower house. Szalasi himself would remain in prison until the following year, and though there was a certain amount of street disorder in Budapest and the larger cities during 1939–40, he had set the Arrow Cross on the legal road to power. That road was now effectively blocked by a semiauthoritarian government. In Hungary, as in Austria, Romania, and elsewhere, the lack of political democracy would be decisive in blocking the political success of a large, broad-based, and popular fascist movement, one that in 1939 could rival the Nazi Party of seven years earlier in proportionate popular support. With access effectively controlled by a nondemocratic government, the Arrow Cross would have to await foreign intervention or military defeat to have an opportunity to seize power.[44]

43. In 1941 twenty-one of the twenty-seven senior generals in the Hungarian army were Magyarized German Swabians, according to A. C. Janos, *The Politics of Backwardness in Hungary, 1825–1945* (Princeton, 1982), 253.
44. This account is drawn mainly from Szöllösi-Janze, *Pfeilkreuzlerbewegung* 101–207, and Nagy-Talavera, *Green Shirts* 94–155. Limited data on the social background of Arrow Cross members and voters may be gleaned from Szöllösi-Janze 134–47; M. Lacko, *Men of the Arrow*

ROMANIA

The situation in Romania was analogous to that in Hungary only with respect to the strength of the Legion of the Archangel Michael (often called the Iron Guard), which at the close of the 1930s became proportionately the third largest fascist movement in Europe, after the German Nazis and the Hungarian Arrow Cross (the Italian Fascists having achieved equivalent size only after Mussolini came to power). Unlike Germany or Hungary, Romania was one of the main beneficiaries of World War I, which doubled the size of the country. Yet this enormous expansion, together with Romania's severe social, economic, and cultural backwardness, posed problems of the utmost severity. The country was faced at one and the same time with the challenge of building a greatly expanded and multiethnic nation, creating a democratic political system, and modernizing one of the weakest economies in eastern Europe. Partial democratization of some institutions only accelerated a kind of national identity crisis and a prolonged search for alternatives.

Interwar Romania was the scene of a "great debate" between westernizers and nativists. The Romanian nativist intellectuals created a sort of Balkan equivalent of *völkisch* culture in Germany, though they were also reminiscent of Russian Slavophiles. In the later nineteenth century the "Junimea," or young conservative nationalists, had carried out a thorough critique of European liberalism and socialism, proposing a distinct Romanian route to a stronger, more modern nation led by an elite presiding over an agrarian society. As in some other eastern European countries, there had developed strong currents of "populism" that espoused a kind of peasant nationalism, equally opposed to liberalism, conservatism, and Marxist socialism.[45]

Anti-Semitism had a stronger popular and intellectual basis in Romania than in possibly any other country. The Jewish minority was comparatively large (4.2 percent of the total population in 1930) and highly diverse. A small minority was prominent in the Romanian economic and financial elite, and many Jews filled middle-class roles, though a certain proportion was virtually impoverished. Nonetheless, Jews were more deeply resented in Romania than almost anywhere else, anti-Semitism of one form or another being more "respectable" among the social and cultural elite than in any other European country.[46] Soon after World War I, discriminatory policies were instituted in Romanian universities.

Cross (Budapest, 1969); idem, "The Social Roots of Hungarian Fascism," in Larsen, Hagtvet, and Myklebust, eds., *Who Were the Fascists?* 395–400; and G. Ranki, "The Fascist Vote in Budapest in 1939," in Larsen, Hagtvet, and Myklebust 401–16.

45. See especially the discussion of the "great debate" in K. Hitchins, *Rumania, 1866–1947* (Oxford, 1994), 292–334.

46. Cf. W. O. Oldson, *A Providential Anti-Semitism* (Philadelphia, 1991).

The new democratic constitution of 1923 introduced universal male suffrage, and by 1926 a mass National Peasant Party had emerged. Two years later it won a large majority in the most democratic election in Romanian history. Yet the Peasant Party soon became divided, producing an only moderately effective government that did not institute any major reforms.

Just as the depression struck, Romania's political equation was fundamentally altered by the return of King Carol, who had abdicated five years earlier. Though this reassumption of royal power had been engineered by a clique of army officers and authoritarian-minded elitists, it was nonetheless accepted by the political parties when Carol promised to observe the constitution. In fact Carol was the most cynical, corrupt, and power-hungry monarch who ever disgraced a throne anywhere in twentieth-century Europe. An admirer of Mussolini, he quickly intervened unconstitutionally in the political process and managed to split the Peasant Party, which he drove from power in 1931. Almost immediately there was talk of a monarchist dictatorship similar to the one introduced in Yugoslavia by King Alexander two years earlier, but Carol quickly found that support for such a maneuver was very limited. For the next year a minority government of notables was led by the ardent nationalist Nicolae Iorga, Romania's leading historian.[47] Another brief government by the National Peasants in 1932–33 was short-lived, internal division having stalemated the only large democratic party. Since these problems stemmed in part from the machinations of an increasingly authoritarian king, by 1933 the political system was in full process of decomposition, with groups in several of the parties splitting off and moving further to the right, as had occurred so recently in Germany. In Romania, as in most of central, southern, and eastern Europe, the postwar democratic breakthrough seemed now to be leading toward a political breakdown.

The chief remaining organization was the Liberal Party, last survivor of the prewar period and the representative of the urban middle and upper classes. It had largely abandoned liberalism, having espoused *neoliberalismul*, a doctrine of "neoliberalism" that stressed more authoritarian and corporative organization under a modernizing elite to create a modern social and economic structure.[48] Thus the Liberals, like King Carol, were moderate conservative authoritarians who had no intention of upholding classic liberal principles. Through the use of the government machinery they created a nominal majority

47. Iorga was a sort of right-wing anti-Semitic liberal. His politics and ideas are explored in R. Ioanid, "Nicolae Iorga and Fascism," *JCH* 27:3 (July 1992): 467–92.

48. The term had first appeared in connection with General Alexandru Averescu, then connoting order and control. The original ideologue of neoliberalism was Stefan Zeletin, who pressed the use of the term "Prin noi înşine" ("Through ourselves alone," or "Sinn Fein" in Romanian). His books *Burghezia romana* (1923) and *Neoliberalismul* (1927) stressed the role of the state, which would have to collect the necessary taxes from the agrarian economy to promote industrialization.

in the elections of 1933, which enabled a succession of Liberal governments to remain in power for the next four years.

By this time the chief doctrinaire of neoliberalism was Mihail Manoilescu, who became the only Romanian political thinker to draw attention abroad, emerging during the 1930s as perhaps the leading theorist of corporatism in Europe. He propounded corporatism as the most useful program of integrated national economics for what would later be called delayed developing nations. An engineer by profession, Manoilescu was first a member of Averescu's earlier People's Party. He abandoned it in 1928 and formed his own National Corporatist League five years later, at which point the Neoliberal government made him head of the national bank. Romania experienced a spurt of industrialization during the next few years, mostly financed by the national bank and other state sources. This did nothing, however, to mitigate the suffering of the ordinary peasant masses. Manoilescu eventually went beyond neoliberalism proper to advocate a single-party corporative system to lead a technocratic industrialization.

Manoilescu drew a distinction between corporatism and fascism, defining the latter as an Italian phenomenon and the former simply as the integration and representation of all the social, economic, and cultural forces of a given country, willing and able to represent its distinct character and needs. In his lexicon, corporatism would nonetheless be "totalitarian," because it would integrate all social and economic forces, but it was not to be rigidly centralized or despotic, permitting limited pluralism and a degree of economic decentralization. This he called pure corporatism, as distinct from Mussolini's state or subordinate corporatism. In his last work, however, he viewed Hitler and Mussolini as differing representatives of national political and economic developmentalism, combining "Rousseau, Danton, and Napoleon." [49]

In addition to the moderately authoritarian Neoliberals, there existed the radically anti-Semitic LANC (described in chapter 5) and the National Agrarian Party of the poet Octavian Goga, also an authoritarian nationalist movement, rather more overtly right radical. A direct effort to imitate Nazism emerged in the National Socialist Party of Romania (PSNR), founded by Colonel Stefan Tatarescu in 1932, yet the only major new political force to appear after the breakup of the National Peasant Party was the Legion of the Archangel Michael, whose founding by Corneliu Zelea Codreanu was briefly described in chapter 5.

The Legion was arguably the most unusual mass movement of interwar

49. Manoilescu's main publications were *Théorie du protectionnisme et de l'échange international* (Paris, 1929), *L'espace corporatif* (Paris, 1934), *Le siècle du corporatisme* (Paris, 1936), and *Der einzige Partei* (Berlin, 1941). See P. C. Schmitter, "Reflections on Mihail Manoilescu," in *Social Change in Romania, 1860–1940*, ed. K. Jowitt (Berkeley, 1978), 117–39.

Europe. It is generally classified as fascist because it met the main criteria of any appropriate fascist typology, but it presented undeniably individual characteristics of its own. Ernst Nolte has written that it "must not only be declared, but also plainly appears, to be the most interesting and the most complex fascist movement, because like geological formations of superimposed layers it presents at once both prefascist and radically fascist characteristics." [50] What made Codreanu especially different was that he became a sort of religious mystic, and though the Legion had the same general political goals as other fascist movements, its final aims were spiritual and transcendental—"The spiritual resurrection! The resurrection of nations in the name of Jesus Christ!" as he put it.[51]

This seemed to be contradicted by the Legion's primary emphasis on life and politics as "war," but Codreanu propounded a doctrine of two spheres: sinful human life which must be the arena of political endeavor, and the reconciled and redeemed spiritual community of nation, ultimately to participate in eternal life. Ordinary human life was a sphere of constant war and eternal struggle, above all against the enemies of the Ţara (Fatherland). The Legionnaire must forgive his personal enemies but not those of the Ţara, who must be punished and destroyed even at the risk of the Legionnaire's personal salvation. Violence and murder were absolutely necessary for the redemption of the nation; if the acts which this required placed in jeopardy the individual soul of the militant who carried them out, his necessary sacrifice was simply the greater. His punishment would consist of the earthly punishment for his deed (which he ought not to avoid) as well as the possible loss of eternal life, the ultimate sacrifice for the Fatherland, which must be accepted with joy. A principal effect of this political theology was a unique death cult, unusually morbid even for a fascist movement.

Self-sacrifice was exalted in all fascist and revolutionary movements, but in the Legion martyrdom was virtually required, accompanied by the theological heterodoxy just outlined. Legionnaires were aware of the uniqueness of their doctrines and of the major differences between their organization and the secular fascist movements, though at the same time they also felt common identity and partially parallel goals with other fascists. Their stress on self-sacrifice led to veritable immolation reminiscent of the most moralistic and idealistic of the Russian socialist revolutionary assassins at the turn of the century. While Ernst Nolte is correct to point out that in single-minded fanaticism Codreanu was the other European fascist leader most like Hitler (whom he also

50. E. Nolte, *Die faschistischen Bewegungen* (Munich, 1966), 227.

51. C. Z. Codreanu, *Eiserne Garde* (Berlin, 1939), 399. Legionnaire doctrine is quoted in the same words—"The ultimate goal of the Nation must be resurrection in Christ!"—in K. Charlé, *Die Eiserne Garde* (Berlin, 1939), 79.

resembled in intense personal magnetism), the Legionnaire martyr complex created a degree of self-destructiveness unequaled in other fascist movements.

The Legion reflected the anti-individualism and emphasis on the collectivity often found in sociopolitical movements in Eastern Orthodox societies, and it has even been termed a kind of heretical Christian sect. What placed it outside even a heretical Christianity, however, was not merely its maniacal insistence on violence but its biological concept of the nation, whose essence supposedly lay in the blood of the Romanian people.

The Legion had little in the way of a concrete program.[52] Codreanu pointed out that a dozen different political programs already existed in Romania, and he proclaimed the need instead for a new spirit, a cultural-religious revolution whose goal was creation of the *omul nou*—the "new man" sought in varying ways by all revolutionary movements, but one that for the Legion would be consubstantial with its interpretation of the Romanian Orthodox Church and the national community. The Legion held that the parliament should be replaced by a corporative assembly based on a "family vote." Its leaders recognized that the country had in some fashion to be developed economically, but they disagreed sharply with the Neoliberal program of rapid industrialization. The high tariff maintained by the government was strongly denounced for increasing living costs among the peasantry. The Legion sought a more national and collective or communal basis for the economy, while abhorring the materialism of capitalism and of socialism. Industrialization per se was not the goal, and it was to be pursued only to the extent necessary for well-being, though, conversely and somewhat contradictorily, the Legion insisted on development of a strong modern army. Legionnaires would later engage in small-scale collective enterprises of their own for public works, retail goods, and restaurants. Codreanu always emphasized that "everything is possible" and, in typical revolutionary and fascist manner, that "everything depends on will."[53] Material conditions were always secondary: "Cry out loud everywhere that the evil, misery and ruin originate in the soul!"[54]

The chief enemies were the leaders of the present corrupt system and the Jews. If the former were immediate targets, Jews constituted the special archenemy, to the extent that the Legion was possibly the only other fascist

52. Professor Nae Ionescu, perhaps the leading Legionnaire ideologue after Codreanu, is quoted as declaring: "Ideology is the invention of the liberals and the democrats." "No one among the theoreticians of totalitarian nationalism creates a doctrine. Doctrine takes shape through the everyday acts of the Legion as it evolves out of the decisions of him whom God placed where he orders." R. Ioanid, *The Sword of the Archangel* (New York, 1990), 83; for a lengthy exposition of Legionnaire ideas, see 98–174.

53. Quoted in A. Heinen, *Die Legion "Erzengel Michael" in Rumänien* (Munich, 1986), 210.

54. Quoted in Nagy-Talavera, *Green Shirts* 309.

movement as vehemently anti-Semitic as German Nazis. Building on preexisting trends that were already powerful in Romania, the Legion encouraged the most extreme policies, to the extent that General Zizi Cantacuzino, one of Codreanu's leading collaborators, declared that the only way to solve the Jewish problem in Romania was simply to kill the Jews.[55]

For several years the Legion remained a tiny sect, a common experience for most fascist movements in the 1920s, lacking both money and support. In 1930 it founded a sort of militia called the Iron Guard, to include all Legionnaires between the ages of eighteen and thirty, and this new formation provided the name by which the Legion was more commonly known in Romanian politics and subsequently in historical study. At the beginning of 1931 the government formally dissolved both the Legion and the Guard, arresting briefly Codreanu and other leading figures. Yet the basic organization continued under a different name, winning only 1.05 percent of the vote in the national elections of June 1931. As the Gruppe Corneliu Zelea Codreanu, it did manage to win two local by-elections, gaining parliamentary representation for the first time. In the subsequent national elections of 1932, however, which were the most honest elections held in Romania during the decade, the main sector of the National Peasants won approximately 40 percent of the vote, while the Legion's support rose to only 2.37 percent, in ninth place among Romanian political organizations, barely ahead of the small Romanian Jewish party. Nonetheless, the democratic National Peasant government which then briefly came to power showed some interest in gaining Legionnaire support, and for the first time the National Peasants began to take a position of limited anti-Semitism.

The influence of Nazism became more noticeable that same year, following the increase in the Nazi vote in the German elections of 1932. From that point Nazi contacts in Romania increased, but primarily with the LANC, the largest extreme anti-Semitic group, and Tatarescu's new National Socialist Party of Romania (PSNR), while a Nazi organization was founded among Romanian Germans. Conversely, Italian Fascists developed contacts with the Legion during the "universal Fascism" program of 1933–34.[56]

In 1933 the Legion was once more allowed to operate legally, growing to twenty-eight thousand members, but it was involved in a number of vicious incidents and several deaths during the late autumn electoral campaign. This provoked a new ban by the government on December 9, leading to the arrest of seventeen hundred Legionnaires. Nonetheless, the growth of support was now rapid, and even in less than free elections the Legion might have

55. According to I. C. Butnaru, *The Silent Holocaust: Romania and Its Jews* (New York, 1992), 60. See also T. I. Armon, "Fra tradizione e rinnovamento: Su alcuni aspetti dell'antisemitismo della Guardia di Ferro," *SC* 11:1 (Feb. 1988): 5–28.

56. J. W. Borejsza, *Il fascismo e l'Europa orientale* (Bari, 1981); T. I. Armon, "Fascismo italiano e Guardia di Ferro," *SC* 3 (1972): 505–27.

Iron Guard militiaman exhibiting the
swastika armband sometimes worn in the
Romanian movement

gained as many as two hundred thousand votes and become the third largest political force in the country. By this point, however, Romanian democracy had essentially broken down, quite apart from the still limited activities of the Legion. The Neoliberal government employed corrupt and coercive practices to register a nominal victory with 51 percent of the vote in the elections of December 20, but for the next four years the Romanian system would function increasingly as a controlled polity with only limited representation, until a moderate authoritarian government was directly instituted in 1938.

The Legion struck back within three weeks. It had already begun to organize direct-action units, appropriately termed *echipa morţii* (death squads); these units developed the fascistic cult of violence more elaborately—and gruesomely—than in any equivalent movement. On December 29 one of them assassinated the Neoliberal prime minister Ion Duca, bringing the arrest of several thousand more Legionnaires. Members of the squad involved, as well as Codreanu and several other top leaders, were soon brought to trial, but verdicts in April 1934 sentenced three of the squad to prison terms while absolving Codreanu.

The relative leniency of these decisions stemmed from the fact that the Romanian system was still semiliberal, but equally from the contradictory tendency of a general movement toward rightist and nationalist authoritarianism, much as in Germany before 1933. Both King Carol and the new prime minister, Gheorghe Tatarescu (brother of the Romanian Nazi leader), hoped to domesticate and exploit the Legion, which acknowledged the monarchy as a fundamental Romanian institution. The government itself tried to form a new parafascist youth group, the Straja Ţarii (Guards of the Fatherland), but its artificiality made its generation of support almost impossible. In July 1935 Professor Cuza's LANC and Octavian Goga's rightist National Agrarian Party fused to form the National Christian Party, a heterogeneous new authoritarian and extreme anti-Semitic movement on the cusp between moderate authoritarianism and the radical right. Its leaders were willing to begin governing under the existing constitution (which was being honored less and less anyway) but aimed at creating a corporative upper house and a smaller, more restricted parliament. The National Christians wore blue shirts and used the swastika emblem of anti-Semitism, but members of their Lancieri (Lancers) militia were clothed in black uniforms and were responsible for more violent anti-Semitic incidents, apparently, than was the Legion. During 1935 there were also formed a National Socialist Christian Peasants Party, a Romanian Sacred Holy League, and a Military Nationalist Front. Radical breakaways from the Legion created separate groups called the Swastika of Fire and the Crusade of Romanianism, the latter a tiny organization which sought to target workers and to inspire socioeconomic transformation. The most nationalist sector of the National Peasant Party—still the plurality, if not majority, party of Roma-

Codreanu in peasant costume, surrounded by followers

nians—broke off to form a more rightist National Front (eventually joining an alliance with the Neoliberals). Even the National Peasants, virtually the only democratic party in the country, began to organize their own political militia in 1936.

The growth of the Legion continued steadily, reaching more than two hundred thousand by late 1937. Normally, to obtain membership, new affiliates in each *cuib* (nest) participated in a grisly ceremony requiring that they suck blood from slashes in the arms of other members. They swore to obey the "six fundamental laws" of the *cuib:* discipline, work, silence, education, mutual aid, and honor. Then they wrote oaths in their own blood, pledging even to kill when so ordered. Members of the death squads, in turn, each contributed some of their blood to a common glass, from which all drank, uniting them in life and death. Legion meetings in peasant villages would open with a religious service in which all participated. If Codreanu were present, he would enter wearing an elaborate white peasant costume astride a white horse. Tall, with an intense gaze and classic features, he was probably the most handsome of the major fascist leaders (bearing, in more mature and serious form, some resemblance to a Hollywood actor of that era, Tyrone Power). This theatricality often had a strong effect on peasant audiences, and Legion support expanded rapidly in parts of the countryside.

In December 1934 the technically illegal movement had been restructured under the guise of the All for the Fatherland movement, nominally led by a retired army general. During that year Codreanu introduced Legionnaire work colonies, and within two years at least fifty special work projects were operating, helping villages to build dams, irrigation facilities, bridges, and churches. Though such projects by political groups were outlawed in 1936, the Legion continued its own canteens and shops.

In August 1936 the government officially dissolved all political militias, and this had some effect in reducing the level of political violence. By the first months of 1937 the king began to realize that persistent efforts to co-opt Codreanu were never going to achieve much effect. That spring more effective measures were taken to put an end to the Legion's work projects, as well as to its labor groups that tried to operate as surrogate trade unions, but the semi-clandestine structure of the Legion itself was tougher to crack. The government in turn tried to co-opt sectors of Legionnaire support, encouraging better relations with the clergy and new church construction, while introducing new laws to control cartels and trusts and to protect workers.

German influence reached a new level during 1937. Though Codreanu and other leaders were aware of the considerable difference between the Legion and Nazism, they were convinced that the future of their movement and of Romania lay with the "national revolutions" led by Hitler and Mussolini. It would be necessary to gain German approval for Romania's expanded territory, won at the expense of Germany's former allies. Codreanu had earlier declared the existing frontiers as adequate for Romania, but since the triumph of Nazism in Germany, Legion spokesmen had shown an increasing tendency to call for the acquisition of "Transnistria" (the southwestern Ukraine). Codreanu had his own plans for a Romanian-led Danubian-Carpathian Federation, though this might conflict to some extent with the goals of the Hungarian Arrow Cross. German support would be crucial, and by the last months of 1937 Codreanu was delivering extremely pro-German speeches, calling for an immediate alliance with Germany and Italy.

In the electoral campaign of December 1937—the last before the war— All for the Fatherland (TPT, the legal cover name for the Legion) formed a pact with the National Peasants, on the basis of a common nationalism and propeasant orientation. Conversely, Legionnaires were involved in nasty street fights with the Lancieri militia of the right radical National Christian Party. In the customarily corrupt and partially manipulated electoral outcome, the Neo-liberal alliance registered a nominal plurality of 35.92 percent, the Peasants 20.4, TPT 15.58, and the National Christians 9.15. Later, Eugen Cristescu, sometime head of the Romanian police, declared that the TPT had in fact received approximately 800,000 votes, or slightly more than 25 percent of the popular vote.[57] If that was indeed the case, then the Legion, with its strong peasant support, was the third most popular fascist movement in Europe, behind the German Nazis and the Arrow Cross, in an approximate tie with the Austrian Nazis. In fact, the 272,000 members which the movement had at that time amounted to 1.5 percent of the Romanian population,[58] compared with 1.3 percent for the NSDAP in January 1933, 0.7–0.8 percent for the PNF in mid-1922, and possibly as much as 2 percent of the total Hungarian population for the Arrow Cross in 1939.

The Legion had begun largely as a student movement. The Legion's leadership cadres were drawn broadly from the middle classes, while the voting base comprised especially peasants, by far the largest social sector in Romania. For example, of ninety-three Legionnaires executed in 1939 whose professional backgrounds can be ascertained, thirty-three were students, and nearly all the rest came from the middle classes, of whom fourteen were lawyers. The hypertrophy of university enrollment in interwar Romania has already been mentioned; associated with that was a massive excess production of lawyers, so that the country came to have one lawyer for every thirteen hundred inhabitants, compared with one for every thirty-six hundred people in Germany.[59] Though many army officers were sympathetic, the military never played as much of a role in the development of the Legion as in some other fascist movements; conversely, the role of the clergy seems to have been much more important than in any other case.

In 1937 the Legion drew support from many different peasant areas but actually did better in the more prosperous, lower-middle-class rural districts. There was no correlation between the TPT vote and the areas of highest illiteracy, infant mortality, or rates of disease. That correlation was much stronger in the case of the National Christians, who lost votes to the Legion generally but did rather better in the more backward northeast. The Legion also drew support from industrializing areas; of twenty-two principal industrial districts surveyed by Armin Heinen, eleven were among those in which the TPT had its greatest success.[60] Of 2,607 ordinary Legionnaires surveyed in jail in 1939, 20.5 percent were unskilled workers, 17.5 percent peasants and farmers, and 14 percent skilled workers, indicating that in the cities a considerable proportion of the activists came from the working classes.[61]

By the close of 1937 Romania had reached the situation of Germany five years earlier, with no majority available. Carol's choice for the role of Franz von Papen was Octavian Goga, leader of the National Christians (though they

57. Ioanid, *Sword of the Archangel* 69.
58. Heinen, *Die Legion* 382.
59. Ibid., 392, 399.
60. Ibid., 411–12.
61. Ioanid, *Sword of the Archangel* 72.

had gained only 9 percent of the vote), who headed a new minority coalition government with the support of one former sector of the Peasant Party and the participation of General Ion Antonescu, Romania's most prestigious military figure, as minister of war. This regime lasted scarcely a month, achieving only the beginning of severe new anti-Semitic legislation.[62] King Carol then decided to follow Papen's earlier ploy in Germany, dissolving parliament at the close of January 1938 and scheduling new elections for March. A way out was suddenly provided through a new pact between the Neoliberals and the National Peasants, which might assure a working majority. But Carol, much more than Hindenburg, had become used to dominating the political scene himself, and he rejected this option, which would have rendered his manipulations superfluous.

Discarding the idea of further elections, on February 10, 1938, the Romanian king carried out a royal coup against the political system, naming a new ministry under Patriarch Miron Cristea, haed of the Romanian Orthodox Church, invested with decree powers. Within a few days it promulgated a new constitution, which in some ways superficially resembled the liberal constitution of 1923 but in fact concentrated power in the hands of the king, creating a situation analogous to the King Alexander regime of Yugoslavia earlier in the decade. The constitution was, however, in other ways comparatively moderate and did set some limits on the government's authority. It was also accompanied by rigorous new laws on public order that increased the powers of the courts and the police. During the course of 1938 the government created an official new political front, the Frontul Renasterii Naţionale (Front of National Rebirth, FRN). This was conceived as a comparatively moderate state authoritarian party that could restrain extreme right radicalism and anti-Semitism. Though other political parties were outlawed, Carol continued to negotiate with leading figures, hoping to draw them into the FRN. The king wavered between plans to have Codreanu murdered and renewed attempts to co-opt him politically, but the latter proved totally impossible. The Legionnaire *Conducator* (Leader) accepted the dictatorship and gave orders to his followers to lie low for the time being until the new arrangement weakened, but Armand Calinescu, the tough new interior minister, was determined to break his power. Codreanu was arrested once more on April 16, and several thousand of his followers were also incarcerated in the days that followed. A military court subsequently sentenced him to ten years of forced labor for subversion.

Acting leadership of the Legion passed to the young lawyer Horia Sima, known more for fanaticism than political judgment. Codreanu realized that the Romanian dictatorship would not hesitate to execute him and ordered Sima to have the Legion desist from violence or other overt actions unless it appeared that his life was in imminent danger. By midautumn Sima seems to have been

---

62. P. Shapiro, "Prelude to Dictatorship in Romania: The National Christian Party in Power, December 1937–February 1938," *Canadian American Slavic Studies* 8 (1974): 51–76.

convinced that the way to deal with this was through a new round of bombings and terrorism that would bring the government to its knees. Codreanu was able to send a dispatch from prison ordering the Legionnaires to desist, but it was too late. On November 30, the "night of the vampires" in Romanian folklore, a detachment of the brutal state Siguranţa removed Codreanu and thirteen other top Legionnaires from prison, carrying them off in trucks. They were then strangled with wires, shot, and dumped in a lime pit at a military prison outside Bucharest.

Sima prepared the Legion for a full-scale insurrection against the Carolist dictatorship, hoping to capitalize on sympathies within the military, but found that these were insufficient. The army remained under discipline, and the Legion, like all other fascist movements, was not strong enough to launch an insurrectionary civil war. The plan for revolt on the sixth of January 1939 had to be canceled, and Sima and hundreds of other leaders and activists fled abroad, mainly to Germany. Once more a rightist authoritarian regime had suppressed a popular fascist movement, as earlier in Austria and concurrently in Hungary. The Legion, which despised democracy, the bourgeoisie, and capitalism, re- quired at least a degree of bourgeois democracy to have the opportunity to build greater support and/or to achieve power.

Despite the government's victory, however, the Legion of the Archangel Michael was by no means destroyed. Though its leaders were either dead, in prison, or abroad, most of the basic membership remained, together with an underground organizational structure. Even Legionnaire terrorism could not be entirely suppressed but remained a secondary factor throughout these months, rather like the persistent terrorist activism of Russian revolutionaries before 1917.[63] Armand Calinescu, the new prime minister who had orchestrated the suppression of the movement, was thus assassinated by Legionnaire gunmen immediately after the beginning of the German invasion of Poland. In retalia- tion, his murderers and other Legionnaire activists were quickly executed, their corpses strung up to rot on lampposts in the center of Bucharest and several other cities.

63. This account of the Legion is based primarily on Heinen, *Die Legion;* Nagy-Talavera, *Green Shirts;* and Ioanid, *Sword of the Archangel.* Eugen Weber has written two important studies: "Romania," in *The European Right,* ed. H. Rogger and E. Weber (Berkeley, 1965), 501–74; and "The Men of the Archangel," *JCH* 1:1 (April 1966): 101–26. T. I. Armon emphasizes the in- coherence of the movement in "La Guardia di Ferro," *SC* 7:3 (Sept. 1976): 507–44. See also Z. Barbu, "Romania," in *European Fascism,* ed. S. J. Woolf (London, 1969), 146–66; and articles by E. Turczynski and S. Fischer-Galati in P. F. Sugar, ed., *Native Fascism in the Successor States, 1918–1945* (Santa Barbara, 1971), 101–23. C. Sburlati, *Codreanu el capitán* (Barcelona, 1970), is a relatively recent hagiography. Codreanu's autobiographical *Pentru legionari* has been translated into several languages (e.g., *Guardia de Hierro* [Barcelona, 1976]). The best general treatment of Romanian politics during this period will be found in H. L. Roberts, *Rumania: Political Problems of an Agrarian State* (New Haven, 1951).

9
The Minor Movements

The movement toward nationalist authoritarianism was steady in interwar Europe, from the March on Rome in 1922. Chronologically, the breakdown of parliamentary government moved as follows: 1922–25, Italy; 1923/1936, Spain; 1926, Poland; 1926, Lithuania; 1926, Portugal; 1926/1936, Greece; 1929, Yugoslavia; 1933, Germany; 1933, Austria; 1938, Romania; 1938, Czechoslovakia. By the time that World War II began, Europe had more authoritarian than parliamentary regimes. Yet with the exceptions of the Soviet Union, Italy, and Germany, there was a tendency to replace the parliamentary government with syncretistic, semipluralist forms of right-wing dictatorship, normally without a developed single-party system and usually without a revolutionary new fascist-type component. That is, authoritarianism normally did not mean fascism, even though it became common for authoritarian regimes to imitate certain aspects of the fascist style.

Though the initial establishment of the Mussolini regime sparked a number of minor imitative fascist or would-be fascist movements in a variety of European countries, none of the new organizations established outside Italy, Germany, and Austria during the 1920s achieved any significance except for the Legion of the Archangel Michael. The major diffusion of fascist movements throughout Europe occurred during the following decade, in the aftermath of Hitler's triumph. Moreover, the growing power of the Nazi regime stimulated rightist movements and right-wing authoritarian regimes to adopt varying degrees of "fascistization"—certain outward trappings of fascist style—to present a more modern and dynamic image, with the hope of attaining broader mobilization and infrastructure.

The characteristics of the many new fascist movements of the 1930s, like those of their predecessors in the preceding decade, varied considerably.

What was common to most of them, beyond a minimum of basic fascist characteristics, was their political failure and complete marginalization. Even at the height of the so-called fascist era, a successful fascist movement was the exception which proved the rule that fascist movements—with their eclectic and revolutionary doctrines, their violence and militarism, their unusually high levels of self-contradiction, and their nonrationalist philosophies—were quite unsuccessful.

ABORTIVE FASCIST MOVEMENTS IN THE DEMOCRACIES

Preconditions for successful fascist movements did not exist in the northern European democracies. There liberal democracy already had deep roots (with the exception of the new states of Czechoslovakia, Finland, and Ireland), and frustrated nationalism was not an issue. Generally the democracies enjoyed higher standards of living, a broader diffusion of property, and greater economic security. Thus, with only one brief exception in Holland, no generically fascist movement could gain more than 2 percent of the vote in general elections in any of the stable democracies of central and northern Europe.

France

France is the home of modern politics in both the negative and positive senses of the term. Though it achieved the first successful large democracy on the European continent, France also shared many of the characteristics of southern European politics: repressive centralization, revolutionary rather than evolutionary patterns of change, radical adversary intelligentsia cultures, class antagonisms, and extremist splinter politics.

Zeev Sternhell has conclusively demonstrated that nearly all the ideas found in fascism first appeared in France.[1] The fusion of radical nationalism with revolutionary and semicollectivist socioeconomic aspirations first occurred there, and in parallel fashion France was the first major country in which the revolutionary left rejected parliamentarianism while supporting a kind of nationalism. Similarly, the effects of the cultural and intellectual revolution of the 1890s extended further in France than in any other country outside the greater German and Italian cultural areas.

What of course was different was simply the general situation of France compared with that of most countries in central and eastern Europe. France was one of the oldest and most successful of all national states, a victor in World War I, a prosperous and in general socially balanced country, and one of the two dominant imperial powers in the world. Ultimately there was little need

---

1. In *La Droite révolutionnaire* and other works cited in chapter 2.

or room for new revolutionary nationalism. For these and other reasons, the consensus among both French and also foreign historians has been that France generally remained free of the "fascist temptation" between the wars. More recently, however, younger scholars have challenged the prevailing consensus, holding that in France fascism and authoritarianism presented a more severe challenge than in any other surviving democracy.[2]

Several of the prewar right authoritarian nationalist groups survived into interwar France. The League of Patriots, the Anti-Semitic League of France, and Action Française had all been formed in the late nineteenth century (see chapter 2), but they were essentially rightist, even reactionary, in orientation. By the 1920s Action Française was the only significant survivor, claiming thirty thousand dues-paying members in 1924 and exerting some influence among sectors of the elite and intelligentsia. Its leader, Charles Maurras, sometimes stressed the differences between Action Française and Italian Fascism, criticizing the latter's radicalism and demagogy, its emphasis on modern mass politics rather than elites, the dubious character of its monarchism, its lack of doctrinal consistency, and its undisciplined use of violence.[3]

The imitation of fascism was first essayed in France by Georges Valois, a young militant who abandoned Action Française as too reactionary and sought to create a mass-mobilizing revolutionary nationalist movement. His Le Faisceau (a literal French translation of Il Fascio), founded in 1925, was able to take advantage of the reaction against the electoral victory of the left in France during the preceding year. It claimed sixty thousand members by the end of 1926, and although the actual number of affiliates was probably less than half that, many of them also organized in the activist "legions" of the movement as militia. Valois was a Social Darwinist but also a moralist and strict antihedonist. Though Le Faisceau sometimes supported trade union strikes and talked about improving worker conditions, most members apparently came from the middle classes. Valois's formula that "nationalism plus socialism equals fascism" was fascistic, but indeed he tried to be a more strictly doctrinaire fascist than the opportunistic Mussolini. Though he sought to combine syndicalism with nationalism, he could not recruit among a comparatively well-organized French left, and with a general shift in French politics toward moderate conservatism, space was increasingly closed off on the opposite side of the spectrum. Wealthy businessmen stopped contributing funds after the end of 1926, and Le Faisceau went into rapid decline, disappearing in April 1928. Most of the limited violence experienced by Le Faisceau was that inflicted on them by Com-

---

2. Especially Zeev Sternhell, Robert Soucy, and William D. Irvine, in works cited in chapter 2 and below in the current chapter.

3. R. Soucy, *French Fascism: The First Wave, 1924–1933* (New Haven, 1986), 1–26; E. Weber, *Action Française* (Stanford, 1962), 113–431.

munists from the left and Action Française from the right. Action Française began a campaign of its own to discredit the movement, and on one occasion its Camelots du Roi attacked a Le Faisceau meeting, knocking Valois to the ground. Valois later moved completely to the left and, as a member of the wartime French resistance, ultimately died in a German concentration camp.[4]

A more moderate right-wing authoritarian nationalism was far more popular in France than fascism. The temporary growth of Le Faisceau was soon exceeded by that of a new authoritarian nationalist youth movement, the Jeunesses Patriotes (Patriot Youth) of Pierre Taittinger. The group had been formed in 1924 as a youth branch of the old League of Patriots (then undergoing its last revival with about ten thousand members). The Jeunesses, like Le Faisceau, was stimulated by the leftist electoral victory of 1924 and soon absorbed the ten thousand or so members of another right authoritarian group called the Legion. In a clash with Communists in Paris in April 1925, four Jeunesses members were killed, three of them students at elite institutions of higher learning. The resulting publicity led to a big increase in recruitment, but only two days after this Taittinger issued orders for members of the Jeunesses militia never to carry guns. Nor did they sport the typical fascistic or revolutionary shirt uniform: their only badge of clothing was the standard blue raincoat of Paris university students. The goal of the Jeunesses was to become a broad youth organization of the right, not a fascist movement. Their 1926 program was comparatively moderate, essentially supporting the status quo, with some reduction of the powers of parliament and provision for a stronger executive. As a moderate right authoritarian movement, the Jeunesses tried to offer something for everyone and welcomed Jewish support, drawing financial backing from sectors of big business. By 1929 they had a nominal 102,000 members, one-quarter of them in Paris, with a student organization called the Phalanges Universitaires (University Phalanxes). The conservative Poincaré government of 1926–27 looked on them with some favor, but after the conservative electoral victory of 1928 the movement eventually declined, and the years 1929–32 were a time of dwindling fortune. In 1933 Taittinger took a more radical turn and began to call for a dictatorship.[5]

As the Jeunesses dwindled, a more clearly right radical league emerged in the Solidarité Française, organized by the perfume king François Coty in 1933. Coty had financed a series of ultranationalist newspapers and journals, some

4. See A. Douglas, *From Fascism to Libertarian Communism: Georges Valois against the French Republic* (Berkeley, 1992); Y. Guchet, *Georges Valois* (Paris, 1975); Soucy, *French Fascism* 87–195; Z. Sternhell, "Anatomie d'un mouvement fasciste: Le Faisceau de Georges Valois," *Revue Française de Science Politique* 26:1 (Feb. 1976): 5–40; and Valois's own *Le fascisme* (Paris, 1926), which dwells on the "French origins of fascism" (5–7).

5. J. Philippet, *Les Jeunesses Patriotes et Pierre Taittinger, 1924–1940* (Paris, 1957); Soucy, *French Fascism* 39–86, 198–216.

of them achieving a wide circulation. Solidarité Française was led by a retired army major. Anti-Semitic and profascist, it was much too rightist to be a fascist movement itself, but it later championed a coup to install an authoritarian regime. At its height in 1934 it claimed to have more than a quarter million members, but the real number of its affiliates may have been little more than ten thousand before the sudden death of its founder, which led to rapid decline.[6]

Though mostly profascist, none of these leagues were generically fascist; all were rightist, nominally Catholic, and culturally traditionalist, ranging from only moderately authoritarian to the extreme radical right.[7] It was the rightist leagues that created France's only "fascist scare" with the riots of February 1934 in Paris. The result of the scare, however, was to magnify French antifascism, which had been vocal and organized ever since 1923, before any fascist or even any major right authoritarian force existed. "Thus, after February 6, 1934, antifascism became the dominant political fact in France, a thousand times more important than fascism."[8] This was a major element in the electoral victory of the Popular Front in May 1936, which then ordered the dissolution of the rightist leagues and their uniformed groups.

Largest and most successful of the new right-wing nationalist movements was the Croix de Feu (Crosses of Fire), organized in 1927 as a veterans' association to promote moral values. A recently retired army officer, Lieutenant Colonel François de la Rocque, took over the leadership in 1931 and converted the group into a more political association with a uniformed militia. By the

---

6. P. Milza, *Le fascisme français* (Paris, 1987), 142–47; A. Chebel d'Appollonia, *L'extrême-droite en France de Maurras à Le Pen* (Brussels, 1988), 201–2.

7. This is the opinion of the majority of analysts, from René Rémond, in *La Droite en France de la première Restauration a la cinquième République*, 2 vols. (Paris, 1968), to Philippe Burrin, in *La dérive fasciste* (Paris, 1986). See also E. Weber, "France," in *The European Right*, ed. H. Rogger and E. Weber (Berkeley, 1965), 71–127, and P. Machefer, *Ligues et fascismes en France, 1919–1939* (Paris, 1974).

Yet another nonfascist right authoritarian group was the Comités de Défense Paysanne (Committees of Peasant Defense), organized in the countryside by Henry Dorgères in 1928, which after 1934 grew into a large force of allegedly as many as four hundred thousand. A nationalist organization to defend farmers, the Committees of Dorgères cooperated with other nationalist and rightist forces and expressed their admiration for Fascist Italy, but their slogan of *Work, Family, Fatherland* was generically conservative and patriotic rather than fascist.

Much more sinister was the Comité Secret d'Action Révolutionnaire (CSAR), known derisively to rivals and enemies as La Cagoule (The Hood), because of its conspiratorial secrecy. During 1936–37 this tiny middle-class right radical group sought through a series of terrorist acts to encourage a military coup. Though it was in contact with a conspiratorial network inside the French army, this campaign failed utterly, its best-known achievements being the murders of several foreign leftists in France. The CSAR's leaders were finally identified and arrested in November 1937, though part of its structure survived. See P. Bourdrel, *La Cagoule* (Paris, 1970); P. Sérant, *Les dissidents de l'Action Française* (Paris, 1978); and P. M. Dioudonnet, *Je Suis Partout, 1930–1944: Les maurrasiens devant la tentation fasciste* (Paris, 1973).

8. J. Plumyène and R. Lasierra, *Les fascismes français, 1923–1963* (Paris, 1963), 42.

end of 1934 it may have had 150,000 members, and under the title Mouvement Social Français it elected 20 deputies to parliament. The members of the Croix de Feu (known to their enemies as *les froides queues,* the cold tails) were successful in part because theirs was a movement of only moderately authoritarian nationalism. De la Rocque was strongly Catholic and preached the "cult of tradition," together with a partially corporative reorganization of the French government to strengthen the executive and reduce the power of parliament. Yet the Croix de Feu did not propose to eliminate elections and spoke of the enfranchisement of women. De la Rocque opposed foreign models, as well as xenophobia, totalitarianism, and extreme statism. He vetoed participation in the riots of February 1934 and was generally more sympathetic to Dollfuss than to Mussolini. The Croix de Feu rather admired Italian Fascism but not Nazism, and its special *dispos* sections (for *disponibles,* or "ready") normally had no weapons. René Rémond, the leading historian of the French right, has dismissed them as an association of *scouting politique* (political boyscouts).[9] De la Rocque sharply discouraged members who sought to turn the movement into a categorically fascist organization, and these people usually left for more extremist groups.

After the official dissolution of all the leagues in June 1936, the Croix de Feu was reorganized as a regular political party called the Parti Social Français (French Social Party, PSF). It soon became the most rapidly growing new party in the country, reaching a nominal (though unverified) membership of eight hundred thousand in 1938. The PSF became the first modern, cross-class, mass-mobilized French rightist party, in some respects a predecessor of the Gaullist movement after 1945. Its initial membership was strongly middle-class, but as the movement grew, farmers made up 25 percent of the total, and an increasing number of workers were mobilized. It drew extensive support from business and finance, sectors of which looked on the PSF as the vehicle for developing a kind of corporative and technocratic authoritarianism.[10] Had elections been held in 1938 or 1939 the PSF would have been a formidable force. During World War II De la Rocque briefly supported the Vichy regime, but then he joined the resistance and was later arrested and deported by the Gestapo.[11]

9. Rémond, *La Droite* 2:222.
10. K.-J. Müller, "French Fascism and Modernization," *JCH* 11:4 (Oct. 1976): 75–107.
11. There is no adequate study of the Croix de Feu and the PSF, but see P. Rudaux, *Les Croix de Feu et le P.S.F.* (Paris, 1967), an account by a former militant, and Milza, *Fascisme français* 133–42. It might also be pointed out that the French war veterans' association, much of whose membership overlapped with the PSF, was considerably more moderate politically than its German counterpart, the Stahlhelm. See A. Prost, *Les anciens combatants et la société française, 1914–1939,* 3 vols. (Paris, 1977).

A dissenting view, arguing rather unconvincingly that the De la Rocque movement was categorically fascist, will be found in R. Soucy, "French Fascism and the Croix de Feu: A Dissenting

The "positive aspects" of fascism also attracted a number of independent young intellectuals and leaders of the moderate left and the Socialist Party during the 1930s. They believed that the left should learn from fascism to become more nationalist, to mobilize more broadly on a multiclass basis, to strengthen the powers of the state, develop economic planning, cultivate youth, and develop a culture of vitalism, to reinvigorate society and foster better relations with Germany. This "fascist influence" for a reformed and democratic antifascist left was expressed by various dissident intellectuals, by some of the Young Turks in the Radical Party and by "neosocialists" in the Socialist Party.[12]

The latter were led by Marcel Déat, in 1930 a rising star in the ranks of French socialism. His book *Perspectives socialistes* (1930) argued the need to mobilize the middle classes to expand the role of the state in planning for a "constructive revolution" for all society. Breaking with his party in 1933 over the issue of an antifascist "national socialism" based on a state corporative planned economy, he insisted that only this sort of "neosocialism" could defeat fascism. His new Socialist Party of France survived less than three years, even though it momentarily carried a small minority of the Socialist parliamentary delegation with it. Déat then joined a new dissident group, the Socialist Republican Union, which formed part of the leftist Popular Front in 1936 but failed to win him a seat in parliament. His neosocialist brand of national socialism remained nonfascist, and indeed antifascist, for some time. Déat would move directly into fascism only after the German occupation.[13]

Only one categorically fascist party emerged in France during this decade, the Francistes of Marcel Bucard, founded in 1933. A former follower of Valois, Bucard declared that "Francisme is to France what Fascism is to Italy." He tried faithfully to copy the Italian formulae, which helps to explain the complete lack of success of his tiny organization. Bucard was the sole French representative invited to the "universal fascism" conference at Montreux in December 1934, and during 1934–35 he was regularly subsidized by the Italian government. During that period of tension between Nazism and Italian Fascism, he declared that Francisme was not anti-Semitic and rejected

---

Interpretation," *JCH* 26:1 (Jan. 1991): 159–88, and W. D. Irvine, "Fascism in France and the Strange Case of the Croix de Feu," *JMH* 63 (1991): 271–95.

12. J.-L. Loubet, *Les non-conformistes des années trentes* (Paris, 1969); and Milza, *Fascisme français* 179–220.

13. The best account of Déat will be found in Burrin, *La dérive fasciste*, but see also D. S. White, *Lost Comrades: Socialists of the Front Generation, 1918–1945* (Cambridge, 1992).

There was considerable congruence between the economic ideas of Déat and those of the Belgian Labor Party leader Hendrik de Man, who later collaborated with the German occupiers but did not become a fascist. See P. Dodge, *Beyond Marxism: The Faith and Works of Henri de Man* (The Hague, 1966), and E. von S. Hansen, *Hendrik de Man and the Crisis in European Socialism, 1926–1936* (Ithaca, 1968).

German racism. After formation of the Rome-Berlin Axis, he quickly switched positions on both issues.[14]

Much more important than the Francistes but less categorically fascist was the Parti Populaire Français organized by Jacques Doriot in 1936. Of all the French ultranationalists, Doriot was the one whose career most nearly approximated that of Mussolini. By 1932 Doriot, of equally modest social background, had become a member of the French Communist Party's Central Committee and head of its youth group. He might reasonably have expected soon to become party secretary, having achieved approximately the same stature as Mussolini in the Italian Socialist Party by 1912. Doriot was equally heterodox and independent, restive with Soviet control, and increasingly critical in public of the social sectarianism of the Communists, whom he urged to cooperate with French Socialists in 1934 to defeat fascism. Doriot's increasingly strident and public dissidence brought his expulsion from the Communist Party in June 1934 just as it was about to initiate part of the fundamental change in its policies—toward the pluralistic Popular Front—that he had demanded. Doriot was forced to the sidelines as the new Popular Front swept to victory in the elections of 1936, but during these months he conceived the project of a great new nationalist party of the people that would attract the dissidents of the left, together with new nationalists, and bring down the Soviet-dominated Communist Party altogether.

The Parti Populaire Français was born soon after the elections of 1936, enjoying considerable financial backing from big business interests, which sought to encourage a popular nationalist anti-Communist force. It grew fairly rapidly, though not so rapidly as the PSF, and at the beginning of 1938 claimed to have three hundred thousand members, though the real figure may have been less than one-third of that. It was a working-class party: 57 percent of the delegates to the first PPF congress in November 1936 were of worker or farmer background. The membership was young, with an average age of thirty-four, and only 20 percent of affiliates were military veterans, unlike the rightist leagues. Nearly 39 percent of the members declared no prior political affiliation, while 33 percent came from the left, especially the Communist Party. There was no particular pattern of regional concentration, except for strong support in the industrial northern suburbs of Paris; support was generally more urban than rural. Yet as time went on the party failed to attract equal growth among workers, and by the time of the second congress in March 1938, the proportion of middle-class delegates had increased to 58 percent, and that of workers had declined to 37 percent.

The PPF did not begin as a specifically fascist movement and had no shirt

---

14. A. Deniel, *Bucard et le Francisme: Les seuls fascistes français* (Paris, 1979).

militia, but it quickly acquired more and more of the trappings of fascism. The ritual of meetings became increasingly elaborate in the fascist mode, with an oath of loyalty to the *chef* (Doriot). By 1938 ceremonies were held in honor of the movement's martyrs (several members killed by Communists), yet the PPF salute only required the raising of the right hand barely above shoulder level, distinct from the full fascist salute. The new state envisaged by the PPF was to be "popular" and authoritarian but decentralized, honoring the family, the community, and the region, with the latter being strongly emphasized. Though nominally anticapitalist as well as antiparliamentary, the PPF had no program of nationalization, propounding a reformist corporatism that would strongly encourage technocratic rationalization. PPF propagandists did encourage an activist and vitalist philosophy and the creation of an *homme nouveau* (new man), and the movement drew the support of some accomplished fascistic intellectuals like Pierre Drieu La Rochelle. Though it did not become a categorically fascist party before the Occupation, the PPF was strongly protofascist from the beginning and maintained relations with the NSDAP, the PNF, and also the Spanish FET. It proclaimed France's role in a "new Europe," even though the dominant place might be that of Nazi Germany—an uncomfortable potential for any French nationalist party. Similarly, though the PPF preached vitalism and activism, together with the military virtues, it was—like all the French nationalist groups from the fascists of Bucard to the most conservative—a "peace party" that discouraged talk of war and sought no particular territorial aggrandizement for France. Most fascist parties in stable, prosperous western European countries with mature colonial empires preached a kind of "peace fascism," unlike their counterparts in central and eastern Europe.

Doriot hoped to lead a broader front of nationalist groups and to that end soon encouraged a sense of Catholic identity as well, but the Front de la Liberté that he attempted to organize in the spring of 1937 was stillborn. (De la Rocque, for example, hoping to attract moderate elements from the leftist Popular Front to his new PSF, refused to participate in a sharply polarized anti-left alliance.) Despite the personal magnetism and pronounced oratorical skill of "le grand Jacques," the heavyset, bespectacled former working-class leader could not sustain the growth of his party for many more months. The following year, 1938, brought the breakup of the Popular Front and the end of any menace from the left, together with a new stress on national unity by consensus moderates in France that discouraged any radical alternatives, fascistic or otherwise. These factors severely restricted the opportunities of the PPF, while Doriot's increasingly dissolute personal life tarnished his image. By the spring of 1939 many of his dissident leftist associates had defected, and a rapidly declining PPF was forced to take a patriotic stand in opposition to Nazi Germany. It had failed to define a distinctively French form of fascism, and in fact the

PPF's transformation into a fully fascist movement would only be completed after 1940.[15]

France remained stable, relatively prosperous, and democratic, the French minicrises of the interwar period being modest in comparison with those of other countries. There was no room for fascism. It was a measure of the relative strength and consensus behind the Third Republic that at various times both French Communists and members of the PPF proclaimed their defense of republican constitutional institutions against each other.

When all is said and done, the main achievements of the tendencies toward fascism in France remained in the sphere in which they had begun two generations earlier—the intellectual and the literary—for whatever strength French fascism possessed in the 1930s lay above all in its writers, such as Pierre Drieu La Rochelle, Robert Brasillach, and others. If there is controversy among scholars regarding the exact extent of fascism in France during the depression, there is general consensus about "the remarkably high level of French fascist literature and thought," for "apart from the work of Gentile, nowhere else in Europe was there a body of fascist ideological writings of comparable quality."[16] Fortunately for France and other countries as well, strong political and social institutions prevented the continued proliferation of literature and ideas from being translated into political fact.

15. The principal studies of Doriot and the PPF are D. Wolf, *Die Doriot-Bewegung* (Stuttgart, 1967); J.-P. Brunet, *Jacques Doriot* (Paris, 1986); Burrin, *La dérive fasciste;* and G. Allardyce, "The Political Transition of Jacques Doriot," Ph.D. diss., State University of Iowa, 1966. A collection of texts and commentaries may be found in B.-H. Lejeune, ed., *Historisme de Jacques Doriot et du Parti Populaire Français*, 2 vols. (Amiens, 1977).

16. Z. Sternhell, *Neither Right nor Left: Fascist Ideology in France* (Berkeley, 1986), 6. Sternhell, in fact, insists that despite the failure of protofascist groups in France, French culture by the 1930s was broadly infected by fascist attitudes and ideas. On the ensuing controversy (including a libel suit against Sternhell), see A. Costa Pinto, "Fascist Ideology Revisited: Zeev Sternhell and His Critics," *European History Quarterly* 16 (1986): 465–83, and R. Wohl, "French Fascism, Right and Left: Reflections on the Sternhell Controversy," *JMH* 63:1 (March 1991): 91–98.

There is an abundant literature on the French fascist intellectuals: P. Sérant, *Le romantisme fasciste* (Paris, 1959); T. Kunnas, *Drieu La Rochelle, Céline, Brasillach et la tentation fasciste* (Paris, 1972); J. Morand, *Les idées politiques de Louis-Ferdinand Céline* (Paris, 1972); W. R. Tucker, *The Fascist Ego: A Political Biography of Robert Brasillach* (Berkeley, 1975); D. Desanti, *Drieu La Rochelle ou le séducteur mystifié* (Paris, 1978); B. L. Knapp, *Céline: Man of Hate* (University, Ala., 1974); J. Hervier, *Deux individus contre la histoire: Pierre Drieu La Rochelle, Ernst Jünger* (Paris, 1978); R. Soucy, *Fascist Intellectual: Drieu La Rochelle* (Berkeley, 1979); M. Balvet, *Itinéraire d'un intellectuel vers le fascisme: Drieu La Rochelle* (Paris, 1984); and, most recently, D. Carroll, *French Literary Fascism* (Princeton, 1995).

The Low Countries

Fascist and protofascist movements had rather more success in the Low Countries, but the difference remained marginal. In Belgium extreme nationalism during the 1920s took the form of a democratic Front Party in Flanders, comprised of Flemish veterans and other activists who demanded Flemish autonomy; also, in the Walloon or French-speaking region, several all-Belgian authoritarian nationalist groups formed. Chief among these were Action Nationale, founded in 1924 on the model of Action Française, and the Légion Nationale, founded by Belgian veterans in 1922, which soon absorbed Action Nationale. In 1927 the leadership of the Légion was taken over by Paul Hoornaert, who sought to model it on the PNF. Though the Légion never had more than four thousand members, it formed a small uniformed fascist-type militia called the Jeunes Gardes (Young Guards) that engaged in limited direct action. The Légion, however, later combated the German occupation, and Hoornaert died in a Nazi concentration camp.

The most notable fascist-type movement in Belgium was the Verdinaso (an acronym standing for Federation of Low Countries National-Solidarists), founded by Joris van Severen in 1931 as a secession from the Flemish Front Party. Verdinaso's goal was the re-creation of the late medieval Burgundian state, uniting the Low Countries together with other territory in northeastern France. It adopted a style, structure, and ideology roughly analogous to Italian Fascism but was strongly hostile to Germany. It apparently never had more than five thousand members, and its dark green–shirted militia, called the Dutch Militant Order, never had more than three thousand activists.

The main force of Flemish nationalism during the 1930s was the schoolteacher Staf de Clercq's VNV (Flemish National Federation), founded in 1933. Unlike Verdinaso, it was neither anti-Semitic nor antiparliamentary and cannot be compared with a fascist movement, being in fact highly Catholic, in an orthodox sense, and antimilitary. Confusion arose from the fact that the German government began to subsidize the VNV in 1937 to weaken Belgian unity. From that time the VNV leadership moved in a protofascist direction, but the party's parliamentary representatives remained more or less democratic.

The key fascist leader in Belgium was Léon Degrelle, a young Catholic publisher, who became dissatisfied with the moderation of Belgian Catholicism and founded his own movement, Christus Rex, in 1935. Rexism was Catholic, authoritarian, and corporatist, with a penchant for direct action, but not categorically fascist. In the national elections of 1936 it attracted considerable attention, winning 11.49 percent of the vote (and considerably more in the French-speaking areas) and electing twenty-one deputies. In the following year Degrelle overreached himself by challenging the prime minister personally in a

Rexist poster publicizing Léon Degrelles

by-election, and he was humiliated when he gained only 20 percent of the vote. From that point, he guided the approximately 12,500 Rexists more and more in the direction of an Italian-type fascism, though it would be difficult to say that the transformation of Rex into a categorically fascist movement was ever completed before 1940. In the process, Degrelle's movement lost seventeen of its twenty-one parliamentary seats in the elections of 1939.[17]

There were a number of Dutch fascist movements, influenced—despite their names—rather more by Italian Fascism than by radical Nazism. The National Socialist Netherlands Workers Party (NSNAP) was founded in 1931. A pale imitation of foreign fascisms, it was in fact relatively moderate and corporatist, accused by rivals of propounding mere "right-wing fascism." The General Dutch Fascist Union was created a year later and called for a *volks-fascisme,* but had difficulty defining this very clearly. It created a minuscule militia but attracted almost no votes in the 1932 elections. It was superseded in 1935 by a new formation, the Black Front, which claimed to be a radical and popular fascist movement. These last movements seem to have drawn a tiny degree of support from the Catholic (potentially more pro-Italian) sectors of the population, but in electoral terms this amounted to only a fraction of 1 percent.

The principal Dutch fascist movement was the National Socialist Movement (NSB), founded by the civil servant Anton Mussert and others in 1931. Again, despite the name, it reflected a more moderate Italian-style fascism, more appropriate to the tolerant and democratic Dutch society. The NSB developed the full panoply of fascism, with elaborate rituals and a party militia, but eschewed racism. Mussert declared that "every good Dutch Jew is welcome in our party." [18] It proposed a corporate economic system and upheld freedom of religion as a Dutch national principle. The NSB was able to take advantage of the depression to gain nearly 8 percent of the vote in the Dutch provincial elections of 1935, the largest vote for a new party in Holland under universal suffrage.

At that point the NSB claimed forty-seven thousand members, but it soon began to decline. Its fascistization began to deepen as some sectors flaunted racist and anti-Semitic doctrines, and Mussert later initiated personal contact with Hitler. Conservative supporters were alienated, while the democratic Dutch parties banded together to block any further growth. As economic conditions improved, the NSB went into steady decline, gaining only 4.2 percent of the vote in the national elections of 1937 and losing most of that in the provincial elections two years later.[19]

17. The only broad treatment is R. Chertok, "Belgian Fascism," Ph.D. diss., Washington University, 1975, which employs an extremely flexible definition of fascism. The best study of the early years of Rex is J.-M. Etienne, *Le mouvement rexiste jusqu'en 1940* (Paris, 1968), which correctly concludes that Rex could not be characterized as fascist in the early period. See J. Stengers, "Belgium," in Rogger and Weber, eds., *European Right* 128–67, and L. Schepens, "Fascists and Nationalists in Belgium, 1919–1940," in *Who Were the Fascists?: Social Roots of European Fascism,* ed. S. U. Larsen, B. Hagtvet, and J. P. Myklebust (Bergen, 1980), 501–16.

18. D. Littlejohn, *The Patriotic Traitors* (London, 1972), 87.

19. Ibid., 84–89; H. van der Wusten and R. E. Smith, "Dynamics of the Dutch National

Sir Oswald Mosley salutes members of the women's section of the British Union of Fascists at a rally in London's Hyde Park, September 9, 1935

Great Britain

The activity of fascist- and Nazi-type parties in the northern European democracies is of interest primarily to those concerned with negative findings. None of the northern European movements mobilized more than 2 percent of the vote, with the exception of the Dutch National Socialists in 1935 and 1937, and none ever found influential allies in other sectors. This is in no way surprising, since nearly all the conditions listed by most analysts as likely prerequisites for the emergence of fascism were lacking in northern Europe. None of the northern democracies except Belgium and Ireland faced significant problems of nationalism, ethnicity, or international status. All save Ireland were prosperous, economically developed, and relatively balanced socially, with well-educated citizens and modern political cultures with parliamentary constitutional traditions. There was neither space nor "need" for revolutionary nationalism.

Socialist Movement (NSB): 1931–1935," in Larsen, Hagtvet, and Myklebust, eds., *Who Were the Fascists?* 524–41.

"Violently expelling the Jewish-Bolsheviks" (Photo reproduced in a Nazi
publication, showing antifascist demonstrators abandoning their barricade
against a BUF march in Cable Street, London, October 5, 1936.)

Hence the British Union of Fascists was essentially a contradiction in
terms, a sort of political oxymoron.[20] It was formed in 1932 by Sir Oswald
Mosley, former rising young leader in the Labor Party whose trajectory as the
"British Mussolini" was similar to that of the Italian leader and of Déat and

20. The BUF had been preceded by a variety of totally insignificant grouplets using the
name fascist: the British Fascisti, the British Empire Fascists, the Fascist League, the National
Fascisti, the Kensington Fascist Party, the Yorkshire Fascists, the Empire Fascist League, and so
on, each pettier and more irrelevant than the other. Most of these were not even generically fascist,
but extreme right-wing groups.

Doriot, save that Mosley made the transition to fascism more rapidly—within only a year or so of leaving the Labor Party. Like other fascist movements in satisfied imperial powers, the BUF never preached war and expansion, but peace and prosperity. Mosley was obsessed with overcoming social, economic, and cultural decadence, and he believed that only the disciplined nationalism and new cultural dynamism of a fascism on the Italian model could achieve it. The BUF was one of the most thoroughly programmatic of all fascist movements, with elaborate corporatist economic proposals. Its thrust was decidedly modernist, paying serious attention to economic theory and concepts of "scientific production," while also espousing equal pay for women. The BUF also preached vitalism and the Shavian superman, while stressing Britain's civilizing and imperial mission in the world "to rescue great nations from decadence, and march together towards a higher and nobler order of civilization." [21]

Originally not anti-Jewish—its strong-arm squads were at first trained by the Jewish boxer "Kid" Lewis—the BUF nonetheless moved to anti-Semitism by 1936 as a corollary of extreme nationalism. In England, however, it was not the Jews but the fascists who were destined for the ghetto, never escaping total insignificance. The handsome, athletic Mosley probably cut the best physical figure of any British (or European fascist) political leader, and his pugilistic skill in taking out a heckler with a single punch was impressive, but it was all for naught. The growing violence that attended BUF activities, even though sometimes engendered by leftist antagonists, was repugnant to most Britons. Parliament passed a Public Order Act, effective at the beginning of 1937, which gave the police broad powers to curtail disorderly political activities, and Mosley—basically committed to legal tactics—had to acquiesce. After a few years of modest growth, the BUF went into serious decline. At one point it may have had fifty thousand members, then dropped away to perhaps as few as five thousand, before climbing back to possibly as many as twenty-five thousand members in 1939. When World War II began, the party was dissolved, and Mosley—protesting his patriotism (probably sincerely)—was imprisoned for most of the duration as a subversive. [22]

21. R. Griffin, *The Nature of Fascism* (London, 1991), 138.

22. The most thorough biography is R. Skidelsky, *Oswald Mosley* (London, 1975). The volume of literature on the BUF is inversely proportionate to the group's significance: C. Cross, *The Fascists in Britain* (New York, 1963); R. Benewick, *Political Violence and Public Order: A Study of British Fascism* (London, 1969); W. F. Mandle, *Anti-Semitism and the British Union of Fascists* (London, 1968); J. D. Brewer, *Mosley's Men: The BUF in the West Midlands* (Aldershot, 1984); R. Thurlow, *Fascism in Britain: A History, 1918–1985* (Oxford, 1987); D. S. Lewis, *Illusions of Grandeur: Mosley, Fascism and British Society, 1931–1981* (Manchester, 1987); and T. Kushner and K. Lunn, *Traditions of Intolerance* (Manchester, 1989). S. Cullen, "The Development of the Ideas and Policy of the British Union of Fascists, 1932–1940," *JCH* 22:1 (Jan. 1987): 115–36, and idem, "Political Violence: The Case of the British Union of Fascists," *JCH* 28:2 (April 1993): 245–67, 513–29, also merit attention.

Ireland

There was no real fascist movement in the new Irish Republic. The nominal candidate for such a role stemmed from the Army Comrades Association, formed in 1932 to oppose the more radical policies of the prime minister, Eamon de Valera. Leadership was assumed the following year by the former national police chief, General Eoin O'Duffy. The name of the association was changed to National Guard, and a blue shirt was adopted as uniform, the group subsequently being known colloquially as the Blue Shirts. It drew support from middle-class farmers and shopkeepers but was essentially a chowder and marching society pressure group that never went beyond a moderately authoritarian corporatism. The Blue Shirts very soon merged into the new Fine Gael Party of nationalist Catholic conservatives, and O'Duffy promised to renounce any dallyings with fascistization. This co-opted most of the Blue Shirts into moderate parliamentary politics. In frustration, O'Duffy in 1935 established a small National Corporate Party that he hoped to develop as a more genuine fascist party. He also initiated contacts with continental fascists, briefly sending an Irish battalion to fight on the Nationalist side in the Spanish Civil War. Both these enterprises were complete failures, and after O'Duffy retired from political life in 1937 the Blue Shirts ceased to exist.[23]

Scandinavia

Numerous right authoritarian or mimetic fascist or national socialist grouplets appeared in Scandinavia. Several different organizations existed in Sweden, and seven in Denmark. Here again the rule that the more different organizations, the more insignificant each is, generally applies. The most important of the Swedish groups, first organized in 1924, took the name Swedish National Socialist Party (SNP) in 1930. Its membership rarely exceeded a thousand, and the party won only 0.6 percent of the national vote in the 1932 elections. By this point there was an increasing tendency to imitate Nazism, though the same trend also produced internal tensions, leading to the formation of the National Socialist Workers Party (NSAP) in 1933, which took a stronger anticapitalist line. An electoral coalition between these two groups gained only 0.7 percent of the vote in the elections of 1936. More popular than the fascist groups were the separate "National Rescue" militias of a moderate right authoritarian

23. M. Manning, *The Blueshirts* (Dublin, 1970). Also worthy of mention is the study by J. J. Barnes and P. P. Barnes which treats perhaps the most unique Irishman associated with fascism: *James Vincent Murphy: Translator and Interpreter of Fascist Europe, 1880–1946* (Lanham, Md., 1987).

Vidkun Quisling

cast, which enrolled thirty thousand members in Norway, eighteen thousand in Sweden, and seven thousand in Denmark.[24]

The chief force in Denmark was the Danish National Socialist Workers Party (DNSAP), organized in 1930 and largely modeled on Nazism. Led by

---

24. U. Lindström, *Fascism in Scandinavia, 1920–1940* (Stockholm, 1985), 32. See also B. Hagtvet, "On the Fringe: Swedish Fascism, 1920–45," in Larsen, Hagtvet, and Myklebust, eds., *Who Were the Fascists?* 715–42. Lindström's study is the broadest treatment but is more concerned with general sociopolitical features of Scandinavia that proved resistant to fascism than with the history of the fascist movements themselves.

Frits Clausen, it experienced severe internal cleavage but by 1939 gained a membership of forty-eight hundred, winning 1.8 percent of the national vote and three seats in parliament.[25]

The Icelandic Nationalist Movement formed in 1933 was essentially Nazi-inspired, preaching racism, anti-Semitism, and a corporatist dictatorship (the corporatist form being largely favored by the Scandinavian parties). It gained 0.7 percent of the vote in the elections of 1934 but failed to win a single seat, even on a municipal council. A membership of three hundred in 1936 marked its high point; it failed even to contest the elections of 1937.[26]

By far the most important of the Scandinavian proto-Nazi movements was Vidkun Quisling's Nasjonal Samling (National Unity) party in Norway. Quisling had earlier been described by some as the most brilliant young officer in the Norwegian army. He served from 1931 to 1933 as defense minister and founded the Nasjonal Samling in the latter year. An abstract theorist, Quisling adopted Nordic racism but believed in the unity of Europe and for some time was pro-British. He propounded a corporative system for Norway and organized a party militia called the Hird. Quisling relied increasingly on the radical youth sector of his party and soon moved closer and closer to Germany, which provided him with funding and also received information from him. Whereas the Danish Nazis relied more on rural support, Quisling drew small numbers of followers from various social sectors and regions, though rather more from urban and middle-class elements than others. Nasjonal Samling claimed to have fifteen thousand members by 1935, but Quisling quickly became the most unpopular public figure in Norway. The party drew 2.2 percent of the national vote in 1933 and 1.84 percent in 1936; membership eventually fell to around eighty-five hundred. Quisling's minuscule rise above the 2 percent barrier was transitory, and the party slowly but steadily lost support.[27]

Switzerland

Switzerland fit perfectly within the northern European pattern. There were philofascist new parties for each of the three language groups: the National

25. H. Poulsen and M. Djursaa, "Social Basis of Nazism in Denmark: The DNSAP," in Larsen, Hagtvet, and Myklebust, eds., *Who Were the Fascists?* 702–14; M. Djursaa, "Who Were the Danish Nazis?" in *Die Nationalsozialisten*, ed. R. Mann (Stuttgart, 1980), 137–54. Danish Nazism was strongest in North Schleswig, where there was a NSDAP-N (National Socialist Danish Workers Party–North Schleswig).

26. A. Gudmundsson, "Nazism in Iceland," in Larsen, Hagtvet, and Myklebust, eds. *Who Were the Fascists?* 743–50.

27. O. K. Hoidal, *Quisling: A Study in Treason* (Oslo, 1989); P. M. Hayes, *Quisling* (London, 1971); and articles by Stein U. Larsen, J. P. Myklebust and Bernt Hagtvet, Hans Hendriksen, S. S. Nilson, and H.-D. Loock in Larsen, Hagtvet, and Myklebust, eds., *Who Were the Fascists?* 586–677.

Front for German speakers, the Union Nationale for French speakers, and the Lega Nazionale Ticinese for Italian speakers.[28] Only the National Front might have been considered a genuine fascist movement. It was of course very small. The upper class was overrepresented in the membership, but in the Schaffhausen district (the only area where the group had any strength) membership was nearly triangulated between farmers (36.5 percent), workers (32.6 percent), and the urban lower middle class (24.6 percent). Its high-water marks were gaining 27 percent of the vote in the Schaffhausen district only and 7.7 percent in the Zurich municipal elections, both in 1933. Aside from a few local seats, its only electoral success was electing a single deputy to the Swiss National Council from Schaffhausen, with 12.2 percent of the district vote in 1935.[29]

Czechoslovakia

The major qualification normally applied to Czechoslovakia between the wars is that it was the only functional democracy east of Germany. This is formally correct, even though both the political system and the economy of this multinational state were Czech-dominated. Little support might have been expected for fascism, and with the eventual exception of the Sudeten German minority, such was indeed the case. There were nonetheless two overtly fascistic Czech parties, the National Fascist League (NOF), organized in 1926 and inspired by Italian Fascism, and the Czech National Camp (Vlajka), which developed in the 1930s. The NOF was led by General Rudolf Gajda, former commander of the Czech Legion in the Russian civil war and briefly Czech chief of staff during 1926. The party was anti-German and anti-Nazi but also anti-Semitic; it was authoritarian on the Italian model, with a youth group and a small trade union organization. A major goal was destruction of Soviet communism, which would be the springboard for coleadership with Poland of a great new authoritarian Pan-Slav federation that would include a post-Communist Russia. Supported by army officers and some middle-class farmers, the NOF found only the most limited backing in southern Bohemia and Moravia. Its leaders preached a kind of national socialism that advocated state purchase of large industrial enterprises and strict state regulation of all profits, with large capital to be expropriated. They also advocated land reform and sought to reinforce rural life. Gajda was elected to parliament in 1929, but a scheme to seize an army barracks in 1933 fizzled, and in elections two years later the NOF drew only 2 percent of the vote, even under the banner of a slightly larger coalition. Vlajka was smaller yet but was quite distinct in its pro-Nazism and strongly

28. See M. Cerutti, *La Svizzera italiana nel ventennio fascista* (Milan, 1986).
29. B. Glaus, *Die Nationale Front* (Zurich, 1969); W. Wolf, *Faschismus in der Schweiz* (Zurich, 1969).

emphasized philosophical vitalism. It may have had thirty thousand members by 1939.[30]

Much more important, though nonfascist, was the Slovak People's Party, the principal force in Slovakia. It moved from being a quasidemocratic Catholic populist party to become a moderate authoritarian Catholic party, and then, during World War II, it shifted more radically toward the right. With the goal of full autonomy (if not independence) for Slovakia, its main strength lay among the Catholic peasantry, and in various elections its share of the Slovak vote varied between 25 and 40 percent. A party militia, the Rodobrana, was formed in 1923, and the radical wing of the party, led by Vojtech Tuka, was strongly profascist, if not itself fascistic.[31]

Categorical fascism in Czechoslovakia developed strongly only among the German minority, which constituted about 20 percent of Czechoslovakia's total population. Whereas the Czech National Socialist Party remained democratic, as well as part of the Czech governing coalition, the old German Workers Party (DAP) of the Sudetenland had evolved into a German National Socialist Workers Party (DNSAP), roughly similar to its Austrian counterpart during the 1920s but prone to increasing Nazification. It began to organize a paramilitary auxiliary in 1929 but was dissolved by the Czech government after Hitler came to power in Germany four years later.

The chief new political force was the Sudeten German Party, led by Konrad Henlein. It was initially oriented more toward Austrian corporatism than Nazism, but the party contained a Nazi wing and later moved increasingly toward Hitlerism. The German minority responded with enthusiasm, giving the party 60 percent of the German vote in the elections of 1935, which resulted in a win of forty-four of the sixty-six German seats in the three-hundred-member Czech parliament. This electoral support increased to no less than 85 percent in the municipal elections of May 1938. After September 1938 the Sudeten party would simply be absorbed into the greater NSDAP.[32]

Finland

Along with Czechoslovakia and Ireland, Finland was the most successful of the new democracies. Parliamentary government was not, however, a novelty

30. J. Zorach, "The Enigma of the Gajda Affair in Czechoslovak Politics in 1926," *Slavic Review* 35:1 (March 1976): 683–98; J. F. Zacek, "The Flaw in Masaryk's Democracy: Czech Fascism, 1927–1942," unpublished.

31. Y. Jellinek, *The Parish Republic: Hlinka's Slovak People's Party, 1939–1945* (Boulder, 1976); idem, "Stormtroopers in Slovakia: The Rodobrana and the Hlinka Guard," *JCH* 6:3 (July 1971): 97–119.

32. R. M. Smelser, *The Sudeten Problem, 1933–1938* (Middletown, Conn., 1975); W. Brügel, *Tschechen und Deutsche, 1918–1938* (Munich, 1967), 238–306. More broadly, on all these groups, see V. Olivova, *The Doomed Democracy* (London, 1972), and J. F. Zacek, "Czechoslovak

in Finland, which had enjoyed considerable autonomy under imperial Russia for much of the nineteenth century, and again after 1906, when universal suffrage was introduced. Finnish affairs were strongly colored by the effects of the revolutionary-counterrevolutionary civil war of 1917–18, won by the Finnish Whites with German assistance and accompanied by brutal repression of Finnish Reds with much loss of life. Stable liberal democracy was quickly attained, though with partial proscription of Communists.

The radical right in Finnish affairs during the 1920s was represented by the Academic Karelia Society (AKS), which preached a national mission to fight Bolshevism and create a greater Finland stretching to the Urals. The AKS stood for a more authoritarian government and a more elitist system, even though a few members urged development of a gradual Finnish state socialism. The society advocated Finnishization, an end to Swedish bilingualism, and a barrier to Swedish "contamination," positing the existence of a Finnish race that mixed Nordic, east Baltic, and Finnish ethnic elements. All this was grounded in a mixture of right-wing Lutheranism and a sort of apodictic "divine law" that justified Finnish expansion. The AKS had considerable influence among some educated young people but remained what its name indicated, a largely "academic" society with only a few thousand members.

A much broader political force emerged in 1929 in the Lapua movement, named for a small town that had been the scene of an anti-Communist riot that year. Lapua was an extreme right-wing counterrevolutionary and authoritarian movement of prosperous farmers and middle-class people from small towns, highly religious in tone and dedicated to the extirpation of Finnish communism, to be followed by the establishment of a more authoritarian, pious, and nationalist government. For two years it enjoyed the cooperation or complaisance of more moderate parties, but an abortive revolt in 1932 led to its being outlawed. All the other middle-class forces (and the Socialists as well) rallied round the parliamentary regime, with the result that Finnish democracy was strengthened rather than weakened.

The Lapua movement was reorganized in 1933 as the People's Patriotic Movement (IKL), a right authoritarian party which advocated drastic corporative restructuring of the society and the economy to achieve a new Finnish "people's community." Its main support came from highly religious and conservative sectors of wealthier farmers and townspeople in western and southwestern Finland, a heartland of old nationalism and Lutheran pietism. Clergymen and other religious leaders were prominent among the followers of a movement that was too religious and ultraconservative to become truly fascist. Though the IKL drew 8.3 percent of the vote in the 1936 elections, it

---

Fascisms," in *Native Fascism in the Successor States, 1918–1945*, ed. P. F. Sugar (Santa Barbara, 1971), 56–62.

could not dent the broad consensus in favor of parliamentary democracy. By 1939 its electoral percentage had declined to 6.6.[33]

A kind of "people's community" did emerge in Finland during the country's heroic resistance to the Soviet Union in World War II, and in 1941 the IKL entered a national unity government coalition. The party was finally dissolved in 1944 under the terms of the peace settlement with Moscow.

SOUTHERN AND EASTERN EUROPE

Aside from the cases studied in previous chapters—those of Italy, Spain, Hungary, and Romania—no other country of southern and eastern Europe developed a major fascist movement, even though one or more efforts were made in every country. With the partial exception of Estonia, all the lands of eastern and southern Europe lived under authoritarian regimes on the eve of World War II, but these regimes served more as a barrier against, rather than an inducement for, fascism.

Portugal

In Portugal a rightist authoritarian regime was established by the military in 1926. In its reorganized form, it survived until overthrown by another military revolt in 1974, nearly half a century later. The Portuguese regime formally repudiated fascism and remained neutral in World War II, until forced to tilt toward the Allies in 1943. The one fascist movement that did develop in Portugal was crushed by the dictatorship itself, as in Austria, Hungary, and Romania.

The weakness of generic fascism in Portugal might at first seem puzzling, since, as the principal investigator of the topic has written, many of the supposed preconditions for fascism existed there, including "modernism and futurism, nationalism, traumas resulting from World War I, a worker offensive, anticommunism, young army officers politicized by the extreme right, the fascism *avant la lettre* of Sidonio Pais, the emergence of mass politics, the crisis of legitimacy of liberalism, and even some real fascists themselves." [34]

The military dictatorship of 1926 was initially supported by a broad array of forces extending temporarily to the moderate left, and its course was for some time unclear. Its components included a certain proportion of conserva-

33. The principal study of the IKL's followers is L. Karvonen, *From White to Blue-and-Black: Finnish Fascism in the Inter-War Era* (Helsinki, 1988). See also M. Rintala, *Three Generations: The Extreme Right Wing in Finnish Politics* (Bloomington, 1962); idem, "Finland," in Rogger and Weber, eds., *European Right* 408–42; A. K. Upton, "Finland," in *European Fascism*, ed. S. J. Woolf (London, 1969), 184–216; and articles by Risto Alapuro and Reijo Keikonen in Larsen, Hagtvet, and Myklebust, eds., *Who Were the Fascists?* 678–701.

34. A. Costa Pinto, *Os camisas azuis* (Lisbon, 1994), 142–43.

tive liberals, but there was also a sector of moderate authoritarian conservatives, and beyond these other more extreme if ill-defined elements of the radical right. Several small groups of the latter eventually coalesced at the beginning of 1928 in the elitist Liga Nacional 28 de Maio, which sought to promote a permanent new authoritarian system.[35]

In 1928 the military dictatorship installed a new finance minister in the person of Dr. Antonio de Oliveira Salazar from Coimbra University, a leading figure among Catholic corporatists.[36] He immediately made himself the system's indispensable administrator, balancing the budget and stabilizing government finance. In 1932 Salazar became prime minister, and from that point he sought to create a permanent new system of institutionalized moderate authoritarianism, introducing in 1933 a new corporative constitution for the Portuguese Republic—the first new corporative constitution in all Europe, anticipating that of Austria by one year. Salazar, who was devoutly Catholic and opposed to any form of radicalism, sought to reconcile economic corporatism and a controlled semiauthoritarian political liberalism by introducing both a corporative chamber for the representation of social and economic interests and a directly elected national assembly. A National Union was organized to support the government, help win elections, and provide new personnel,[37] but elections were held regularly, even though they were carefully controlled. Church and state remained separate. Salazar's system might best be described as one of "authoritarian corporatism" or even of "authoritarian corporative liberalism."[38]

The Liga Nacional 28 de Maio had hoped to avoid exactly this sort of semimoderate outcome, which it feared would be excessively liberal. It may

35. A. Costa Pinto, "A Direita Radical e a Ditadura Militar: A Liga Nacional 28 de Maio (1928–1933)," in *Conflict and Change in Portugal*, ed. E. de Sousa Ferreira and W. C. Opello Jr. (London, 1985), 23–39.

36. On the background of Catholic corporatism in Portugal, see M. Braga da Cruz, *As origens da democracia cristã e o salazarismo* (Lisbon, 1980).

37. M. Braga da Cruz, *O partido e o estado no salazarismo* (Lisbon, 1988).

38. The phrase is derived in part from Marcello Caetano, last leader of the regime, and is developed in M. Braga da Cruz, "Notas para uma caracterização política do salazarismo," *Análise Social* 72 (1982): 897–926. The principal history of the Salazar regime is *O Estado Novo (1926–1974)*, by Fernando Rosas, which constitutes volume 7 of the *História de Portugal* edited by J. Mattoso (Lisbon, 1994). The best accounts in English will be found in T. Gallagher, *Portugal: A Twentieth-Century Interpretation* (Manchester, 1983), 38–190, and R. A. H. Robinson, *Contemporary Portugal* (London, 1979), 32–193. The two broadest treatments of the development of Portuguese corporatism are M. de Lucena, *A evolução do sistema corporativo português* 2 vols. (Lisbon, 1976), and H. J. Wiarda, *Corporatism and Development: The Portuguese Experience* (Amherst, 1977). But see P. C. Schmitter, *Corporatism and Public Policy in Authoritarian Portugal* (Beverly Hills, 1975), and brief studies in L. S. Graham and H. M. Makler, eds., *Contemporary Portugal* (Austin, 1979). The best collection of recent Portuguese studies will be found in *O Estado Novo*, 2 vols. (Lisbon, 1987). Antonio Costa Pinto provides an excellent analysis of the diverse interpretations of the Portuguese regime in *O Salazarismo e o fascismo europeu: Problemas de interpretação nas ciencias sociais* (Lisbon, 1982).

have had ten thousand members by the beginning of 1932, but Salazar got it under control rather easily by placing one of his own government administrators in charge of it, and the organization faded away in 1933, its remnants joining Salazar's own National Union.

Meanwhile, a movement of generic Portuguese fascism was being developed in 1931–32 that even more vehemently opposed the establishment of a merely moderate and conservative authoritarian system. It was initiated by students dissatisfied with both the rightist character of the Liga Nacional and the moderation of Salazar's administration, and was officially constituted in September 1932 as Portuguese National Syndicalism under Rolão Preto, a former leader of monarchist integralism who had moved "left." Preto declared that "nationalism can no longer signify 'Tradition'—but a breaking of the mold— a break with the old ideological restraints so that the spirit may fly and rise ever higher." [39] The National Syndicalists adopted blue shirts and generally identified themselves with fascism, even though Preto sometimes claimed that he was "beyond Fascism and Hitlerism," since they divined a totalitarian state whereas National Syndicalists sought to synthesize their movement with Portuguese Catholic values and "our dignity as free men." [40] The Blue Shirts proclaimed their own revolution, emphasizing social transformation, though in the vaguest of terms. In practice, they welcomed contacts with other fascist movements and, despite an occasional remark by Preto, seem to have identified almost completely with Italian Fascism, while holding their distance from Nazism and condemning the excesses of the Romanian Legion of the Archangel Michael. Relations with the Spanish Falange were somewhat conflictive. Ramiro Lesdema feared that the Blue Shirts were potentially reactionary, while Preto himself criticized the Falangist leader José Antonio Primo de Rivera as perhaps too "capitalist." Moreover, the Portuguese had certain designs on Spanish Galicia, whereas some, at least, of the Falangists believed that the Spanish should rule the entire peninsula.[41] This uneasy relationship was somewhat similar to that between the Arrow Cross in Hungary and the Legion of the Archangel Michael in Romania.

Like some other radical new organizations, the National Syndicalists considered themselves a movement rather than a party. They grew fairly rapidly during 1933 and at their high point may have had twenty-five thousand members, whereas the government's National Union then had only about twenty thousand. Militancy was centered in Lisbon and in the conservative northern cities of Braga and Bragança. Of those members for whom data are available, the largest minority came from the working class, followed by white-collar employees and students, and next by shopkeepers, petty entrepreneurs, and

---

39. J. Medina, *Salazar e os fascistas* (Lisbon, 1979), 239.
40. Costa Pinto, *Camisas azuis* 215.
41. Ibid., 215–23.

farmers. There was also a not inconsiderable membership among junior army officers. By contrast, the National Union was made up more of professional men, landowners, and other conservative middle-class elements.[42] In political background, the largest single sector of leaders and militants stemmed from the old Integralist movement, and more than a few local National Syndicalist centers seemed interested in a monarchist restoration, which tended to dilute genuine fascist identity. The National Syndicalists organized small *brigadas de choque* (shock brigades) but rarely engaged in direct action.

Salazar made clear his rejection of fascist "pagan caesarism" and its "new state which knows no juridical or moral limits."[43] Catholic leaders also strongly denounced National Syndicalism. While inaugurating his Estado Novo (New State) in 1933, Salazar put strong pressure on the Blue Shirts, closing their newspaper and firing some of their leaders who held government positions, tightly censoring their activity. He also created his own student organization, the Accão Escolar Vanguarda (Student Action Vanguard, AEV), to outflank them with a more moderate youth group.[44] Salazar then permitted the National Syndicalists to hold a national congress in November 1933, indicating a willingness to co-opt them if they would moderate their position and renounce a categorical fascism. By the first months of 1934 he had succeeded to some extent in splitting the movement; those who broke off were then incorporated in many cases into positions within the regime (where for the remainder of the decade some of them constituted a sort of de facto fascistic pressure group within the state syndical system). On July 29, 1934, Salazar announced dissolution of the National Syndicalist organization. The government's note rejected their fascistic "exaltation of youth, the cult of force through so-called direct action, the principle of the superiority of state political power in social life, the propensity for organizing masses behind a single leader."[45]

At the same time Salazar felt a need to give a somewhat more dynamic, mobilized appearance to his system. This was provided initially by the AEV, which also, somewhat contradictorily, maintained contact with the CAUR organization in Rome promoting "universal fascism." The only Portuguese representative at the CAUR's conference at Montreux in December 1934 was Antonio Eça de Quieroz, a leader of the AEV (and son of Portugal's leading novelist). His presence created an anomaly, the only case of a delegate who was not representing an ostensible fascist movement in opposition to the government in power in his home country. Eça de Queiroz was even announced as the delegate of the "National Syndicalists, led by Salazar." It is not clear

42. Ibid., 260–303.
43. Quoted in A. Ferro, *Salazar* (Lisbon, 1933), 148.
44. A. Costa Pinto and A. Ribeiro, *A Accão Escolar Vanguarda* (Lisbon, 1980).
45. *Diario de Noticias* (Lisbon), July 29, 1934, quoted in Costa Pinto, *Camisas azuis* 361, and in J. Ploncard d'Assac, *Salazar* (Paris, 1967), 107.

whether Salazar had ever approved the initiative, and during 1935 relations with the CAUR lapsed, while the AEV itself was downgraded.[46] The Portuguese government condemned Mussolini's invasion of Ethiopia, and a Portuguese diplomat chaired the League of Nations committee charged with coordinating economic sanctions against Italy.

The regular National Syndicalists meanwhile maintained a clandestine existence, though a number of their militants were placed under arrest. Preto helped to organize an extremely heterogeneous conspiracy against the Portuguese regime. This was led by the National Syndicalists and by a small circle of monarchists but was also supported by some right-wing republicans and even a few Socialists and anarchists interested simply in toppling the existing regime. Preto may have hoped for decisive support from the military, but the revolt of September 10, 1935, was backed by only a small sector of the armed forces and failed completely, leading to the effective repression of the National Syndicalists.[47] Fascism in Portugal had suffered the same fate as its counterparts in Austria, Hungary, and Romania.

Salazar had nonetheless already indicated a willingness to consider a few of the trappings of fascism, and the Spanish Civil War, which broke out in July 1936, carried his Estado Novo a little further in that direction. The Spanish conflict drastically radicalized the atmosphere in the peninsula, leading the Portuguese regime to create a full-scale youth movement, Mocidade Portuguesa (Portuguese Youth), and a paramilitary auxiliary, the Legião Portuguesa, both of which used the fascist salute. Though the Mocidade was immediately given a primarily Catholic coloring, the Legião was more political and looked like a regular fascist militia. By 1939 it had fifty-three thousand members, though only about thirty thousand were active. The chief political organization of the regime was nonetheless the National Union, which particularly dominated local administration, and after the close of the Spanish Civil War the Legião was downgraded.[48]

In Portugal fascism played no role in either the overthrow of the parliamentary regime or the construction of the new authoritarian system, functioning instead as a movement of opposition against the moderation of the latter. After 1935 National Syndicalism could survive only as a tiny semiclandestine sect; former Blue Shirts within the regime were not very influential, with the partial exception of their influence in the syndical system. Salazar personally rejected the support of a fascist movement, was hostile to genuine fascist

---

46. S. Kuin, "O Braço Longo de Mussolini: Os 'Comitati d'Azione per l'Universalità di Roma' em Portugal (1933–1937)," *Penélope* 11 (1993): 7–20.

47. Costa Pinto, *Camisas azuis* 276–82.

48. J. da Silva, *Legião Portuguesa* (Lisbon, 1975); C. Oliveira, *Portugal e a Guerra Civil de Espanha* (Lisbon, 1988); L. N. Rodrigues, "A Legião Portuguesa no espectro político nacional (1936–1939)," *Penélope* 11 (1993): 21–36.

culture, and rejected any concept of a charismatic *Führerprinzip*, as well as cultural modernization in general and any priority for accelerated economic development. He similarly rejected militarism and aggressive new imperialism as simply opposed to Portuguese interests, which should center on law and order to maintain the empire already held. Though he briefly employed certain organizational and choreographic trappings of fascism, he was categorical in his rejection of its most distinctive and determining features. Salazar's ideology was that of Catholic corporatism, and though his moderation prevented him from formally reunifying church and state, the Estado Novo should be seen as a new Catholic corporative regime analogous to that of Dollfuss in Austria.

After the opposition of the regime itself—which was decisive—the possibilities of a fascism in Portugal were limited by other basic factors: the relatively low level of mobilization in a country where genuine mass politics had never fully emerged; the comparative weakness of the threat from the worker left (compared with Italy, Germany, Austria, or Spain); the fact that Portugal had been on the winning side in World War I, so that any lingering traumas from that conflict had dissipated by the late 1920s; an imperial position which was satisfied and defensive, concerned only to retain the empire already occupied; and finally the essentially agrarian structure of the society, less amenable to mass mobilization (even though fascist movements had mobilized agrarian support in Italy, Austria, Hungary, and Romania).

Greece

Greece, a small southern European country that for long had been even weaker than Portugal, was nonetheless characterized by one of the most severe irredentist problems in Europe. The so-called Megali Idea of territorial expansion had been a persistent feature of Greek life since the original liberation of southern Greece from Ottoman rule early in the nineteenth century. Moreover, Greece's defeat in the war with Turkey in 1921–23 and the resultant mass influx of poverty-stricken refugees created huge national problems and a strong sense of status deprivation.

Greece thus seemed to possess some of the major variables necessary for fascism, yet it lacked other political, cultural, and social constituents. Greek political organization remained remarkably stable on the level of ordinary society and was solidly based—despite the large refugee minority—on a large moderate left and a large moderate right. Most cultural life was either liberal-progressive or semitraditionalist, so that truly radical new ideas got little hearing. Nationalist radicalism remained largely in the hands of the Liberals. Despite a major land reform concluded in the mid-1920s, the social framework of most of the nation's agrarian majority had not yet been drastically transformed. The older patterns of clientelist networks survived well into the twentieth century.[49] Even the Liberals depended on them, so that direct mass mobilization was still not a primary feature of political life. The persistence of such factors thus precluded the opening of new space for a fascist movement, despite kaleidoscopic changes of government.

Finally, the disaster of 1922–23 had a certain purgative effect, while the goal of including nearly all Greeks within the independent homeland had itself been realized. Turkey was too formidable a foe to challenge again, especially after the great powers had indicated their lack of support. There was no remaining Greek-inhabited *irredenta* to focus further ambitions, so a new fascistic nationalism could only have developed strongly in a dependent relationship with other powers. After 1923, however, Greece was less challenged by the existence of irredentist territory and also drew less encouragement from other powers for possible changes or ambitions than at any time since 1830. Until the threat developed from Italy at the close of the 1930s, Greece's international situation had thus become depressurized to a much greater degree than during the preceding century.

Greece's politics were nonetheless among the most unstable in Europe, exceeded before 1926 only by the parliamentary republic in Portugal, and by none during the decade that followed. Such extreme instability stemmed from several factors, beginning with acute polarization between liberal republicanism and conservative monarchism, more persistent than equivalent polarization in any southern European or Balkan country. A second factor was persistent domination by the clientelist structure of politics, which limited the effects of the nominal universal male suffrage in effect since 1864. The combination of these factors helps to account for the "circular" effect in Greek politics between 1917 and 1936, with rapid alternation between short-lived civilian and temporary military governments, in a manner more extreme even than Portugal and more similar to a Latin American country than to anything else in Europe. Another factor, which played much less significant a role in southwestern Europe, was the sometimes decisive influence of foreign affairs and military involvement, as during 1917–23.

The Greek crisis during the depression was primarily political, for after 1932 the depression rapidly came to an end, as the government ceased payments on the foreign debt and industrial production rose rapidly. Yet the *ethnikos dichasmos* (national schism) once more became profound. After the monarchist conservatives re-won power, the Liberals boycotted the 1935 elections. General Georgios Kondyles, one of the senior officers who had acted to end the monarchy more than a decade earlier, then led a coup to restore it. By this point the military had become more insubordinate in Greece than anywhere else in

49. This aspect of Greek political structure is particularly emphasized in Nicos P. Mouzelis's stimulating *Politics in the Semi-Periphery: Early Parliamentarism and Late Industrialization in the Balkans and Latin America* (New York, 1986).

Europe, and there was increasing talk about the failure of the parliamentary system, even among the Liberals.

In April 1936 another interim government was needed after the failure of the two main parties to reach any agreement, and King George appointed a caretaker ministry under the right-wing nationalist general Ioannis Metaxas, even though his party had won no more than 4 percent of the vote in national elections three months earlier. After a series of large strikes, Metaxas declared an emergency and seized full powers of government, to the exclusion of parliament. He at first instituted a ministry composed of "businessmen, bankers and technocrats . . . , a coalition of experts and professors." [50]

In the following month, however, he proclaimed a "New State" to replace the parliamentary system. A corporative framework of state economic regulation was subsequently announced, though never more than partially implemented. Trade unions were administered by the state, while extensive governmental regulations, replete with price controls, channeled and distorted the economy. Social insurance was expanded somewhat, and broad debt relief for the peasantry was announced, although in fact industry and finance prospered a good deal more than the peasants. All political parties were dissolved, though Metaxas made no effort to create a new one of his own. The only mass organization he developed was the National Youth Organization (EON), created in November 1936. Within two years it had reached a nominal membership of one million, thus including the great majority of Greek youth. The EON had only a limited paramilitary dimension, though some effort was made to create Worker Battalions. As the months passed, more and more of the older conservative bureaucrats were eliminated in favor of new, more radical personnel.

On August 4, 1938, the second anniversary of the inauguration of the dictatorship, Metaxas "declared himself political dictator for life, with the approval of the crown. His 'New State' proclaimed a gospel of 'Hellenism' that would lift Greece out of centuries of decline into a 'Third Civilization' (following classical Greece and the Byzantine empire)," though he defined the Hellenic race through culture and history rather than biology.[51] He sought its basis not in modern vitalism but in Sparta and the Greek past, announcing that "we owe it therefore to revert backwards in order to rediscover ourselves," a process that required the leadership of a new elite.[52] Though the regime used the fascist salute and sometimes employed the term *totalitarian*, it was neither generically fascist nor structurally totalitarian. The absence of any revolutionary doctrine or potential, or of political mass mobilization, left it a primarily bureaucratic form of authoritarianism that ideologically relied a great deal on religion. There was little indication of popular support, nor was there much

50. M. Mazower, *Greece and the Inter-War Economic Crisis* (Oxford, 1991), 290.
51. J. V. Kofas, *Authoritarianism in Greece: The Metaxas Regime* (Boulder, 1983), 62.
52. Ibid.

overt opposition. Metaxas's greatest successes lay in strengthening the military and developing effective police control, creating a rather brutal prison camp system that soon contained several thousand prisoners.

This essentially right radical authoritarian system was accepted by the monarchy, by the British government (Greece's traditional ally), and even by major Liberal émigrés as the most effective system that could be hoped for as Europe moved toward another major war. Metaxas believed that Europe needed a nationalistic and antiliberal new order, and he tried to draw nearer to both Germany and Italy, while loosening ties with Britain. He nonetheless rejected the label of fascism, telling a British official that "Portugal under Dr. Salazar, not the Germany of Hitler or the Italy of Mussolini, provided the nearest analogy." [53] Though he was both more militarist and rather more radical than Salazar, this statement was not misleading. Metaxas's regime and country withstood direct Italian invasion in 1940; had he not died of illness in January 1941 and his country been overrun by the Wehrmacht three months later, his regime might have endured for some time.

The only categorically fascist force in Greece was George Mercouris's Greek National Socialist Party. Mercouris followed somewhat the same career line as Valois and Preto, save that his previous political activity had been more important, since he had twice been a cabinet minister with the conservative monarchists and also a member of the delegation to the League of Nations. Overcome by the vertigo of fascism in the mid-1930s, he launched an imitative political organization which failed to draw significant support.[54]

Poland

Polish government after 1926 constituted another eastern European case of domination by a right authoritarian system. Unlike most of its counterparts, however, the Polish regime governed its country for more than a decade and tended to become increasingly rigorous and dictatorial, though not fundamentally fascist. Josef Pilsudski, the creator and leader of the Polish regime, was not a believer in thoroughgoing dictatorship. Like Mussolini and various fascist leaders, he had begun his career as a Socialist, but he had always been fundamentally a nationalist. The regime which he created was politically semipluralist; it at first eschewed anti-Semitism and maintained a certain degree of civil rights. In 1928 his regime created an umbrella-type political group, the BBWR (Nonparty Bloc for the Support of the Government), to bring together for electoral purposes a variety of parties and organizations willing to support

53. Ibid., 186. See also H. Cliadakis, "Le régime de Metaxas et la Deuxième Guerre Mondiale," *Revue d'Histoire de la Deuxième Guerre Mondiale* 107 (July 1977): 19–38.
54. Thus the most famous member of his family would subsequently be his daughter Melina Mercouri, the well-known actress and left populist politician of the 1980s, sometime minister of the extraordinarily corrupt Papandreou Socialist government.

the regime, including several Jewish organizations. It won a plurality but far from a majority of the vote in largely but far from entirely free elections that year. The Sanacja (Purification), or Pilsudskiite supporters, comprised various sectors of moderates, Catholic conservatives, nationalist social groups, and especially the military. Leaders of the latter—the Colonels, as they were called—increasingly took over the government after Pilsudski's health declined in 1930. Government became more repressive, particularly with regard to the Ukrainian and White Russian minorities. A new constitution in 1935 greatly increased the powers of the presidency while reducing those of parliament, but direct elections were still retained. By the time of Pilsudski's death that year, the main opposition parties were boycotting the regime's increasingly controlled political processes.[55]

In Poland the main sector of radical nationalists was not, however, Pilsudski's Sanacja but the National Democrat Party of western Poland. The National Democrats were largely middle-class in social background, Catholic, fanatically nationalist, and anti-Semitic. They sought an extreme nationalist authoritarian system and an even more repressive policy toward the ethnic minorities who formed a third of the entire population. They constituted the main Polish radical right as distinct from Pilsudski's moderate authoritarianism, tending to admire Fascist Italy but also later being somewhat influenced by Nazi racism. After establishment of the Pilsudski regime, the National Democrats developed a more extreme right radical force, the Camp of Great Poland (OWP), which by 1928 was virtually dominated by its youth movement. Though partially reunited with other National Democrats in a new National Party, the OWP still stood apart, urging a strongly religious new corporative authoritarian system, preferably under a restored monarchy. By early 1933 the OWP claimed a quarter of a million followers, was very strong in the universities, and began to talk of a coup.[56] The government dissolved it at this point, but the result was a yet more radical new organization, the Camp of National Radicalism (ONR), now influenced more by Nazism than Italian Fascism, which was similarly shut down the following year. The National Radicals would reappear, but in the meantime a more explicitly fascist-type offshoot appeared, Falanga, based on the ONR youth.

Falanga was probably the only clear-cut fascist organization of any significance in Poland. Its name was derived from Spanish Falangism, but as might be expected from a National Democrat offshoot, its Catholicism was more extreme than that of its Spanish counterpart. Falanga insisted that "God is the highest end of man," a statement more reminiscent of Codreanu than

55. A. Polonsky, *Politics in Independent Poland, 1921–1939* (Oxford, 1972), is the principal study of this period.

56. W. Kozub-Ciembroniewicz, "La ricezione ideologica del fascismo italiano in Polonia negli anni 1927–1933," *SC* 24:1 (Feb. 1993): 5–17.

of José Antonio Primo de Rivera.[57] Falanga, which apparently never had more than about two thousand members, also emphasized radical subordination of the economy to a program of national socialism.[58]

The Colonels who ran Poland's government after 1935 accentuated state control and authoritarianism. The more radical among them foresaw a great new world upheaval that would finish liberalism; their goal was a drastic "reconstruction of the state and of social life demanded by the historic moment and those deep transformations of which we are conscious near us and throughout the world." [59] State investment in and regulation of the economy rapidly increased, until by 1939 the Polish government owned about 20 percent of all capital in industrial joint-stock companies and 40 percent of the country's banking capital.[60]

A second project was to develop a more integrated state party in place of the BBWR that could mobilize mass support. This was entrusted to a relatively inept Colonel, Adam Koc, who in February 1937 began to build a new organization, the Camp of National Unity (OZN). This was conceived in many ways as an equivalent of other efforts to create government parties or political fronts by authoritarian regimes in eastern or southern Europe, but Koc was so impressed by Falanga and its leader, Boleslaw Piasecki, that he placed Piasecki's chief lieutenant in charge of the OZN youth section, the League of Young Poland. OZN began to preach a new kind of corporative authoritarian system and was able to incorporate some of the diverse groups that had composed the now defunct BBWR, enabling Koc to claim, albeit with considerable exaggeration, a membership of two million by early 1937. Yet some of the more moderate sectors of the old BBWR refused to affiliate, because of the highly authoritarian and protofascist appearance of OZN. By October Koc and other OZN leaders were advocating the immediate transformation of Poland into a one-party state, accompanied by a drastic purge of all opposition leaders. This was too much for the more moderate elements in the government. By early 1938 Koc was forced to resign, and the link with Falanga was severed. The new leader was Colonel Zygmunt Wenda, a more conservative military commander who turned OZN partly in the direction of a paramilitary organization for national defense. With the full backing of the regime, OZN scored a victory in the generally free but partially boycotted parliamentary elections of 1938,

57. E. D. Wynot Jr., *Polish Politics in Transition: The Camp of National Unity and the Struggle for Power, 1935–1939* (Athens, Ga., 1974), 88. See also P. S. Wandycz, "Fascism in Poland, 1918–1939," in Sugar, ed., *Native Fascism* 92–97.

58. This helps to explain why Falanga's leader, Boleslaw Piasecki (who in 1938 liked to be called Il Duce), could after 1945 be used as a major puppet by the Communist regime for a kind of Catholic peace and socialism movement. See L. Blit, *The Eastern Pretender* (London, 1965).

59. Quoted in Wynot, *Polish Politics* 85.

60. Polonsky, *Politics* 353–54.

and its new directors continued to develop plans for a more restrictive one-party system. The open municipal elections of December 1938, in which OZN bested the Socialists by only 29 to 27 percent, constituted only a temporary frustration.

During the final months before the German invasion, the government accelerated the policy which it sometimes called guided democracy. The proto-fascist characteristics of OZN were not accentuated, and by midsummer several other nationalist groups had agreed to join its ranks. As the international crisis deepened, even the opposition parties were willing to form a coalition with the government, but the Colonels seemed bent on accentuating state central-ization and authoritarianism, which they considered an ineluctable choice for a country trapped between Nazi Germany and the Soviet Union.[61]

Finally, it might be noted that, like several other multinational states, Poland had to face minority nationalist movements which sometimes exhibited authoritarian and protofascist characteristics. Nazism became strong among the German minority in western Poland during the late 1930s, while, to the east, the Organization of Ukrainian Nationalists (OUN)—one of several Ukrai-nian nationalist groups—functioned increasingly as a right radical terrorist movement and was more and more influenced by Nazism.

The Baltic States

Some parallels existed between the situations in the three Baltic states and that in Poland. A moderate right authoritarian government was established in Lithuania by military coup at the close of 1926. Its president was Antanas Smetona of the National Christian Democratic Party, while the leader of the ultranationalist Tautinninkai movement, a history professor named Augustinas Voldemaras, became prime minister. The Tautinninkai grew increasingly radi-cal, having already inspired Lithuania's seizure of the coastal city of Memel in 1923. It sought territorial expansion and repressive measures against the Jewish, Russian, and Polish minorities. The most radical sector formed a proto-fascist group, the Iron Wolf Association, with the support of Voldemaras, and by 1929 there were rumors of a coup. At that point Smetona forced Volde-maras from power and temporarily moderated his government, but it moved in a more authoritarian direction by 1931, giving increased power to the main section of the Tautinninkai. Even this was inadequate for the most extreme followers of Voldemaras, who, with the support of junior officers and the Iron Wolf, attempted a "march on Kaunas" (the Lithuanian capital) in 1934 that was suppressed by the military, with numerous arrests.

61. The best account of OZN and the final phase will be found in Wynot, *Polish Politics* 177–267.

This rebellion, together with a number of local peasant revolts, stimulated Smetona to take greater power. The main sector of the Tautinninkai was given a virtual monopoly of political organization, and a new constitution in 1936 increased the powers of the president (including the control of elections) and authorized corporative organization of the economy. Smetona was now called the Leader of the People, and Lithuania had become a de facto one-party state, though along right radical rather than fascist lines. Once more, however, a fascist or protofascist movement, the Iron Wolf Association, had been repressed by a right authoritarian system.[62]

By contrast, the moderate regimes of what Georg von Rauch calls authoritarian democracy in Estonia and Latvia were installed simply as preventive or preemptive authoritarianism in 1934 by the moderate forces. In Estonia, the most progressive and democratic of the Baltic states, the main nationalist force was the Estonian War of Independence Veterans League (EVL), a paramilitary organization composed originally of those who had fought Communists and Russians in 1917–18. The EVL was based mainly on the lower middle class (probably the largest single social sector in Estonia) and had no elaborate ideology or any connection with foreign fascist movements. Its goal was simply a more authoritarian and nationalist regime in Estonia. After the League won absolute majorities in local elections in the three largest cities at the beginning of 1934, the recently elected constitutional president, Konstantin Päts, seized emergency powers, disbanding the EVL and arresting many of its leading figures. In 1935 a National Association was formed to replace political parties, and a series of state corporative institutions were introduced, but a new constitution which took effect in 1938 reduced the powers of the presidency, and by 1939 some liberties had been restored.[63]

Similarly, in Latvia the government of Karlis Ulmanis in 1934 seized authoritarian powers to outlaw the Thunder Cross, a protofascist movement organized the preceding year. Like Päts, Ulmanis developed state corporative institutions during the next three years to regulate many aspects of Latvian affairs. He failed, however, to carry out the partial return to liberalism which occurred in Estonia.[64] Both these regimes exercised policies of very moderate

62. G. von Rauch, *The Baltic States: The Years of Independence, 1917–1940* (Berkeley, 1974), 161–65; L. Sabaliunas, *Lithuania, 1939–1941* (Bloomington, 1972).

63. T. Parming, *The Collapse of Liberal Democracy and the Rise of Authoritarianism in Estonia* (London, 1975); A. Kasekamp, "The Estonian Veterans' League: A Fascist Movement?" *Journal of Baltic Studies* 24:3 (Fall 1993): 263–68.

64. J. von Hehn, *Lettland zwischen Demokratie und Diktatur* (Munich, 1957); Rauch, *Baltic States* 151–61. The Thunder Cross, with its gray shirts and black berets, employed the swastika emblem and was clearly influenced by Nazism, even though politically it was strongly anti-German. It reemerged for a period under the German occupation after 1941.

There were several other small right radical and protofascist political groups in Latvia. Whereas the Estonian EVL had been influenced by the Finnish radical right, the equivalent forces in Latvia looked more to Germany and Poland. Among them were the tiny Latvian National

authoritarianism and may well have had the support of a majority of the population in their countries. Their preemptive strategies may indeed have averted worse ills; beyond that, their main achievement was to maintain a remarkably positive rate of economic growth in the late 1930s.

Yugoslavia

Following the assassination of King Alexander in 1934, Yugoslavia soon returned to a semicontrolled system of parliamentary government under a monarchist regency. Milan Stojadinović, prime minister from 1935 to early 1939, made a new effort at authoritarian mass mobilization, forming in 1935 the Yugoslav Radical Union. This state-sponsored organization was inspired by earlier efforts to form government-based parties in eastern and southern Europe, and it nominally brought together Serb, Slovene, and Bosnian Muslim groups, among others. The goal was to organize the YRU throughout Yugoslavia, even in the smallest local districts; members would wear green shirts and address Stojadinović as Vodja, or "Leader." He normally denied that the organization had any fascist goals, but in 1938 he assured the Italian foreign minister, Ciano, that his erstwhile moderate authoritarian movement would in the future develop along the model of Italian Fascism. There was, however, very little "Yugoslav" nationalism, and any success of this ambiguous organization would depend on state sponsorship. That came to an end when the Yugoslav regent dismissed Stojadinović in 1939, in effect dissolving the movement, and moved toward a compromise with the opposition that would make possible a more representative government.[65]

During the 1930s many different nationalist groups and movements were active within Yugoslavia. Some endeavored to promote a general Yugoslav nationalism, but most were devoted to the concrete nationalism of either Serbs, Croatians, or Slovenes. The most radical was Yugoslav Action, originally created in 1930 to support the Alexander dictatorship, which preached an authoritarian corporative system and a planned economy. Yugoslav Action eventually grew more independent and more radical. Though it denied any connection with fascism, it was suppressed by the government in 1934.

A new group, Zbor (Convention), was organized the following year by some of the more right-wing elements from Yugoslav Action, together with small groups of Serbs and Slovenes. Zbor was essentially a right radical movement that propounded a general Yugoslav nationalism, a corporative authoritarian regime, and maintenance of the status quo and neutrality in foreign af-

Socialist Party, the National Revolutionary Work Force, and the Association of Legionnaires (the latter apparently inspired by the Pilsudski regime). All these organizations were animated by strong antipathy toward the various national minorities which existed in each small Baltic country.

65. J. B. Hoptner, *Yugoslavia in Crisis, 1934–1941* (New York, 1962), 33–135.

fairs. Its leader, Dimitrije Ljotić, came from a prominent Serb family and was such a frequent churchgoer (said to be very uncommon among Serbian politicians) that when the government decided to arrest him for political excesses, it charged him with religious mania and briefly shipped him off to an asylum. Zbor drew its main support from Serbs but got only about 1 percent of the general vote in the Yugoslav elections of both 1935 and 1938. By 1940 it had developed contacts with Nazi Germany and, after fomenting several incidents, was suppressed by the government before the close of the year.[66]

Among the myriad of nationalist groups in Yugoslavia, the most seriously protofascist was the small Ustasha (Insurgent) movement of radical Croatian nationalists, organized by the Zagreb lawyer Ante Pavelić in 1929. It was responsible—together with Macedonian terrorists—for the assassination of King Alexander in 1934. Small and conspiratorial during the 1930s, the movement developed increasingly ambitious goals and protofascist characteristics, aiming at an independent, extremist, and highly authoritarian Croatia. It was repressed by the Yugoslav government, but once the government was overthrown by Germany in 1941 the Ustashi would be handed the government of an autonomous Croatia and would develop into one of the most destructive of all the fascist-type movements.

In summary, there was little democracy in interwar Yugoslavia but also very little genuine fascism. The two most radical movements, the Ustashi and Zbor, were effectively repressed by a semiauthoritarian regime. This was the common experience of the great majority of fascist or extreme right radical movements in eastern and southern Europe.

Bulgaria

Bulgaria, like Greece and Portugal, seemed to possess a number of the prerequisites for significant fascist mobilization. As the so-called Prussia of the Balkans, it had been at war almost continuously between 1912 and 1918, suffering great social and economic stress as well as loss of life. Defeated twice within five years, it was despoiled of territory after both the Second Balkan War of 1913 and World War I. Yet the only mass movement to emerge in postwar Bulgaria was the Agrarian Union—a peace movement par excellence—which in turn was overthrown by military revolt in 1923.

For the next eleven years Bulgaria lived under a nineteenth-century-style oligarchic parliamentary regime that restricted power. The fact that land was more evenly divided in Bulgaria than anywhere else in the Balkans encouraged social stability and some degree of political quiescence. During these

---

66. See the articles by Dimitrije Djordjević and Ivan Avakumović in Sugar, ed., *Native Fascism* 123–43.

years a number of small right radical and/or protofascist groups emerged. The only one to achieve any support at all was the Ratnitsi (Warriors), followed by the Bulgarian National Legions of General Christo Lukov. Groups called the National Fascist Zadruga and the Bulgarian National Socialist Workers Party also appeared briefly.

Right radical army officers formed their own conspiratorial organization called Zveno (the Link), which seized power temporarily in a coup of 1934. Their government proved ineffective, whereupon King Boris arranged a royalist takeover the following year that inaugurated a controlled but still semipluralist parliamentary regime more like that which existed in Poland than the Bulgarian system before 1934. The veiled royalist regime governed down to the time of the king's death in 1943. Though Boris repressed both the Communist and peasant left and the protofascist right (dissolving the Ratnitsi in April 1939), his government felt the need to draw nearer to Germany and Italy in foreign policy.[67]

Bulgaria thus followed the standard "Balkan model" of a rightist authoritarian system under the crown, the royalist superstructure being the main difference compared with countries in southwestern and northeastern Europe, even though in Greece the crown played no more role in affairs than in Italy. In Bulgaria once more a protofascist movement had been repressed by a right authoritarian regime.

By 1939 the majority of European political systems were authoritarian, and of these the most common form was a comparatively moderate rightist authoritarian regime, which in the Balkans was to some extent under royalist leadership. What was much less common was a fascist movement of any real significance in any given country, for neither in the more developed and democratic countries of the northwest nor in the more backward lands of the east and south did conditions exist which were appropriate for fascist movements. When fascist movements did emerge, they were usually repressed without great difficulty by the rightist regimes, and this was even the case with broadly popular forces such as the Arrow Cross and the Legion of the Archangel Michael.

67. E. Nolte, *Die Krise des liberalen Systems und die faschistischen Bewegungen* (Munich, 1968), 194–200; R. Solliers, "Notes sur le fascisme bulgare," in *Etudes sur le fascisme*, by M. Bardèche et al. (Paris, 1974), 166–73; articles by Djordjević and Avakumović in Sugar, ed., *Native Fascism* 125–43; M. L. Miller, *Bulgaria during the Second World War* (Stanford, 1975); S. Groueff, *Crown of Thorns: The Reign of King Boris III of Yugoslavia, 1918–1943* (Lanham, Md., 1987). For further references, see N. Poppetrov, "Die bulgarische Wissenschaft über die Probleme des bulgarischen Faschismus," *Bulgarian Historical Review* 14:1 (1986): 78–93.

10
Fascism Outside Europe?

Whether or not political forces with the primary characteristics of European fascism have emerged elsewhere has been a problematic question for some analysts, though it has posed no problem for the observer who assumes that any form of anti-Marxian authoritarianism is intrinsically fascist. Primary candidates for a non-European fascism have been variously identified in Japan, South Africa, Latin America, and the Middle East.

JAPAN

The issue has been most acute in the case of Japan, because of its aggressiveness in World War II and its association with Germany and Italy. The existence of "Japanese fascism" was detected by Soviet writers as early as 1934,[1] and most Marxist commentators have applied this interpretation to Japanese government and institutions of the 1930s ever since.[2] A slightly different formulation has been made by other Japanese and Western social scientists, who point to the growing bellicosity and authoritarianism of the Japanese regime during those years and argue that fascism is a valid label to define regimes that become aggressive and authoritarian during the industrialization of a non–state socialist system.[3]

---

1. O. Tanin and E. Yohan [pseuds.], *Militarism and Fascism in Japan* (New York, 1934).
2. Cf. references in G. M. Wilson, "A New Look at the Problem of 'Japanese Fascism,' " in *Reappraisals of Fascism*, ed. H. A. Turner Jr. (New York, 1975), 199–214, and T. Furuya, "Naissance et développement du fascisme japonais," *Revue d'Histoire de la Deuxième Guerre Mondiale* 86 (April 1972): 1–16.
3. This approach takes diverse forms in such works as R. A. Scalapino, *Democracy and the Party Movement in Prewar Japan* (Berkeley, 1953); R. Storry, *The Double Patriots* (Boston,

George M. Wilson has argued that the concept of "Japanese fascism" is mistaken, insofar as no political movement arose to seize power and formal Japanese constitutional authority remained nominally intact, while a certain amount of political pluralism, together with parliamentary elections, continued to exist.[4] Gregory J. Kasza, the keenest Western analyst of Japanese authoritarianism, has further expanded this critique. He summarizes the arguments of those who reject the concept of a Japanese fascism under five categories:

1. The concept is inadequately defined.
2. It suffers from what one Japanese scholar called the deficiency theory: that is, the absence of a single party, a Duce or Führer, and so on.
3. It has been applied indiscriminately, without differentiating between various groups and sectors.
4. It has sometimes been motivated by political and/or wartime, rather than scholarly, concerns.
5. It is particularly closely identified with Marxist interpretations of recent Japanese history.[5]

Those who continue to employ the concept of Japanese fascism readily admit differences from Europe, and so they often modify the term as "military fascism" or "emperor-system fascism." Opponents stress instead the continuation of traditional authoritarianism, similarities between Japan and other third world and developmental dictatorships, and the fact that the Japanese system was an emergency wartime expedient, or else they adopt a radical nominalism which defines the Japanese system as uniquely Japanist or Japanese right

---

1957); idem, "Japanese Fascism in the Thirties," *Wiener Library Bulletin* 20:4 (Autumn 1966): 1–7; and M. Masso, "The Ideology and Dynamics of Japanese Fascism," in *Thought and Behavior in Modern Japanese Politics*, ed. I. Morris (London, 1963), 25–83. Ivan Morris has edited a compendium of some of the main interpretations under the title *Japan, 1931–1945: Militarism, Fascism, Japanism?* (Boston, 1963).

The most recent formulation of this approach by an American scholar will be found in A. Gordon, *Labor and Imperial Democracy in Prewar Japan* (Berkeley, 1991). See also H. P. Bix, "Rethinking 'Emperor-System Fascism': Ruptures and Continuities in Modern Japanese History," and G. McCormack, "Nineteen-Thirties Japan: Fascism?" both in *Bulletin of Concerned Asian Scholars* 14:2 (April–June 1982): 2–14, 15–34.

One of the most extended discussions in Japanese is Yamaguchi Yasushi, *Fuashizmu* (Tokyo, 1979), which argues for the concept, distinguishing between fascist ideologies, movements, and regimes. According to G. J. Kasza, " 'Fascism from Above'? The Renovationist Right in Wartime Japan," forthcoming, 24–25, Yamaguchi finds a common identity in the negatives of anti-Marxism, antiliberalism, anticapitalism, anti-internationalism and anti–status quo.

4. Wilson, "New Look"; P. Duus and D. Okimoto, "Fascism and the History of Prewar Japan: The Failure of a Concept," *Journal of Asian Studies* 39:1 (Nov. 1979): 65–76.

5. Kasza, " 'Fascism from Above'?" 2–5. The categories presented represent my summary of Kasza's analysis.

authoritarian. Kasza observes that "the key question is whether the differences between the Japanese and European cases warrant abandoning the fascist concept in describing Japan, or whether the similarities demand its retention. Neither alternative is really suitable: both the similarities and the differences are substantial, and whatever conceptual apparatus is employed, it should not lose sight of either." [6] He points out that whereas in Europe fascism was most common as a movement, second as an ideology, and only third and last as a regime, "in Japan this order of scholarly interest must be turned on its head. European fascism had its greatest impact on Japan's political regime, a secondary impact on political thought, and its least significant impact on political movements." [7]

Both imperialism and racist concepts have a long history in modern Japan, but during the fascist era the main radical nationalist pressure came from small radical nationalist circles and from radical elements of the military.[8] The principal influence from abroad was that of Nazi Germany, and this primarily affected only elites. Before 1937 none of the small ultranationalist societies transformed themselves into significant parties or movements, but some of their spokesmen and theorists might be generally described as national socialists (though not "Nazis"). They formed part of the general phenomenon of the 1920s and 1930s known as *kakushin,* or "radical reformism," which produced a great variety of nationalist reform doctrines.

The most prominent theorist was the precocious Kita Ikki, in his youth a socialist. His *Plan for the Reorganization of Japan,* written in 1919 and published four years later, propounded a new system of authoritarian nationalist corporatism, though permitting a form of subordinated electoral democracy. This regime would follow a policy of national socialism, nationalizing large industries and fostering economic modernization. It would implement a modern welfare program that would raise the status of workers and permit a limited degree of worker control in industry. Wealth would be both expanded and redistributed, with estates divided among tenant farmers (along lines similar to the American occupation land reform of 1946). Above all, the new Japan would not scruple to use military force to free Asia from Western imperialism, seeking an economic alliance with the United States while confronting and defeating the Soviet Union and Britain. Ultimately Japan would become the leader of mankind, opening the way to a higher humanity that would realize the redemption foretold in the prophecy of the Second Coming of Christ. Kita had

6. Ibid., 6.

7. Ibid., 6–7.

8. On the development of Japanese nativist thought, see H. D. Harootunian, *Things Seen and Unseen: Discourse and Ideology in Tokugawa Nativism* (Chicago, 1988). Donald Calman, in *The Nature and Origins of Japanese Imperialism* (London, 1992), presents a possibly extreme reading of nineteenth-century Japanese imperialism and racism.

no plan for a party movement or mass mobilization; his new system would rely on military leadership to institute an organic authoritarian state. During the last two decades of his life, Kita was personally a devout Nichiren Buddhist, following a Japanese nationalist variant of that religion.[9]

There were other theorists, such as Takabatake Motoyuki, a former leftist who had translated Marx, as well as small grouplets of national socialists. Their goals were certainly revolutionary, sometimes including a state socialism that would nationalize most of the economy and the willingness to encourage violent change, but their influence was limited. The national socialists in toto edited only seven of the fifty-nine nationalist journals in Japan in 1932 and only five of ninety in 1935.[10] Some of those most interested in economic issues had little concern for militarism and imperialism, even though they advanced a secular doctrine of the state, unusual under Japanese Shinto. Most of the national socialists, however, did not espouse secular principles of political legitimacy, accepting the Shintoist emperor system, and scarcely any had a doctrine of secularist revolutionary culture.

Revolutionary national socialism was much less common than the right-wing nationalism developed by several dozen small groups during the 1920s. Kasza has divided these in turn into the moderate or idealist right and the more radical or renovationist right. The moderate or idealist right sought to restore the dominance of a bureaucratic nondemocratic constitutional monarchy, somewhat as it had existed before the 1920s. Most of the idealist right did not seek a completely new order but rather change and spiritual renewal within the old order, which would be reformed and made more conservative and authoritarian. These people had few concrete new economic and political proposals and were basically nonviolent and legalistic.

The radical right was most visible among younger army officers. They formed small conspiratorial groups, often with vague goals, and made little effort to mobilize political support. They took literally their oath to the emperor; a key concept was "restoration of the Showa emperor," meaning a strong authoritarian government. They were in a general sense encouraged also by the trend within the Japanese army during the 1920s away from the older military thinking in favor of the new "Imperial Army system," which relied on vitalist doctrines, the cult of the will, and the primacy of morale as guarantors of what began to be called the inevitable victory.[11]

9. G. M. Wilson, *Radical Nationalist in Japan: Kita Ikki, 1883–1937* (Cambridge, Mass., 1969).

10. G. J. Kasza, "Fascism from Below? A Comparative Perspective on the Japanese Right, 1931–1936," *JCH* 19:4 (Oct. 1984): 607–27; idem, *The State and the Mass Media in Japan, 1918–1945* (Berkeley, 1988).

11. L. A. Humphreys, *The Way of the Heavenly Sword: The Japanese Army in the 1920's* (Stanford, 1994).

What both sets of rightists had in common were ultranationalism, antiparliamentarianism, moderate social and economic reform, a reliance on elites, and an emphasis on foreign expansion, together with the exaltation of the emperor (though the radical right would go much further in breaking the law and changing the form of the state). Probably the most important new right radical group was the Cherry Blossom Society, organized in 1930 among officers on the general staff and in the War Ministry. By that time nationalist doctrines were expanding rapidly on several levels; several thousand workers were being organized in new "Japanist" or nationalist trade unions, and by the spring of 1931 the parliamentary government was preparing new social legislation that would increase the role of the state.

What some Japanese historians call the Fifteen Years' War began in 1931 with the first political assassinations by right radicals. They killed a prime minister and several other notables and helped to promote the Mukden Incident and the beginning of military aggression on the mainland. A new sect of military radicals quickly emerged called the Land-Loving School (later the National Principle group). Inspired by the right radical intellectual Gondo Seikyo, they held that the Japanese were a true race superior to all others, whose rural, preindustrial way of life had been superior to the decadently modern. All power must be restored to the throne to create a radical new government that would abolish inequities and restore national principles. This sect of radicals held that modernizing renovationist rightists were mere "fascists" who sought to preserve the existing oligarchies and expand the power of the existing corrupt institutions. The latter could only be overthrown by a wave of assassinations, and this idea in 1932 produced the death of another prime minister and several other leaders.[12] Though this group was quickly repressed, the events of 1931–32 initiated the destabilization of the Japanese government, which henceforth would veer increasingly toward nationalism and militarism, with coalition "national governments" replacing regular parliamentary leadership. The final round of direct military radicalism occurred in 1936 with further assassinations, after which discipline was more sternly imposed.[13] Even before these incidents, right radicals had generally begun to renounce violent change, and the 1936 repression (which also brought the execution of Kita Ikki the following year) produced a major decline in publication of right radical journals, few of which, it might be noted, ever invoked European models.[14]

The last year of partial democracy in Japan was 1937, which saw in-

---

12. J. Crowley, *Japan's Quest for Autonomy* (Princeton, 1966), 172–77. Cf. T. R. H. Havens, *Farm and Nation in Modern Japan: Agrarian Nationalism, 1870–1940* (Princeton, 1974).

13. B.-A. Shillony, *Revolt in Japan: The Young Officers and the February 26, 1936, Incident* (Princeton, 1973).

14. Kasza observes that of 712 "rightist" books investigated by the police in 1936, only 11 dealt with Hitler and Mussolini, mostly from a critical perspective ("Fascism from Above?" 12).

creased membership in trade unions and a sizable strike wave, with the Social Masses Party (the Japanese socialists) reaching its highest levels in the elections of 1935 and 1937. Yet even the spokesmen for the Social Masses made it clear that the party accepted key aspects of "Japanism," including imperial expansion and state coordination of economic affairs and planning, and only sought fair treatment for labor within this context.

The two most protofascist of the right radical groups in 1936–37 were Kingoro Hashimoto's Great Japan Youth Party and Seigo Nakano's Eastern Way Society. As Kasza notes, "neither was a fascist movement," but they "were the closest approximations." [15] The Great Japan Youth Party sought to promote social and economic change, but the Eastern Way Society was the only right radical group to achieve any degree of popular support, gaining 2.1 percent of the vote in the parliamentary elections of 1937 and 3.0 percent in 1942 (when it had to run against an official government slate). Its members wore black shirts, and its leader was sometimes called the Japanese Hitler. Though he had talked with notables in both Italy and Germany, Seigo Nakano denied, doubtless correctly, that he was a fascist. The Eastern Way Society repudiated political violence and accepted the monarchy, together with traditional cultural and moral values, but sought mass mobilization to achieve a one-party state that would manage the economy. After criticizing the government during wartime, Seigo Nakano was disgraced in 1942 and committed suicide.[16]

With this exception, the Japanese right radicals' unremitting elitism and disinterest in popular mobilization was more reminiscent of early nineteenth-century European liberals than of Italian or German rightists during the 1930s. It should be remembered that mass politics had only timidly begun to enter Japan during the 1920s and that full participation had never been achieved, that labor organization was very weak (at their peak, only 8 percent of industrial workers were in trade unions), that traditional culture remained very strong, that Japan had had only the most limited participation in World War I, and finally that the police simply had greater power there than in most European countries.[17]

The beginning of full-scale war with China in 1937 marked, at least in retrospect, a point of no return. Government authority expanded steadily, particularly with the National Mobilization Law of 1938, which gave the state unprecedented civil and economic authority. The government had sponsored a national youth organization ever since 1915, and several women's groups had been added in more recent years. In 1938 a Central Alliance for the Mobilization of the National Spirit was formed as an umbrella association for ninety-four

15. Ibid., 13.
16. Ibid., 13–15.
17. Ibid., 18–21. Cf. R. H. Mitchell, *Thought Control in Prewar Japan* (Ithaca, 1976).

national associations (of veterans, municipal mayors, trade unions, and so on). Though Prince Konoye, the first regular wartime prime minister, resigned at the beginning of 1939, by the following year he had launched a proposal for a "new political order" which would mean an end to the independence of the political parties and the formation of a yet stronger government.[18]

His brain trust, the Showa Research Association, had since 1935 developed designs for an end to the old order, of parliamentary government and capitalism, stressing the priority of the national community. The Showa intellectuals, led by Ryu Sintaro, Royama Masamichi, and Miki Kiyoshi, were modernizers and technocrats who encouraged more effective state planning and regulation, buttressed by a spirit of unity, self-sacrifice, and national expansion. They believed that a modern industrial society could best be structured and represented by extreme state corporatism, resting on a broad program of mobilization. For them, a new world war was inevitable, but they also conceded that a major new political movement could not be created under wartime conditions.

Their charge, however, had been to find new policies conceived "from an antifascist viewpoint."[19] Royama had denounced what he termed the violent "fascism" of the right radical rebels in 1936, correctly citing big business as a leading opponent of "fascism." As Miles Fletcher says of the Showa Association:

> These intellectuals did not imitate some aspects of fascism. Although they longed for a strong leader . . . , they did not implicitly call for a charismatic dictator. . . . Such an idea would have prompted immediate charges of lese majesty. Nor did these writers glorify struggle and violence for their own sake, as was often the case with European fascism. European fascists often referred to the glory of the Roman Empire or the savagery of the *Volk* to stress the values of struggle and martial valor. Royama, Ryu, and Miki did not emphasize those qualities, despite the presence of the samurai as a convenient reference.[20]

Instead, they emphasized a legal transition based on traditional values. The spiritual basis of their new system was to be the emperor doctrine combined with Confucian humanism. Everything was to be administered from above, with no exaltation of youth.

Soon after Konoye returned as prime minister in mid-1940, the government created a new political umbrella association, the Imperial Rule Assistance Association (IRAA). Though all political parties had patriotically declared their dissolution, they were immediately allowed to reconstitute themselves

18. Y. Oka, *Konoe Funimaro* (Tokyo, 1983). This book is in English.
19. W. M. Fletcher III, *The Search for a New Order: Intellectuals and Fascism in Prewar Japan* (Chapel Hill, 1982), 96.
20. Ibid., 156.

under the IRAA, which was not itself a party but simply "an instrument of bureaucratic control" administered by provincial prefects.[21] The parliament still held the power of the purse and, in fact, would not initially approve the IRAA's budget until terms were met to allow the parties to survive. Parliament never voted against the government on military measures, but some deputies were not afraid to vote against other bills.

Japanese authoritarianism was a complex amalgam of state bureaucrats, conservative economic leaders, and military praetorians, though with the military becoming more dominant after the formation of General Hideki Tojo's government in the fall of 1941. Yet Tojo was far from a military dictator. Radical rightists criticized his cabinet for being too weak and disunified, and it has been argued that Tojo held less personal power than Churchill or Roosevelt. The military did attempt to create a new Great Japan Imperial Rule Assistance Young Men's Corps as a sort of paramilitary and political force of young men. This was an outgrowth of the Young Adults Group formed some years earlier to combat leftists, which had a membership of 1.5 million in 1941. The updated version was established in January 1942; apparently Tojo and his military colleagues planned to use it to present a large slate of candidates in the upcoming parliamentary elections. The conservatives in charge of the regular parties managed to thwart this, setting up the IRAA candidacies themselves. The Young Men's Corps won only forty seats, though a grand total of forty thousand were elected to various levels of local and provincial bodies.[22]

Nazi Germany was nonetheless a major inspiration to Japanese bureaucrats and ideologues with regard to regulating the economy and dissolving autonomous interest groups. New Japanese associations tended structurally to parallel German state cartels, as did the formation of a general state association of workers, a state women's association, a new state youth organization, and a state agricultural association. The Japanese Cabinet Information Bureau was patterned directly on the German Ministry of Propaganda, though conversely the Greater Japan Industrial Patriotic Association was only formed in 1942, combining capital and labor organizations, with some autonomy for the former. Both the two major Japanese industrial organizations survived the war intact, so that in this area Japanese wartime institutions resembled those of Fascist Italy more than Nazi Germany. Whereas the German state particularly emphasized state organizations for industry, agriculture, and youth, the most extensive Japanese state organizations were formed for local society, women, and youth.[23] One way in which the Japanese mobilization was broader than

21. Kasza, "Fascism from Above?" 37. Cf. G. M. Berger, *Parties Out of Power in Japan, 1931–1941* (Princeton, 1977).

22. These data are taken from chapter 6 of Kasza's *Administered Mass Organizations* (forthcoming).

23. The conclusions are drawn from Kasza, *Administered Mass Organizations.*

that of Germany was in state sponsorship of neighborhood, town, and village associations. There was even more compaction of individual entities, for "newspapers and magazines were reduced from over 30,000 in 1937 to 2,500 in 1944; banks from 426 to 59, large textile mills from 271 to 44." [24] Yet there was never any ambition merely to copy the German system, and no translation of *Mein Kampf* could be distributed in Japan because of its racial statements. Major differences remained: Japan lacked a charismatic all-powerful dictator, a Nazi Party, and an SS,[25] and it never developed a general concentration camp system for dissidents.[26]

The highest governmental authority remained the cabinet, not any single figure or even the military. General Tojo was eventually forced to resign in favor of a more moderate general as prime minister in 1944, and this, "the first and almost the only orderly change of government among the major belligerent nations in World War II [except for that of England in 1940], was achieved smoothly, with no violence, no arrests and no clashes." [27] The IRAA was itself replaced by two other umbrella organizations in the last three years of the war.

Japan had evolved a somewhat pluralistic authoritarian system which exhibited some of the characteristics of fascism, but it did not develop fascism's most distinctive and revolutionary aspects. Japan was never subjected to the same degree of radicalization, for Imperial Japan on the eve of World War II in many ways approximated the development of Germany's Second Reich more than it did Hitler's nation. Japan was much less industrialized and had never fully achieved democratic mass mobilization. The executive authority of the emperor reigned de jure if not de facto, and institutions remained highly elitist within a society that was still to a large degree deferential. It may be argued that Japan was still too traditional and conservative, as well as too non-Western, to be receptive to a genuine fascism. Despite the assassinations, ultranationalist hysteria, and radical pressures of the 1930s, and despite the great extension of state power, pluralism was never entirely destroyed. Patriotic nongovernmental forces won 34 percent of the vote in the parliamentary elections of 1942. Ben-Ami Shillony concludes that

24. Kasza, "Fascism from Above?" 41.

25. The only recent comparative study is P. Brooker, *The Faces of Fraternalism: Nazi Germany, Fascist Italy, and Imperial Japan* (Oxford, 1991), which concludes that a greater degree of "mechanical solidarity" was achieved in Japan. However, Andrew Gordon, in *Labor and Imperial Democracy in Prewar Japan*, points out that during the war the real wages of German workers fell only 2 percent (before the final phase), while between 1939 and 1944 those of Japanese workers fell 33 percent. In his judgment, this led to a higher degree of absenteeism, job-switching, slowdowns, and shoddy work.

26. Ben-Ami Shillony, in *Politics and Culture in Wartime Japan* (Oxford, 1981), points out that in 1945 there were only twenty-five hundred political prisoners.

27. Ibid., 67.

a closer observation of the wartime years has shown that Japan was not an ideological disciple of the Axis. Although militarily tied to totalitarian powers, her
society was, in many respects, freer than those of the Soviet Union or Kuomintang China, both of which ostensibly fought on the side of democracy. The
Japanese regime was restrictive, narrow-minded, and stifling, but it was not a
dictatorship. Intellectuals and writers were subjected to many pressures, but they
still retained a degree of influence. Western culture, although denigrated and vili-
fied, continued to exert a fascination, and these pro-Western feelings . . . could
not be erased.[28]

CHINA

Most of China was governed during the fascist era by Chiang Kai-shek's
Kuomintang (KMT), which is normally classified as a multiclass populist or
"nation-building" party but not a fitting candidate for fascism (except by old-
line Communists). In the aftermath of the Japanese aggression of 1931, a number of new patriotic societies were formed in China. The most important of
these was the Blue Shirts, a secret elite organization formed within the KMT in
1932, which recognized Chiang as leader. The Blue Shirts sought to mobilize
a stronger nationalist movement that would unite elite and masses, increase
China's strength, and accelerate industrial growth. They subsequently formed
a larger movement, the Chinese Renaissance Society, which had at least a hundred thousand members in widely scattered parts of China. By 1934 the Blue
Shirts had gained more favor from Chiang, who granted them temporary control of political indoctrination in the army and partial control of the general
educational system. The Blue Shirts also helped mobilize popular resistance
when the main phase of the war with Japan began in 1937.[29] They were, however, dissolved by Chiang in 1938, possibly because of competition with the
KMT itself.

Lloyd Eastman has called the Blue Shirts, whose members admired European fascism and were influenced by it, a Chinese fascist organization.[30] This is
probably an exaggeration. The Blue Shirts certainly exhibited some of the characteristics of fascism, as did many nationalist organizations around the world,
but it is not clear that the group possessed the full qualities of an intrinsic fascist
movement. Sun Yat-sen, founder of the KMT, believed in a one-party system

28. Ibid., 177.
29. M. H. Chiang, *The Chinese Blue Shirt Society* (Berkeley, 1985); M. E. Lestz, "Gli
intellettuali del Fuxingshe: Fascismo e dittatura del partito in Cina, 1932–1937," *SC* 18:2 (April
1987): 269–86.
30. L. E. Eastman, *The Abortive Revolution* (Cambridge, Mass., 1974), 31–84; idem,
Seeds of Destruction: Nationalist China in War and Revolution, 1937–1945 (Berkeley, 1984); idem,
"Fascists in Kuomintang China: The Blue Shirts," *China Quarterly* 49:1 (Jan. 1972): 1–31.

of guided democracy and state-directed industrialization and modernization as early as the 1920s, before any fascist influence could have been felt.[31] The Blue Shirts probably had some affinity with and for fascism, a common feature of nationalisms in crisis during the 1930s, but it is doubtful that they represented any clear-cut Asian variant of fascism.

SOUTH AFRICA

Of all peoples outside Europe, the Afrikaner society of South Africa may have registered the greatest degree of popular support for something approaching European-type fascism during the middle and late 1930s. Reasons for the appeal of radical nationalism to the Afrikaner population are in some respects obvious: recent memories of foreign conquest in the Boer War, constraints of the British imperial system (mild though they were), and the strong sense of minority status within the greater British system ethnically and politically and among the greater South African population racially. Moreover, about one-sixth of the Afrikaner population was originally of German, rather than Dutch, background.

The South African branch of the Nazi Auslandsorganisation (Organization Abroad, AO) was set up in 1932, and a number of small native fascist or proto-fascist groups were founded in the next year or so. Clearly the most important was Louis Weichardt's South African Gentile National Socialist Movement, which formed a militia called the Greyshirts. This in turn produced several splinter groups, the most notable being J. S. von Moltke's South African Fascists, whose Junior Nationalists wore orange shirts.[32]

A nonfascist moderate authoritarian right was represented by Daniel Malan's "Purified" Nationalist Party, which divided from the main Afrikaner Nationalist Party in 1934 over the latter's alliance with the liberal United Party. Some months earlier, in December 1933, a more right radical South African National Democratic Party (also known as the Blackshirts) had been organized. The Blackshirts and the South African Fascists reached an electoral agreement with the Malan party in 1937, but the Greyshirts ran their own slate in three districts in the parliamentary elections the following year, failing to elect a single deputy. Then with the coming of the war in 1939, the United Party split, with the liberal Jan Smuts taking over the government as a pro-

31. A. J. Gregor and M. H. Chiang, "*Nazionalfascismo* and the Revolutionary Nationalism of Sun Yat-Sen," *Journal of Asian Studies* 39:1 (Nov. 1979): 21–37.

32. The main study is P. J. Furlong, *Between Crown and Swastika: The Impact of the Radical Right on the Afrikaner Nationalist Movement in the Fascist Era* (Hanover, N.H., 1991), 1–26. Also useful is S. Uren, "Fascism and National Socialism in South Africa," M.A. thesis, University of Wisconsin–Madison, 1975.

British prime minister. Most of the Afrikaner Nationalist wing reunited with Malan in a reunified right-wing Afrikaner National Party.

The volume of Nazi propaganda in South Africa was considerable and was apparently effective in stimulating anti-Semitism among Afrikaner rightists.[33] South African Jews made a significant target because of their numbers and prominence: in 1936 they totaled about ninety-five thousand, or 4.75 percent of the white population, making them one of the largest Jewish minorities in the world.

The most important of all the South African right radical or protofascist groups, the paramilitary Ossewabrandwag (Ox-Wagon Sentinel, OB), was founded in 1938. The goal of the OB was to create a mass *Volksbeweging,* or people's movement, strongly pro-German in sentiment. The OB maintained a militia called the Stormjaers. It was pro-Nazi and somewhat anticapitalist, preaching a syncretic "Calvinist" racial and corporative republic, authoritarian in structure. Its most prominent leader was the former cabinet member J. H. J. Van Rensburg, who became head in 1941. The next two years saw the zenith of OB activism, with many incidents of violence, sabotage, and even bank robberies, though apparently only one death resulted. In 1941 a German agent attempted to provoke a coup with the support of the Stormjaers but was soon captured. OB leaders were interned, but the organization had penetrated deep into the military and especially the police. During the last two years of the war the OB was less violent but more strident, even declaring itself "national socialist." Nonetheless, the religiosity of most members created tension with the categorical fascists and prevented the movement from playing a more overtly fascistic role.[34] Though a clear break had existed between the OB and the Afrikaner National Party since 1941, the latter did cooperate temporarily with the Greyshirts in 1944. In the interim, the former cabinet minister Oswald Pirow created the New Order movement, which split off from the Afrikaner National Party in 1942, carrying sixteen deputies with it. The New Order also looked toward a protofascist system, perhaps more along Italian than German lines, but could not avoid marginalization. After 1945 the OB also faded away, its members mostly drifting back into the reunified National Party. The Greyshirts changed their name in 1949 to the White Workers Party, but this did not avoid an accelerated movement of members into the National Party.

The main achievement of the protofascists and right radicals in South Africa was not to create a successful movement of their own but to move the National Party after 1945 further toward the right and extreme racism, and toward the doctrine and system which after 1948 became apartheid, involv-

---

33. R. Citino, *Germany and the Union of South Africa in the Nazi Period* (Westport, Conn., 1991), covers the years to 1939.

34. G. C. Visser, *OB: Traitors or Patriots?* (Johannesburg, 1976).

ing some reduction of the power of parliament and of civil rights for whites as well.[35] The apartheid system was nonetheless primarily rooted in Afrikaner history, not that of central Europe; despite partial revamping of the political system, it remained a "racial democracy," not an authoritarian system, with regular competitive elections, a constitutional legal structure, most civil rights for whites, much spontaneous popular participation in political and other organizations, and no one-man rule. The literature which classifies the "South African Reich"[36] and "Afrikaner fascism"[37] is taxonomically confused.[38]

LATIN AMERICA

The world region where continental European politics have been most copied is Latin America. Given the frequently authoritarian character of Latin American governments and the rise of nationalism there between the wars, it might have seemed the most likely locale for the emergence of significant non-European fascisms. Such was not the case, however. A variety of new movements with the term *fascism* in their titles did appear, but all without exception quickly came to naught. Though some of the new dictatorships of the 1930s were favorably disposed toward Italian Fascism or Nazism and permitted or occasionally even encouraged profascist propaganda, their own structure and doctrines were different. Only one large fascist-type movement appeared—and quickly failed—while the only comparable new phenomenon to enjoy some success was the highly equivocal phenomenon of Peronism.

Several reasons may be advanced for the weakness, indeed virtual absence, of categorical fascism in Latin America: the generally low rate of political mobilization, a generation or more behind even the most backward European countries; the noncompetitive nature of nationalism in most Latin American countries, which were not threatened with direct foreign domination and conquest or wars (hence war and competitive nationalism have largely been absent as catalysts or mobilizing factors); as a corollary of the first factor, the customary elitist-patronal domination of political processes, and hence the capacity of dominant and less radical groups, as in eastern Europe, to suppress revolutionary nationalism; the multiracial composition of many Latin American societies, which blurs radical nationalist identity and usually creates internal

35. T. D. Moodie, *The Rise of Afrikanerdom* (Berkeley, 1975). Moreover, Furlong (*Between Crown and Swastika*) points out that one prime minister and several cabinet ministers met with Oswald Mosley in the 1960s and that several major figures in the National Party maintained contacts with neo-Nazis in West Germany.

36. B. Bunting, *The Rise of the South African Reich* (Harmondsworth, 1969).

37. H. Simpson, *The Social Origins of Afrikaner Fascism and Its Apartheid Policy* (Uppsala, 1980).

38. Furlong, *Between Crown and Swastika* 244–64, is quite convincing in this regard.

divisions and complexes that fortify the status quo; political dominance of the military, which chokes off other violent political manifestations; weakness of the pre-1960 revolutionary left, which could thus not serve as a stimulus; the tendency of Latin American nationalists after 1930 to reject both Europe and North America, turning either to populist nativism or to some variant of the Hispanic tradition; the inappropriateness of the national socialist–national syndicalist economics of autarchy to countries so dependent on the world economy as those of Latin America; and the development of a rather distinct Latin American mode of radical multiclass nationalism in the form of populist movements, such as the Peruvian APRA and the Bolivian MNR (some might add the Mexican PRI).[39]

One of the interesting minor cases concerned the National Socialist Movement (MNS), or Nacis, as they were called for short, in Chile. Founded by the Chileno-German Jorge González von Mareés in 1932, *nacismo* was in part inspired by German National Socialism but developed its own characteristics. Under the tutelage of its chief ideologue, Carlos Keller, it stood for a corporatist but economically radical national socialism, and for a more strongly centralized and presidentialist republic. While forming a paramilitary Tropas Nacistas de Asalto (TNA), the Nacis declared for the defense of Western Christian civilization and the family. Though the Nacis defined Chile as a European-type country with qualities different from and superior to the rest of Latin America, they declared their opposition to imperialism and their support for the international interests of other South American states. In 1937 González von Mareés publicly criticized Hitler for having become a tyrant, and by the following year he had rejected ties or comparisons with Nazism or Fascism, declaring his own movement to be democratic. Though formally anti-Semitic, González von Mareés admitted that there was no "Jewish problem" in Chile and theoretically espoused freedom of religion. In the parliamentary elections of 1937 the Nacis got 3.5 percent of the vote but did better in the worker districts of some large cities, and they gained 4.6 percent of the total vote in the municipal elections of April 1938. They faced the usual problem of protofascist movements: how to break in from the outside as a novel force against both right and left.

González von Mareés rejected violence for its own sake but advocated it as a "defensive necessity." An attempted coup against the rightist government of Jorge Alessandri in September 1938 was easily repressed, and fifty-four captured Nacis were then massacred in cold blood in much the same way that the rightist regime in Romania was dispatching Legionnaires. At this point the

39. A somewhat different list of factors, on which I have drawn in part, is offered by Alistair Hennessy, in "Fascism and Populism in Latin America," in *Fascism: A Reader's Guide*, ed. W. Lacqueur (Berkeley, 1976), 255–62. On Latin American populism, see G. Hilliker, *The Politics of Reform in Peru: The Aprista and Other Mass Parties of Latin America* (Baltimore, 1971).

Nacis decided to support Aguirre Cerda, presidential candidate of the leftist Chilean Popular Front, and gave him the margin of votes needed for a very narrow victory. One historian writes, "Strangely enough, the cult of violence of the MNS promoted the cause of liberal democracy in Chile in the nineteen thirties."[40] There seems little doubt that a movement originally inspired by German Nazism—if always nonracist and nonimperialist—had evolved into something different. Theoretical anti-Semitism was dropped, and the movement even featured one Jewish leader by 1938.[41] By 1941 the MNS had been reconstituted as the Popular Socialist Vanguard but was already in decline, having failed to find political space and no longer offering so distinct an alternative as in 1938.

Various attempts were made to form violent nationalist or radical antileftist mass movements in Mexico, but most had the characteristics of the radical right more than of European fascism. The Gold Shirts of General Nicolás Rodríguez, organized in 1934, were violent, anti-Semitic, antileftist, and authoritarian and directly aped German and Italian styles, but their goals were essentially counterrevolutionary and rightist. They were easily controlled by a government that was itself developing into a one-party, semicorporatist system. Only one Mexican president, Plutarco Elías Calles, in the early 1930s seems to have toyed with the idea of fascistizing aspects of the Mexican regime. Acción Revolucionaria Mexicana (ARM), an auxiliary force that he encouraged, was later associated with the Gold Shirts in an abortive revolt against a subsequent administration in 1938 (the Cedillo Rebellion).

The main counterrevolutionary mass movement, however, was the Cristeros, a major Catholic peasant force that, together with its successors in the Unión Nacional Sinarquista (UNS), became the largest single popular movement in early twentieth-century Mexico. This group launched a successful revolt against religious persecution in west central Mexico between 1926 and 1929 that finally forced the government to terms. The Cristeros were essentially a peasant self-defense force, and in their struggle it was the government which played the role of fascists.[42] The subsequent Sinarquista movement that began

40. M. Sznajder, "A Case of Non-European Fascism: Chilean National Socialists in the 1930s," *JCH* 28:2 (April 1993): 269–96.

41. Sznajder observes that "Chilean Nacism stood somewhere between fascism and the radical right" (ibid.). This would be fairly typical of the main Latin American attempts to approximate fascism. See also M. Potashnik, "Nacismo: National Socialism in Chile, 1932–1938," Ph.D. diss., UCLA, 1974.

42. After the Cristeros laid down their arms, the Mexican government violated its agreement, resuming religious persecution two years later. Over the years, some fifteen hundred Cristeros, including most of the leaders, were murdered by government forces. The Cristeros had at one time formed their own National Liberation government, but this was ultimately disavowed by Church leaders. Some Cristeros were former Zapatistas and eventually adopted a position of radical Christian democracy. See J. Meyer, *The Cristero Rebellion* (Cambridge, 1976), and D. C. Bailey, *Viva Cristo Rey!* (Austin, 1973).

in 1937 was rather more middle-class. The Sinarquistas became the largest mass party of the time, with more than half a million members by 1943. The Sinarquistas were Catholic, ultranationalist, and supporters of the Hispanic tradition, as opposed to the leftism and anti-Hispanism of the Mexican regime. Sinarquistas advocated a corporative style of government and organization, more equitable distribution of wealth, and land reform for poor peasants. The movement was nonviolent and did not respond to numerous killings carried out by the authorities. The Mexican government tried alternately to repress and co-opt the UNS, which dwindled after 1945 as the government itself moved more toward the right.[43]

Two of the more notable fascistic ideologues of Latin America were active in Peru during the 1930s. José Riva Agüero developed the broader reputation, but though he categorically endorsed fascism in Italy and Spain, his own position was essentially that of the Catholic radical right. Riva was highly elitist (even by Peruvian standards) and championed the Catholic and Hispanic traditions. Genuinely nearer European fascism was Raul Ferrero Rebagliati, son of an Italian immigrant, who encouraged broader nationalist mobilization. The only political movement of any significance in Peru that invoked European fascism, at least to some extent, was the Unión Revolucionaria, a nationalistic, populist, and authoritarian movement founded by the dictator Luis Sánchez Cerro before his assassination in 1933. Only after that point did the Unión Revolucionaria, then out of power, make some effort to approximate fascism. It developed a militia called the Black Shirts, whose members used the fascist salute, but after failure in the elections of 1936 steadily lost support.[44]

In some ways the most likely candidate for a "fascist situation" during the 1930s was Bolivia, one of the least developed Latin American countries and the only one during this period to have decisively lost an international war, the Chaco conflict with Paraguay from 1932 to 1935. Bolivia's national frustration led to a search for new alternatives, some of the most attractive of which seemed to be found in Italy and Germany. With leftist groups very weak, the idea of some sort of Bolivian "national socialism" became increasingly popular, even among the small non-Marxist Bolivian Socialist Party. An unstable new radical coalition came to power under Colonel David Toro in 1936, composed of radical officers, war veterans subsequently organized as a "Legion," and small socialist and labor groups. Toro's goal was "military socialism," which aimed at corporative economic organization, a new system of national syndicalism, and a partially corporative parliament. Toro fell from power in 1937, but his successor was a fellow officer, Germán Busch, who developed a

43. J. Meyer, *Le Sinarquisme: Un fascisme mexicain? 1937–1947* (Paris, 1977).

44. J. I. López Soria, ed., *El pensamiento fascista (1930–1945)* (Lima, 1981); O. Ciccarelli, "Fascism and Politics in Peru during the Benavides Regime, 1933–1939: The Italian Perspective," *Hispanic American Historical Review* 70:3 (1990): 405–32.

new social constitution and a prosyndical labor code, together with vague ideas about making government more charismatic and authoritarian, before committing suicide in 1939. All this was less than a Bolivian fascism, but the influence of Italian and German ideas was often admitted by Bolivian leaders.[45]

Military socialism and the influence of central European fascism set the background for the rise of revolutionary populism in the Movimiento Nacionalista Revolucionaria (MNR), whose leaders would also be frank about the impact which European fascism had on their thinking. Founded in 1940, the MNR originally adopted concepts of national socialism for a Bolivia defined as a proletarian nation, Italian-style. It sought at first to nationalize basic industries and create a thoroughgoing national syndicalism, looking on Italy and Germany as allies in revolutionizing the international division of power and wealth. The MNR formed an alliance with an organization of radical officers, RADEPA, which was also pro-Axis in orientation. A military junta headed by Major Gualberto Villarroel, which seized power in La Paz in December 1943, immediately adopted a pro-Axis policy and included three of the most fascistic leaders of the MNR in its cabinet. Though the international situation prompted Villarroel to oust them in the following year, he remained close to the most fascistic sector of the MNR until he was overthrown by the opposition in 1946. The MNR, however, soon largely defascistized itself and finally achieved power on its own in 1952 to begin a Bolivian populist revolution, one of only three socioeconomic revolutions in Latin America during the second half of the century.[46]

It might be mentioned that there is also a "Falange" in Bolivia, as for so many years in Spain. Founded in 1937 and inspired at least in part by the Spanish fascist organization, the Falange Socialista Boliviana (FSB) became much more of a Catholic corporatist and antisocialist right authoritarian movement, though, like its Spanish namesake, it originally relied on support among students. It played a major role in the opposition to the MNR revolution after 1952 and gained 15 percent of the vote in the national elections four years later. An effort to seize power by force failed in 1959, costing the life of the party's leader. Though its support later declined, the FSB has remained active, dividing into several factions, including a "Falangist left," with each wing

45. See F. Gallego, *Los orígenes del reformismo miitar en América Latina: La gestión de David Toro en Bolivia* (Barcelona, 1991); idem, *Ejército, nacionalismo y reformismo en América Latina: La gestión de Germán Busch en Bolivia* (Barcelona, 1992); and two articles by Herbert Klein in the *Hispanic American Historical Review:* "David Toro and the Establishment of 'Military Socialism' in Bolivia," 45:1 (Feb. 1965): 25–52, and "Germán Busch and the Era of 'Military Socialism' in Bolivia," 47:2 (May 1967): 166–84.

46. See two broader works by Klein: *Parties and Political Change in Bolivia, 1880–1952* (London, 1969), 228–402, and *Bolivia: The Evolution of a Multi-Ethnic Society* (New York, 1992), 192–226.

subsequently allied on varying occasions with some of the later Bolivian military governments. The FSB is probably the longest-lasting example in Latin America of a party founded in the 1930s, partly on the basis of European fascism, that subsequently came to occupy the space of the radical right in the accelerated politicosocial dynamics of the postfascist era.[47]

During the 1930s diverse new radical right and protofascist groups were most common in Argentina and Brazil, particularly the latter. One Brazilian historian has identified the Legião do Cruzeiro do Sul, founded in 1922, followed within the decade by the Legião de Outubro, the Partido Nacional Sindicalista, the Partido Fascista Nacional, the Legião Cearense do Trabalho, the Partido Nacionalista of São Paulo, the Partido Nacional Regenerador, the Partido Socialista Braziliero, and the Partido Fascista Braziliero.[48] The only one to achieve broader significance, and in fact to become the only large Latin American party that in most respects approximated European fascism, was the Ação Integralista Brasileira (Brazilian Integralist Action, AIB) of Plinio Salgado, founded in 1932. Its name betrayed origins in French and Portuguese Catholic-monarchist doctrine of the radical right, but it was also inspired in some measure by Italian Fascism. The Integralists sought to achieve an authoritarian and corporatist state (an "integral state") that would foster a new multiracial—if anti-Semitic—*Brasilidade,* a new Brazilian "race" defined in cultural and historical rather than ethnobiological terms. Members of the movement wore green shirts and combined the fascist salute with the Brazilian Indian greeting of "Anauê." Salgado himself was semimystical and identified his movement with religion and the sanctity of the family. Several Catholic bishops made favorable pronouncements concerning the AIB, and a number of priests were active in midlevel leadership, including the subsequently famous Helder Cámara. There was a large Protestant minority among the members and regional and local leaders, chiefly among the Germans in southern Brazil. Salgado held that humanity had passed through three great cultural phases and that *Brasilidade,* paralleled by the European fascist movements, would develop the creativity of nations and would create a new empire—even if only of spirit and doctrine—as the principles of the "fourth humanity" swept through the Western Hemisphere. The movement was extremely hierarchical and centralized under the charismatic leadership of Salgado. Most of the members and even the provincial and local leaders were under thirty. The AIB's elite came from the upper middle and middle classes, though local-level leaders came from the

47. I have found no study of the FSB, but its program is set forth in two books by Rodolfo Surcou Macedo: *Hacia la revolución integral* (La Paz, 1961) and *Conozca Falange Socialista Boliviana* (La Paz, 1972).

48. E. Carone, *Revoluções do Brazil contemporáneo* (São Paulo, 1975), 113–14. The Integralist ideologue Gustavo Barroso presents a yet broader survey in his *O Integralismo e o mundo* (Rio de Janeiro, 1936).

lower middle class and below. The largest sector of members came from the urban lower middle classes, but there was also a proportion of worker and artisan members, together with small farmers and farmworkers, mainly from areas where landownership was more broadly based.

Though the term *totalitarian* was used by Integralists, their leaders were uncomfortable with the paganism and extreme statism of most European fascism. Salgado avoided the latter term and always emphasized the originality and strictly Brazilian identity of his movement, while Miguel Reale, the AIB's national secretary for doctrine, stressed that the Brazilian "integral state" would differ from European fascism in its greater respect for the "rights of the human person." Whereas fascism tended to be "vitalist," integralism emphasized the "spiritual." Between 1935 and 1938 the Integralists became the first popular mass movement in Brazilian history and generated more support than any other protofascist movement in Latin America, with at least two hundred thousand members and allegedly more than twice that number. The AIB was not a mere copy of anything in Europe, but it did carry most of the distinguishing characteristics of European fascism, though more of the western than the central or eastern European fascisms. Its members were citizens of a territorially satisfied state, and thus the movement was nearer the "peace fascisms" of the West than the ultraviolent, extreme militarist varieties.[49]

At that time Brazil, like many other countries in Latin America and southern and eastern Europe, was governed by a moderate authoritarian regime, in this case led by Getulio Vargas. In November 1937 he announced the constitution of an Estado Novo (New State), inspired more by the Portuguese regime of the same name than by Italy. The Integralists then met the same fate at the hand of Vargas that the Portuguese National Syndicalists had under Salazar. Vargas officially dissolved the movement in December. The AIB's first insurrectionary conspiracy, in March 1938, fizzled, and the coup that was attempted two months later was crushed, bringing the definitive suppression of the movement.[50]

The Latin American case which has drawn by far the most attention, how-

49. The principal studies are H. Trindade. *Integralismo* (São Paulo, 1974), and Trindade's slightly updated *La tentation fasciste au Bresil dans les années trente* (Paris, 1988). In addition, see J. Chasin, *O Integralismo de Plinio Salgado* (São Paulo, 1978); J. Medeiro, *Ideologia autoritaria no Brasil, 1930–1945* (Rio de Janeiro, 1978); G. Vasconcelos, *Ideologia curupira: Análise do discurso integralista* (São Paulo, 1979); E. R. Broxson, "Plinio Salgado and Brazilian Integralism," Ph.D. diss., Catholic University, 1973; and S. Hilton, "Ação Integralista Brasileira," *Luso-Brazilian Review* 9:2 (Dec. 1972): 3–29. J. C. Parente, *Anauê: Os camisas verdes no poder* (Fortaleza, 1986), and J. A. de Sousa Montenegro, *O Integralismo no Ceará* (Fortaleza, 1986), both deal with the background of the AIB in Ceará, a region of major strength.

50. See R. M. Levine, *The Vargas Regime: The Critical Years, 1934–1938* (New York, 1970). It might be noted that after 1945 the Integralist movement reemerged in more moderate form, and several former Integralists assumed roles in the military regime established in 1964.

ever, is that of Argentine Peronism. Well before Perón, Argentina was the home of the most continuous and the most ideologically developed radical right in Latin America, which patterned its ideas on earlier counterparts in Spain and France. Beginning with the Argentine Patriotic League at the beginning of the century, this southwestern European–style radical right has maintained a continuous political and ideological presence in Argentina, assuming a variety of different forms down to the present time.[51] Compared with the persistence of the radical right, efforts to organize a National Fascist Party in 1923 and an Argentine Fascist Party in 1932 were ephemeral.[52] Similarly, the widespread publicity just before and during World War II about the German Nazi menace in Argentina and the danger of a "Fourth Reich" was the product of wartime hysteria and of British government disinformation, designed to stir up concern in Washington.[53]

The first Argentine dictatorship of this century was the military regime of General José Uriburu from 1930 to 1932, which also attempted a little of the style and substance of Italian Fascism. Uriburu hoped to install a corporative regime and organized a militia called the Legión Cívica, but all this proved too radical for Argentine society.[54] During World War II, however, the Argentine government—which had extensive and hegemonic designs of its own—was more sympathetic to Germany and Italy than was any other major government in the Western Hemisphere. A profascist military group, the Grupo de Oficiales Unidos (GOU), seized control in 1943, imposing temporary dictatorship and a policy initially more favorable to the Axis.[55]

This provided the background to Peronism, a related yet quite distinct

51. S. McGee Deutsch, *Counterrevolution in Argentina: The Argentine Patriotic League* (Lincoln, 1986).

52. The Argentine radical right is ably surveyed in S. McGee Deutsch and R. Dolkart, eds., *The Argentine Right* (Wilmington, Del., 1993), and D. Rock, *Authoritarian Argentina* (Berkeley, 1993). Alberto Spektorowski, in "The Ideological Origins of Right and Left Nationalism in Argentina, 1930–1943," *JCH* 29:1 (Jan. 1994): 155–84, analyzes the differences between left populist and right radical nationalism, while M. C. Nascimbene and M. I. Neuman, in "El nacionalismo argentino, el fascismo y la inmigración en la Argentina (1927–1943): Una aproximación téorica," *Estudios Interdisciplinarios de America Latina y el Caribe* 4:1 (Jan.–June 1993): 115–40, articulate the differences between the Catholic right and fascism.

53. This is exhaustively demonstrated in R. C. Newton, *The "Nazi Menace" in Argentina, 1931–1947* (Stanford, 1992).

54. A. Rouquié, *Poder militar y sociedad política en la Argentina* (Buenos Aires, 1983), 1:223–52.

55. E. Díaz Araujo, *La conspiración del '43: El GOU, una experiencia militarista en la Argentina* (Buenos Aires, 1971). For the broader political history of the military, see, in addition to the basic work by Rouquié, R. Potash, *The Army and Politics in Argentina, 1928–1945* (Stanford, 1969); M. Goldwert, *Democracy, Militarism and Nationalism in Argentina, 1930–1966* (Austin, 1972); and, for the period 1930–43, M. Falcoff and R. Dolkart, eds., *Prelude to Perón: Argentina in Depression and War, 1930–1943* (Berkeley, 1976).

development which here refers to the nine years in power of Juan Domingo Perón (1946–55), not to the subsequent history of the Peronist party. Though Perón first emerged as a leading figure in the GOU, he took office in 1946 as the legally elected president of the republic. The uniqueness of Peronism is that its main support stemmed from the mass organization of Argentine labor fomented by Perón's government. The Peronist regime of 1946–55 was a personal government of limited authoritarianism that tolerated a considerable degree of pluralism. Its twin pillars were nationalism and social reform, encouraging industrial development on the one hand and income redistribution on the other, with the ultimate goal of making Argentina the dominant power in South America. Perón had been a military attaché in Fascist Italy and later admitted that he had been influenced by Fascism, but after 1945 he strove to create an independent position. The ideology of the regime was termed *justicialism,* and it attempted a synthesis of the four principles of idealism, materialism, individualism, and collectivism. Perón defined European fascism as an exaggerated combination of idealism and collectivism that excluded individualism and a salutary materialism, a definition that as far as it goes is not necessarily inaccurate. At one point he declared, "Mussolini was the greatest man of our century, but he committed certain disastrous errors. I, who have the advantage of his precedent before me, shall follow in his footsteps but also avoid his errors." [56]

Many analysts of the Peronist case have concluded that Peronism in power did indeed have most of the characteristics that they variously impute to fascism, even though its military-syndical base made it an unusual example. The regime was, of course, like nearly all new Latin American systems, eclectic; one of Perón's advisers, speechwriters, and syndical theorists was José Figuerola, a Spaniard who had earlier served as labor adviser to the Spanish dictator Miguel Primo de Rivera in the late 1920s.

Though the Peronist political party was organized by 1949 with announced aspirations of becoming a *partido único* (single party), Perón never established a complete and rigid dictatorship. He relied on the support of organized labor, middle-class nationalists, much of the industrialist class, and a significant part of the army officer corps. Having displaced and alienated the formerly dominant landlord class, he had to balance the appeals and discontents of various sectors to sustain his power. Inflation, corruption, and economic slowdown, together with his demagogic and distributive social policies, eventually united the upper classes against him. A feud with the Church and mounting national and institutional frustrations turned most of the military against the regime and led to Perón's overthrow in 1955.[57]

56. G. Blanksten, *Perón's Argentina* (Chicago, 1953), 279.
57. The literature on Peronism is now extensive. See particularly, in addition to Blanksten's *Perón's Argentina,* R. J. Alexander, *The Perón Era* (New York, 1951); P. Lux-Wurm, *Le Péro-*

A careful assessment reveals that Peronism had most but not all the characteristics of European fascism. It was for a long time not an organized political movement, and even after Perón was in power it could not define a new system. Perón did express the fascist negatives and to a certain degree built on cultural and philosophical values akin to European fascist movements, with expansive goals in foreign affairs. The aim of a single-party regime was conceived but never effectively implemented. Perón's "leftist" demagogy and worker mobilization scarcely made him unfascist, as some naively contend, but he did not project the fascist insistence on an organic new national hierarchy that could discipline society. The ways in which Perón fell short of a European fascist model stemmed from his personal, national, and historical circumstances. In military-dominated Latin American political society, abrupt changes were produced only by the army, and from that basis it was necessary to try to develop a radical new movement from the top downward. Rising to prominence after 1945 and with only limited power at his disposal, Perón purposefully moderated the extent and timing of his ambitions and does not seem to have conceived a full-scale European fascist model as feasible in a country like Argentina after World War II. The crucial use of female leadership in the form of Doña Evita, central to his mobilization process, was also a notable deviation from fascist (and traditional Latin American) style.[58]

---

nisme (Paris, 1965); P. Waldmann, *Der Peronismus, 1943–1955* (Hamburg, 1974); and, on the historical background, Falcoff and Dolkart, eds., *Prologue to Perón*. On the social base, see P. H. Smith, "The Social Base of Peronism," *Hispanic American Historical Review* 52.1 (Feb. 1972): 55–73, and idem, "Social Mobilization, Political Participation, and the Rise of Juan Perón," *Political Science Quarterly* 84.1 (March 1969): 30–49. For further bibliography, see M. Ben Plotkin, "Perón y el peronismo: Un ensayo bibliográfico," *Estudios Interdisciplinarios de América Latina y el Caribe* 2:1 (1991): 113–36.

58. In chapter 5 of *Political Man* (New York, 1969), Seymour M. Lipset termed Peronism a "fascism of the left." The fascist categorization is largely accepted by Paul M. Hayes, in *Fascism* (London, 1972), and by H.-U. Thamer and W. Wippermann, in *Faschistische und neofaschistische Bewegungen* (Darmstadt, 1977). Other works that tend to include Peronism in the fascist category are C. S. Fayt et al., *La naturaleza del peronismo* (Buenos Aires, 1967); C. H. Waisman, *Reversal of Development in Argentina: Postwar Counterrevolutionary Policies and Their Structural Consequences* (Princeton, 1987); and P. H. Lewis, "Was Perón a Fascist? An Inquiry into the Nature of Fascism," *Journal of Politics* 42:1 (Feb. 1980): 242–56. George Blanksten regards Peronism as nearer to being fascist than nonfascist.

On the other hand, Gino Germani distinguishes (in my opinion correctly) between European fascism and Argentine "national populism," even though he fails to define their full typological or morphological differences in his *Authoritarianism, Fascism, and National Populism* (New Brunswick, N.J., 1978). Other works which conclude that Peronism was not fascist include A. Ciria, *Perón y el Justicialismo* (Buenos Aires, 1971); C. Buchrucker, *Nacionalismo y peronismo* (Buenos Aires, 1987); R. D. Crassweller, *Perón and the Enigmas of Argentina* (New York, 1987); and E. Kenworthy, "The Function of the Little Known Case in Theory Formation; or, What Peronism Wasn't," *Comparative Politics* 6 (Oct. 1973): 16–45. Torcuato di Tella, in *El sistema político argentino y la clase obrera* (Buenos Aires, 1964), 54–64, recognizes many similarities between Peronism and fascism but prefers to call the former "Bonapartist."

THE UNITED STATES

As in Latin America, the various populist, nativist, and rightist movements in the United States during the 1920s and 1930s fell distinctly short of fascism.[59] The Ku Klux Klan, which enjoyed a brief apogee between 1920 and 1924, was ultraconservative and not receptive to fascistic radicalism.[60] Huey Long—feared in some circles as the American Duce—was the most important in a long line of southern demagogues and in 1934–35 the most important politician in the country after Franklin Roosevelt, but he was a southern populist who sought to promote a kind of egalitarianism, and his Share Our Wealth clubs never developed into a political movement.[61] The only theoretical precondition for fascism which existed in the United States was ethnoracial tension, and the only aspects of prefascist culture which flourished were racialist and eugenicist doctrines, from the 1880s to the 1920s.[62] Yet these doctrines actually began to go into abeyance by the 1930s, perhaps due to the persistence of effective segregation and the immigration restrictions of 1924.[63] Some of the special groups which existed during these years were inspired more by biblical and apocalyptic ideas, as in the case of the Silver Legion of William Dudley Pelley, than by European fascist doctrines.[64]

Of the new American secret societies and extremist groups, the most extensive was the Black Legion, an offshoot of the Klan dating from approxi-

59. The best brief evaluation is P. H. Amann, "Les fascismes américains des années trentes: Aperçus et reflexions," *Revue d'Histoire de la Deuxième Guerre Mondiale* 126 (1982): 47–75. There is an extensive literature, much of it in unpublished doctoral dissertations, inversely proportional to the significance of the topic. Morris Schonbach, in *Native American Fascism during the 1930s and 1940s* (New York, 1987), treats a broad gamut of groups. See also L. K. Gerber, "Anti-Democratic Movements in the United States since World War I," Ph.D. diss., University of Pennsylvania, 1964, and F. Duprat and A. Renault, *Les fascismes américains, 1924–1941* (Paris, 1976). Seymour M. Lipset and Earl Raab, in *The Politics of Unreason, 1790–1970* (New York, 1970), present a history of the American extreme right.

60. W. P. Randel, *The Ku Klux Klan* (Philadelphia, 1965); K. T. Jackson, *The Ku Klux Klan in the City, 1915–1930* (New York, 1967); D. Chalmers, *Hooded Americanism* (New York, 1981).

61. The lengthiest biography is T. H. Williams, *Huey Long* (New York, 1969), while I. P. Hair, *The Kingfish and His Realm* (Baton Rouge, 1991), is more critical. See also F. Hobson, *Tell about the South* (Baton Rouge, 1983), 255–56, 334.

62. T. F. Gossett, *Race—The History of an Idea in America* (Dallas, 1963); O. Handlin, *Race and Nationality in American Life* (Boston, 1948); M. H. Haller, *Eugenics: Hereditarian Attitudes in American Thought* (New Brunswick, N.J., 1963); I. A. Newby, *Jim Crow's Defense: Anti-Negro Thought in America, 1900–1930* (Baton Rouge, 1965).

63. E. Barkan, *The Retreat of Scientific Racism* (New York, 1992).

64. D. B. Portzline, "William Dudley Pelley and the Silver Legion of America," Ed.D. diss., Ball State University, 1965; J. M. Werly, "The Millenarian Right," Ph.D. diss., Syracuse University, 1972; L. P. Ribuffo, "Protestants on the Right," Ph.D. diss., Yale University, 1976; Schonbach, *Native American Fascism* 303–15.

mately 1925 and founded by an eccentric small-town physician named W. J. Shepard. During the early and middle 1930s the Legion may have had a membership of as many as sixty thousand spread over a half dozen midwestern states and as far east as Pennsylvania. It committed numerous acts of arson and bombing, though the latter seem to have been primarily directed against dissident members. While the Black Legion leaders talked of seizing Washington *manu militari*, they in fact had little organization and scarcely more ideology. The Legion was a Protestant nativist group strong on religion and short on political thought. It had no public organization as a political movement and no allies. Prosecution of several of its more violent members brought massive publicity by 1936—including a Hollywood movie starring Humphrey Bogart as a Legionnaire—and the society collapsed.[65]

An almost equally implausible candidate for the "American Mussolini" was Father Charles E. Coughlin, the "radio priest," who broadcast regularly on Detroit (and subsequently national) radio, beginning in 1926. From weekly sermons Father Coughlin soon branched out into far-reaching social and political commentary of a radical and demagogic nature. Breaking with Roosevelt in 1934, he founded a National Union for Social Justice that at one point claimed to have five million members. However, his subsequent Unionist Party candidate in the 1936 presidential election gained fewer than a million votes. From that point on Coughlin became directly apologetic for Hitler, Mussolini, and Franco, as well as overtly anti-Semitic. By 1938 his followers were organizing local Christian Front paramilitary groups. Coughlin was the most important direct apologist for fascism in the United States, but as a priest he could not form an effective political movement to represent the ideology which he espoused, and he was finally completely silenced by the Church hierarchy at the beginning of 1942.[66]

Thus the only real American "fascist party" was probably the German-American Bund, which aspired to be a slightly watered-down Nazi Party for the United States. Despite such gestures as combining pictures of George Washington with swastika emblems at its meetings, the Bund never succeeded in establishing American credentials. Only briefly did it have as many as fifteen thousand members; of these, about two-thirds were German immigrants, and most of the rest were naturalized Germans. There was also a significant contingent of the Fasci all'Estero organized among Italian Americans, and a much

65. P. H. Amann, "Vigilante Fascism: The Black Legion as an American Hybrid," *Comparative Studies on Society and History* 25:3 (July 1983): 490–524.

66. G. T. Marx, *The Social Basis of the Support of a Depression Era Extremist: Charles E. Coughlin* (Berkeley, 1962); C. J. Tull, *Father Coughlin and the New Deal* (Syracuse, 1965); D. H. Bennett, *Demagogues in the Depression: American Radicals and the Union Party, 1932–1936* (New Brunswick, N.J., 1969); and S. Marcus, *Father Coughlin* (Boston, 1973).

smaller section of the Nazi Auslandsorganisation, but neither could play a role in American affairs.[67]

THE MIDDLE EAST

Though they have drawn less attention from students of comparative attempted fascisms than have groups in Japan, South Africa, or Latin America, the radical Arab nationalist groups of the 1930s and after were at least as much influenced by European fascism as movements in any other part of the world. This was strongly encouraged by Rome and Berlin. From an early date Mussolini chose to present himself as a promoter of Arab nationalism, above all as a tool for the expansion of Italian influence. The Fascist regime had him proclaimed a "hero of Islam" and "defender of Islam" in Italian Libya, where a parallel Libyan Arab Fascist Party was created. If Mussolini supported Zionists to some extent as a lever against the British Empire, both he and Hitler subsidized Haj Amin el Husseini, the violently anti-Jewish grand mufti of Jerusalem. Anti-Jewish feeling mounted in parts of the Middle East during the 1930s, as the Fascist and Nazi regimes and doctrines made increasing sense to many Arab nationalists. King Abdul Aziz of Saudi Arabia sought German arms and contacts and was favorably received. Various delegations of Syrians and Iraqis attended the Nürnberg party congresses, and there were several different Arabic translations of *Mein Kampf*.[68] Both the German and Italian regimes were active in propaganda in the Arab world, and there was much pro-German sentiment in Egypt.

At least seven different Arab nationalist groups had developed shirt movements by 1939 (white, gray, and iron in Syria; blue and green in Egypt; tan in Lebanon; white in Iraq), though most of these groups would not be called generically fascist. The three most directly influenced by European fascism would seem to have been the Syrian People's Party (PPS, also sometimes known as the Syrian National Socialist Party), the Iraqi Futuwa youth movement, and the Young Egypt movement (also known as the Green Shirts). All three were nonrationalist, anti-intellectual, and highly emotional, and all three were territorially expansionist, with Sami Shawkat, the Futuwa ideologue, envisioning the "Arab nation" as eventually covering half the globe (though by conversion

---

67. L. V. Bell, *In Hitler's Shadow: The Anatomy of American Nazism* (Port Washington, N.Y., 1973); S. A. Diamond, *The Nazi Movement in the United States, 1924–1941* (Ithaca, 1974); D. M. McKale, *The Swastika Outside Germany* (Kent, Ohio, 1977); G. Salvemini, *Italian Fascist Activities in the United States* (Staten Island, 1977).

68. The Lebanese Pierre Gemayel is said to have founded his Christian Phalange Party after returning from a Nürnberg congress. The nomenclature was drawn from fascism, though the Phalange was not a generically fascist movement. See D. Pryce-Jones, *The Closed Circle* (New York, 1989), 182–208.

and leadership, not military conquest). All believed in the basic superiority of their own peoples, with Antun Saadeh, leader of the People's Party, defining Syrians as a distinct and naturally superior race, the product, however, not of a pure biology but of the creative fusing of the many different ethnoracial strains in Syrian history. His PPS sought complete control of Syria, but Young Egypt and Futuwa (which in fact was created with the assistance of the Iraqi minister of education) proposed to work with existing forces. All three emphasized military virtues and power and stressed self-sacrifice, though only Futuwa, which looked especially to the army, believed in what it called the art of death. All three praised Italian Fascism and German National Socialism, but none had fully developed programs (though the Syrian party came closest). Both Young Egypt and the Syrian party were essentially elite groups, with little structure for mobilization. Futuwa had broader goals, planning to enroll all Iraqi youth of both sexes. The only potentially charismatic figure among these organizations may have been Saadeh in Syria, but his achievements were modest. In sum, none of these were developed fascist movements, and none reproduced the full characteristics of European fascism.[69]

Nonetheless, European fascism was taken more seriously in the Middle East than anywhere else in the world except Japan, Bolivia, and South Africa. This influence would live on long after 1945. By the 1980s the regimes of Gadhafi in Libya and of Saddam Hussein in Iraq would have more characteristics of a classic fascist regime than any others in the world.

GENERIC FASCISM: A UNIQUELY EUROPEAN PHENOMENON

Thus it seems that the full characteristics of European fascism could not be reproduced on a significant scale outside Europe. The specific preconditions encountered in Europe but not present or not jointly present on other continents were intense nationalist-imperialist competition among newer independent nations, formed mostly in the 1860s; liberal democratic systems still in their first generation of development, not yet consolidated though beyond the control of conservative elites; opportunity for mobilized nationalism on a mass scale as an independent force not restricted to elites or an institutionalized oligarchy; and a new cultural orientation stemming from the cultural and intellectual revolution of 1890–1914.

Japan was intensely nationalist-imperialist and one of the new states of the 1860s that was striving to expand in the imperial order, but it lacked the opportunity for radical new social and political mobilization by independent groups. Though nominally under a parliamentary regime, the Japanese polity

69. E. Marston, "Fascist Tendencies in Pre-War Arab Politics: A Study of Three Arab Political Movements," *Middle East Forum* (May 1959): 19–22, 33–35.

was much more subject to the domination of the state and special elites. Moreover, Japan's distinctive culture remained semitraditionalist and not receptive to all the radical new ideas associated with fascism. Latin American nationalism was considerably weaker, and the Latin American polities were normally subject to oligarchic domination. With partial exceptions in Argentina, Brazil, and Bolivia, the cultural attitudes and values accompanying fascism had received little exposure. South Africa had a much more fully European type of polity, but its international problems were in the process of resolution, its culture less secularized, and its political expressions channeled to some extent by British institutions. The large black majority deflected the utility of a national socialist approach to radical nationalism, so that a more conservative kind of nationalism became dominant. The Middle East was generally under western European tutelage and lacked the national independent or political development to give full expression to new political forms.

It is consequently doubtful that a typology derived from European fascism can be applied to non-European movements or regimes with full accuracy or specificity. As two of the most assiduous European students of fascism, Ernst Nolte and Renzo De Felice, have insisted, fascism was a historical phenomenon primarily limited to Europe during the era of world wars.

11
World War II: Climax and Destruction of Fascism

Fascism was the most overtly militarist of all the modern revolutionary ideologies in its style, rhetoric, and goals. In practice it was no more violent than Marxism-Leninism and in fact did not promote so high a degree of structural militarism as contemporary and subsequent Communist regimes, but the fascist movements and regimes (with some minor exceptions) placed a high positive evaluation on violence, emphasizing its necessary creative role as intrinsic to their doctrine of the "new man," and usually proclaimed national war as the highest commitment and test of a nation. By contrast, Marxist-Leninist regimes qualified violence as an indispensable means to an end—while gratuitously employing it en masse—and almost always preached peace as ideal and goal, while massively militarizing their systems in practice. Just how violent and aggressive individual fascist movements and regimes were, however, often depended on circumstances. The weaker ones employed much less violence, while those in either weak or satisfied countries did not necessarily promote war as practical policy. Mussolini was a relatively good citizen for more than a decade and only turned to aggression in 1935, and then in Africa, not in Europe.

No such equivocation characterized Adolf Hitler. Not merely did Nazism preach war and violence as a necessary form of activity to bring out the intrinsic qualities of the master race, but Hitler held specific goals that required major war as soon as possible. While some historians have doubted whether Hitler possessed a grand design, it is clear from his words and writings that he sought to acquire vast *Lebensraum* in the east for the accomplishment of the racial revolution and the full construction of the Thousand-Year Reich, in the process destroying the Soviet Union and totally eliminating France as a power

355

factor in the west. The extent of these ambitions, together with the racial war involved, constituted the revolutionary or ultra-"fascist" quality of Nazi expansionism, compared with the more limited expansionist goals of traditional German foreign policy.[1]

The causes of World War II were basically twofold: the mutual competition of power politics and imperial interests, compounded by the effects of the new revolutionary ideologies in Germany, Italy, Japan, and the Soviet Union. The chief aggressors were the "new nations of the 1860s," latecomers who had failed to achieve imperial status equivalent to the main powers of western Europe, or to the United States and the Soviet Union. Nonetheless, the ambitions of Germany, Italy, and Japan would not have provoked such a war had it not been for the rise to power of Hitler, Mussolini, and the Japanese military, who felt impelled to achieve historic greatness and revolutionary goals through foreign conquest. War was also a necessity of Marxist-Leninist ideology, which saw the path to the expansion of communism arising from the results of a "second imperialist war" which would wear down the capitalist world.

The only kind of operational plan which Hitler seems to have possessed was to proceed in a general way through fairly obvious phases of the expansion of German power. The first involved the consolidation of the regime at home and rearmament, followed by the expansion of German power in central and east central Europe, climaxed by major struggles to destroy the Soviet Union in the east and, if necessary, France in the west. The sequence in which the last two decisive developments might take place was not rigidly determined and would depend on events.[2]

Despite the brutality of his designs, Hitler expected to find indispensable allies and/or complicity abroad. The most important would be the British Empire, which he proposed to support in exchange for the return of the old German colonies and a free hand on the Continent.[3] Anglo-Saxon "racial cousins" were not targets of Nazi expansionism and racial revolution, and in some undetermined fashion they might be helpful allies in the eventual ultimate struggle for world power, probably directed against the mongrelized United States by a greatly expanded Reich of the future, even after Hitler's own death.[4] Italy

---

1. Similarly, Nazism broke with the tradition of nationalist "geopolitics" before 1933, the former having been grounded in cultural, historical, and environmentalist doctrines rather than racialism. M. Bassin, "Race contra space: The conflict between German *Geopolitik* and National Socialism," *Political Geography Quarterly* 6:2 (April 1987): 115–34.

2. The best overall treatment of Hitler's expansionist policies is N. Rich, *Hitler's War Aims*, 2 vols. (New York, 1973–74).

3. K. Hildebrand, *Vom Reich zum Weltreich: Hitler, NSDAP und koloniale Frage, 1919–1945* (Munich, 1969).

4. A. Hillgruber, "England's Place in Hitler's Plans for World Dominion," *JCH* 9:1 (Jan. 1974): 6–22.

would be the only significant ally on the Continent for ideological and geographic reasons, as first explained in *Mein Kampf*. More broadly, Hitler expected support from fascistic elements, and from rightists, anti-Communists, and anti-Semites in various countries, though these played no specific role in his planning. Certainly he did not even remotely envisage the situation of Germany's being almost alone against the other major powers, the circumstance that had developed by 1943.[5]

Long-range military planning was less than clear-cut. In 1934 Hitler declared to his generals that Germany would have to be ready for offensive warfare within eight years, for "short decisive blows first to the west and then to the east would be necessary."[6] Yet there was no exact scheme for any specific sequence of operations. In the best scenario both Britain and France might stand aside while Germany took over east central Europe and then destroyed the Soviet Union. Alternately, by 1936 Hitler was hoping for war between Japan and the Soviet Union, which would make his task easier. Military strategy was never predicated merely, as some have said, on short *Blitzkrieg* operations alone, for the *Blitzkrieg* strategy was only somewhat haltingly developed in 1938–39. The general concept was rather for a large-scale (though never complete) economic conversion to sustain a lengthy period of war, involving major fortifications and vast mobilization of resources and synthetic products, ultimately resulting in the creation of a major high seas fleet as well.[7]

Hitler defended the institutional integrity of the military as the technical organizers of this process against the political inroads of the Nazi Party, but nonetheless he was determined to extend his personal authority further. The opportunity was provided by a personnel crisis in the military command (the Blomberg-Fritsch affairs) in January 1938, which resulted in Hitler's becoming officially commander in chief of the Wehrmacht (armed forces), with more pliant generals now holding the senior commands.[8] This was immediately fol-

5. On the development of Hitler's diplomacy, the key works are G. Weinberg, *The Foreign Policy of Hitler's Germany*, 2 vols. (Chicago, 1970–80), and H. A. Jacobsen, *Nationalsozialistische Aussenpolitik, 1933–1938* (Frankfurt, 1968), while K. Hildebrand, *The Foreign Policy of the Third Reich* (London, 1973), is perhaps the best brief summary. For foreign policy in earlier years, see G. Stoakes, *Hitler and the Quest for World Domination: Nazi Ideology and Foreign Policy in the 1920s* (Leamington Spa, 1987), and, on the party abroad, D. H. McKale, *The Swastika Outside Germany* (Kent, Ohio, 1977).

6. Quoted in W. Carr, *Arms, Autarky and Aggression* (London, 1979), 36–37.

7. German military expenditure as a percentage of GNP increased as follows: 1932, 3%; 1933, 3%; 1934, 6%; 1935, 8%; 1936, 13%; 1937, 13%; 1938, 18%; 1939, 23. J. Noakes and G. Pridham, eds., *Nazism, 1919–1945* (Exeter, 1984), 2:297–98.

8. The complex relationship between the Nazi Party, the regime, and the military is treated in the works of K. J. Müller: *Das Heer und Hitler: Armee und nationalsozialistische Regime, 1933–1940* (Stuttgart, 1960), *General Ludwig Beck* (Boppard, 1980), and *Armee und Drittes Reich, 1933–1939* (Paderborn, 1987).

lowed by extension of more complete Nazi control over the Foreign Ministry, together with the naming of a Nazi foreign minister, Joachim von Ribbentrop.

Significant acceleration began in 1936, encouraged by the limited Western reaction to the remilitarization of the Rhineland (in effect, of all Germany's western frontier, in violation of the Treaty of Versailles) in March of that year. Hitler subsequently declared that an acceleration in rearmament and foreign expansion would be required for domestic purposes as well, to distract attention from mounting economic difficulties, to integrate the people more fully under the regime, and to expedite their Nazification. This trend both paralleled and exceeded the strategy of Mussolini, which sought the completion of the Fascist revolution through foreign expansion.

The acceleration of rearmament in 1936 did set an earlier timetable, requiring the German army to be operational by October 1, 1939, even though total rearmament would not be completed for several years after that point. The Four-Year Plan for economic and military expansion adopted in mid-1936 was designed to have Germany prepared for "total war" and as self-sufficient as possible by 1940, even though some of its key targets were not met.

Direct expansion began with the annexation of Austria in March 1938. Though this had always been Hitler's goal, there is no indication of any timetable or even any precise strategy involved. Hitler's decision was precipitated by internal developments in Austria that would have stiffened anti-Nazi resistance and caught him momentarily by surprise. Once the annexation of Austria had been accomplished both more rapidly and more easily than anticipated, he turned his attention to multinational Czechoslovakia, whose large German minority was both a major target of and a major justification for expansion. By May 30, 1938, Hitler was determined to eliminate Czechoslovakia as an entity, even though his army was far from fully prepared and Czechoslovakia possessed a well-equipped modern force on sound defensive terrain. Thus he gave his commanders orders to be ready for offensive action by October 1, for, from Hitler's point of view, Czechoslovakia presented him with the best possible case; an invasion might be presented as the national self-determination of the German minority, denied any such right in 1919. This was also the moment of greatest internal political danger for Hitler, since General Ludwig Beck, chief of the general staff, led an active military conspiracy to depose him if he led Germany into another major international war. That depended on a vigorous response from Britain and France; their quasisurrender at the famous Munich Conference late in September avoided war and handed over all the Sudetenland to Germany immediately. It disarmed the German military conspirators, bringing Beck's resignation and greater Hitlerian authority over the army command. Nonetheless, at first it was an actual frustration for Hitler, for it deprived him of the opportunity to launch a "justified" and "moral" war. He also admitted

"All the people say yes" (Nazi poster for the plebiscite on the annexation of Austria, April 10, 1938.)

that, in view of the anxiety and dismay shown by much of the German populace during the crisis, Germany was not yet prepared psychologically and politically for war. There had been too much demagogy about "National Socialism means peace"; the resumption of general military conscription in 1935 had never been popular.

Though Hitler promised his commanders that he would not again involve Germany in a major two-front war such as had brought its defeat in 1918, the other two major powers on the Continent—the Soviet Union and France—both had to be dealt with. For Hitler, the main enemy was the Soviet Union, because of its size and power, because of its competing revolutionary ideology (considered the greatest threat to National Socialism), and because it occupied the vital *Lebensraum* of the east. Poland lay between Germany and the Soviet Union, but for complex reasons Hitler had somewhat less hatred of Poland than of Czechoslovakia. At the beginning of 1939 he offered Poland a kind of satellite status with a view toward assisting eventual hostilities against their common Soviet enemy to the east. Contrary to the frequently subscribed notion, Hitler did not in the short term require the total subjugation of all the various national groups in eastern Europe. He would settle initially in some cases for a semivoluntary subordination consonant with German policies. After his offer to Poland was spurned, Hitler came to the conclusion that the country must be destroyed. The situation was greatly complicated by the fact that, despite Britain's acquiescence over Austria and Czechoslovakia, he had failed completely in his fundamental goal of a general understanding or quasialliance with Britain. As German pressure on Poland increased, Britain's position stiffened, returning to the classic policy of maintaining a balance of power on the Continent and denying overall hegemony to any one power. During March and April 1939 Britain and France took the step (unprecedented for Britain) of offering general security guarantees to both Poland and Romania. If implemented, these guarantees meant that a German attack on Poland would mean general war with Britain and France as well, and this was definitely not what Hitler had planned.

Hitler was prepared at some point to go to war with France, which he hoped could eventually be attacked and defeated, if the need arose, in isolation. More serious was war with Britain, which contradicted his racial doctrines and general strategy. Hitler had firm and relatively clear ultimate goals and was a master opportunist in the adoption of short-term tactics. His weakness, as Rainer Zitelmann observes, lay in his inability to conceive a practical strategy that would connect his immediate tactics with achievement of his long-range goals. Though he understood little about Britain, he perceived that there was scant enthusiasm there for a war with Germany and concluded that Britain would not go to war if it became clear that the Soviet Union would not take up arms against Germany in the east. To clear the decks, he negotiated the Nazi-Soviet Pact of August 1939—the diplomatic bombshell of the century—in which the two revolutionary powers that had sworn undying politial and ideological enmity signed a ten-year pact of friendship and nonaggression, a broad new economic trade agreement, and a secret protocol to divide most of eastern Europe between them. This strategy was directed at deterring Britain and France from going to war with Germany in the absence of any Russian support. Hitler was therefore deeply chagrined when, on September 3, two days after the German invasion of Poland, both Western powers declared war on Germany. For the first time, Hitler's strategy—devious and breathtaking though it was—had failed, and strategic failure in the face of brilliant tactical success would later become characteristic.

The beginning of the European war was greatly facilitated by Soviet policy, which found nothing repugnant about a secret deal with Hitler for the elimination of independent states. For Stalin, the pact seemed a brilliant stroke, since a deal with Hitler was much more useful for his two main goals of immediate Soviet security and the general destabilization of Europe. By contrast, Britain and France merely sought to maintain the status quo and offered the Soviet Union no easy conquests whatever. Though Stalin may have had no illusions about the ultimate durability of the new relationship, the Soviet government made clear in its Comintern circular of September 1939 that stimulation of the "second imperialist war" was in the interests of the Soviet Union and of world revolution, while maintaining the peace was not.[9] Not only could the German pact provide the Soviet Union with territory and nominal security, it would destabilize the situation generally by strengthening the weaker side, which is how Stalin viewed Germany. By supporting Hitler, Stalin could weaken the dominant imperial powers—Britain and France—and unleash a war against them by Hitler, which would even the odds and improve the strategic situation of the Soviet Union.[10]

Though it shocked the world, the pact thus made more sense—at least in some respects—from the Soviet side. There was certainly no moral problem in the relationship, for to this point the Soviet regime had been responsible for infinitely more deaths than had Nazi Germany—indeed, the greatest liquidation of the citizens of any state in world history, amounting to the deaths of

9. Quoted in A. C. Brown and C. B. MacDonald, *On a Field of Red: The Communist International and the Coming of World War II* (New York, 1981), 508.

10. Rolf Ahmann, in "Soviet Foreign Policy and the Molotov-Ribbentrop Pact of 1939: An Enigma Reassessed," *Storia delle Relazioni Internazionali* 5:2 (1989): 349–69, argues that Stalin perceived Nazi Germany (even with Italian assistance) as weaker than the Western powers down to the fall of France in June 1940. Bianka Pietrow, in "Stalins Politik bis 1941," in *Streit um Geschichtsbild*, ed. R. Kühnl (Cologne, 1987), 140–43, tends to concur.

The literature on Nazi-Soviet relations has become extensive. Among recent accounts that take the standard view, relatively favorable to Stalin, are J. Haslam, *The Soviet Union and the Struggle for Collective Security in Europe, 1933–1939* (London, 1984); A. Read and D. Fisher, *The Deadly Embrace* (New York, 1988); I. Fleischhauer, *Der Pakt* (Frankfurt, 1990); and G. Roberts, *The Unholy Alliance* (Bloomington, 1989), based partly on Soviet secondary sources.

The principal revisionist accounts, more critical of Soviet policy, are E. Gnedin, *Iz istorii otnoshenii mezhdu SSSR i fashistskoi Germaniei* (New York, 1977); J. Hochman, *The Soviet Union and the Failure of Collective Security, 1934–1938* (Ithaca, 1984); and the earlier J. McSherry, *Stalin, Hitler and Europe: The Origins of World War II, 1933–1939* (Cleveland, 1968).

thirty million or more people as the result of state policies,[11] even including the tentative introduction of mobile gas vans to kill kulaks.[12] Soviet support was essential to Hitler's designs during 1939–40 and took a variety of forms,[13] even though Stalin in turn prepared feverishly for rapid Soviet military expansion, potentially against Germany.[14]

Even though Germany was well short of its maximal rearmament level, Hitler was convinced that by mid-1939 he enjoyed a "window of opportunity" favorable to German expansion that would not last more than a few years. The reluctance of Britain and France to fight was obvious, and they had been at first slow to rearm. Conversely, the Soviet Union had vast resources at its disposal which would mean that in the future it would become stronger yet. Thus Hitler became convinced that in the period 1939–43 Germany would enjoy its greatest relative advantage, which could only decrease in subsequent years. Added to this was concern for his own health, which had begun to decline somewhat with advancing age. He seems to have felt that he might not live long (which was quite correct), so he must begin to accomplish his major goals as soon as possible.

Marxist historiography has subsequently sought to explain Hitler's decision for war as driven above all by economic pressures and the desire to increase profits, arguing that the depletion of resources in 1938–39 required a war of conquest to make them good.[15] Analysts have also asserted that the participation of German industrial firms and cartels in the economic exploitation of conquered areas demonstrated their dominance in the Third Reich. The first argument confuses effect with cause. The condition of the German economy did not itself dictate war—there was no autonomous German economy at that point—but rather the economy was in straitened circumstances because for

11. For tentative quantifications, see I. G. Dyadkin, *Unnatural Deaths in the USSR, 1928–1954* (New Brunswick, N.J., 1983), and R. J. Rummel, *Lethal Politics: Soviet Genocide and Mass Murder since 1917* (New Brunswick, N.J., 1990).

12. This has not been fully established. Cf. P.G. Grigorenko, *Memoirs* (New York, 1982), 209.

13. See especially D. W. Pike, "Aide morale et matérielle de l'URSS a l'Allemagne Nazie," *Guerres Mondiales* 160 (1990): 113–22.

14. B. Pietrow, *Stalinismus, Sicherheit und Offensive: Das "Dritte Reich" in der Konzeption der sowjetischen Aussenpolitik, 1933–1941* (Melsungen, 1983). Two recent works that seek to establish that Stalin was preparing to attack Germany in the summer of 1941 are E. Topitsch, *Stalin's War* (New York, 1987), and V. Suvorov, *Icebreaker: Who Started the Second World War?* (London, 1990).

15. J. Dülffer, "Der Beginn des Krieges, 1939: Hitler, die innere Krise und das Mächtesystem," *Geschichte und Gesellschaft* 2:4 (1976): 443–70; F. Forstmeier and H.-E. Volkmann, eds., *Wirtschaft und Rüstung am Vorabend des Zweiten Weltkrieges* (Düsseldorf, 1975); T. W. Mason, *Arbeiterklasse und Volksgemeinschaft* (Opladen, 1975); idem, "The Domestic Dynamics of Nazi Conquests: A Response to Critics," in *Reevaluating the Third Reich*, ed. T. Childers and J. Caplan (New York, 1993), 161–93.

three years Hitler had been subordinating normal economic interests to intense preparation for war. Nonetheless, "the German economy was not unmanageable in 1939," but simply under a stress whose degree has been somewhat exaggerated.[16] Sectors of German industry then later participated in the exploitation of conquered territory on much the same basis on which they operated at home, as subordinate economic units (albeit with important privileges within that category), not as dominant or even fully autonomous ones.

Hitler had no intention of starting a world war in 1939, nor did he ever plan to be involved in any Europe-wide or worldwide conflict. He hoped to be able to isolate his foes and destroy them one at a time. After eliminating Poland, he could then have turned on his new partner in crime. He could have attacked the Soviet Union in 1940 (or more likely in the year or so following), while still preserving peace in the west. The decision for a broader European war on September 3, 1939, was thus made in London and Paris, partly to preserve the balance of power; the choice also stemmed from a kind of moral conviction that Hitlerism was so evil and dangerous that it must be stopped. This was something that Hitler—within his own amoral and racially obsessed mental universe—simply could not understand. Yet the British and French governments admitted that they had no means with which to influence the campaign in Poland, which ended within one month with the destruction of Poland as an independent state and its partition between the invading German and Soviet armies.

Hitler then once again proposed peace to Britain and France on the basis of the status quo (though with regard to Poland conceding only the possibility of a small rump Polish state under German tutelage). Once this was not accepted, he prepared to launch an all-out attack on France as soon as possible, convinced that the defeat of France would bring peace with Britain, leaving him free to consummate his grand design, destruction of the Soviet Union. It was his great good fortune that the invasion was delayed innumerable times until May 1940, for at first neither Hitler nor his generals had any strategy with which to gain a rapid victory by an outnumbered German army that had still not completed its planned rearmament. Only the belated adoption—by Hitler's personal decision—of a new plan for a *Blitzkrieg* breakthrough and encirclement made it possible to shatter the Anglo-French front with lightning speed and knock France out of the war. Victory in the west was accompanied by

---

16. See P. Hayes, "Polyocracy and Policy in the Third Reich: The Case of the Economy," in Childers and Kaplan, eds., *Reevaluating the Third Reich* 190–210. See also J. Fest, "Hitlers Krieg," *Vierteljahrshefte für Zeitgeschichte* 38:3 (1990): 359–73; K. Hildebrand, "Le forze motrici di politica interna agenti sulla politica estera nazionalsocialista," *SC* 5:2 (June 1974): 201–22; and, for a review of the literature on the origins of the war with respect to Berlin and Rome, G. Schreiber, "Politik und Kriegführung im zeichen von Nationalsozialismus und Faschismus," *Neue Politische Literatur* 35:2 (1990): 179–94.

a new escalation of National Socialist propaganda about a young and healthy revolutionary "people's Germany" defeating aged and decadent Western capitalist plutocracies. Norway, Denmark, Belgium, Holland, and Luxembourg were also conquered in the dramatic spring of 1940, yet the new British government under Winston Churchill still refused to accept the obvious and make peace. Moreover, after it managed to give Hitler his first military defeat in the aerial battle of Britain a few months later, Hitler decided he did not wish to risk a direct amphibious assault on Britain, so contrary to his preferred strategic goals.[17]

Instead, Hitler decided that the time had come for Germany's most decisive military operation, the destruction of the Soviet Union. As a "friend," though not officially an ally, of Nazi Germany during 1939–40, the Soviet Union had taken advantage of Hitler's role as "icebreaker" to occupy the eastern half of Poland, all three of the Baltic republics, the southeastern corner of Finland, and the northeastern part of Romania.[18] (Moreover, during their two-year occupation of eastern Poland, the Soviets managed to kill Polish citizens at *six times* the rate carried out by Nazi policy in western Poland.[19]) By this point Mussolini liked to convince himself that the Soviet regime had become "nationalist" as well as "socialist," in fact virtually "fascist," and some Nazis said the same.[20] However that may have been, the Soviet regime had carried out extensive conquests on Germany's eastern frontier and through the autumn of 1940 pressed Hitler for further concessions. It seemed to become stronger and stronger through its own accelerated military expansion while Hitler remained bogged down in what was, from his point of view, an irrational conflict with Britain. Finally Hitler convinced himself that only the possibility of future assistance from the Soviet Union prevented the British government from making peace. The attack nonetheless had to be delayed six weeks to permit the German Balkan *Blitzkrieg* of April 1941 that overran Yugoslavia and

---

17. On Anglo-German maneuverings during these months, see J. Costello, *Ten Days to Destiny: The Secret Story of the Hess Peace Initiative and British Efforts to Strike a Deal with Hitler* (New York, 1991).

18. "Icebreaker of the revolution" was standard Soviet terminology for the disruptive effect of the "second imperialist war."

19. During the first two years of Polish occupation (before the major mass liquidations), the Germans killed about 120,000 people and the Soviets at least 400,000. Since the population of the Soviet-occupied territory was barely more than half that of the German-dominated area, the differential rate of slaughter was approximately 600 percent. J. T. Gross, *Revolution from Abroad: The Soviet Conquest of Poland's Western Ukraine and Western Belorussia* (Princeton, 1988), 228–29.

20. Conversely, it was always painful for the Soviets to recognize the Nazis as "National Socialists," theoretically so near Soviet nomenclature. Soviet commentary and propaganda always emphasized the generic term *fascist* for Nazis, save during the years of friendship, between 1939 and 1941, when *fascist* was banned.

Greece in order to rescue Mussolini's military forces and protect Germany's southeastern flank.

When the great invasion of the Soviet Union was launched on June 22, 1941, massed Red Army units were caught in forward offensive formation on the border, completely out of position for the defensive battle that Hitler forced on them. He announced the campaign to his generals as not merely another great power conflict but a "war of racial annihilation" that would unleash "the most voracious beast of prey the world has ever seen." [21] Yet the military and manpower resources of the Soviet Union were greater than those of Germany, and given the confusion of targets and priorities in the German advance, it proved impossible to knock out the Red Army in a five-month campaign during 1941, though its losses were the greatest ever suffered by an army in an equivalent period at any time in history.

Just as the German advance ground to a halt outside Moscow, Japan attacked the United States at Pearl Harbor. The American government was doing all it could to assist Britain and the Soviet Union short of entering the war, and Hitler therefore accepted what he saw as the logic of this situation by declaring war on the United States, converting the European conflict into a world war. Since, in Hitler's general scheme, Germany was not to become involved in a world war with the United States for a full generation or more and since it is by no means clear, at that juncture, that the American government would have taken the initiative in declaring war on Germany as it had in 1917, historians have asked ever since why Hitler took the plunge.

Though he had never had any illusion that Germany at that time could win a great world war of attrition similar to World War I, Hitler maintained a primarily Eurocentric focus. He was convinced that the main phase of conflict would soon be decided in Europe, where German arms would be able to defeat the Soviet Union before the close of the next year. Following the signature of the Tripartite Pact earlier between Germany, Italy, and Japan, he had found the Japanese leaders reluctant to attack the Soviet Union but increasingly drawn toward an attack on the United States.[22] He was concerned to tie down American military power in the Pacific in the short term while the major conflict was decided in Europe. Thus the German declaration of war was intended, in Hitler's thinking, simply to face the facts. The United States had already become an enemy, and declarations of war by Germany and Italy would encourage the Japanese government to keep American forces fully engaged in the Pacific while Germany defeated the Soviet Union. Though Hitler respected to some extent the "Aryan" component of the American population, as he did American industry and technology, he held that in general American society

21. Quoted in E. Nolte, *Three Faces of Fascism* (New York, 1966), 526.
22. See J. M. Meskill, *Hitler and Japan* (New York, 1964).

Japanese ambassador Kurusu, Ciano, and Hitler signing the Tripartite Pact in Berlin, September, 1940

was hopelessly mongrelized in racial terms and would be unable during the next year or more to make a decisive military contribution against two major enemies across two different oceans.[23] The gamble on which this was all predicated—winning the war against the Soviet Union in 1942—soon became the most serious of Hitler's blunders. Much more decisively than in 1939–40, his long-range strategy had foundered on the shoals of his impatient short-term opportunist tactics.

Thenceforth the Third Reich would face an increasingly desperate struggle of attrition on multiple fronts against enemies with greatly superior economic and demographic resources. Soon there was little hope of German victory, but Hitler maintained iron determination. He hoped to divide his enemies and achieve a separate peace on one front or the other, conducting secret negotiations with Stalin once more during 1943–44. This time, however, Hitler stubbornly refused to pay Stalin's price, and thus the unnatural alliance of the Western democracies and the Soviet Union held firm, almost inevitably grinding the Third Reich down into defeat. That it survived until May 1945 against such heavy odds was due to Hitler's determination, the iron grip of the Nazi

23. S. Friedlander, *Prelude to Downfall: Hitler and the United States, 1939–1941* (New York, 1967); G. L. Weinberg, "Hitler's Image of the United States," *American Historical Review* 69:4 (July 1964): 1006–21.

dictatorship, the regime's ability to inspire self-sacrifice, the ruthless pillaging of the resources of occupied Europe, and the superior military skills of the German army, outnumbered but never outclassed.

Because of the discipline and determination with which the German army fought and its institutional separation from the NSDAP, there has always been some tendency to draw a distinction, and not always incorrectly, between Nazis and soldiers in the Third Reich. Yet recent research has suggested that the distinction has been exaggerated. Most German soldiers were not Nazis, yet the functioning of the German army was increasingly influenced by Nazi brutality and racialism. Discipline was much more harsh than in World War I. In that conflict, the German army executed only forty-eight of its troops for disciplinary infractions, the lowest rate of any of the large European armies. Yet in World War II, between thirteen thousand and fifteen thousand German soldiers were executed by their own army, equivalent to the loss of nearly two divisions, a rate equaled only by Stalin's Red Army, likewise brutal and prone to atrocity. Troop behavior toward civilians in Hitler's "war of racial annihilation" in the east was often violent in the extreme, approximately as bad as that of Red Army units in eastern Europe and eastern Germany.[24] As the war advanced, the German army was forced into increasingly primitive conditions, lacking proper transport and supplies.[25] This relative immiserization and primitivization were reflected in atrocious behavior, particularly in the Waffen-SS but also in other units. The Nazification of the German army never became complete, but in the later phases the process was expedited by copying a main feature of Soviet practice, when "National Socialist guidance officers," a Nazi equivalent of political commissars, began to be attached to some units.[26]

As in World War I, many of the military innovations in the Second World War were introduced by Germany. These began with the successful strategies of *Blitzkrieg* and tactical bombing and were extended to long-range rockets and the first jet aircraft. But just as in World War I it was the Allies who developed the tank, so it was the Allies who developed strategic bombing and finally the ultimate weapon of the atomic bomb. Though Germany (and also Japan) had

24. O. Bartov, *Hitler's Army* (New York, 1991); idem, *The Eastern Front, 1941–1945: German Troops and the Barbarisation of Warfare* (London, 1985); C. W. Sydnor, *Soldiers of Destruction: The SS Death's Head Division, 1933–1945* (Princeton, 1977); T. Schulte, *The German Army and Nazi Policies in Occupied Russia* (Oxford, 1989); C. Streit, *Keine Kameraden: Die Wehrmacht und die sowjetische Kriegsgefangenen, 1941–1945* (Stuttgart, 1978).

25. The *"Blitzkrieg* army" in fact relied in large measure on horses for transport beyond rail heads. See R. L. Di Nardo and A. Bay, "Horse-Drawn Transport in the German Army," *JCH* 23:1 (Jan. 1988): 129–42.

26. R. L. Quinnett, "The German Army Confronts the NSFO," *JCH* 13:1 (Jan. 1978): 53–64; M. Messerschmidt, *Die Wehrmacht im NS-Staat: Zeit der Indoktrination* (Hamburg, 1969).

an atomic project, it was far behind that of the United States and was developed more slowly, at least in part because of ideological prejudices against "Jewish physics."[27]

THE NAZI PARTY AND THE HOME FRONT

In the final years before the war the Nazi Party had actually suffered some decline in general esteem among the German people, even while Hitler's stock rose. Thus when the Führer announced in 1939 that party membership was being opened to new recruits until 10 percent of the total population was enrolled, it proved impossible to meet that total, to the surprise and consternation of NSDAP leaders. New members tended to come somewhat more from the ranks of blue-collar workers than before, though this group still remained a minority, while the proportion of new white-collar members stayed about the same and that of civil servants and small shopkeepers declined. During the years 1939–42 new members stemmed disproportionately from the middle-agd; overall the average age of NSDAP members had increased from thirty-two or thirty-three in 1933 to forty-five or forty-six by 1942. In 1942 general recruitment was halted once more, and Hitler announced that henceforth new members would come primarily from the Hitler Youth and military veterans. Female membership nonetheless increased rapidly during the war. It had amounted to 16.5 percent of the total in 1939, whereas nearly 35 percent of all new members in 1942–44 were female.[28]

Support and new recruits declined most strikingly among the elite, from the upper classes socially through university professors and students to civil

27. There were numerous practical problems as well. See M. Walker, *German National Socialism and the Quest for Nuclear Power, 1939–1949* (New York, 1989), and idem, "National Socialism and German Physics," *JCH* 24:1 (Jan. 1989): 63–90.

The two best general accounts of World War II are P. Cavalcoressi and G. Wint, *Total War*, 2 vols. (New York, 1979), and G. L. Weinberg, *A World at Arms* (New York, 1993), while H. P. Willmott, *The Great Crusade* (New York, 1989), is the best recent military history. On the war in Europe, see G. Wright, *The Ordeal of Total War, 1939–1945* (New York, 1968). The outstanding German account is the multivolume *Germany and the Second World War*, 5 vols. to date (Oxford, 1991–), written by a team of specialists. See also M. Cooper, *The German Army, 1933–1945* (New York, 1978), and, on the key campaigns, N. Bethell, *The War Hitler Won* (London, 1972); T. Taylor, *The March of Conquest: German Victories in Western Europe, 1940* (London, 1959); R. Lewin, *The Life and Death of the Afrika Korps* (London, 1977); A. Seaton, *The Russo-German War, 1941–45* (London, 1971); and B. I. Fugate, *Operation Barbarossa* (Novato, Calif., 1984). Concerning Hitler's military leadership and ultimate aims, see P. E. Schramm, *Hitler: The Man and the Military Leader* (Chicago, 1971); Rich, *Hitler's War Aims;* and J. Thies, *Architekt der Weltherrschaft: Die "Endziele" Hitlers* (Düsseldorf, 1976).

28. M. H. Kater, *The Nazi Party: A Social Profile of Members and Leaders, 1919–1945* (Cambridge, Mass., 1983), 116–38.

servants and lawyers. All these social sectors saw their own interests increasingly circumscribed and in some cases superseded under the Third Reich. The only elite sector to retain a generally favorable attitude toward Nazism was the big businessmen, because of guaranteed profits and the opportunity to expand into occupied territories.

The regime reached the all-time height of its popularity in the second half of 1940 in a society momentarily delirious with joy over its stunning victory against France. By 1940 even Communist workers were volunteering for the army, and it has been accurately observed that there was more evidence of a "workers' opposition" during the war in Britain than in Germany. Some organized opposition to the regime did exist, but it was very limited and significant only among a small sector of the military. Police pressure was important in this and continued to mount; by late 1941 the Gestapo was arresting approximately fifteen thousand people a month in Germany, more than ten times the rate of 1935.[29]

Party popularity nonetheless, and not too surprisingly, plummeted during the war. As local party units began to be given increasing responsibility in wartime administration and local mobilization, they became responsible for many local problems, particularly from 1942 on, and they became the targets of growing ire. Nearly half the NSDAP membership was eventually mobilized into the armed forces, but elite sectors, once in the military, more often than not got themselves assigned to occupation duty. During the war the party leadership tended to ossify, and the bosses simply lacked the training, experience, and ability to handle the increasingly complex tasks in war mobilization and the administration of the home front that were being thrust on them in the later stages of the war. By 1943 mounting corruption among Nazi leaders made the party look bad compared with the remarkable achievements of the wartime army and industry. Only Hitler's prestige remained comparatively undiminished, and he did for the most part loyally stand behind the old party leaders, but the decline in prestige was such that by 1944 party members were known on occasion to hide their party badges and even sometimes to deny membership.

During the victorious years of the war, Hitler encouraged the Labor Front to prepare bold plans for sweeping changes in welfare and insurance, as well as in the salary structure of German labor. The latter was to be based exclusively on productivity, but to be adjusted for all social classes and professions, not just labor, to achieve greater de facto social equality, together with special educational and incentive programs for the more talented workers to rise to higher roles. This would achieve "true socialism" for the first time in the world, according to the vision of Hitler and the German Labor Front's Institute of Labor Science. The new plan for "Social Work of the German People"

29. K. D. Bracher, *The German Dictatorship* (New York, 1970), 418.

would provide for the entire population unprecedented welfare, insurance, and pension rights. It was to be accompanied by the most massive worker housing program in the world, to transform a "nation of proletarians" into a true "master race." The Führer hoped to begin the first stages of this great scheme while the fighting yet raged, but in 1942 financial pressures forced all these improvements to be shelved for the duration, though costly plans for the reorganization and expansion of the social insurance system were still being proposed as late as 1944.[30]

It has usually been argued that the greatest wartime failure of the Third Reich—aside of course from Hitler's faulty overall strategy—was the relative undermobilization of the economy for military production until 1942–43, by which point the war had virtually been lost. There is perhaps some truth to this, though the interpretation has been somewhat exaggerated. Hitler's electoral victories had been based in part on promises of better economic conditions, and as full employment and relative prosperity had returned to Germany in the late 1930s, he was reluctant to commit the German economy to total mobilization—despite the rapid rise of arms expenditures from 1936—so as to limit at least somewhat the impact on living standards. Instead, the Third Reich had followed a strategy which produced military goods in breadth—a certain amount of each kind—but not in depth, which would have cost even more. Hitler's initial strategy was to plan for one-front campaigns that would end relatively quickly. Even so, Germany produced more military goods between 1937 and 1939 than did any other power save the Soviet Union. What has been called into question was the failure to move into a program of "total war" production before 1942–43. At that point the new director of the expanded Reich Ministry for Armaments was Hitler's personal architect, Albert Speer, who presided over sharp increases in production.[31] By streamlining procedures, avoiding duplication and waste, and incorporating greatly expanded resources, Speer managed to triple German production between 1942 and 1944, despite destruction from Allied bombing. Even so, centralization and efficiency were hampered by the multiplicity of overlapping state boards which Hitler had created, while Nazi Party leaders sometimes insisted on maintaining as high a level of consumer goods as possible.[32]

Previous evaluations of German mobilization have sometimes been distorted, for military production in fact rose steadily even before 1942 and living

30. The principal study is M.-L. Recker, *Nationalsozialistische Sozialpolitik im Zweiten Weltkrieg* (Munich, 1985). Cf. R. Zitelmann, *Hitler* (Bari, 1992), 170–74.

31. For a revised estimate of Speer, see M. Schmidt, *Albert Speer: Das Ende eines Mythos* (Bern, 1982).

32. L. Herbst, *Der total Krieg und die Ordnung der Wirtschaft* (Stuttgart, 1982), is a reliable study.

standards were being steadily depressed. Paul Hayes has found that "German military expenditure rose at a virtually steady rate from 1938–39 to 1943–44" and that "between 1938 and 1941, the regime forced down per capita civilian consumption within Germany by 20 percent and per capita consumer goods by 22 percent and raised the output of producer goods by 28 percent."[33] Before 1943 Germany had spent a greater proportion of its national product on military expenditures over a longer period than any power save the Soviet Union, and according to Hayes's estimates it finally caught up with the Soviet Union in that year.

Analysts have suggested more recently that the problem was not that Hitler and other Nazi leaders rejected total mobilization at an early stage, but that at first they failed to realize all that was involved. Hitler, Himmler, and the party secretary, Bormann, all emphasized ideological mobilization, while Goebbels went further than any other in stressing the social aspects—rather in the nature of emulating Soviet structure and practice.[34] By the end of 1941 Hitler was impressed by the Soviet capacity for military mobilization and production in depth, and he came increasingly to admire Soviet state socialism as an economic model, one that should be emulated by the Third Reich.[35] Total mobilization was not fully attempted, however, until Joseph Goebbels was made Reich plenipotentiary for total war in July 1944. For the first time a serious effort was made to mobilize women, while old men, teenagers, and even children over ten were mobilized for economic and militia service, a *Volkssturm* (people's storm or people's army) of the very young and very old being created as an internal militia force. Though revealed as increasingly corrupt and discredited, the Nazi Party apparatus was given new powers for broad mobilization of the home front, with increased police authority, finally including that of summary execution of civilians. Only during this last phase of wartime emergency is it possible to speak of "totalitarian" structural control, as Hannah Arendt and other students have recognized.

National Socialist doctrine held that a woman's place was in the home, and Hitler long rejected any plan for the economic mobilization of women. The goal until well after the war began was to have fewer, not more, women in the workplace. This policy was somewhat concealed by global statistics which indicated a higher percentage of German women actually employed than in most other countries, a tendency which predated Nazism. During the first part of the

33. Hayes, "Polyocracy and Policy" 196.

34. See E. Hancock, *National Socialist Leadership and Total War, 1941–45* (New York, 1991).

35. To encourage industrialists, however, he would still halfheartedly promise them that the state's share of the economy would not increase after the war was over. On this issue, see R. Zitelmann, *Hitler: Selbstverständnis eines Revolutionärs* (Hamburg, 1987), and his biography *Hitler* 183–89.

war, however, the percentage of women in the labor force actually declined, evidently due to the large-scale receipt of military dependents' benefits. For the first time in 1943, women between the ages of seventeen and forty-five were required to register for possible compulsory labor, but even then most were at first exempted. Only in mid-1944 did the regime turn in desperation to the serious mobilization of women. By that time nearly 47 percent of employment-age German women were employed. Women made up well over half the German labor force, a percentage exceeded only in the Soviet Union.[36]

The chief replacement for German men in the labor force was the increasing number of contract and forced laborers from abroad. Recruitment of foreign labor began early in the war, with labor conscription in conquered territories subsequently reaching massive proportions. Eventually foreign contract and forced laborers came to total nearly eight million (including women as well as men).[37]

German people in general continued to work and to fight with a discipline, determination, and courage worthy of a better cause. It is doubtful if Nazi ideology per se ever had much to do with it. What had achieved the high standing of the Hitler regime had been its successes in the economy and in international and military affairs. What kept Germans at their posts was not so much the effectiveness of National Socialist ideological propaganda[38] as patriotism, the rigors of an ever more severe police state, and pure fear of what would happen if Germany lost such a total and destructive war.[39] The Führer mythos seems to have survived relatively intact among a large proportion of the population, even as the Nazi Party itself became increasingly despised.[40]

THE ROLE OF THE SS

The most powerful Nazi organization was the SS, whose leadership of the racial revolution gave it a special role in Germany's expansion. It had become a large and complex institution, harboring various shadings of internal opinion, but the higher SS and police leadership structure (HSSPF) under Heinrich Himmler was reasonably well organized.[41]

36. Hancock, *National Socialist Leadership* 159, 288.

37. E. L. Homze, *Foreign Labor in Nazi Germany* (Princeton, 1967).

38. This is the conclusion of David Welch, in *The Third Reich: Politics and Propaganda* (New York, 1993).

39. Concerning attitudes on the home front, see M. Steinert, *Hitler's War and the Germans* (Athens, Ohio, 1977); C. Whiting, *The Home Front: Germany* (Chicago, 1982); and E. R. Beck, *Under the Bombs* (Lexington, Ky., 1986).

40. I. Kershaw, *The "Hitler Myth"* (Oxford, 1987). Dieter Rebentisch, in *Führerstaat und Verwaltung im Zweiten Weltkrieg* (Wiesbaden, 1989), argues that, contrary to the standard opinion, Hitler continued to play a relatively active role in the administration of domestic affairs.

41. R. B. Birn, *Die Höheren SS- und Polizeiführer: Himmlers Vertreter im Reich und in den besetzten Gebieten* (Düsseldorf, 1986).

During the war Himmler led "a systematic SS process of power accumulation through the whole of society," dominating much of the Occupation in western as well as nearly all eastern Europe.[42] The role of the SS was particularly prominent in the future *Lebensraum* territories of the east, where it set up an elaborate police structure and led much of the antipartisan warfare and nearly all the rounding up of Jews and other prisoners, enslaving or liquidating millions.[43] A long-range goal was to make the SS a major economic power as well, with a "European Ministry of Economy" to be built of the numerous SS economic enterprises in Germany and the conquered territories.[44] When Himmler was named head of the Ersatzheer (Home Army) late in 1944, his authority only increased.

The most important single new SS wartime initiative was the Waffen-SS. Originating in 1935, the Waffen-SS expanded into division-sized military units in 1938–39. There is no indication that Himmler schemed to have the Waffen-SS replace the entire army, as is sometimes alleged, but he did plan for the SS to take over the political aspect of military affairs and, after the attempt on Hitler's life on July 20, 1944, developed the goal of reconstructing the entire army command on the basis of the SS leadership after the war. In September 1943 Hitler allegedly remarked that the SS was the best single instrument that he would leave his successor, and the institution that should develop the military organization of the *Volksdeutsche* (ethnic Germans) outside Germany.[45] Thus the leading historian of the Waffen-SS has judged that "Himmler succeeded within a few years in laying the political basis to secure for the SS after the hostilities *one if not the* leading position in the territories of eastern, northern and western Europe conquered by Germany."[46]

At its height in 1944 the Waffen-SS numbered nearly 600,000 troops, and in the final German call-up of the class of 1928 in February 1945 were awarded the 95,000 best-conditioned of a total of 550,000 new recruits. The great irony and contradiction of Waffen-SS membership was that the military force which had originated as the ultimate racial elite not merely enlisted large numbers of *Volksdeutsche* (not in itself contradictory) but also had continuously to lower its own manpower standards, during the latter part of the war creating large-scale units made up of non-German, eventually even non-European, volunteers, from northern, western, and eastern Europe. Generally *Volksdeutsche* and members of foreign Waffen-SS units were not eligible to

42. B. Wegner, *The Waffen-SS* (Oxford, 1990), xiii.
43. H. Krausnicj and H.-H. Wilhelm, *Die Truppe des Weltanschauungskrieges: Die Einsatzgruppen der Sicherheitspolizei und des SD, 1938–1942* (Stuttgart, 1981).
44. Cf. A. Speer, *Infiltration* (New York, 1981).
45. On the SS role with ethnic Germans in eastern Europe, see V. O. Lumans, *Himmler's Auxiliaries: The Volksdeutsche Mittelstelle and the German National Minorities of Europe, 1933–1945* (Chapel Hill, 1993).
46. Wegner, *Waffen-SS* 364–65.

Recruitment poster for the Waffen SS "Wallonie" Brigade in Belgium, 1942

join the SS proper, save for those in the all-Scandinavian Viking Division, but were projected to serve as the basis of expanded military power and recruitment in non-German areas.[47] The increasingly diverse national membership of the Waffen-SS was featured in the tendency to present Germany's struggle as that of "European civilization" against Asian Bolshevism, though it made

47. For a descriptive military account, see G. H. Stein, *The Waffen-SS* (Ithaca, 1966). There are also narratives of the main foreign units, such as J. Mabire, *Les SS français*, 3 vols. (Paris, 1973–75). P. H. Buss and A. Mollo, *Hitler's Germanic Legions: An Illustrated History of the Western European Legions with the SS, 1941–43* (London, 1978), is somewhat popularized.

nonsense of strict racial policy.[48] Moreover, in contrast to the iron discipline of the regular Waffen-SS, there were cases of mutiny, refusal to fight, and even wholesale desertion among a number of *Volksdeutsche* and foreign Waffen-SS detachments.

Inevitably, the higher SS leadership also failed to live up to the stereotype. From mid-1943 Himmler and other top SS figures, like the main Nazi leaders generally, began to look for a political solution to the war. This was mostly unknown to Hitler, who continued to give Himmler increasingly important posts in keeping with the tendency toward total war and total mobilization. Himmler was thus made Reich interior minister in August 1943, but there he proved that he had no coherent concept of total war. Thus it was the more determined and resolute Goebbels who became Reich plenipotentiary for total war in July 1944, after the near-fatal attempt on Hitler's life. Himmler was next placed in charge of the Ersatzheer, to organize a new home militia. After he failed in that task, the job was handed to the more truly fanatical and energetic Goebbels in December. Himmler then quickly failed successively in new responsibilities as head first of the Army Group Upper Rhine and then of the Army Group Vistula, absurd assignments for the militarily almost illiterate SS leader. During the last years of the war Himmler came secretly to differ from both Hitler and Goebbels in his preference for striking a deal with the Western powers, in the interest of which he was willing to sacrifice ideological considerations. In September–October 1944 he even gave orders to stop killing Jews in order to be more presentable to the Western powers, though these orders were not made generally effective.[49]

THE NAZI NEW ORDER

Hitler's startling victories between 1938 and 1941 gave him control of the greater part of continental Europe, something unprecedented since the height of Napoleon's power, and with it the opportunity to begin the drastic realignment of peoples and states which he sought. The basic goal was an enormously expanded Germany to the east, which would quickly become a great superpower of well over a hundred million people and the breeding ground of the racial revolution. But even in Hitler's mind that would take more than one generation, and in the meantime there was a desperate war to be fought and allies to be sustained.

48. Such concepts were adjusted in various ways. By 1944 the SS more and more used the terminology of "Nordic" rather than "Germanic" racism, to include as many northern and central European peoples as possible.

The apologetic works of H. W. Neulen propound the notion that the foreign Waffen-SS volunteers developed a positive concept of "Eurofascism" that would not be led by Germans alone: see his *Eurofaschismus und der Zweite Weltkrieg* (Munich, 1980) and *An deutscher Seite: Internationale Freiwillige von Wehrmacht und SS* (Munich, 1985).

49. On the roles of Himmler and Goebbels in the later phases of the war, see Hancock, *National Socialist Leadership* 127–87.

Table 11.1. The Nazi New Order

1. Direct Annexations: Austria; Czech Sudetenland; Danzig; Polish West Prussia, Poznan, and Silesia; Luxembourg; Belgian Eupen and Malmedy; French Alsace and Moselle; northern Slovenia; Yugoslav Banat

2. Direct German Administration:
   a) Civil: Polish Government General, "Ostland" (Baltic area). Ukraine. Norway, Holland
   b) Military: Belgium and part of northern France, forward military districts in the Soviet Union

3. Tutelary Satellite or Puppet Regimes: Protectorate of Bohemia-Moravia; Croatia. Serbia. Montenegro, Greece, Italian Social Republic (1943–45)

4. Satellites: Denmark, Finland, Hungary, Romania, Slovakia, Bulgaria, Vichy France, Italy (1941–43)

5. Neutrals:
   a) Friendly neutrals: Spain, Switzerland, Sweden
   b) Distant neutrals: Portugal, Ireland, Turkey

Even Hitler did not propose that most of Europe—at least for the time being—could be taken over directly by Germany. He recognized the need for certain allies, for acquiescent satellite states, and for friendly neutrals. Ideally, these would be ordered according to the Nazi racial hierarchy, but in practice their roles and identities would be determined by politics and geography. Altogether, allies, satellites, and the upper administrations in some of the occupied territories produced a new configuration of states under German leadership and/or domination that the Nazi press sometimes hailed as the new "united states of Europe."

Italy was Germany's ally from the beginning, though it only entered the war in June 1940. When Hitler invaded the Soviet Union in the following year, he acquired three new eastern allies for that campaign: Romania, Hungary, and Finland. Romania was the most committed and ambitious anti-Soviet ally, while the association with Finland was only circumstantial, since that country sought simply to recover the territory seized by Stalin in 1940. Bulgaria was a friendly state without ever becoming a full ally, cooperating economically, receiving a slice of Yugoslavia, and allowing its territory to be freely used for the transit of German troops. In addition, German expansion created two new satellite states, Slovakia (1939) and Croatia (1941), while the rump state of Vichy France, left independent in the southern half of France, was at least a semisatellite.[50] Occasional puppet administrations, like that of Quisling in Norway, were also sometimes installed in occupied states.

There were five neutral countries on the Continent—Spain, Sweden, Switzerland, Portugal, and Turkey. Of these, Spain was never fully neutral be-

.50. The allies and satellites are treated in B. Mueller-Hildebrand, *Germany and Its Allies in World War II* (Washington, D.C., 1980), and M. Mourin, *Le drame des Etats satellites de l'Axe* (Paris, 1957).

cause of the Franco regime's semifascist structure. After the fall of France, Franco's policy changed from neutrality to "nonbelligerence," tilted in favor of the Axis. It only moved back to technical neutrality late in 1943.

Official German annexation of conquered territory was comparatively limited during the war, though after a final German victory this would have been greatly extended. In the west, three small Belgian territories taken from Germany in 1919 were reannexed in 1940, while in the east, other districts were directly annexed from western Poland, northwestern Czechoslovakia, and northwestern Yugoslavia. In addition, Luxembourg and the French provinces of Alsace and part of Lorraine were treated administratively as though they were part of the Reich and would have been officially incorporated after a final German victory.

The most leniently treated of the Nazi conquests were the "Nordic" lands of Denmark, Norway, and Holland. The Danes were at first allowed to retain their own regular autonomous government, though this was finally eliminated late in 1943. Norway was administered by a Nazi Gauleiter, Joseph Terboven, though a puppet Norwegian government was later created under the Norwegian fascist Vidkun Quisling, whose name became synonymous with treason during World War II. Holland, like Denmark and Norway, was also considered to be susceptible to full Germanization. It was also governed by a civilian Nazi administrator who created a simulacrum of internal Dutch autonomy. By contrast, the more "Latin" areas of Belgium and occupied northern France were directly administered by military government.

In the east, Czechoslovakia and Yugoslavia were dissolved. Southwestern Yugoslavia was placed under Italian military occupation, the northeast under that of Germany, with a Croatian Ustashi satellite state governing the main part of Croatia and a puppet Serbian protofascist administration governing part of Serbia. Most of Poland, apart from the two large provinces in the west directly annexed by the Reich, was administered by a Nazi governor as the Government General of Poland. Administration of the huge occupied territories in the western Soviet Union was chaotic. Two special Reich commissariats were created for Ostland (the former Baltic states) and the Ukraine, but at the same time in these and in other occupied Soviet districts there were overarching military occupation authorities, special German economic agencies, and the SS racial and police administration.

Nazi administration was interested in finding collaborators and puppets but did not seek them primarily among native fascists. When these were employed, they were normally given little authority, even in controlled puppet situations. Stable conservatives and rightists were preferred: they were easier to deal with and also enjoyed greater credibility among the conquered peoples. Only in Norway and to a lesser extent in Holland was nominal (not real) authority given to a puppet fascist leader in a directly occupied country. Among satellites such as Romania and Slovakia, Hitler consistently favored right authoritarians over native fascists. In Croatia power was given to the native Usta-shi only after the role had been rejected by the leading conservative politician. Somewhat extreme but not unrepresentative was the policy of the Czech puppet government installed in Prague in 1939, one of whose first acts was to ban General Gajda's Czech Fascist Community as potentially subversive.[51]

On October 7, 1939, as soon as the conquest of Poland was completed, Heinrich Himmler was appointed head of a new Reich Commissariat for the Strengthening of Germandom (RKFDV). Its task was the clearing of inferior races from conquered territory and the establishment of new German settlers as forerunners of the racial revolution. Initially about one million Poles were removed from the former western Polish provinces that were incorporated into Germany, their places taken by a smaller number of German immigrants. The plan was later to pursue even more drastic procedures in the main part of Poland and particularly in the western territories of the Soviet Union. Since nearly all the population of Germany was being mobilized in one way or another for the war, new Germanic inhabitants were found among the *Volksdeutsche* whose ancestors in earlier generations had settled in various parts of eastern Europe. Eventually nearly a million of these *Volksdeutsche* were settled in newly incorporated territories.[52]

There were also plans for the Germanization of much of western Europe. Scandinavians, Dutch, and the Flemish population of Belgium were generally considered fellow Nordics and racially redeemable, as were a minority of the blond population in Czechoslovakia, Poland, and the Baltic states. The Latin peoples of southwestern Europe occupied an intermediate category, inferior to Nordics but still acceptable in subordinate roles. For the bulk of the population of eastern Europe, however, the future was to be one of virtual slave labor, of massive resettlement, and in many cases of wholesale extermination.

The economic program of the New Order consisted of almost unrelieved exploitation, in which nearly all the rest of Europe would labor (though in varying degrees) for the sustenance of Germany and its war effort. All occupied Western countries (again with the exception of Denmark) were required to pay full occupation costs, but economic assets were not normally confiscated unless the owners were Jews or in the resistance. However, throughout western Europe German occupation systematically regulated and manipulated economic assets and production so that a sizable part of all production went to Germany for very low costs and sometimes none at all. In the east, economic exploitation was much more direct, extensive, and ruthless, driving down living standards

51. F. Bertin, *L'Europe de Hitler*, 3 vols. (Paris, 1976–77), provides a broad treatment. See also E. Collotti, *L'occupazione nazista in Europa* (Rome, 1964).

52. R. Koehl, *RKFDV: German Resettlement and Population Policy* (Cambridge, Mass., 1957).

even further. As most of Germany's able-bodied adult male population under forty was conscripted for military service, labor shortages within the German economy became extreme. The gap was filled by steadily increasing the importation of foreign laborers, at first using contract workers and prisoners of war and later rounding up huge numbers of forced laborers, until eventually nearly eight million—many treated little better than slaves—had been employed in German agriculture and industry, where they came to make up at least 20 percent of the total labor force.[53] The number of free and forced laborers working directly or indirectly for the German economy in the occupied territories was of course much greater.

EUROPEAN CIVILIZATION OR REVOLUTIONARY WORLD ORDER?

The propaganda framework of Axis expansion varied considerably during the course of the war, reflecting the ambiguities of Italian Fascist and German National Socialist ideology, as well as the contradictory relationship between the two. For most of the 1930s the goals and language of both Italian and German expansion had been couched in moderate terms—normal imperial expansion for the one, vital national interest for German-speaking people for the other. Both Mussolini and Hitler held that military expansion was part of a grander revolutionary process, and in Germany this came to the forefront during the western campaign of 1940, described sometimes as one of youthful and revolutionary National Socialism against the decadent, individualistic, plutocratic-capitalist West. For Hitler, revolution came even more to the fore with the revolutionary race war unleashed by the attack against the Soviet Union, though in occupied Europe this was presented as a crusade of European civilization against Asian Bolshevism. Such themes became even more prominent later in the war,[54] paralleled in Rome by the presentation of *Romanità* as the leader of European culture against the barbarous outer world.[55]

At the same time, a major subtheme employed outside Europe portrayed the Axis powers as creators of a new revolutionary world order that would break the hegemony of the nineteenth-century Western empires. This propaganda was especially directed toward the Arab world but was occasionally also echoed by the Germans in eastern Europe.[56] Thus small Italian and German air

53. Homze, *Foreign Labor.*

54. Cf. E. Nolte, *Der europäische Bürgerkrieg, 1917–1945: Nationalsozialismus und Bolschewismus* (Hamburg, 1987). This became a major theme among surviving fascists after the war, as in M. Bardèche, *Qu'est-ce que le fascisme?* (Paris, 1961).

55. D. Cofrancesco, "Il mito europeo del fascismo (1939–1945)," *SC* 14:1 (Feb. 1983): 5–45. This seems to have been taken seriously primarily by Fascist intellectuals.

56. An Italian Foreign Ministry paper of January 1942 speculated about the construction of an Italian-led "commonwealth" of east Mediterranean and Middle Eastern, mostly Arab, states.

units assisted the Rashid Ali revolt against British hegemony in Iraq in April 1941, yet neither power was in a position to play this card fully. Earlier, Mussolini had encouraged Zionism as a factor to weaken the British Empire in the eastern Mediterranean.[57] Ultimately Japan went much further in the Far East to encourage new Asian nationalisms against the Western colonial powers.[58]

Within occupied Europe, the theme of "defending European civilization" against Bolshevism and other barbarisms was sounded more and more as the war continued, especially to encourage foreign military volunteering. The latter paradoxically reached its greatest extent among the "submen" of the Soviet Union, among whom more than a million military auxiliaries were organized, including many thousands of troops who were not Europeans.[59]

THE HOLOCAUST

Fascism was one of the two most atrocious political movements of modern times, and its greatest single atrocity was the mass liquidation of the Jewish population of German-occupied Europe, a process unique in human history and now generally known from the usage of Jewish writers and historians as the Holocaust. This program of mass murder was a direct and logical consequence of the extreme racial anti-Semitism of Hitler and most of the Nazi core group. Though it was necessary for propaganda purposes to tone down the party's anti-Semitism in the mass German electoral campaigns of 1930–33, and though for similar reasons Hitler never announced a complete program

---

R. De Felice, *Il fascismo e l'Oriente* (Bologna, 1988), 68–71. On Italian policy, see also J. Bessis, *La Méditerranée fasciste* (Paris, 1981); R. W. Melka, "The Axis and the Arab Middle East, 1930–1945," Ph.D. diss., University of Minnesota, 1966; and G. Procacci, *Dalla parte d'Etiopia: L'aggressione italiana vista dai movimenti anticolonialisti d'Asia, d'Africa, d'America* (Milan, 1984). For Germany, see L. Hirszowicz, *The Third Reich and the Arab East* (London, 1966); H. Tillmann, *Deutschlands Araberpolitik im Zweiten Weltkrieg* (Berlin, 1965); J. B. Schechtman, *The Mufti and the Fuehrer* (New York, 1965); M. Hauner, *India in Axis Strategy* (London, 1981); and A. Kum'a N'Dumbe III, *Hitler voulait l'Afrique* (Paris, 1980).

57. De Felice, *Il fascismo e l'Oriente* 125–86. For a brief period the terrorist Zionist Stern Gang in Palestine sought to collaborate with the Axis, misunderstanding the categorical nature of Hitler's anti-Semitism. J. Heller, *The Stern Gang* (London, 1994).

58. J. Lebra, *Japanese-Trained Armies in Southeast Asia* (New York, 1977). Ba Maw, leader of independent postwar Burma, later wrote: "We must never forget the tremendous spell that Hitler and the Axis countries cast over the east generally. It was almost hypnotic. The Axis leaders were believed to be irresistible. They would create a new world order . . . and the east as a whole was longing for some kind of really new order." Ba Maw, *Breakthrough in Burma: Memoirs of a Revolution, 1939–1946* (New Haven, 1968), 23.

59. On the main Russian auxiliary force, see C. Andreyev, *Vlassov and the Russian Liberation Movement* (New York, 1987), and R. B. Burton, "The Vlassov Movement of World War II: An Appraisal," Ph.D. diss., American University, 1963. On the non-Europeans, see Joachim Hoffmann, *Die Ostlegionen, 1941–1943: Turkotataren, Kaukasier und Wolgafinnen im deutschen Heer* (Freiburg, 1976).

for dealing with the "Jewish problem," extreme measures of discrimination, accompanied by acts of terror, were carried out against Jews during the first months of the Nazi regime. Nonetheless, in the initial years persecution of Jews was for political purposes kept within limits, and at first a surprising number of Jews made little effort to flee. After the initial outbursts in 1933, the next systematic nationwide violence was the riots of Kristallnacht (Glass Night, for shattered glass) of November 9–10, 1938, after the murder of a Nazi diplomat in Paris by a young Jew.[60]

Complete documentation of Hitler's plans and decisions did not survive the war, so historians continue to debate the precise timing, decision-making process, and initial scope of what became known as the *Endgültige Auslösung*, the Final Solution. Outbreak of war in 1939 brought much of the large Jewish population of Poland under German control and initiated a progressive radicalization of Hitler's policies. There were speculations during 1940 about mass deportations of Jews to Madagascar, with Himmler even observing that Soviet policies of mass extermination were repugnant to German culture. Britain's refusal to make peace and its control of the sea lanes dashed any serious consideration of such a policy, which was quickly superseded by that of concentrating the Jewish population in large ghettos in Polish cities. The "war of racial extermination" against the Soviet Union in 1941 further increased the number of Jews in occupied territory, with the total under German control and in allied and satellite states reaching six million or more. Special *Einsatzgruppen* (operation units) of the SS were organized to carry out mass killings, and these, together with their auxiliaries, had already slaughtered more than a million Jews by the end of 1941. This process was considered too slow and inefficient, and by the beginning of 1942 a decision had been taken to construct six special mass *Vernichtungslagern* (extermination camps) in Poland, not to be confused with the ordinary concentration camps, in which many Jews had already died. There the central phase of what had now been labeled the Final Solution began early in 1942 and continued uninterruptedly down to the time of the occupation of this territory by the Red Army in 1944–45. More than four million Jews were killed, eventually bringing the total number of Jews slaughtered to approximately five and a half to six million. It was the greatest single act of genocide in world history.[61]

60. K. A. Schleunes, *The Twisted Road to Auschwitz* (Chicago, 1970), and U. D. Adam, *Judenpolitik im Dritten Reich* (Düsseldorf, 1972), treat German policy prior to the war.

61. The principal accounts are R. Hilberg, *The Destruction of the European Jews*, 3 vols. (New York, 1985); L. Yahil, *The Holocaust* (New York, 1990); L. Dawidowicz, *The War against the Jews* (New York, 1986); Y. Bauer, *A History of the Holocaust* (New York, 1982); and M. Gilbert, *The Holocaust* (New York, 1985). Its historiography is ably treated in M. R. Marrus, *The Holocaust in History* (Hanover, NH, 1987), and L. Dawidowicz, *The Holocaust and the Historians* (Cambridge, Mass., 1981).

On the Nazi decision-making process (which remains murky) and the leaders, see C. Brown-

The total scope of Nazi liquidation was greater yet, amounting to approximately ten million lives in German-occupied Europe. The only other ethnic group to be treated on somewhat the same terms as Jews were Gypsies, of whom several hundred thousand were killed, though the total number of Poles executed or murdered in large groups was much greater, amounting to nearly three million.[62] In addition to the ten million people killed in direct executions and liquidations, more than three million Soviet prisoners of war died in German camps of starvation and disease,[63] and nearly four million slave laborers in eastern Europe and Germany died of overwork or other abuse. This ghastly record exceeded that of any equivalent phase even of Stalinism in the Soviet Union.[64]

The Holocaust and the other mass deaths and liquidations were a direct consequence of Hitlerian doctrine, of the primacy and autonomy of politics and ideology. These deaths served no military purpose and in fact weakened the German war effort by diverting military and other resources. In Hitler's eyes, this was all worth it, because even if Germany could not win the war, an almost equally important goal was to rid Europe of Jews and of as many others considered to be racially undesirable as possible.

ITALIAN FASCISM IN WAR AND DEFEAT

Mussolini had long claimed that war was the final test of any nation and would be the final standard of Fascism. Martial rhetoric was fundamental to his movement and his regime, for he made it clear that he intended to lead Italy to military expansion and the creation of a new Roman Empire. Thus during the decade before 1939 Italy had been more widely engaged in conflict than any

---

ing, *Fateful Months* (New York, 1985); idem, *The Path to Genocide* (New York, 1992); P. Burrin, *Hitler and the Jews* (New York, 1994); G. Fleming, *Hitler and the Final Solution* (Berkeley, 1984); R. Breitman, *The Architect of Genocide: Himmler and the Final Solution* (New York, 1991); F. Weinstein, *The Dynamics of Nazism: Leadership, Ideology and the Holocaust* (New York, 1980); D. Cesarani, ed., *The Final Solution* (New York, 1994); S. Friedlander, ed., *Probing the Limits of Representation: Nazism and the "Final Solution"* (Cambridge, Mass., 1992); E. Jäckel and J. Rohwer, eds., *Der Mord an den Juden im Zweiten Weltkreig: Entschlussbildung und Verwirklichung* (Stuttgart, 1985); W. Schneider, ed., *Vernichtungspolitik* (Hamburg, 1991); and G. Aly and S. Heim, *Vordenker der Vernichtung* (Hamburg, 1991). There is an ongoing journal titled *Holocaust and Genocide Studies*, edited by Y. Bauer.

62. B. Wytwycky, *The Other Holocaust* (Washington, D.C., 1980); Lukas, *Forgotten Holocaust* (Lexington, Ky., 1986).

63. Streit, *Keine Kameraden;* G. Hirschfeld, ed., *The Policies of Genocide: Jewish and Soviet Prisoners of War in Nazi Germany* (New York, 1986). Streit found that 3.3 million of the total 5.7 million Soviet POWs died in German captivity (9–10, 128).

64. The most global study is R. J. Rummel, *Democide: Nazi Genocide and Mass Murder* (New Brunswick, N.J., 1992), which tallies approximately 16 million Nazi "killings" in "cold blood," including a minimum of 5,291,000 Jewish deaths.

other state in the world, with the possible exception of Japan. A murderous campaign to pacify Libya in the early 1930s, resulting in the deaths of many tens of thousands of Libyans, was followed by the conquest of Ethiopia in 1935–36 and extensive intervention in the Spanish Civil War between 1936 and 1939. Arguably Italy should have been well prepared for World War II, but events quickly showed that this was not the case.

Despite his pompous rhetoric and expansive ambitions, Mussolini had not intended to involve Italy in major wars against major powers. He thought of colonial campaigns in Africa and limited operations in the Mediterranean and Balkans against small states, knowing that Italy lacked the resources to build a war machine equal to that of the four major powers. Moreover, the Fascist regime had been based on a tacit institutional compromise that largely respected the autonomy of the armed forces, particularly the army and navy, which were dominated by upper-class bureaucrats more interested in holding high position than in preparing for high combat. Mussolini himself had much less knowledge of military affairs than Hitler and made little effort to create a truly coordinated command. Though Italy's military spending comprised a larger percentage of the national product than did that of Germany during 1935–36, it was reduced considerably during 1937–38, as much money was invested in developing the infrastructure of Ethiopia. Moreover, no amount of spending would have enabled Italy to develop armed forces equal to the great powers, for its industrial base was still much too small. In 1939 Italy produced only 2.4 million tons of steel, compared with 22.5 million for Germany and 13.4 million for Britain. The interservice rivalry and bureaucratic routinism within the armed forces forestalled any coordinated planning, and the combination of all these weaknesses precluded any large-scale development of the most modern and sophisticated weaponry. The Fascist state also failed to coordinate overall use of economic resources efficiently. Neither Italian generals nor business leaders sought war, and the establishment of the Anglo-French partial blockade with the outbreak of war in 1939 was extremely damaging to an economy dependent on foreign trade and severely deficient in raw materials.

Mussolini's attitude toward Hitler was an ambivalent mixture of fear and envy. He was impressed by German military strength, but his insistence on signing the military alliance of May 1939 (the Pact of Steel) demonstrated that he sought political more than military goals. He hoped to become the principal ally of the strongest military power in the world, not to be immediately involved in a great war. Mussolini had helped to initiate the Munich negotiations of September 1938 that preserved a fragile peace (and earned him renewed popularity in Italy), and he was told by German leaders in May 1939 that Germany would not be ready for major war for four more years. He even seems to have cherished the expectation that the alliance would provide him with leverage to restrain Hitler. Subsequently, he was appalled by the Nazi-Soviet Pact, which he termed "criminal," and then opted for "nonbelligerence" (neutrality with a tilt toward Germany) after the invasion of Poland.

Mussolini began to worry that Hitler would soon grow too powerful, and he would have preferred a negotiated settlement. Italian diplomacy briefly conducted soundings about the possibility of a "neutral bloc" of southern European states, before dropping the idea.[65] After the Soviet Union attacked Finland in the "Winter War" of 1939–40, the Italian regime took a strongly pro-Finnish position, sending military matériel. By January 1940 a virtual rupture of relations had occurred with Moscow, though Hitler later took the initiative in helping to restore them.[66] A new commercial accord was signed with France soon after the war began, and during the next months Italy provided France with powder, explosives, mines, and airplanes at commercial rates, with France having contracted for as many as five hundred planes by the spring of 1940.[67] Mussolini even sent to the governments of the Low Countries what information he possessed about the German attack in the west just before it was launched in the spring of 1940. Moreover, at that point the French government, part of Britain's cabinet, and the American president, Roosevelt, all favored concessions to Italy to guarantee continued nonbelligerence.

The incipient collapse of France only a few weeks after the German invasion placed Mussolini in a quandary. It now appeared that Hitler was about to win a stunning victory that would make him master of western Europe, while Italy—despite all its Fascist pageantry of war—stood peacefully on the sidelines. Moreover, Mussolini had had to ignore the terms of his own military alliance with Germany when he had declared nonbelligerence, and he now seemed to be exposed as a hollow braggart unwilling to fight, with Italy once more, as in 1914, "the whore of Europe," refusing to honor its alliances. Even worse, from a practical point of view, if Italy failed to enter the conflict, the country would gain no profit from the peace settlement likely to be dictated by Germany and would be weaker than ever by comparison with a victorious Reich, which would no longer have any reason to favor its de facto nonally. Consequently Mussolini declared war on an almost defeated France on June 10, 1940, in a situation very similar to Stalin's invasion of Poland in mid-September 1939, but without the Soviet rhetoric about merely being engaged in a "peacekeeping occupation." It appeared that, playing a "jackal's role," Italy was merely giving an already mortally wounded France a final stab in the back. Even so, the attempt by Italian forces to advance was halted by French units for

65. F. Manzari, "Projects for an Italian-led Balkan Bloc of Neutrals, September–December 1939," *Historical Journal* 13:4 (1970): 767–88.

66. G. Petracchi, *Da San Pietroburgo a Mosca: La diplomazia italiana in Russia, 1861–1941* (Rome, 1993), 337–73.

67. W. I. Shorrock, *From Ally to Enemy: The Enigma of Fascist Italy in French Diplomacy* (Kent, Ohio, 1988), 274.

some time, and in the subsequent peace settlement Hitler ignored Mussolini's request for Nice, Corsica, and Tunisia, granting Italy only a modest strip of territory along its northwestern border.

Mussolini's Parallel War

Though Mussolini wanted to be associated in a minor way with Hitler's campaigns for reasons of prestige and greater influence at the peace table, his own strategy was conceived as waging a *guerra parallela,* a "parallel war," entirely in Italy's own interests, to build a stronger position and greater security for Italy in the future. Thus he dispatched an Italian air corps to assist the Luftwaffe in the battle of Britain but focused his attention on North Africa, where he hoped to make Italy the dominant power, perhaps as a base for expansion into the Middle East. Yet he found the Italian forces—at least according to their own commanders—too weak to launch an immediate offensive against British Egypt, and he complained bitterly about Hitler's refusal to give the war against England greater priority.

He soon concluded that it would be easier to expand Italy's sphere in the southern Balkans, where it would only have to fight small and weak states. Thus after Hitler moved troops into Romania in October 1940 to protect Romanian oil fields and to prepare for the invasion of the Soviet Union, Mussolini precipitately decided to invade Greece on October 28 to create Italy's own sphere to the south. There was no time for a major Italian buildup, the invasion route lay over difficult mountain terrain, and the autumn weather quickly turned bad (negating Italian air power), but Mussolini had calculated that Greek forces were in no condition to resist and would be subverted by several leading generals and politicians who had for some time been on the payroll of Italian intelligence. In fact, the major achievement of the Metaxas dictatorship had been to strengthen the Greek army, which halted the Italian invasion in a matter of days and after some weeks began to throw the Italian forces back into Albania. The ensuing stalemate, which lasted into the following spring, was a bitter blow to Fascist pride. Mussolini glumly concluded that the "Fascist new man" had not been created, at least in sufficient numbers, and that Italians were still an "inferior race" who at best had to be purged through suffering.[68]

Only Hitler could rescue Mussolini. After Britain moved forces into Greece and a military coup in Belgrade produced a new Yugoslav government more hostile to Germany, he did so with a lightning invasion of Yugoslavia and Greece in April 1941, which quickly overran both countries. Mussolini's

---

68. J. J. Sadkovich, "The Italo-Greek War in Context: Italian Priorities and Axis Diplomacy," *JCH* 28:3 (July 1993): 439–64; M. Knox, *Mussolini Unleashed, 1939–1941* (Cambridge, 1982); M. Cervi, *The Hollow Legions* (New York, 1971).

Greek nightmare was over, but his regime had lost its strategic independence, and he was in danger of falling from ally to satellite. Italy later sent a large army corps to the Russian front and provided the bulk of the manpower and matériel for the Axis campaigns of Field Marshal Erwin Rommel in Libya and Egypt during 1941–42, but the "parallel war" was over. It was of little use that Mussolini had continued quietly to fortify Italy's northeastern frontier during 1941 to protect against a future conflict with Germany. Italy was now trapped in the long war with major powers that Mussolini had sought to avoid and had effectively lost its freedom of action to Germany. Hence a saying soon developed among many Italians: "If England wins, we will lose, but if Germany wins, we are lost."

Italy was prepared neither militarily nor economically for a long war. Shortages of raw materials became acute, and though military production increased somewhat, overall industrial output faltered and civilian living standards declined rapidly. The Italian armed forces lacked the equipment for the level of combat which they faced in Russia and in North Africa, nor was the military leadership of a quality to face such challenges. Though many Italian units and troops fought bravely, the Italian army was not able to function at a level comparatively as high as during World War I, under a liberal regime. Whereas German military discipline became much more severe, that of the Italian forces moved in the opposite direction. Capital punishment had been imposed more frequently in the Italian than in the German army in the earlier conflict, but in World War II it became rare. Morale was actually much worse on the home front, however, than in the armed forces. Unlike the situation in Germany, the government in Italy seemed unable to command or coerce the full cooperation of industrialists and entrepreneurs. During 1942 civilian attitudes became increasingly gloomy.[69]

The Fascist Party proved of little benefit to the regime in its growing crisis. The Fasci di Combattimento had, at least on paper, reached a membership of 3.6 million by October 1941, and its ranks later swelled to nearly 5 million by the pro forma inclusion of many military personnel. More than half the population belonged to some sort of Fascist organization.[70] In fact,

---

69. The best brief analysis is J. J. Sadkovich, "Understanding Defeat: Reappraising Italy's Role in World War II," *JCH* 24:1 (Jan. 1989): 27–61. See also L. Ceva, *La condotta italiana della guerra* (Rome, 1975).

70. At their height on October 28, 1941, the Fascist organizations reported the following memberships: Fasci di Combattimento, 3,619,848; Gruppi Universitari Fascisti, 119,713; Gioventù Italiana del Littorio, 8,495,929 (about 20 percent of them girls); Fasci Femminili, 845,304; Massaie Rurali, 1,656,941; Operaie Lavoranti a Domicilio, 616,286; Studenti Stranieri, 763; Other groups, 7,926,838 (including about 4 million in the Operazione Nazionale Dopolavoro and 1 million in the veterans' association), for a total of 23,281,622. These data are drawn from G. B. Guerri, ed., *Rapporto al Duce* (Milan, 1978), 6. During the following year these figures increased to 4,770,770 for the Fasci, 159,297 for the GUF, 8,754,589 for the GIL, 1,027,409 for the Fasci

Mussolini was not able to mobilize these masses effectively for the war effort or the defense of the regime. For approximately a decade he had been building the power of the state, consistent with the policy he had adopted as early as December 1922 of relying primarily on the state apparatus. Though the party organization was given certain new responsibilities for the home front after the war began, these were more limited than those given the Nazi Party in Germany. The Fascist militia (MVSN) did provide more than four hundred thousand men for the armed forces, but they were the very opposite of the Waffen-SS. Only about twenty-five thousand were of the quality to be directly incorporated into front-line combat units, the rest being assigned to rear units and occupation forces.[71] The new offices and agencies which were created for the PNF during the war seem for the most part only to have added to the confusion, inefficiency, and corruption. By 1942 popular attitudes toward the PNF were probably even more negative than those of German civilians toward the Nazi Party, with growing complaints of abuse of power and irresponsibility. The minority of hard-line radicals in the party urged Mussolini to impose a drastic new policy of "revolutionary war" that would give the party real power and fully Fascistize Italian institutions, but he had no faith in such an expedient at this point.[72]

Mussolini did want to reform the PNF but was not sure how. As a sign of his displeasure during the grim winter of 1940–41, he had packed many overweight, middle-aged *gerarche* off to the Greek front—much to their dismay—but that was merely a theatrical gesture. Though he had no intention of using the party to run the state, he still hoped to have it carry out the education of the youth and eventually create a Fascist cultural revolution. Mussolini recognized in theory the need for a purge to reduce the party once more to an elite of the young and active, but he had gone too far in the opposite direction. In May 1943 he did appoint a more vigorous and younger secretary-general, Carlo Scorza, partly to placate the hardliners, but when Scorza made a series of new proposals to have the PNF take over direction of the major institutions for "revolutionary war," Mussolini rejected the whole idea.[73] The rhetorical movement to the left, which Mussolini had initiated in 1935–36, was extended somewhat further in 1941–42 under the pressure of the war. There was increasing denunciation of the selfishness of the bourgeoisie, little of which went beyond talk. Mussolini found it impossible to accomplish in time of war what he had failed to do during peacetime.

Femminili, and 2,491,792 for the Massaie Rurali. R. De Felice, *Mussolini l'alleato*, 2 vols. (Turin, 1990), 2:969.

71. De Felice, *Mussolini l'alleato* 1:26–27.

72. *Revolutionary War* was the title of a new book by Ugo Spirito, the most left-wing of the major Fascist theorists, whose publication Mussolini refused to authorize.

73. De Felice, *Mussolini l'alleato* 2:988–1040.

Mussolini had plunged into the conflict because he was convinced it would be a short war that required immediate participation in order to benefit. Subsequently he seemed to favor a longer war that might leave Germany more exhausted even if victorious, yet conversely he recognized that the longer it continued, the more difficult things would become for Italy and for his regime. Thus he seems to have been much more receptive than Hitler to Stalin's first overtures for a separate peace in October 1941, renewed periodically for the next two years.[74] He tried to retain aspects of the original goals of "parallel war" by dabbling with the notion of converting it, at least on a level of all-out propaganda, into a war of "national liberation" for colonial peoples subjugated by British and French imperialism. Such an idea conflicted with the reality of Italy's own African empire, but much of this territory was swiftly being lost to the British military advance. As late as 1942 Hitler still opposed the destruction of the British Empire, and some Italian Fascists lamented the "extreme imperialism" of the Nazis' own conquests, which contradicted the Axis's rhetoric of liberation and a revolutionary new order, as well as the "civilizing mission" dear to the self-image of Italian imperialism. Germans, in turn, grumbled that the need to preserve Italian Libya prevented the Axis from making an all-out appeal to Muslim nationalists in the eastern Mediterranean. As late as 1942 Mussolini tried to convince Hitler to win broader support by issuing a Continental Charter—the response of Mussolini, ever the propagandist, to the earlier Atlantic Charter of Roosevelt and Churchill—which would rally the peoples of Europe on behalf of national sovereignty, integrity, and equal rights.[75] This was acceptable enough to Mussolini outside his own coveted sphere, but of course it contradicted the very essence of Hitler's policy.

Between 1940 and 1942 the ideologues of Italian Fascism developed their own concepts of the struggle as a "social" and "revolutionary" war to create a new "hierarchy of peoples" and new standards of international justice. This transcended even traditional *italianità* to embrace a "new order" of Fascist *civiltà imperiale* (imperial civilization), though the formulation remained largely rhetorical and abstract and produced little concrete application.[76]

Though the Italian military had committed numerous atrocities in Africa, and to a lesser extent in Yugoslavia,[77] the Italian authorities did not follow up on Mussolini's earlier anti-Semitic legislation to join in the Nazi hunt for Jews.

74. Ibid., 1254–55. On these soundings, see P. Kleist, *Entre Hitler et Staline (1939–1945)* (Paris, 1953); I. Fleischhauer, *Die Chance des Sonderfriedens: Deutsch-sowjetische Geheimgespräche, 1941–1945* (Berlin, 1986); and V. Mastny, *Russia's Road to the Cold War* (New York, 1979), 73–85.

75. De Felice, *Mussolini l'alleato* 1:464–66.

76. The best presentation of these ideas will be found in E. Gentile, "La nazione del fascismo: Alle origini della crisi dello Stato nazionale in Italia," *SC* 24:6 (Dec. 1993): 833–87.

77. Cf. F. Potocnik, *Il campo di sterminio fascista: L'isola di Rab* (Turin, 1979).

World War II   389

Approximately the opposite occurred, for Jews generally found safe haven in Italy, as well as in the Italian occupation zones in Yugoslavia and southeastern France. The Italian army was especially notable for its protection of Jews, but many members of the Fascist Party did the same. Of Italy's approximately 47,000 Jews, 44,500 or so fell under the scope of Fascist anti-Semitic legislation. Of these, 7,682 were killed by the Germans after the loss of Italian independence, but the rest were protected, often under dire conditions, by Italians of the most diverse backgrounds and circumstances. The ultimate survival rate of the Jews in Italy—83 percent—was exceeded only in Denmark, where most Jews were simply smuggled out of the country to safety. Moreover, the survival rate for Jews who made it to Italian-occupied territories elsewhere was approximately as high.[78]

After the Allied landing in French Northwest Africa in November 1942, the war came ever closer to Italy. Soon afterward, the rulers of Hungary, Romania, and Bulgaria began to contact Rome about the possibility of negotiating a separate peace with the United States and Britain. Instead, in the months that followed, Mussolini desperately urged Hitler to undertake a reconcentration of forces and a reversal of strategy, beseeching the Führer to make some sort of agreement or at least a truce with Stalin on the eastern front, so that the "revolutionary totalitarian forces" could concentrate against the "capitalist plutocracies" in the Mediterranean, but Hitler would have none of that.

By the spring of 1943 most Italians could see the handwriting on the wall. Italian servicemen fought with courage and, under a lighter discipline than in World War I, registered fewer cases of desertion and self-inflicted wounds than in the earlier conflict, but the home front was demoralized. Business leaders and other conservatives urged a negotiated peace and withdrawal from the war, which the Church was also known to favor. Support for the regime was collapsing, as few Italians believed the war was connected with any vital interest, but for Mussolini the die was cast. He believed that he had no choice but to hold on grimly and hope for some remarkable reversal of fortune. For years he had been marked by manic-depressive tendencies, and the one-time strutting Duce was now sunk deep in depression. Even part of his own military command began to conspire to withdraw Italy from the war, and the political opposition—dormant as recently as 1942—began to revive, as a series of major strikes shook northern industry in March and April 1943. The tormented Duce had never reciprocated Hitler's own feelings of strong personal esteem. He knew the war was lost but could find no way to break with the Germans. During the first months of 1943 he seemed to prefer a separate peace with the

78. J. Steinberg, *All or Nothing: The Axis and the Holocaust, 1941–43* (London, 1990); S. Zuccotti, *The Italians and the Holocaust* (New York, 1988); D. Carpi, *Between Hitler and Mussolini: The Jews and the Italian Authorities in France and Tunisia* (Boston, 1994).

Soviet Union but made private indications that he would not necessarily reject one with the United States and Britain. By June Mussolini did give some signs that he might change course within a few more months. In the meantime, he kept asking Germany for more and more economic and military assistance, even though he knew this was virtually impossible. Both Mussolini and King Victor Emmanuel were extremely sensitive about Italy's reversal of alliances in World War I and wanted to avoid giving the appearance of another betrayal. Thus it has been argued that Mussolini was seeking to document the case that it was Germany who would no longer assist Italy, making a drastic change in policy look like the fault of the Germans. If so, however, Mussolini took no concrete steps whatsoever to begin making contacts for an Italian withdrawal from the war.

When Anglo-American forces invaded Sicily on July 9, it was clear that their entry into the Italian peninsula would not be long delayed. A number of top generals and other figures close to the king had begun to conspire, and contacts were now also made with moderate leaders of the political opposition and with several moderate Fascist chiefs. Most of the increasingly anxious Fascist *gerarchi* themselves wanted change, though there was no internal agreement among them. The ultras such as party secretary Scorza and Roberto Farinacci sought a more drastic dictatorship under the direct control of fellow Fascist ultras (and closely linked with Germany), while others sought a new but more moderate Fascist government. The leader who now came to the fore was Dino Grandi, one of the most moderate of the veteran *gerarchi,* who had been foreign minister between 1929 and 1932. As Mussolini reluctantly agreed to the first meeting of the Fascist Grand Council in four years, Grandi began to lobby other worried members and also reached an understanding with King Victor Emmanuel, the legal head of state.

At the Grand Council meeting on July 24, 1943, Mussolini refused all significant changes but was otherwise strangely passive, offering little defense of his policies during a lengthy debate. As the discussion droned on into the small hours of the morning, Grandi (who was carrying concealed hand grenades, in the event of violence) took advantage of a short break to collect signatures for a motion calling for the king to reassume the powers of government, which finally carried by a vote of nineteen to seven.[79] When Grandi first presented the motion, Mussolini calmly requested him to consider with full seriousness a measure which the Duce said might well be the end of Fascism. Otherwise he showed little reaction to a measure which gave the timid and skeptical king—

79. See P. Nello, *Un fedele disubbediente: Dino Grandi da Palazzo Chigi al 25 luglio* (Bari, 1993), and Grandi's memoir, *25 luglio: Quarant'anni dopo,* ed. R. De Felice (Bologna, 1983). Two quite different motions were also presented by the two leading hardliners, Scorza and Farinacci, but lacked adequate support. See C. Scorza, *La notte del Gran Consiglio* (Milan, 1968).

a stickler for nominal legality—authorization from the state party to depose him. When he then called on Victor Emmanuel on the afternoon of the twenty-fifth, the king told Mussolini that he was being dismissed as prime minister. Immediately afterward he was placed under military arrest.[80]

A new non-Fascist (but not officially anti-Fascist) government was formed under Marshal Pietro Badoglio, former head of the army general staff, which slowly and clumsily proceeded to negotiate an arrangement with the Allies for Italy's withdrawal from the war. Announcement of this came on September 8, 1943, the eve of the first Allied landings in southern Italy proper, and was immediately followed by German military occupation of virtually the entire peninsula.[81] The overthrow of Mussolini thus marked the end of the Fascist regime in Rome, but it would not be the end of Italian Fascism itself or the horrors of war, for Italy would now become the scene of twenty months of intense combat and of a vicious new civil war between the remnants of Fascism and the Italian anti-Fascist opposition.

THREE SATELLITE REGIMES

The Nazi New Order was flanked by several allies in eastern Europe who, with the partial exception of Finland, sank to satellite status. In addition, new satellite and puppet regimes emerged in states created by German expansion. New regimes produced by indigenous political forces, as in Slovakia and Vichy France, are here categorized as satellite regimes, in contrast to puppet governments directly appointed or created by German initiative. Whereas the puppet governments were in most cases led by native fascists appointed by the Nazis, none of the satellite regimes were led by fascist forces, with the partial exception of a brief interlude in Romania in 1940–41.

Legionnaire Fascism and Military Right Radicalism in Satellite Romania

The brutal police action of the Carolist regime in Romania had suppressed the Legion of the Archangel Michael but had not destroyed it. The Legion remained a powerful underground movement as the Carolist regime was being overtaken and undermined by international events. Though the Anglo-French guarantees of April 1939 had sought to preserve Romanian independence, the Nazi-Soviet Pact and the occupation of Poland in effect placed Romania within

---

80. The best account of the events of July 24–25 will be found in De Felice, *Mussolini l'alleato* 2:1089–410. Perhaps the best previous one was G. Bianchi, *Perchè e come cadde il fascismo* (Milan, 1970).

81. This is described in detail in J. Schröder, *Italiens Kriegsaustritt, 1943: Die deutschen Gegenmassnahmen* (Göttingen, 1969).

the German sphere of influence. Hitler had been angered by King Carol's murder of Codreanu and other Legionnaire leaders in 1938, but his overriding concern was that Romania become a reliable satellite of Germany in preparation for its eventual confrontation with the Soviet Union.

This was not likely to happen as long as the Romanian government was dominated by Carol, whose regime had become identified with the former Anglo-French hegemony. The authoritarian government appointed in 1938 had failed to rally much genuine support, and after the German triumph in the west in June 1940, Carol became increasingly desperate. He officially renounced Romania's alignment with Great Britain and scrapped the relatively moderate and ineffective Front of National Rebirth, replacing it with a more radical Party of the Nation, designed as a so-called totalitarian unity party that could also incorporate the support of the Legion.

Under the Carolist dictatorship the Legion had lost little of its popular support, but its greatest weakness was leadership. The main replacement for Codreanu, a lawyer named Horia Sima, was an extremist who preferred terrorism and possessed little political or administrative ability. He brushed aside more moderate or better-qualified figures, though he was never able to command the same unqualified support from the Legionnaires enjoyed by the charismatic Codreanu. After the fall of France, Sima and other exiled Legionnaires secretly began to return from Germany. In July he and his colleagues decided to accept Carol's offer; Sima and two other Legion leaders accepted cabinet positions in the Romanian government, though a month later Sima resigned because of strong pressure from within the Legion for the king's abdication. The Second Vienna Award was then announced by the German government in August, stripping Romania of most of the large region of Transylvania, which was handed over to Hungary. This provoked massive protest from the Romanian public, and Carol's regime reached its nadir. A poorly organized coup attempt by the Legion on September 3 failed, but the government could no longer survive.

In desperation Carol turned to General Ion Antonescu, the most prestigious figure in the military command, who enjoyed good relations with the Legion. Antonescu agreed to form a government but demanded dictatorial powers. These were granted by the king, who did not realize that the new dictator had reached agreement with other political leaders to demand the king's abdication. Carol then had no alternative but to consent, abdicating in favor of his son Prince Michael.

The new Romanian dictator was an ultranationalist right radical rather than a genuine fascist, and he sought to create a strong new authoritarian state that would abolish parliament and make Romania an influential middle-sized power in eastern Europe. On September 6 Michael ascended the throne and immediately ratified Antonescu's full powers as the new Leader of the Roma-

Horia Sima *(right)*, Codreanu's successor as leader of the Legion, with Marshal Ion Antonescu and military dignitaries, in Bucharest, September, 1940

nian State, a kind of military Mussolini. Antonescu would have preferred a Carol-type union of all the major political parties under his authoritarian rule, but the National Peasants and also, to some extent, the Liberals remained pro-British, anti-Nazi, and unwilling to abandon parliamentary government altogether, though they expressed their acceptance of the general's rule during this national emergency.

Antonescu therefore turned to the Legion as the only national force that shared his extreme nationalism, authoritarianism, and pro-German orientation. He negotiated a coalition with the Legion and on September 15 announced formation of a "National Legionnaire State." The Legion became the sole political party of Romania, and Sima entered the government as Antonescu's vice-premier. Other Legionnaires held five ministerial posts, including those in foreign affairs, interior, education, and religion. What Antonescu had in mind was an arrangement similar to that created by Franco in Nationalist Spain in 1937. He himself would retain ultimate power, and he made it clear that the Legion would not hold power over the state itself.

Nonetheless, the Legion was now the principal force in the new government and thus, to a degree at least, had become the fourth fascist-type party to come to power. Though Antonescu was also proclaimed the honorary Conducator (Leader) of the Legionnaire movement, the situation differed from that in Spain because the Legion remained essentially autonomous under its own directors, with Sima still as "Commander," and thus held a significant share of power without being totally dominated by the state. The result was an uneasy dyarchy between the military dictator and the subordinate yet autonomous party.

Antonescu sought to build a "national totalitarian state" in consonance with the Nazi New Order, signing Hitler's Tripartite Pact and soon permitting German troops to enter Romania. There is no indication that he saw the compromise with the Legion as a final political solution, but under the new system the Legionnaires held many provincial and local administrative positions, as well as the power to name local police chiefs. They took control of propaganda and organized an endless series of public ceremonies and marches. A wave of terror was launched against Jews and political enemies, the local *case verzi* (green houses, or party headquarters) all over Romania becoming interrogation and torture chambers, with the party in alliance with the regular police. Sima reintroduced the Legionnaire Worker Corps to replace trade unions, and a new Worker Guard militia was created. The Legion began to create its own cadres of parallel government institutions and to develop its own police. Within a few weeks "Romanianization commissars" with broad economic powers were appointed throughout the country, and Legionnaire administrators were given sweeping authority over industry. Sima and the other party leaders sought to apply "national socialist" principles but generally lacked any economic or technical expertise; their "economic revolution" soon produced mounting chaos. Wealthy Jews were despoiled of property, with major corruption becoming a feature of Legionnaire administration. So many new members flocked to the state party that Sima began to take measures to reduce recruitment. Yet all this was not enough for the Legionnaire leaders, who accused the dictator of being insufficiently "totalitarian" and of tolerating other influences. They determined to seek total power.

General Antonescu nonetheless retained overall command of the Romanian state and direct control of the armed forces, as well as the paramilitary gendarmerie and the national police center. After the Legion massacred in prison those being held for Codreanu's murder, and murdered several prestigious national figures as well, Antonescu officially dissolved the parallel "Legionnaire police" and demanded to be recognized as absolute commander of the Legion, like Franco in the Spanish Falange, rather than merely honorary Conducator. When Sima, the Commander, and other Legionnaire bosses refused, Antonescu recognized that a showdown was inevitable. Legionnaire propaganda declared that the bourgeoisie would have no future in Romania, and there was now talk of a St. Bartholomew's Day immolation of all potential competing politicians.

Legionnaire popularity was, however, becoming rapidly eroded, due to the excesses and incompetence of the Legion's rule. Even the workers, the special targets of Legionnaire propaganda, were becoming disillusioned, for Legionnaire "national socialism" subordinated labor to hierarchical control and created mounting economic disarray that provided no advantages to workers. Antonescu therefore decided to bide his time a bit longer until the Legion had become fully discredited and then eliminate it altogether.[82]

By January 1941, 170,000 German troops were stationed in Romania in preparation for the forthcoming invasion of the Soviet Union, and Antonescu realized that he could not move decisively against the Legion without Hitler's approval. On January 14 he flew to Germany, and he talked intermittently with the Führer for several days. A genuine personal rapport seems to have developed between the two, and Hitler came to hold Antonescu in higher regard than any other allied eastern European leader. Antonescu assured Hitler of his loyalty and his support of Germany's policy in eastern Europe, particularly as against the Soviet Union. After his account of the disaster which coalition with the Legion had become, Hitler recommended that Antonescu seize full command of the Legion himself, but in any event he assured the Romanian dictator of his support in resolving the situation.[83]

Returning to Bucharest, Antonescu soon faced new demands by the Legionnaires, who were apparently themselves being encouraged by other Nazi functionaries in Berlin. He acted quickly to terminate the "Romanianization commissions" which had created economic chaos and also replaced the Legionnaire provincial governors. This goaded the Legion into a full-scale revolt on January 21, in which they took over many local government and communication centers while unleashing a vicious pogrom in the main Jewish quarter of the capital.[84] Antonescu waited for two days, reconfirmed his understanding with Hitler, and then initiated a counteroffensive at 5:00 A.M. on the twenty-third, quickly regaining control of the situation. No fascist movement was ever in a position to take on an organized army, and the Legionnaire militia was defeated rather easily. Once more a fascist movement had been quelled by a right authoritarian regime, this time in the most extreme example of all such confrontations. Antonescu outlawed the Legion and on February 15, 1941,

---

82. The best studies of the Antonescu-Legionnaire coalition are A. Heinen, *Die Legion "Erzengel Michael" in Rumänien* (Munich, 1986), 415–53; N. M. Nagy-Talavera, *The Green Shirts and the Others* (Stanford, 1970), 309–30; and K. Hitchins, *Rumania, 1866–1947* (Oxford, 1994), 451–68. See also I. C. Butnaru, *The Silent Holocaust: Romania and Its Jews* (New York, 1992), 68–88.

83. The definitive account of German-Romanian relations in this period is A. Hillgruber, *Hitler, König Carol und Marschall Antonescu: Die deutsch-rumänischen Beziehungen, 1938–1944* (Wiesbaden, 1965).

84. The best eyewitness account of these horrors will be found in the final chapter of R. St. John, *Foreign Correspondent* (New York, 1957).

officially abolished the National Legionnaire State. Through its excesses and incompetence, the Legion had become "paradoxically the first fascist movement to fall in a Europe where Germany reigned supreme."[85] Though Hitler might have preferred that Antonescu not go quite that far, his chief concern was a disciplined and reliable satellite for the forthcoming invasion of the Soviet Union, which Antonescu guaranteed. The Romanian dictator arrested 9,000 Legionnaires (including 218 priests). A total of 1,842 were sentenced to varying terms by military courts, and 20 were executed for murder.[86] Once again a fascist movement had been defeated by the authoritarian right.

For the next three and a half years, Antonescu ruled as a right radical nationalist dictator with the support of the military, his principal civilian auxiliaries being the Goga-Cuza "National Christian" anti-Semites. His regime was accepted more readily, at least, than the capricious tyranny of the Legion, and his forces joined with the German army in the invasion of the Soviet Union. Romania was rewarded with the return of Bukovina and Bessarabia, stolen by Stalin in 1940, and the occupation of a southwestern corner of the Ukraine between the Bug and Dniester Rivers, christened with the neologism "Transnistria."

Romania's army fought rather better in World War II than in World War I, but its most gory deed was the wholesale slaughter of Jews in the newly occupied territories—a genocide operationally separate from the Nazi Final Solution. Carried out by Romanian soldiers and police, this nonautomated holocaust killed between two hundred thousand and three hundred thousand Jews and was by far the greatest liquidation of Jews by non-German forces.[87] Late in 1942, however, this most horrendous of Antonescu's policies began to shift. He turned to a new strategy of releasing some Jews for ransom and even showed a measure of contrition. Jews within Romania were often sent to labor camps, but Antonescu refused to hand the great majority of them over to the SS. After Romania's defeat he was executed in 1946 as a war criminal, while many thousands of Legionnaires were welcomed en masse into the Romanian Communist Party, probably the largest wholesale migration of former fascists into a Communist group anywhere in eastern Europe.[88]

85. Nagy-Talavera, *Green Shirts* 82. Hitler later complained that "Antonescu ought to have made the Legion the basis of his power—after shooting Horia Sima." *Hitler's Secret Conversations* (New York, 1962), 227.

86. Hitchins, *Rumania* 469.

87. The principal description in English is in Butnaru, *Silent Holocaust*.

88. Sima and other Legionnaire leaders who fled to Germany in 1941 had been interned just like Pavelić and the émigré Ustashi in Italy after 1934. Following the overthrow of Antonescu in August 1944 and Romania's reversal of alliances, Hitler set up a puppet Legionnaire Romanian government-in-exile under Sima in Vienna, but this group had difficulty attracting other collaborators. Before the end of the war a regiment was formed under its banner of some seven thousand Romanian POWs who had been captured by the Germans. Heinen, *Die Legion* 459–63.

The postwar Communist regime later revived extreme nationalism and flaunted the old Legionnaire slogan *Totul pentru Ţara* (All for the Fatherland). As it turned out, Romanian nationalism also survived communism. In April 1991 the newly democratic Romanian parliament rose to observe a minute of silence on the forty-fifth anniversary of the execution of Antonescu. Two months later, on the fiftieth anniversary of the invasion of the Soviet Union in which Antonescu's forces had joined, much of the Romanian media hailed the memory of "Romania's greatest anti-Communist," whom some considered the greatest Romanian of the century.[89]

The Vichy Regime and French Fascism

The most important new regime to emerge in the countries defeated or occupied by Germany, and the only one in that category with any degree of independence (however limited), was the new French regime at Vichy. Limited by the terms of the surrender to no more than central and southeastern France, or about half the country, the new regime under the eighty-four-year-old Marshal Philippe Pétain was legally voted power to govern by decree in the final meeting of the last democratically elected parliament of the Third Republic. It created no new political party but rested on a broad ad hoc coalition of moderates, conservatives, and rightists. Its name was derived from the choice of the south central resort town of Vichy as seat of government, a selection resulting from geographic location and the large amount of available hotel space there.

In the wake of France's shocking defeat, the Vichy regime reflected a broad consensus on the need for patriotic reform, declaring a "national revolution." This amounted to corporatist restructuring of governmental policies and new economic regulations which emphasized coordination and modernization, together with an effort at a sort of cultural revolution based on conservative values and larger families. Religious instruction was restored in public schools, physical education emphasized, and alcohol discouraged, the motto being *Work, Family, Fatherland*. In the judgment of a leading historian, Vichy's blend of conservatism, neotraditionalism, and modernist technocracy "to an extent unique among the occupied nations of Western Europe, . . . went beyond mere administration . . . to carry out a domestic revolution in institutions and values."[90]

Vichy was a regime of moderate right authoritarianism (though with increasing right radical overtones) that identified with Franco and Salazar rather than with Hitler and Mussolini. The aged Pétain clearly functioned as a national

89. See the account in P. Hockenos, *Free to Hate: The Rise of the Right in Post-Communist Europe* (New York, 1993), 167–207.
90. R. O. Paxton, *Vichy France* (New York, 1972), 20.

father figure in the wake of disaster to turn the French from the errors of their recent ways and restore traditional values, but his government also sought to foster new forms of economic and social development. Catholicism provided perhaps the most important single element, but conservatives and rightists were also flanked by a new sector of neoliberals, who sought to use the "national revolution" to purge liberalism of democratic excess and restore an earlier elitism, while still retaining a partially representative republic. Equally important were the specialists and technocrats placed in charge of restructuring economic policy, whose work charted new directions in planning and expansion that had a decisive influence on the postwar period. "There is hardly an aspect of social structure that did not move Vichy toward the modernizers' model" in society and economics, for "it was during Vichy that the apostles of growth moved from oddity to commonplace."[91] Cultural life remained comparatively unrestricted and in certain fields was quite active.[92] The new textbooks that were produced for public schools proved in many cases to be more scientific, objective, and balanced than the old texts and were sometimes retained by the democratic Fourth Republic after the war.

The Vichy regime evolved through a series of phases, with characteristics that were partly distinct but often overlapping and contradictory.[93] The initial phase of "national revolution" lasted from July 1940 into the early months of 1941. The second or more mature phase made up two years from 1941 to 1943, marked by increasing authoritarianism and also greater technocracy. A General Secretariat of Youth was created almost immediately, and the state sponsored several different youth organizations, though the Catholic Church and other conservative influences blocked formation of a single national youth group. The new veterans' organization, the Légion Française des Combattants, numbered 650,000 by early 1941 but was generally moderate in tone. Most fundamental was simply the growth of the state apparatus itself (which rather contradicted the conservative values of the "national revolution"), whose bureaucracy increased by 65 percent in three years.

Genuine French fascists and protofascists mostly remained in the German northern occupation zone, whose center was Paris, realizing that they would

91. Ibid., 353, 356.

92. J.-P. Rioux, ed., *La vie culturelle sous Vichy* (Brussels, 1990); M. Serra, *Una cultura dell'autorità: La Francia di Vichy* (Bari, 1980).

93. While Paxton's is perhaps the best single work, the literature on Vichy is extensive. Among the more important accounts are M. Ferro, *Pétain* (Paris, 1987); H. Michel, *Pétain et le régime de Vichy* (Paris, 1986); W. D. Halls, *The Youth of Vichy France* (Oxford, 1981); D. Peschanski and L. Gervereau, *La propaganda sous Vichy* (Paris, 1990); J.-P. Azéma and F. Bédarida, eds., *Vichy et les français* (Paris, 1992); J. F. Sweets, *Choices in Vichy France* (New York, 1986); H. Rousso, *The Vichy Syndrome* (Cambridge, Mass., 1991); and A. Chebel d'Appollonia, *L'extrême-droite en France de Maurras à Le Pen* (Brussels, 1988), 224–73.

draw more support from Nazis than Pétainists. The major exception at first was Marcel Déat, who only began to complete the transition from "neosocialism" to genuine fascism after the French defeat. As early as the end of July 1940, Déat presented the Vichy government with a plan to organize a single state party, but this drew opposition from all sectors, ranging from repentant neo-liberals to the radical right of Charles Maurras. Within two months Déat also moved to Paris. One more effort was made by a motley coalition of rightists and protofascists to present a second project for the creation of a single state party at the beginning of 1941, but this was also vetoed.[94]

Even as greater features of technocracy were being introduced into economic administration, the regime took a more authoritarian turn with a key speech by Pétain in August 1941. He announced the official suppression of political parties (which in the preceding year had languished without use), the creation of a new system of special courts and a new national police, together with more central control of local police. Obligatory labor service laws were developed in 1942–43 to facilitate mobilization of young people for work in Germany. The first anti-Semitic legislation was introduced as early as October 1940 and was followed by increasingly stringent measures, defined in family and racial rather than religious terms and ending with French police doing the work of the SS in rounding up tens of thousands of Jews to be handed over to the administrators of the Final Solution.[95] Vichy was not a fascist regime, but its Jewish policy was much more destructive than that of Italian Fascism; by early 1943 incidents developed near the boundary between the two regimes in southeastern France in which Jews hunted by the Vichy police were protected by the Italians.

Vichy was the only regime in occupied Europe with which the government of the Third Reich maintained completely formal diplomatic relations, as with a sovereign state. It retained France's huge colonial empire overseas and one of the world's larger navies, though its army was limited by the armistice to fewer than seventy-five thousand men. Its leaders were prepared for a more complete collaboration with Hitler's New Order (carrying on a limited civil war with de Gaulle's Free French in part of French Africa during 1941–42), and it was Hitler who decided not to concede any greater partnership to Vichy. He sought to grant the defeated French no more than he thought minimally necessary to hold them in line until the final victory was won over Britain and the Soviet Union, planning to exact much more in the hour of a final victory.[96]

94. The best analysis of the relationship between the Vichy regime and categorical fascism is M. Cointet-Labrousse, *Vichy et le fascisme* (Brussels, 1987).

95. P. Webster, *Pétain's Crime: The Complete Story of French Collaboration in the Holocaust* (Chicago, 1990).

96. See E. Jäckel, *La France dans l'Europe de Hitler* (Paris, 1968).

In the long run, Vichy's efforts to cooperate with Hitler drew little reward, did not appreciably lighten the German yoke on France, and may even have made it easier for the Third Reich to exploit massively the French economy.

While Pétain's government followed its tortuous and contradictory course, the fascist leaders were headquartered in Paris. The only clear-cut French fascist movement of the 1930s, Marcel Bucard's Parti Franciste, remained active. Francisme had been inspired more by Italy than by Germany and in its first years had a few Jewish members, but was virulently anti-Semitic during the Occupation. It preached total collaboration with the Third Reich and proclaimed its "socialist" radicalism but in fact never had more than a few thousand members. Its most destructive work was the participation in special police units against the resistance during the later phases of occupation.[97]

The Parti Populaire Français eventually reemerged as the largest group, when Jacques Doriot completed his transition to full fascism under German occupation in 1940–41. At first he played both sides, proclaiming loyalty to Pétain and obtaining a seat in the marshal's appointive National Council, while drawing subsidies from both Vichy and the Germans in Paris. The latter authorized the revival of the PPF in the occupied zone in April 1941, and from that point Doriot worked to make of it a major "revolutionary and totalitarian fascist party," as he put it. It had gained as many as thirty thousand members by 1942, making it the largest of the wartime French fascist parties, though the active cadres may never have surpassed seven thousand. The social profile remained much the same: young, male, urban, lower middle class, and worker, drawn especially from the regions of Paris and Lyons, together with Marseilles and Corsica. Though most were new recruits, 22 percent were former Communists, 26 percent former rightists. More than any other collaborationist fascist, Doriot was of direct use in the German war effort, helping to raise the unit of French volunteers to fight on the eastern front, the Légion des Volontaires Français (LVF). Yet this unit, even though it was supported by other fascist groups, seems only to have contributed about four thousand fighting men, mostly consigned to secondary combat functions. The German authorities carefully limited the amount of support and recognition given Doriot, preferring to keep the French groups divided. The PPF did become the only French fascist party to seize power of a sort, since its leaders in Tunis, together with other collaborationists, managed to take over the civil government of Tunisia in support of the Wehrmacht's defense of that region from November 1942 to May 1943.

Marcel Déat initiated what became the second largest of the French movements when he launched the Rassemblement National Populaire (RNP) in Paris in January 1941. What principally distinguished the RNP from the PPF was that Déat's new party continued ideologically to reflect its leader's socialist origins

97. A. Deniel, *Bucard et le Francisme: Les seuls fascistes français* (Paris, 1979), 137–279.

and thus became the most "left fascist" of these little movements, whereas the PPF, despite (or because of) its significant contingent of former Communists, tried to approximate Nazism more completely. Déat directly invoked the heritage of the French revolution and emphasized corporative economic planning, syndicalist organization, and administrative and educational reform, much more than direct action and militarization. He seems not to have taken subsidies from big business and never to have lost altogether his initial orientation toward internationalism and a kind of "peace fascism." In his future fascist utopia, Déat still proposed to retain universal suffrage on the municipal level, and he took a more moderate anti-Semitic position than his more ultrafascist rivals. Philosophically and ideologically, he may never have completed the full transition to fascism, for he seems metaphysically and epistemologically to have remained a historical materialist. Déat's "left fascism" was tolerated and even supported by the German authorities as a useful ploy to draw part of the French left toward the Third Reich. At its height in 1942, the RNP may have had twenty thousand members (concentrated in the Paris region), but the figure dropped to ten thousand the following year. Though like other fascist parties it formed its own militia, the RNP seemed halfhearted about violence.[98]

In addition to these three groups, there were a number of other very tiny would-be French fascist parties. The most important was the so-called Mouvement Social Revolutionnaire of Eugène Deloncle, which eventually formed small militia or police groups that engaged in terrorist acts and battled the resistance. Other little grouplets included the Parti Français National Collectiviste of Pierre Clémenti, the Parti National-Socialiste Français of Christian Message, and the Croisade Français du National Socialisme, led by M. Bernard de la Gatinais.[99]

The crisis of the final year of German occupation imposed a more semifascist orientation on the Vichy regime as well. Pétain's government had originally been charged by the outgoing parliament in the summer of 1940 with the preparation of a new constitution. In January 1941 Pétain had created a new National Council with 213 appointed members to prepare this document. The ultimate draft was not ready until 1943, and it proposed a parliament based on family, not universal, suffrage with a corporative economic structure.

98. The best account of Doriot and Déat during this phase will be found in P. Burrin, *La dérive fasciste* (Paris, 1986), and J.-P. Brunet, *Jacques Doriot* (Paris, 1986).

99. More data on these and the other fascist groups will be found in P. Ory, *Les collaborateurs, 1940–1945* (Paris, 1976); M. Cotta, *La collaboration, 1940–1944* (Paris, 1964); G. Hirschfeld and P. S. Marsh, eds., *Collaboration in France* (New York, 1989); B. M. Gordon, *Collaboration in France during the Second World War* (Ithaca, 1980); and P. Milza, *Le fascisme français* (Paris, 1987), 250–74. See also E. Dejonghe, ed., *L'Occupation en France et en Belgique, 1940–1944*, 2 vols. (Lille, 1987), and J. F. Sweets, "Hold That Pendulum! Redefining Fascism, Collaborationism and Resistance in France," *French Historical Studies* 15:4 (1988): 731–58.

Local and regional government would be based on partial direct elections but generally dominated by indirect and corporative procedures. Pétain would remain chief of state for life, with successors holding the office for ten years and having the power to dominate the legislative branch. By November 1943, as the military situation of Germany deteriorated, the Pétain government decided that it would be prudent to try to reestablish historical legitimacy by recalling the old parliament and obtaining its approval for at least part of this reform, particularly the authorization to strengthen the executive branch.[100] The Vichy zone had been under direct German military occupation since the Allied landing in North Africa in November 1942, and the German authorities vetoed Pétain's effort to regain legitimacy as soon as they learned of it. From that point he remained a mere figurehead. In a cabinet reorganization at the beginning of 1944, two fascists were brought in to hold the portfolios of security and information,[101] and Déat was made labor minister in March.[102]

During the Allied liberation of France in the summer of 1944, the Vichy government and the collaborationist elite, with a few thousand followers, was moved to Sigmaringen in southwestern Germany. There two different power centers developed, a Governmental Commission led by Déat and several other figures, and a Committee of French Liberation that Doriot was authorized to form in January 1945. By that time Doriot clearly had the main backing of the German government and the SS, and he busied himself with the dispatch of spies and preparations for guerrilla warfare in liberated France. He was in the process of forcing the other Vichy residues into backing his own committee when he was suddenly killed by an Allied strafing attack on a German road in February 1945.[103]

The Slovak Republic

The Slovak Republic created under Hitler's protection out of the destruction of Czechoslovakia in March 1939 may be considered to some extent a more backward and rightist, clerical version of Vichy. It was based on the Slovak People's Party, a Catholic nationalist-populist movement founded at the close of World War I, highly religious in culture and moderately right authoritarian in political complexion. In the elections of 1935 it had gained 30 percent of

100. The Pétain regime generally enjoyed the support of most French political opinion during its first two years, but this had shifted in 1942 to an *attentiste* position and by 1943 clearly favored the Allies. See P. Laborie, *L'opinion française sous Vichy* (Paris, 1990).

101. The security minister was Joseph Darnand, leader of the Milice, a special militia police which brutally combated the resistance and persecuted Jews and presumed enemies. See J. Delperrie de Bayac, *Histoire de la Milice* (Paris, 1969).

102. A. Brissaud, *La dernière année de Vichy (1943–1944)* (Paris, 1965).

103. On the final phase, see H. Rousso, *Pétain et la fin de la collaboration* (Brussels, 1984).

the vote in Slovakia, not far from its average in recent contests, making it the plurality but not the majority party in Slovakia. Extremist sectors had become completely right radical and even protofascist, maintaining relations with the Nazis and with other fascist parties in neighboring countries. An autonomous Slovak government within Czechoslovakia had been created on December 1, 1938, as part of the aftermath of the Munich settlement. This government was completely dominated by the Slovak People's Party and soon abolished all other political groups save for those representing the large Hungarian and small German national minorities. Three and a half months later Hitler prompted it to declare Slovak independence, giving him an excuse for military occupation of what was left of the Czech territories. A treaty of March 23, 1939, recognized Slovakia to be under the "protection" of the Third Reich, though "independent."

Nominally absorbing all other Slovak political groups, the People's Party was renamed the Party of National Unity. The Slovak constitution of July 1939 acknowledged its basis in "divine law" and proclaimed a "Christian national community." It revised fundamental laws in the spirit of Dollfuss and Salazar rather than Mussolini and Hitler. The powers of the president were not unlimited, with authority being shared with a State Council. The socioeconomic philosophy of "Christian solidarism" on which the state was based eventually produced an effort to coordinate social and economic institutions into an overarching corporative structure, but this met considerable opposition and was eventually vetoed by Hitler himself.

Dr. Josef Tiso, the Catholic prelate who became the first president in October 1939, was ultimately successful in keeping the regime under rightist clerical control, though not without challenges. The first prime minister was Vojtech Tuka, also the leading protofascist. The party had organized a militia in 1938, named the Hlinka Guard after the party's founder, but Tuka in 1923 had organized a black-shirted Rodobrana (Defense of the Fatherland) to serve as a party militia in imitation of Italian Fascism, though that had lasted only four years. When he became prime minister, he revived the Rodobrana as the elite of the larger Hlinka Guard. To check Tuka, Tiso placed the Guard under his own personal control in May 1940, but at a conference with Hitler two months later, he was forced to allow Tuka to take over the Foreign Ministry as well and to name another leading protofascist, Alexander Mach, as minister of the interior and head of the Guard. From that point Tuka and Mach worked to Nazify the party, Tuka publicly calling for a "national socialist" system in Slovakia in 1941. In the meantime the Slovak government had signed Hitler's Tripartite Pact and in June 1941 declared war on the Soviet Union, sending fifty thousand troops to fight with the Wehrmacht. The party became directly influenced by Nazi racism and increasingly propounded racial identity as a doctrine of Slovak nationalism, contradicting its Catholic basis. Yet Tiso eventually gained the upper hand, exploiting Tuka's own calls for greater state leadership and authority to extend the powers of the presidency to such an extent that in October 1942 he cemented his ascendancy over Tuka and Mach. Hitler seems to have accepted the fact that greater stability could be provided by the majority clerical wing of the party, and in 1943 the leadership of the Hlinka Guard was absorbed into the party secretariat, under Tiso's control.[104]

Thus satellite Slovakia provided yet another example of Hitler's preference for reliable rightist regimes that would avoid trouble, for he explicitly ratified the power of the clerical conservatives to the ultimate detriment of the protofascist radicals. The Slovak army officer corps was among the more anti-fascist of Slovak institutions, though the anti-German revolt of August 1944 that sought to free Slovakia from the Nazi sphere was promoted primarily by the liberal and Communist political opposition. Even after Germany occupied Slovakia in the final phase of fighting, however, Hitler made no effort to place the protofascists in control.

THREE PUPPET REGIMES

Hitler placed fascists in charge of puppet governments in occupied territory only as a last resort, when more legitimate or popular moderate political forces were not available. This was most strikingly the case in Croatia, in occupied Italy after the fall of Fascism, and in Hungary during the final phase of resistance to the Red Army.

The Croatian Ustashi State

The most gruesome of the Nazi puppet regimes, and the only one to rival the Third Reich itself in bloodthirstiness, was the Ustashi state in occupied Croatia. The Ustasha (Insurgent) movement represented the most extreme form of Croatian nationalism to have emerged from the conditions of royal Serbian centralization and oppression in interwar Yugoslavia. Its founder, Dr. Ante Pavelić, was a young lawyer and sometime leader in the senior Croatian nationalist movement, the Party of Rights. In 1929, when King Alexander imposed a direct dictatorship, Pavelić decided that a more militant organization was necessary, since Croatia's majority party, the Croatian Peasant Party, was essentially moderate and democratic. Thus he founded the Ustasha–Hrvatska Revolucionarna Organizacija (Insurgency–Croatian Revolutionary Organization, UHRO) to spearhead militant and armed struggle. More moderate nationalists created a broader clandestine national militia, the Croatian Home Defense

104. Y. Jellinek, *The Parish Republic: Hlinka's Slovak People's Party, 1939–1945* (Boulder, 1976); and J. K. Hensch, *Die Slowakei und Hitlers Ostpolitik* (Cologne, 1965).

(Hrvatski Domobran, HD), together with a common front of Croatian parties, the Croatian Union (HS), with which Pavelić cooperated until 1936.

As Poglavnik, or "Leader," of the Ustashi (Insurgents, in the plural), Pavelić developed a charter of principles in 1932. This defined the goal of the movement as the achievement of an independent Croatian state, to be accomplished by a general *ustanak*, or armed "insurgency," of the Croatian people, led by the Ustashi, who would direct the new state. *Ustástvo* based itself on a tradition of hard-line Croatian nationalism dating from the late nineteenth century, aiming at a greater Croatia that would include Dalmatia and much of Bosnia as well as Croatia proper. Catholic identity was considered of fundamental importance, though the Ustashi were not members of a Catholic or clerical movement per se. They propounded a nationalist mystique which viewed Croatia as the historic bulwark of the Christian West, first against Oriental nomads, then against Turkish invaders, and now against "Eastern" Slavic tyranny and communism. Thus they preached the warrior virtues and the necessity of struggle, based on the distinct identity and superiority of Croatians as against Serbs and other "Eastern" peoples. The Croatian warriors were considered a peasant people in social structure, so the future state should be founded on the peasantry. The social norm should be the *zadruga,* or peasant family commune, which was to be erected into the foundation of a new, basically anticapitalist economic system, though one that would admit private property.

A peculiar racial theory was later evolved according to which Croatians were both "Western" and "Gothic," not "Eastern" and "Slavic" (this also had the advantage of better aligning Croats with the Nazi racial hierarchy). Ustashi racism was, however, by no means exclusively biological and was originally designed to include Serbs long resident in Croatia who would accept Catholicism, as well as Bosnian Muslims on the same terms. The basic concept—at least in the early years—was cultural and ethnic along Italian "racial" lines, rather than biological in the Nazi version. Toward the end of the movement's first decade, Croatian racism also became increasingly anti-Semitic.[105]

During the early 1930s the Ustashi were a very small group with perhaps no more than two thousand members (though with twice that number of supporters among Croatian émigrés in the Western Hemisphere) and did not yet possess a fully developed ideology. The terrorism which they employed was no novelty in Yugoslavia, for the Yugoslav state and its allies sponsored repression and certain forms of state terrorism, particularly from 1928–29, and also promoted Yugoslav terrorist activities inside Italy. The Ustashi initiated direct action in 1931 with a series of bombings and several murders—directed against

105. See the outline of doctrine presented in J. J. Sadkovich, *Italian Support for Croatian Separatism, 1927–1937* (New York, 1987), 133–62.

bridges, railways, and the Yugoslav police—climaxed by a small guerrilla raid at Lika in the following year. Yet the Yugoslav dictatorship had little difficulty in repressing this small group, while its agents sought to murder Ustashi and other Croat leaders abroad. Pavelić and his followers eventually decided to strike down the head of state. In collusion with IMRO, the Macedonian terrorist organization, three Ustashi agents were the direct accomplices of the IMRO assassins who murdered King Alexander and the French foreign minister in Marseilles in October 1934.[106]

This dramatic assassination turned out to be the climax of the movement's prewar activity, for Pavelić was unable to obtain any support from the Peasant Party—Croatia's majority force—for his violent designs. Though the Peasant Party continued to develop its clandestine Domobran, or Home Defense, militia, it was committed to passive resistance. Whereas in its first years the Ustashi had been a Balkan terrorist and insurgency organization that was no more than protofascist, Pavelić broke completely with Croatian moderates by 1936 and moved the group toward a more overtly fascist and anti-Semitic position. He himself was forced to operate from exile, depending on the largesse of the Italian and Hungarian governments, but reaction to the assassination in 1934 brought closing of the Ustashi centers in those two countries. Soon the movement had been virtually shut down, with 500 activists interned abroad under lenient conditions (including 235 with Pavelić in Italy). Though a larger skeletal network existed in Croatia, it was unable to sustain a terrorist campaign. Whereas in the first years Pavelić had tried to convince Western governments that an independent Croatia would be a force for peace and stability in the Balkans, many Ustashi sought inspiration in Fascist Italy. By 1936–37 Pavelić had, during his Italian internment, come to identify the Ustashi fully with a Fascist and Nazi New Order and increasingly aligned his movement with an overtly fascist ideology, mixed with romantic peasantism and a Croatian brand of "national Catholicism." Meanwhile, the émigré Ustashi group in Germany, led by Dr. Branimir Jelić, maneuvered to carry the movement in a more racial, Nazi-influenced direction. After the *Sporazum,* or Compromise, of 1939 that for the first time gave Croats approximately equal rights and representation in Yugoslavia, the underground Ustashi, with a possible membership of thirty to forty thousand in a total Croat population of six million, endeavored to increase terrorism and other forms of subversion.

Defeat of Yugoslavia by the German *Blitzkrieg* of April 1941 opened the way for nominal Croatian independence, and Hitler and Mussolini agreed on the total obliteration of the Yugoslav state. In keeping, however, with Hitler's

106. J. J. Sadkovich, "Terrorism in Croatia, 1929–1934," *East European Quarterly* 22:1 (March 1988): 55–79.

preference for the rule of reliable conservatives or rightists, the leadership of the new Croat state was first offered to Vladko Macek, head of the majority Croatian Peasant Party. It was only his refusal to play Quisling that induced Hitler then to give power to Pavelić and the Ustashi. Even so, much of Dalmatia was detached for annexation by Italy, and all of remaining Croatia was divided into Italian and German zones of military occupation, so that the Ustashi state never enjoyed the degree of nominal territorial sovereignty of satellite Slovakia, even though it joined the Tripartite Pact and participated in the invasion of the Soviet Union. In a separate agreement, Mussolini officially guaranteed the independence and territorial integrity of the new state, though Hitler soon made it clear that he intended to exercise the major influence in Croatia.

Pavelić was thus released from his long if reasonably comfortable internment in Italy to become Poglavnik of the Independent State of Croatia (NDH), which he established as a one-party regime, proclaiming an indissoluble mystical bond between Poglavnik and nation. Ustashi ranks swelled with the incorporation of tens of thousands of followers of the Peasant Party. The Peasant Party itself was soon outlawed, though the numerous Peasant officials in local administration were mostly retained if they were willing to swear allegiance. The remnants of the Peasant Party themselves divided, some becoming pro-Ustashi, others becoming neutralists, and some eventually supporting the opposition Communist Partisans. The Ustashi seem to have recruited especially well among the lower-class urban population, gaining the support also of many students and some Croatian intellectuals, as well as a surprising number of the strongly nationalist Croatian Catholic clergy. The Ustashi were not, however, an officially Catholic movement, and because of its extremism and puppet status, the NDH was never officially recognized by the Vatican.

The constitution of the new state defined Croatians as a distinct race, and by 1942 the NDH had begun to develop a national labor syndicate, together with the outline of "chambers of professional association" that would form part of a corporative economic system. The regime declared opposition to both capitalism and communism, recognizing the Croatian peasantry as the basis of the people and upholding the traditional semicommunal *zadruga* as its paradigm of economic condominion. A consultative assembly was eventually convened in Zagreb in 1942, preparatory to forming a regular corporative parliament, but the concept seemed troublesome to Pavelić and he never implemented it.[107] In fact the greatly swollen Ustasha organization was strongly divided by internal rivalries, never becoming fully unified or developing a fully crystallized ideology or state system. For security it took over the former Peas-

---

107. Y. Jellinek, "An Authoritarian Parliament: The Croatian State Sabor of 1942," *Canadian Slavonic Papers* 22:2 (June 1980): 259–73.

Ante Pavelić, Ustashi chief and "Poglavnik" of the Independent State of Croatia, meets Italian foreign minister Ciano in Venice, December 15, 1941

ant Party militia institution, Domobran, developing it into a larger territorial defense force, and formed elite detachments of some fifteen thousand Ustashi militants as a special force.

The most striking feature of the NDH was its extraordinary ethnic violence. Within a matter of weeks the Ustashi shock units began to apply themselves to the forcible conversion, expulsion, and/or mass extermination of the large Orthodox Serbian minority within Croatia, which amounted to well over 20 percent of the total population, in excess of a million people. Though some were allowed simply to flee or to convert to Catholicism, untold numbers were soon being murdered wholesale in gruesome mass slaughters, sometimes apparently even with the blessing and/or participation of individual members of the clergy (especially a number of Franciscan monks). The Ustashi also moved swiftly to carry out their miniature "Final Solution" without any very direct prompting from the Nazis, massacring all the thirty to forty thousand Jews in Croatia, except for a few thousand who managed to flee to safety in the Italian zone.

It will never be possible to determine exactly how many Serbs and others (including Jews and Gypsies) were killed in the only other example of fascistic violence proportionately equivalent to that of the Nazis themselves. The total proportionate loss of life in Yugoslavia during World War II was the third highest for any country in Europe, after Poland and the Soviet Union, even though the official postwar Yugoslav government figure of 1.7 million unnatural deaths, or 12 percent of the total population, is probably inflated. Most of this vast toll of victims, whose total may be rather closer to 1 million than the official statistic, were killed in the extraordinary set of civil wars, guerrilla wars, and antiguerrilla campaigns that wracked the Yugoslav territories during World War II. Three distinct civil wars and one international conflict, waged both consecutively and simultaneously, pitted Communist Partisans and Serbian nationalist Chetniks against the Axis occupation forces, and sometimes also against the collaborationist units of the Serbian puppet leader General Milan Nedić (who administered central Serbia for the Germans), as well as against the Serbian and Bosnian units of the protofascist Zbor movement. Meanwhile, both Partisans and Chetniks waged their own conflicts against the Ustashi, while ultimately saving most of their energy to fight each other.[108] The bloody struggles that have attended the breakup of Yugoslavia since 1991 had their origins partly in these many-sided conflicts during World War II.

108. The Chetniks were a right radical, essentially monarchist and authoritarian, Serbian force that carried out a number of ethnic massacres of their own. They had their own plans for "ethnic cleansing" after the war, which the Communist takeover frustrated. See J. Tomasevich, *War and Revolution in Yugoslavia, 1941–1945: The Chetniks* (Stanford, 1975), 256–61.

Perhaps the main controversy coming out of this many-sided conflict concerned the extent to which both the Partisans and the Chetniks concentrated on the anti-Axis struggle, rather than fighting their internal civil wars. The Partisans also carried out thousands of cold-blooded executions but supposedly devoted more of their energy to fighting the Axis, though it remains difficult to determine exactly how much. The Chetniks eventually engaged in armistices with Axis forces to concentrate on the Communist menace, but they were hampered in all their activities by being denied the arms from the Western allies that flowed in to supply the Partisans, who also engaged in tacit truces with the Axis occupiers. The bulk of the literature takes a pro-Partisan stance, but two recent revisionist books that give the Chetniks more credit are D. Martin, *The Web of Disinformation* (New York, 1990), and M. Lees, *The Rape of Serbia* (New York, 1990). The standard works are Tomasevich, *War and Revolution,* and M. J. Milazzo, *The Chetnik Movement and the Yugoslav Resistance* (Baltimore, 1975).

The total number of Serbs liquidated by the Ustashi may have reached the startling figure of 250,000.[109] The NDH operated as many as twenty-four concentration camps, most of them small, but the chief camp at Jasenovać, where tens of thousands of Jews and Serbs died, functioned as a sort of Ustashi Auschwitz. A system of thirty-four special courts, which had the power to hand down death sentences to be executed within three hours, was created, but many of the Serbs were killed in village massacres, with the Ustashi on several occasions herding hundreds into a local Orthodox church, boarding up the doors and windows, and setting the building afire. There seemed to be special animus against educated Serbs, akin to the initial Nazi persecution of the Polish intelligentsia in 1939–40. By contrast, the attitude toward Bosnian Muslims was more accepting. Though they were expected to convert to Catholicism, they were categorized by some Ustashi ideologues as racially the "purest Croatians." By 1942 Pavelić and his henchmen began to tire of their gory labors. Finding it too much of a struggle to drive out all Serbs, the NDH created a separate autocephalous Croatian Orthodox Church under a White Russian prelate that was to be akin to the Galician Uniate Church, in communion with Rome and thus providing an acceptable identity for Serbs in Croatia.

Hitler had not been eager to give power to Pavelić, and the virtual chaos which Ustashi policy created in parts of Croatia within only a few months confirmed his suspicions. By the autumn of 1941 he was prepared to depose the Ustashi Poglavnik, again offering the leadership of the NDH to the Peasant Party chieftain Macek, but once more Macek refused to cooperate. Hitler therefore left Pavelić in power for lack of an alternative. The Poglavnik in fact during the middle of the war increasingly neglected his responsibilities to spend more and more time writing novels, purging the Croatian vocabulary of non-Croatian elements, and trying to construct a perpetual-motion machine. Eventually, when the war was lost to Germany, two NDH government figures made a secret effort to negotiate an independent peace for Croatia on their own, but they were discovered and executed by Pavelić. In the spring of 1945 the German forces made a last stand in Croatia, supported by 150,000 (mostly

---

109. The most detailed recent demographic study is by the Serb Bogoljub Kočević, *Zrtve drugog svetskog rata u Jugoslaviji* (London, 1985), which presents the following ethnic losses: Serbians, 487,000 (6.9 percent of their total population); Croatians, 207,000 (5.4%); Montenegrins, 50,000 (10.4%); Muslims, 86,000 (6.8%); Slovenes, 32,000 (2.5%); Macedonians, 7,000 (0.9%). Thus the total of "Yugoslavs" killed was 869,000, or 5.9 percent of the total population. To these figures Kočević adds: other Slavs, 12,000 (3.9%); other Balkan nationalities, 13,000 (1.3%); and "others", 120,000 (9.9%), raising the grand total to 1,014,000 (5.9%).

The highest rate of losses among the non-Yugoslav minorities were among Jews (60,000 [77.9%]), Gypsies (27,000 [31.4%]), and Germans (26,000 [4.8%]). Lower figures for nearly all the above groups have been calculated by the Croatian statistician Vladimir Zerjavić, in *Opsesije i megalomanije oko Jasenovca i Bleiburga* (Zagreb, 1992), but these appear less reliable.

Domobran) Croatian troops under German command. During the final rout Pavelić managed to escape (making his way to Argentina), but 50,000 or more Croatian troops were not so fortunate, being slaughtered in mass executions by the newly dominant Yugoslav Communists.[110]

Some scholars have concluded that the Ustashi were too divided and ideologically immature to have ever become more than protofascists, and indeed it is not clear that they possessed a vision of a categorically fascist-type revolution and a "new man" other than as a staunch Catholic peasant nationalist, albeit of extreme and bloodthirsty qualities. The murderousness of the Ustashi did not by itself qualify them to be considered generic fascists, since the great majority of the movements and regimes of this century to have engaged in large-scale killings were either Marxist-Leninists or nonfascist nationalists. Their ghastly distinction was to have become the leaders of the only other regime in occupied Europe to rival the Nazis themselves as mass murderers.

The Italian Social Republic

The German army was prepared to act when Italy's armistice with the Allies was publicly announced on September 8, 1943, and within a few days it seized control of almost the entire peninsula, disarming and interning the remaining units of the Italian army, whom the new Badoglio government in Rome left without leadership. On September 12 Mussolini himself was rescued from internment on Gran Sasso Mountain by a special SS commando unit and flown to Germany. Hitler then decided that Mussolini should lead a new purified Fascist government to assist the German war effort and soon returned him to Italy to begin the task. In fact, Italy was to be governed by German military

---

110. S. Guldescu and J. Prcela, eds., *Operation Slaughterhouse: Eyewitness Accounts of Postwar Massacres in Yugoslavia* (Philadelphia, 1970); F. Nevistić and V. Nikolić, *Bleiburska tragedija hrvatskoga naroda* (Munich, 1976); and "La Tragedia de Bleiburg," a special number of *Studia Croatica* (Buenos Aires, 1963), present the Croatian version of these mass murders.

The principal research on the Ustashi and the NDH is in Serbo-Croatian: B. Krizman, *Ante Pavelić i Ustase* (Zagreb, 1978); idem, *Pavelić izmedu Hitlera i Mussolinija* (Zagreb, 1980); idem, *Ustase i Treći Reich,* 2 vols. (Zagreb, 1983); and F. Jelić-Butić, *Ustase i NDH* (Zagreb, 1972).

The scholarly literature on the NDH in Western languages is limited. Of use are L. Hory and M. Broszat, *Der kroatische Ustascha-Staat, 1941–1945* (Stuttgart, 1964); E. Paris, *Genocide in Satellite Croatia, 1941–1945* (Chicago, 1960); M. Ambri, *I falsi fascismi* (Rome, 1980), 129–97; K. Meneghello-Dinčić, "L'état 'Oustacha' de Croatie (1941–1945)," *Revue d'Histoire de la Deuxième Guerre Mondiale* 74 (April 1969): 46–49; F. Tudman, "The Independent State of Croatia as an Instrument of the Occupation Powers in Yugoslavia, and the People's Liberation Movement in Croatia from 1941 to 1945," in *Les systèmes d'occupation en Yugoslavie, 1941–1945* (Belgrade, 1963), 135–262; Y. Jellinek, "Nationalities and Minorities in the Independent State of Croatia," *Nationalities Papers* 8:2 (1984): 195–210; and also J. A. Irvine, *The Croat Question* (Boulder, 1993), 93–102, 130–31.

administration like many other parts of occupied Europe, while the north-eastern territories which Italy had incorporated from Austria-Hungary in 1919 were immediately placed under complete German administration, preparatory to their eventual annexation by the Reich.

Mussolini would initially have preferred to have been allowed to retire to Switzerland, but he accepted Hitler's assignment apparently out of some combination of inertia, fear, and a lingering ambition to vindicate Fascism or possibly to regain some shred of sovereignty or honor. He was aware that to a large extent he was merely acting out a role, and he once remarked to a subordinate that it would be better to be sent to a German concentration camp than to continue as a puppet, but continue he did. His residence was established at a villa near Salò by Lake Garda on the northern frontier, effectively under German control. He was virtually a prisoner of the SS, who restricted his communications and controlled all his travel.[111]

The new regime was theoretically to embody true Fascism restored to its revolutionary origins, freed of its conservative compromises with the monarchy and the bourgeoisie. The resulting "Italian Social Republic" was also known as the Salò regime, from the location of its Foreign Ministry and the proximity of Mussolini's residence. In fact, it had no capital of its own, with ministries and offices scattered over eight cities and its leader under virtual house arrest. Before fleeing to Allied territory, the Badoglio government had dissolved the National Fascist Party in one of its first acts. A new Revolutionary Fascist Party began to be organized in September under German occupation, and then held its first and only congress in Verona (center of German military administration in Italy) in November 1943. It quickly enrolled about a quarter million members, roughly the same number as the original party in 1922. At the congress a new party manifesto declared Mussolini Capo della Republica (Head of the Republic), with power to appoint all ministers, but also announced that a new republican chamber was in some fashion to be elected by the people. Though the right to private property was guaranteed, all public services were to be governed by parastate agencies, and in all larger industrial enterprises joint councils of workers, technicians, and administrators were to supervise production and the distribution of profits. Uncultivated or improperly developed land was to be confiscated and given to landless farmworkers or farmer cooperatives.

"Socialization" of some sort was to be the goal of the Social Republic, and economic terms were formalized in a decree of February 1944. All larger enterprises were henceforth to be governed by a complex new administrative

---

111. The best account of the peculiar Hitler-Mussolini relationship is F. W. Deakin, *The Brutal Friendship* (London, 1962).

structure composed of four parts: assemblies made up equally of representatives of workers and shareholders, a management council of similar composition, a worker college or council, and a director. This represented Mussolini's revenge against the bourgeoisie and the rightist elite whom he believed had thwarted Fascism.[112] It was not a full socialism or genuine worker control, but even this was too much for German occupation authorities, who feared it would disrupt Italian production for the Reich. These and most other economic reforms of the Social Republic were therefore largely or completely stymied by the German command.[113]

The Social Republic nonetheless gained the support of a certain minority of Italians, resting on the remaining hard-core Fascists as well as a cadre of opportunists—and even in some cases misguided patriots[114]—willing to collaborate with the new masters. The members of the old army had been rounded up and disarmed by the Germans, who shipped about 600,000 of them to Germany, mostly for forced labor. The Salò regime managed to draft about 500,000 men for a new army, partly trained and completely controlled by the German authorities, who employed it only for rearguard security. While soldiers in these units deserted in droves, another 300,000 recruits were militarized for forced labor in Germany.[115] The old Fascist militia (MVSN) was reconstituted as the National Republican Guard, whose 345,000 men functioned as a largely ineffective paramilitary force.[116] Various diehard Fascist leaders organized other semiautonomous paramilitary units, by far the most important of which were the approximately 40,000 men organized into the fifty brigades of the elite Black Brigades, under the direction of the new party secretary, Alessandro Pavolini.[117]

The German occupation and the formation of the neo-Fascist puppet government led to a new conflict with the patriotic resistance forces, composed of Communists, Socialists, Christian Democrats, and liberals. By 1944 this conflict had become an Italian civil war between anti-Fascists on the one hand and German troops and Fascist forces on the other. Partisan bands of the resistance attacked government installations and small German convoys and

112. As Nolte says of Mussolini, "The *finalità* of Marxism continued to live in him, even if he was not aware of it" (*Three Faces* 310).
113. E. Collotti, *L'amministrazione tedesca dell'Italia occupata, 1943–1945* (Milan, 1963); S. Bertoldi, *Tedeschi in Italia* (Milan, 1964).
114. Cf. the *Lettere dei caduti della R.S.I.* (Rome, 1976).
115. G. Pansa, *L'Esercito di Salò* (Milan, 1970); G. Pisanò, *Storia delle Forze Armate della Repubblica Sociale Italiana* (Rome, 1962).
116. S. Setta, *Renato Ricci: Dallo squadrismo alla Repubblica Sociale Italiana* (Bologna, 1986), is a biography of its leader.
117. R. Lazzero, *Le Brigate Nere* (Milan, 1983).

also ambushed Fascist leaders and police. German troops and particularly the Black Brigades responded with ferocious reprisals, those of the latter being so excessive that even German military commanders occasionally protested. Altogether, the partisans would lose nearly forty thousand men, but they inflicted not inconsiderable losses on the Fascist paramilitary units and on the German forces. Five thousand of the German troops were killed, and many more were wounded in partisan attacks during the summer of 1944. Thousands of civilians were slaughtered, mostly in direct reprisals that in several cases wiped out entire villages.[118]

Though supported by tens of thousands of Fascist diehards, the Italian Social Republic was but a minor, radicalized version of the historic Fascist regime that could not have survived twenty-four hours without German military occupation. With its social reforms largely blocked by the Nazis, it completely failed to convince ordinary society, particularly the industrial workers who were pressed ever harder under the most difficult circumstances, to produce for the occupation authorities. The experience of the Salò regime discredited Mussolini more than the twenty years of Fascist government which preceded it.[119] He was finally seized by partisans when attempting to escape with German military units at the end of April 1945 and summarily executed together with his mistress, their corpses hung upside down in a public square in Milan.[120] Though the postwar prosecution of Fascists was generally mild, the initial reprisals at the end of the war were not.[121] The best estimates conclude that the resistance forces carried out twelve to fifteen thousand summary executions between April and June 1945.[122] Such killings continued at a much lower rate into 1947. Most of those executed were Fascists, though a certain number were simply anti-Communists liquidated for political reasons.

118. C. Pavone, *Una guerra civile* (Turin, 1991). Pavone accurately defines the conflict in northern Italy as simultaneously a national patriotic war, a civil war, and a kind of class war. Also useful is the dissertation by W. L. Myers, "Revolution and Retribution: The Theory and Practice of Revolutionary Justice in the Italian Fascist Republic of Salò," Ph.D. diss., University of Colorado, 1989.

119. The principal accounts in English are Deakin, *Brutal Friendship*, and R. Dombrowski, *Mussolini: Twilight and Fall* (London, 1956), but there is an extensive literature in Italian. Perhaps the best treatment is G. Bocca, *La Repubblica di Mussolini* (Bari, 1977), but see also E. Cione, *Storia della Repubblica Sociale Italiana* (Rome, 1951); G. Perticone, *La Repubblica di Salò* (Rome, 1947); F. Bellotti, *La Repubblica di Salò* (Milan, 1974); P. P. Poggio, ed., *La Repubblica sociale italiana* [*sic*] *1943–1945* (Brescia, 1986); and the pen portraits in S. Bertoldi, *Salò* (Milan, 1976). The attempt to create a new current of Catholic (if schismatic) neo-Fascism is treated in A. Dordoni, "*Crociata italica*" (Milan, 1976), and Fappani-Molinari [*sic*], *Chiesa e Repubblica di Salò* (Turin, 1981).

120. C. Bianchi and F. Mezzetti, *Mussolini aprile 1945* (Milan, 1979).

121. R. P. Domenico, *Italian Fascists on Trial, 1943–1948* (Chapel Hill, 1991); L. Mercuri, *L'epurazione in Italia, 1943–1948* (Cueno, 1988).

The Arrow Cross Regime in Hungary, 1944–1945

The final satellite regime founded by Hitler, and only the third to be placed directly under a national fascist leadership, was the Arrow Cross government in Hungary. Following the striking success of the Arrow Cross and its Hungarian national socialist allies in the Hungarian elections of 1939, the Horthy regime moved effectively to repress the danger. With Ferenc Szalasi in prison, the Arrow Cross became increasingly divided between moderates and revolutionaries, though with the moderates generally in control. After the outbreak of war in Europe, the government increased its own discretionary powers and extended greater censorship, restricting Arrow Cross activities. Uncertain leadership and the internal division in the movement combined with governmental pressure to initiate a fairly rapid decline in membership. In a local by-election in November 1939, only six months after an impressive national showing, the Arrow Cross ticket lost nearly half its earlier votes, and this decline continued in several by-elections during 1940. The government's own political party became increasingly active, and the regime adopted new anti-Soviet and anti-Jewish measures which, with the formal restrictions on opposition political meetings, further discouraged Arrow Cross activity. All this only underscored the paradoxical need of fascistic parties for democratic conditions in which to develop.

After Hitler's dramatic military victories in 1940, however, the Hungarian regime thought it prudent to release Szalasi. Regaining freedom in September, he immediately fused the Arrow Cross with the other principal fascistic group, the Hungarian National Socialist Party of Laszlo Baky and Fidel Palffy, which, with fifteen deputies, stood as the second largest opposition party in parliament. Thus the expanded Arrow Cross, momentarily gaining new adherents on the crest of Hitler's triumphs, counted a total parliamentary delegation of forty-six.

A few weeks later the former prime minister Bela Imredy broke with the ruling party and formed a new right radical Party of Hungarian Renewal. This was based on small sectors of the upper and middle classes who found the Arrow Cross too radical and plebeian, and it proposed to replace the existing system with a one-party corporate state, strongly anti-Semitic and tied to Germany. The Imredy group was the heir of the original so-called Szeged fascists of Gyula Gömbös. Within a year the National Socialists of Baky and Palffy, less socially revolutionary and rather more biologically racist than the Arrow Cross core, broke once more with the latter and later merged with the Imredy party to form a new Hungarian Renewal–National Socialist Party Union. The

122. This is the conclusion of Bocca (*La Repubblica* 338–39), who correlates diverse estimates.

new formation proposed an elite takeover of the Hungarian government that would reject social revolution and eschew mass mobilization, while acting in concert with Germany. Hitler's representatives tended to back the new party, distrusting Szalasi as too radical and disruptive, all the more because he refused to renounce his goal of incorporating "Swabians" (members of the German ethnic minority in Hungary) into the Arrow Cross. Himmler sought to promote the organization of Swabians into their own Hungarian-German Volksbund, and in general German authorities preferred to see a smoother inside takeover by a right radical elite, led presumably by Imredy, to a more disruptive (potentially even somewhat anti-German) Arrow Cross revolution.[123]

The growth in Arrow Cross membership in mid-1940 proved transitory, for, with continuing wartime restrictions on political activity and persistent internal division, the decline was soon resumed. By 1942 the Szalasi mythos seems to have become seriously damaged, even within the movement, for he was increasingly revealed as inept and unrealistic. Though the revised program of what was now officially the Arrow Cross Party announced the need for "adjustment to the New Order desired by the Axis Powers" to the extent compatible with Hungarism, Szalasi viewed Hitler as merely a "pseudo–National Socialist" and denounced the new Imredy-Palffy party as a lackey of German imperialism. Nor did he favor the initial German invasion of the Soviet Union; like any committed revolutionary, he was certain that the enactment of his utopia would carry all before it, and so at first he held that if "true National Socialism" were instituted in Hungary and Germany, its success would be so compelling that the Soviet Union would simply crumble in its shadow. Once the die was cast, however, and the Horthy regime had also entered the war as a German ally, Szalasi recognized the decisiveness of the *Weltanschauungskrieg* (war of ideologies) on the eastern front and declared that all true Hungarians must support it.

Internal conflict persisted. The Arrow Cross set up its own "scientific" biological racial office in 1942, but the latter was forced to recognize that Hungarians constituted a mixed race, which in turn was praised because of its comprehensiveness. On the religious front, radicals developed plans to create a kind of Hungarian national church, partially based on Catholic doctrine but totally free from the Vatican. More and more of the remaining moderates and upper-class members drifted away, but the revolutionaries were also often unhappy, chafing under the absence of direct action, which Szalasi refused to approve in wartime. So many party deputies crossed over that by the last months of 1942 the Hungarian Renewal–National Socialist Union counted forty-four parliamentary deputies, only eighteen remaining loyal to the Arrow

123. M. Szöllösi-Janze, *Die Pfeilkreuzlerbewegung in Ungarn* (Munich, 1989), 250–74.

Cross. Szalasi himself admitted by the end of the following year that actual party membership had dropped to no more than ninety thousand. With the war reaching a critical point, 1944 was announced as the "year of decision" for the movement, and some modest success was registered by an all-out effort to regain membership.

As the eastern front moved nearer Hungary, German forces entered the country in March 1943. Henceforth Hungary would be not an ally but a satellite under de facto occupation, and Horthy was pressured to appoint a more right radical, pro-German government under Döme Sztojay. Imredy, Palffy, and several other members of the party soon became cabinet members. German authorities attempted to encourage formation of a grand Imredy–National Socialist–Arrow Cross coalition as the new government's political support, but Szalasi refused to participate. Progressively losing contact with reality, he busied himself with a plan to reorganize Europe into ethnic "tribes," with Hitler as "supreme tribal leader," Mussolini as "deputy tribal leader," Szalasi as "tribal leader for Hungary," and so on.

During the summer of 1944, as the German position deteriorated on every front, the Hungarian chief of state, Admiral Horthy, tried to regain the initiative. The Sztojay-Imredy cabinet was replaced by a more moderate government under General Geza Lakatos. This was composed exclusively of ministers from the government party, and all other political groups were officially dissolved.

For the past three years the Arrow Cross leaders had tried stubbornly to retain whatever strength they could, determined not to suffer the fate of the Legion of the Archangel Michael in neighboring Romania. Szalasi had largely avoided direct action, insisting that the movement must achieve power by legal means. By September 1944 the situation was becoming so desperate for all concerned that for the first time the German authorities were willing to give their main support to the Arrow Cross. Szalasi managed to convince himself that a coup to seize power from Horthy with German support was now acceptable, since the regent's well-known efforts to seek a negotiated exit from the war amounted to a betrayal of the Tripartite Pact and an act of treason against Hungary itself in the *Weltanschauungskrieg*.

Early in October Hitler finally decided that he must forcibly remove Horthy and replace him with Szalasi, but events were precipitated on the fifteenth by the government's negotiation of a deal with the oncoming Soviet forces. German units seized control of the Hungarian government on October 16, installing Szalasi as prime minister and also as acting head of state in place of Horthy. The former appointment had supposedly been approved by Horthy before his deposition, while a submissive parliament, which had the legal power to name an emergency head of state, ratified the latter a few days later.

Szalasi formed a cabinet of fourteen ministers, half chosen from the

Ferenc Szalasi, followed by Arrow Cross militiaman, in Budapest, October 16, 1944

Arrow Cross and half from the various rightist parties (including also the right wing of the old government party). Though he now enjoyed decree powers, Szalasi continued to show a rather fastidious concern for legitimacy. A rump parliament was maintained, even if it met only once a week to approve decrees issued by the government. Protests could still be registered by spokesmen for the various rightist groups. In November the Arrow Cross and the Hungarian Renewal–National Socialist Party were officially reunited, but a true merger never took place, and both groups preserved their separate identities. In Budapest local sections of the Arrow Cross and others got out of control, conducting sporadic pogroms against the Jews. Well over half the Jewish population of Hungary had been deported to the death camps by the SS under the Sztojay government, and of the remaining 250,000, about 50,000 more were deported during Szalasi's regime.[124] By December the government was forced to evacuate Budapest and to set up a new capital in western Hungary, where it administered only about 25 percent of Hungarian territory.

Like Hitler, Szalasi rapidly increased the appointment of special commissioners in charge of new agencies or programs, eventually naming more than fifty. It quickly became clear that the Arrow Cross could not produce enough competent administrators to man the state apparatus, but more and more were appointed anyway, and in January Szalasi named by decree twenty-six new Arrow Cross deputies to fill some of the vacancies in the rump parliament. Confusion, incompetence, and overlapping proliferated.

Little effort was apparently made to recruit new members for a party that now amounted to scarcely more than 1 percent of the population. In a manner somewhat analogous to Mussolini, Szalasi now envisioned the party's main role as that of a special "Hungarian Order" to educate the masses and incorporate them in a true National Socialism. Thus, despite the extreme military crisis with half the country already occupied by the Red Army, members were exempted from military service. Szalasi deemed it more important to create a special "Administrative Staff of the Leader of the Nation" from among the party elite to serve as a kind of shadow government, looking over the shoulders of the ministers. A total of thirteen Arrow Cross bureaus were established to parallel the official ministries; some of these scarcely got started, though several had to be restricted so as to limit interference with the government.

124. The large Jewish minority in Hungary, including the residents of reannexed lands in Transylvania, amounted to 762,000. During a period of seven weeks under Sztojay (from May 16 to July 8), approximately 437,000 were deported, and further deportations occurred before Sztojay was removed. Under Szalasi, another 50,000 were deported, and hundreds were killed in pogroms. Altogether, about 255,000 Jews survived in Hungarian territory or in deportation (primarily in the former category). The key study is R. L. Braham, *The Politics of Genocide: The Holocaust in Hungary*, 2 vols. (New York, 1992).

Szalasi refused to abandon his voluminous literary activities, devoting much of his time to a definitive book on Hungarist ideology, as well as to the elaborate composition of theoretical laws for his future Hungarist state. His work habits were poor, and other time was diverted to useless side trips to corners of his shrinking domain, the main business of government being conducted by his vice-premier, Jeno Szöllösi. His grand scheme for the future envisioned a one-party state, though he theoretically provided that, when the task of Hungarism had been completed, there could be a moderate opposition party and also a catchall "minorities party."

The new economic structure was to be entitled "Corporate Order of the Working Nation." Szalasi had earlier rejected both the Italian system—which failed to alter capitalism very much—and the Nazi economic framework, which in his judgment was not true National Socialism. He simply added the *Führerprinzip* to the liberal model, however, without building true corporations. There were to be a total of fourteen corporations, and once achieved, this system would initiate an international relationship among the "Working People of the World." Mining and energy were to be nationalized, and other large industries "controlled" by the state. Amid the chaos and disaster in which Szalasi's government functioned, his economic policies still met considerable opposition from the right, and no more than four corporations were ever organized. For Szalasi, nothing was more important than winning the workers, and he did begin to create "factory councils" dominated by Arrow Cross members in some of the larger firms within his tiny territory. These were to be formed in all factories with twenty or more employees.

No matter how desperate the circumstances, Szalasi refused theoretically to compromise Hungarian sovereignty. He never yielded completely to the Germans on the principle of not including German-Hungarians within the Arrow Cross, and he tried to retain nominal command of all Hungarian military units, even including *Volksdeutsche* members of the Waffen-SS. Among his schemes was a project to create a new Arrow Cross–led Hungarian army on the basis of his own version of the Waffen-SS.

By the end of March 1945 the Red Army had driven Szalasi's administration out of Hungary and into German territory, where he was later captured. Like nearly all the top fascist leaders in prison after the war, he was subsequently executed for war crimes.[125]

---

125. The best account of the Szalasi government in a Western language will be found in Szöllösi-Janze, *Pfeilkreuzlerbewegung* 283–432.

PUPPET FASCISTS IN NORTHWESTERN EUROPE

Of the Nazi puppets in the occupied countries of northwestern Europe, the most notorious was the Norwegian Vidkun Quisling, whose name has become a synonym for such a role. Quisling's Nasjonal Samling had completely failed to mobilize significant support before the war. Nonetheless, he seized the initiative during the initial German conquest of Norway in April 1940 and was allowed to form a Nasjonal Samling government under the Occupation. This was dissolved by Hitler within no more than six days after it became apparent that Quisling had scarcely any support. The real governor was the newly appointed Reichskommissar Joseph Terboven, who administered Norway with the assistance of an Administrative Council of Norwegian technical experts. In September 1940 Terboven replaced this body with a State Council enjoying broader administrative powers and declared the Nasjonal Samling the only political party allowed to function. Subsequently Nasjonal Samling representatives held nine of the thirteen State Council seats, and party membership increased from fifteen thousand to nearly forty-three thousand by April 1942.[126]

On February 1, 1942, Quisling was restored to "power" as minister-president of Norway ("minister-president" was the German designation for the head of a provincial government). He administered his country on Germany's behalf for the remainder of the war but was met by widespread passive resistance and totally failed in his goal of inculcating a "new mentality." When all urban workers were declared members of a new Nasjonal Samling Labor Front, so much chaos resulted that Hitler chose to cancel the order. Similar efforts to establish compulsory participation in a Nasjonal Samling youth front and to include all teachers in a Nasjonal Samling teachers' front met equal resistance. Quisling's function was to administer his country for the benefit of the Reich, but his own mobilization goals were almost entirely thwarted.[127]

In Denmark, by contrast, there was no significant puppet. Technically Denmark was never at war and did not contest the German occupation. It was allowed to retain a nominal neutrality and to maintain its own internal autonomy and sovereignty within the military sphere of the New Order. Thus there was no interference with the Danish government's arrest of 350 Danish Nazis after troublesome demonstrations in December 1940. The Danish government did play a somewhat Pétain-like role, giving Germany eight torpedo boats in February 1941, later announcing formation of a volunteer corps to fight against the Soviet Union, and also signing the Anti-Comintern Pact. Vichy

126. H. D. Loock, *Quisling, Rosenberg und Terboven: Zur Vorgeschichte und Geschichte der nationalsozialistischen Revolution in Norwegen* (Stuttgart, 1970).

127. O. K. Hoidal, *Quisling: A Study in Treason* (Oslo, 1989); P. M. Hayes, *Quisling* (London, 1971); A. Milward, *The Fascist Economy in Norway* (Oxford, 1972).

France never did the latter, an action that proved very unpopular among Danish political leaders. Danish autonomy was terminated after major strikes and demonstrations in August 1943 in which ninety-seven were killed. At that point the tiny Danish army was dissolved, and most of the navy fled to Sweden. For the remainder of the war internal administration was supervised by the secretaries-general of the government ministries. The main Danish Nazi group, led by Frits Clausen, did manage to expand slightly, but even so it gained less than 2 percent of the vote in the 1943 parliamentary elections. During the last two years of the war its place was increasingly taken by a black-uniformed group known as the Schalburg Corps, modeled on the SS, but this had scarcely as many as a thousand members.[128]

Holland was governed by a German Reichskommissar, Arthur Seyss-Inquart but produced more collaborationists proportionately than any other northwestern European country under the Occupation. As in Belgium and later in Denmark, routine government administration in Holland was supervised by the secretaries-general of the government ministries, and the regular civil administration was maintained, with new state propaganda and cultural offices added. As in Norway, the ruler (Queen Wilhelmina) and the legitimate government had fled abroad, but soon after the German conquest a new "Netherlands Union" sprang up with goals analogous to those of Vichy, seeking both to collaborate and to protect Dutch interests. Within seven months it claimed a nominal eight hundred thousand members but showed too much devotion to Dutch priorities and was restricted by the Reichskommissar. A prey to internal contradictions, it soon declined and was dissolved in December 1941.

Anton Mussert's Dutch National Socialist Movement (NSB) had undergone steady decline in the years before the Occupation, its membership dropping from forty-seven thousand at the end of 1935 to twenty-nine thousand by the spring of 1940. This figure increased to about fifty thousand six months after occupation. Mussert, despite his movement's name, was more of a moderate Italian or western European–style fascist than a Nazi, and at first he was denied any special role in the Occupation. The German authorities preferred to maintain a sort of competition between the NSB, the smaller National Socialist Party of Dutch Workers, and the exiguous National Fascist Front. In September 1940 Mussert naively submitted to Hitler a plan for a "Nordic Federation" led by the Führer, in which Holland would enjoy autonomy, flanked by a "Latin Federation" led by Mussolini. Mussert's recipe for an autonomous Holland within the New Order was an authoritarian state that would still be governed by law and would recognize freedom of religion. In December 1941 the NSB was recognized as the sole legal political party in Holland. Increasingly Mussert's more radical lieutenant, Rost van Tonningen, came to the fore, espousing a

128. E. Thomsen, *Deutsche Besatzungspolitik in Dänemark, 1940–1945* (Düsseldorf, 1971).

more socialistic orientation and extreme racism, proposing the incorporation of Holland into a Greater Germany. He thus became the main NSB associate of the SS, who dominated so much of German administration in the later stages of the Occupation.

Mussert's increasing complaints were rewarded when he was given the honorific title of Leader of the Netherlands People in December 1942, after which a Political Secretariat of State of the NSB was set up as a sort of shadow government. Mussert chose, however, not to head the secretariat, and Seyss-Inquart therefore named figures from the van Tonningen sector of the party. NSB members were given an increasing number of positions in local administration, and by 1943 seven of the eleven Dutch provinces had NSB commissars. A Nazi-style Dutch Labor Front was created in April 1942 to replace the outlawed trade unions but enjoyed only limited success. The NSB maintained its own militia and a fairly elaborate roster of secondary associations. Though greatly manipulated by the Germans, "the NSB was a real force in the life of the Dutch community, and its activities were often the focus of more attention than were the activities of the German authorities." [129] Approximately half a million Dutch workers were sent for labor service in Germany, and seventeen thousand young Dutchmen volunteered for the Waffen-SS, one of the highest recruitment rates in occupied Europe. Thus the ethnic, linguistic, and cultural affinities between Holland and Germany helped to generate a greater degree of collaboration, and even of partial fascistization, than in the rest of western Europe. The influence of Mussert began to wane in mid-1943, but the radical wing of his party then came to the fore, supported by the SS and plumping for direct incorporation into Germany. In the last phase of the war, some forty thousand NSB members and their families fled with the retreating Germans, but Mussert refused to run. At the very end he conducted a purge of the ultra-Nazis in the NSB, expelling van Tonningen. After the liberation there were more than 120,000 arrests of collaborationists, proportionately the highest figure in western Europe, and Mussert was among the much smaller number executed. [130]

In Belgium the degree of collaboration was less than in Holland, but the roster of participating organizations was somewhat more complex, due especially to the tension between the two main ethnolinguistic sectors of the Belgian population, the French-speaking Walloons and the Flemish. German administration was headed by a *Militärbefehlshaber* (military commander for Belgium and northeastern France), with civil administration supervised by the secretaries-general of the regular ministries in the Belgian bureaucracy (the

129. W. Warmbrunn, *The Dutch under German Occupation, 1940–1945* (Stanford, 1963), 83.

130. G. Hirschfeld, *Nazi Rule and Dutch Collaboration* (New York, 1988), and Y. Durand, *Le nouvel ordre européen nazi, 1938–1945* (Brussels, 1990), 78–80, 164–69, 208–14, 231–33.

same arrangement as in Holland). The only Belgian organization that had assumed fascist characteristics during the 1930s had been the tiny Verdinaso, which sought a common authoritarian system for both Belgium and Holland. Its leader, Joris van Severen, was imprisoned at the beginning of hostilities and killed by Belgian soldiers during their retreat.[131]

German policy in Belgium was preoccupied with the Flemish sector of the population, considered a redeemable Germanic people who might be closely associated with the Reich.[132] The main Flemish nationalist party, Staf de Clercq's Flemish National Federation (VNV), was not a fascist movement but an eclectic populist party that had a broad following. The German authorities concentrated their support on the VNV, by 1941 giving its representatives control of several Belgian ministries and appointing VNV members to many regional positions in Flanders. The party grew considerably, claiming one hundred thousand members by early 1942 (very possibly an exaggeration) and expanding its various auxiliary organizations.

The main radical nationalist force in French-speaking Wallonia was Léon Degrelle's Rexist movement, which had been in decline before the war even as it moved further toward the radical right. Rexists served their country faithfully during the brief military campaign and then were ignored by the German administration. By the close of 1940, however, Degrelle decided to adopt a policy of full collaboration and transform his party into a New Order fascist-type movement. This cost Rex a significant proportion of the fifteen to twenty thousand members it had had at the outbreak of the war, though membership was rebuilt to the level of ten thousand or so by 1943. Degrelle decided to emphasize military participation in the Third Reich's "European crusade" on the eastern front, forming a volunteer legion of Walloons in 1941 that was transformed into a Waffen-SS brigade at the end of the following year, while Flemish volunteers formed their own separate unit. Rex also developed a domestic militia, the Formations de Combat, and organized a variety of auxiliary groups, including a labor corps, and two other paramilitary formations to assist in German guard duty and in police work.

For most Belgians, and especially the great majority of Walloons, German occupation soon revived memories of similar harsh experiences under German rule during World War I, so that an initial mood of resignation[133] was followed

131. In the absence of its founder, Verdinaso tried to strike deals with other collaborationist groups but later faded away. The right-radical Légion Nationale formed a joint action pact with Verdinaso in August 1940 but subsequently moved in the opposite direction, becoming antifascist, royalist, and Belgicist.

132. W. Wagner, *Belgien in der deutschen Politik während des Zweiten Weltkrieges* (Boppard, 1974).

133. J. Gotovitch and J. Gérard-Libois, *L'an quarante: La Belgique occupée* (Brussels, 1971).

by 1942 by a broad consensus favoring various forms of opposition and resistance.[134] Loyalty of the Rexists to the Third Reich was rewarded late in 1941 when German authorities began to give Rexists an increasing number of posts in local government and administration, until by 1943 they governed nearly all the larger French-speaking cities. All this in turn drew upon the small cadres of Rex the increasing hatred of most Belgians, and during the course of the war several hundred Rexists (and sometimes also members of their families) were assassinated by the resistance. Degrelle spent a large part of his time on the eastern front, where he compiled a distinguished combat record that drew generous praise from Hitler. Ideologically, Rex underwent increasing Nazification. Degrelle eventually invented an equivalent Germanic identity for Walloons as well as Flemish speakers and declared Belgium part of "Germanic space," but this renunciation of a distinct Belgian identity made Rexists the more hated. Rex's narrow recruitment base lay among small sectors of the urban middle and working classes, but as the war continued its propaganda increasingly accentuated the call to "social revolution" through authoritarian mobilization, racial identity, and corporative economic reorganization, making a special effort to recruit workers. There was a mounting tendency to ape the SS, until Rex became one of the most "Germanized" of all collaborationist movements. By 1944 Degrelle espoused a kind of "Eurofascism" whereby the Nazi cause had become that of all racially superior elements regardless of prewar nationality.[135]

The VNV moved in the opposite direction. Hendrik Elias, who succeeded de Clercq after the latter's sudden death in 1942, turned the Flemish movement in a more moderate and conciliatory direction, defascistizing rather than fascistizing it. This only encouraged the VNV's one-time German backers to look elsewhere, and by 1943 the Flemish movement was becoming increasingly demoralized. Two small new Nazi-type movements in Flanders, De Vlag and the SS-Vlaanderen, provided extremist competition. The SS-Vlaanderen and a tiny Flemish Nationalist Workers Party sought direct annexation by the Reich, and during the later phases of the war De Vlag and the SS-Vlaanderen received strong support from the German authorities and particularly the SS, organizing military volunteers and forming small paramilitary police units. After fleeing Belgium in the autumn of 1944, these two proto-Nazi groups were permitted

134. G. Jacquemyns, *La société belge sous l'occupation allemande* (Brussels, 1945). John Gillingham, in *Belgian Business in the Nazi New Order* (Ghent, 1977), treats economic collaboration.

135. Martin Conway, in *Collaboration in Belgium: Léon Degrelle and the Rexist Movement in Belgium, 1940–1944* (New Haven, 1993), provides a detailed study, suggesting that in 1943–44 Rex had about 8,000 regular members, 600–850 in the Formations de Combat, 1,850 men in the Waffen-SS, 1,500 men doing guard duty, 2,000 children and adolescents in the youth groups, 300–500 men in the paramilitary police, 1,600 men in the auxiliary German transport corps, and 600–700 women in three women's groups (220).

to form a brief Flemish government-in-exile in Hanover. Between 1944 and 1949 approximately fifty-seven thousand people were prosecuted for collaboration in Belgium (proportionately rather more in Flanders than in Wallonia) and fifty-three thousand convicted, overall a distinctly lower rate of indictment and conviction than in Holland.[136] Degrelle alone among the major figures survived, flying in a small plane at the very end of the war from German-occupied Norway to a crash landing at the water's edge of the northern Spanish coast, a dramatic escape that reflected his daredevil adventurism. He was allowed to remain in Spain, where he became a reasonably prosperous businessman, later emerging in print to falsify history and to serve as a kind of living oracle to various European neofascist and right radical groups.

PUPPET FASCISTS IN EASTERN EUROPE

Czechoslovakia was the first country to undergo German occupation, and during the final months of the Czech Republic its leaders had turned the Czech system in a more authoritarian direction. Shortly after the Munich settlement the Czech parliament passed legislation to facilitate the transition to a more unified political structure. The main parties merged into an umbrella organization, the Party of National Unity, and later a formal censorship was imposed. All this was swept away, however, when German troops entered Prague in mid-March 1939.

The main Czech-inhabited territory was transformed into the Protectorate of Bohemia-Moravia, under the "protection" of the Reich. Konstantin von Neurath, a senior diplomat, became Reich protector, though the existing Czech administration was allowed to continue internal administration. It created a National Solidarity Movement as an all-Czech party that would renounce parliamentary democracy and announced by May 1939 that 98.4 percent of adult Czech males were registered, but this was simply a kind of all-purpose Czech front to facilitate collaboration and not a fascist party.

The preexisting petty Czech fascist parties were themselves expected to enter the NSM. The largest of these, the National Fascist Community (NOF), had made an effort to take over the new Czech government as German troops entered Prague, but the Germans refused to support so insignificant a group. The NOF soon disbanded itself, the Czech puppet administration apparently having successfully bribed its leader. Two even smaller fascist organizations, the National Socialist Workers and Peasants Party (or "Green Swastika"),

---

136. For general surveys of resistance and collaboration, see J. Willequet, *La Belgique sous la botte: Résistances et collaborations, 1940–1944* (Brussels, 1986), and Durand, *Le nouvel ordre* 801–81, 153–64, 204–8, 233–37.

active primarily in Moravia, and the National Socialist Guard of Slavonic Activists, drew even less support.[137]

The only Czech fascist party that generated greater activity was Vlajka, founded by a philosophy professor named Mares who sought to develop a Nazi-type organization on the basis of extreme philosophical vitalism. Vlajka had thirteen thousand members in 1939, and it formed a small militia called Svato-pulk Guards. It called for a full national socialist system in Bohemia-Moravia and carried out assaults on Jews, but when Vlajka members and remnants of the NOF rioted in May 1939, the Czech puppet administration was allowed to use the police against them. Four months later Vlajka renounced its semicom-pulsory membership in the NSM. When the Reich protector finally decided to dissolve the NSM in August 1940, the Svatopulk Guards tried to take over its headquarters, but once again the Germans refused support. Vlajka subse-quently went into irremediable decline, like its other Czech fascist competitors, though its remnants formed a new group called Activists, who supported full Nazification.[138]

There was very little Czech resistance to the German occupation, which, though harsh, was less so than elsewhere in east central Europe. In Septem-ber 1940 Hitler ruled that the "greater part of the Czech people" were racially redeemable and assimilable, and the following month a report from the Nazi Race and Settlement Head Office found that "the racial picture of the Czech people is considerably more favorable today than that of the Sudeten German population." [139]

In Greece the occupation puppet government continued in domestic ad-ministration much of the system of the former right radical dictatorship of Me-taxas. The Greek National Socialist Party of George Mercouris, which had had scarcely ten thousand members in 1936, failed to develop and soon faced the competition of an even more radical offshoot, the National Socialist Political Organization (ESPO). In addition, several small right radical nationalist groups also collaborated with the Occupation and sometimes formed anti-Communist police units.

The Greek Communist insurgency (ELAS) developed increasing strength and was successful in eliminating most of the competing conservative resis-tance groups. It also managed to decapitate several of the right radical nation-alist organizations by attentats and ambushes against their headquarters and leaders. Its most spectacular blow against Greek adversaries was its bombing

137. J. F. Zacek, "The Flaw in Masaryk's Democracy: Czech Fascism, ca. 1927–1942," unpublished, and V. Mastny, *The Czechs under Nazi Rule* (New York, 1971), 57–60.
138. Mastny, *Czechs* 62–63, 157–58.
139. Ibid., 128, 132.

of ESPO's Athens headquarters in September 1942, which killed forty-three Germans and twenty-nine ESPO members, including the latter's founder, a Dr. Sterodimos. ESPO had been actively recruiting right-wing former Greek officers and soldiers to create a Greek Legion of the Waffen-SS, but this ambition was never realized. ESPO itself soon had to be dissolved for lack of support.[140]

In occupied Serbia, the right radical Zbor (Convention) movement of Dimitrije Ljotić evolved into a more clearly fascist-type organization. Zbor had initially emphasized religion and work but had never gained more than 1 percent of the vote under its banner of a somewhat contradictory "Yugoslav nationalism." Ljotić seems always to have been a poor political tactician, and his movement was suppressed under the more representative Yugoslav government of 1939–41. During the Occupation, Zbor emphasized therapeutic violence and the organization of youth. Ljotić attempted to create "proletarian divisions" led by Zbor commissars to assist the Germans but only managed to form one small Volunteer Corps. Initially composed of about thirty-six hundred men, it was later expanded and seems to have compiled a comparatively good military record in combat against the Serbian Chetniks and Communist Partisans.[141] Ljotić was killed in a highway accident during his attempted flight from Yugoslavia in April 1945.

In the occupied territories of the Soviet Union, German forces sometimes obtained the collaboration of a number of right radical nationalist anti-Soviet groups, the most important of them in the Ukraine. Since the main part of the Ukraine had been organized after 1920 as a Soviet Socialist Republic with no autonomous political life, organized Ukrainian nationalism had been confined to Galicia (the western Ukraine), part of interwar Poland. There were a surprising number of Ukrainian nationalist groups, but clearly the most important was the Organization of Ukrainian Nationalists (OUN), founded in 1929. The principal Western historian of Ukrainian nationalism has judged that "the theory and teachings of the Nationalists were very close to Fascism, and in some respects, such as the insistence on 'racial purity,' even went beyond the original Fascist doctrines." [142] This was particularly the case with the stronger, more radical and youthful sector split off by Stepan Bandera (commonly referred to as the OUN-B). The OUN adopted a program of integral and authoritarian

140. H. Richter, *Griechenland zwischen Revolution und Konterrevolution (1936–1946)* (Frankfurt, 1973); J.-L. Houdros, *Occupation and Resistance: The Greek Agony, 1941–1944* (New York, 1963); H. Mavrocordatis, "Le fascisme en Grèce pendant la guerre (1941–1944)," in *Etudes sur le fascisme,* by M. Bardèche et al. (Paris, 1974), 98–102. The best general account of occupied Greece is M. Mazower, *Inside Hitler's Greece* (New Haven, 1993).

141. See the articles by Dimitrije Djordjević and Ivan Avakumović in P. F. Sugar, ed., *Native Fascism in the Successor States, 1918–1945* (Santa Barbara, 1971), 123–43.

142. J. A. Armstrong, *Ukrainian Nationalism* (New York, 1963), 280.

nationalism, emphasizing direct action and a romantic, mystical, nonrational, and vitalistic ideology. It stressed the distinct racial identity and racial purity of Ukrainians compared with inferior surrounding peoples, such as Russians. By 1944 the OUN had developed a national socialist (though not Nazi) program that propounded state ownership of heavy industry and transport, together with natural resources. Yet the OUN never adopted a fully and explicitly fascist program, and its 1944 conference endorsed "popular-democratic procedures," "freedom of thought," "the rule of law," and "civil rights for all national minorities." [143] It sought vainly to foster an independent Ukraine during World War II, sometimes collaborated with the Germans, and then became the main force behind the Ukrainian People's Army, an irregular national liberation force that did battle with the Soviet occupiers in the forest and countryside until as late as 1950.

PRO-AXIS SEMINEUTRALS: BULGARIA AND SPAIN

The royalist regime in Bulgaria occupied the most anomalous position of any in Europe during World War II. In March 1941 it signed the Tripartite Pact with Germany's allies but did not declare war on the Soviet Union or participate in the German invasion. Nonetheless, acting on Churchill's all-out policy of "the worse, the better," Great Britain declared war on Bulgaria on December 6, 1941, followed by the United States six months later. In February 1940 King Boris appointed a more pro-German government and then in Hitler's partial dismemberment of Romania received the territory of southern Dobrudja in return. Following the German conquest of Greece and Yugoslavia, Bulgaria was also given control of Macedonia. In September 1941 the docile Bulgarian parliament further increased the powers of the executive branch. That year the government enacted a state labor law, created a state youth organization, and began anti-Semitic legislation.

The relatively most successful of several right radical and protofascist organizations in Bulgaria during prewar years had been the Ratnitsi, or Warriors,[144] and the Union of Bulgarian National Legions, founded by General Christo Lukov. The Ratnitsi had been officially dissolved as a menace by the government in 1939 but not destroyed, whereas the Legions gained at least a little German support during the war and managed to expand somewhat. The Communist opposition nonetheless grew stronger during 1943 and launched a terrorist campaign that included among its successes the assassination of Lukov.

143. Ibid., 163–64.
144. Technically, the group was called Warriors or Fighters for the Advancement of the Bulgarian National Spirit.

The regency that followed the sudden death of Boris in September 1943 made clumsy efforts to achieve recognition of Bulgaria's neutrality, since it had never taken the initiative of declaring war on or attacking any other country. As the Red Army entered the Balkans, however, the Soviet Union declared war on Bulgaria on September 5, 1944. Four days later the army officers' group Zveno (the Link) carried out a coup against its own government in order to form a Popular Front regime with the Communists and others, erroneously thinking that this would earn better treatment from Stalin. The new regime began to hunt down members of right radical and protofascist groups, though the Zveno officers themselves would later be dismissed by the Communists as mere "left fascists." In Vienna German authorities sponsored a Bulgarian government-in-exile under the right radical leader Professor Tsankov, and a separate Macedonian equivalent under the Macedonian nationalist terrorist (IMRO) leader Ivan Mihailov. Though one Bulgarian SS regiment was formed to fight in Yugoslavia, the new Bulgarian Popular Front government committed twelve divisions to the war against Germany. Thus Bulgaria, which received at varying times declarations of war from Britain, the United States, and the Soviet Union, engaged in its only significant military action on the side of these former enemies. During this final phase of the war and afterward, hundreds, possibly thousands, of "fascists" were condemned and executed by new Communist-style "people's courts" in Bulgaria.[145]

In Spain the Franco regime, thanks partly to its favorable geographic location, managed to maneuver much more successfully. It achieved power through its final victory in the Spanish Civil War (April 1939), which would not have been possible without the military assistance of Italy and Germany. Though not himself an ideological fascist sensu stricto, Franco strongly identified with the Axis and with a "new order" of nationalist organic and authoritarian regimes in Europe. In the final days of the Civil War, he had signed Germany's Anti-Comintern Pact and then withdrew Spain from the League of Nations. Yet the approach of general war in the following summer was an alarming prospect, both because of Spain's weak and exposed position and because the object of Hitler's invasion—the Polish state—was itself a nationalist semiauthoritarian and Catholic regime that had certain things in common with the new Spanish system. Franco therefore followed a policy which he labeled "adroit prudence" and declared Spain's neutrality in the opening phase of the European war.

At that point Franco theoretically wielded greater formal power within his own country than did Hitler, Stalin, or Mussolini in theirs. These three leaders

145. M. L. Miller, *Bulgaria during the Second World War* (Stanford, 1975); R. Solliers, "Notes sur le fascisme bulgare," in Bardèche et al., *Etudes* 166–73; N. Poppetrov, "Ideino-politicheskite skhvashtaniia na 'Suiuz Natsionalni Legioni' i 'Ratnitsi za Napreduka na Bulgarshtinata' v godinite na Vtorata Svetovna Voina," *Istoricheski Pregled* 47:6 (1991): 53–67.

were at least theoretically restrained by political structures and laws (however insignificant in practice), whereas Franco was dictator of Spain by conquest with theoretically unlimited powers. His regime was an eclectic mixture of a right-wing military elite, a fascist state party (the Falange, or FET), and various sectors of conservatives and monarchists, all buttressed by the strong support of a revitalized, neotraditional Catholicism—a unique blend without an exact parallel in any other country.

The FET claimed a nominal male membership of 650,000, which swelled to an all-time high of 900,000 by 1942, making it officially by far the largest political organization in Spanish history. It was in charge of building the state syndical (labor) organization, of organizing youth, and of developing state propaganda, while providing much of the personnel for the new government bureaucracy. Nonetheless, the Falange was even more subordinate than the Fascist Party in Italy. Its national youth organization remained restricted, at no time organizing more than about 17.5 percent of Spanish boys and 8.5 percent of girls, while its militia organization was similarly reduced and kept under strict army control. The most influential force, after Franco himself, was the military command. Between 1938 and 1945 senior officers held 46 percent of all ministerial appointments and 37 percent of other top governmental positions, compared with 38 and 30 percent, respectively, for Falangists.[146] Franco's limitation of Falangist influence and his obvious disinterest in carrying out a thoroughgoing "national syndicalist revolution" (the original Falangist goal) led to an abortive Falangist plot to assassinate him in 1940.[147] Though most Falangists served loyally, an undercurrent of Falangist opposition lingered to the end of the regime.[148]

Franco's foreign policy changed rather drastically with the fall of France. Much as Mussolini hastened to enter the war at that point, Franco also wanted to be on the winning side. Spain's official position was changed from neutrality to technical "nonbelligerence" (the same as Italy's policy between September 1939 and June 1940), clearly tilted toward the Axis. At the same time, Britain had not yet been defeated, and its control of the Atlantic could wreak havoc with a war-ravaged Spanish economy heavily dependent on imports. During the second half of 1940 Franco therefore made clear to Hitler his willingness to enter the war on the side of the Axis, provided that Germany would guarantee extensive military and economic assistance, as well as the cession to Spain of

146. See my *The Franco Regime, 1936–1975* (Madison, 1987), 231–65, and P. Preston, *The Politics of Revenge: Fascism and the Military in 20th Century Spain* (London, 1990).

147. This is recounted in A. Romero Cuesta, *Objetivo: Matar a Franco* (Madrid, 1976).

148. S. M. Ellwood, *Spanish Fascism in the Franco Era* (London, 1987); J. Onrubia Revuelta, ed., *Historia de la oposición falangista al régimen de Franco en sus documentos* (Madrid, 1989).

Serrano Súñer, Franco, and Mussolini at Bordighera, February 12, 1941

much of French Northwest Africa, including all of Morocco and northwestern Algeria. This Hitler would not do, since he could not afford to alienate his important satellite of Vichy France or to ignore Italian ambitions in North Africa. The decision that Spain would not enter the war was thus in a sense made by Hitler rather than Franco.

Falangists lead a mass anti-Soviet demonstration in the center of Madrid on June 24, 1941, two days after Germany's invasion of the USSR

Ramón Serrano Súñer while Spanish Minister of the Interior, 1940

Falangists became more assertive in Spanish affairs during 1941–42, when German military victory seemed imminent. This led to two internal crises in May 1941 and August–September 1942, each adroitly handled by Franco to maintain the same eclectic balance of forces within his regime.[149] The German invasion of Russia momentarily sparked keen enthusiasm for it seemed to re-establish the terms of the Spanish Civil War between the revolutionary left and the authoritarian right. A "Blue Division" (named for the Falangist shirt color) of twenty thousand volunteers subsequently fought with the German army on the eastern front for nearly two years, and remnants of it remained with the German forces until the very end near the Führer bunker in Berlin.[150] Conversely, the fall of Mussolini was a sobering blow to Franco, and in the autumn of 1943 Spain resumed official neutrality.[151] Hitler occasionally toyed with the notion of

149. P. Preston, *Franco* (London, 1993), 432–73.

150. The Blue Division may have generated more literature than any other division in any army of World War II. For a guide, see C. Caballero Jurado and R. Ibáñez Hernández, *Escritores en las trincheras: La División Azul en sus libros, publicaciones periódicas y filmografía (1941–1988)* (Barcelona, 1989).

151. J. Tusell and G. G. Queipo de Llano, *Franco y Mussolini* (Barcelona, 1985).

a German-backed Spanish conspiracy to unseat Franco (whom he came to term a "Latin charlatan") in favor of a Falangist-dominated, completely pro-Nazi government, but he found no effective opportunity.[152]

As early as 1942 a process of relative defascistization of the Spanish regime had begun, culminating in the years 1945–47 with the nominal redefinition of the Spanish state as a corporative, Catholic monarchy. Regime spokesmen first began to redefine political doctrine to downplay the significance of the term *totalitarian* in the Falangist program. In September 1942 Franco relieved his pro-Fascist brother-in-law, Ramón Serrano Súñer, as foreign minister, replacing him with a politically more neutral general. In the following year a corporative parliament, rather similar to that of Mussolini's regime, was introduced, as a gesture toward some degree of representation beyond a purely dictatorial executive. Defascistization was accelerated with the decline of Nazi Germany in 1944. By the following year it was forbidden to make the slightest comparison between Spain on the one hand and Italy or Germany on the other. The fascist salute, official since 1937, was now outlawed, the FET budget reduced, Falangist activities drastically curtailed, and the organization left without a secretary-general. Though the "National Movement," as the FET was now antiseptically called, was not dissolved, the regime labored mightily to recast its image as that of a Catholic, organic, and corporative system, based on church, profession, municipality, and family—a system that supposedly had never favored the Axis or sought to imitate it politically. By 1947 the Spanish state was officially reconstituted as a monarchy—though without a king. Franco served as regent for life. In fact, the process of defascistization would continue for another thirty years, down to the time of Franco's death in 1975, as one vestige after another of the fascist era was slowly but eventually dismantled.[153]

A major factor in the totally different outcomes in Bulgaria and in Spain, where a more fascistized semineutral regime nonetheless survived, was simply geographic location. The former lay in the path of the advancing Red Army in the east, whereas the Western Allies—despite deep antipathy to Franco and his regime—were not willing to intervene militarily in a country with which they were not at war. Stalin, needless to say, possessed no such scruples. Though ostracized by all major powers for several years after 1945, Franco and his regime were nonetheless able to maintain domestic control of Spain, until the outbreak of the Cold War relieved the pressure and altered the scenario, even-

---

152. K.-J. Ruhl, *Spanien im Zweiten Weltkrieg: Franco, die Falange und das "Dritte Reich"* (Hamburg, 1975). For other studies of Spanish domestic politics during these years, see J. L. Garcia Delgado, ed., *El primer franquismo: España durante la Segunda Guerra Mundial* (Madrid, 1989), and J. Tusell et al., eds., *El régimen de Franco (1936–1975)*, vol. 1 (Madrid, 1993).

153. Payne, *Franco Regime* 343–621.

tually enabling Franco to negotiate a strategic military pact with the United States in 1953.

THE DESTRUCTION OF FASCISM AND NATIONAL SOCIALISM

In its final phase, more than ever before, fascism presented itself as an all-European movement, indeed the only pan-Europeanist movement (in the form adopted by propaganda after 1941). Though this managed to convince a small minority, it was too self-contradictory and too contradicted by circumstances to appeal to most Europeans. At the very end, fascist spokesmen in the SS and in some of the other fascist groups took refuge in what they considered the indestructibility of the fascistic and racial ideal. This was the position taken by the SS journal *Das Schwarze Korps* at the beginning of April 1945, though its acceptance of material defeat had to be disavowed at Goebbels's insistence.[154] Hitler's own final statements were, not surprisingly, contradictory. On the one hand, he declared that the future lay with the "stronger Eastern peoples" who had, with Western aid, defeated the Wehrmacht, yet on the other, he continued to hold to his philosophical and racial principles, declaring that the subordination of the superior German people would be only temporary. Their racial and cultural superiority would eventually in some fashion win out. Near his dying breath, he responded to a subordinate's query about what there was left to work for with the standard revolutionary reference to the "new man," the higher form of human being.

Fascism and National Socialism, like all other institutionalized modern authoritarian systems in Europe to that time, were neither overthrown from within nor eroded in power but destroyed from the outside by military defeat. The fate of nearly all European fascist movements had become increasingly bound to Nazi Germany, which established such control or hegemony over them that the fascists—the most extreme nationalists in European history—paradoxically in most cases lost their own national sovereignty in the process. The pitiful puppet position of Mussolini symbolized what was in fact a common situation. Fascism, arguably the most self-contradictory of all modern revolutionary and utopian movements, had become its own self-negation and, militarily, in the form of Hitler's own virtual "all or nothing" formulation, its own self-destruction. Nearly all fascist movements, with only a few minor exceptions, had appealed to war as the ultimate test, the nation's most validating mission. To have failed in the final test of what was largely—even though not exclusively—a fascist war put the seal on the inviability and self-destructiveness of the fascist enterprise. It was appropriate that the most

154. Cf. H. Trevor-Roper, ed., *The Goebbels Diaries* (London, 1978), 311.

philosophically militaristic of all modern movements [155] should meet complete military disaster, and that a struggle which took the form of such total and extreme warfare itself should undergo a destruction almost equally complete.

Even though the great majority of fascist movements had been altogether unsuccessful in peacetime as well, the final defeat was so thorough and unconditional that fascism was itself discredited to a degree unprecedented among major modern political movements. The processes of defascistization, de-Nazification, and prosecution of collaborators carried out so unevenly all across Europe would not in themselves punish or proscribe most fascists, at least among the rank and file, [156] but the political discrediting of the movement and ideology was so definitive that the settlement and aftermath of World War II would be quite different from the aftermath of World War I. Even though the years after 1945 seemed to be witnessing yet another armed truce of a different sort than that of interwar Europe, they would in fact constitute a unique and distinctive kind of historical transition to a very different era.

155. The reference here is to fascist doctrine and the will to go to war, not to the most extensive institutional structures of militarization, which would of course be found in Communist regimes.

156. Nominally the most extreme and thorough theoretical defascistization was the massive Stalinist purge in the reconquered territories of the Soviet Union. It carried off millions of people to the Gulag, many hundreds of thousands of whom died as a direct result. Very few of these, however, were genuine fascists. Any defascistization was merely incidental to a sweeping purge determined to eliminate any potential vestige of dissidence. All over Soviet-occupied eastern Europe, most rank-and-file former fascist party members, together with many lower-level leaders, were welcomed to fill the ranks of the initially exiguous local Communist parties. The psychological transition seems to have been an easy one, for obvious reasons. On de-Nazification in western Germany, see E. Davidson, *The Trial of the Germans* (New York, 1966); B. F. Smith, *The Road to Nuremberg* (New York, 1981); and A. Tusa, *The Nuremberg Trial* (New York, 1984).

Proportionately the most extensive prosecutions of collaborators in western Europe occurred in Holland and Belgium. The greatest number of executions outside the Soviet Union, however, took place in Italy and France, where thousands of fascists and collaborators were killed summarily by political vigilante groups and Communist squads. Estimates of the total killed in France range from as many as 40,000 to a low of 7,306, the latter calculation being presented by Peter Novick, in *The Resistance versus Vichy* (New York, 1968). There is a partial consensus regarding an approximate figure of 10,000 or more, as in H. R. Lottman, *The Purge: The Purification of French Collaborators after World War II* (New York, 1986), and several others. Probably the most reliable is P. Bourdrel, *L'épuration sauvage*, 2 vols. (Paris, 1988), which lists a total of 163,000 prosecutions in France. These resulted in 26,289 prison sentences, 10,434 commitments to hard labor, 2,777 life sentences, and 7,037 death sentences, of which 791 were legally carried out. The number of summary executions was much greater: Bourdrel estimates them as a minimum of 10,000 and a maximum of 20,000.

PART II
Interpretation

12
Interpretations of Fascism

Ever since the March on Rome, analysts and other writers have sought to formulate an interpretation or theory capable of explaining fascism. As the only genuinely novel form of radicalism emerging from World War I, and one that seemed to involve multiple ambiguities if not outright contradictions, fascism did not obviously lend itself easily to monocausal explanations or simple theories—though that did not deter many commentators. The first attempts to provide an interpretation came from Italian opponents, such as Luigi Salvatorelli and other liberals, and from Socialists and Communists. The issue was addressed by the Comintern as early as 1922, and indeed the main activity in generalizing the concept was carried on by Communists and other leftists, for purposes of promoting antifascism. The term *fascist* was being widely applied in some European countries, especially Spain, by the early 1930s; it was increasingly applied as a pejorative for political opponents, though on a few occasions some accepted it as a badge of honor. It became widely used in the Soviet Union, both as a term with which to smear opponents and also as a basic synonym for German National Socialism, the latter an awkward term that struck too close to home for Communist comfort. The Italian Communist dissident Angelo Tasca early observed that to define fascism was to write its history, and after 1945 Western historiography concentrated on monographic study of individual countries and movements. Subsequently the "fascism debate" of the 1960s and 1970s, touched off especially by Ernst Nolte's *Der Faschismus in seiner Epoche* (1963), refocused scholarly attention on the general concept, but no consensus has ever been achieved concerning an explanatory interpretation or theory, or even a complete and precise definition.

The principal interpretations of fascism have been directed toward defining the underlying nature of this presumed genus of politics, toward its over-

441

all significance, or, more commonly, toward its principal sources or causes.[1] The main interpretations may for the sake of convenience be summarized in thirteen categories, with the understanding that these concepts are not mutually exclusive but in some cases may draw upon each other. Fascism has been considered a violent, dictatorial agent of bourgeois capitalism; a unique radicalism of the middle classes; a twentieth-century form of "Bonapartism"; a typical manifestation of twentieth-century totalitarianism; a new form of "authoritarian polyocracy"; a cultural revolution; a product of cultural, moral, or sociopsychological pathologies; a product of the rise of amorphous masses; a consequence of unique national histories; a reaction against modernization; a product of the struggle for modernization or a stage of socioeconomic growth; and a unique metapolitical phenomenon. Finally, some analysts have denied that any such general phenomenon as generic fascism can be defined or identified.

Before briefly examining each of these interpretations, we should face the fact that few of those who attempt to develop a causal theory or explanatory concept of fascism define exactly what they mean by the term or specifically identify which parties or movements they seek to interpret, beyond a primary reference which is normally to National Socialism alone. The absence of an empirical definition of what is meant by *fascism* has been an obstacle to conceptual clarification.

---

1. The principal studies of the interpretations of fascism are W. Wippermann, *Faschismustheorien* (Darmstadt, 1989); Renzo De Felice, *Interpretations of Fascism* (Cambridge, Mass., 1977); A. J. Gregor, *Interpretations of Fascism* (Morristown, N.J., 1974); G. Schulz, *Faschismus-Nationalsozialismus: Versionen und theoretische Kontroversen, 1922–1972* (Frankfurt, 1974); H. Grebing, *Aktuelle Theorien über Faschismus und Konservatismus* (Stuttgart, 1974); R. Saage, *Faschismustheorien* (Munich, 1976); G. Schreiber, *Hitler: Interpretationen, 1923–1983* (Darmstadt, 1984); F. Perfetti, *Il dibattito sul fascismo* (Rome, 1984); L. Bossle et al., *Sozialwissenschaftliche Kritik am Begriff und an der Erscheinungsweise des Faschismus* (Würzburg, 1979); M. A. Saba, *Il dibattito sul fascismo* (Milan, 1976); L. L. Pera, *Il fascismo dalla polemica alla storiografia* (Florence, 1975); and P. Ayçoberry, *The Nazi Question* (New York, 1981). Two good summaries and analyses of the historiography and interpretations in Italy and Germany down to 1985 concerning the two main movements and regimes are E. Gentile, "Fascism in Italian Historiography: In Search of an Individual Historical Identity," *JCH* 21:2 (April 1986): 179–208, and in the same issue, W. Hofer, "Fifty Years On: Historians and the Third Reich" 225–51.

The chief anthologies are De Felice's *Il fascismo: Le interpretazioni dei contemporanei e degli storici* (Rome, 1970); E. Nolte, ed., *Theorien über den Faschismus* (Cologne, 1967); T. Pirker, ed., *Komintern und Faschismus 1920 bis 1940* (Stuttgart, 1965); P. Alatri, *L'antifascismo italiano* (Rome, 1961); C. Casucci, *Il fascismo* (Bologna, 1961); L. Cavalli, ed., *Il fascismo nell'analisi sociologica* (Bologna, 1975); J. Jacobelli, *Il fascismo e gli storici oggi* (Bari, 1988); W. Abendroth et al., *Faschismus und Kapitalismus* (Frankfurt, 1967); R. Kühnl, ed., *Texte zur Faschismusdiskussion 1* (Reinbek, 1974), which presents mainly Marxist theories; and idem, ed., *Faschismustheorien: Texte zur Faschismusdiskussion 2* (Reinbek, 1979), which presents other interpretations.

FASCISM AS A VIOLENT, DICTATORIAL AGENT OF BOURGEOIS CAPITALISM

The notion that fascism is primarily to be understood as the agent of "capitalism," "big business," "finance capital," the "bourgeoisie," "state monopoly capitalism" (Stamokap), or some conceivable combination thereof is one of the oldest and most widely disseminated interpretations, having for many decades served as the official Communist theory of fascism. It was formulated to some extent even before Italian Fascism was organized (to explain Mussolini's defection from orthodox socialism) and began to be given currency, with primary reference to Italy, as early as 1923 in the formulations of the Hungarian Communist Gyula Šaš and the Russian German Sandomirsky.[2] Though dissident or more critical-minded Communists would later offer more complex and sophisticated interpretations,[3] the "agent theory" was adopted as the official Third International interpretation of fascism (including German National Socialism) in 1924 and was officially codified by 1935 in the definition of *fascism* as "the open terrorist dictatorship of the most reactionary, most chauvinist, and most imperialist elements of finance capital."[4] Leading Western Marxist exponents of the concept in the 1930s were R. Palme Dutt and Daniel Guérin.[5]

The Communist agent theory also bore with it the concept of a sort of "panfascism," which held that after fascism appeared as the instrument of finance capital, all other forces "serving" capitalism were also "objectively fascist." This included not merely all right authoritarian forces and regimes but also, most prominently and insidiously, social democrats who "collaborated" with capitalist forces in democratic systems. Thus as early as 1924 Socialists became "social fascists"—objectively the most dangerous "fascists" of all because they purportedly represented the workers. The "panfascist" and "social fascists" doctrines were only partially altered in 1935, after the Soviet leadership began to take the danger of genuine fascism more seriously and to measure the alternatives more objectively.

The agent theory reached its height of elaboration and refinement after

2. G. Šaš, *Der Faschismus in Italien* (Hamburg, 1923); G. Sandomirsky, *Fashizm*, 2 vols. (Moscow, 1923).

3. Fritz Sternberg theorized that the fascist state represented the highest stage of imperialism and those sectors of capitalism most oriented toward imperialism, in his *Der Faschismus an der Macht* (Amsterdam, 1935). See Gruppe Arbeiterpolitik, eds., *Der Faschismus in Deutschland: Analysen der KPD-Opposition aus den jahren 1928 bis 1933* (Frankfurt, 1973), and the excellent summary in Wippermann, *Faschismustheorien* 43–49.

4. W. Wippermann, *Zur Analyse des Faschismus: Die sozialistischen und kommunistischen Faschismustheorien, 1921–1945* (Frankfurt, 1981); Pirker, ed., *Komintern und Faschismus;* D. Beetham, ed., *Marxists in Face of Fascism* (Totowa, N.J., 1984).

5. R. Dutt, *Fascism and Social Revolution* (London, 1934); D. Guérin, *Fascisme et grand capital* (Paris, 1936).

World War II, particularly in East Germany, where "Stamokap" was official doctrine. The interpretation of Nazism, in particular, became a major source of difference between scholars in the two Germanies, though some in West Germany also adopted the agent theory.[6] This reached a crescendo in the decade 1965–75, the time of the last major phase of Marxist hysteria in the Western world.[7]

The reductio ad absurdum of all agent theories was formed almost simultaneously in the Soviet Union, when some of the rapidly multiplying Russian anti-Semitic ideologues developed the notion that fascism, most prominently Nazism, had itself been a "Jewish plot." According to Trofim Kichko and certain other Russian anti-Semitic mythomaniacs,

> The idea of Judaism is the idea of world fascism. The Old Testament was fascist; so were Moses, King Solomon, and virtually all other Jewish leaders from the very beginning. The Jews had always been chauvinist aggressors and mass murderers. . . . Hitler and the other Nazi leaders had been mere puppets in their hands. . . . They had connived with Hitler at the destruction of poor Jews during the Second World War, but the number . . . killed had been grossly exaggerated. The aim of this intrigue was to get international sanction for the establishment of the state of Israel. But Israel was a mere sideshow; the real aim was world domination.[8]

6. There is a good summary in the 1976 edition of Wippermann, *Faschismustheorien* 19–37, 49–55. See also the analysis in Gregor, *Interpretations* 128–70, and W. Wippermann, "The Post-War German Left and Fascism," *JCH* 11:4 (Oct. 1976): 185–219. Slightly revised and more sophisticated versions of the agent theory may be found in B. Lopukhov, *Fashizm i rabochoe dvizhenie v Italii, 1919–1929* (Moscow, 1968); A. Galkin, "Capitalist Society and Fascism," *Social Sciences: USSR Academy of Sciences* 2 (1970): 128–38; R. Kühnl, *Formen bürgerlicher Herrschaft* (Hamburg, 1971); and M. Vajda, *Fascism as a Mass Movement* (London, 1976). The last major collection of Stamokap writings was D. Eichholtz and K. Gossweiler, eds., *Faschismusforschung: Positionen Probleme Polemik* (East Berlin, 1980).

For more sophisticated interpretations of the influence of major industry in the Third Reich, see D. Stegmann, "Zum Verhältnis von Grossindustrie und Nationalsozialismus, 1930–1933," *Archiv für Sozialgeschichte* 13 (1973): 399–482; D. Petzina, *Autarkiepolitik im Dritten Reich: Der nationalsozialistische "Vierjahresplan"* (Stuttgart, 1968); idem, *Die deutsche Wirtschaft in der Zwischenkriegszeit* (Wiesbaden, 1977); and R. Neebe, *Grossindustrie, Staat und NSDAP, 1930–1933* (Göttingen, 1981). Two of the broader theoretical treatments of the economic interpretations of fascism (though, as always, primarily Nazism) are A. Kuhn, *Das faschistische Herrschaftssystem und die moderne Gesellschaft* (Hamburg, 1973), and N. Kadritzke, *Faschismus und Krise* (Frankfurt, 1976).

The definitive demolishing of the agent theory of Nazism will be found in H. A. Turner Jr., *German Big Business and the Rise of Hitler* (New York, 1985).

7. A good critique of New Left neo-Marxist concepts of fascism may be found in H. A. Winkler, *Revolution, Staat, Faschismus* (Göttingen, 1978).

8. W. Laqueur, *Black Hundred: The Rise of the Extreme Right in Russia* (New York, 1993), 106.

This became the ultimate agent theory. Such interpretations had themselves become a part of the very delusion they purported to explain.

FASCISM AS THE EXPRESSION OF A UNIQUE RADICALISM OF THE MIDDLE CLASSES

A different social-class concept of fascism has been suggested by several observers and scholars who did not see fascism as the agent of a bourgeoisie but rather as the vehicle of sectors of the middle classes, previously denied status among the national elite, to forge a new national system that would give them a more salient role. This interpretation was first suggested by Luigi Salvatorelli in his *Nazionalfascismo* (1923), when he underscored the role of the "humanistic petite bourgeoisie"—civil servants, the professionally educated—seeking to restructure the Italian state and society against both the higher capitalist bourgeoisie and the workers.[9] His interpretation has drawn considerable support from the leading student of Italian Fascism, Renzo De Felice, and also from the official historian of that movement, Gioacchino Volpe.[10] It largely coincides with the thesis of Seymour Lipset that fascism is the "radicalism of the center."[11]

This approach explains the social recruitment of part of the base of certain major fascist parties and also accounts for certain aspects of the fascist program. Yet it is limited in its explanatory ability, for it fails to account for the number of fascist supporters outside the middle classes in such diverse countries as Germany, Hungary, and Romania. Nor is it able to explain the full nature and extent of radical goals among leaders as different as Hitler, Déat, Piasecki, and Codreanu. The "radicalism of the middle classes" thus accounts for one of the most important strands of fascism but is inadequate to provide a general theory of fascism.

---

9. The Italian Socialist Giovanni Zibordi was in fact one of the first analysts to define Fascism as a "counterrevolution" that did not primarily mobilize the traditional right but rather the broader middle classes, particularly the lower-middle stratum, as he emphasized shortly before the March on Rome. Zibordi, "Critica socialista del fascismo," in *Il fascismo e i partiti politici: Studi di scrittori di tutti partiti* (Bologna, 1922), 1–61, condensed in Nolte, ed., *Theorien* 79–87.

The importance of the mobilization of the middle classes (and even of some workers) for Italian Fascism was also underlined by Clara Zetkin in her speech to the Comintern executive in June 1923 (Nolte 88–11) and was stressed in the subsequent analyses of the Italian Communists Gramsci and Togliatti (see chapter 4).

10. De Felice, *Interpretations* 130, 174–92; idem, *Fascism: An Informal Introduction to Its Theory and Practice* (New Brunswick, N.J., 1976); G. Volpe, *Storia del movimento fascista* (Milan, 1939), 46–47.

11. S. M. Lipset, "Fascism—Left, Right and Center," in his *Political Man* (New York, 1960), chap. 5.

FASCISM AS A TWENTIETH-CENTURY FORM OF "BONAPARTISM"

The inaccuracy of the mere "agent" theory became clear to more perceptive and objective observers, including some Marxists, during the first years of Italian Fascism.[12] The interpretation of "Bonapartism" by Marx and Engels following the establishment of the Second Empire as an authoritarian system in France under Louis-Napoleon in 1852 was invoked by the Austrian Socialist Julius Braunthal at the close of 1922 to explain how in a situation of sociopolitical fragmentation ("equilibrium of social forces") a new force might create independent state power that did not rest solely on the interests of one social class, even though in the economic realm it might guarantee the "class interests of the bourgeoisie." [13] The "Bonapartist" interpretation was further elaborated by the dissident German Communist August Thalheimer, who explained fascism as the product of a political and social crisis in which traditional forms of class domination were no longer effective and in which competing forces canceled each other out, allowing a new form of dictatorship to free itself of class domination. Though fascism might benefit some sectors more than others, it served as a political force above all and could enjoy a transitory independent success until the weight of other factors shifted against it.[14]

Subsequent variations on or reiterations of the Bonapartist theory were made by quite a number of other Socialist writers, especially the Austrian Otto Bauer and the German Rudolf Hilferding.[15] Later theorists of the postwar Soviet bloc such as Alexander Galkin and Mihaly Vajda also incorporated aspects of this interpretation. Not surprisingly, there was general agreement among those who employed the Bonapartist theory that the "independence of the state" was greater in Nazi Germany than in Fascist Italy.[16]

12. On the original Marxist concept, see W. Wippermann, *Die Bonapartismustheorie von Marx und Engels* (Stuttgart, 1983).

13. J. Braunthal, "Der Putsch der Fascisten" [*sic*], *Der Kampf* 15 (1922): 320–33, cited in Wippermann, *Faschismustheorien* 30–31.

14. A. Thalheimer, "Ueber den Faschismus," *Gegen den Strom*, nos. 2–4 (Jan. 1930), reprinted in De Felice, *Il fascismo* 272–95. See M. Kitchen, "August Thalheimer's Theory of Fascism," *Journal of the History of Ideas* 34:1 (Jan.–March 1973): 67–78.

15. See the references in Wippermann, *Faschismustheorien* 30–32.

16. J. Dülffer, "Bonapartism, Fascism and National Socialism," *JCH* 11:4 (Oct. 1976): 109–28; L. Mangoni, "Per una definizione del Fascismo: I concetti di Bonapartismo e Cesarismo," *Rivista Italiana Contemporanea* 135 (1979): 18–52; and the discussion in Kuhn, *Das faschistische Herrschaftssystem*. The theory has been applied to east central Europe by Miklos Lacko, in "Zur Frage der Besonderheiten des südosteuropäischen Faschismus," in *Fascism and Europe: An International Symposium* (Prague, 1970), 2:1–22, and to Castro's rise in Cuba by Samuel Farber, in *Revolution and Reaction in Cuba, 1933–1960* (Middletown, Conn., 1977). For a discussion of the broader applications of the theory, see K. Hammer and P.-C. Hartmann, eds., *Der Bonapartismus* (Munich, 1976).

FASCISM AS A TYPICAL MANIFESTATION OF
TWENTIETH-CENTURY TOTALITARIANISM

It was logical that the achievement of power by the leader of a revolutionary authoritarian movement in Italy, with the potential to create a radical new kind of dictatorship, should be compared with the extreme revolutionary dictatorship already in power in the Soviet Union. Liberal critics such as Mario Missiroli and Luigi Salvatorelli were in 1922–23 the first to comment on the similarity of the revolutionary qualities of Fascism to communism, while in his *Il Fascio: Sinn und Wirklichkeit des italienischen Fascismus*, published in 1924, the German Social Democrat Fritz Schotthöfer proclaimed Fascism and Bolshevism to be "brothers in the spirit of violence," resembling each other like "two opposing armies." That same year Otto Bauer also pointed out the similarities between the two movements, one having established, and the other seeking to establish, a complete dictatorship independent of the domination of individual social classes.[17] This was soon remarked upon by many commentators, and later Leon Trotsky moved beyond his first analysis of fascism (a variation on the Bonapartist thesis) to proclaim the fundamental similarity between Hitler's "total state" and the Soviet state: like features included complete dictatorship, terrorism, centralized bureaucracy, and the elimination of proletarian power. Trotsky, however, could not fully adopt a "general totalitarianism" position because he remained certain that the German bourgeoisie had largely preserved its economic power.[18]

Even social democrats felt constrained to emphasize strongly the allegedly capitalist character of fascism,[19] so that the "general totalitarianism" theory was primarily developed by non-Marxist liberals and conservatives, who suffered from no ideological requirement to engage in economically reductionist arguments. The first liberal commentator who endeavored systematically to establish the typological similarities was Francesco Nitti, in his *Bolschewismus, Fascismus und Demokratie* [*sic*], published in 1923.[20] Luigi Sturzo was even more categorical, defining Bolshevism as "left Fascism" and Fascism as "right Bolshevism."[21] German conservatives such as Waldemar Gurian and Friedrich Meinecke took much the same position.[22]

17. O. Bauer, "Das Gleichgewicht der Klassenkämpfe," *Der Kampf* 17 (1924): 57–67.

18. L. Trotsky, *The Class Nature of the Soviet State* (London, 1937).

19. Only in 1939, on the very eve of the war, did German Social Democrats such as Rudolf Hilferding and Curt Geyer recognize the Third Reich as a total dictatorship to which theories of class domination could no longer apply. Wippermann, *Faschismustheorien* 39–40.

20. The original Italian version, *Bolscevismo, fascismo e democrazia*, appeared in New York the following year.

21. L. Sturzo, *Italien und der Faschismus* (Cologne, 1926).

22. Walter Gerhart [pseud. of Waldemar Gurian]. *Um des Reiches Zukunft* (Freiburg,

A complete and systematic theory of totalitarianism would not be developed until after 1945, when the specter of a Europe dominated by Hitlerism was replaced by that of one dominated by Stalinism. The interpretation formed by some Western political theorists suggested that fascism in general, but more specifically German National Socialism, did not constitute an absolutely unique category or genus but was merely one typical manifestation of the broader and even more sinister general phenomenon of twentieth-century totalitarianism, which would endure long after the specific fascist movements and regimes had expired. The most precise statement of this approach was *Totalitarian Dictatorship and Autocracy,* published in 1956 by Carl J. Friedrich and Zbigniew Brzezinski. It found the distinguishing characteristics of totalitarianism to be an all-encompassing revolutionary ideology, a mass party numbering approximately 10 percent of the total population, a policy of continuing mass terror, a monopoly of military and other armed power, constant manipulation of mass media, and central economic control.[23]

The totalitarianism concept enjoyed considerable vogue during the 1950s, though more as an interpretation of Communist than of fascist regimes. Subsequent years, however, brought increasing criticism. Hannah Arendt's *The Origins of Totalitarianism* (1951) had excepted Mussolini's government from the category of true totalitarian systems, undercutting the concept that generic fascism tended toward totalitarianism.[24] In a major article, Wolfgang Sauer later drew attention to common features of Fascism and National Socialism, together with their differences from Communist systems, casting further doubt on any broad concept of general totalitarianism.[25] By the late 1960s analysts encountered increasing difficulty in defining totalitarianism at all, and many questioned its existence as a continuous, comparable category of political systems.[26] The model would, however, continue to be used by other scholars.[27]

1932); F. Meinecke, "Nationalsozialismus und Bürgertum," in *Werke* (Stuttgart, 1969), 2:441–45. See also W. Wippermann, "Friedrich Meineckes 'Die deutsche Katastrophe'—Ein Versuch zur deutschen Vergangenheitsbewältigung," in *Friedrich Meinecke heute,* ed. M. Erbe (Berlin, 1982), 101–21.

23. See also C. J. Friedrich, ed., *Totalitarianism* (New York, 1954).

24. She also conceded that Nazi Germany only approximated structural totalitarianism by degrees, and only began to approach the full model during 1944–45.

25. W. Sauer, "National Socialism: Totalitarianism or Fascism?" *American Historical Review* 73:2 (Dec. 1967): 404–22.

26. Cf. H. Spiro, "Totalitarianism," *International Encyclopedia of the Social Sciences* (New York, 1968), vol. 16. A. Perlmutter, *Authoritarianism* (New Haven, 1981), is more nuanced.

27. The best comparative taxonomy and analysis will be found in J. J. Linz, "Totalitarian and Authoritarian Regimes," in *Handbook of Political Science,* ed. F. Greenstein and N. Polsby (Reading, Mass., 1975), 3:175–411.

Among the most useful studies are W. Ebenstein, *Totalitarianism* (New York, 1962); S. Neumann, *"Permanent Revolution": Totalitarianism in an Age of International Civil War* (London,

During the final thaw in the Soviet bloc in the 1980s, scholars in Communist lands who analyzed the central European fascist regimes were increasingly impressed by the similarity of the authoritarian institutions under fascism to those in the Soviet bloc. They began spontaneously to revive the theory of general totalitarianism, possibly even exaggerating it in the process. The main product of this syndrome was the book *Fashizmut* (Fascism), published by the leading Bulgarian dissident, Zheliu Zhelev, in 1982 but immediately withdrawn and suppressed by Bulgarian censorship. This comparative study of the regimes in Germany, Italy, and Spain suffered from the lack of full access to the comparatively rich Western bibliography, yet Zhelev arrived at an interpretation of general totalitarianism in some respects remarkably similar to that of Friedrich and Brzezinski and audaciously extended it to include the Soviet model as well.[28]

THE FASCIST REGIME AS A NEW FORM OF "AUTHORITARIAN POLYOCRACY"

Early interpretations tended to portray the Italian and German regimes either as agents of capitalism or as new forms of radical and centralized dictatorship, though the analyses of several Socialists and one or two dissident Communists did advance the perception of a possible delimitation of power between political and economic forces, as in the Bonapartist theory. This latter line of analysis was carried further in Ernst Fraenkel's *The Dual State* (1941), which interpreted the Third Reich as an uneasy symbiosis of Nazism and capitalism, the former tending toward domination, intervention, and expansion, the latter preserving elements of earlier structures and a more traditional normative life. Fraenkel concluded that the expansionist, violent, and domineering tendencies

---

1965); H. Buchheim, *Totalitarian Rule* (Middletown, Conn., 1968); B. Seidel and S. Jenkner, eds., *Wege der Totalitarismusforschung* (Darmstadt, 1968); M. Jänicke, *Totalitäre Herrschaft: Anatomie eines politischen Begriffes* (Berlin, 1971); H. Löffler, *Macht und Konsens in den klassischen Staatsutopien: Eine Studie zur Ideengeschichte des Totalitarismus* (Wärzburg, 1972); M. Greiffenhagen, R. Kühnl, and J. B. Müller, *Totalitarismus* (Munich, 1972); W. Schlangen, *Die Totalitarismus-Theorie* (Stuttgart, 1976); M. Curtis, *Totalitarianism* (New Brunswick, N.J., 1979); K. Löw, ed., *Totalitarismus und Faschismus* (Munich, 1980); idem, *Totalitarismus* (Berlin, 1988); E. Menza, ed., *Totalitarianism Reconsidered* (Port Washington, N.Y., 1981); and S. P. Soper, *Totalitarianism: A Conceptual Approach* (Lanham, Md., 1985).

The concept enjoyed a revival in France during the 1970s and 1980s, in such works as J.-F. Revel, *La tentation totalitaire* (Paris, 1975); idem, *Comment les democraties finissent* (Paris, 1983); J.-J. Walter, *Les machines totalitaires* (Paris, 1982); A. Glucksman, *La force du vertige* (Paris, 1983); and G. Hermet, P. Hassner, and J. Rupnik, *Totalitarismes* (Paris, 1984).

28. The book was subsequently reprinted in Bulgarian by Social Science Monographs (Boulder, 1990). Like several other leading dissidents in eastern Europe, Zhelev went on to election as president of his country after the downfall of communism.

of Nazism led both to the weakening of capitalism and to Nazism's own self-destruction. This interpretation took a more complex form in Franz Neumann's *Behemoth* (1944), which defined the self-proclaimed Nazi "total state" as in fact resting on four competing pillars or power blocs: the party, the military, the bureaucracy, and the economic leadership.

Such an approach was developed and refined by West German historians such as Martin Broszat, Hans Mommsen, and Peter Hüttenberger in the late 1960s and 1970s, crystallizing in Hüttenberger's concept of a Nazi "polyocracy." [29] This refers to the competition between semiautonomous structures of the military, the economic elite, the bureaucracy, and the party, together with various combinations of leaders, interest groups, or subsectors of these forces. One of the most widely read neo-Marxist works of those years, Nikos Poulantzas's *Fascisme et dictature* (1972), also tended in this direction.[30] It viewed fascism as an "exceptional regime" of capitalism and rejected the Bonapartist thesis for attributing too much autonomy and central power to the fascist state. Poulantzas viewed fascist regimes as segmented between bureaucratic, political, and economic power blocs, which represented distinct classes and power groups. The perception of the limitations of state power was also reenforced by studies of local and regional affairs under Nazism[31] and by the development of *Alltagsgeschichte* (the history of everyday life) in the 1970s and 1980s.[32]

The interpretation of Nazi Germany, in particular, as a sort of polyocracy was contested not merely by advocates of the totalitarian thesis but also by those who emphasized the "intentionalist" approach to the Third Reich, which rested on the priority of Hitler's ideological aims and *Zielstrebigkeit* (goal fixation), together with his virtually absolute overarching authority, even for the most extreme policies.

FASCISM AS CULTURAL REVOLUTION

One of the clearest, most forceful, and most cogent interpretations of fascism is George L. Mosse's presentation of fascism as a new form of cultural revolution. He has interpreted it as the effort to develop a new ideology and culture and to create a revolutionary "new man" in place of the materialist, prag-

29. M. Broszat, *The Hitler State* (Munich, 1969; English trans., London, 1981); H. Mommsen, *Beamtentum in Dritten Reich* (Stuttgart, 1966); P. Hüttenberger, "Nationalsozialistische Polykratie," *Geschichte und Gesellschaft* 2:4 (1976): 417–42.

30. The English translation is N. Poulantzas, *Fascism and Dictatorship: The Third International and the Problem of Fascism* (Atlantic Highlands, N.J., 1975).

31. The first notable publication in this subfield was E. N. Peterson, *The Limits of Hitler's Power* (Princeton, 1969).

32. Perhaps the best example is D. Peukert, *Inside Nazi Germany: Conformity, Opposition and Racism in Everyday Life* (New Haven, 1987).

matic, and liberal culture of the nineteenth century. Mosse's approach is based on a non-Hegelian concept of a kind of dialectic between myth and objective reality; he rejects the interpretation advanced by certain Marxists and liberals of a sudden explosion of the irrational. National Socialism is here seen as the actualization and crystallization of elements of a specific tradition in German history since the war of liberation against Napoleon, though not inherent in German history from earlier times. Fascism was thus not merely reactionary but rather a specific kind of revolution from the right that was based on race and a combination of mystical, even semioccult, concepts that were employed to nationalize and mobilize the masses. Fascist culture made a strong appeal to the past and simultaneously to the creation of a new race of heroes, even though in practice most of its national and racial values were based on bourgeois or traditional morality. A major aspect of fascist technique was to actualize these concepts through new forms of public aesthetics and liturgy. All fascist movements sought to create a new sense of fulfillment for the masses through community and comradeship, and a new social hierarchy based on function rather than status.[33]

FASCISM AS A PRODUCT OF CULTURAL, MORAL, OR SOCIOPSYCHOLOGICAL PATHOLOGIES

Other interpretations pay much less attention to the cultural content of fascism and focus instead on what the analysts perceive as the cultural, moral, or sociopsychological pathogens in the prefascist environment, which they infer to have been responsible for producing fascism. Several distinguished German and Italian historians have viewed fascism as the product of a unique moral and cultural crisis ending in collapse, while theories developed by a number of analysts (mainly German and American) have regarded fascism as the product of underlying authoritarian and pathological sociocultural patterns and values.

Fascism as the Product of Cultural or Moral Breakdown

Certain historians of culture in Germany and Italy, led by such figures as Benedetto Croce and Friedrich Meinecke, have interpreted fascism as the product of

---

33. G. L. Mosse, *The Crisis of German Ideology: Intellectual Origins of the Third Reich* (New York, 1964); idem, *Nazi Culture* (New York, 1966); idem, *Germans and Jews* (New York, 1970); idem, *The Nationalization of the Masses* (New York, 1975); idem, *Masses and Man* (New York, 1980); and numerous shorter publications. A succinct summary will be found in Perfetti, *Il dibattito* 19–22.

J. W. Mannhardt, *Der Faschismus* (Munich, 1925), one of the first German studies of Italian Fascism, took a somewhat congruent approach, defining Fascism as the creator of a new "spiritual-moral power."

cultural fragmentation and moral relativism in European values from the late nineteenth century on.[34] According to their approach, the crisis of World War I and its aftermath, producing intense economic dislocation, social conflict, and cultural anomie, resulted in a kind of spiritual collapse that permitted novel forms of radical nationalism to flourish. One of the most cogent contemporary statements of this interpretation was made before World War II by Peter Drucker.[35] A somewhat more extreme variant was that of Hermann Rauschning, who maintained that cultural and political deterioration had produced a condition of cultural and moral nihilism.[36] The principal Marxist contribution to this approach was made by Georg Lukács, who, while not abandoning the agent theory, agreed with aspects of Mosse's later interpretation and also to some extent with the emphasis of Croce and Meinecke. Lukács viewed National Socialism as the product of a specific irrational German cultural process, leading from romanticism through vitalist doctrines, pseudoscientism, antiscientism, and a love of mythmaking to cultural and social fascism.[37]

Fascism had a clear intellectual genealogy, but the weakness of the moral crisis approach alone is that it only tries to explain which conditions permitted fascist concepts and movements to develop, without accounting for their specific ideas, values, forms, or goals. By contrast, in his *Ideology of Fascism* (1969), A. James Gregor argues that Italian Fascism developed a coherent ideology that was not the product of nihilistic collapse but rather the consequence of new cultural, political, and sociological ideas developed in western and central Europe during the late nineteenth and early twentieth centuries.

Fascism as the Product of Underlying Authoritarian and Pathological Sociocultural Patterns

A number of related but not identical concepts were advanced by psychological and social analysts to account for fascism through underlying patterns of authoritarian and pathological sociocultural attitudes. This approach, more intuitive than empirical, first achieved notice through the extreme Freudian psychosexual explanation presented in Wilhelm Reich's *The Mass Psychology of Fascism*, which appeared in German in 1934 and subsequently in English twelve years later. Reich viewed fascism as the product of sexual repression

---

34. References to and evaluations of Croce's writings on fascism will be found in Gregor, *Interpretations* 29–32. Selections from Meinecke, Hans Kohn, and Gerhard Ritter in this vein are presented and discussed in De Felice, *Il fascismo* 391–437.

35. P. Drucker, *The End of Economic Man* (New York, 1939).

36. H. Rauschning, *Die Revolution des Nihilismus* (Zurich, 1938; English trans., New York, 1939).

37. G. Lukács, *Wie ist die faschistische Philosophie in Deutschland entstanden?* (Budapest, 1982), first published in 1933; idem, *Die Zerstörung der Vernunft* (Berlin, 1954).

in bourgeois society when combined with compensatory and aggressive impulses. He thus interpreted fascism as the "natural" consequence of bourgeois society, which was grounded in sexual repression, but thought it capable of involving other social classes as well. Since the culture of "bourgeois society" was the product of centuries of Western civilization, the number of potential fascists would seem to have been vast. This notion, of course, totally failed to explain why most bourgeois societies did not produce significant fascist movements; its presumption that such repression was worst in Germany was not tested in any way, and its extension to Italy seems ludicrous.[38]

More important interpretations would later be presented by former members of the Frankfurt School for Social Research. As associates of this well-known institute, the Frankfurt School writers had not taken fascism very seriously before 1933; as dissident German Marxists, they assumed that the triumph of the socialist revolution was inevitable and that Germany more than Russia represented the "world-historical future." Only later in exile did they study fascism more seriously, but they clung to their old idée fixe concerning Germany as representing the wave of the future. Thus fascism would be a danger to other major societies during the "final phase" of capitalism.[39]

A new sociocultural interpretation by one of their associates which drew considerable attention was Erich Fromm's *Escape from Freedom* (1941). Fromm contended that fascism should be seen as the product of decaying central European middle-class society, whose family structure encouraged sadomasochistic personal authority relationships. Fromm also laid emphasis on feelings of isolation, impotence, anomie, and frustration.

Theodor Adorno, Max Horkheimer, and other sociologists of the Frankfurt School placed heavy stress on the influence of a generally authoritarian and rigid culture, which produced a specific personality type they labeled the "authoritarian personality."[40] This was held to have created strong attitudes that were anti-Semitic, ethnocentric, conservative, and antidemocratic and to have flourished especially, but not only, in central Europe in the early twentieth century. In various writings Horkheimer combined analyses of economic structures and psychological models with speculations about the bourgeois family, insecurity, and various economic forces, resulting in the self-destruction of reason and its replacement by a subjective or "perverse reason" in society that

---

38. Since Reich, there have been many attempts to present a speculative psychological or psychohistorical interpretation of Hitler and of National Socialism. Most of these are surveyed in G. M. Kren, "Psychohistorical Interpretations of National Socialism," *German Studies Review* 1:3 (1978): 150–72. A more empirical background study in German male attitudes was later presented in K. Theweleit, *Männerphantasien*, 2 vols. (Frankfurt, 1977–78: English trans., 1989).

39. See the discussion in S. Turner and D. Käsler, eds., *Sociology Responds to Fascism* (London, 1992), 1–5.

40. T. Adorno et al., *The Authoritarian Personality* (New York, 1950).

encouraged irrational trends. The last offshoot of the Frankfurt School was the philosophy of Herbert Marcuse, who later achieved a certain prominence with the new left of the late 1960s. Marcuse held that fascism constituted an extension of the terms of production found in capitalism, representing the culmination of certain trends within it.[41] Rather than presenting an interpretation of fascism, Marcuse seemed simply to reflect the kind of thinking that had made up fascism in the first place.

The American sociologists Harold Lasswell and Talcott Parsons attempted a more empirically grounded analysis. Lasswell's psychological interpretation stressed the standard themes of middle-class insecurity and resentment.[42] Parsons, meanwhile, developed a broadly based approach that sought to combine the effects of psychological insecurity, economic and social rationalization, social anomie, the loss of familiar symbols, general alienation, a reaction against capitalism and rationalist thought, together with general conditions of recent German history, society, culture, and economics.[43]

Parsons's study did involve many verifiable factors, but in general the weakness of most of these theories lay in their purely speculative and unverifiable content, particularly in the cases of Fromm and Reich, and most especially in the reductionist nature of the latter's sexual ideas, which cannot be rendered methodologically applicable to the main problems. The "authoritarian personality" inventory is more empirical, but subsequent investigation has been unable to substantiate any clear assumptions about middle classes or central European personality traits in this period, and one empirical study not surprisingly found Communist personalities as "authoritarian" as those of fascists.

FASCISM AS THE PRODUCT OF THE RISE OF AMORPHOUS MASSES

A somewhat related sociological interpretation has considered fascism the product of unique qualitative changes in society as the traditional class structure gave way to large, undifferentiated, and atomized populations—the "masses" of urban industrial society. This idea was first advanced by José Ortega y Gasset and in varying ways has been reformulated by Emil Lederer, Talcott Parsons,

---

41. There is a useful summary in R. Trifiletti Saldi, "La Scuola di Francoforte," in Cavalli, ed., *Il fascismo* 85–121. For a broader analysis that deals especially with Horkheimer, see M. Wilson, *Das Institut für Sozialforschung und seine Faschismusanalysen* (New York, 1982).

42. H. D. Lasswell, "The Psychology of Hitlerism," *Political Quarterly* 4 (July–Sept. 1933): 373–84; idem, *A Study of Power* (Glencoe, Ill., 1950).

43. T. Parsons, "Some Sociological Aspects of the Fascist Movements" and "Democracy and Social Structure in Pre-Nazi Germany," in his *Essays in Sociological Theory* (Glencoe, Ill., 1954), 124–41, 104–23.

and Hannah Arendt, and perhaps most cogently by William Kornhauser.[44] It emphasizes the irrational, anti-intellectual, and visceral nature of the fascist appeal to "mass man" and thus parallels and complements the "cultural breakdown" theories.

This approach tends, however, to obfuscate the extent to which practical ideological content and cogent appeals to tangible interests figured in the programs and practices of fascist movements, as well as the extent to which many of their supporters were still identified and definable as members of structured social or institutional sectors. Moreover, it fails to distinguish between the nature of "mass society" in the central European context and any other mass framework of industrialized society.

FASCISM AS THE CONSEQUENCE OF UNIQUE NATIONAL HISTORIES

Various writers and historians have sought to portray Fascism and Nazism as unique Italian and German disorders, stemming from defective cultural and social values and institutions rooted in the earlier histories of these countries.[45] Such an approach cannot be totally discounted, but its proponents have lost support because of the relative superficiality of the analyses of the two national histories involved, analyses which failed to make adequate comparisons with other countries that had similar characteristic and problems, whether or not to a lesser degree.

It is clearly useful to isolate those nations which produced significant fascist movements to determine exactly what they had in common, and this will be attempted in chapter 15. The earlier literature, however, has lacked objectivity and analytic specificity.

FASCISM AS A REACTION AGAINST MODERNIZATION

The old argument that fascism was merely irrational and incomprehensible in normal terms was given a new twist in later years by Western scholars who interpreted it as an expression of resistance to "modernization"—however

---

44. J. Ortega y Gasset, *The Revolt of the Masses* (New York, 1932); E. Lederer, *The State of the Masses* (New York, 1940); Parsons, "Some Sociological Aspects"; H. Arendt, *The Origins of Totalitarianism* (New York, 1951); W. Kornhauser, *The Politics of Mass Society* (New York, 1959).

45. For example, on Italian Fascism, see D. M. Smith, *Italy: A Modern History* (Ann Arbor, 1959). The literature on Nazism flourished, especially during World War II. Leading examples are E. Vermeil, *Doctrinaires de la révolution allemande* (Paris, 1939); idem, *Germany's Three Reichs* (New York, 1969); W. M. McGovern, *From Luther to Hitler: The History of Fascist-Nazi Political Philosophy* (New York, 1941); and P. Viereck, *Metapolitics: From the Romantics to Hitler* (Boston, 1941).

variously defined. They saw fascism as primarily opposed to central features of Western liberal society such as urbanization, industrialization, liberal education, rationalist materialism, individualism, social differentiation, and pluralist autonomy and so categorized fascism as inherently opposed to modernization "itself." Henry A. Turner Jr. provided the clearest statement of this point of view,[46] while Wolfgang Sauer interpreted fascism as the political movement of "losers" in the modernization process. Barrington Moore Jr., employing a highly elastic definition of fascism, has argued that it was the product of an aberrant and distorted modernization process controlled by rural, martial elites—though this thesis is difficult to demonstrate empirically.[47] Ernst Nolte maintained that fascism was, among other things, the expression of resistance to modern "transcendence," a philosophical concept perhaps not unrelated to that of modernization in the social sciences.

Another interpretative approach recognizes that fascism adopted fully modern methods and technology but holds that these were embraced for essentially antimodern ends. This argument is presented in Jeffrey Herf's *Reactionary Modernism* (1984), which particularly emphasizes the fascination with technology. Detlev Peukert was more concerned with Nazi social and cultural policies, modern in style and technique but, in his interpretation, regressive in content.[48] Hans-Dieter Schäfer has applied a similar approach to Nazi popular culture, and these ambiguities have been discussed in works by Hans-Ulrich Thamer and Horst Matzerath and Heinrich Volkmann.[49]

FASCISM AS MODERNIZATION OR A STAGE OF
SOCIOECONOMIC GROWTH

A directly opposite interpretation not merely underlines the modern technology of fascism but also emphasizes its fundamentally modernizing functions and goals. Such an approach was perhaps first essayed by Franz Borkenau, who in 1933 interpreted Italian Fascism as a sort of "developmental dictatorship."[50]

46. H. A. Turner Jr., "Fascism and Modernization," *World Politics* 24:4 (July 1972): 547–64, reprinted in *Reappraisals of Fascism*, ed. H. A. Turner Jr. (New York, 1975), 117–39.

47. B. Moore Jr., *Social Origins of Dictatorship and Democracy* (Boston, 1966).

48. D. Peukert, *Volksgenossen und Gemeinschaftsfremde* (Cologne, 1982).

49. H.-D. Schäfer, *Das gespaltene Bewusstsein: Deutsche Kultur und Lebenswirklichkeit, 1933–1945* (Frankfurt, 1984); H.-U. Thamer, *Verführung und Gewalt: Deutschland, 1933–1945* (Berlin, 1986); H. Matzerath and H. Volkmann, "Modernisierungstheorie und Nationalsozialismus," in *Theorien in der Praxis des Historikers*, ed. J. Kocka Göttingen, 1977), 86–116.

50. F. Borkenau, "Zur Soziologie des Faschismus," in Nolte, ed., *Theorien* 156–81.

It should be noted that over the decades some of the Marxist interpreters, such as "Giulio Acquila" (G. Šaš), Mihaly Vajda, and Alexander Galkin, have also recognized that Italian Fascism promoted modernization and economic development. Vajda has written that Fascism constituted.

At the time this was a relatively isolated interpretation, but the concept re-emerged twenty years after the defeat of Nazi Germany and was influenced by general ideas concerning the political and structural imperatives of economic modernization, together with the recent experiences of newly emerging countries.

The stages of growth concept holds that the process of modernization and industrialization has frequently tended to produce severe internal conflict as the balance of power shifts between or threatens various social and economic groups. Those who lean toward this approach differ from the Marxists in not reducing the conflict to a capital versus labor struggle but defining it more broadly through a large range of social and structural forces and national interests.

Two leading exponents of this approach are A. F. K. Organski and Ludovico Garruccio (a pseudonym). Organski has suggested that the potential for fascism arises at the point at which the industrial sector of the economy first begins to equal in size and labor force that of the primary sector, creating the potential for severe conflicts that also elicit aggressive nationalism and authoritarian government.[51] The trouble with this concept is that its author did not refine it sufficiently to make it uniquely applicable to Italy and other countries undergoing a "fascist" experience, and as such it cannot be applied to Germany (nor does its author attempt to do so). Most countries passing through that stage of growth have never experienced anything that could be called fascism.

Perhaps the most serious effort to understand fascism via broad comparative patterns of modernization is Garruccio's *L'industrializzazione tra nazionalismo e rivoluzione* (1969). It suggests that what was known as fascism was the central European variant of a common experience of crisis, normally issuing in authoritarian government, that has accompanied the effort of modern nations (or, in the case of Russia, empires) to establish their identity and power on a modern basis, to overcome internal conflict, and to complete their social and economic modernization. This concept is extremely suggestive and may help to explain the relationship of fascism to communism and to third world developmental dictatorships, but it fails to identify or explain the unique historical features of European fascism.

Both the sociologist Ralf Dahrendorf and the social historian David Schoenbaum have emphasized the modernizing effects of the Third Reich and

---

in fact, the "only progressive solution" for Italy in 1922, socialism having become "reactionary." Vajda, "Crisis and the Way Out: The Rise of Fascism in Italy and Germany," *Telos* 12 (Summer 1972): 3–26. Galkin largely concurred, declaring that Fascism was "inherently revolutionary in the case of Italy" ("Capitalist Society").

51. A. F. K. Organski, *The Stages of Political Development* (New York, 1965); idem, "Fascism and Modernization," in *The Nature of Fascism*, ed. S. J. Woolf (London, 1968), 19–41.

the war experience on German society.[52] They do not regard National Socialism as having instituted a planned and conscious attempt at modernization but have argued that the effects of Hitlerian rule, especially combined with the profound alterations wrought by World War II, had undeniably modernizing effects on German society.

Other analysts are willing to concede the point, though primarily with regard to Italy, and distinguish between "two faces" of fascism. The first, in certain underdeveloped countries, had the goal and also the effect of accelerating modernization, while the second, in Germany and in certain other countries, was regressive and fundamentally antimodern.[53]

Renzo De Felice, the foremost historian of Italian Fascism, largely agrees with this approach. He views Italian Fascism as having progressivist and revolutionary origins, stemming from the Enlightenment and the French Revolution, while regarding Nazism as antimodernist and regressive. De Felice considers Fascism to have been the vehicle of the emerging lower middle class—a typical product of modernization—and distinguishes firmly between the movement and the regime (the latter being "the politics of Mussolini"). The Fascist movement was thus revolutionary insofar as it mobilized masses for a "new society" and a "new man," which the Fascist regime also attempted to achieve through the typically modern means of education.[54]

A. James Gregor has taken the boldest position of all, at least with regard to Italian Fascism. He has argued that it developed a coherent ideology based on a stable core of new social, political, and philosophical ideas,[55] and that Fascism, more than communism, was in diverse manifestations the typical revolution of the twentieth century, being the first to introduce coherent new concepts and techniques of national revolution, accelerated development, and

52. R. Dahrendorf, *Society and Democracy in Germany* (London, 1968); D. Schoenbaum, *Hitler's Social Revolution* (New York, 1966).

53. A. Cassels, "Janus: The Two Faces of Fascism," *Canadian Historical Papers, 1969* 166–84, reprinted in Turner, ed., *Reappraisals of Fascism* 69–92; idem, *Fascism* (New York, 1974). Otto-Ernst Schüddekopf recognized in Italian Fascism an "anti-reactionary mass movement" which produced what was at least in part a "dictatorship for development." Schüddekopf, *Revolutions of Our Time: Fascism* (New York, 1973), 99, 112. Miklos Lacko also draws this distinction with regard to Hungary and certain other underdeveloped countries in "Zur Frage."

54. Particularly in M. A. Ledeen, ed., *Intervista sul fascismo* (Bari, 1975), translated as *Fascism: An Informal Introduction to Its Theory and Practice* (New Brunswick, N.J., 1976). G. Amendola, *Intervista sul fascismo* (Bari, 1976), was part of the Marxist rejoinder. On the resulting controversy, see M. A. Ledeen, "Renzo De Felice and the Controversy over Italian Fascism," *JCH* 11:4 (Oct. 1976): 269–82, and B. W. Painter, "Renzo De Felice and the Historiography of Italian Fascism," *American Historical Review* 95:2 (April 1990): 391–405.

Ernst Nolte has distinguished between what he calls the "normal fascism" of Italy and the "radical fascism" of Germany.

55. A. J. Gregor, *The Ideology of Fascism* (New York, 1969).

integrated dictatorship.[56] Italian Fascism is specifically identified as a prototype of the mass-mobilizing developmental dictatorship designed to achieve a broad threshold of modernization, and thus a model for Spain, Greece, and various "third world" countries that achieved a significant level of development under authoritarianism.[57]

FASCISM AS A UNIQUE METAPOLITICAL PHENOMENON

Some of the most profound students of fascism have refused to categorize it in simple political, social, or economic terms, seeing fascism rather as a unique historical phenomenon that attempted to synthesize or symbolize the special features of a distinct early twentieth-century historical trend. Thus Ernst Nolte has dismissed most of the earlier interpretations as dealing with factors that are either secondary or irrelevant. He has viewed fascism primarily as a meta-political phenomenon, that is, as the product of certain political, cultural, and ideological aspirations arising at the turn of the century and aiming to create a radically new order, with new values and doctrines of its own, rejecting existing projects of "transcendence," and seeking an alternate revolution of the right. For him, fascism is a product of the era of world wars and of Bolshevism, seeking to counteract the latter by adopting some of its forms and techniques.[58]

Though few scholars have accepted Nolte's exact formulation, other leading figures have suggested congruent metapolitical interpretations of their own. Almost simultaneously with the publication of Nolte's first book on fascism, Eugen Weber suggested that fascism was a unique and specific revolutionary project in its own right.[59] George L. Mosse, the leading historian of Nazi and pre-Nazi culture,[60] interprets fascism as a revolution of the right with transcendental goals of its own and specific, not merely reactive or opportunistic, cultural and ideological content.[61] Somewhat similarly, the Catholic philosopher

56. A. J. Gregor, *The Fascist Persuasion in Radical Politics* (Princeton, 1974); idem, "Fascism and Modernization: Some Addenda," *World Politics* 26:3 (April 1974): 370–84.

57. A. J. Gregor, *Italian Fascism and Developmental Dictatorship* (Princeton, 1979).

58. E. Nolte, *Three Faces of Fascism* (New York, 1966). Nolte later reacted positively to the criticism that he may have inflated the category of generic fascism and presented it as the basic foe of democracy, emphasizing in writings of the 1970s and 1980s that fascism was only one aspect of totalitarianism, the earliest and most ultimately destructive form of which was Soviet communism, without which, in fact, fascism might not have been possible.

59. E. Weber, *Varieties of Fascism* (New York, 1964). See also his article "Revolution? Counterrevolution? What Revolution?" *JCH* 9:2 (April 1974): 3–47, reprinted in *Fascism: A Reader's Guide,* ed. W. Laqueur (Berkeley, 1976), 435–67.

60. See the following works by Mosse: *Crisis of German Ideology; Nazi Culture; Germans and Jews; Nationalization;* and "The Genesis of Fascism," *JCH* 1.1 (April 1966): 14–26.

61. G. L. Mosse, *Nazism: A History and Comparative Analysis of National Socialism* (New Brunswick, N.J., 1978). Mosse's review of Nolte, probably the best critique of the latter, appeared

Augusto Del Noce sees fascism as the revolutionary form of certain European nationalisms during the "first age of secularization," when modern secularism was still capable of projecting idealistic and semitranscendent goals and before the complete victory of materialism and consumerism. He interprets Italian Fascism as the competitor of Leninism and the more radical German National Socialism as the competitive counterpart of Stalinism, thus constituting two different phases of twentieth-century radicalism.[62]

Roger Griffin's interpretation both parallels and diverges from that of Nolte. For Griffin, fascism was an epochal revolutionary movement of palingenetic populist ultranationalism. It was not the agent of any other force or the reflection of any particular social class but was produced by specific historical, political, social, and cultural conditions, arising ideologically from the crisis of the fin de siècle. It achieved significance only in a few countries characterized by powerful preexisting nationalist forces, limited experience with liberal democratic institutions, and major crises in the interwar period that opened significant new political space. The psychological and psychosocial mainsprings of fascism were not merely fear or insecurity and were in some respects the opposite of "nihilism," being derived from the need for meaning, value, and self-transcendence, as in all major religious or ideologically revolutionary movements. As an extreme expression of European nationalisms in a certain historical era, it could not be expected to reappear unless similar conditions recur, which is not likely. Griffin's interpretation of fascism is too rich to be adequately summarized in brief, and of all scholarly discussions it is one of those most worth a complete reading.[63]

Yet another interpretation sees fascism—and sometimes all modern utopian revolutionary movements—as "political religions," gnostic, mystic, and totalist, beyond normal political concepts and arguments. This was specifically applied to Italian Fascism and German National Socialism, as well as Soviet communism, by the Austrian philosopher Eric Voegelin in his *Politische Religionen* (1938), published on the eve of the Nazi entry into Vienna.[64] In a similar vein, James Rhodes has interpreted National Socialism as "a modern millenarian revolution."[65]

Some neofascists after 1945 argued that fascism was above all a "myth,"

---

in the *Journal of the History of Ideas* 24:4 (Oct.–Dec. 1966): 621–25. J. P. Stern, in *Hitler: The Führer and the People* (Glasgow, 1975), tends to agree with Mosse.

62. A. Del Noce, *L'Epoca della secolarizzazione* (Milan, 1970), 111–35; idem, "Per una definizione storica del fascismo," in his *Il problema storico del fascismo* (Florence, 1970), 11–46.

63. R. Griffin, *The Nature of Fascism* (London, 1991), esp. 182–237.

64. Later translated as E. Voegelin, *Political Religions* (Lewiston, N.Y., 1986).

65. J. M. Rhodes, *The Hitler Movement: A Modern Millenarian Revolution* (Stanford, 1980).

a new system of ideals and values.[66] Certainly in its ultimate form, fascism constituted the most extreme moral and cultural revolution of the twentieth century. It was the only ideology which reversed the doctrines of egalitarianism present or latent in both capitalism and socialism.[67]

THE DENIAL THAT GENERIC FASCISM CAN BE DEFINED

Finally, some analysts of a nominalist turn of mind have concluded that generic fascism is a projection of the imagination, the various allegedly fascist movements being too dissimilar to form a common category. Depending on how rigidly or uniformly the category of generic fascism is defined, they may be right. The most direct statement of this position has been made by Gilbert Allardyce,[68] but in varying degrees it has been supported by Karl D. Bracher and Renzo De Felice (who do not deny the possibility of constructing analytically an abstract common "fascist minimum" but doubt its utility), John Lukacs, and others.[69]

---

66. M. Bardèche, *Qu'est-ce que le fascisme?* (Paris, 1961).

67. Cf. G. Locchi, *La esencia del fascismo* (Barcelona, 1984). Locchi claims that this was ultimately admitted by Max Horkheimer (18).

68. G. Allardyce, "What Fascism Is Not: Thoughts on the Definition of a Concept," *American Historical Review* 84:2 (April 1979): 367–88. Much the same argument may be found in B. Martin, "Zur Tauglichkeit eines übergreifenden Faschismus-Begriff," *Vierteljahrshefte für Zeitgeschichte* 1 (1981): 48–73, and M. Geyer, "The State in National Socialist Germany," in *Statemaking and Social Movements*, ed. C. Bright and S. Harding (Ann Arbor, 1984), 193–232.

69. This judgment is also sometimes made with regard to subsectors of the putative common genus of fascism. Thus Mario Ambri, in *I falsi fascismi* (Rome, 1980), would remove the movements and wartime regimes in Hungary, Romania, and Croatia from any category of generic fascism because of the differences in doctrine, genesis, basis, and development. Specifically with regard to National Socialism, Fred Weinstein, in *The Dynamics of Nazism: Leadership, Ideology and the Holocaust* (New York, 1980), argued that the heterogeneity of Nazism made it impossible to verify—indeed more likely disproved—all objective explanations based upon social causation, economics, regions, or quantification, as well as mere psychoanalytic insights, social science theories, or a single explanatory concept applied to the entire movement. The same conclusion might be applied to any interpretation or generic theory of fascism.

Conversely, the late Tim W. Mason, in "Whatever Happened to Fascism?" *Radical History Review* 49 (1991): 89–98, criticized the abandonment of a general concept of fascism by scholars during the 1980s.

13
Generic Fascism?

Not merely has the interpretation or search for causes of fascism generated immense controversy and widely discordant theories, but there is a persistent tendency among historians to conclude that no such unified genus of political movements as a general fascism ever existed. The nominalist position is in some respects on firm ground, for proponents are able to point out significant individual characteristics and differences—some of them genuinely important—between the principal cases that are studied.

More probably, a rigorous "either-or" approach toward the problem of generic fascism is fundamentally misleading. That is, the common reduction of all putative fascisms to one single generic phenomenon of absolutely common identity is inaccurate, while a radically nominalist approach which insists that all radical nationalist movements of interwar Europe were inherently different, though correct in the narrow technical sense that not one was a carbon copy of any other, has the opposite defect of ignoring distinctive similarities.

Italian Fascists at first denied any intrinsic similarity between their movement and new authoritarian nationalists in Germany or elsewhere. Mussolini, rather typically, failed to adopt a firm and consistent position one way or the other. As early as 1921 he suggested to a Romanian admirer that like-minded activists might form a Romanian equivalent of Fascism (and in fact an ephemeral Romanian Fascist Party was formed in 1923), and in 1923 he responded to the flattery of his first formal state visitors, the king of Spain and the Spanish dictator Primo de Rivera, by suggesting that Fascism did present a series of generalizable characteristics that might be reproduced elsewhere. But when Mussolini visited Germany that same year, he found it politic to deny any fundamental similarity between Fascism and the German authoritarian nationalist groups. In 1925 Giuseppe Bastianini presented an enthusiastic report to the

Fascist Grand Council, saying that there were already groups in forty different countries which either called themselves fascist or were so termed by others. Yet in the following year Mussolini denied any real similarity to or connection with those who were sometimes called Hungarian fascists, and so it went. In March 1928 he made his famous statement, "Fascism is not for export." [1]

In effect Mussolini always wavered between the notion that Fascism had developed a new style, a new set of beliefs, values, and political forms, that might constitute the basis of Italian hegemony in a broader European fascism. He realized that such ambitions were imprudent, would be difficult to achieve, and would always face conflict and contradiction with would-be fascists elsewhere, who would press their own national interests and exhibit marked national idiosyncracies.

Hitler's approach, at least vis-à-vis Italy, was more firm, practical, and consistent. He clearly became convinced, at least from the time of the March on Rome, that Fascism and National Socialism shared a common destiny. Though not considered identical in the sense of point-by-point similarity, they were deemed historical equivalents in their respective countries. While Hitler maintained that general conviction from beginning to end, he did not try to develop a worldwide concept of generic national socialism and did not normally call German National Socialism "fascist." Since the core of Nazism was race, the most specific counterparts of Nazism were to be found less in political forms and characteristics than in the most firm supporters of the Aryan racial principle and Aryan racial revolution, wherever they might be. In the process of Europe-wide racial revolution, however, Hitler soon became convinced that a combination of political characteristics and national interests dictated that Italy would be the most natural immediate ally of a National Socialist Germany. If this conclusion was in one sense contradictory, Hitler proved fully consistent in its prosecution and for some time even respected Italian control of the Alto Adige (the northeastern corner of Italy, inhabited by German-speaking people). This position was much appreciated. By 1928, if not before, the NSDAP was one of several authoritarian nationalist groups being subsidized by the Italian state.[2]

Hitler's unswerving admiration for Mussolini and by extension (but more weakly) for Fascism was not necessarily shared by other leading Nazis. The ideologist Alfred Rosenberg was interested in an international association of kindred movements but increasingly deprecated the racial confusion and intermittent philo-Semitism of the Fascists. Some of the more radical Nazis rejected the Mussolini regime for other reasons—especially for being too conservative

---

1. See especially M. Michaelis, "I rapporti tra fascismo e nazismo prima dell' avento di Hitler al potere (1922–1933)," *Rivista Storica Italiana* 85:3 (Sept. 1973): 544–600.

2. Ibid., 597–600.

or allegedly capitalist. In varying ways and degrees, Gregor Strasser, Goebbels, and Himmler shared these aversions. (The conviction that Fascist corporatism was too capitalist or conservative would be a common criticism later among national syndicalists or national socialists in Spain, France, Japan, and elsewhere.) Strasser also considered the *Führerprinzip* to have been pioneered by Mussolini (in a sense that was correct) and resented it as a "fascist" foreign import.[3]

In general, nonetheless, Mussolini and certain other Fascist leaders turned increasingly, if not unswervingly, toward contact with and support for other nationalist groups abroad. Subsidies in the late 1920s were one aspect of this policy, the strongly pro-Nazi stance of the anti-Semitic Fascist journal *Il Tevere* another. The new Fascist review *Antieuropa,* founded in 1929, was directed especially toward the universality of fascist-type radical nationalism, but at first its editors harbored no illusions about absolute generic identity or a fascist international. The hypernationalism of parallel groups, if nothing else, would bring them into mutual conflict so that "they could not be friends."[4]

The collapse of the Spanish regime of Primo de Rivera was something of a blow to Mussolini, but he hailed the big electoral victories of Hitler that began in 1930. While Hitler declared that National Socialism marked a "fascistization" of Germany (admittedly not his normal terminology), Mussolini applauded the advance of what he eventually termed "German fascism" and its victory in 1933, despite an earlier preference for the more conservative Stahlhelm.

By 1934 the Italian regime was promoting "universal fascism," while increasingly dissociating itself from German National Socialism. That year marked the peak of the war of words in which all the negative features of Nazism and the differences between it and Fascism were underscored and sometimes exaggerated.[5] Mussolini put all this behind him with the formation of the Axis, even though he and most other top Fascist leaders never completely lost their distrust of the Nazis. In Germany, lesser Nazi leaders remained scornful of Fascism for its limitations, conservatism, and lack of full revolutionary potential.

In sum, the top Fascists and Nazis realized that they had a lot in common and represented a new departure compared with previous political groups, but they were uncertain just how far any mutual identity extended and remained conscious of major, some thought decisive, differences. The original Italian Fascists were unable to solve either the political or the conceptual problem of generic fascism, even when they made a concerted effort to affirm and define it in the mid-1930s.

3. Ibid., 582–83.
4. Ibid., 575, 584–86.
5. This is treated in chapter 7.

LIMITATIONS OF THE GENERIC CONCEPT:
THE VARIETIES OF FASCISM

The suggested typological description of common features of a generic fascism is useful only for limited purposes of comparison and distinction. On occasion the differences between fascistic movements—whether political or ideological—seemed almost as important as the similarities. When employing an inductive inventory of characteristics of generic fascism, one should understand that individual movements potentially possessed further beliefs, goals, and characteristics of major importance that did not necessarily contradict the common features but went beyond them. For these reasons, the typological description may serve as an analytic or heuristic device but should not be used as a monolithic, reified taxonomic category.[6] It may help us to understand the common traits of the most radical forms of a generation of European nationalism, conditioned by unique cultural, political, and social influences, but these cannot provide the full historical definition of each of the movements. They may, however, serve to underscore the historical uniqueness of fascism if we are able to conclude that neither before 1919 nor after 1945 have significant political movements existed that share the full cluster of fascist characteristics.

Some scholars perceived early that European fascism was not uniform but included a variety of distinct subtypes. They have defined this problem diversely. Eugen Weber distinguished two general subtypes or tendencies among fascist movements, the "fascist" proper, or Italian, and the "national

6. Hence the term *generic* has been used simply for general illustration and in conformity with verbal convention. To try to apply exact taxonomic language, which is usually derived from biological references, would probably lead to greater uncertainty and confusion, since we do not have sufficient understanding of political movements to demonstrate that they conform to or differ from each other with the taxonomic regularity or distinctness observable in the biological world. The term *generic fascism* is used only in a tentative sense and is not intended to indicate that fascistic movements constituted a specific, delimited "genus" altogether distinct from other possible "genera" of political movements, or that there was a necessarily direct and identifiable genetic relationship between them.

If generic fascism is to be categorized, in a tentative and limited way, in comparison with other nonparliamentary movements, then it might be identified as one of the major types of revolutionary mass movements that have emerged since the 1790s, of which at least six general types can be identified: Jacobin (1792–1871 or 1917), leading to the radical republican movements of southern Europe in the nineteenth and early twentieth centuries; anarchist (1835–1939); Socialist (1868–1939) (R. Luxembourg, Mensheviks, PSI, Austro-Marxists, PSOE); Leninist (1903–); Fascist (1919–45); and populist (1890–).

The latter is the most amorphous genus of the entire family, presumably embracing the Russian SRs, the Stambuliski peasant party, the early Mexican PRI or its immediate antecedents, APRA, the Bolivian MNR, the early Kuomintang, and probably a number of other third world movements.

One might possibly add a seventh category of mass counterrevolutionary movements with some radical goals of their own, most notably the Spanish Carlists.

socialist," contending that the Italian type was pragmatic (and hence more moderate, even conservative) and the national socialist type more theoretically motivated and fanatical, hence more radical and destructive. More recently, Alan Cassels suggested a kind of dichotomy between southwest European fascists and central European national socialists in their modernizing and regressive tendencies.[7] Wolfgang Sauer distinguished between three different "subtypes of fascism": the "original Mediterranean"; the "various and not too long-lived regimes" of east central Europe, as "a mixed, or not full-fledged variation; and German Nazism as a special form."[8]

There is substance to most of these distinctions, especially in the case of Weber's basic duality, but none of them are sufficiently detailed to make allowance for all the major subtypes. Since fascism was grounded in extreme nationalism, national movements sensitively reflected institutional, cultural, social, and spiritual differences in their own countries, producing many national variations. A minimum of five varieties can be identified (though other analysts might make the list considerably longer):

1. Paradigmatic Italian Fascism, pluralist, diverse, and not easily definable in simple terms. Forms to some extent derivative appeared in France, England, Belgium, Austria, Hungary, Romania, and possibly even Brazil.
2. German National Socialism, sometimes defined as the most extreme or radical form of fascism, the only fascistic movement to achieve a total dictatorship and so to develop its own system. Somewhat parallel or derivative movements emerged in Scandinavia, the Low Countries, the Baltic States, and Hungary, and, more artificially, in several of the satellite states during the war. The Italian and German types were the two dominant forms of fascism.
3. Spanish Falangism. Though to some extent derivative from the Italian form, it became a kind of Catholic and culturally more traditionalist fascism that was more marginal.
4. The Romanian Legionary or Iron Guard movement, a mystical, kenotic form of semireligious fascism that represented the only notable movement of this kind in an Orthodox country. It was also marginal.
5. Szalasi's "Hungarist" or Arrow Cross movement, somewhat distinct from either the Hungarian national socialists or Hungarian proponents of a more moderate and pragmatic Italian-style movement. For a short time, perhaps, it was the second most popular fascist movement in Europe.

Since fascist politics was a novel and late-blooming form, a large proportion of fascist leaders and even ordinary activists began their political careers

7. A. Cassels, *Fascism* (New York, 1974).

8. W. Sauer, "National Socialism: Totalitarianism or Fascism?" *American Historical Review* 73:2 (Dec. 1967): 404–22.

in association with nonfascist groups, usually either of the radical left or the Catholic or authoritarian right. The transformation that issued in fascist politics and organization was rarely instantaneous and complete. Sometimes a long evolutionary period of five years and more was required for the transformation into fascism, and sometimes that metamorphosis was never complete, stopping short at the boundary of a kind of partial protofascism. Thus amid the tensions of the 1930s many groups and movements were denounced as fascist, when they did not fully exhibit the characteristics of generic fascism but were simply moving toward certain aspects of fascist doctrine or style; or they may have merely begun to exhibit a few of the external trappings of fascist organizations, as was frequently the case with rightist groups, without actually adopting the radical spirit, doctrines, and goals of generic fascism. The undeniable vertigo produced by fascist politics during the depression decade induced displays of window dressing in marginally related groups that were frequently accepted for the real thing. Not only did such window dressing confuse analysts and historians of a subsequent generation, but it also confused the original fascists themselves, when Mussolini's regime began to move toward a broader doctrine of "universal fascism" and then was faced with the problem of identifying kindred fascist or sympathetic and fascistizing or fascistizable elements in other countries.[9]

THE DISTINCTIONS BETWEEN FASCIST MOVEMENTS AND REGIMES

Another major source of confusion in defining generic fascism has stemmed from the failure to distinguish between fascist movements and regimes. Most fascist parties failed to develop beyond the movement stage, and even in Italy the Fascist movement never assumed full power to develop a complete regime-system. One of the many paradoxes of fascist movements was that though they aspired to destroy the liberal political system (or more exactly, its residues) and to introduce a peculiarly apolitical style of militarized politics, they were nonetheless constrained to function in large measure as a regular political force within liberal or semiliberal political systems. This was due in part to their need to rely on portions of the middle classes, and to the fact that such mobilized national-integrative movements could develop only in countries that had already achieved a not inconsiderable degree of social and political development, which brought with it electoral parliamentary systems that had to be coped with. Thus fascist movements were never able to function as revolutionary-insurrectionist forces in the Leninist-Maoist style—the means

9. See M. A. Ledeen, *Universal Fascism* (New York, 1972); and R. De Felice, "I movimenti fascisti nel mondo," in his *Mussolini il Duce*, vol. 1, *Gli anni del consenso, 1929–1936* (Turin, 1974), appendix 8.

whereby all independent Communist parties that established their own regimes have come to power.

The fact that fascist movements were forced to work out their militarized style of politics largely within a middle-class parliamentary framework exposed them to major contradictions and normally made it difficult for them to work with existing parliamentary groups. Even in the most favorable situations, radical authoritarian movements or coalitions aiming at a new dictatorship have great, normally insurmountable, difficulty in passing the "40 percent barrier." This is true of such diverse movements as German National Socialism, Austro-Marxism, parliamentary communism in southwestern Europe, and the Allende coalition in Chile. Fascist movements, at any rate, were always dependent on allies in the final drive for power. Most of them failed to find effective allies, and the majority of those who did were in varying ways overwhelmed by their allies, whether these allies were the more conservative right or, during the war, the maximal fascist regime of Germany.

Thus in the absence of a plurality of generically fascist regimes and systems, it is possible to refer only to a number of semifascist or would-be fascist regimes, while in turn distinguishing between the character and structure of each type and subtype both among themselves and in comparison with diverse kinds of conservative (or at least nonsocialist) nonfascist authoritarian regimes. In general, the genus to which these refer is not that of fascist systems but rather of syncretic or mixed national authoritarian regimes of the twentieth century, of which the protototalitarian National Socialist regime in Germany may be considered the most extreme or atypical variation.

Rather than an anomaly, as Anglo-American theorists long considered it, the syncretic national authoritarian system was for some time the most common new political form of the twentieth century and became more common than either liberal parliamentary or totalitarian socialist systems. Within this general group at least seven different types can be identified:

1. The Hitler regime as the most extreme expression of generic fascism and the only completely fascist regime-system. It moved toward the elimination of all pluralism and by its last year of life had nearly achieved that. The fact that the Hitler regime represented the only fully fascist-controlled system, however, should not be interpreted as a demonstration that it realized the inherent tendencies of all fascist movements, for it represented only one specific form.

2. The Mussolini regime, created in large measure on the basis of the original Fascist movement, but in fact established and developed as a more limited and even semipluralist dictatorship in which the party was largely subordinated to the state and system rather than merely to the leader. The state itself failed to realize its own theoretical aspirations toward totalitarianism (and

in practice gave a less than total meaning to the term), as many analysts have recognized.

3. Satellite fascist and authoritarian regimes established by or through the Nazi imperium during World War II. The only ones that could be called genuine fascist regimes were those of the Ustashi and Arrow Cross, and these were more nearly puppet than genuine satellite regimes. The two which fit the latter category were those of Vichy France and Slovakia, and their political systems were not fascist but more similar to those in categories 5 and 6 below.

4. Syncretic dictatorships based on a nonfascist leadership principle, derived from military command or traditional legitimacy (or both) and a semi-pluralist national coalition but combining a significant fascist party component. The chief examples would be Spain from 1937 to 1945 and Romania from 1940 to 1941 (or 1944).

5. Syncretic, semipluralist authoritarian regimes lacking a mass-based government or a distinctive new party system which strove to develop a semi-bureaucratic semifascist movement from the top downward but normally failed in the enterprise. Examples would be Yugoslavia, 1929–39; Poland, 1937–39; Romania, 1938–40; Lithuania in the 1930s; and to some extent Greece, 1936–41. The case of Peronist Argentina bears a slight analogy with this type.

6. Conservative or praetorian bureaucratic-national regimes that were semi-pluralist and eschewed major new efforts at mobilization. Examples would be Spain, 1923–30 (and in a partial sense again after 1945); Brazil under Vargas; the new Latin American dictatorships of the 1960s and 1970s; the Greece of the Colonels, 1967–74; and various third world military regimes.

7. Limited authoritarian regimes that preserved certain liberal and parliamentary forms, such as Hungary under Horthy, the original Pilsudski regime in Poland (1926–35), Mexico under the PRI, the Latvian and Estonian regimes of the mid-1930s, Bulgaria from 1933 to 1944, and certain third world "guided democracies." [10]

Given these limitations, it is doubtful that fascism can be generically defined through a regime structure that was typically and fully fascist. Even the Hitler regime—the only one completely dominated by a fascist-type party and its leader for a full decade or more—failed to last long enough to achieve a complete and finished structure.

The concept "fascist regime" may therefore be employed only in a very

10. The most complete taxonomic analysis is J. J. Linz, "Totalitarian and Authoritarian Regimes," in *Handbook of Political Science*, ed. F. Greenstein and N. Polsby (Reading, Mass., 1975), 3:175–411.

loose and general sense, by analogy with the new style of dictatorship introduced by Mussolini. Thus many prefer to call fascist any non-Marxist authoritarian system based on a single party and attempting to regulate a mixed economy. Within this very loose framework one may identify a considerable number of "fascist regimes" both before and after World War II. Few of them, however, have had much to do with fascist movements or the historic culture of fascism.

14
Fascism and Modernization

In chapter 12 we saw that one of the principal controversies in the interpretation of fascism has concerned its relationship to modernization. As the only uniquely new political phenomenon of the early twentieth century, fascism has been thought by some to have been in some way related to the major processes of modernization under way in Europe at that time. There is, however, no agreement among historians as to the character of that relationship. As one Italian scholar has recently observed:

> There is now a widespread consensus among political sociologists that fascism is in some way or another connected with a pathological interaction between modernity and backwardness. That in other words it is one of the possible permutations of modernization.
>
> There is however less unanimity on the chief characteristics of such modernization. To what category of "perverse modernity" does it belong?[1]

One way of accounting for fascism has been to suggest that it was a modern phenomenon that was nonetheless strongly, perhaps principally, informed by antimodern attitudes and values. Though James Burnham early claimed fascism as one aspect of the modern managerial revolution, for Talcott Parsons fascism represented a radical form of resistance to modernization.[2] The most sagacious statement of this thesis was made by Henry Turner.[3] Such interpreta-

---

1. Marco Revelli, in *The Social Basis of European Fascist Movements*, ed. D. Mühlberger (New York, 1987), 1.
2. J. Burnham, *The Managerial Revolution* (New York, 1941); T. Parsons, "Some Sociological Aspects of the Fascist Movement," in his *Essays in Sociological Theory* (Glencoe, Ill., 1954), 124–41.
3. H. A. Turner Jr., "Fascism and Modernization," *World Politics* 24:4 (1972): 547–64, reprinted in *Reappraisals of Fascism*, ed. H. A. Turner Jr. (New York, 1975), 117–39. It should be

tions have been derived primarily but not exclusively from the German case and refer to National Socialism's opposition—real or perceived—to emancipation, egalitarianism, rationalism, scientism, urbanism, industrialism, and feminism. Fascism in general would thus be understood as the kind of radical mass movement that was primarily opposed to modernism, as distinct from communism and certain others that have purportedly prompted modernization. As in all monocausal and unireferential concepts of fascism, this one is too limited to deal adequately with so complex a movement, but since it lies near the center of many discussions of fascism, it merits more detailed examination.

During the past generation, modernity itself has become a very complex and controversial topic. On the one hand, it is declared by some to lie already in the past, the late twentieth century having become "postmodern." On the other hand, the easy assumptions about the correlation between modernization and progress have been called increasingly into question. There has developed a more general recognition that not all modernization brings "progress."

To render the concepts intelligible, we may begin by defining modernization as industrialization, urbanization, secularization, and rationalization. These four processes are central to what most social scientists have referred to as modernization. Several general theorists of modernization, it should be noted, have tended to view fascism as positively related to the modernization process, though their discussion of fascism is too general and limited to be of much use.[4] Let us therefore start by examining the programs, doctrines, and propaganda in some of the main fascist movements and then proceed to the actual policies and performance of the only two noteworthy fascist regimes.

The case of paradigmatic Italian Fascism seems clear enough during its first phase. The chief group of Fascist doctrinaires stemmed from revolutionary syndicalism, and at the core of their break with Marxism was not merely the principle of nationalism but also the concept of relative class coordination in achieving greater overall productivity and a modernized economy. The original Fascist program stood for economic modernization combined with more equal distribution, the reduction of traditional elites, ruthless secularization, voting rights for women, and the rapid renovation of Italian culture. In the arts, early Italian Fascism was completely identified with the avant-garde.

Within two years early Fascism lost its quasileftist identity, but the shift to

---

noted, however, that Turner questions the generic approach and suggests that the relationship in an underdeveloped country like Italy may have been quite different from the German case.

See also H. Mommsen, "Nationalsozialismus als vorgetäuschte Modernisierung," in *Der historische Ort des Nationalsozialismus,* ed. W. Perle (Frankfurt, 1990), 31–46, and M. Rauh, "Anti-Modernismus im nationalsozialistischen Staat," *Historisches Jahrbuch* 107 (1987): 94–121.

4. For example, D. Apter, *The Politics of Modernization* (Chicago, 1965); C. E. Black, *The Dynamics of Modernization* (New York, 1966); and A. F. K. Organski, *The Stages of Political Development* (New York, 1965). It should be noted that Organski refers primarily to Italy, where he believes that Fascism permitted the "forced accumulation" necessary for industrialization.

accommodate the right did not involve opposition to modernization. Though extreme secularism would no longer be emphasized in the same way, Fascism nonetheless remained secularist and fundamentally anticlerical. The renewed emphasis on multiclass cooperation was not opposed to modern development but was stressed as an indispensable prerequisite for it. In Fascist terms, Lenin was denounced not for being a revolutionary but for practicing a mere uniclass proletarian state collectivism, inadequate to promote the full forces of modern development.

Renzo De Felice tends to see Fascism as a genuinely modern and also modernizing force, in certain respects heir to key impulses of the French Revolution. De Felice finds these qualities strongest in the movement phase of Fascism, though also present in varying degrees within the subsequent Mussolini regime.[5]

The attitudes of early National Socialism were more ambivalent. Germany was much more urban and industrialized, and a wide current of *völkisch* cultural norms had already developed in reaction. National Socialism broadly identified with this form of ethnicist-environmentalist culture, which had little counterpart in Italy at that time. *Grossstadtfeindlichkeit* was not a Nazi invention but was fully exploited, while the threat of "bigness" in industrial and commercial organization was vigorously combated.

Yet emphasizing these aspects alone considerably distorts the general perspective. National Socialism in fact made an effort, surprisingly successfully, to appeal to all major sectors of German society, so that the ideals of the rural and the small-scale coexisted with profoundly contradictory and distinct tendencies. Ian Kershaw correctly concludes that "recent research on the social basis of Nazi support before 1933 has, in fact, completely undermined earlier generalizations about the backward-looking, reactionary (in a literal sense) nature of Nazism's mass backing, and has emphasized the strong, dynamic motivation for radical social change and undeniable 'modern' tendencies and aspirations among the socially heterogeneous support for the NSDAP."[6] Jürgen Falter, the leading German analyst of the Nazi electoral campaigns, has shown that the Nazis came closer than any other German political party to being a true *Volkspartei*, with members and voters from every class, and that the proportion of new supporters who came from the left was considerably larger than previously estimated.[7]

---

5. See the eight volumes of De Felice's classic biography of Mussolini (Turin, 1965–90), as well as his interview with Michael Ledeen, *Intervista sul fascismo* (Bari, 1975), and his commentaries in his massive edition of interpretations, *Il fascismo: Le interpretazioni dei contemporanei e degli storici* (Rome, 1970).

6. I. Kershaw, *The Nazi Dictatorship: Problems and Perspectives of Interpretation* (London, 1985), 134.

7. See, inter alia, J. Falter, "War die NSDAP die erste deutsche Volkspartei," in *Nationalsozialismus und Modernisierung*, ed. M. Prinz and R. Zitelmann (Darmstadt, 1991), 21–47;

The programs of fascist movements varied widely with regard to major aspects of modernity and the process of modernization. The notion that the more backward the country the more concerned its own fascists were with questions of development does not seem to be accurate. The two parties that most emphasized economic theory and development were arguably two of the most sophisticated in two of the most advanced countries: Sir Oswald Mosley's British Union of Fascists and Marcel Déat's Rassemblement National Populaire. It is clear that a major aspect of fascism's attraction for Mosley lay in his belief that it would provide the most useful means of overcoming what he saw as the economic stagnation and demodernization of Britain. The first categorical French fascist movement, Georges Valois's Le Faisceau, emphasized modernization, rationalization, planning, technology, and a new mass prosperity to be built by radical national syndicalism. Jacques Doriot's Parti Populaire Français also to some extent stressed the role of technology. The Spanish Falange recognized the need for economic modernization in its program, though it had difficulty identifying concrete proposals to bring this about. The culture of modernity was rejected most strongly by the Romanian Legion of the Archangel Michael, which in theory sought a resacralization of life (rather like an Islamic neofundamentalist movement), yet even the Legion recognized the need for modern economic development and industrialization.

Much has been made—or at least attempted—concerning the bases of social support of the fascist movements. Such inquiries do not in and of themselves decisively prove anything concerning the relationship between fascism and modernization. Italian Fascists primarily mobilized sectors of the middle classes, with an important agrarian component. National Socialism relied proportionately less on the middle classes, having more worker support and proportionately even more support among farmers. The Legion of the Archangel Michael was a movement of students and peasants, the Spanish Falange was for long primarily a movement of students, and the Arrow Cross mobilized a sector of the workers and numerous poor peasants. The social sector proportionately most susceptible to lending support to fascist movements would seem to have been university students, presumably a modern and modernizing class.

It is of course more useful to discuss the policies and priorities of the two fascist regimes than to engage in abstract debates concerning points of programmatic theory or propaganda. That the Mussolini government in power maintained a vigorous and effective program of modernization is a view propounded with especial vigor by A. James Gregor.[8] There is no doubt that Italian

---

J. Falter and R. Zintl, "The Economic Crisis of the 1930s and the Nazi Vote," *Journal of Interdisciplinary History* 19 (1988): 55–85; and J. Falter and D. Hänisch, "Die Anfälligkeit von Arbeitern gegenüber der NSDAP bei den Reichstagswahlen, 1928–1933," *Archiv für Sozialgeschichte* 26 (1986): 179–216.

8. Gregor's thesis finds full expression in his *Italian Fascism and Developmental Dictator-*

state policy during the first years of the regime stressed rationalization and economic development, and the 1920s were a period of rapid growth for Italy as for most of the Western world. Critics have pointed to the decline in workers' real income which took place in that decade, yet other scholars have observed that this was offset in part or even wholly by a substantial increase in fringe benefits. More conclusive was the survey of eating habits which "found, for the first time in Italian history, that in the North the upper classes were consuming fewer calories per day than the poorer ones—a sure sign of prosperity." "Army recruits grew taller each year, another good index of better hygiene and diet," even though recruits came disproportionately from the underdeveloped south. "Welfare spending rose from 1.5 billion lire in 1930 to 6.7 billion lire by 1940, i.e. from 6.9 percent to 20.6 percent of all state and local tax receipts," indicating that even during the period of massive new military expenditure, welfare programs—normally considered a sort of index of modernization—rapidly increased.[9]

There was nothing especially leftist or revolutionary about Fascist economic policy.[10] No fully "corporate system" was ever developed, and most of the time private business, especially big business, was given considerable latitude. Direct state investment in industry and finance began only as an emergency measure during the depression, with the introduction of the IRI (Institute for Industrial Reconstruction) in 1933. By the end of the decade the IRI possessed 17.8 percent of the capital assets of Italian industry, placing Italy in a virtual tie with Poland for the second largest proportion of state holdings among European countries.[11]

Gregor, after noting basic Fascist priorities toward nationalism and war in the 1930s, concludes,

---

ship (Princeton, 1979). See also his *The Fascist Persuasion in Radical Politics* (Princeton, 1974) and, for briefer presentation, his "Fascism and Modernization: Some Addenda," *World Politics* 26:3 (April 1974): 370–84. This approach was suggested to some extent by Franz Borkenau in 1933 and was employed tentatively in more recent work by the Hungarian historian Mihaly Vajda. It has been advanced by Italian scholars in M. Abrate et al., *Il problema storico del fascismo* (Florence, 1970), and L. Garruccio [pseud.], *L'industrializzazione tra nazionalismo e rivoluzione* (Bologna, 1969). The productivist and modernizing goals of early Fascism have been pointed out by Roland Sarti, in "Fascist Modernization in Italy: Traditional or Revolutionary?" *American Historical Review* 75:4 (April 1970): 1029–45, and E. R. Tannenbaum, "The Goals of Italian Fascism," *American Historical Review* 74:4 (April 1969): 1183–204.

9. M. Clark, *Modern Italy, 1871–1982* (London, 1984), 268, 267.

10. For further debate about Italian Fascism and revolution, see the chapters by Leo Valiani ("Il fascismo; controrivoluzione e rivoluzione") and Dino Cofrancesco ("Fascismo; destra o sinistra?") in *Fascismo e nazionalsocialismo*, ed. K. D. Bracher and L. Valiani (Bologna, 1986), 125–51, 107–24.

11. R. Sarti, *Fascism and the Industrial Leadership in Italy, 1919–1940* (Berkeley, 1971), 123.

For all that, by 1937 Italy had become a modern industrial nation. For the first time in its history, industrial production outstripped that of agriculture. Italy had recovered from the depression with an overall volume of output (1913 = 100) that achieved a level of 153.8 by 1938, compared with the 132.9 attained in 1929—a performance at least comparable to that of Germany, whose index was 149.9, and the United Kingdom, whose index was 158.3, and considerably better than that of France, which languished at 109.4. In point of fact, Fascist Italy maintained a level of industrial development at least equal to that of its more resource-favored neighbors while it was attempting to create a measure of self-sufficiency that required enormous commitments in terms of resources and investment capital. While the extensive cartelization of Italian industry and the abundance of relatively cheap labor afforded little intrinsic incentive for technological innovation and industrial modernization, output per man in Fascist Italy rose from the index 126.3 (1913 = 100) in 1929 to 145.2 in 1938, an output performance that surpassed that of any other industrial or industrializing nation save Norway and Switzerland. Similarly, during the same period, output per man-hour in Fascist Italy was superior to the performance in almost every other European nation with the exception of Norway.[12]

Gianni Toniolo, perhaps the leading economic historian of the Fascist period, has collected economic growth figures for the entire Fascist era before World War II which place the Italian performance on a more mediocre level, as indicated in table 14.1. Different weightings can produce different outcomes. The pre-Fascist decade was itself a period of both crisis and growth. The comparison with Switzerland is irrelevant, while the slightly better performance of Britain in this comparison is due to relatively rapid growth in the later 1930s. The poorer performance of France is due to stagnation during the early 1930s following rapid development in the preceding decade.

Conversely, if one examines Paul Bairoch's data for the two decades 1913–33, the performance of the Italian economy has a different appearance (table 14.2). If one looks only at the trough of the depression, the perspective alters yet again, and Italy's performance becomes almost exactly equivalent to the European norm (table 14.3). Pierluigi Ciocca, generally critical of Fascist economic policy, concurs, finding that between 1929 and 1933 Italian GNP dropped by 5.4 percent and that industrial production fell 22.7 percent, compared with the general western European averages of 7.1 percent and 23.2 percent respectively.[13] After the new economic growth spurred by rearmament and war in the second half of the 1930s is included, the general Italian economic performance during the depression decade of annual industrial growth is 1.7. Less than Germany's and considerably less than Sweden's, it was only

12. Gregor, *Developmental Dictatorship* 161.
13. P. Ciocca, "L'economia nel contesto internazionale," in *L'economia italiana nel periodo fascista*, ed. P. Ciocca and G. Toniolo (Bologna, 1976), 36.

Table 14.1. Western European Economic Growth, 1922–1938

Geographic Division	Average Annual Percentage Rate
Switzerland	4.1
Germany	3.8
Western Europe as a whole	2.5
United Kingdom	2.2
Italy	1.9
France	1.4

Source: G. Toniolo, L'economia dell'Italia fascista (Bari, 1980), 6.

Table 14.2. Economic Production in Real Terms Per Capita in 1933 (1913 = 100)

Geographic Division	Index
France	121.7
Sweden	120.0
Italy	111.6
Spain	109.8
Europe as a whole	102.0
United Kingdom	99.9
Germany	94.6

Source: P. Bairoch, "Europe's Gross National Product (1800–1975)," Journal of European Economic History 5:2 (Fall 1976): 297.

Table 14.3. Index of Net Production in Real Terms Per Capita in 1933 (1929 = 100)

Geographic Division	Index
Sweden	97.4
United Kingdom	95.9
Italy	95.2
Europe as a whole	95.1
Germany	93.0
France	86.2

Source: Bairoch, "Europe's Gross National Product" 297.

slightly below the western European norm and stood well above the figure of −2.8 for liberal democratic France.[14]

As had already been clear in the second half of the 1920s, what was distinctive about Fascist economic policy was not that it was opposed to industrialization and modernization but that it was aimed toward autarchy, self-sufficiency, and the growth of industries such as chemicals and metallurgy that

14. Cf. D. Lomax, The Inter-War Economy of Britain, 1919–1939 (London, 1970).

might be more useful for military growth (all these trends paralleled those in the Soviet Union as well). The much-heralded imposition of the Quota Novanta that deflated the lira in 1926 was partly a matter of international prestige but was also the first dramatic demonstration of the turn away from an export-led economy such as had fueled the relative boom of the first half of the 1920s. This fundamental economic priority of the regime may be considered "antimodern," compared with the terms of economic growth for the world economy before 1914, during the 1920s, and after 1950, but it was a fundamental characteristic shared not merely with Nazi Germany but also with the Soviet Union and many nationalist and Communist dictatorships of the century. Moreover, Fascist Italy did sustain an increase in domestic food production during the 1930s, unlike the modern revolutionary model of the Soviet Union.

It is not to the point to argue, as critics do, that the rate of Italian economic development was higher before 1914 or after 1947, for the difficult interwar period, with its major international depression, cannot be readily compared with the booms before World War I or after World War II. Compared with other economies at similar stages of development during that same historical period, the Italian system performed reasonably well.[15] Conversely, the great Stalinist industrialization in the Soviet Union was achieved by catastrophic exploitation of the rural economy and hugely disproportionate human and economic investment—hardly a superior performance, since per capita Soviet income did not exceed the 1928 level until 1953. Moreover, of the four industrial states that increased production rapidly in the late 1930s, three—Germany, Japan, and the Soviet Union—did so in large measure on a burgeoning military industrial complex. Despite Mussolini's blustering rhetoric about considering Italy "in a permanent state of war," he never made truly major investments in military production until these years.

Industrialization is but one major index of modernization. One of the most unique features of the Italian regime in its own time was its emphasis on ecology, on the *ridimensionamento* of national socioeconomic structure, which aimed at controlling urbanization, improving environmental conditions, promoting reforestation, and keeping a large percentage of the rural population in the countryside. Such concepts had become all the rage by the 1980s, but they have somehow been held to be "antimodern" when promoted by Fascism in the 1930s, rather than prescient and precocious. In some ways fascistic ecology seems to have been a sophisticated presentiment of the problems of twentieth-century urbanization and industrialization, long before social democrats became seriously aware of such problems.

15. A sober empirical critique will be found in A. Hughes and M. Kolinsky, " 'Paradigmatic Fascism' and Modernization: A Critique," *Political Studies* 24:4 (Dec. 1976): 371–96, and in the economic articles in A. Acquarone and M. Vernassa, eds., *Il regime fascista* (Bologna, 1974).

The Fascist regime also carried out fundamental reorganization of the Italian banking system and the state's civil, commercial, and penal codes. These reforms have long survived Fascism and formed part of the basic postwar structure after 1945. They can all be considered fundamental achievements in institutional updating and modernization.

The record in some of the basic social programs, however, was quite different. The Fascist educational reform introduced by Giovanni Gentile was clearly classicist rather than modernizing, devoted much more to the humanities than to the sciences. The last major Fascist reform, Giuseppe Bottai's Carta della Scuola in 1939, had the effect of rationalizing and streamlining somewhat the Italian educational system but did not really overcome the limitations of the 1923 law.[16] Basic primary education expanded considerably under Fascism, as under all modernizing regimes, but so did the scope of Catholic education—theoretically a hindrance to modern secularization (though in fact probably more functional in promoting basic modernization than much of Fascist educational policy).

Even more unsuccessful were the regime's efforts to establish a more austere, militarily disciplined, and prolific society. Mussolini eventually developed the notion that a creative future depended on general austerity, on people "eating less." If modernization means hedonism and consumerism, then the heroic and military spirit of austerity sought by Fascism was clearly antimodern. Equally unsuccessful were the perverse attempts to raise the national birthrate, which generally continued to decline. Only in the promotion of sports and leisure activities did the regime achieve a greater measure of success.[17]

The balance is neither one of unalloyed modernization nor of pure antimodernism, but a complex mixture distinct from either of these. In industrialization and technology, Fascist Italy was at least moderately successful. The broader Fascist cultural ideals, rebelling against the priorities of the nineteenth century, were opposed to urbanism, rationalism, and true secularism (however anticlerical and anti-Christian), devoted to achieving a new twentieth-century counterculture that was modernist in some ways but Roman and military in others.

Those who hold that fascism was generally antimodernist are usually referring, however, not to Fascist Italy but to Nazi Germany. More precisely, discussions of fascism and modernization have tended to revolve around the extent to which major social and economic transformations occurred during

16. T. Koon, *Believe, Obey, Fight: Political Socialization of Youth in Fascist Italy, 1922–1943* (Chapel Hill, 1985); M. Barbagli, *Educating for Unemployment: Politics, Labor Markets, and the School System—Italy, 1859–1973* (New York, 1982); L. Minio-Paluello, *Education in Fascist Italy* (London, 1946); M. Ostenc, *L'Education en Italie pendant le Fascisme* (Paris, 1980).

17. Cf. V. de Grazia, *The Culture of Consent: Mass Organization of Leisure in Fascist Italy* (Cambridge, 1981).

the twelve-year Hitler regime, scarcely a single year of which was lived in absolute normalcy. The three years of recovery from the depression (1933–36) were followed by three years of rapid rearmament (1936–39), succeeded in turn by endless war which eventually came close to total mobilization.

The two best-known proponents of the concept of the Third Reich as a socially modernizing regime are Ralf Dahrendorf and David Schoenbaum. Dahrendorf has argued that the National Socialist system produced "a social revolution" that carried out "the break with tradition and thus a strong push toward modernity" by breaking down social barriers inherited from the Wilhelmian era.[18] Schoenbaum's *Hitler's Social Revolution* makes the same point, though noting that the social change was sometimes more oriented toward psychological status than concrete social structure. Nonetheless, he concludes that there occurred "a revolution of class and a revolution of status at the same time" that, at least in regard to status, amounted to "the triumph of egalitarianism" in the national *Volksgemeinschaft*.[19] These views are echoed by the more recent study of Werner Abelshauser and Anselm Faust, who see the Third Reich as "a catalyst of modernization."[20] All these interpretations run directly counter to Marxist theories and also to the evaluations of Western liberal scholars who view National Socialism as inherently antimodernist.

A more nuanced approach has been adopted by Horst Matzerath and Heinrich Volkmann, who view National Socialism not so much as an attempt to solve the problems of modernization through antimodernism as an effort toward a utopian third course. Though in some respects it did promote social modernization, this is viewed as contradictory, nonrational, and dysfunctional, achieving only a "pseudomodernization."[21] Some commentators have concluded that the basic structure and group loyalties within German society were changed comparatively little and that the pattern of income distribution altered hardly at all. They see changes which did take place as the inevitable result of further industrialization and not of any radical reform or revolution.[22]

There is now a tendency for the most recent scholars to agree with Schoenbaum that National Socialism effected some change in psychological social status, while disagreeing with the idea of any major change in social struc-

18. R. Dahrendorf, *Society and Democracy in Germany* (London, 1968), 403.

19. D. Schoenbaum, *Hitler's Social Revolution* (New York, 1966), 272–73.

20. W. Abelshauser and A. Faust, *Wirtschafts und Sozialpolitik: Eine national-sozialistische Sozialrevolution?* (Tübingen, 1983).

21. H. Matzerath and H. Volkmann, "Modernisierungstheorie und Nationalsozialismus," in *Theorien in der Praxis des Historikers*, ed. J. Kocka (Göttingen, 1977), 100.

22. Thus Jens Albers, comparing various socioeconomic indicators of the Third Reich and the Federal Republic, finds that the decisive accelerations took place under the latter. Albers, "Nationalsozialismus und Modernisierung," *Kölner Zeitschrift für Soziologie und Sozialpsychologie* 41 (June 1989): 346–65.

ture itself. During the entire Nazi period, truly major shifts occurred only at the very end, under the impact not of Nazi policy per se but of total war and massive defeat. Detlev Peukert has made the more sophisticated point that National Socialism's main contribution to a later phase of German modernization may well have lain in the atomization of society through depoliticization. This had the effect of encouraging Germans to withdraw into the personal and private sphere, contributing subsequently to the individual economic drive and consumerism central to the postwar *Wirtschaftswunder*.[23]

One aspect of Nazi policy that appears strikingly antimodern is the area of education. The subordination of scientific and rational criteria to political values was especially notable here. A feature such as the expansion of physical education might at first seem typically modern, but its extension to include 15 percent of all school time, with boxing becoming a required subject for boys in upper grades, seems nonrational. The decline in discipline and learning standards had already become marked by the early part of the war.

What happened in the universities was even more striking, since 60 percent of undergraduates in 1931 had supported the Nazi Student League, perhaps the highest pro-Nazi proportion of any sector of society. Nearly 15 percent of the university faculty were dismissed, and as many as 18 percent in the natural sciences. The total university student body shrank from 128,000 in 1933 to only 58,000 in 1939.

There was another side to the Nazi record, however, for while the secondary and university curricula declined, effort was made to expand unified, secular, modern state elementary schools, and there was strong encouragement for certain kinds of new work in the natural and social sciences.[24] Applied sociology and social research expanded considerably, some of the new research units carrying over to the postwar Federal Republic.[25] The demands of war

23. D. Peukert, *Inside Nazi Germany: Conformity, Opposition, and Racism in Everyday Life* (New Haven, 1987), 241–42. Peukert further declares: "Nazism arose as an aimless rebellion against the thrust toward modernization that had been bound up with the crisis of the 1920s; once in power, however, it absorbed and came to terms with the technologies and trends of modernity" (248). "In fact, the long-term trends characteristic of a modern industrial society, which had been interrupted by the world economic crisis, continued to run their course. Many of these trends were deliberately encouraged by the National Socialists; others were pragmatically accepted; yet others persisted in contradiction of the NSDAP's scheme and, so to speak, behind the party's back. In this sense we cannot properly speak of 'Hitler's social revolution,' even though the resultant effect of this parallelogram of mainly destructive forces was that a more 'modern' society emerged from the ruins of the Third Reich at the end of the war" (247).

24. Cf. F. Sonnenberger, "Die vollstreckte Reform—Die Einführung der Gemeinschaftsschule Bayern, 1935–1938," in Prinz and Zitelmann, eds., *Nationalsozialismus* 172–98.

25. C. Klingemann, "Social-Scientific Experts—No Ideologues: Sociology and Social Research in the Third Reich," in *Sociology Responds to Fascism*, ed. S. Turner and D. Käsler (London, 1992), 127–54.

soon produced a change in attitude toward the work of physicists and the "new physics,"[26] and further encouragement was given to biological research.[27] The professions of psychology and psychiatry were active under the Nazi framework,[28] with greater attention to social history and social science approaches,[29] and to new applied research on eastern Europe.[30] The notion that Hitler merely made a desert of the modern sciences is in fact wide of the mark.

Nazi policy toward women appeared so sexist and traditionalist that it has almost without exception been held to be clearly antimodernist. Yet to the extent that an effort was made to mobilize women at all, it might be considered in one sense modernizing. By 1937 official policy discouraging the employment of women had been partially reversed, and female employment rose from 11.5 million in 1933 to 12.7 million by May 1939, though the latter figure was insufficient to meet the need. The percentage of women among university students rose from 17 percent in 1933 to 20 percent in 1939 and 40 percent in 1940, and the percentage of women doctors rose from 5.6 in 1930 to 7.6 in 1939. The regime was clearly successful in raising the birthrate—presumably a token of antimodernism—and remained sufficiently true to its principles that compulsory women's labor was not introduced until 1943, very late in the day for Germany.

The regime's concern for environmentalism and environmental planning might be considered precocious and postmodern, rather than antimodern. In general, Nazi environmentalism probably merits much the same commentary as that in Fascist Italy. It was honored much more in theory than in practice, but the concept in various respects was ahead of the times.

No one has attempted to deny that certain fundamental processes of modernization, such as urbanization and industrialization, accelerated under National Socialism. This has usually been ascribed to the natural requirements for a strong state and war machine, with the assumption that such modernization contradicted Nazi principles and would have been reversed in the event of a final military victory.

In fact, Hitler and most other top Nazi leaders never envisioned any Nazi

---

26. A. D. Beyerchen, *Scientists under Hitler: Politics and the Physics Community in the Third Reich* (New Haven, 1977); M. Walker, *German National Socialism and the Quest for Nuclear Power, 1939–1949* (New York, 1989); idem, "National Socialism and German Physics," *JCH* 24:1 (Jan. 1989): 63–90.

27. P. Weingart, J. Kroll, and K. Bayertz, *Rasse, Blut und Gene: Geschichte der Eugenik und Rassenhygiene in Deutschland* (Frankfurt, 1988).

28. U. Geuter, *Die Professionalisierung der deutschen Psychologie im Nationalsozialismus* (Frankfurt, 1984); H.-W. Schmuhl, "Reformpsychiatrie und Massenmord," in Prinz and Zitelmann, eds., *Nationalsozialismus* 239–68.

29. W. Oberkrome, "Reformansätze in der deutschen Geschichtswissenschaft der Zwischenkriegszeit," in Prinz and Zitelmann, eds., *Nationalsozialismus* 216–39.

30. M. Burleigh, *Germany Turns Eastward: A Study of "Ostforschung" in the Third Reich* (Cambridge, 1988).

"Morgenthau Plan" of deindustrialization for the Reich. Hitler always appreciated the central importance of modern industry, and the whole scheme of *Lebensraum* was oriented toward guaranteeing vast deposits of raw materials and agricultural resources so that the German heartland might be even more heavily industrialized in the future. This was accompanied throughout by steady encouragement of rationalization and technological improvement in productive processes.[31]

Social policy and planning reflected many of the same features and emphases. The growth in fringe benefits, increasing opportunities for workers, a trend toward relatively increasing social equality, planning for an elaborate and more egalitarian welfare state, sophisticated new city planning and architectural projects—all reflected the institutionalized policies of a more modern (and in strictly individual aspects "progressive") structure of society.[32] This society was to become increasingly totalitarian and exclusionary, and the cost in lives and suffering to establish it was super-Stalinesque, but the project was not one of a return to a rural and premodern structure of society.

Any evaluation of the modernism of National Socialism must consider not only individual domestic policies but even more the Hitlerian grand design of *Lebensraum* and racial revolution. It would be absurd to label the Hitlerian revolution as traditional, reactionary, "feudal," or premodern. All of Hitler's political and social ideas had their origin in variants of the eighteenth-century Enlightenment—the revolt against traditional culture in the name of a revolutionary secularism, the belief in a secular natural law and a naturalistic Deist concept of God, the rejection of the traditional Christian concept of the unity of mankind in favor of racial division, the emphasis on a combination of biological inequality and social equality, the distinction between the productive and unproductive, the emphasis on the people and the national group, the Rousseauian general will of the people, the optimistic belief in progress and a higher humanity, and the cult of will.[33] All these Hitlerian beliefs were fundamen-

31. A. Ritschl, "Die NS-Wirtschaftsideologie—Modernisierungsprogramm oder reaktionäre Utopie?" and M. Prinz, "Die soziale Funktion moderner Elemente in der Gesellschaftspolitik des Nationalsozialismus," both in Prinz and Zitelmann, eds., *Nationalsozialismus* 48–70, 267–96. Similarly, Anson Rabinbach has drawn attention to "the expansion of technical rationality to all aspects of the production process in the Four-Year Plan" and the "emphasis on production and the glorification of technology as ends in themselves." Rabinbach, "The Aesthetics of Production in the Third Reich," *JCH* 11:4 (Oct. 1976): 43–64.

32. See the articles by Ronald Smelser, Rolf Messerschmidt, Werner Durth, Hans-Dieter Schäfer, Berhard R. Kroener, and Michael Prinz, together with the other studies which they cite, in Prinz and Zitelmann, eds., *Nationalsozialismus*.

33. This was perhaps first pointed out by Marcel Déat. in *Révolution française et révolution allemande* (Paris. 1943). but has only been fully developed in Lawrence Birken's *Hitler as Philosophe: Remnants of the Enlightenment in National Socialism* (Westport, Conn.. 1995).

George L. Mosse formulates this as part of the "new politics" of the nationalistic masses, stemming from eighteenth-century doctrines of popular sovereignty in which the people worship

tal postulates in modern philosophy and culture, though not every aspect of them was shared by all modern thinkers. Hitler was himself a stern derider of premodern "superstition." His own ideas had been radicalized by the new doctrines of late nineteenth-century German extremist nationalism and the cultural crisis of the fin de siècle, but none of this involved a reversion to traditional, premodern thought. Nazi racism was conceivable only in the early twentieth century and at no previous time in human history. The naturalistic racial anthropology of Hitler was purely a modern concept without any premodern parallels.

Much of modern culture is based on a cult of the will, which Hitler carried to an absolute extreme. The very concept of National Socialism as the "will to create a new man" was a typically modern, antitraditional idea. The same might be said of the Nazi search for extreme autonomy, a radical freedom for the German people. Hitler carried the modern goal of breaking the limits and setting new records to an unprecedented point. For no other movement did the modern doctrine of man as the measure of all things rule to such an extent.[34]

The ultimate horror of truly large-scale genocide or mass murder is a prototypical development of the twentieth century, from Turkey to Russia to Germany to Cambodia to Africa. The unique Nazi contribution was to modernize the process as never before or after, to accomplish the mass murder more efficiently and surgically than other great liquidators in the Soviet Union or Cambodia have done. Nor was Hitler's genocidal program any more or less "rational," since the goal of mass murder is always political, ideological, or religious and not a matter of practical economic ends.

National Socialism in fact constituted a unique and radical kind of modern revolutionism. Karl Bracher, for example, has identified the following revolutionary qualities of National Socialism:

1. A supreme new leadership cult of the Führer as the "artist genius."
2. The effort to develop a new Social Darwinist structure of state and society.
3. The replacement of traditional nationalism by racial revolution.
4. Development of a new system (of sorts) of state-regulated national socialism in economics.
5. Implementation of the organic status revolution for a new national *Volksgemeinschaft*.
6. The goal of a completely new kind of racial imperialism on a world scale.
7. Stress on new forms of advanced technology in the use of mass media and

---

themselves as a national group or race and are ultimately directed not by laws or parliaments but by secular natural religion. Mosse, *The Nationalization of the Masses* (New York, 1975), 1–20.

34. Here I must refer again to Steven E. Aschheim's unpublished seminar paper, "Modernity and the Metapolitics of Nazism," University of Wisconsin, 1975. See also Z. Bauman, *Modernity and the Holocaust* (Cambridge, 1989).

mass mobilization, a cult of new technological efficiency, new military tactics and technology, and an emphasis on aerial and automotive technology.[35]

This list might be refined and made even more detailed, but it covers the main points. For those interested in national liberation movements as an index of modernity, it should be remembered that during World War II the promotion of national liberation movements among colonial and minority peoples around the world was almost exclusively the work of the Tripartite powers.[36]

The most extensive reappraisal is that carried out by Rainer Zitelmann, who emphasizes Hitler's oft-expressed ultimate determination to overthrow the materialist capitalist-bourgeois order as well as the modernizing character of his utopia. For Zitelmann, Hitler had no real interest in defending private property and eventually planned a series of economic nationalizations that would revalue the position of the working class and, even more important, subject economics to politics. He had only a tactical and temporary interest in peasant and preindustrial society and never sought a primarily agrarian utopia, as charged by many. Zitelmann concludes that the character of the new *Lebensraum* in the east in Hitlerian thinking has been misunderstood, for it was to be primarily a source of food and raw materials, serving to reinforce the industrial character of the German heartland.[37]

Fascism was nothing if not modernist, despite its high quotient of archaic or anachronistic warrior culture. Its primary concern was neither antimodernism nor modernization per se, for it promoted many new aspects of modernization while combating or seeking fundamentally to readjust others.[38] Fascism was above all a product of the new culture and intense international Social Dar-

35. K. D. Bracher, *Zeitgeschichtliche Kontroversen um Faschismus Totalitarismus Demokratie* (Munich, 1976), 60–78; idem, "Il nazional-socialismo in Germania: Problemi d'interpretazione," in Bracher and Valiani, eds., *Fascismo* 31–54. The list presented above represents my own reformulation, not an exact transcription of Bracher. See also J. Ellul, *Autopsy of Revolution* (New York, 1971), and E. Weber, "Revolution? Counterrevolution? What Revolution?" *JCH* 9:2 (April 1974): 3–47, reprinted in *Fascism: A Reader's Guide*, ed. W. Laqueur (Berkeley, 1976), 435–67.

36. This is not to overlook Franklin Roosevelt's vigorous opposition to western European imperialism while acquiescing in Soviet imperialism. Cf. W. R. Louis, *Imperialism at Bay* (New York, 1978).

37. R. Zitelmann, *Hitler: Selbstverständnis eines Revolutionärs* (Hamburg, 1987); Prinz and Zitelmann, eds., *Nationalsozialismus.*

38. Eric Dorn Brose has underscored the diversity of the fascists themselves: "There does not exist a modernist or antimodernist Nazism or Fascism, if viewed from the perspective of attitudes toward technology. Instead it seems evident that there were numerous and competing traditions in both parties that constrained both Hitler and Mussolini to be tolerant on these doctrinal questions. Each movement possessed 1) reactionary modernists and technocrats; 2) enthusiasts of a return to the land and technophobes; and 3) charismatic leaders who left a place for the machine in a 'reformed' postindustrial world." Brose, "Il nazismo, il fascismo e la tecnologia," *SC* 18:2 (April 1987): 387–405.

winism of the early twentieth century, normally (though not in every instance) wedded to war and fundamental international changes. Its pagan warrior mentality sometimes conflicted with the norms and processes of modernization, but fascist states eagerly incorporated major functions of rationalization and modern development. These were fundamental and irresolvable contradictions of the most contradictory of all the revolutionary mass movements.

Perhaps the key relationship between fascism and modernization lay in the fact that fascism achieved significance only among the second-phase latecomers in the European state and industrial systems of the nineteenth and early twentieth centuries. Even Germany was a latecomer in political modernization and imperial expansion, though it generated great momentum in industry and technology. Fascism had little appeal in the older established polities and economic systems of northern and northwestern Europe, exerting its maximal appeal in the new nations of the 1860s and 1870s, to whom it offered an acceleration of power, unity, and expansion. Nonetheless, its most distinctive values concerning the revalorization of violence, war, and intense nationalism strove for a martial utopia and a distinctive kind of modernity, apart from traditionalism, liberal capitalism, or Communist materialism. Fascism sought to accelerate many, but not all, aspects of modernization while rejecting and modifying others en route to the abortive realization of its separate nationalist-racialist utopia.[39] Ultimately, what was most modern of all about fascism was that it "was a very 'modern' form of tyranny" distinct from all others.[40] Whatever gains it realized in accelerated modernization of social, economic, and technological structures "stand in no remotely comparable relation to the costs" which it exacted.[41]

39. For further discussion, see R. Griffin, *Modernity under the New Order: The Fascist Project for Managing the Future* (1994).

40. Robert Smelser, in Prinz and Zitelmann, *Nationalsozialismus* 91.

41. Ibid., 327, quoting Michael Prinz.

15
Elements of a Retrodictive
Theory of Fascism

The search for an adequate theory or interpretation of fascism has generally ended in failure, so that over the years the residue left by such discussions has come to resemble, in MacGregor Knox's phrase, the remains of a desert battle-field littered with abandoned or burned-out wrecks. Most theories of fascism can be easily shown to lack general or even specific validity. They mostly tend toward the monocausal or reductionist and can either be disproved or shown to be inadequate with greater or lesser ease. Moreover, most of those who deal with fascism are not primarily concerned with a common or comparative category of diverse movements and/or regimes but refer exclusively or primarily to German National Socialism, which reduces the scope and application of such arguments.

It is doubtful that there is any unique hidden meaning in, cryptic explanation of, or special "key" to fascism. It was an epochal European revolutionary movement of the early twentieth century of great complexity, fomented by the new ideas and values of the cultural crisis of the fin de siècle and the ideology of hypernationalism. Fascism possessed distinctive political and social doctrines, as well as economic approaches, but these did not stem from any one source and did not constitute an absolutely discrete new economic doctrine. Fascist movements differed more widely among themselves than was the case with various national movements among other political genera. Fascism was not the agent of any other force, class, or interest or the mere reflection of any social class, but was produced by a complex of historical, political, national, and cultural conditions, which can be elucidated and to some extent defined. Above all, fascism was the most revolutionary form of nationalism in Europe

487

to that point in history, and it was characterized by its culture of philosophical idealism, willpower, vitalism, and mysticism and its moralistic concept of therapeutic violence, strongly identified with military values, outward aggressiveness, and empire.

On the basis of broad inductive study of the principal fascist movements, it should be possible to arrive at the constituents of a kind of retrodictive theory of fascism—that is, an elucidation of the particular circumstances that would have to have existed in an early twentieth-century European country in order for a significant fascist movement to have developed. Such movements—gaining the support of as much as about 20 percent or more of the electorate—emerged in only five countries: Italy, Germany, Austria, Hungary, and Romania. The only other two lands where significant fascist movements developed were Spain and Croatia, but the growth of Spanish fascism developed only after incipient civic breakdown and then civil war—circumstances of such crisis as to cloud the issue there—whereas in Croatia the Ustashi had remained a comparatively small movement before Hitler overran Yugoslavia and awarded power to Pavelić as a second choice.

The elements of such a retrodictive theory would include many factors, including the cultural, political, social, economic, and international (table 15.1). Obviously not all these factors existed in every case where a significant fascist movement developed, but the great majority of them did, and the absence of certain factors may explain the ultimate failure of one or two of the stronger movements.

The cultural roots of fascism lay in certain ideas of the late nineteenth century and in the cultural crisis of the fin de siècle. The chief doctrines involved were intense nationalism, militarism, and international Social Darwinism in the forms that became widespread among the World War I generation in greater central Europe, coupled with the contemporary philosophical and cultural currents of neoidealism, vitalism, and activism, as well as the cult of the hero. Fascism developed especially in the central European areas of Germany, Italy, and the successor states of Austria-Hungary most affected by these cultural trends. It was also to be found in varying degrees outside greater central Europe, but elsewhere fascism was more effectively counterbalanced by opposing cultural influences. The impact in France may have been nearly as great as in central Europe, since some of these concepts originated there. Yet the overall effect in France was less, because the ideas were counterbalanced by other elements and because the overall sense of crisis was less acute. Moreover, most of the other variables were scarcely present in France. The case of Romania is somewhat peculiar, for the fin de siècle crisis seems initially to have been less intense there. Among the smaller Romanian intelligentsia, nonetheless, the general sense of crisis grew after World War I. A Marxist response was ineffective for domestic political and for geopolitical reasons, while more

Table 15.1. Elements of a Retrodictive Theory of Fascism

Cultural Factors

1. Comparatively strong influence of the cultural crisis of the fin de siècle
2. Preexisting comparatively strong currents of nationalism
3. Perceived crisis in cultural values
4. Strong influence (or challenge) of secularization

Political Factors

1. A comparatively new state, not more than three generations old
2. A political system that temporarily approximates liberal democracy but has existed for no more than a single generation
3. A fragmented or seriously polarized party system
4. A significant prior political expression of nationalism
5. An apparent danger, either internally or externally, from the left
6. Effective leadership
7. Significant allies
8. In order to triumph, a government that is at least semidemocratic at the time of direct transition to power

Social Factors

1. A situation of pronounced social tension or conflict
2. A large sector of workers and/or peasants-farmers that are either unrepresented, underrepresented, or outside the main party system
3. Major middle-class discontent with the existing party system because of either underrepresentation or major party/electoral shifts
4. Existence of a Jewish minority

Economic Factors

1. Economic crisis either of dislocation or of underdevelopment, caused by or nominally imputable to war, defeat, or "foreign" domination
2. A sufficient level of development in politics and economics to have neutralized the military

International Factors

1. A serious problem of status humiliation, major status striving, and/or underdevelopment
2. Existence of a fascist role model

moderate nationalist populism proved ineffective. Spain was another peripheral country in which the effect of the fin de siècle crisis was weaker, and in fact fascism had little presence there before the final breakdown of 1936.

Fascism could not become a major force in countries where a reasonably significant nationalist ideology or movement had not preceded it, at least by half a generation if not more. So radical and intense a doctrine could gain momentum only as the second stage in ongoing nationalist agitation and mobilization. This was the case in each example of a vigorous fascist movement, while the virtual absence of any previously mobilized nationalism in Spain was a major handicap for the Falange that could not be overcome under seminormal political conditions.

Fascism seems also to have required the kind of cultural space opened by a process of secularization or, in one or two cases, the challenge of a kind of secularization not otherwise being met. In most of the more heavily secularized countries, conversely, fascism was not a challenge either because the secularization process had been effectively completed or because most of the other preconditions did not exist. In a number of central European countries, fascism was able to take advantage of the space left by secularization, and it was less successful in nonsecularized areas. In Spain, political Catholicism sought to meet the challenge of leftist secularization directly, and under seminormal political conditions it had no need of fascism. In Romania, however, fascism itself provided perhaps the main political challenge to secularization, creating a hybrid religious fascism, though necessarily of a semiheretical character. The core fascist movements were anticlerical and fundamentally even antireligious, but this was not so much the case in the geographically and developmentally more peripheral areas. As the main example of a nominally religious or Christian fascism, the Legion of the Archangel Michael was the most anomalous of fascist movements, for the somewhat heretical or potentially schismatic character of its mysticism nonetheless did not obviate its peculiar religiosity.

In every case, the significant fascist movements emerged in comparatively new states, none more than three generations old. In general, fascism was a phenomenon of the new countries of the 1860s and 1870s—Italy, Germany, Austria, Hungary, and Romania—their unsatisfied status strivings, defeats, or frustrations, and late-developing political systems. Fascism has sometimes been called the product of a decaying liberal democracy, but that notion can be misleading. In no case where a liberal democratic system had been established either before World War I or had existed for a full generation did the country succumb to fascism. This, rather, was a significant phenomenon only in certain relatively new countries during the period in which they were just making, or had very recently made, the initial transition to a liberal democracy that was as yet unconsolidated. Simultaneously, and again seemingly paradoxically, conditions approximating liberal democracy were in fact necessary for fascist movements to develop and flourish. They did not function as Communist-style insurrections but as broad European nationalist movements which required the liberty to mobilize mass support—liberty offered only by conditions equivalent to, or closely approaching, liberal democracy.

Another, and fairly obvious, requirement was fragmentation, division, or sharp polarization within the political system. Countries with stable party systems, such as Britain, France, and the Low Countries, were largely immune to fascism. The larger fascist parties required not merely some preparation of the soil by a preexisting movement of intense nationalism but also significant fragmentation or cleavage among the other forces. A partial exception to this stipulation might appear to be the rise of the Arrow Cross in Hungary during the late 1930s, in a situation in which Horthy's government party still enjoyed a nominal majority. In this case, however, the system was one of only semiliberal democracy at best. The elitist ruling party was increasingly unpopular and maintained its status to that point only by sharp electoral restrictions, accompanied by some corruption. Fascism (or more precisely the multiple national socialisms, in the Hungarian nomenclature) thus became the main vehicle for a deeply felt popular protest that had few other means of expression. The structure of the Hungarian electoral system stood apart from that of most other European parliamentary regimes.

The existence of a menace from the left—either real or perceived—has often been held necessary for the rise of fascist movements, and this is generally correct. Italian Fascism could probably never have triumphed without the specter, and the reality, of revolutionary social maximalism. Germany was the home of the strongest Communist party in Europe outside the Soviet Union, always perceived as a serious threat by many. In the minds of others, the broad base of support enjoyed by German Social Democrats only added to the problem. The even greater strength of socialism in Austria was at first a basic catalytic factor there, while the Spanish Civil War represented the ultimate in left-right polarization.

Conversely, the left would not seem at first glance to have played an equivalent role in Hungary and Romania, but certain other features of politics in these countries must also be kept in mind. At the beginning of the interwar period, Hungary was briefly the only country outside the Soviet Union ruled by a revolutionary Communist regime. This colored Hungarian politics for the next generation, exacerbating anticommunism and antileftism in general and also helping to create the conditions in which only a radical nonleftist movement such as Hungarian national socialism would have both the freedom and the appeal to mobilize broadly social discontent. In Romania, the Communist Party was effectively suppressed and the Socialists weak, but Romania now shared a new border with the Soviet Union, which never in principle recognized the Romanian occupation of Bessarabia. Anticommunism thus remained a significant factor in Romanian affairs, and Soviet seizure of Bessarabia and Bukovina in 1940 (together with Hitler's award of much of Transylvania to Hungary) created the condition of extreme trauma in which Antonescu and then the Legion could come to power.

Fascist movements were no different from other political groups in needing effective leadership. In fact, because of their authoritarian principles they required a strong leader—with at least some degree of ability—more than did more liberal forces. Not all the leaders of the larger fascist movements were charismatic or efficient organizers, Szalasi being perhaps the best negative example. But in many cases leadership was a factor in helping to determine the relative success of the movement, even though other conditions were more determinative. The difference between the relative success of a Mosley and a Szalasi did not lie in their respective talent and ability but in the totally distinct conditions of their two countries.

Leadership was more important the higher any particular fascist movement rose. It became vital for any serious attempt to take power, except in the cases where Hitler simply awarded authority to puppets of limited ability such as Pavelić and Szalasi. When Horia Sima, a relatively incompetent leader, was awarded a share of power in Romania, he was unable either to consolidate or to expand it. Given the inability of fascist parties to employ insurrectionary tactics because of the institutionalized character of European polities, allies were in every case essential for taking power. No fascist leader ever seized power exclusively on his own, as leader of a fascist movement and no more. Since semilegal tactics were required, and even the most popular fascist movement never gained an absolute majority, allies—who almost always came from the authoritarian right—were indispensable in bringing a fascist leader to power and even to some extent in helping to expand that power.

Though fascism battened on the weakening of democracy and consensus, it was important for such movements that relative pluralism and some degree of a representative process be preserved up to the time of initially taking power. Without conditions of at least relative freedom—even if not the purest constitutional democracy—a fascist leader could not expect to be able to take power (again, with the standard exception of Hitler's puppets). Authoritarian government closed the door to fascism in Austria and Portugal, in Vichy France, and in a number of eastern European countries. Authoritarian government also controlled and limited the participation of fascists in power in Romania and Spain, subordinating them in the latter and eventually eliminating them altogether in the former.

As far as international circumstances are concerned, significant fascist movements took root in countries suffering from severe national frustration and/or ambition, or in some cases a combination of both. The classic examples of fascist movements battening on a national sense of status deprivation and defeat were the national socialisms, German and Hungarian. To a lesser degree, the whole complex arising from the sense of a *vittoria mutilata* (mutilated victory) in Italy stimulated the growth of Mussolini's movement, though it was not necessarily the prime cause thereof. In Spain, the Falange finally benefited not merely from the challenge of the revolutionary left in 1936 but also from the strong, if paranoid, perceptions of the roles of foreign ideologies and powers therein. Once more the Romanian case seems anomalous, for, despite an ignominious military effort, Romania was one of the biggest winers in World War I, doubling in size and being awarded more territory than it could digest. The deprivation perceived by Romanians did not stem from military defeat or loss of territory (as in Germany and Hungary) but from the failure to achieve dignity, development, and national unity or integration, from the perception of a breakdown in culture and institutions as much as in politics.

Another international factor of importance was the existence abroad of a fascist role model, at least in the case of nearly all the movements except for those in Germany and Italy. To prosper, any fascist movement had to develop autochthonous roots, but foreign examples were factors in encouraging the majority of them, for only in Italy and Germany did they develop absolutely on their own. Conversely, it was of course also true that a fascist movement primarily (rather than only secondarily) dependent on foreign example, ideology, inspiration, or funding was not likely to develop much strength of its own, and thus all the purely mimetic movements—with the exception of Austrian Nazism and perhaps the partial exception of Spanish Falangism—failed.

No aspect of the analysis of fascist movements has generated more controversy than the issue of social bases and origins. It is true that fascism had little opportunity in stable societies not undergoing severe internal tensions. A significant degree of internal stress or social conflict was a sine qua non, but that is about as far as agreement has gone. There is relative consensus that the lower middle class was the most decisive social stratum for fascism, but even this has been somewhat exaggerated. Italian Fascism, for example, had approximately as much support from workers, farmers, and farm laborers during its rise as it did from the lower middle class, the mesocratic stratum coming to dominate membership only after formation of the dictatorship. The decisiveness of different social classes varied from case to case and country to country. The lower middle class was ultimately the most important social sector for the movements in Germany, Austria, Italy, and probably Spain. In these cases, the failure to represent or incorporate the lower middle sectors adequately in the liberal system was important, together with the fragmenting of middle-class parties in Germany and Spain.

In Hungary and Romania, the role of the middle and upper classes was significant primarily for the leadership. The ordinary members were more likely to be peasants and workers. In these countries, it was the failure to incorporate or represent the lower classes that provided available space for mass social recruitment.

In the majority of cases, the existence of a Jewish minority was important for the development of the movement as well. In Italy, on the other hand, this proved to be irrelevant, the Fascist Party itself being disproportionately Jewish. In Poland and Lithuania, conversely, the presence of Jewish minorities as large or even larger than those in Hungary and Romania did not "elicit" significant fascist movements, though a great deal of less lethal anti-Semitism existed. Once again, no single factor is of crucial importance by itself, but only insofar as it converged, or was unable to converge, with other influences.

In economic structure, influence, or development, no single key common to all significant fascist movements can be found. Such a movement was powerful in one of the best educated and most advanced of European countries, and also in one of the most backward and illiterate. Those seeking to explain the social and economic basis of Hitlerism have often referred to the very high German unemployment statistics of 1930–33, but equally high unemployment existed in various other countries that did not develop significant fascist movements, and the percentage of unemployed was almost as high in the democratic America of Hoover and Roosevelt.

The only economic common denominator was that in every country in which a strong fascist movement was found, there existed a broad perception that the present economic crisis stemmed not merely from normal internal sources but also from military defeat and/or foreign exploitation. The further down the development ladder, the greater the economic hatred of the "capitalist plutocracies."

One factor concerning the level of development that was more clear-cut was the need for the country to have achieved a plateau in economic and political development in which the military was no longer a prime factor in political decisions. Otherwise the Mussolini and Hitler governments would probably have been vetoed as both irrelevant and even as harmful by a politically dominant military. Such military powers largely throttled fascism in eastern Europe.

Not one of the factors providing elements for a retrodictive theory was of any great significance by itself, or even in combination with one or two others. Only if the majority of them converged in a given country between the wars was it possible for a truly fascistogenic situation to develop.

To recast the retrodictive design in simpler and shorter terms, then, we can say that the necessary conditions for the growth of a significant fascist movement involved strong influence from the cultural crisis of the fin de siècle in a situation of perceived mounting cultural disorientation; the background of some form of organized nationalism before World War I; an international situation of perceived defeat, status humiliation, or lack of dignity; a state system comparatively new that was entering or had just entered a framework of liberal democracy; a situation of increasing political fragmentation; large sectors of workers, farmers, or petit bourgeois that were either not represented or had lost confidence in the existing parties; and an economic crisis perceived to stem in large measure from foreign defeat or exploitation.

Fascism was, as Nolte, Mosse, Weber, and Griffin have explained, a revolutionary new epochal phenomenon with an ideology and a distinctive set of ambitions in its own right. It was also the product of distinctive national histories, being primarily confined to the new nations of the 1860s—new state systems that had failed to achieve empire and status, and in some cases even reasonable economic development. Sufficient conditions existed for strong fascisms in those countries alone, the only exception being the sudden rise of fascism in Spain amid the unique civil war crisis of 1936—itself sufficient explanation of this apparent anomaly in the Europe of the 1930s.

Conversely, sufficient conditions for the growth of fascist movements have ceased to exist since 1945, even though the number of neofascist or putatively neofascist movements during the past half century has been possibly even greater than the number of genuine fascist movements during the quarter century 1920–45. This final anomaly in the history of so seemingly bewildering and contradictory a political phenomenon will be explored in the Epilogue.

To call the entire period 1919–45 an era of fascism may be true in the sense that fascism was the most original and vigorous new type of radical movement in those years, and also in the sense that Germany for a time became the dominant state in Europe. The phrase is inaccurate, however, if it is taken to imply that fascism became the dominant political force of the period, for there were always more antifascists than fascists. Antifascism preceded fascism in many European countries, and among Italian Socialists—in their opposition to Mussolini's early "social chauvinism"—it almost preceded the original Fascism itself. Down to 1939, antifascists, both voters and activists, always outnumbered fascists in Europe as a whole.

Crises and semirevolutionary situations do not long persist, and fascist movements lacked any clear-cut social class or interest basis to sustain them. Their emphasis on a militarized style of politics, together with their need for allies, however temporary the association, greatly restricted their opportunities as well as their working time, requiring them to win power in less than a generation and in some cases within only a few years. The drive of a fascist movement toward power threatened the host polity with a state of political war (though normally not insurrectionary civil war) quite different from normal parliamentary politics. No system can long withstand a state of latent war, even if a direct insurrection is not launched. It either succumbs or overcomes the challenge. In the great majority of cases the fascist challenge was repelled, though sometimes at the cost of establishing a more moderate authoritarian system. At any rate, the 0.7 percent of the popular vote won by the Spanish Falange in the 1936 elections was much nearer the norm than the 38 percent won by the Nazis in 1932.

Epilogue
Neofascism: A Fascism
in Our Future?

Fascism failed to achieve world significance as a driving force of the twentieth century, but, as Ernst Nolte earlier concluded, it did acquire an epochal significance in Europe during the era of World War II. Even in Europe, however, it failed to develop broad popular support in most countries. Its total defeat in 1945, followed by the enormous changes which took place in the years that followed, meant that the same forms of fascism could not be effectively revived. Absolute military disaster put an end to the imperial ambitions of the new states of the 1860s, while the bipolarization of the Cold War ended the "international anarchy" of early twentieth-century Europe. The suppression of political freedom by communism in the East and the development of broadly stable democracy in the West denied political space to radical alternatives, while the long and unprecedented prosperity of western Europe that began around 1950 greatly eased social tensions. In the postwar world the major competing ideological forces shared a common humanist materialism, to the exclusion of either the older idealism or vitalism. The triumph of a hedonist and consumerist materialism increasingly cut the ground from under calls to revolutionary asceticism and idealism—whether fascist or Communist. This was accentuated by the general crisis of authority in the Western world, together with broadly accepted norms of equality and growing social individualism and atomization. All the preconditions of fascism discussed in chapter 15 disappeared in postwar Europe.

Yet, though fascism had disappeared as a force, fascists in greatly diminished numbers remained. As the most distinctive new radicalism of the century, fascism had left a seemingly permanent, if very limited, cultural residue. Thus even more fascist and right radical grouplets and organizations have appeared during the past half century than in the so-called era of fascism be-tween the wars.[1] Partly because of their very weakness they have emphasized international contacts and interassociation more than did the classic fascist movements, and they have found counterparts in the United States and many different parts of the world. Moreover, with the collapse of communism, fascist and right radical groups have become increasingly active in Russia and eastern Europe.

During the second half of the twentieth century it has been more common for serious students to classify the main forces of authoritarian nationalism in Europe under the rubric of "the radical right." Following American social science usage, this terminology entered Germany in the 1950s and has been commonly employed since.[2] The need to adjust to a radically different climate of affairs has meant that those groups which hope to compete electorally in stable democracies have had to modify their positions considerably, so that, un-like historic fascists or the more genuine neofascists, they stand explicitly at the far right of the political spectrum. Economic prosperity, nominal egalitarian-ism, and the welfare state have eliminated the more revolutionary kind of social appeal used by historic fascism, so that the newer right radical movements ap-peal rather more to established interests and do not propound any revolutionary changes in social structure. Moreover, even the more radical and genuinely neofascist groups sometimes accept the rightist designation for themselves— which no genuine fascist would have done in the 1920s. In an age of mass egalitarianism their message does not play as revolutionary a role. For conve-nience's sake, the tripartite taxonomy of fascist, radical right, and moderate authoritarian right used throughout this book may still be applied to the sec-ond half of the century, though with the general understanding that those few groups which have achieved any real electoral success will fit more into a right-

1. Among the general works that have sought to cover neofascism are the following: D. Eisenberg, *Fascistes et nazis d'aujourd'hui* (Paris, 1963); A. Del Boca and M. Giovana, *Fascism Today: A World Survey* (New York, 1969); G. Gaddi, *Neofascismo in Europa* (Milan, 1974); F. Laurent, *L'orchestre noir* (Paris, 1978); J.-M. Théolleyre, *Les neo-nazis* (Paris, 1982); M. N. Filatov and A. I. Ryabov, *Fashizm 80x* (Alma Ata, 1983); K. von Beyme, ed., "Right-Wing Ex-tremism in Western Europe," a special number of *West European Politics* 11:2 (1988); U. Backes, *Politischer Extremismus in demokratische Verfassungsstaaten: Elemente einer normativen Rahmen-theorie* (Opladen, 1989); M. Kirfel and W. Oswalt, eds., *Die Rückkehr der Führer: Modernisierter Rechtsradikalismus in Westeuropa* (Vienna, 1989); F. Gress, H.-G. Jaschke, and K. Schönekäs, *Neue Rechte und Rechtsextremismus in Europa* (Opladen, 1990); G. Harris, *The Dark Side of Europe: The Extreme Right Today* (Edinburgh, 1990); C. T. Husbands, *Race and the Right in Con-temporary Politics* (London, 1991); P. Hainsworth, ed., *The Extreme Right in Europe and America* (London, 1991); G. Ford, ed., *Fascist Europe* (London, 1993); and P. H. Merkl and L. Weinberg, *Encounters with the Contemporary Radical Right* (Boulder, 1993).

2. This has been pointed out in C. T. Husbands, "The State's Response to Far-Right Ex-tremism," in *The Radical Right in Western Europe*, ed. J. Munholland (forthcoming).

ist than into a true neofascist category. At the same time, it should be borne
in mind that there has been considerable infiltration, double membership, and
liaison activity, so that the degree of interconnection between many of these
small groups has been considerably greater than that between the wars.[3]

The number of neofascist and right radical or authoritarian groups has
actually increased, in bewildering and kaleidoscopic variety, following the
basic rule of thumb "The more insignificant, the more of them." As Roger
Griffin has put it, these organizations are characterized by "organizational
complexity and ideological heterogeneity."[4] They have constantly undergone
the fragmentations and multiple subfragmentations to which extreme radical
groups, whether left or right, are prone.[5] Many are no more than tiny agitational
circles; others are very small, purely clandestine organizations.

Even among the more genuinely neofascist groups, there are a number of
differences from the historic movements. One is that the "myth of Europe"
coexists with the nationalist myth to offer a new concept of transcendence for a
broader, more interdependent world. Neofascism has more often than not been
"Eurofascism," not in the sense of being moderate and parliamentary, as in so-
called Eurocommunism, but in the sense of a fundamental appeal to the myth
of "Aryan Europe" or some other definition of the ideal European identity as a
basic frame of reference. Some neofascists and new radical rightists also give
greater attention to doctrine and theory than their predecessors, though this is
true in only a minority of the groups. Finally, among the genuine neofascists,
terrorism plays a more important role than it did in historic fascism. Ordinary
terrorism, as distinct from street fighting and group actions (what the Germans
called *zusammenstösse*), was rare in historic fascism. Its frequent presence
among neofascist grouplets is a reflection of the latter's extreme weakness and
lack of political prospects—similar to the situation among their leftist terrorist
counterparts.

The true neofascist organizations, as distinct from the right radical political parties, propound much the same vitalist, nonrationalist, and violent creeds
as their ideological forebears—often to an exaggerated extent—and in some
cases advocate even more revolutionary social and economic changes, but this
only further ensures their total marginalization. They have preached a kind of

3. A slightly more elaborate taxonomy will be found in R. Eatwell, "Neo-Fascism and the
Right: Conceptual Conundrums?" in Munholland, ed., *Radical Right*. Roger Griffin presents a yet
more complex scheme, very cogently drawn, in *The Nature of Fascism* (London, 1991), 161–69.
For further differentiation between genuinely neofascist parties and the new right radical groups,
see P. Ignazi, "Nuovi e vecchi partiti di estrema destra in Europa," *Rivista Italiana di Scienza
Politica* 22:2 (Aug. 1992): 293–333.

4. Griffin, *Nature of Fascism* 170.

5. The most extensive listing and classification of such groups through the mid-1980s has
been provided by Ciaran O'Maoláin, in *The Radical Right: A World Directory* (London, 1987).

"liberation nationalism" against the former American-Russian hegemony in Europe, with the goal of a collaborative new Europe based on "Eurofascism," sometimes building on the myth of the "pan-European" Waffen-SS of the later years of World War II.

Thus a full taxonomy of authoritarian nationalism would begin with moderate groups that advocate only a certain number of restrictions to achieve a very moderate degree of national authoritarianism. Since these are directed primarily against immigrants, such groups can function within the sphere of liberal parliamentarianism. Beyond them are the right radical organizations which cannot profess—and in many cases do not genuinely seem to want to profess—fascist extremism within stable democracies. They instead propound more drastic changes to make the existing systems more nationalist and authoritarian.

Several different kinds of neofascists can be identified. The basic tendency has been for the authentic neofascists to become neo-Nazi rather than neofascist in the non-Nazi sense. They often present themselves as "national revolutionaries" who preach creation of a new national community with individual free enterprise, autonomous cooperative groups of producers, and nationalization of key industries and public services (sometimes advocating "comanagement" of workers and owners in industry). They have demanded the freeing of Europe from Americans and Soviets, placing emphasis on the family, the municipality, and national syndicates. To their left stand a small minority of "left fascists" who advocate more extreme forms of national socialism, with such variants as "anarchofascists" and one or more grouplets of "Nazi-Maoists." The tendency toward "social racism" is present among most and is also an overlapping feature of parliamentary right radical parties. On the fringe are to be found discussion circles that engage in a kind of profascist propaganda without fully committing themselves politically. "Holocaust denial" groups are one example.[6] Yet another distinctive feature of the second half of the century has been the various "neofascist internationals," though none have developed into significant forces. These have ranged from the European Social Movement of the 1950s through the European New Order association and the Young Europe affiliation of the two following decades, the American and British-led World Union of National Socialists of the same period, and the World Alliance of National Revolutionaries formed in the late 1970s.[7]

The most immediate concern about neofascism after 1945 focused on the Federal Republic in West Germany, whose citizens after 1949 enjoyed the

6. See R. Eatwell, "The Holocaust Denial: A Study in Propaganda Technique," in *Neo-Fascism in Europe*, ed. L. Cheles, R. Ferguson, and M. Vaughan (London, 1991), 120–46.

7. The neofascist internationals are treated in E. Cadena, *La ofensiva neo-fascista* (Barcelona, 1978), 213–49.

democratic organizational rights denied their fellow countrymen in the Soviet zone. A study of the population in the American zone prior to 1949 concluded that 15 to 18 percent of the adult population might be categorized as unreconstructed Nazis.[8] A survey by the West German Institut für Demoskopie in 1953 found that this sector had shrunk to 5 percent,[9] and yet another survey three years later reduced the figure to only 3 percent[10] (though the accuracy of these studies might be questioned by some). These figures may or may not have been too low, but it is indisputable that unreconstructed Nazi sympathies declined sharply in West Germany during the first postwar decade.

Nonetheless, many small circles were eager to revive extreme nationalist and even directly neo-Nazi politics, though their support was limited. By 1948 there were four such organizations, and the number increased to at least twelve by 1951. The only one of any significance was the Socialist Reich Party (SRP), an organization that restricted itself to legal activity but operated on the cusp between a right radical and an only slightly veiled neo-Nazi party. It scored a notable success in winning as much as 11 percent of the vote in its first national campaign in 1950. The SRP failed, however, to effect a merger with the other two largest right radical parties and then was officially dissolved by the West German government in 1952 for having become too overtly neo-Nazi.[11] Its membership then splintered in many directions; one scholar has counted the existence of as many as seventy-four different grouplets by the end of the year, a figure that was reduced to only eleven by 1955.[12]

The space of the SRP was mainly occupied by two somewhat more moderate right radical parties, the National Democratic Party (NPD) and the German Reich Party (DRP). The NPD was distinctly the larger, having more than fifty-six thousand members at its height in 1959, but it never received the 5 percent minimum in national elections to qualify as a parliamentary minority group.[13]

8. A. Ashkenasi, *Modern German Nationalism* (Cambridge, Mass., 1976), 59.

9. C. Emmet and N. Muhlen, *The Vanishing Swastika* (Chicago, 1961), 9.

10. According to R. C. Lewis, *A Nazi Legacy* (New York, 1991), 31. This is the most succinct recent overall guide in English to the postwar German radical right.

11. C. Büsch and P. Furth, *Rechtsradikalismus in Nachkriegsdeutschland: Studien über die "Sozialistische Reichspartei" (SRP)* (Berlin, 1957).

12. H.-H. Knütter, *Ideologien des Rechtsradikalismus im Nachkriegsdeutschland* (Bonn, 1961), 31.

13. On the NPD, see K. B. Tauber, *Beyond Eagle and Swastika* (Middletown, Conn., 1967); H. Maier and H. Bott, *Die NPD* (Munich, 1968); J. D. Nagle, *The National Democratic Party* (Berkeley, 1970); and also Lewis, *Nazi Legacy* 44–62. Other useful studies which treat the organizations of these years include M. Jenke, *Die Nationale Rechte* (Berlin, 1967); H. Gerstenberger, *Der revolutionäre Konservatismus* (Berlin, 1969); H.-D. Klingemann and F. U. Pappi, *Politischer Radikalismus* (Munich, 1972); W. Gessenharte, H. Fröchling, and B. Krupp, *Rechtsextremismus als normativ-praktisches Forschungsproblem* (Weinheim, 1978); M. Sattler, *Rechtsextremismus in der Bundesrepublik: Die "Alte," die "Neue" Rechte und der Neonazismus* (Opladen, 1980); and W. Graf, ed., *"Wenn ich die Regierung wäre . . .": Die rechtsradikale Bedrohung* (Berlin, 1984).

The most recent organization to create a neofascist scare during the final phase of a separate West Germany was the Republican Party, which won 7.5 percent of the vote in the West Berlin municipal election of 1989. The *Republikaner* had equivalent showings in a few other local elections but gained scarcely more than 1 percent of the vote in the first all-German national election of 1990. They have vehemently and convincingly denied being members of a neofascist party and propose no drastic alternative political system, focusing on an authoritarian tightening of restrictions on immigrants, ethnic minorities, criminals, and other marginal sectors.[14] As a moderate right authoritarian party, the RP more nearly resembles the old Spanish CEDA or some of the moderate interwar French rightist groups than it does either the PNF or the NSDAP. It also reflects the fact that any ultranationalist organization which seeks to mobilize electoral support must become, or appear to become, increasingly moderate.

There was an increase in genuine neo-Nazi activity during the 1980s and 1990s, when more than a score of such grouplets were formed. This most recent phase has been characterized by neo-Nazi youth violence, particularly in the form of the "skinhead" phenomenon, and by the disproportionate growth of neo-Nazi sentiment in the former East Germany after unification. (The latter development is in no way contradicted by the surveys which showed political attitudes in the East to be generally more "leftist" than in the West.) The largest of the new groups was the Free German Labor Party (Freiheitliche Deutsche Arbeiterpartei, FDAP), which may have had as many as five hundred members at the beginning of 1989. None of the newest neo-Nazi groups had either an electoral following or any political significance in themselves, but some engaged in acts of violence and terrorism that generated considerable publicity, and many were in contact with other neo-Nazi groups in western Europe and the United States. In 1988 a report issued by the West German government estimated that the "total number of identified right-wing extremists" in sixty-nine right radical and neo-Nazi organizations was approximately 25,000, of whom fewer than 10 percent belonged to genuine neo-Nazi groups. Of these, some 220 had been identified as active in political violence.[15] These figures have increased somewhat in recent years.

14. On the *Republikaner,* there are C. Leggewie, *Die Republikaner* (Berlin, 1989); L. A. Müller, *Republikaner, NPD, DVU, Liste D . . .* (Göttingen, 1989); H.-G. Jaschke, *Die Republikaner* (Bonn, 1990); and H.-J. Veen, N. Lepszy, and P. Mnich, *The Republikaner Party in Germany* (Washington, D.C., 1993), which generally view it as having the potential to become a much more extremist right radical party.

15. Cited in Lewis, *Nazi Legacy* 8, 85, which also presents a list of the principal neo-Nazi groups as of 1987 (137). Recent German studies include R. Stöss, *Die extreme Rechte in der Bundesrepublik* (Opladen, 1989); W. Benz, ed., *Rechtsextremismus in der Bundesrepublik* (Frankfurt, 1989); K.-H. Klaer, M. Ristau, B. Schoppe, and M. Stadelmaier, *Die Wähler extremen Rechten,* 3 vols. (Bonn, 1989); W. Bergmann and R. Erb, eds., *Antisemitismus in der*

The chief homeland of neofascism during the second half of the century, however, has been the homeland of paradigmatic historical fascism—Italy. Though the democratic Italian republic was founded on antifascism, there are several reasons for the comparatively greater strength of neofascism in Italy. One is simply that, despite the broad wave of summary executions by political and vigilante groups at the close of the war (whose victims may have totaled twelve to fifteen thousand—something without parallel in Germany), subsequently there was much less effort at systematic defascistization than was the case under the occupying powers in Germany. Foreign military occupation in Italy was both much briefer and also much less complete. A second factor is that it was easier for would-be neofascists in Italy to feel that Fascism itself had not been so much defeated and discredited as that it had fallen victim to Hitler, creating an alibi for shifting blame. A third potential factor was the remarkable institutional continuity between Fascist Italy and democratic Italy: the republic retained the four basic legal codes enacted between 1931 and 1942, the enormous state capitalist Institute for Industrial Reconstruction (which dominated much of industry and finance), and the arrangement with the Catholic Church, Mussolini's Lateran Pacts becoming Article 7 of the republican constitution. Even the 1931 regulations on ordinary police regulation were retained. A fourth factor had to do with the greater fragmentation and seeming weakness of postwar Italian democracy, faced with much more severe internal and social problems than in Germany. A final factor is that German neo-Nazism never found anyone to provide the same degree of intellectual leadership as did Julius Evola in Italy.

Down to the time of his death in 1974, Evola stood as the leading intellectual of neofascism and/or the radical right in all Europe. Scion of an aristocratic Roman family, Evola had been a teenage artillery officer in World War I and subsequently became the leading representative of artistic Dadaism in Italy, the first expression of his lifelong revolt against rationalist and materialist bourgeois culture. Dadaism represented but a brief phase, after which he was drawn to idealist philosophy and radical elitism, though Evola never joined the Fascist Party and never held a government position under Mussolini. While producing a lengthy series of books criticizing contemporary culture and politics, he also criticized Fascism for its demogogic, plebeian, and statist qualities.[16]

Evola enveloped a highly elitist and cyclical view of history in which

---

politischen Kultur nach 1945 (Opladen, 1990); C. Butterwege and H. Isola, eds., Rechtsextremismus im vereinten Deutschland (Berlin, 1990); B. Bailer-Galanda, Die Neue Rechte (Vienna, 1990); H. Engelstädter and O. Seiffert, Die schleichende Gefahr: Europa, die Deutschen, Nationalismus und Neofaschismus (Berlin, 1990); and G. Paul, ed., Hitlers Schatten verblasst: Die Normalisierung des Rechtsextremismus (Bonn, 1990).

16. Years later this critique was fully developed in Evola, Il fascismo: Saggio di una analisi critica dal punto di vista della destra (1970).

leadership in society and culture passed from priests to warriors to merchants and finally to slaves (in contemporary socialism and communism). His two most important early works were *Imperialismo pagano* (1928) and *La rivolta contro il mondo moderno* (1934), in which he outlined his philosophy of "heroic pessimism" and the need to restore traditional values under a ruthless elitism. Since history was totally cyclical, the modern world was headed for ultimate crisis and extinction. Materialism, hedonism, and egalitarianism would result in catastrophe but also the opportunity to restore true values. This process would have to be led by a revolutionary elite who would create an "organic state" that corresponded to higher reality; as a living entity, it would replace the mechanical totalitarian system of Mussolini, which was a lifeless structure of bureaucratic control and had no means with which to reproduce itself and/or replace its leader. The genuine "new order" would be a *civiltà solare*—a "civilization of the sun" which would reestablish a pagan humanism of the natural order. Italy he viewed as an essentially pagan blend of the Nordic and the Mediterranean, a land and culture of synthesis which gave it the creative potential to play a leading role in achieving the new "solar civilization."

Not all these ideas were completely developed by the 1930s, and Evola was largely ignored in Fascist Italy by all save some of the most radical sectors of Fascism (though Mussolini seems to have held his intellectual dynamism in some esteem). He considered Germany a second spiritual home and was much appreciated by German extreme rightists and also by elements of the SS, for Evola had begun to develop a doctrine of race before such a *svolta* had been adopted by Mussolini. Evola's racism nonetheless anticipated the eventual Fascist doctrine of 1938 in being based on culture, psychology, and the "spiritual," as he put it, rather than on biology.[17] He was himself seriously injured in an Allied bombing raid on Vienna; true to his doctrines of the heroic, he had refused to take refuge in a bomb shelter. Though he assisted in the first phase of the reconstruction of Fascism in 1943, Evola still refused to join the reorganized Fascist Party and was critical of the Salò regime for its persistent demagogy and pseudoegalitarianism. Throughout he remained uncompromisingly pagan and anti-Christian, sharply criticizing the Mussolini regime for its compromises with the Church.

Strictly speaking, therefore, Evola had never been a complete Fascist and was never a full neofascist, but after the war he became the intellectual leader of the most extreme radical right. Though anti-Jewish, he later considered Hitler's demonic anti-Semitism to have been a "demagogic aberration."[18] What made

17. This was begun in writings of the early 1930s, climaxed by Evola's *Sintesi di dottrina della razza* (1941).

18. Quoted in R. Drake, *The Revolutionary Mystique and Terrorism in Contemporary Italy* (Bloomington, 1989), 64.

Evola so attractive both to genuine neofascists and to the radical right after the war was the fact that he developed eloquently and incisively an alternative concept of history and of culture, based on uncompromising antidemocratism, elitism, mysticism, and the call for a revolutionary elite to create a hierarchic, organic new order, structured on socioeconomic corporation. The goal, as in Fascist doctrine, was to achieve a "new man" with a "soul of steel" capable of "transcendence against temporality," who would live a "warrior epic" imbued with "legionary spirit." In all this there lay a scarcely veiled encouragement of terrorist action against the present rotting order.[19] Evola thus provided inspiration for a wide range of right radical, neofascist, and even neo-Nazi groups in Italy.

The first neofascist organization was the Fasci d'Azione Rivoluzionaria (reviving the name used by revolutionary left interventionists of 1915), organized in May 1945 as soon as the war ended. In following years it members engaged in varying kinds of direct action, including terrorism, remaining a small clandestine group that finally ceased operations altogether and dissolved in May 1951.[20] Conversely, the first regular political organization inspired to some extent by Fascism was the Uomo Qualunque (Common Man) movement, which appeared in southern Italy at the end of the war. Uomo Qualunque was vague in program and had more the character of a moderate right authoritarian populist movement than a neofascist one. Though it gained 5.3 percent of the vote for the Italian constituent assembly in 1946, it soon faded away.[21]

The main political force in postwar Italy inspired by Fascism was the Movimento Sociale Italiano (Italian Social Movement, MSI), founded in December 1946. Unlike the clandestine Fasci, the MSI was conceived as a regular political organization to participate in elections and theoretically observe legality. Its official program was not the reassertion of historic Fascism but a more moderate stance adjusted to postwar circumstances. Thus technically it was more a movement of the parliamentary authoritarian or semiauthoritarian right than of genuine neofascism, even though the Fascist nature of much of its inspiration was obvious. What made it more a movement of the radical rather than the moderate authoritarian right was not its official doctrines but the overlapping membership and special relationship with other right radical and neofascist groups. The MSI stood for strong nationalism, a more assertive foreign policy to realize Italy's "mission," support for Catholicism as the

19. Good brief discussions of Evola will be found in Drake, *Mystique* 114–34, and in Cadena, *La ofensiva* 48–61. A. Romualdi, *Julius Evola: L'uomo e l'opera* (Rome, 1971), and G. F. Lami, *Introduzione a Evola* (Rome, 1980), are admiring treatments.

20. P. G. Murgia, *Il vento del Nord: Storia e cronaca del fascismo dopo la Resistenza (1945–1950)* (Milan, 1975); M. Tedeschi, *Fascisti dopo Mussolini* (Rome, 1950); R. Chiarini and P. Corsini, *Da Salò a Piazza della Loggia: Blocco d'ordine, neofascismo, radicalismo di destra a Brescia (1945–1974)* (Milan, 1983).

21. S. Setta, *L'Uomo Qualunque, 1944–1948* (Bari, 1975).

Table E.1. MSI's Percentage of the Vote
in National Elections, 1948–1989

Year	Percentage
1948	1.9
1953	5.9
1958	4.8
1963	5.1
1968	4.5
1972	8.7
1976	6.1
1979	5.3
1983	6.8
1987	5.9
1989	5.5

Source: R. Chiarini, "The 'Movimento Sociale Italiano': A Historical Profile," in *Neo-
Fascism in Europe,* ed. L. Cheles, R. Ferguson, and M. Vaughan (London, 1991), 19–
42.

state religion, and the creation of a corporative worker state achieving full partnership between capital and labor.

By 1953 it had become the most successful neofascist or right radical party in Europe, with 5.9 percent of the national vote, and it would maintain this relative position for several decades. The MSI's varying share of the Italian popular vote is presented in table E.1. Its geographic basis, however, was the opposite of that of the historic PNF, for nearly half the MSI's voting support was drawn from the backward south, the most conservative part of Italy.

To expand its appeal during the 1950s the party moved a little more toward the right center, supporting Italian membership in NATO and abandoning—for the time being—most ties to right radical direct action groups. Growing support from conservative monarchists encouraged this trend, as did passage by the Italian parliament of the "Scelba Law" as a constitutional amendment forbidding any future re-creation of the PNF under whatever name. The decades of the 1950s and 1960s were a time of intermittent collaboration with moderate centrist forces, punctuated by periods of greater hostility and moments of challenge by the MSI in local areas and over selected issues. This in turn led to increasing controversy within the party and on its fringes, as several sectors of militants sought a more radical line and a number of new splinter right radical parties were formed, particularly in the mid-1960s.[22]

22. Examples include the Italian People's Party, founded by the former Fascist militant Arconovaldo Bonaccorsi, the National Democratic Party, and the National Party of Labor.

Categorical neofascism developed outside the organizational structure of the MSI, though there were sometimes links. The first important new group was Ordine Nuovo (New Order), which was begun as a series of study groups within the MSI in 1953. Led by the journalist Pino Rauti, Ordine Nuovo left the MSI three years later to become a separate organization and eventually claimed as many as ten thousand members. It became the intellectual center of Italian neofascism, inspired both by Evola and by more genuine proponents of a categorical neofascism. During the 1960s an even more extreme group split from Ordine Nuovo, alleging that the latter lacked the will to act and to create the "new man." This became L'Avanguardia Nazionale (National Avant-garde), led by Stefano della Chiae, though it survived for only a limited period as a distinct organization.

The growth of radical agitation, disorder, and political violence which began in 1965 and intensified during 1968–69 created conditions propitious for the proliferation of small conspiratorial neofascist and neo-Nazi groups, which were numerous and active for the next decade and more.[23] MSI students participated in tumultuous university demonstrations, riots, and other disorders, but terrorism was carried out by the smaller new extremist groups.[24] The great majority of the bombings, assassinations, and other acts of violence were the work of the Red Brigades and the many other Marxist-Leninist revolutionary organizations, but the terrorism of the neofascists and neo-Nazis was proportionately much more lethal. Though most ordinary neofascist violence was carried out against the political left and the great majority of the bombings were directed against property rather than human targets, nearly all the mass actions of pure terrorism resulting in multiple deaths were also their work.

23. See S. Tarrow, *Democracy and Disorder: Protest and Politics in Italy, 1965–1975* (Oxford, 1989).

24. Ordine Nuovo rejoined the MSI in 1969, but a minority split off to create the Movimento Politico Ordine Nuovo. These elements remained the largest neofascist group until final dissolution of Ordine Nuovo by the Italian judiciary in 1973. A radical splinter, Ordine Nero (Black Order), was active in bombings for the next five years. In addition to these organizations and L'Avanguardia Nazionale, other neofascist and neo-Nazi groups (many of them involved in terrorism) were Terza Posizione (Third Position), Nuclei Armati Rivoluzionari (Armed Revolutionary Nuclei), Movimento Popolare Rivoluzionario (People's Revolutionary Movement), Movimento d'Azione Rivoluzionario (Movement of Revolutionary Action), the Squadre d'Azione Mussoliniani (Mussolini Action Squads), Comunità Organica del Popolo (Organic Community of the People), Costruiamo l'Azione (Let's Build Action), Movimento Tradizionale Romano (Roman Traditional Movement), Movimento Nazionale Proletario (Proletarian National Movement), Giovane Europa (Young Europe), the "anarcho-fascist" Gruppi Nazionali Proletari (National Proletarian Groups), Gruppi Dannunziani (D'Annunzian Groups), which collaborated with the Croatian neo-Ustashi, and the Comitato di Difesa Publica–Sinistra Nazionale (Committee of Public Defense–National Left). Altogether between the 1960s and 1980s a total of sixty-four neofascist, neo-Nazi, and right radical groups and circles linked in some manner with terrorism were identified.

These began with the huge explosion in Milan in 1969 and continued through the Bologna train station blast of 1980, which killed eighty people in one blow. Individual assassinations also occurred from time to time. As this continued, more terrorist groups developed links with the massive Italian structures of organized crime. There were also links with subversive elements in the army and police command which generated several conspiracies to seize power, including one abortive effort at a coup d'état in Rome.[25] Throughout these years the MSI maintained its official distance from the neofascist terrorist groups, though some of its members kept covert links.

In 1969 the former Fascist Giorgio Almirante began a lengthy period as MSI leader and ended the tactic of intermittent dialogue with the Christian Democrats. He initiated the *strategia del doppio binario* (double-pronged strategy) of seeking to unite the conservative sectors of the northern middle class with the lower and lower middle classes of the south, to enable the MSI to replace the Demo-Christians as Italy's principal conservative force. This initially seemed to produce results. The party gained 13.9 percent of the total vote in Italy's municipal elections of 1971 and did even better in the south. Merger with the main monarchist party (henceforth the acronym would be MSI-DN) helped it to win 8.7 percent in the national parliamentary elections the following year—its best showing to date. In Italy's highly fragmented party system, this placed it virtually in a tie with the Socialists for third place, after the Christian Democrats and the Communists.

The hopes raised in 1971–72, however, were quickly dashed. The Christian Democrats moved gingerly in the direction of greater cooperation with the Communists, while the MSI was wracked by internal divisions. Like the other major national parties, it had developed its own auxiliary organizations among young people, students, trade unionists, women, and others, creating a total membership of nearly half a million in all its organizations, but these auxiliaries harbored a wide variety of tendencies. Radical militants demanded more direct action, conservatives stressed moderation, and the lower-class and lower-middle-class populist currents insisted on more attention to economic issues. During the remainder of the decade the MSI vote steadily declined.

A moderate recuperation took place in the 1980s, as terrorism was overcome on both left and right and some of the splinter extremists returned to the party. The MSI became increasingly pragmatic and in turn found the

25. On the entire spectrum, see L. B. Weinberg, *After Mussolini: Italian Neo-Fascism and the Nature of Fascism* (Washington, D.C., 1979); D. Barneri, *Agenda nera: Trent'anni di neofascismo in Italia* (Rome, 1976); P. Guzzanti, *Il neofascismo e le sue organizzazioni paramilitari* (Rome, 1972); F. Ferraresi, ed., *La destra radicale* (Milan, 1984); and the brief synthesis in V. S. Pisano, *The Dynamics of Subversion and Violence in Contemporary Italy* (Stanford, 1987), 50–56. By 1985 a total of 180 right radical and neofascist terrorists were in prison, 40 more had already completed their sentences, and another 68 had been identified but not apprehended.

highly corrupt anti-Communist administrations led by Christian Democrats and Socialists more willing to collaborate. Though the party still officially affirmed Italy's Fascist past as a historic legacy, the MSI's program espoused a moderate rightist kind of corporatism.[26]

With the collapse of the postwar Italian party system in 1993 under the weight of massive and ubiquitous corruption and the indictment of several hundred leading political and economic figures, a new political era began. At the very close of the year the MSI became part of a broader Alleanza Nazionale (National Alliance) with former right-wing Christian Democrats and other conservatives.[27] Under the direction of the younger and more pragmatic MSI leader Gian Franco Fini, the Alleanza took a stance of moderate rightism. In the parliamentary elections of 1994, this enabled the Alleanza to form a broad right-center alliance with Silvio Berlusconi's new Forza Italia and the Lega Lombarda, giving it 13.5 percent of the popular vote. This relative victory, much higher than anything registered by the old MSI at the national level, was virtually repeated in the balloting for the European parliament which soon followed and enabled the Alleanza to gain a share of national power, taking three cabinet positions in Berlusconi's coalition government.

Government entry raised a new "fascist scare" in Italian politics and in western European affairs generally by June 1994. Unlike the old MSI, however, the Alleanza Nazionale does not invoke the positive valorization of the Fascist past per se, though it is respectful of the person of Mussolini. While acknowledging the Duce as a "great statesman," Fini has declared Fascism to be "not repeatable." The Alleanza positions itself as a parliamentary and nationalist right-wing party, calling for a stronger central government, the streamlining of the bureaucracy, the recovery of part of Istria from Yugoslavia, the welcoming of east central European countries into NATO, controls on immigration, aid to Middle Eastern and North African countries to reduce immigration, tougher anti-Mafia laws, and the "reconquering" of southern Italy. Only rather gingerly does it affirm possible corporative reform of part of Italy's representative institutions, in economics if not in politics.[28] By mid-1994 it was poised on the cusp between the moderate authoritarian right and a nationalist parliamentary conservatism.

Spain is the European country that experienced the second largest vol-

26. The principal studies of the MSI are P. Ignazi, *Il polo escluso: Profilo del Movimento Sociale Italiano* (Bologna, 1989), and idem, "La cultura politica del Movimento Sociale Italiano," *Rivista Italiana di Scienza Politica* 19:3 (Dec. 1989): 43–65. See also P. Rosenbaum, *Il nuovo fascismo: Da Salò ad Almirante. Storia del MSI* (Milan, 1975).

27. In its last independent contest, the MSI won 16.4 percent of the vote in 428 municipal elections held in December 1993.

28. MSI-DN, Assamblea Congressuale, "Documento base per la commissione 'Valori e Solidarietà,' " Jan. 1994. (I wish to thank Luca De Caprariis for obtaining this document for me.)

ume of right radical and neofascist terrorism during the 1970s and 1980s, but right radical politics overall has been much weaker in Spain. The return to democracy in Spain began only after the death in November 1975 of General Franco, who had progressively defascistized his regime during the preceding thirty years but nonetheless sustained a rightist authoritarian system to the very end. Several small neo-Falangist *grupúsculos*, nominally in opposition to the Franco regime, were first organized in the late 1950s and 1960s. Their number increased rapidly in the 1970s, especially after the death of Franco, but those which contested the first democratic parliamentary elections in 1977 gained less than 2 percent of the vote, after which their support declined even further. In democratic Spain as under the democratic republic of 1931–36, most new political violence came from the left: the Basque nationalist terrorist movement ETA itself eventually carried out nearly a thousand political murders over a period of more than twenty years. Right radical, neo-Falangist, and neo-Nazi terrorism in Spain was primarily a feature of the key transition period of 1976–81. During those years such elements committed forty-six murders and many more attacks on property, but proportionately more of their activists were arrested in Spain than in Italy. The Spanish authorities rounded up 141 during 1981 alone.[29] Though, as in Italy, scores of new groups were formed in Spain, their average size and strength was even smaller than in Italy.[30] No moderate right authoritarian force, such as the MSI, emerged in Spain with any ability to attract any electoral following whatsoever.

In France neofascist and right radical terrorism played very little role, but the intellectual and doctrinaire influence exerted by such groups in France was second only to that in Italy, while the leading French right nationalist party came to generate greater electoral support in the 1980s than any equivalent movement in western Europe. During the first two decades after the war, a variety of small neofascist and right radical groups were organized in France, each more insignificant than the other. They did, however, play roles in the "Europeanist" dimension of neofascism and in propagating doctrines of "social racism." During the early 1960s the OAS (Organization of the Secret Army), a conspiratorial terrorist organization formed by dissident military and French-Algerian colonist ultras, managed to create certain minor problems, but it was repressed with a ruthlessness greater than that exhibited by any other democracy.[31]

29. According to data appearing in *Cambio 16* (Madrid), Aug. 30, 1982.

30. The most recent account of Spanish neofascism is M. Sánchez Soler, *Los hijos del 20-N: Historia violenta del fascismo español* (Madrid, 1993).

31. F. Duprat, *Les mouvements d'extrême droite en France depuis 1944* (Paris, 1972); R. Chiroux, *L'extrême droite sous la Ve République* (Paris, 1974); M.-J. Chombart de Lauwe, *Complots contre la democratie* (Paris, 1981); J. Algazy, *La tentation néo-fasciste en France* (Paris, 1984); R. Badinter et al., *Vous avez dit Fascismes?* (Paris, 1984).

The doctrinaires who came to command the greatest cultural attention were the writers and thinkers of the *nouvelle droite* (new right) of the 1970s and 1980s. They were formed around a study center known as GRECE (Groupement de Recherche et d'Etudes pour une Civilisation Européenne, Group of Research and Studies for a European Civilization), and their leading figure, Alain de Benoist, won a prize from the Académie Française for a book of essays. Generally denounced, they nonetheless exerted a certain fascination within the French intelligentsia for their bold contradiction of contemporary norms.

The *nouvelle droite* is extremely elitist, hierarchical, and antiegalitarian but rejects the mysticism and idealism of an Evola, affirming the importance of science in modern life and relying heavily on the new sociobiology. Unlike the classic right, the new right maintains a religious position that is exclusively pagan, opposing equally Marxism and "Judaeo-Christianity." It attempts to create a political and philosophical program on the basis of a certain kind of human anthropology, which gives it an intellectuality and rigor normally lacking in vitalist neofascism.[32]

The first popular antisystem movement of the right in postwar France was the group led by Pierre Poujade in the early 1950s. Poujade, however, was a right-wing populist who failed to develop a consistent political organization.[33] More important in later years was Jean-Marie Le Pen, whose Front National became an electoral force in the 1980s. The Front National is a rightist-nationalist movement opposed to immigration, foreign minorities, crime, disorder, and modern egalitarianism, which is held to contradict the natural organic hierarchy of human life. Thus it stands for an organic and more hierarchical national community. In five different elections between 1984 and 1989 (two for the French parliament, two for the European parliament, and one for the presidency), candidates of the Front National won from 10 to 15 percent of the national vote, though its parliamentary representation has varied drastically, going down from thirty-two to one after the elections of 1987. In 1993 it gained 12.5 percent of the popular vote but no assembly seat.[34]

Neofascism is of very scant importance in the smaller democracies of northern Europe. Proportionately the largest number of small right radical and neofascist groups appears to have been formed in Belgium (reflecting the Flemish-Walloon ethnic tension, at least to some extent). They have scored a few minor local electoral successes.[35]

32. A.-M. Duranton-Crabol, *Visages de la Nouvelle Droite: La GRECE et son histoire* (Paris, 1988).

33. S. Hoffman, *Le mouvement Poujade* (Paris, 1956).

34. E. Plénel and A. Rollat, eds., *L'effet Le Pen* (Paris, 1984); E. Roussel, *Le cas Le Pen: Les nouvelles droites en France* (Paris, 1985); J. Chatain, *Les affaires de M. Le Pen* (Paris, 1987); N. Mayer and P. Perrineau, eds., *Le Front National à découvrir* (Paris, 1989).

35. Michel Géoris-Reitshof's brief *Extrême droite et néo-fascisme en Belgique* (Brussels, 1962) presented a taxonomy of the right, reactionary right, and neofascist groups.

In England Oswald Mosley survived the war. Always among the most intellectual of national fascist leaders, he later stressed doctrine and theory even more. The Union Movement which he founded in 1948 did not propose a categorical neofascism but occupied a differentiated position on the radical right. Much more categorical was Colin Jordan's National Socialist Movement, though it later changed its title. The only right radical British organization of any note has been the National Front, created by the fusion of various right radical groups (some of them close to neo-Nazism) in 1967. It reached 17,500 members by 1974, but its electoral appeal peaked only a few years later and then rapidly declined. By 1984 membership was down to three thousand.[36]

If it is clear that, on the one hand, neofascism and the radical right have created a kind of permanent subculture in most western European countries, on the other it is equally clear that they have been doomed to a ghettolike existence of electoral insignificance, escaped only by sporadic, desperate essays in terrorism which lead nowhere. The Western world has been inoculated against fascism, and all the cultural trends of the second half of the century have militated against it. Even a major new economic crisis will probably be inadequate to give it life, for its competitors are more sophisticated and it lacks any broad philosophical basis in terms credible to the ordinary population.

But of course for many years a legion of leftist journalists and commentators, as well as a large chorus of professional anti-Americanists, have been certain that in the Western world neofascism would soon become strongest, even predominant, in the United States rather than Europe. Once more they are doomed to disappointment, their most common fate. Though the black leader Marcus Garvey once claimed to have "invented" a fascism for black Americans, we have seen that the interwar United States harbored scarcely any fascist-type movements for black or white, with the main exception of the imported German-American Bund.

The situation in some respects has been more promising for would-be fascistologists in the second half of the century, for a large number of small neo-Nazi and white supremacist right radical groups have been formed in the United States. Though all are very small, more than a few have engaged in violence. Similarly, several black extremist groups have created forms of right radical black nationalism, though not of categorical black neofascism. Not a single one of these has come remotely close to developing any political significance, though the black extremist groups have become proportionately stronger than the white ones. Moreover, not one has proved effective in converting itself

---

36. The National Front harbored a diversity of currents from the comparatively moderate to direct neo-Nazism. See N. Fielding, *The National Front* (London, 1981); C. T. Husbands, *Racial Exclusionism and the City: The Urban Support of the National Front* (London, 1983); R. Thurlow, *Fascism in Britain: A History, 1918–1985* (Oxford, 1987), 274–89; and G. Gable, "The Far Right in Contemporary Britain," in Cheles, Ferguson, and Vaughan, eds., *Neo-Fascism* 244–63.

into any kind of more moderate mass political organization that could compete for votes.[37] As hard as it may be for the left to accept the fact, neofascism is even weaker in the United States than in western Europe.

Nor has Latin America—home to recurring cycles of authoritarianism, revolutionism, and terrorism—done much better in re-creating classic fascism. The new wave of rightist dictatorships of the 1960s and 1970s excited considerable speculation among commentators about a new "Latin American fascism," yet aside from Communist Cuba all these regimes were right-wing military systems without any elaborate ideology and without any mobilized political basis. Their economic and security policies were more sophisticated than those of traditional military regimes, yet they were much more adequately described by the new appellation of military "bureaucratic authoritarianism"[38] than by "fascism."[39] A good many new fascistic and right radical circles have been organized here in the past two generations, as in most other parts of the world, yet, as usual, their number has been inversely proportional to their significance. The only right radical movement to survive from the end of the fascist era through the subsequent period has been the right radical Falange Socialista Boliviana, a minor force in Bolivian affairs. Though the Movimiento Nacional Revolucionario did come to power by revolution in Bolivia by 1952, by that time it had lost most of its early fascistic coloration and characteristics.

In developed countries outside Europe, the search for the equivalents of fascism has often turned toward Japan and South Africa. In chapter 10 we saw that interwar Japan failed to develop any direct political equivalent of European fascism, even though the semipluralist Japanese system of the 1930s did achieve a partial functional equivalent of it in practice. Since 1945 Japan has been largely demilitarized and has drastically realtered its priorities. The country nonetheless harbors many small fringe religious and political groups, including a few that are neofascist and many more that are right radical nationalist. By the mid-1980s at least fifty radical nationalist associations with some 120,000 members were identified.[40] One of the most influential right radicals was the multimillionaire gambling czar Ryoichi Sasakawa, a major financier of

---

37. Conceivably the organization that has come the closest—and that's not saying much—is Lyndon LaRouche's National Caucus of Labor Committees, which has placed a very few members in minor local offices. Yet the NCLC has only some, not most, of the characteristics of a fascist movement. See D. King, *Lyndon LaRouche and the New American Fascism* (New York, 1989).

38. G. O'Donnell, *Modernization and Bureaucratic-Authoritarianism* (Berkeley, 1973). Fundamental works in this area include D. Collier, ed., *The New Authoritarianism in Latin America* (Princeton, 1979); A. Rouquié, *The Military and the State in Latin America* (Berkeley, 1987); J. M. Malloy, ed., *Authoritarianism and Corporatism in Latin America* (Pittsburgh, 1977); and F. B. Pike and T. Stritch, eds., *The New Corporatism* (South Bend, Ind., 1974).

39. See H. Trindade, "La question du fascisme en Amérique Latine," *Revue Française de Science Politique* 33:2 (April 1983): 281–312.

40. O'Maoláin, *Radical Right* 176–77.

such groups and apparently also a man with strong *yakuza* (organized crime) connections. Yet Japan is similar to most other countries in that nearly all these circles and organizations are small and without influence.

Probably the largest of the extremist-nationalist groups in Japan is Ryubo Okawa's Institute for Research in Human Happiness, whose title is an interesting commentary on the forms such forces must take in the postfascist era of hedonism and materialism. His book *Nostradamus: Fearful Prophecies* foresees a Japan dominant in the twenty-first century after having defeated both Russia and the United States, able to make China "a slave" and Korea "a prostitute." [41] Okawa's institute has been said to have two million followers, but it has not been able to become a very significant political force. Democracy has more shallow roots in Japan than in most European countries, and Japanese nationalism is latently stronger also than in most European countries. The revolution that would create a true neofascist potential is not in sight, however, as the country continues to evolve further in the direction of Western hedonism and materialism.

South Africa long seemed more promising to those looking for a contemporary fascism. It possessed the most racist system in the world and in earlier years proportionately more citizens who sympathized with Nazism than in any other country outside Europe. A sector of the radical right even split off from the dominant National Party to form a more extreme Reconstituted National Party in 1969, followed four years later by a yet more extreme Afrikaner Resistance Movement, which eventually claimed fifty thousand members and had a militia called the Storm Falcons. Indeed, there was little doubt that in the Afrikaans-speaking population there was greater sympathy for more extreme forces and measures than in most developed countries. Yet throughout the postwar period South Africa remained a "racial democracy" for whites and not a completely authoritarian system of any kind. This, plus the pressures of the times and the black majority, eventually forced a basic change, so that by 1994 South Africa had suddenly become a multiracial democracy, though it was far from certain that it would be able to develop effectively as one. Nonetheless, for the time being this was a severe blow to explorers for neofascism. Certainly the future potential for extremist politics remains greater there than in any other developed country with the exception of Russia so that the future remains uncertain.

If effective neofascism stubbornly refused to blossom in democratic and capitalist countries, some analysts eventually looked to the Communist regimes, most of which became increasingly nationalist from the 1950s on. A number of them relied on powerful variants of the *Führerprinzip*, extreme ethnocentric nationalism, and racism (as well as the ultimately grotesque in

41. *Wisconsin State Journal* (Madison), Oct. 20, 1991.

antimodernism in the case of the Khmer Rouge in Cambodia). This might seem like the fascistization of communism. There is no doubt that fascism and communism have shared fundamental characteristics, and for many years Soviet spokesmen delighted in applying the same terms to the People's Republic of China as to Nazi Germany: "bourgeois nationalism," "voluntarism," "subjectivism," "anti-intellectualism," "military-bureaucratic degeneration," "subservient obedience" of the masses, "petit bourgeois" economic policies, and "autarchic" policies that try to place "surplus population" on "foreign territories." They concluded that "the Maoist approach in no way differs from fascism."[42] Parallel lists for Castro's Cuba by more serious analysts would include the pragmatic development a posteriori of ideology, government by the charismatic cult of personality and the leadership principle, extreme nationalism, voluntarism, militarism, adventurism, and expansionism, the cult of myths and heroes, emphasis on peasantism, and violent struggles against the plutocracies. Accurate though most of these technical comparisons are, they do not define doctrines and regimes that possess all the defining characteristics of fascism, though in many ways similar to fascism. Communist regimes have remained faithful to the Leninist-Stalinist principles of complete state bureaucracy, theoretical (if not practical) revolutionary internationalism, complete state collectivism (with the exception of China), and philosophical materialism. These are cardinal principles absolutely opposed to fascism.

Yet others have suggested that the future of fascism has lain beyond the developed world and would be more important for new states emerging after 1945, as it was originally for the new nations of the 1860s. One of the prime group of candidates has been the new African dictatorships of the past generation. Such qualities as extreme nationalism, racism, ethnocentrism, nominally one-party systems, charismatic leadership, elaborate use of myths and national religiosity, and various forms of "African socialism" have seemed to approximate the fascist typology.[43] Closer inspection, however, casts grave doubt on this analysis. As Paul Hayes has written, "Many of the characteristics of European fascism may be found in certain of the African countries, though it is rare for any number to be found at the same time in one place."[44] The leader-

42. These terms are taken from A. Malukhin, *Militarism—Backbone of Maoism* (Moscow, 1970), 33 and throughout, cited in an unpublished paper by A. James Gregor.

43. See A. J. Gregor, "African Socialism and Fascism: An Appraisal," *Review of Politics* 29:3 (July 1967): 353–99, and idem, *The Fascist Persuasion in Radical Politics* (Princeton, 1974), 406–9. A broader application may be found in A. J. Joes, *Fascism in the Contemporary World* (Boulder, 1978); idem, "Fascism: The Past and the Future," *Comparative Political Studies* 7:1 (April 1974): 107–33; and idem, "The Fascist Century," *Worldview* 21:5 (May 1978): 19–23.

44. P. M. Hayes, *Fascism* (London, 1972), 208. Maurice Bardèche, one of the few noteworthy fascist intellectuals to make an effort at defining fascism after the passing of the fascist era, has insisted convincingly that so-called third world fascisms are "false fascisms." The differences that he emphasizes are above all cultural. Bardèche, *Qu'est-ce que le fascisme?* (Paris, 1961).

ship principle there resembles the former *caudillaje* sultanates of the Caribbean much more than that of Italy or Germany. The single parties normally do not turn out to be much in the way of organized parties, and the political economy falls short of any organized national syndicalism or state-regulated economy in the central European forms.[45] Finally, the philosophical culture of Fascism and Nazism is largely lacking. About all that one can say is that the Fascist example of a one-party nationalist dictatorship may have been the original precedent for such regimes, but any specific and complete typology of European fascism has not been reproduced. Moreover, the wave of later African dictatorships in the 1970s was overtly Leninist-Stalinist, seeking to implement Russian-derived norms of complete state bureaucracy and a state collectivism as nearly total as circumstances permitted. These were regime goals quite distinct from fascism.

As one approaches the Middle East, however, the trail becomes warmer. This is an area originally impacted to some extent by paradigmatic European fascism. Some of the new nationalist regimes which developed in the Middle East during the second half of the century exhibited more of the characteristics of fascism than those of any other part of the world. A first example was the Egyptian regime under Nasser, with its *Führerprinzip,* "Arab socialism," a state sector of the economy approaching 40 percent, and bellicosity toward Israel. Yet the Nasser regime failed to formulate a distinctive new philosophy or culture, and its only state party was the rather amorphous Arab National Union, more like something to be found under a Balkan monarchy of the 1930s than the Arrow Cross or the Legion of the Archangel Michael. It was never consistently anti-Communist, or for that matter very coherent in any form.[46] In a subsequent phase under Anwar Sadat, Egypt turned resolutely toward peace.

At first glance a better case might be made for the Libyan dictatorship of Mu'ammar al-Gadhafi, established in 1969. Though the dictator of a major oil-exporting country, Gadhafi is a fanatical Muslim antimaterialist who has sought to create a new communitarian system. His *Green Book* of 1978 presented Gadhafi's "third universal theory," which preached "true democracy" by means of direct organic links between the leader and the masses. Thus what began as a military regime has been converted into a charismatic dictatorship structured in theory on direct popular revolutionary committees and people's congresses. The regime is based on a form of Islamic puritanism, but its religiosity is heterodox, rejecting the Muslim Sunna and the doctrines of the Islamic teaching class in order to augment its own authority. "Brother Colonel" has renounced capitalism, preaching pan-Arabism and a form of "Arab socialism," while his interest in militarism, violence, and adventurism abroad has

45. A. Hughes and M. Kolinsky, " 'Paradigmatic Fascism' and Modernization: A Critique," *Political Studies* 24:4 (Dec. 1976): 371–96.

46. Cf. J. Lacouture, *Nasser* (London, 1973). On the profascist leanings of Nasser's generation, see J. P. Jankowski, *Egypt's Young Rebels: "Young Egypt," 1933–1952* (Stanford, 1975).

been amply demonstrated. Aspects of all this are somewhat reminiscent of fascism, but the Libyan regime constitutes a unique personal blend of notions that is sui generis and has sometimes been labeled anarcho-Leninist. Gadhafi theoretically rejects the state and bureaucratization, while in fact operating a state dictatorship characterized by more than a little bureaucratic corruption. In recent years he has moderated various policies and has moved somewhat nearer orthodox Islam. His regime's nominal grounding in the Koran identifies it as a variant of the Islamic fundamentalist systems, rather than a secular fascist-type state.

Perhaps a better candidate yet is the regime of Saddam Hussein in Iraq, its leader known among other things by George Bush's appellation in 1990 as "The Hitler of Our Time." The Iraqi dictatorship is a product of the Baath movement of "Arab socialism" created originally in Syria by Michel Aflaq and others after the fall of France in 1940. Its goal was a national renaissance of Arabs on the basis of a kind of national socialism and a new ideology to "represent the Arab spirit" against Western liberalism and "materialist communism."[47] The Baath movement eventually became stronger in Iraq than in Syria, though basically as a conspiratorial elite rather than as a true fascist-style mass movement. An ultranationalist coup in Baghdad enabled Saddam Hussein in 1968 to become the head of a regime which he soon turned into a personal dictatorship based on an extreme "cult of personality" (or *Führerprinzip*).

Unlike some other extremist nationalist Arab movements, Baath was always inherently secular (Aflaq himself had been reared a Christian) and only paid lip service to Islam as the religion of Arabs. Shiite fundamentalism thus eventually became one of its major foes. In addition to the cult of leadership, the Iraqi regime developed an extremely authoritarian system, its police and intelligence services rigorously trained by eastern European Communist technicians. It has stressed the palingenesis of the "Arab spirit" in a more secular and political manner than have the Shiite fundamentalist revolutionaries, with the goal of creating a "new Arab" not defined by religious fundamentalism. Though preserving private property, the state has played a dominant role in its own form of *Zwangswirtschaft,* and any independent role of the bourgeoisie has been vigorously combated. The regime has undertaken broad mobilization of youth and also to some extent of women, another feature distinct from the fundamentalists, with mass mobilization carried out only under state auspices after consolidation of the dictatorship. Like nearly all states of the second half of the twentieth century, it has employed peace rhetoric but in practice developed one of the most extensively militarized systems in the world, its elite "Republican Guard" units forming a vague analogy with the Waffen-SS.

The regime is intensely anti-Western, anti-Jewish, and anti-Israeli, and

47. Michel Aflaq, as quoted in S. al-Khalil, *Republic of Fear* (Berkeley, 1989), 191.

it proclaimed a "new order" with its own "ethnic cleansing" or liquidation of minorities. Hussein's goal of military expansion was dramatically demonstrated in his two brutal invasions of Iran and Kuwait, perhaps the two initiatives of the later twentieth century most reminiscent of classic Hitlerism. In the process, pan-Arabism has increasingly given way to ultra-Iraqism, with a striving for new Iraqist cultural and art forms, a specific sense of "modern *Romanità*" through identification with the ancient Mesopotamian empires (including the literal reconstruction of the city of Babylon), and one of the all-time ultimates in Hitlerian-Stalinist architecture in the grandiose and grotesque Victory Arch in Baghdad. There will probably never again be a reproduction of the Third Reich, but Saddam Hussein has come closer than any other dictator since 1945.[48]

Fascism was, after all, the only major new ideology of the early twentieth century, and it is not surprising that a variety of its key features reemerged in radical movements and national authoritarian regimes in later times and other regions, even though the profile of the new forces is on balance distinct. Many nationalist authoritarian regimes have some of the characteristics of fascism, just as all Communist regimes have had and still have some of the characteristics of Fascism. These features include:

1. Permanent nationalistic one-party authoritarianism, neither temporary nor a real prelude to internationalism.
2. The charismatic leadership principle, incorporated by many different kinds of regimes.
3. The search for a synthetic ethnicist ideology, distinct from liberalism and Marxism.
4. An authoritarian state system and political economy of corporatism or partial socialism, more limited and pluralist than the Communist model.
5. The philosophical principle of voluntarist activism, unbounded by any philosophical determinism.

In these respects fascism was fundamental to revolution, nationalism, and dictatorship in the twentieth century. To that extent its influence will continue to be felt into the twenty-first century.

Concern about the "return" of fascism, however, has mounted since the collapse of the Soviet empire and the reunification of Germany in 1989. This has been fed by several different sources. One is the growing activism and violence of "skinheads" and other small neofascist and neo-Nazi groups, par-

---

48. In addition to the work cited in the previous note, see al-Khalil's *The Monument: Art, Vulgarity and Responsibility in Iraq* (Berkeley, 1991); A. Baram, *Culture, History and Ideology in the Formation of Ba'thist Iraq, 1968–1989* (New York, 1991); and CARDRI, *Saddam's Iraq* (London, 1989).

ticularly as directed against immigrants and aliens. A second is the growth in electoral support for parliamentary rightist parties that promote xenophobia, various forms of neonationalism, authoritarian measures, and a tougher policy on immigration and ethnic minorities. Yet another is the growth of neofascism and the radical right in former Communist countries, most gravely in the case of the Russian Federation.

The concern is not so much with the absolute re-creation of the Hitler and Mussolini regimes, which most analysts recognize is a historical and political impossibility—quite unlike the cloning abroad for decades of Marxist-Leninist regimes. Rather, as one German commentator wrote, "Today there is little prospect for fascism to succeed in its traditional accustomed form in Europe or the USA. Yet the danger is great and growing that a new kind of fascism vaguer in contours can again" develop power.[49]

How great is this danger? In the Western world, very slight. The enormous cultural, social, and economic changes, together with the lengthy development of democratic systems, makes anything genuinely resembling a historic fascism almost impossible. All the genuine neofascist and neo-Nazi groups remain tiny circles of fringe activists. The right radical parties are stronger, but only in Italy and France have they any significant support, and that is limited. The more broadly they seek to mobilize, the more moderate they are forced to become. Even in South Africa, whose political future remains so uncertain, the genuine right radicals are very seriously outnumbered. A complete breakdown that would result in authoritarian rule either by blacks or whites cannot be discounted, but to govern at all a new regime would have to follow pragmatic rather than doctrinaire fascist policies.

Religious fundamentalist movements have great potential for the expansion of authoritarian politics, particularly in the Middle East and in India. In the mid-1990s there is probably more concern about the growth of a strong new authoritarian force in India than in any other nominally established democracy. Groups such as Shiv Sena and particularly the RSS (Communion of National Volunteers), with its millions of followers and militia group several hundred thousand strong, undoubtedly have great potential for religiously based authoritarian nationalism.[50] These Hindu fundamentalists speak of a "greater India" and domination of the entire Indian Ocean. It is possible that India could become the first country with a fifty-year-old nominally democratic system to succumb to an expansive new authoritarianism, though the transcendent religious references and very distinct cultural background of the fundamentalists would make of it something different from historic fascism.

Within Europe the major question marks, at the end of the twentieth

49. F. Hacker, *Das Faschismus-Syndrom* (Düsseldorf, 1990), 130.
50. See, among others, T. Basu et al., *Khaki Shorts, Saffron Flags* (Hyderabad, 1993).

century as at its beginning, remain the Balkans and the lands of the former Soviet Union, especially Russia. There are neofascist and right radical groups in all former Communist countries,[51] but they have significant potential only in parts of former Yugoslavia—mainly Serbia—and perhaps Romania, where the nonfascist but murderous former dictator Ion Antonescu has apparently become the hero of the century.[52] Slobodan Milosevíc seems to have made the transition in Serbia from secretary of the Communist Party in a Communist dictatorship to head of a violent, militarist, and expansionist nationalist regime that has acquired aspects of fascist style in its mass atrocities and "ethnic cleansing." Yet for all its crimes, the Serbian system at the time of writing remains semipluralist, with a not insignificant public opposition, and has not been completely transformed into a one-party dictatorship.

Clearly the most sinister figure in European politics outside Serbia is Vladimir Zhirinovsky, head of the new Russian Liberal Democratic Party, which is neither liberal nor democratic but won 25 percent of the vote in the first free and open Russian parliamentary elections. By the early 1990s Russia hosted a wide variety of right radical and even in some cases neofascist groups,[53] but the only one to achieve a mass following is Zhirinovsky's organization. He has set a new world record for saying the most outrageous and provocative things, and he sometimes deliberately plays the role of a kind of menacing buffoon, which has led some to dismiss him as a clown. Zhirinovsky's *Mein Kampf,* a small book entitled *Poslednii brosok na iug* (Last Push to the South, 1993), reveals an enormous, potentially highly unstable, ambition and a scheme to compensate Russia for its loss of the Soviet empire by the reannexation of most of the former tsarist domains under a new Russian dictatorship. Further *Lebensraum* is to be achieved by throttling the danger of Islamic expansionism, not merely by controlling central Asia but by advancing directly "to the south" to dominate Turkey, Iran, and Afghanistan. This sounds like a sort of design for World War III.

For some time analysts have been busy comparing the new Russian Republic with the German Republic of Weimar, and there are alarming similarities. While Zhirinovsky himself has developed no very consistent ideology of any kind—fascist or otherwise—other than authoritarian Russian nationalism

51. The first survey in book form is P. Hockenos, *Free to Hate: The Rise of the Right in Post-Communist Europe* (New York, 1993).

52. J. Geran Pilon, *The Bloody Flag: Post-Communist Nationalism in Eastern Europe. Spotlight on Romania* (New Brunswick, N.J., 1992).

53. The best account to date is W. Laqueur, *Black Hundred: The Rise of the Extreme Right in Russia* (New York, 1993). Useful earlier works include J. B. Dunlop, *The New Russian Revolutionaries* (Boston, 1976); idem, *The Faces of Contemporary Russian Nationalism* (Princeton, 1984); A. Yanov, *The Russian New Right* (Berkeley, 1978); idem, *The Russian Challenge and the Year 2000* (New York, 1987); and "Pamyat," a special number of *Nationalities Papers* 19:2 (Fall 1991).

and imperialism, Russian variations on historic fascist, Nazi, and right radical and anti-Semitic doctrines are being developed by others. The greatest danger of reversion to an authoritarian nationalist-imperialist past would thus seem to be found in the eastern Orthodox countries of eastern Europe, whose history and culture have to some extent isolated them from the massive changes that have occurred in the past two generations in almost all the rest of Europe.

Specific historic fascism can never be re-created, but the end of the twentieth century may witness the rise of both new and partially related forms of authoritarian nationalism, particularly in eastern Europe, Africa, and Asia.

Bibliography

Index

Bibliography

BOOKS

Primary Sources

Anonimo Nero. *Camerata dove sei? Rapporti con Mussolini ed il Fascismo degli anti-fascisti della prima Repubblica*. Rome, 1976.
Arrese, J. L. de. *La revolucíon social del nacionalsindicalismo*. Madrid, 1940.
Barnes, J. S. *The Universal Aspects of Fascism*. London, 1928.
Barroso, G. *O Integralismo e o mundo*. Rio de Janeiro, 1936.
Bertele, A. *Aspetti ideologici del fascismo*. Turin, 1930.
Bottai, G. *Vent'anni e un giorno*. Naviglio, 1949.
Codreanu, C. Z. *Guardia de Hierro*. Barcelona, 1976.
Drumont, E. *La France juive*. 1886.
Evola, J. *Saggi sull'idealismo magico*. Rome, 1925.
Evola, J. *Teoria dell'individuo assoluto*. Turin, 1927.
Evola, J. *Sintesi di dottrina della razza*. 1941.
Evola, J. *Il fascismo: Saggio di una analisi critica dal punto di vista della destra*. 1970.
Fantini, O. *L'universalità del Fascismo*. Naples, 1933.
Federzoni, L. *Italia di ieri per la storia di domani*. Verona, 1967.
Gentile, G. *Origini de dottrina del fascismo*. Rome, 1927.
Gentile, G. *Fascismo e cultura*. Milan, 1928.
Gil Robles, J. M. *No fue posible la paz*. Barcelona, 1968.
Grandi, D. *25 luglio: Quarant'anni dopo*, ed. R. De Felice. Bologna, 1983.
Grigorenko, P. G. *Memoirs*. New York, 1982.
Gumplowicz, L. *Der Rassenkampf*. Innsbruck, 1883.
Hitler's Secret Conversations. New York, 1962.
Lettere dei caduti della R.S.I. Rome, 1976.
Manoilescu, M. *Théorie du protectionnisme et de l'échange international*. Paris, 1929.
Manoilescu, M. *L'espace corporatif*. Paris, 1934.
Manoilescu, M. *Le siècle du corporatisme*. Paris, 1936.
Manoilescu, M. *Der einzige Partei*. Berlin, 1941.
Marx, K. *The Eighteenth Brumaire of Louis Napoleon*. New York, 1970.

Mousseaux, G. des. *Le Juif, le judaïsme et la judaisation des peuples chrétiens*. Paris, 1869.

Mussolini, B. *My Autobiography*. London, 1928.

Mussolini, B. *Memoirs, 1942–1943*, ed. R. Klibansky. London, 1949.

Mussolini, B. *Opera omnia di Benito Mussolini*, ed. E. and D. Susmel. 36 vols. Florence, 1951–63.

Nazi Conspiracy and Aggression. Vol. 7. Washington, D.C., 1948.

Nordau, M. *Entartung*. 1892.

Onrubia Revuelta, J., ed. *Historia de la oposición falangista al regimen de Franco en sus documentos*. Madrid, 1989.

Palmieri, M. *The Philosophy of Fascism*. Chicago, 1936.

Panunzio, S. *Diritto, forza e violenza: Lineamenti di una teoria della violenza*. Bologna, 1921.

Panunzio, S. *Lo stato di diritto*. 1922.

Panunzio, S. *Teoria generale dello Stato fascista*. Padua, 1939.

Partito Nazionale Fascista. *Mostra della Rivoluzione Fascista*. Rome, 1990.

Perkins, F. *The Roosevelt I Knew*. New York, 1946.

Salvemini, G. *Italian Fascist Activities in the United States*. Staten Island, 1977.

Salvemini, G. *Le origini del fascismo in Italia*. Milan, 1979.

Salvemini, G., et al. *Non mollare* (1925). Florence, 1955.

Seillière, E. [pseud.]. *Der demokratische Imperialismus*. Berlin, 1907.

Seillière, E. [pseud.]. *Introduction a la philosophie de l' imperialisme*. Paris, 1911.

Seilleère, E. [pseud.]. *Les Mystiques du néo-romanticisme*. Paris, 1911.

Seillière, E. [pseud.]. *Mysticisme et domination*. Paris, 1913.

Sorel, G. *Réflexions sur la violence*. 1908.

Spinetti, G. S. *Fascismo universale*. Rome, 1933.

Starhemberg, E. R. von. *Between Hitler and Mussolini*. London, 1942.

Valois, G. *Le fascisme*. Paris, 1926.

Zeletin, S. *Burghezia romana*. 1923.

Zeletin, S. *Neoliberalismul*. 1927.

Secondary Sources

Abelshauser, W., and A. Faust. *Wirtschafts- und Sozialpolitik: Eine national-sozialistische Sozialrevolution?* Tübingen, 1983.

Abendroth, W., et al. *Faschismus und Kapitalismus*. Frankfurt, 1967.

Abraham, D. *The Collapse of the Weimar Republic: Political Economy and Crisis*. Princeton, 1981.

Abramovitch, R. *The Soviet Revolution*. New York, 1962.

Abrate, M. *Benedetto Croce e la crisi della società italiana*. Turin, 1966.

Abrate, M., et al. *Il problema storico del fascismo*. Florence, 1970.

Ackermann, J. *Heinrich Himmler als Ideologe*. Göttingen, 1970.

Acquarone, A. *L'Organizzazione dello Stato Totalitario*. Turin, 1965.

Acquarone, A., and M. Vernassa, eds. *Il regime fascista*. Bologna, 1974.

Adam, U. D. *Judenpolitik im Dritten Reich*. Düsseldorf, 1972.

Adamson, W. L. *Avant-Garde Florence: From Modernism to Fascism*. Cambridge, Mass., 1993.

Adorno, T., et al. *The Authoritarian Personality.* New York, 1950.

Agursky, M. *The Third Rome: National Bolshevism in the USSR.* Boulder, 1987.

Akademiya Nauk SSSR. *Fashizm i antidemokratischeskie rezhimy v Evrope. Nachalo 20-x godov—1945 g.* Moscow, 1981.

Alatri, P. *Le origini del fascismo.* Rome, 1956.

Alatri, P. *Nitti, D'Annunzio e la questione adriatica.* Milan, 1959.

Alatri, P. *L'antifascismo italiano.* Rome, 1961.

Alatri, P. *Gabriele D'Annunzio.* Turin, 1983.

Alberghi, P. *Il fascismo in Emilia Romagna.* Modena, 1989.

Alberi, A. C. *Il teatro nel fascismo.* Rome, 1974.

Albertoni, E. A. *Gaetano Mosca.* Milan, 1978.

Albright, W. F. *History, Archaelogy and Christian Humanism.* New York, 1964.

Alexander, R. J. *The Perón Era.* New York, 1951.

Alff, W. *Der Begriff Faschismus und andere Aufsätze.* Frankfurt, 1971.

Algazy, J. *La tentation néo-fasciste en France.* Paris, 1984.

al-Khalil, S. *Republic of Fear.* Berkeley, 1989.

al-Khalil, S. *The Monument: Art, Vulgarity and Responsibility in Iraq.* Berkeley, 1991.

Allen, W. S. *The Nazi Seizure of Power: The Experience of a Single German Town.* New York, 1984.

Alltagsgeschichte der NS-Zeit: Neue Perspektive oder Trivialisierung? Munich, 1984.

Alter, P. *Nationalism.* London, 1989.

Aly, G., and S. Heim. *Verdenker der Vernichtung.* Hamburg, 1991.

Ambri, M. *I falsi fascismi.* Rome, 1980.

Amendola, G. *Intervista sul fascismo.* Bari, 1976.

Andreyev, C. *Vlassov and the Russian Liberation Movement.* New York, 1987.

Angebert, J.-M. *The Occult and the Third Reich.* New York, 1974.

Apter, D. *The Politics of Modernization.* Chicago, 1965.

Arendt, H. *The Origins of Totalitarianism.* New York, 1951.

Arisi Rota, A. *La diplomazia del ventennio.* Milan, 1990.

Armstrong, J. A. *Ukrainian Nationalism.* New York, 1963.

Aronson, S. *Reinhard Heydrich und die Frühgeschichte von Gestapo und SD.* Stuttgart, 1971.

Aschheim, S. E. *The Nietzsche Legacy in Germany, 1890–1990.* Berkeley, 1992.

Ashkenasi, A. *Modern German Nationalism.* Cambridge, Mass., 1976.

Ayçoberry, P. *The Nazi Question.* New York, 1981.

Azéma, J.-P., and F. Bédarida, eds. *Vichy et les français.* Paris, 1992.

Azpiazu, J., S. J. *The Corporate State.* St. Louis, 1951.

Backes, K. *Hitler und die bildenden Künste.* Cologne, 1988.

Backes, U. *Politischer Extremismus in demokratische Verfassungsstaaten: Elemente einer normativen Rahmentheorie.* Opladen, 1989.

Badinter, R., et al. *Vous avez dit Fascismes?* Paris, 1984.

Baer, G. *The Coming of the Italo-Ethiopian War.* Cambridge, Mass., 1967.

Bailer-Galanda, B. *Die neue Rechte.* Vienna, 1990.

Bailey, D. C. *Viva Cristo Rey!* Austin, 1973.

Balvet, M. *Itinéraire d'un intellectuel vers le fascisme: Drieu La Rochelle.* Paris, 1984.

Ba- Maw. *Breakthrough in Burma: Memoirs of a Revolution, 1939–1946.* New Haven, 1968.

Bankier, D. *The Germans and the Final Solution.* Oxford, 1992.

Baram, A. *Culture, History and Ideology in the Formation of Ba'thist Iraq, 1968–1989.* New York, 1991.

Barbagli, M. *Disoccupazione e sistema scolastico in Italia.* Bologna, 1974.

Barbagli, M. *Educating for Unemployment: Politics, Labor Markets, and the School System—Italy, 1859–1973.* New York, 1982.

Bardèche, M. *Qu'est-ce que le fascisme?* Paris, 1961.

Barkai, A. *Nazi Economics.* New Haven, 1990.

Barkan, E. *The Retreat of Scientific Racism.* New York, 1992.

Barneri, D. *Agenda nera: Trent'anni di neofascismo in Italia.* Rome, 1976.

Barnes, J. J., and P. P. Barnes. *James Vincent Murphy: Translator and Interpreter of Fascist Europe, 1880–1946.* Lanham, Md., 1987.

Barnett, V. *For the Soul of the People: Protestant Protest against Hitler.* New York, 1993.

Barnouw, D. *Weimar Intellectuals and the Threat of Modernity.* Bloomington, 1978.

Barros, J. *The Corfu Incident of 1923.* Princeton, 1965.

Barrows, S. *Distorting Mirrors: Visions of the Crowd in Late Nineteenth-Century France.* New Haven, 1981.

Bartolotto, G. *Fascismo e nazionalsocialismo.* Bologna, 1933.

Bartov, O. *The Eastern Front, 1941–1945: German Troops and the Barbarisation of Warfare.* London, 1985.

Bartov, O. *Hitler's Army.* New York, 1991.

Basu, T., et al. *Khaki Shorts, Saffron Flags.* Hyderabad, 1993.

Batkay, W. M. *Authoritarian Politics in a Transitional State: Istvan Bethlen and the Unified Party in Hungary, 1919–1926.* New York, 1982.

Battistrada, L., and F. Vancini. *Il delitto Matteotti.* Bologna, 1973.

Bauer, Y. *A History of the Holocaust.* New York, 1982.

Bauman, Z. *Modernity and the Holocaust.* Cambridge, 1989.

Beck, E. R. *Under the Bombs.* Lexington, Ky., 1986.

Beetham, D., ed. *Marxists in Face of Fascism.* Totowa, N.J., 1984.

Bell, D. *The Cultural Contradictions of Capitalism.* New York, 1976.

Bell, J. D. *Peasants in Power: Alexander Stamboliski and the Bulgarian Agrarian Union, 1899–1923.* Princeton, 1977.

Bell, L. V. *In Hitler's Shadow: The Anatomy of American Nazism.* Port Washington, N.Y., 1973.

Bellamy, R. *Modern Italian Social Theory.* Stanford, 1987.

Bellotti, F. *La Repubblica di Salò.* Milan, 1974.

Ben-Ami, S. *Fascism from Above: The Dictatorship of Primo de Rivera in Spain, 1923–1930.* Oxford, 1983.

Bendersky, J. *Carl Schmitt: Theorist for the Reich.* Princeton, 1983.

Benedetti, U. *Benedetto Croce e il fascismo.* Rome, 1967.

Benewick, R. *Political Violence and Public Order: A Study of British Fascism.* London, 1969.

Bennecke, H. *Hitler und die SA.* Vienna, 1962.

Bennett, D. H. *Demagogues in the Depression: American Radicals and the Union Party, 1932–1936*. New Brunswick, N.J., 1969.

Benz, W., ed. *Rechtsextremismus in der Bundesrepublik*. Frankfurt, 1989.

Berger, G. M. *Parties Out of Power in Japan, 1931–1941*. Princeton, 1977.

Berghahn, V. R. *Der Stahlhelm*. Düsseldorf, 1966.

Bergmann, K. *Agrarromantik und Grosstadtfeindlichkeit*. Meisenheim am Glan, 1970.

Bergmann, W., and R. Erb, eds. *Antisemitismus in der politischen Kultur nach 1945*. Opladen, 1990.

Berselli, A. *L'opinione pubblica inglese e l'avvento del fascismo (1919–1925)*. Milan, 1971.

Bertin, F. *L'Europe de Hitler*. 3 vols. Paris, 1976–77.

Bertoldi, S. *Tedeschi in Italia*. Milan, 1964.

Bertoldi, S. *Salò*. Milan, 1976.

Bertoni, R. *Il trionfo del fascismo nell'URSS*. Milan, 1937.

Bessel, R. *Political Violence and the Rise of Nazism: The Storm Troopers in Eastern Germany, 1925–1934*. New Haven, 1974.

Bessel, R. *Germany after the First World War*. New York, 1993.

Bessis, J. *La Méditerranée fasciste*. Paris, 1981.

Bethell, N. *The War Hitler Won*. London, 1972.

Betti, C. *L'Opera Nazionale Balilla e l'educazione fascista*. Florence, 1984.

Beyerchen, A. D. *Scientists under Hitler: Politics and the Physics Community in the Third Reich*. New Haven, 1977.

Bianchi, C., and F. Mezzetti. *Mussolini aprile 1945*. Milan, 1979.

Bianchi, G. *Perchè e come cadde il fascismo*. Milan, 1970.

Billington, J. S. *Fire in the Minds of Men: Origins of the Revolutionary Faith*. New York, 1980.

Birken, L. *Hitler as Philosophe: Remnants of the Enlightenment in National Socialism*. Westport, Conn., 1995.

Birn, R. B. *Die Höhern SS- und Polizeiführer: Himmlers Vertreter im Reich und in den besetzten Gebieten*. Düsseldorf, 1986.

Black, C. E. *The Dynamics of Modernization*. New York, 1966.

Blackbourn, D., and G. Eley. *The Peculiarities of German History*. Oxford, 1984.

Blackburn, G. W. *Education in the Third Reich*. Albany, 1985.

Blanksten, G. *Perón's Argentina*. Chicago, 1953.

Blinkhorn, M. *Carlism and Crisis in Spain, 1931–1939*. Cambridge, Mass., 1975.

Blit, L. *The Eastern Pretender*. London, 1965.

Boca, A., and M. Giovana. *Fascism Today: A World Survey*. New York, 1969.

Bocca, G. *La Repubblica di Mussolini*. Bari, 1977.

Bock, G. *Zwangssterilisation im Nationalsozialismus*. Opladen, 1986.

Boissel, J. *Victor Courtet (1813–1867) premier théoricien de la hiérarchie des races*. Paris, 1972.

Bongiorno, J. A. *Fascist Italy and the Disarmament Question, 1928–1934*. New York, 1992.

Borejsza, J. W. *Il fascismo e l'Europa orientale*. Bari, 1981.

Borrás, T. *Ramiro Ledesma Ramos*. Madrid, 1972.

Bortoletto, G. *Fascismo e nazionalsocialismo*. Bologna, 1933.

Bossle, L., et al. *Sozialwissenschaftliche Kritik am Begriff und an der Erscheinungsweise des Faschismus.* Würzburg, 1979.

Bott, H. *Die NPD.* Munich, 1968.

Botz, G. *Gewalt in der Politik: Attentate, Zusammenstösse, Putschversuche, Unruhen in Österreich, 1918–1934.* Munich, 1976.

Botz, G. *Nationalsozialismus in Wien: Machtübernahme und Herrschaftssicherung, 1938/39.* Obermayer, 1988.

Bourdrel, P. *La Cagoule.* Paris, 1970.

Bourdrel, P. *L'épuration sauvage.* 2 vols. Paris, 1988.

Bowen, R. H. *German Theories of the Corporate State.* New York, 1947.

Boyer, J. W. *Political Radicalism in Late Imperial Vienna: Origins of the Christian Social Movement, 1848–1897.* Chicago, 1981.

Bozzetti, G. *Mussolini direttore dell' "Avanti."* Milan, 1979.

Bracher, K. D. *Die Auflösung der Weimarer Republik.* Villingen, 1964.

Bracher, K. D. *The German Dictatorship.* New York, 1970.

Bracher, K. D. *Zeitgeschichtliche Kontroversen um Faschismus Totalitarismus Demokratie.* Munich, 1976.

Bracher, K. D., W. Sauer, and G. Schulz. *Die nationalsozialistische Machtergreifung.* 3 vols. Frankfurt, 1979.

Braham, R. L. *The Politics of Genocide: The Holocaust in Hungary.* 2 vols. New York, 1992.

Bramsted, E. K. *Goebbels and National Socialist Propaganda, 1925–1945.* London, 1965.

Brandão, J. *Sidonio.* Lisbon, 1983.

Branwell, A. *Blood and Soil: Richard Walther Darré and Hitler's "Green Party."* Bourne End, Bucks., 1985.

Breitling, R. *Die nationalsozialistische Rassenlehre.* Meisenheim am Glan, 1971.

Breitman, R. *The Architect of Genocide: Himmler and the Final Solution.* New York, 1991.

Brennan, J. H. *The Occult Reich.* New York, 1974.

Brenner, H. *Die Kunstpolitik des Nationalsozialismus.* Reinbek, 1963.

Brewer, J. D. *Mosley's Men: The BUF in the West Midlands.* Aldershot, 1984.

Brissaud, A. *La dernière année de Vichy (1943–1944).* Paris, 1965.

Brissaud, A. *Mussolini.* 3 vols. Paris, 1983.

Broglio, F. M. *Italia e Santa Sede dalla Grande Guerra alla Conciliazione.* Bari, 1966.

Brooker, P. *The Faces of Fraternalism: Nazi Germany, Fascist Italy, and Imperial Japan.* Oxford, 1991.

Brooke-Shepherd, G. *Dollfuss.* London, 1961.

Broszat, M. *The Hitler State.* London, 1981.

Broszat, M. *Die Machtergreifung.* Munich, 1984.

Broszat, M., ed. *Bayern in der NS-Zeit.* 6 vols. Munich, 1977–83.

Browder, G. C. *Foundations of the Nazi Police State: The Formation of Sipo and SD.* Lexington, Ky., 1990.

Brown, A. C., and C. B. MacDonald. *On a Field of Red: The Communist International and the Coming of World War II.* New York, 1981.

Browning, C. *Fateful Months.* New York, 1985.

Browning, C. *The Path to Genocide*. New York, 1992.

Brügel, W. *Tschechen und Deutsche, 1918–1938*. Munich, 1967.

Brunet, J.-P. *Jacques Doriot*. Paris, 1986.

Brüning, H. *Memoiren*. Frankfurt, 1975.

Buchheim, H. *Totalitarian Rule*. Middletown, Conn., 1968.

Buchrucker, C. *Nacionalismo y peronismo*. Buenos Aires, 1987.

Bullock, A. *Hitler: A Study in Tyranny*. New York, 1964.

Bunting, B. *The Rise of the South African Reich*. Harmondsworth, 1969.

Burden, H. *The Nuremberg Party Rallies, 1923–39*. New York, 1967.

Burgwyn, H. J. *The Legend of the Mutilated Victory: Italy, the Great War, and the Paris Peace Conference, 1915–1919*. Westport, Conn., 1993.

Burleigh, M. *Germany Turns Eastward: A Study of "Ostforschung" in the Third Reich*. Cambridge, 1988.

Burleigh, M., and W. Wippermann. *The Racial State: Germany, 1933–1945*. New York, 1991.

Burnham, J. *The Managerial Revolution*. New York, 1941.

Burns, M. *Rural Society and French Politics: Boulangism and the Dreyfus Affair, 1866–1900*. Princeton, 1984.

Burrin, P. *La dérive fasciste*. Paris, 1986.

Burrin, P. *Hitler and the Jews*. New York, 1994.

Büsch, C., and P. Furth. *Rechtsradikalismus in Nachkriegsdeutschland: Studien über die "Sozialistische Reichspartei" (SRP)*. Berlin, 1957.

Busi, F. *The Pope of Antisemitism: The Career and Legacy of Edouard-Adolphe Drumont*. Lanham, Md., 1986.

Busino, G. *Gli studi su Vilfredo Pareto oggi*. Rome, 1974.

Buss, P. H., and A. Mollo. *Hitler's Germanic Legions: An Illustrated History of the Western European Legions with the SS, 1941–43*. London, 1978.

Butnaru, I. C. *The Silent Holocaust: Romania and Its Jews*. New York, 1992.

Butterwege, C., and H. Isola, eds. *Rechtsextremismus im vereinten Deutschland*. Berlin, 1990.

Caballero Jurado, C., and R. Ibáñez Hernández. *Escritores en las trincheras: La División Azul en sus libros, publicaciones periódicas y filmografía (1941–1988)*. Barcelona, 1989.

Cadena, E. *La ofensiva neo-fascista*. Barcelona, 1978.

Cagnetta, M. *Anticristi e impero fascista*. Bari, 1979.

Calman, D. *The Nature and Origins of Japanese Imperialism*. London, 1992.

Cambó, F. *En torn del feixisme italià*. Barcelona, 1925.

Cambó, F. *Las dictaduras*. Barcelona, 1929.

Canali, M. *Cesare Rossi*. Bologna, 1991.

Cancogni, M. *Storia del squadrismo*. Milan, 1959.

Cancogni, M. *Gli squadristi*. Milan, 1980.

Canfora, L. *Matrici culturali del fascismo*. Turin, 1980.

Cannistraro, P. V. *La fabbrica del consenso: Fascismo e mass media*. Bari, 1975.

Cannistraro, P. V., ed. *Historical Dictionary of Fascist Italy*. Westport, Conn., 1982.

Cannistraro, P. V., and B. Sullivan. *Il Duce's Other Woman*. New York, 1993.

Cantagalli, R. *Storia del fascismo fiorentino, 1919–1925*. Florence, 1972.

Caplan, J. *Government without Administration*. Oxford, 1988.

Caracciolo, N. *Tutti gli uomini del Duce*. Milan, 1982.

Cardoza, A. L. *Agrarian Elites and Italian Fascism: The Province of Bologna, 1901–1926*. Princeton, 1983.

CARDRI. *Saddam's Iraq*. London, 1989.

Carini, C. *Giacomo Matteotti*. N.p., 1984.

Carlini, A. *Filosofia e religione nel pensiero di Mussolini*. Rome, 1974.

Caro, K., and W. Oehme. *Schleichers Aufstieg*. Berlin, 1933.

Carocci, G. *La politica estera dell'Italia fascista (1925–1928)*. Bari, 1968.

Carone, E. *Revoluções do Brazil contemporáneo*. São Paulo, 1975.

Carpi, D. *Between Hitler and Mussolini: The Jews and the Italian Authorities in France and Tunisia*. Boston, 1994.

Carr, W. *Arms, Autarky and Aggression*. London, 1979.

Carr, W. *Hitler: A Study in Personality and Politics*. New York, 1979.

Carré, J. M. *Les écrivains français et le mirage allemand (1800–1940)*. Paris, 1947.

Carroll, B. A. *Design for Total War: Arms and Economics in the Third Reich*. The Hague, 1968.

Carroll, D. *French Literary Fascism*. Princeton, 1995.

Carsten, F. L. *The Reichswehr and German Politics, 1918–1933*. New York, 1966.

Carsten, F. L. *Fascist Movements in Austria from Schönerer to Hitler*. London, 1977.

Casali, L., ed. *Bologna, 1920: Le origini del fascismo*. Bologna, 1982.

Casanova, A. *Il '22: Cronaca dell'anno piu nero*. Milan, 1972.

Cassels, A. *Mussolini's Early Diplomacy*. Princeton, 1970.

Cassels, A. *Fascism*. New York, 1974.

Cassese, S. *La formazione dello Stato amministrativo*. Milan, 1974.

Castillo, J. del, and S. Alvarez. *Barcelona, objetivo cubierto*. Barcelona, 1958.

Casucci, C. *Il fascismo*. Bologna, 1961.

Catalano, F. *Potere economico e fascismo: La crisi del dopoguerra (1919–1921)*. Lerici, 1964.

Catalano, F. *L'impresa etiopica e altri saggi*. Milan, 1965.

Catalano, F. *La nascita del fascismo (1918–1922)*. Milan, 1976.

Catalano, F. *Fascismo e piccola borghesia*. Milan, 1979.

Cavalcoressi, P., and G. Wint. *Total War*. 2 vols. New York, 1979.

Cavalli, L. ed. *Il fascismo nell'analisi sociologica*. Bologna, 1975.

Cavandoli, R. *Le origini del fascismo a Reggio Emilia*. Rome, 1972.

Cederna, A. *Mussolini urbanista: Lo sventramento di Roma negli anni del consenso*. Bari, 1981.

Ceicel, R. *The Myth of the Master Race: Alfred Rosenberg and Nazi Ideology*. London, 1972.

Ceplair, L. *Under the Shadow of War: Fascism, Anti-Fascism and Marxists, 1918–1939*. New York, 1987.

Cereja, F. *Intellettuali e politica dall'epoca giolittiana all 'affermazione del fascismo*. Turin, 1973.

Cerutti, M. *La Svizzera italiana nel ventennio fascista*. Milan, 1986.

Cervi, M. *The Hollow Legions*. New York, 1971.

Cesarani, D., ed. *The Final Solution*. New York, 1994.

Cesari, M. *La censura del periodo fascista*. Naples, 1978.

Ceva, L. *La condotta italiana della guerra*. Rome, 1975.

Chalmers, D. *Hooded Americanism*. New York, 1981.

Chapman, B. *Police State*. London, 1970.

Charlé, K. *Die Eiserne Garde*. Berlin, 1939.

Chasin, J. *O Integralismo de Plinio Salgado*. São Paulo, 1978.

Chatain, J. *Les affaires de M. Le Pen*. Paris, 1987.

Chebel d'Appollonia, A. *L'extrême-droite en France de Maurras à Le Pen*. Brussels, 1988.

Chiang, M. H. *The Chinese Blue Shirt Society*. Berkeley, 1985.

Chiara, P. *Vita di Gabriele D'Annunzio*. Milan, 1978.

Chiarini, R., and P. Corsini. *Da Salò a Piazza della Loggia: Blocco d'ordine, neofascismo, radicalismo di destra a Brescia (1945–1974)*. Milan, 1983.

Childers, T. *The Nazi Voter*. Chapel Hill, 1983.

Childers, T., ed. *The Formation of the Nazi Constituency, 1919–1923*. Totowa, N.J., 1986.

Chiodo, M., ed. *Geografia e forme del dissenso sociale in Italian durante il fascismo (1928–1934)*. Cosenza, 1990.

Chiroux, R. *L'extrême droite sous la Ve Republique*. Paris, 1974.

Chiurco, G. A. *Storia della rivoluzione fascista, 1919–1922*. 5 vols. Florence, 1929.

Chombart de Lauwe, M.-J. *Complots contre la democratie*. Paris, 1981.

Cione, E. *Storia della Repubblica Sociale Italiana*. Rome, 1951.

Ciria, A. *Perón y el Justicialismo*. Buenos Aires, 1971.

Citino, R. *Germany and the Union of South Africa in the Nazi Period*. Westport, Conn., 1991.

Ciucci, G. *Gli architetti e il fascismo*. Turin, 1989.

Clark, M. *Modern Italy, 1871–1982*. London, 1984.

Clarke, J. C., III. *Russia and Italy against Hitler: The Bolshevik-Fascist Rapprochement of the 1930s*. Westport, Conn., 1991.

Clough, R. T. *Futurism*. New York, 1961.

Clough, S. B. *France: A History of National Economics*. New York, 1964.

Codreanu, C. Z. *Eiserne Garde*. Berlin, 1939.

Cohn, N. *Warrant for Genocide: The Myth of the Jewish World Conspiracy*. London, 1967.

Cointet-Labrousse, M. *Vichy et le fascisme*. Brussels, 1987.

Colarizzi, S. *Dopoguerra e fascismo in Puglia*. Bari, 1971.

Colby, J., et al. *Between Two Wars*. Celtic Court, Bucks., 1990.

Collier, D., ed. *The New Authoritarianism in Latin America*. Princeton, 1979.

Collier, R. *Duce!* New York, 1971.

Collotti, E. *L'amministrazione tedesca dell'Italia occupata, 1943–1945*. Milan, 1963.

Collotti, E. *L'occupazione nazista in Europa*. Rome, 1964.

Combs, W. L. *The Voice of the SS: A History of the SS Journal "Das Schwarze Corps."* New York, 1986.

Conway, J. S. *The Nazi Persecution of the Churches, 1933–1945*. New York, 1968.

Conway, M. *Collaboration in Belgium: Léon Degrelle and the Rexist Movement in Belgium, 1940–1944*. New Haven, 1993.

Cooper, M. *The German Army, 1933–1945.* New York, 1978.

Cordova, F. *Arditi e legionari dannunziani.* Padua, 1969.

Cordova, F. *Le origini dei sindacati fascisti.* Bari, 1974.

Cordova, F., ed. *Uomini e volti del fascismo.* Rome, 1980.

Corner, P. *Fascism in Ferrara.* Oxford, 1974.

Corni, G. *Hitler and the Peasants, 1930–1939.* New York, 1990.

Corsini, P. *Il feudo di Augusto Turati: Fascismo e lotta politica a Brescia, 1922–1926.* Milan, 1988.

Costello, J. *Ten Days to Destiny: The Secret Story of the Hess Peace Initiative and British Efforts to Strike a Deal with Hitler.* New York, 1991.

Cotta, M. *La collaboration, 1940–1944.* Paris, 1964.

Coverdale, J. F. *Italian Intervention in the Spanish Civil War.* Princeton, 1975.

Craig, G. *The Germans.* New York, 1984.

Crasweller, R. D. *Perón and the Enigmas of Argentina.* New York, 1987.

Crispoli, E. *Il secondo futurismo.* Turin, 1962.

Cross, C. *The Fascists in Britain.* New York, 1963.

Crowley, J. *Japan's Quest for Autonomy.* Princeton, 1966.

Cruz, M. Braga da. *As origens da democracia cristã e o salazarismo.* Lisbon, 1980.

Cruz, M. Braga da. *O partido e o estado no salazarismo.* Lisbon, 1988.

Cunsolo, R. S. *Italian Nationalism.* Melbourne, Fla., 1990.

Curtis, M. *Three against the Third Republic: Sorel, Barrès, and Maurras.* Princeton, 1959.

Curtis, M. *Totalitarianism.* New Brunswick, N.J., 1979.

Czichon, E. *Wer verhalf Hitler zur Macht?* Cologne, 1967.

Dahm, W. *Der Mann der Hitler die Ideen gab.* Munich, 1958.

Dahrendorf, R. *Society and Democracy in Germany.* London, 1968.

Dalla Tana, L. *Mussolini massimalista.* Salsomaggiore, 1964.

D'Amoja, F. *Declino e prima crisi dell'Europa di Versailles: Studio sulla diplomazia italiana ed europa (1931–1933).* Milan, 1967.

Daniels, R. V., ed. *The Stalin Revolution.* Boston, 1965.

Dansette, A. *Le Boulangisme.* Paris, 1947.

Davidson, E. *The Trial of the Germans.* New York, 1966.

Davidson, E. *The Making of Adolf Hitler.* New York, 1977.

Dawidowicz, L. *The Holocaust and the Historians.* Cambridge, Mass., 1981.

Dawidowicz, L. *The War against the Jews.* New York, 1986.

Deakin, F. W. *The Brutal Friendship.* London, 1962.

Déat, M. *Révolution française et révolution allemande.* Paris, 1943.

de Castris, A. L. *Egemonia e fascismo: Il problema degli intellettuali negli anni trenta.* Bologna, 1981.

Dedijer, V. *The Road to Sarajevo.* London, 1967.

De Felice, R. *Mussolini il rivoluzionario, 1883–1920.* Turin, 1965.

De Felice, R. *Mussolini il fascista.* 2 vols. Turin, 1966.

De Felice, R. *Sindacalismo rivoluzionario e fiumanesimo nel carteggio De Ambris-D'Annunzio.* Brescia, 1966.

De Felice, R. *Il fascismo: Le interpretazioni dei contemporanei e degli storici.* Rome, 1970.

De Felice, R. *Le interpretazioni del fascismo*. Rev. ed. Bari, 1971.

De Felice, R. *La Carta del Canaro nei testi di Alceste de Ambris e di Gabriele D'Annunzio*. Bologna, 1973.

De Felice, R. *Mussolini il Duce*. Vol. 1, *Gli anni del consenso, 1929–1936*. Turin, 1974.

De Felice, R. *Intervista sul fascismo*. Bari, 1975.

De Felice, R. *Fascism: An Informal Introduction to Its Theory and Practice*. New Brunswick, N.J., 1976.

De Felice, R. *Interpretations of Fascism*. Cambridge, Mass., 1977.

De Felice, R. *D'Annunzio politico, 1918–1938*. Bari, 1978.

De Felice, R. *Mussolini il Duce*. Vol. 2, *Lo Stato totalitario, 1936–1940*. Turin, 1981.

De Felice, R. *Hitler e Mussolini: I rapporti segreti (1922–1933)*. Florence, 1983.

De Felice, R. *Intellettuali di fronti al fascismo*. Rome, 1985.

De Felice, R. *Il fascismo e l'Oriente*. Bologna, 1988.

De Felice, R. *Storia degli ebrei italiani sotto il fascismo*. Turin, 1988.

De Felice, R. *Mussolini l'alleato*. 2 vols. Turin, 1990.

De Felice, R., ed. *L'Italia fra tedeschi e alleati: La politica estera fascista e la seconda guerra mondiale*. Bologna, 1973.

De Felice, R., ed. *Futurismo, cultura e politica*. Turin, 1988.

De Felice, R., ed. *Bibliografia orientativa del fascismo*. Rome, 1991.

De Felice, R., and L. Goglia. *Mussolini: Il mito*. Bari, 1983.

De Grand, A. J. *Bottai e la cultura fascista*. Bari, 1978.

De Grand, A. J. *The Italian Nationalist Association and the Rise of Fascism in Italy*. Lincoln, 1978.

De Grand, A. J. *Italian Fascism*. Lincoln, 1982.

de Grazia, V. *The Culture of Consent: Mass Organization of Leisure in Fascist Italy*. Cambridge, 1981.

de Grazia, V. *How Fascism Ruled Women: Italy, 1922–1945*. Berkeley, 1991.

Deist, W. *The Wehrmacht and German Rearmament*. Toronto, 1981.

Dejonghe, E., ed. *L'Occupation en France et en Belgique, 1940–1944*. 2 vols. Lille, 1987.

Del Boca, A. *La guerra d'Abissinia, 1935–1941*. Milan, 1966.

Del Boca, A., and M. Giovana. *Fascism Today: A World Survey*. New York, 1969.

Del Noce, A. *L'Epoca della secolarizzazione*. Milan, 1970.

Delperrie de Bayac, J. *Histoire de la Milice*. Paris, 1969.

Delzell, C. F. *Mussolini's Enemies*. Princeton, 1961.

Demers, F. J. *Le origini del fascismo a Cremona*. Bari, 1979.

Deniel, A. *Bucard et le Francisme: Les seuls fascistes français*. Paris, 1979.

Denkler, H., and K. Prümm, eds. *Die deutsche Literatur im Dritten Reich*. Stuttgart, 1976.

De Rosa, G. *Giolitti e il fascismo in alcune sue lettere inedite*. Rome, 1957.

Desanti, D. *Drieu La Rochelle ou le séducteur mystifié*. Paris, 1978.

Deschner, G. *Reinhard Heydrich*. New York, 1981.

Diamond, S. A. *The Nazi Movement in the United States, 1924–1941*. Ithaca, 1974.

Díaz Araujo, E. *La conspiración del '43: El GOU, una experiencia militarista en la Argentina*. Buenos Aires, 1971.

Diehl, J. M. *Paramilitary Politics in Weimar Germany*. Bloomington, 1978.

Diehl-Thiele, P. *Partei und Staat im Dritten Reich.* Munich, 1969.

Digeon, C. *La crise allemande de la pensée française, 1870–1914.* Paris, 1959.

Diggins, J. P. *Mussolini and Fascism: The View from America.* Princeton, 1972.

Dioudonnet, P. M. *Je Suis Partout, 1930–1944: Les maurrasiens devant la tentation fasciste.* Paris, 1973.

Dodge, P. *Beyond Marxism: The Faith and Works of Henri de Man.* The Hague, 1966.

Dombrowski, R. *Mussolini: Twilight and Fall.* London, 1956.

Domenico, R. P. *Italian Fascists on Trial, 1943–1948.* Chapel Hill, 1991.

Dordoni, A. *"Crociata italica."* Milan, 1976.

Dornberg, J. *Munich, 1923.* New York, 1982.

Dorpalen, A. *Hindenburg and the Weimar Republic.* Princeton, 1964.

D'Orsi, A. *La rivoluzione antibolscevica.* Milan, 1985.

Dorso, G. *Mussolini alla conquista del potere.* Turin, 1949.

Doty, C. S. *From Cultural Rebellion to Counterrevolution: The Politics of Maurice Barrès.* Athens, Ohio, 1976.

Douglas, A. *From Fascism to Libertarian Communism: Georges Valois against the French Republic.* Berkeley, 1992.

Dragnich, A. *Serbia, Nikola Pasic, and Yugoslavia.* New Brunswick, N.J., 1974.

Drake, R. *Byzantium for Rome: The Politics of Nostalgia in Umbertian Italy, 1878–1900.* Chapel Hill, 1980.

Drake, R. *The Revolutionary Mystique and Terrorism in Contemporary Italy.* Bloomington, 1989.

Droz, J. *Histoire de l'antifascisme en Europe, 1923–1939.* Paris, 1985.

Drucker, P. *The End of Economic Man.* New York, 1939.

Dunlop, J. B. *The New Russian Revolutionaries.* Boston, 1976.

Dunlop, J. B. *The Faces of Contemporary Russian Nationalism.* Princeton, 1984.

Dupeux, L. *"Nationalbolschewismus" in Deutschland, 1919–1933.* Munich, 1985.

Duprat, F. *Les mouvements d'extrême droite en France depuis 1944.* Paris, 1972.

Duprat, F., and A. Renault. *Les fascismes américains, 1924–1941.* Paris, 1976.

Durand, Y. *Le nouvel ordre européen nazi, 1938–1945.* Brussels, 1990.

Duranton-Crabol, A.-M. *Visages de la Nouvelle Droite: La GRECE et son histoire.* Paris, 1988.

Dutt, R. P. *Fascism and Social Revolution.* London, 1934.

Dyadkin, I. G. *Unnatural Deaths in the USSR, 1928–1954.* New Brunswick, N.J., 1983.

Eastman, L. E. *The Abortive Revolution.* Cambridge, Mass., 1974.

Eastman, L. E. *Seeds of Destruction: Nationalist China in War and Revolution, 1937–1945.* Berkeley, 1984.

Eatwell, R., and A. Wright, eds. *Contemporary Political Ideologies.* London, 1993.

Ebenstein, W. *Totalitarianism.* New York, 1962.

Edmondson, C. E. *The Heimwehr and Austrian Politics, 1918–1936.* Athens, Ga., 1978.

Eichholtz, D., and K. Gossweiler, eds. *Faschismusforschung: Positionen Probleme Polemik.* East Berlin, 1980.

Eisenberg, D. *Fascistes et nazis d'aujourd'hui.* Paris, 1963.

Eksteins, M. *Rites of Spring: The Great War and the Birth of the Modern Age.* New York, 1989.

Elbow, M. H. *French Corporative Theory, 1789–1948.* New York, 1953.

Eley, G. *Reshaping the German Right.* New Haven, 1980.

Eley, G. *From Unification to Nazism.* Boston, 1986.

Ellul, J. *Autopsy of Revolution.* New York, 1971.

Ellwood, S. M. *Spanish Fascism in the Franco Era.* London, 1978.

Emmet, C., and N. Muhlen. *The Vanishing Swastika.* Chicago, 1961.

Engelstädter, H., and O. Seiffert. *Die schleichende Gefahr: Europa, die Deutschen, Nationalismus und Neofaschismus.* Berlin, 1990.

Etienne, J.-M. *Le mouvement rexiste jusqu'en 1940.* Paris, 1968.

Etlin, R. A. *Modernism in Italian Architecture, 1890–1940.* Cambridge, Mass., 1991.

Evans, R. J. *Rethinking German History: Nineteenth Century Germany and the Origins of the Third Reich.* London, 1987.

Eyck, E. *A History of the Weimar Republic.* 2 vols. Cambridge, Mass., 1962–64.

Falcoff, M., and R. Dolkart, eds. *Prelude to Perón: Argentina in Depression and War, 1930–1943.* Berkeley, 1976.

Fappani-Molinari. *Chiesa e Repubblica di Salò.* Turin, 1981.

Farber, S. *Revolution and Reaction in Cuba, 1933–1960.* Middletown, Conn., 1977.

Farquharson, J. *The Plough and the Swastika, 1928–1945.* London, 1976.

Faust, A. *Der Nationalsozialistische Deutsche Studentenbund.* 2 vols. Düsseldorf, 1976.

Faye, J. P. *Langages totalitaires.* Paris, 1972.

Fayt, C. S., et al. *La naturaleza del peronismo.* Buenos Aires, 1967.

Fedele, S. *Storia della Concentrazione Antifascista (1927–1934).* Milan, 1976.

Fein, H. *Genocide: A Sociological Perspective.* London, 1993.

Feldman, G. D. *The Great Disorder: Politics, Economics, and Society in the German Inflation, 1914–1924.* New York, 1993.

Ferrão, C. *O Integralismo e a República.* 3 vols. Lisbon, 1964–65.

Ferraresi, F., ed. *La destra radicale.* Milan, 1984.

Ferro, A. *Salazar.* Lisbon, 1933.

Ferro, M. *Pétain.* Paris, 1987.

Fest, J. *The Faces of the Third Reich.* New York, 1970.

Fest, J. *Hitler.* New York, 1974.

Field, G. G. *Evangelist of Race: The Germanic Vision of Houston Stewart Chamberlain.* New York, 1981.

Field, G. L. *The Syndical and Corporative Institutions of Italian Fascism.* New York, 1938.

Fielding, N. *The National Front.* London, 1981.

Filatov, M. N., and A. I. Ryabov. *Fashizm 80x.* Alma Ata, 1983.

Fischer, C. *Stormtroopers.* London, 1983.

Fischer, C. *The German Communists and the Rise of Nazism.* New York, 1991.

Fischer, F. *From Kaiserreich to Third Reich.* New York, 1986.

Fischer, R. *Entwicksstufen des Antisemitismus in Ungarn, 1867–1939.* Munich, 1988.

Fischer, W. *Die Wirtschaftspolitik des Nationalsozialismus.* Hanover, 1961.

Fisichella, D. *Analisi del totalitarismo.* Messina, 1976.

Fleischhauer, I. *Die Chance des Sonderfriedens: Deutsch-sowjetische Geheimgespräche, 1941–1945*. Berlin, 1986.

Fleischhauer, I. *Der Pakt*. Frankfurt, 1990.

Fleming, G. *Hitler and the Final Solution*. Berkeley, 1984.

Fletcher, W. M., III. *The Search for a New Order: Intellectuals and Fascism in Prewar Japan*. Chapel Hill, 1982.

Florinsky, M. T. *Fascism and National Socialism*. New York, 1936.

Foard, D. W. *The Revolt of the Aesthetes: Ernesto Giménez Caballero and the Origins of Spanish Fascism*. New York, 1989.

Ford, G., ed. *Fascist Europe*. London, 1993.

Fornari, H. *Mussolini's Gadfly: Roberto Farinacci*. Nashville, 1971.

Forstmeier, F., and H.-E. Volkmann, eds. *Wirtschaft und Rüstung am Vorabend des Zweiten Weltkrieges*. Düsseldorf, 1975.

Forsyth, D. J. *The Crisis of Liberal Italy*. New York, 1993.

Fraenkel, E. *The Dual State*. New York, 1941.

Francesca, S. *La politica economica del fascismo*. Bari, 1972.

Franck, L. *Il corporativismo e l'economia dell'Italia fascista*. Turin, 1990.

Franz-Willing, G. *Die Hitler-Bewegung, 1919–1922*. Hamburg, 1962.

Franz-Willing, G. *Krisenjahre der Hitlerbewegung: 1923*. Preussich Oldendorf, 1975.

Friedlander, H. *The German Revolution of 1918*. New York, 1992.

Friedlander, S. *Prelude to Downfall: Hitler and the United States, 1939–1941*. New York, 1967.

Friedlander, S., ed. *Probing the Limits of Representation: Nazism and the "Final Solution."* Cambridge, Mass., 1992.

Friedrich, C. J., ed. *Totalitarianism*. New York, 1954.

Fritzsche, P. *A Nation of Flyers*. Cambridge, Mass., 1992.

Fucci, F. *Ali contro Mussolini: I raid aerei antifascisti degli anni trenta*. Milan, 1978.

Fucci, F. *Le polizie di Mussolini*. Milan, 1985.

Fugate, B. I. *Operation Barbarossa*. Novato, Calif., 1984.

Furlong, P. J. *Between Crown and Swastika: The Impact of the Radical Right on the Afrikaner Nationalist Movement in the Fascist Era*. Hanover, N.H., 1991.

Gaddi, G. *Neofascismo in Europa*. Milan, 1974.

Gaeta, F. *Nazionalismo italiano*. Naples, 1965.

Gallagher, T. *Portugal: A Twentieth-Century Interpretation*. Manchester, 1983.

Gallego, F. *Los orígenes del reformismo militar en América Latina: La gestión de David Toro en Bolivia*. Barcelona, 1991.

Gallego, F. *Ejército, nacionalismo y reformismo en América Latina: La gestión de Germán Busch en Bolivia*. Barcelona, 1992.

Gamm, H.-J. *Der braune Kult: Das Dritte Reich und seine Ersatzreligion*. Hamburg, 1962.

Ganapini, L., ed. *La storiografia sul fascismo locale nell'Italia nordorientale*. Udine, 1990.

García Delgado, J. L., ed. *El primer franquismo: España durante la Segunda Guerra Mundial*. Madrid, 1989.

Garruccio, L. [pseud.]. *L'industrializzazione tra nazionalismo e rivoluzione*. Bologna, 1969.

Gasman, D. *The Scientific Origins of National Socialism: Social Darwinism in Ernst Haeckel and the German Monist League.* New York, 1971.

Geehr, R. S. *Karl Lueger.* Detroit, 1990.

Geifman, A. *Thou Shalt Kill: Revolutionary Terrorism in Russia, 1894–1917.* Princeton, 1993.

Gellately, R. *The Gestapo and German Society.* Oxford, 1990.

Gelott, L. S. *The Catholic Church and the Authoritarian Regime in Austria, 1933–1938.* New York, 1990.

Gentile, E. *"La Voce" e l'età giolittiana.* Milan, 1972.

Gentile, E. *Le origini dell'ideologia fascista.* Bari, 1975.

Gentile, E. *Mussolini e "La Voce."* Florence, 1976.

Gentile, E. *Il mito dello Stato Nuovo.* Bari, 1982.

Gentile, E. *Storia del Partito Fascista, 1919–1922.* Bari, 1989.

Gentile, E. *Il culto del Littorio.* Bari, 1993.

Géoris-Reitshof, M. *Extrême droite et néo-fascisme en Belgique.* Brussels, 1962.

Geran Pilon, J. *The Bloody Flag: Post-Communist Nationalism in Eastern Europe. Spotlight on Romania.* New Brunswick, N.J., 1992.

Gerhart, Walter [pseud. of Waldemar Gurian]. *Um des Reiches Zukunft.* Freiburg, 1932.

Germani, G. *Authoritarianism, Fascism, and National Populism.* New Brunswick, N.J., 1978.

Germany and the Second World War. 5 vols. to date. Oxford, 1991–.

Gerra, F. *L'impresa di Fiume.* 2 vols. Milan, 1974.

Gerstenberger, H. *Der revolutionäre Konservatismus.* Berlin, 1969.

Gessenharte, W., H. Fröchling, and B. Krupp. *Rechtsextremismus als normativ-praktisches Forschungsproblem.* Weinheim, 1978.

Geuter, U. *Die Professionalisierung der deutschen Psychologie im Nationalsozialismus.* Frankfurt, 1984.

Ghirardo, D. *Building New Communities: New Deal America and Fascist Italy.* Princeton, 1989.

Gilbert, M. *The Holocaust.* New York, 1985.

Giles, G. *Students and National Socialism in Germany.* Princeton, 1985.

Gillingham, J. *Belgian Business in the Nazi New Order.* Ghent, 1977.

Gillingham, J. *Industry and Politics in the Third Reich.* New York, 1985.

Gil Pecharromán, J. *Conservadores subversivos: La derecha autoritaria alfonsina (1913–1936).* Madrid, 1994.

Giovannini, C. *L'Italia da Vittorio Veneto all'Aventino.* Bologna, 1972.

Giraldi, G. *Giovanni Gentile.* Rome, 1968.

Giudice, G. *Mussolini.* Turin, 1971.

Glaser, H. *The Cultural Roots of National Socialism.* Austin, 1978.

Glaus, B. *Die Nationale Front.* Zurich, 1969.

Glucksman, A. *La force du vertige.* Paris, 1983.

Gnedin, E. *Iz istorii otnoshenii mezhdu SSSR i fashistskoi Germaniei.* New York, 1977.

Goldwert, M. *Democracy, Militarism and Nationalism in Argentina, 1930–1966.* Austin, 1972.

Golomstock, I. *Totalitarian Art.* New York, 1990.

Golsan, R., ed. *Fascism, Aesthetics and Culture.* Hanover, N.H., 1992.

Gómez Navarro, J. L. *El régimen de Primo de Rivera*. Madrid, 1991.

Goodrick-Clarke, N. *The Occult Roots of Nazism: Secret Aryan Cults and Their Influence on Nazi Ideology. The Ariosophists of Austria and Germany, 1890–1935*. London, 1985.

Gordon, A. *Labor and Imperial Democracy in Prewar Japan*. Berkeley, 1991.

Gordon, B. M. *Collaboration in France during the Second World War*. Ithaca, 1980.

Gordon, H. J., Jr. *Hitler and the Beer Hall Putsch*. Princeton, 1972.

Gordon, S. *Hitler, Germans and the Jewish Question*. Princeton, 1984.

Gossett, T. F. *Race—The History of an Idea in America*. Dallas, 1963.

Gotovitch, J., and J. Gérard-Libois. *L'an quarante: La Belgigue occupée*. Brussels, 1971.

Graf, W., ed. *"Wenn ich die Regierung wäre . . .": Die rechtsradikale Bedrohung*. Berlin, 1984.

Graham, L. S., and H. M. Makler, eds. *Contemporary Portugal*. Austin, 1979.

Graml, H. *Anti-Semitism and Its Origins in the Third Reich*. London, 1992.

Grebing, H. *Aktuelle Theorien über Faschismus und Konservatismus*. Stuttgart, 1974.

Greenfeld, L. *Nationalism: Five Roads to Modernity*. Cambridge, 1992.

Gregor, A. J. *The Ideology of Fascism*. New York, 1969.

Gregor, A. J. *The Fascist Persuasion in Radical Politics*. Princeton, 1974.

Gregor, A. J. *Interpretations of Fascism*. Morristown, N.J. 1974.

Gregor, A. J. *Sergio Panunzio: Il sindacalismo ed il fondamento razionale del fascismo*. Rome, 1978.

Gregor, A. J. *Italian Fascism and Developmental Dictatorship*. Princeton, 1979.

Gregor, A. J. *Young Mussolini and the Intellectual Origins of Fascism*. Berkeley, 1979.

Gress, F., H.-G. Jaschke, and K. Schönekäs. *Neue Rechte und Rechtsextremismus in Europa*. Opladen, 1990.

Grieffenhagen, M., R. Kühnl, and J. B. Müller. *Totalitarismus*. Munich, 1972.

Griffin, R. *The Nature of Fascism*. London, 1991.

Griffin, R. *Modernity under the New Order: The Fascist Project for Managing the Future*. 1994.

Grimaldi, U., and G. Bozzetti. *Farinacci, il piú fascista*. Milan, 1972.

Gross, J. T. *Revolution from Abroad: The Soviet Conquest of Poland's Western Ukraine and Western Belorussia*. Princeton, 1988.

Groueff, S. *Crown of Thorns: The Reign of King Boris III of Yugoslavia, 1918–1943*. Lanham, Md., 1987.

Gruchmann, L. *Justiz im Dritten Reich, 1933–1940*. Munich, 1988.

Grunberger, R. *A Social History of the Third Reich*. London, 1971.

Gruppe Arbeiterpolitik, eds. *Der Faschismus in Deutschland: Analysen der KPD-Opposition aus den jahren 1928 bis 1933*. Frankfurt, 1973.

Gualerni, G. *La politica industriale fascista, 1922–1935*. Milan, 1956.

Gualerni, G. *Industria e fascismo*. Milan, 1976.

Guchet, Y. *Georges Valois*. Paris, 1975.

Guérin, D. *Fascisme et grand capital*. Paris, 1936.

Guerri, G. B. *Giuseppe Bottai, un fascista critico*. Milan, 1976.

Guerri, G. B. *Galeazzo Ciano*. Milan, 1979.

Guerri, G. B. *Italo Balbo*. Milan, 1984.

Guerri, G. B., ed. *Rapporto al Duce*. Milan, 1978.

Guillaumin, C. *L'idéologie du racisme*. Paris, 1972.

Guldescu, S., and J. Prcela, eds. *Operation Slaughterhouse: Eyewitness Accounts of Postwar Massacres in Yugoslavia*. Philadelphia, 1970.

Gumbel, E. J. *Vier Jahre Politischer Mord*. Berlin, 1923.

Guzzanti, P. *Il neofascismo e le sue organizzazioni paramilitari*. Rome, 1972.

Hachtmann, R. *Industriearbeit im "Dritten Reich."* Göttingen, 1989.

Hacker, F. *Das Faschismus-Syndrom*. Düsseldorf, 1990.

Hafner, S. *Anmerkungen zu Hitler*. Munich, 1978.

Hagopian, M. *The Phenomenon of Revolution*. New York, 1974.

Hainsworth, P., ed. *The Extreme Right in Europe and America*. London, 1991.

Hair, I. P. *The Kingfish and His Realm*. Baton Rouge, 1991.

Hale, O. J. *The Captive Press in the Third Reich*. Princeton, 1984.

Halle, L. J. *The Ideological Imagination*. London, 1971.

Haller, M. H. *Eugenics: Hereditarian Attitudes in American Thought*. New Brunswick, N.J., 1963.

Halls, W. D. *The Youth of Vichy France*. Oxford, 1981.

Hamilton, R. F. *Who Voted for Hitler?* Princeton, 1982.

Hammer, K., and P.-C. Hartmann, eds. *Der Bonapartismus*. Munich, 1976.

Hancock, E. *National Socialist Leadership and Total War, 1941–45*. New York, 1991.

Handlin, O. *Race and Nationality in American Life*. Boston, 1948.

Hanfstaengel, E. *Hitler: The Missing Years*. London, 1957.

Hansen, E. von S. *Hendrik de Man and the Crisis in European Socialism, 1926–1936*. Ithaca, 1968.

Harootunian, H. D. *Things Seen and Unseen: Discourse and Ideology in Tokugawa Nativism*. Chicago, 1988.

Harris, G. *The Dark Side of Europe: The Extreme Right Today*. Edinburgh, 1990.

Harris, H. S. *The Social Philosophy of Giovanni Gentile*. Urbana, 1960.

Harsch, D. *German Social Democracy and the Rise of Nazism*. Chapel Hill, 1993.

Haslam, J. *The Soviet Union and the Struggle for Collective Security in Europe, 1933–1939*. London, 1984.

Hauner, M. *India in Axis Strategy*. London, 1981.

Hauner, M. *Hitler: A Chronology of His Life and Times*. New York, 1983.

Havens, T. R. H. *Farm and Nation in Modern Japan: Agrarian Nationalism, 1870–1940*. Princeton, 1974.

Hay, J. *Popular Film Culture in Fascist Italy*. Bloomington, 1987.

Hayes, C. J. H. *The Historical Evolution of Modern Nationalism*. New York, 1931.

Hayes, C. J. H. *Nationalism: A Religion*. New York, 1960.

Hayes, P. *Industry and Ideology: IG Farben in the Nazi Era*. Cambridge, 1987.

Hayes, P. M. *Quisling*. London, 1971.

Hayes, P. M. *Fascism*. London, 1972.

Hayward, N. F., and D. J. Morris. *The First Nazi Town*. New York, 1988.

Hehn, J. von. *Lettland zwischen Demokratie und Diktatur*. Munich, 1957.

Heiber, H. *Goebbels*. New York, 1972.

Heinen, A. *Die Legion "Erzengel Michael" in Rumänien*. Munich, 1986.

Heller, J. *The Stern Gang*. London, 1994.

540   Bibliography

Helmreich, E. C. *The German Churches under Hitler*. Detroit, 1979.
Hensch, J. K. *Die Slowakei und Hitlers Ostpolitik*. Cologne, 1965.
Herbst, L. *Der Totale Krieg und die Ordnung der Wirtschaft*. Stuttgart, 1982.
Herf, J. *Reactionary Modernism*. New York, 1984.
Hermet, G., P. Hassner, and J. Rupnik. *Totalitarismes*. Paris, 1984.
Hertz-Eichenrode, D. *Wirtschaftskrise und Arbeitbeschaffung: Konjunkturpolitik 1925/ 26 und die Grundlagen der Krisenpolitik Brünings*. Frankfurt, 1982.
Hervier, J. *Deux individus contre la histoire: Pierre Drieu La Rochelle, Ernst Jünger*. Paris, 1978.
Hewitt, A. *Fascist Modernism*. Stanford, 1993.
Hibbert, C. *Benito Mussolini*. London, 1962.
Hiden, J., and J. Farquharson. *Explaining Hitler's Germany: Historians and the Third Reich*. Totowa, N.J., 1983.
Hilberg, R. *The Destruction of the European Jews*. 3 vols. New York, 1985.
Hildebrand, K. *Vom Reich zum Weltreich: Hitler, NSDAP und koloniale Frage, 1919– 1945*. Munich, 1969.
Hildebrand, K. *The Foreign Policy of the Third Reich*. London, 1973.
Hillgruber, A. *Hitler, König Carol und Marschall Antonescu: Die deutsch-rumänischen Beziehungen, 1938–1944*. Wiesbaden, 1965.
Hilliker, G. *The Politics of Reform in Peru: The Aprista and Other Mass Parties of Latin America*. Baltimore, 1971.
Hinz, B. *Art in the Third Reich*. New York, 1979.
Hirsch, M., et al., eds. *Recht, Verwaltung und Justiz im Nationalsozialismus*. Cologne, 1989.
Hirschfeld, G. *Nazi Rule and Dutch Collaboration*. New York, 1988.
Hirschfeld, G., ed. *The Policies of Genocide: Jewish and Soviet Prisoners of War in Nazi Germany*. New York, 1986.
Hirschfeld, G., and L. Kettenacker, eds. *Der "Führerstaat."* Stuttgart, 1986.
Hirschfeld, G., and P. S. Marsh, eds. *Collaboration in France*. New York, 1989.
Hirszowicz, L. *The Third Reich and the Arab East*. London, 1966.
Hitchins, K. *Rumania, 1866–1947*. Oxford, 1994.
Hobson, F. *Tell about the South*. Baton Rouge, 1983.
Hochman, J. *The Soviet Union and the Failure of Collective Security, 1934–1938*. Ithaca, 1984.
Hockenos, P. *Free to Hate: The Rise of the Right in Post-Communist Europe*. New York, 1993.
Hoepke, K.-P. *Die deutsche Rechte und der italienische Faschismus*. Düsseldorf, 1968.
Hoffman, P. *The History of the German Resistance, 1933–1945*. Cambridge, Mass., 1977.
Hoffman, P. *German Resistance to Hitler*. Cambridge, Mass., 1988.
Hoffman, S. *Le mouvement Poujade*. Paris, 1956.
Hoffmann, H. *Hitler Was My Friend*. London, 1955.
Hoffmann, Joachim. *Die Ostlegionen, 1941–1943: Turkotataren, Kaukasier und Wolga- finnen im deutschen Heer*. Freiburg, 1976.
Hoffmann, Josef. *Der Pfrimer-Putsch*. Vienna, 1965.
Höhne, H. *The Order of the Death's Head*. London, 1969.

Hoidal, O. K. *Quisling: A Study in Treason*. Oslo, 1989.

Homze, E. L. *Foreign Labor in Nazi Germany*. Princeton, 1967.

Hoptner, J. B. *Yugoslavia in Crisis, 1934–1941*. New York, 1962.

Horn, W. *Führerideologie und Parteiorganisation in der NSDAP, 1919–1933*. Düsseldorf, 1975.

Hory, L., and M. Broszat. *Der kroatische Ustascha-Staat, 1941–1945*. Stuttgart, 1964.

Host-Venturi, G. *L'impresa fiumana*. Rome, 1976.

Houdros, J.-L. *Occupation and Resistance: The Greek Agony, 1941–1944*. New York, 1963.

Hovannisian, R. G., ed. *The Armenian Holocaust: A Bibliography Relating to the Deportations, Massacres, and Dispersion of the Armenian People, 1915–1923*. Cambridge, Mass., 1978.

Hovannisian, R. G., ed. *The Armenian Genocide in Perspective*. New Brunswick, N.J., 1987.

Hull, D. S. *Film in the Third Reich*. Berkeley, 1969.

Humphreys, L. A. *The Way of the Heavenly Sword: The Japanese Army in the 1920's*. Stanford, 1994.

Husbands, C. T. *Racial Exclusionism and the City: The Urban Support of the National Front*. London, 1983.

Husbands, C. T. *Race and the Right in Contemporary Politics*. London, 1991.

Hüttenberger, P. *Die Gauleiter*. Stuttgart, 1969.

Ignazi, P. *Il polo escluso: Profilo del Movimento Sociale Italiano*. Bologna, 1989.

Il trauma dell'intervento, 1914–1919. Florence, 1968.

Ioanid, R. *The Sword of the Archangel*. New York, 1990.

Iraci, A. *Arpinati l'oppositore di Mussolini*. Rome, 1970.

Irvine, J. A. *The Croat Question*. Boulder, 1993.

Irvine, W. D. *The Boulanger Affair Reconsidered*. New York, 1989.

Irving, D. *Göring*. London, 1989.

Isnenghi, M. *L'educazione dell'italiano: Il fascismo e l'organizzazione della cultura*. Bologna, 1979.

Italia y la guerra civil española. Madrid, 1986.

Jäckel, E. *Hitler's Weltanschauung*. Middletown, Conn., 1972.

Jäckel, E. *Hitler in History*. Hanover, N.H., 1984.

Jäckel, E. *Hitlers Herrschaft*. Stuttgart, 1986.

Jäckel, E. *La France dans l'Europe de Hitler*. Paris, 1968.

Jäckel, E., and J. Rohwer, eds. *Der Mord an den Juden im Zweiten Weltkrieg: Entschlussbildung und Verwirklichung*. Stuttgart, 1985.

Jackson, K. T. *The Ku Klux Klan in the City, 1915–1930*. New York, 1967.

Jacobelli, J. *Il fascismo e gli storici oggi*. Bari, 1988.

Jacobitti, E. E. *Revolutionary Humanism and Historicism in Modern Italy*. New Haven, 1981.

Jacobsen, H. A. *Nationalsozialistische Aussenpolitik, 1933–1938*. Frankfurt, 1968.

Jacquemyns, G. *La société belge sous l'occupation allemande*. Brussels, 1945.

James, H. *The German Slump*. New York, 1986.

Jamin, M. *Zwischen den Klassen: Zur Sozialstruktur der SA-Führerschaft*. Wuppertal, 1984.

Jänicke, M. *Totalitäre Herrschaft: Anatomie eines politischen Begriffes.* Berlin, 1971.

Jankowski, J. P. *Egypt's Young Rebels: "Young Egypt," 1933–1952.* Stanford, 1975.

Janos, A. C. *The Politics of Backwardness in Hungary, 1825–1945.* Princeton, 1982.

Jarausch, K. H. *The Four Power Pact.* Madison, 1965.

Jaschke, H.-G. *Die Republikaner.* Bonn, 1990.

Jelić-Butić, F. *Ustase i NDH.* Zagreb, 1972.

Jellinek, Y. *The Parish Republic: Hlinka's Slovak People's Party, 1939–1945.* Boulder, 1976.

Jenke, M. *Die Nationale Rechte.* Berlin, 1967.

Jenks, W. *Vienna and the Young Hitler.* New York, 1960.

Jennings, J. R. *Georges Sorel.* London, 1985.

Jetzinger, F. *Hitler's Youth.* London, 1958.

Jiménez Campos, J. *El fascismo en la crisis de la Segunda República española.* Madrid, 1979.

Jocteau, G. C. *La magistratura e i conflitti di lavoro durante il fascismo.* Milan, 1978.

Joes, A. J. *Fascism in the Contemporary World.* Boulder, 1978.

Jones, L. E. *German Liberalism and the Dissolution of the Weimar Party System, 1918–1933.* Chapel Hill, 1988.

Kadritzke, N. *Faschismus und Krise.* Frankfurt, 1976.

Karvonen, L. *From White to Blue-and-Black: Finnish Fascism in the Inter-War Era.* Helsinki, 1988.

Kasza, G. J. *The State and the Mass Media in Japan, 1918–1945.* Berkeley, 1988.

Kasza, G. J. *Administered Mass Organizations.* Forthcoming.

Kater, M. H. *Das "Ahnenerbe" der SS, 1933–1945.* Stuttgart, 1974.

Kater, M. H. *Studentenschaft und Rechtsradikalismus in Deutschland, 1918–1933.* Hamburg, 1975.

Kater, M. H. *The Nazi Party: A Social Profile of Members and Leaders, 1919–1945.* Cambridge, Mass., 1983.

Kater, M. H. *Doctors under Hitler.* Chapel Hill, 1989.

Katz, S. T. *The Holocaust in Historical Context.* Vol. 1, *The Holocaust and Mass Death before the Modern Age.* New York, 1994.

Kaufmann, W. H. *Monarchism in the Weimar Republic.* New York, 1953.

Kele, M. *Nazis and Workers.* Chapel Hill, 1972.

Kelley, A. *The Descent of Darwin: The Popularization of Darwinism in Germany, 1860–1914.* Chapel Hill, 1981.

Kent, P. C. *The Pope and the Duce.* London, 1981.

Kershaw, I. *Popular Opinion and Political Dissent in the Third Reich: Bavaria, 1933–1945.* New York, 1983.

Kershaw, I. *The Nazi Dictatorship: Problems and Perspectives of Interpretation.* London, 1985.

Kershaw, I. *The "Hitler Myth."* Oxford, 1987.

Kershaw, I., ed. *Weimar: Why Did German Democracy Fail?* New York, 1990.

Kindermann, G.-K. *Hitler's Defeat in Austria, 1933–1934: Europe's First Containment of Nazi Expansionism.* Boulder, 1988.

King, D. *Lyndon LaRouche and the New American Fascism.* New York, 1989.

Kirfel, M., and W. Oswalt, eds. *Die Rückkehr der Führer: Modernisierter Rechtradikalismus in Westeuropa.* Vienna, 1989.

Kirkpatrick, I. *Mussolini: A Study in Power.* New York, 1964.

Kirschenmann, D. *"Gesetz" im Staatsrecht und in der Staatslehre des Nationalsozialismus.* Berlin, 1970.

Kissenkoetter, U. *Gregor Strasser und die NSDAP.* Stuttgart, 1978.

Klaer, K.-H., M. Ristau, B. Schoppe, and M. Stadelmaier. *Die Wähler der extremen Rechten.* 3 vols. Bonn, 1989.

Klein, B. *Germany's Economic Preparations for War.* Cambridge, Mass., 1959.

Klein, H. *Parties and Political Change in Bolivia, 1880–1952.* London, 1969.

Klein, H. *Bolivia: The Evolution of a Multi-Ethnic Society.* New York, 1992.

Kleist, P. *Entre Hitler et Staline (1939–1945).* Paris, 1953.

Klemperer, K. von. *Germany's New Conservatism.* Princeton, 1957.

Klemperer, K. von. *Ignaz Seipel.* Princeton, 1972.

Klingemann, H.-D., and F. U. Pappi. *Politischer Radikalismus.* Munich, 1972.

Kluge, U. *Der oesterreichische Ständestaat, 1934–1938.* Munich, 1984.

Knapp, B. L. *Céline: Man of Hate.* University, Ala., 1974.

Knox, M. *Mussolini Unleashed, 1939–1941.* Cambridge, 1982.

Knütter, H.-H. *Ideologien des Rechtsradikalismus im Nachkriegsdeutschland.* Bonn, 1961.

Kočević, B. *Zrtve drugog svetskog rata u Jugoslaviji.* London, 1985.

Koch, H. W. *Sozialdarwinismus.* Munich, 1973.

Koch, H. W. *The Hitler Youth.* New York, 1976.

Koch, H. W. *Der deutsche Bürgerkrieg: Eine Geschichte der deutschen und österreichischen Freikorps, 1918–1923.* Berlin, 1978.

Koch, H. W. *In the Name of the Volk: Political Justice in Hitler's Germany.* New York, 1989.

Kocka, J. *Facing Total War: German Society, 1914–1918.* Cambridge, Mass., 1985.

Kocka, J. *Bildungsbürgertum im 19. Jahrhundert.* Vol. 4. Stuttgart, 1990.

Kocka, J., ed. *Bürgertum im 19. Jahrhundert: Deutschland im europäischen Vergleich.* 3 vols. Munich, 1990.

Koehl, R. *RKFDV: German Resettlement and Population Policy.* Cambridge, Mass., 1957.

Koehl, R. L. *The Black Corps: The Structure and Power Struggle of the Nazi SS.* Madison, 1983.

Kofas, J. V. *Authoritarianism in Greece: The Metaxas Regime.* Boulder, 1983.

Kohn-Branstedt, E. *Dictatorship and Political Police.* London, 1945.

Kolb, E. *The Weimar Republic.* London, 1988.

Koon, T. H. *Believe, Obey, Fight: Political Socialization of Youth in Fascist Italy, 1922–1943.* Chapel Hill, 1985.

Koontz, C. *Mothers in the Fatherland.* New York, 1987.

Kornhauser, W. *The Politics of Mass Society.* New York, 1959.

Koshar, R. *Social Life, Local Politics and Nazism: Marburg, 1880–1935.* Chapel Hill, 1986.

Kovacs, M. *The Politics of the Legal Profession in Interwar Hungary.* New York, 1987.

Krausnicj, H., and H.-H. Wilhelm. *Die Truppe des Weltanschauungskrieges: Die Einsatzgruppen der Sicherheitspolizei und des SD, 1938–1942*. Stuttgart, 1981.

Krieger, L. *The German Idea of Freedom*. Chicago, 1957.

Krizman, B. *Ante Pavelić i Ustase*. Zagreb, 1978.

Krizman, B. *Pavelić izmedu Hitlera i Mussolinija*. Zagreb, 1980.

Krizman, B. *Ustase i Treči Reich*. 2 vols. Zagreb, 1983.

Kube, A. *Pour le mérite und Hakenkreuz: Hermann Göring im Dritten Reich*. Munich, 1986.

Kuhl, S. *The Nazi Connection: Eugenics, American Racism, and German National Socialism*. New York, 1993.

Kuhn, A. *Das faschistische Herrschaftssystem und die moderne Gesellschaft*. Hamburg, 1973.

Kühnl, R. *Die nationalsozialistische Linke 1925 bis 1930*. Meisenheim am Glan, 1966.

Kühnl, R. *Formen bürgerlicher Herrschaft*. Hamburg, 1971.

Kühnl, R., ed. *Texte zur Faschismusdiskussion 1*. Reinbek, 1974.

Kühnl, R., ed. *Faschismustheorien: Texte zur Faschismusdiskussion 2*. Reinbek, 1979.

Kum'a N'Dumbe, A., III. *Hitler voulait l'Afrique*. Paris, 1980.

Kunnas, T. *Drieu La Rochelle, Céline, Brasillach et la tentation fasciste*. Paris, 1972.

Kuper, L. *Genocide: Its Political Use in the Twentieth Century*. New Haven, 1982.

Kushner, T., and K. Lunn. *Traditions of Intolerance*. Manchester, 1989.

Labini, P. S. *Saggio sulle classe sociali*. Bari, 1975.

Laborie, P. *L'opinion française sous Vichy*. Paris, 1990.

Lacko, M. *Men of the Arrow Cross*. Budapest, 1969.

Lacomba, J. A. *La crisis española de 1917*. Madrid, 1970.

Lacouture, J. *Nasser*. London, 1973.

La cultura italiana negli anni trenta '30–'45. 2 vols. New York, 1984.

La Francesca, S. *La politica economica del fascismo*. Bari, 1972.

Lami, G. F. *Introduzione a Evola*. Rome, 1980.

Landauer, C. *Corporate State Ideologies*. Berkeley, 1983.

Landy, M. *Fascism in Film*. Princeton, 1986.

Lane, B. M. *Architecture and Politics in Germany, 1918–1945*. Cambridge, Mass., 1968.

Lang, J. von. *Der Hitler-Junge: Baldur von Schirach*. Hamburg, 1988.

Lang, J. von. *The Secretary Martin Bormann*. New York, 1989.

Laqueur, W. *Young Germany*. New York, 1962.

Laqueur, W. *Russia and Germany*. New York, 1963.

Laqueur, W. *Black Hundred: The Rise of the Extreme Right in Russia*. New York, 1993.

Laqueur, W., ed. *Fascism: A Reader's Guide*. Berkeley, 1976.

Large, D. C., ed. *Contending with Hitler*. New York, 1992.

Larsen, S. U., B. Hagtvet, and J. P. Myklebust, eds. *Who Were the Fascists?: Social Roots of European Fascism*. Bergen, 1980.

Lasswell, H. D. *A Study of Power*. Glencoe, Ill., 1950.

Laurent, F. *L'orchestre noir*. Paris, 1978.

Lazzero, R. *Le Brigate Nere*. Milan, 1983.

Lebovics, H. *Social Conservatism and the Middle Classes in Germany, 1914–1933*. Princeton, 1969.

Lebra, J. *Japanese-Trained Armies in Southeast Asia.* New York, 1977.

Ledeen, M. A. *Universal Fascism.* New York, 1972.

Ledeen, M. A. *Intervista sul fascismo.* Bari, 1975. Trans. as *Fascism: An Informal Introduction to Its Theory and Practice.* New Brunswick, N.J., 1976.

Ledeen, M. A. *The First Duce.* Baltimore, 1977.

Lederer, E. *The State of the Masses.* New York, 1940.

Lee, S. E. *The European Dictatorships, 1918–1945.* London, 1987.

Leed, E. J. *No Man's Land: Combat and Identity in World War I.* New York, 1979.

Lees, M. *The Rape of Serbia.* New York, 1990.

Leggewie, C. *Die Republikaner.* Berlin, 1989.

Lejeune, B.-H., ed. *Historisme de Jacques Doriot et du Parti Populaire Français.* 2 vols. Amiens, 1977.

Leoni, F. *La stampa nazionalista.* Rome, 1965.

Leoni, F. *Origini del nazionalismo italiano.* Naples, 1965.

Leoni, F. *Il dissenso nel fascismo dal 1924 al 1939.* Naples, 1983.

Leontaritis, G. B. *Greece and the First World War, 1917–1918.* New York, 1990.

Leopold, J. A. *Alfred Hugenburg.* New Haven, 1978.

Levine, R. M. *The Vargas Regime: The Critical Years, 1934–1938.* New York, 1970.

Levy, R. S. *The Downfall of the Anti-Semitic Political Parties in Imperial Germany.* New Haven, 1975.

Lewin, R. *The Life and Death of the Afrika Korps.* London, 1977.

Lewis, D. S. *Illusions of Grandeur: Mosley, Fascism and British Society, 1931–1981.* Manchester, 1987.

Lewis, J. *Fascism and the Working Class in Austria, 1918–1934.* New York, 1991.

Lewis, R. C. *A Nazi Legacy.* New York, 1991.

Lewy, G. *The Catholic Church and Nazi Germany.* New York, 1964.

Lindström, U. *Fascism in Scandinavia, 1920–1940.* Stockholm, 1985.

Lipset, S. M. *Political Man.* New York, 1969.

Lipset, S. M., and E. Raab. *The Politics of Unreason, 1790–1970.* New York, 1970.

Littlejohn, D. *The Patriotic Traitors.* London, 1972.

Locchi, G. *La esencia del fascismo.* Barcelona, 1984.

Löffler, H. *Macht und Konsens in den klassischen Staatsutopien: Eine Studie zur Ideengeschichte des Totalitarismus.* Wärzburg, 1972.

Lohalm, U. *Völkischer Radikalismus: Die Geschichte des Deutschvölkischen Schutz- und Trutzbundes, 1919–1923.* Hamburg, 1970.

Lomax, D. *The Inter-War Economy of Britain, 1919–1939.* London, 1970.

Lombardi, P. *Per le patrie libertà: La dissidenza fascista tra "mussolinismo" e Aventino (1923–1925).* Milan, 1990.

Lönne, K.-E. *Faschismus als Herausforderung: Die Auseinandersetzung der "Roten Fahne" und des "Vorwärts" mit dem italienischen Faschismus, 1920–1933.* Cologne, 1981.

Loock, H. D. *Quisling, Rosenberg and Terboven: Zur Vorgeschichte und Geschichte der nationalsozialistischen Revolution in Norwegen.* Stuttgart, 1970.

López Soria, J. I., ed. *El pensamiento fascista (1930–1945).* Lima, 1981.

Lopukhov, B. *Fashizm i rabochee dvizhenie v Italii, 1919–1929.* Moscow, 1968.

Lottman, H. R. *The Purge: The Purification of French Collaborators after World War II.* New York, 1986.

Loubet, J.-L. *Les non-conformistes des années trentes.* Paris, 1969.

Louis, W. R. *Imperialism at Bay.* New York, 1978.

Löw, K. *Totalitarismus.* Berlin, 1988.

Löw, K., ed. *Totalitarismus und Faschismus.* Munich, 1980.

Lucena, M. de. *A evolução do sistema corporativo português.* 2 vols. Lisbon, 1976.

Ludendorff, E. *Weltkrieg droht auf deutschen Boden.* Munich, 1930.

Luebbert, G. M. *Liberalism, Fascism or Social Democracy.* New York, 1991.

Lukács, G. *Die Zerstörung der Vernunft.* Berlin, 1954.

Lukács, G. *Wie ist die faschistische Philosophie in Deutschland entstanden?* Budapest, 1982.

Lukas, R. *Forgotten Holocaust.* Lexington, Ky. 1986.

Luks, L. *Entstehung der kommunistischen Faschismustheorie.* Stuttgart, 1985.

Lumans, V. O. *Himmler's Auxiliaries: The Volksdeutsche Mittelstelle and the German National Minorities of Europe, 1933–1945.* Chapel Hill, 1993.

Lussu, E. *Marcia su Roma e dintorni.* Rome, 1945.

Luti, G. *La letteratura nel ventennio fascista.* Florence, 1972.

Lux-Wurm, P. *Le Péronisme.* Paris, 1965.

Luza, R. *Austro-German Relations in the Anschluss Era.* Princeton, 1975.

Lyttelton, A. *The Seizure of Power: Fascism in Italy, 1919–1929.* New York, 1973.

Lyttelton, A., ed. *Italian Fascism from Pareto to Gentile.* London, 1973.

Mabire, J. *Les SS français.* 3 vols. Paris, 1973–75.

Macartney, C. A. *October Fifteenth: A History of Modern Hungary, 1929–1945.* 2 vols. Edinburgh, 1957.

Macciocchi, M. *La donna nera.* Milan, 1976.

Machefer, P. *Ligues et fascismes en France, 1919–1939.* Paris, 1974.

MacKenzie, D. *Apis: The Congenial Conspirator.* Boulder, 1989.

Macrakis, K. *Surviving the Swastika: Scientific Research in Nazi Germany.* New York, 1993.

Maddison, A. *Economic Growth in the West.* New York, 1965.

Madureira, A. *O 28 de maio.* Lisbon, 1978.

Maier, C. S., et al. *The Rise of the Nazi Regime.* Boulder, 1985.

Maier, H., and H. Bott. *Die NPD.* Munich, 1968.

Malloy, J. M., ed. *Authoritarianism and Corporatism in Latin America.* Pittsburgh, 1977.

Malukhin, A. *Militarism—Backbone of Maoism.* Moscow, 1970.

Mancini, E. *The Struggle of the Italian Film Industry during Fascism, 1930–1935.* Ann Arbor, 1985.

Mandle, W. F. *Anti-Semitism and the British Union of Fascists.* London, 1968.

Mangoni, L. *L'interventismo della cultura.* Bari, 1974.

Mannhardt, J. W. *Der Faschismus.* Munich, 1925.

Manning, M. *The Blueshirts.* Dublin, 1970.

Manning, R. *Rehearsal for Destruction.* New York, 1967.

Manstein, P. *Die Mitglieder und Wähler der NSDAP, 1919–1933.* Frankfurt, 1988.

Manvell, R., and H. Fraenkel. *Heinrich Himmler.* London, 1965.

Marcon, H. *Arbeitsbeschaffungspolitik der Regierung Papen und Schleicher*. Frankfurt, 1974.

Marcus, S. *Father Coughlin*. Boston, 1973.

Marrus, M. R. *The Holocaust in Italy*. London, 1988.

Martin, D. *The Web of Disinformation*. New York, 1990.

Marx, G. T. *The Social Basis of the Support of a Depression Era Extremist: Charles E. Coughlin*. Berkeley, 1962.

Maser, W. *Die Frühgeschichte der NSDAP*. Frankfurt, 1965.

Maser, W. *Adolf Hitler*. New York, 1973.

Masgaj, Paul. *Action Française and Revolutionary Syndicalism*. Chapel Hill, 1979.

Mason, T. W. *Arbeiterklasse und Volksgemeinschaft*. Opladen, 1975.

Mason, T. W. *Social Policy in the Third Reich*. Providence, 1993.

Mastny, V. *The Czechs under Nazi Rule*. New York, 1971.

Mastny, V. *Russia's Road to the Cold War*. New York, 1979.

Mavrogordatos, G. T. *Stillborn Republic*. Berkeley, 1983.

Mayer, A. J. *Dynamics of Counterrevolution in Europe, 1870–1956*. New York, 1971.

Mayer, N., and P. Perrineau, eds. *Le Front National à découvert*. Paris, 1989.

Mayer-Tasch, P. C. *Korporativismus und Autoritarismus*. Frankfurt, 1971.

Mazower, M. *Greece and the Inter-War Economic Crisis*. Oxford, 1991.

Mazower, M. *Inside Hitler's Greece*. New Haven, 1993.

Mazzatosta, T. M. *Il regime fascista tra educazione e propaganda (1935–1943)*. Bologna, 1978.

McGee Deutsch, S. *Counterrevolution in Argentina: The Argentine Patriotic League*. Lincoln, 1986.

McGee Deutsch, S., and R. Dolkart, eds. *The Argentine Right*. Wilmington, Del., 1993.

McGovern, W. M. *From Luther to Hitler: The History of Fascist-Nazi Political Philosophy*. New York, 1941.

McGrath, W. J. *Dionysian Art and Populist Politics in Austria*. New Haven, 1974.

McKale, D. M. *The Nazi Party Courts*. Lawrence, Kans., 1974.

McKale, D. M. *The Swastika Outside Germany*. Kent, Ohio, 1977.

McNeil, W. C. *American Money and the Weimar Republic*. New York, 1985.

McSherry, J. *Stalin, Hitler and Europe: The Origins of World War II, 1933–1939*. Cleveland, 1968.

Medeiro, J. *Ideologia autoritaria no Brasil, 1930–1945*. Rio de Janeiro, 1978.

Medina, J. *Salazar e os fascistas*. Lisbon, 1979.

Meinck, G. *Hitler und die deutsche Aufrüstung, 1933–1939*. Wiesbaden, 1959.

Melograni, P. *Il trauma dell'intervento, 1914–1919*. Florence, 1968.

Melograni, P. *Storia politica della grande guerra*. Bari, 1971.

Melograni, P. *Gli industriali e Mussolini*. Milan, 1972.

Melson, R. *Revolution and Genocide: On the Origins of the Armenian Genocide and the Holocaust*. Chicago, 1992.

Menza, E., ed. *Totalitarianism Reconsidered*. Port Washington, N.Y., 1981.

Mercuri, L. *L'epurazione in Italia, 1943–1948*. Cueno, 1988.

Merker, R. *Die bildenden Künste im Nationalsozialismus*. Cologne, 1983.

Merkl, P. H. *Political Violence under the Swastika: 581 Early Nazis*. Princeton, 1975.

548   Bibliography

Merkl, P. H. *The Making of a Stormtrooper*. Princeton, 1980.
Merkl, P. H., and L. Weinberg. *Encounters with the Contemporary Radical Right*. Boulder, 1993.
Meskill, J. M. *Hitler and Japan*. New York, 1964.
Messerschmidt, M. *Die Wehrmacht im NS-Staat: Zeit der Indoktrination*. Hamburg, 1969.
Meyer, J. *The Cristero Rebellion*. Cambridge, 1976.
Meyer, J. *Le Sinarquisme: Un fascisme mexicain? 1937–1947*. Paris, 1977.
Michaelis, M. *Mussolini and the Jews*. Oxford, 1978.
Michalka, W., ed. *Die nationalsozialistische Machtergreifung*. Paderborn, 1984.
Michel, H. *Pétain et le régime de Vichy*. Paris, 1986.
Miège, J. L. *L'imperialismo coloniale italiano dal 1870 ai nostri giorni*. Milan, 1976.
Migone, G. C. *Gli Stati Uniti e il fascismo*. Milan, 1980.
Miguel Medina, C. de. *La personalidad religiosa de José Antonio*. Madrid, 1975.
Milazzo, M. J. *The Chetnik Movement and the Yugoslav Resistance*. Baltimore, 1975.
Miller, M. L. *Bulgaria during the Second World War*. Stanford, 1975.
Milward, A. *The Fascist Economy in Norway*. Oxford, 1972.
Milza, P. *L'Italie fasciste devant l'opinion française*. Paris, 1967.
Milza, P. *Le fascisme français*. Paris, 1987.
Milza, P., and S. Berstein. *Le fascisme italien, 1919–1945*. Paris, 1980.
Minio-Paluello, L. *Education in Fascist Italy*. London, 1946.
Miró, F. *Cataluña, los trabajadores y el problema de las nacionalidades*. Mexico City, 1967.
Misefari, E. *Il quadrumvio col frustino: Michele Bianchi*. Cosenza, 1977.
Mitchell, O. C. *Hitler's Nazi State*. New York, 1989.
Mitchell, R. H. *Thought Control in Prewar Japan*. Ithaca, 1976.
Mockler, A. *Haile Selassie's War: The Italian-Ethiopian Campaign, 1935–1941*. New York, 1985.
Mohler, A. *Die konservative Revolution in Deutschland, 1918–1933*. Darmstadt, 1972.
Molinelli, R. *Per una storia del nazionalismo italiano*. Urbino, 1966.
Mommsen, H. *Beamtentum in Dritten Reich*. Stuttgart, 1966.
Montenegro, J. A. de Sousa. *O Integralismo no Ceará*. Fortaleza, 1986.
Montero, J. L. *La CEDA*. 2 vols. Madrid, 1977.
Monticone, A. *Il fascismo al microfono*. Rome, 1978.
Moodie, T. D. *The Rise of Afrikanerdom*. Berkeley, 1975.
Moore, B., Jr. *Social Origins of Dictatorship and Democracy*. Boston, 1966.
Morand, J. *Les idées politiques de Louis-Ferdinand Céline*. Paris, 1972.
Morodo, R. *Orígenes ideológicos del franquismo: Acción Española*. Madrid, 1985.
Morris, I., ed. *Japan, 1931–1945: Militarism, Fascism, Japanism?* Boston, 1963.
Moses, J. A. *The Politics of Illusion: The Fischer Controversy in German History*. London, 1975.
Mosley, L. *The Reich Marshal*. London, 1974.
Mosse, G. L. *The Crisis of German Ideology: Intellectual Origins of the Third Reich*. New York, 1964.
Mosse, G. L. *Nazi Culture*. New York, 1966.
Mosse, G. L. *Germans and Jews*. New York, 1970.

Mosse, G. L. *The Nationalization of the Masses.* New York, 1975.

Mosse, G. L. *Nazism: A History and Comparative Analysis of National Socialism.* New Brunswick, N.J., 1978.

Mosse, G. L. *Toward the Final Solution.* New York, 1978.

Mosse, G. L. *Masses and Man.* New York, 1980.

Mosse, G. L. *Nationalism and Sexuality.* New York, 1985.

Mosse, G. L. *Fallen Soldiers.* New York, 1990.

Mosse, G. L. *Confronting the Nation.* Hanover, N.H., 1993.

Mourin, M. *Le drame des Etats satellites de l'Axe.* Paris, 1957.

Mouzelis, N. P. *Politics in the Semi-Periphery: Early Parliamentarism and Late Industrialization in the Balkans and Latin America.* New York, 1986.

Mueller-Hildebrand, B. *Germany and Its Allies in World War II.* Washington, D.C., 1980.

Mühlberger, D. *Hitler's Followers.* London, 1991.

Mühlberger, D., ed. *The Social Basis of European Fascist Movements.* New York, 1987.

Müller, I. *Hitler's Justice: The Courts of the Third Reich.* Cambridge, Mass., 1991.

Müller, K. J. *Das Heer und Hitler: Armee und nationalsozialistische Regime, 1933–1940.* Stuttgart, 1960.

Müller, K. J. *General Ludwig Beck.* Boppard, 1980.

Müller, K. J. *Armee und Drittes Reich, 1933–1939.* Paderborn, 1987.

Müller, L. A. *Republikaner, NPD, DVU, Liste D . . .* Göttingen, 1989.

Muñoz Alonso, A. *Un pensador para un pueblo.* Madrid, 1969.

Muret, C. T. *French Royalist Politics since the Revolution.* New York, 1933.

Murgia, P. G. *Il vento del Nord: Storia e cronaca del fascismo dopo la Resistenza (1945–1950).* Milan, 1975.

Nagle, J. D. *The National Democratic Party.* Berkeley, 1970.

Nagy-Talavera, N. M. *The Green Shirts and the Others.* Stanford, 1970.

Navajas Zubeldía, C. *Ejército, Estado y sociedad en España (1923–1930).* Logrono, 1991.

Neebe, R. *Grossindustrie, Staat und NSDAP, 1930–1933.* Göttingen, 1981.

Nellessen, B. *Die verbotene Revolution.* Hamburg, 1963.

Nello, P. *L'avanguardismo giovanile alle origini del fascismo.* Bari, 1979.

Nello, P. *Dino Grandi.* Bologna, 1987.

Nello, P. *Un fedele disubbediente: Dino Grandi da Palazzo Chigu al 25 luglio.* Bari, 1993.

Neulen, H. W. *Eurofaschismus und der Zweite Weltkrieg.* Munich, 1980.

Neulen, H. W. *An deutscher Seite: Internationale Freiwillige von Wehrmacht und SS.* Munich, 1985.

Neumann, F. *Behemoth: The Structure and Practice of National Socialism, 1933–1944.* New York, 1944.

Neumann, S. *"Permanent Revolution": Totalitarianism in an Age of International Civil War.* London, 1965.

Nevistić, F., and V. Nikolić. *Bleiburska tragedija hrvatskoga naroda.* Munich, 1976.

Newby, I. A. *Jim Crow's Defense: Anti-Negro Thought in America, 1900–1930.* Baton Rouge, 1965.

Newton, R. C. *The "Nazi Menace" in Argentina, 1931–1947.* Stanford, 1992.

Nicholls, A. J. *Weimar and the Rise of Hitler*. New York, 1991.

Nicosia, F. R., and L. D. Stokes. *Germans against Nazism*. New York, 1991.

Nieddu, L. *Dal combattentismo al fascismo in Sardegna*. Milan, 1979.

Nin, A. *Las dictaduras de nuestro tiempo*. Madrid, 1930.

Nitti, F. *Bolscevismo, fascismo e democrazia*. New York, 1924.

Noakes, J. *The Nazi Party in Lower Saxony, 1921–1933*. London, 1971.

Noakes, J., and G. Pridham, eds. *Nazism, 1919–1945*. 2 vols. Exeter, 1984.

Noel, L. *Les illusions de Stresa: L'Italie abandonnée a Hitler*. Paris, 1975.

Nolte, E. *Die faschistischen Bewegungen*. Munich, 1966.

Nolte, E. *Three Faces of Fascism*. New York, 1966.

Nolte, E. *Die Krise des liberalen Systems und die faschistischen Bewegungen*. Munich, 1968.

Nolte, E. *Der europäische Bürgerkrieg, 1917–1945: Nationalsozialismus und Bolschewismus*. Hamburg, 1987.

Nolte, E., ed. *Theorien über den Faschismus*. Cologne, 1967.

Nova, F. *The National Socialist Fuehrerprinzip and Its Background in German Thought*. Philadelphia, 1943.

Novick, P. *The Resistance versus Vichy*. New York, 1968.

Nowak, K. *Euthanasie und Sterilisierung im "Dritten Reich."* Göttingen, 1980.

Nusser, H. G. W. *Konservative Wehrverbände in Bayern, Preussen und Oesterreich, 1918–1933*. Munich, 1973.

Nye, R. A. *The Origins of Crowd Psychology: Gustave Le Bon and the Crisis of Mass Democracy in the Third Republic*. London, 1975.

Nye, R. A. *The Anti-Democratic Sources of Elite Theory: Pareto, Mosca, Michels*. London, 1977.

Nye, R. A. *Madness and Politics in Modern France: The Medical Concept of National Decline*. Princeton, 1984.

Nyomarkay, J. *Charisma and Factionalism in the Nazi Party*. Minneapolis, 1967.

O'Donnell, G. *Modernization and Bureaucratic-Authoritarianism*. Berkeley, 1973.

O Estado Novo. 2 vols. Lisbon, 1987.

Oka, Y. *Konoe Funimaro*. Tokyo, 1983.

Oldson, W. O. *A Providential Anti-Semitism*. Philadelphia, 1991.

Oliveira, C. *Portugal e a Guerra Civil de Espanha*. Lisbon, 1988.

Olivova, V. *The Doomed Democracy*. London, 1972.

O'Maoláin, C. *The Radical Right: A World Directory*. London, 1987.

O'Neill, R. J. *The German Army and the Nazi Party*. London, 1964.

Organski, A. F. K. *The Stages of Political Development*. New York, 1965.

Orlow, D. *The History of the Nazi Party, 1919–1945*. 2 vols. Pittsburgh, 1969.

Ortega y Gasset, J. *The Revolt of the Masses*. New York, 1932.

Ory, P. *Les collaborateurs, 1940–1945*. Paris, 1976.

Osgood, S. M. *French Royalism since 1870*. The Hague, 1970.

Ostenc, M. *L'Education en Italie pendant le Fascisme*. Paris, 1980.

Ostenc, M. *Intellectuels italiens et fascisme (1915–1929)*. Paris, 1983.

Overy, R. J. *The Nazi Economic Recovery, 1932–1938*. London, 1982.

Overy, R. J. *Göring, the Iron Man*. London, 1984.

Pabón, J. *Cambó*. 3 vols. Barcelona, 1952–69.

Padfield, P. *Himmler: Reichsführer-SS*. New York, 1990.

Palomares Lerma, G. *Mussolini y Primo de Rivera: Política exterior de dos dictaduras mediterráneas*. Madrid, 1989.

Paluello, L. M. *Education in Fascist Italy*. London, 1946.

Pansa, G. *L'Esercito di Salò*. Milan, 1970.

Parente, J. C. *Anauê: Os camisas verdes no poder*. Fortaleza, 1986.

Pareti, L. *I due imperi di Roma*. Catania, 1938.

Paris, E. *Genocide in Satellite Croatia, 1941–1945*. Chicago, 1960.

Parlato, G. *Il sindacalismo fascista*. Vol. 2, *Dalla "grande crisi" alla caduta del regime (1930–1943)*. Rome, 1989.

Parming, T. *The Collapse of Liberal Democracy and the Rise of Authoritarianism in Estonia*. London, 1975.

Passerini, L. *Fascism in Popular Memory*. Cambridge, 1987.

Passerini, L. *Mussolini immaginario*. Bari, 1991.

Pastor, M. *Los orígenes del fascismo en España*. Madrid, 1975.

Patrucco, A. *Italian Critics of Parliament, 1890–1918*. New York, 1992.

Paul, G., ed. *Hitlers Schatten verblasst: Die Normalisierung des Rechtsextremismus*. Bonn, 1990.

Pauley, B. F. *Hahnenschwanz und Hakenkreuz: Steirischer Heimatschutz und österreichischer Nationalsozialismus, 1918–1934*. Vienna, 1972.

Pauley, B. F. *Hitler and the Forgotten Nazis: A History of Austrian National Socialism*. Chapel Hill, 1981.

Pauley, B. F. *From Prejudice to Persecution: A History of Austrian Anti-Semitism*. Chapel Hill, 1992.

Pavone, C. *Una guerra civile*. Turin, 1991.

Paxton, R. O. *Vichy France*. New York, 1972.

Payne, S. G. *The Franco Regime, 1936–1975*. Madison, 1987.

Payne, S. G. *Spain's First Democracy: The Second Republic, 1931–1936*. Madison, 1993.

Pera, L. L. *Il fascismo dalla polemica alla storiografia*. Florence, 1975.

Perfetti, F. *Il nazionalismo italiano dalle origini alla fusione col fascismo*. Bologna, 1977.

Perfetti, F. *Il dibattito sul fascismo*. Rome, 1984.

Perfetti, F. *Sergio Panunzio: Il fondamento giuridico del fascismo*. Rome, 1987.

Perfetti, F. *Fascismo monarchico*. Rome, 1988.

Perfetti, F. *Fiumanesimo, sindacalismo e fascismo*. Rome, 1988.

Perfetti, F. *Il sindacalismo fascista*. Rome, 1988.

Perfetti, F. *La Camara dei Fasci e delle Corporazioni*. Rome, 1991.

Perlmutter, A. *Authoritarianism*. New Haven, 1981.

Perloff, M. *The Futurist Moment*. Chicago, 1986.

Perry, D. M. *The Politics of Terror: The Macedonian Revolutionary Movements, 1893–1903*. Durham, N.H., 1988.

Perticone, G. *La Repubblica di Salò*. Rome, 1947.

Peschanski, D., and L. Gervereau. *La propaganda sous Vichy*. Paris, 1990.

Petersen, J. *Hitler-Mussolini: Die Entstehung der Achse Berlin-Rom, 1933–1936*. Tübingen, 1973.

Peterson, E. N. *The Limits of Hitler's Power*. Princeton, 1969.

Petracchi, G. *La Russia rivoluzionaria nella politica italiana: Le relazioni italiano-sovietiche, 1917–1925*. Rome, 1982.

Petracchi, G. *Da San Pietroburgo a Mosca: La diplomazia italiana in Russia, 1861–1941*. Rome, 1993.

Petrovich, M. B. *A History of Modern Serbia, 1804–1918*. 2 vols. New York, 1976.

Petzina, D. *Autarkiepolitik im Dritten Reich: Der nationalsozialistische "Vierjahresplan."* Stuttgart, 1968.

Petzina, D. *Die deutsche Wirtschaft in der Zwischenkriegszeit*. Wiesbaden, 1977.

Peukert, D. *Volksgenossen und Gemeinschaftsfremde*. Cologne, 1982.

Peukert, D. *Alltagsgeschichte der NS-Zeit: Neue Perspektive oder Trivialisierung?* Munich, 1984.

Peukert, D. *Inside Nazi Germany: Conformity, Opposition, and Racism in Everyday Life*. New Haven, 1987.

Peukert, D. *The Weimar Republic: The Crisis of Classical Modernity*. New York, 1992.

Peukert, D., and J. Reulecke, eds. *Die Reihen fast Geschlossen: Beiträge zur Geschichte des Alltags unterm Nationalsozialismus*. Wuppertal, 1981.

Pfetsch, F. *Die Entwicklung zum faschistischen Führerstaat in der politischen Philosophie von Robert Michels*. Karlsruhe, 1964.

Philippet, J. *Les Jeunesses Patriotes et Pierre Taittinger, 1924–1940*. Paris, 1957.

Pica, A. *Mario Siroli*. Milan, 1955.

Pick, D. *Faces of Degeneration: A European Disorder, c. 1848–c. 1918*. Cambridge, 1989.

Pietrow, B. *Stalinismus, Sicherheit und Offensive: Das "Dritte Reich" in der Konzeption der sowjetischen Aussenpolitik, 1933–1941*. Melsungen, 1983.

Pike, F. B., and T. Stritch, eds. *The New Corporatism*. South Bend, Ind., 1974.

Pini, G., and D. Susmel. *Mussolini: L'Uomo e l'opera*. 4 vols. Florence, 1953–55.

Pinto, A. Costa. *O Salazarismo e o fascismo europeu: Problemas de interpretacão nas ciencias sociais*. Lisbon, 1992.

Pinto, A. Costa. *Os camisas azuis*. Lisbon, 1994.

Pinto, A. Costa, and A. Ribeiro. *A Accão Escolar Vanguarda*. Lisbon, 1980.

Pipes, R. *The Russian Revolution*. New York, 1990.

Pipes, R. *Russia under the New Regime: Lenin and the Birth of the Totalitarian State*. New York, 1994.

Pirker, T., ed. *Komintern und Faschismus 1920 bis 1940*. Stuttgart, 1965.

Pisanò, G. *Storia delle Forze Armate della Repubblica Sociale Italiana*. Rome, 1962.

Pisano, V. S. *The Dynamics of Subversion and Violence in Contemporary Italy*. Stanford, 1987.

Plehwe, F.-K. von. *Reichskanzler Kurt von Schleicher: Weimars Letzte Chance gegen Hitler*. Esslingen, 1983.

Plénel, E., and A. Rollat, eds. *L'effet Le Pen*. Paris, 1984.

Ploncard d'Assac, J. *Salazar*. Paris, 1967.

Plumyène, J., and R. Lasierra. *Les fascismes français, 1923–1963*. Paris, 1963.

Poggio, P. P., ed. *La Repubblica sociale italiana [sic], 1943–1945*. Brescia, 1986.

Pois, R. A. *National Socialism and the Religion of Nature*. New York, 1986.

Poliakov, L. *The Aryan Myth*. New York, 1971.

Pollard, J. F. *The Vatican and Italian Fascism, 1929–1932*. Cambridge, 1985.

Polonsky, A. *Politics in Independent Poland, 1921–1939*. Oxford, 1972.

Pool, J., and S. Pool. *Who Financed Hitler?* New York, 1978.

Potash, R. *The Army and Politics in Argentina, 1928–1945*. Stanford, 1969.

Potocnik, F. *Il campo di sterminio fascista: L'isola di Rab*. Turin, 1979.

Poulantzas, N. *Fascism and Dictatorship: The Third International and the Problem of Fascism*. Atlantic Highlands, N.J., 1975.

Preston, P. *The Politics of Revenge: Fascism and the Military in 20th Century Spain*. London, 1990.

Preston, P. *Franco*. London, 1993.

Preti, L. *Impero fascista, africani ed ebrei*. Milan, 1968.

Preti, L. *Mussolini giovane*. Milan, 1982.

Pridham, G. *Hitler's Rise to Power: The History of the NSDAP in Bavaria, 1923–1933*. London, 1973.

Prinz, M. *Vom neuen Mittelstand zum Volksgenossen*. Munich, 1986.

Prinz, M., and R. Zitelmann, eds. *Nationalsozialismus und Modernisierung*. Darmstadt, 1991.

Procacci, G. *Dalla parte d'Etiopia: L'aggressione italiana vista dai movimenti anticolonialisti d'Asia, d'Africa, d'America*. Milan, 1984.

Proctor, R. W. *Racial Hygiene: Medicine under the Nazis*. Cambridge, Mass., 1988.

Prost, A. *Les anciens combatants et la société française, 1914–1939*. 3 vols. Paris, 1977.

Pryce-Jones, D. *The Closed Circle*. New York, 1989.

Puhle, H. J. *Von der Agrarkrise zum Präfaschismus*. Wiesbaden, 1972.

Puhle, H. J. *Agrarische Interessenpolitik und preussischer Konservatismus im wilhelmischen Reich, 1893–1914*. Bonn, 1975.

Pulzer, P. *The Rise of Political Anti-Semitism in Germany and Austria*. Cambridge, 1988.

Quartararo, R. *Politica fascista nelle Baleari (1936–1939)*. Rome, 1977.

Quartararo, R. *Roma tra Londra e Berlino: La politica estera fascista dal 1930 al 1940*. Rome, 1980.

Radek, K. *Der Kampf der Kommunistische Internationale gegen Versaille und gegen die Offensive des Kapitals*. Hamburg, 1923.

Rainero, R. *La rivendicazione fascista sulla Tunisia*. Milan, 1978.

Randel, W. P. *The Ku Klux Klan*. Philadelphia, 1965.

Ranfagni, P. *I clerico-fascisti*. Florence, 1975.

Rauch, G. von. *The Baltic States: The Years of Independence, 1917–1940*. Berkeley, 1974.

Rauschning, H. *Die Revolution des Nihilismus*. Zurich, 1938. English trans., New York, 1939.

Rauti, P., and R. Sermonti. *Storia del Fascismo*. 6 vols. Rome, 1976–78.

Read, A., and D. Fisher. *The Deadly Embrace*. New York, 1988.

Rebentisch, D. *Führerstaat und Verwaltung im Zweiten Weltkrieg*. Wiesbaden, 1989.

Recker, M.-L. *Nationalsozialistische Sozialpolitik im Zweiten Weltkrieg*. Munich, 1985.

Redman, T. *Ezra Pound and Italian Fascism*. New York, 1990.

Reichel, P. *Der schöne Schein des Dritten Reiches*. Munich, 1991.

Rein, G. A. *Bonapartismus und Faschismus in der deutschen Geschichte.* Göttingen, 1960.

Rémond, R. *La Droite en France de la première Restauration a la cinquième République.* 2 vols. Paris, 1968.

Rempel, G. *Hitler's Children: The Hitler Youth and the SS.* Chapel Hill, 1989.

Renouvin, B. *Charles Maurras, l'Action Française et la question sociale.* Paris, 1982.

Repaci, A. *La marcia su Roma.* Milan, 1972.

Repaci, A. *Sessant'anni dopo: 28 ottobre 1922, il giorno che stravolse Italia.* Milan, 1982.

Repaci, A. *Da Sarajevo al "maggio radioso."* Milan, 1985.

Retallack, J. N. *Notables of the Right: The Conservative Party and Political Mobilization in Germany, 1876–1914.* Boston, 1988.

Reuth, R. G. *Goebbels.* New York, 1993.

Revel, J.-F. *La tentation totalitaire.* Paris, 1975.

Revel, J.-F. *Comment les democraties finissent.* Paris, 1983.

Reventlow, E. von. *Völkisch-kommunistische Einigung?* Leipzig, 1924.

Rhodes, J. *The Hitler Movement: A Modern Millenarian Revolution.* Stanford, 1980.

Rich, N. *Hitler's War Aims.* 2 vols. New York, 1973–74.

Richard, L. *Le Nazisme et la culture.* Paris, 1978.

Richter, H. *Griechenland zwischen Revolution und Konterrevolution (1936–1946).* Frankfurt, 1973.

Ridley, F. F. *Revolutionary Syndicalism in France.* Cambridge, 1970.

Rimbotti, L. L. *Il fascismo di sinistra.* Rome, 1989.

Rintala, M. *Three Generations: The Extreme Right Wing in Finnish Politics.* Bloomington, 1962.

Rioux, J.-P., ed. *La vie culturelle sous Vichy.* Brussels, 1990.

Ripepe, E. *Gli elitisti italiani.* Pisa, 1974.

Rizzo, F. *Giovanni Amendola e la crisi della democrazia.* Rome, n.d.

Rizzo, G. *D'Annunzio e Mussolini.* Rome, 1960.

Roberts, D. D. *The Syndicalist Tradition and Italian Fascism.* Chapel Hill, 1979.

Roberts, G. *The Unholy Alliance.* Bloomington, 1989.

Roberts, H. L. *Rumania: Political Problems of an Agrarian State.* New Haven, 1951.

Robertson, E. M. *Mussolini as Empire-Builder: Europe and Africa, 1932–1936.* New York, 1977.

Robinson, R. A. H. *The Origins of Franco's Spain.* London, 1970.

Robinson, R. A. H. *Contemporary Portugal.* London, 1979.

Rocco, M. *Come il fascismo divenne una dittatura.* Milan, 1952.

Rochat, G. *L'esercito italiano da Vittorio Veneto a Mussolini.* Bari, 1967.

Rochat, G. *Militari e politici nella preparazione della campagna d'Etiopia, 1932–1936.* Milan, 1971.

Rochat, G. *Il colonialismo italiano.* Turin, 1974.

Rochat, G. *Gli arditi della grande guerra.* Milan, 1981.

Rochat, G. *Italo Balbo.* Turin, 1986.

Rock, D. *Authoritarian Argentina.* Berkeley, 1993.

Rogari, S. *Santa Sede e fascismo.* Bari, 1977.

Rogger, H., and E. Weber, eds. *The European Right.* Berkeley, 1965.

Röhrich, W. *Robert Michels von sozialistischsyndikalistischen zum faschistischen Credo.* Berlin, 1972.

Romero, Cuesta, A. *Objetivo: Matar a Franco.* Madrid, 1976.

Romualdi, A. *Julius Evola: L'uomo e l'opera.* Rome, 1971.

Rosar, W. *Deutsche Gemeinschaft: Seyss-Inquart und der Anschluss.* Vienna, 1971.

Rosas, F. *O Estado Novo (1926–1974).* Vol. 7 of *Historia de Portugal*, ed. J. Mattoso. Lisbon, 1994.

Rose, P. L. *Revolutionary Antisemitism in Germany from Kant to Wagner.* Princeton, 1990.

Rosenbaum, P. *Il nuovo fascismo: Da Salò ad Almirante. Storia del MSI.* Milan, 1975.

Rosengarten, F. *The Italian Anti-Fascist Press (1919–1945).* Cleveland, 1968.

Rosenhaft, E. *Beating the Fascists? The German Communists and Political Violence, 1929–1933.* Cambridge, 1983.

Rossi, C. *Il Tribunale Speciale.* Milan, 1952.

Rotchie, J. M. *German Literature under National Socialism.* Totowa, N.J., 1983.

Roth, J. J. *The Cult of Violence: Sorel and the Sorelians.* Berkeley, 1980.

Rothschild, J. *Pilsudski's Coup d'Etat.* New York, 1966.

Rothschild, J. *Eastern Europe between Two World Wars.* Seattle, 1974.

Rouquié, A. *Poder militar y sociedad política en la Argentina.* 2 vols. Buenos Aires, 1983.

Rouquié, A. *The Military and the State in Latin America.* Berkeley, 1987.

Roussel, E. *Le cas Le Pen: Les nouvelles droites en France.* Paris, 1985.

Rousso, H. *Pétain et la fin de la collaboration.* Brussels, 1984.

Rousso, H. *The Vichy Syndrome.* Cambridge, Mass., 1991.

Roveri, A. *Le origini del fascismo a Ferrara, 1918–1921.* Milan, 1974.

Rudaux, P. *Les Croix de Feu et le P.S.F.* Paris, 1967.

Rudel, M. *Karl Marx devant le Bonapartisme.* Paris, 1960.

Ruhl, K.-J. *Spanien im Zweiten Weltkrieg: Franco, die Falange und das "Dritte Reich."* Hamburg, 1975.

Rumi, G. *Alle origini della politica estera fascista, 1918–1923.* Bari, 1968.

Rummel, R. J. *Lethal Politics: Soviet Genocide and Mass Murder since 1917.* New Brunswick, N.J., 1990.

Rummel, R. J. *Democide: Nazi Genocide and Mass Murder.* New Brunswick, N.J., 1992.

Rummel, R. J. *Death by Government: Genocide and Mass Murder since 1900.* New Brunswick, N.J., 1994.

Rusinow, D. I. *Italy's Austrian Heritage, 1919–1946.* Oxford, 1969.

Rutherford, W. *Hitler's Propaganda Machine.* New York, 1978.

Rüthers, B. *Die unbegrenzte Auslegung: Zum Wandel der Privatrechtsordung im Nationalsozialismus.* Frankfurt, 1973.

Rutkoff, P. M. *Revanche and Revisionism: The Ligue des Patriotes and the Origins of the Radical Right in France, 1882–1900.* Athens, Ga., 1981.

Saage, R. *Faschismustheorien.* Munich, 1976.

Saba, M. A. *Gioventù Italiana del Littorio: La stampa dei giovani nella guerra fascista.* Milan, 1973.

Saba, M. A. *Il dibattito sul fascismo.* Milan, 1976.

Sabaliunas, L. *Lithuania, 1939–1941*. Bloomington, 1972.

Sabbatucci, G. *I combattenti nel primo dopoguerra*. Rome, 1974.

Sadkovich, J. J. *Italian Support for Croatian Separatism, 1927–1937*. New York, 1987.

Sánchez Diana, J. M. *Ramiro Ledesma Ramos*. Madrid, 1975.

Sánchez Soler, M. *Los hijos del 20-N: Historia violenta del fascismo español*. Madrid, 1993.

Sandomirsky, G. *Fashizm*. 2 vols. Moscow, 1923.

Santarelli, E. *Origini del fascismo (1911–1919)*. Urbino, 1963.

Santarelli, E. *Storia del movimento e del regime fascista*. 3 vols. Rome, 1967.

Santarelli, E. *Ricerche sul fascismo*. Urbino, 1971.

Santarelli, E. *Fascismo e neofascismo*. Rome, 1974.

Sapelli, G. *Fascismo, grande industria e sindacato: Il caso di Torino, 1929/1935*. Milan, 1975.

Saracinelli, M., and N. Totti. *L'Italia del Duce: L'informazione, la scuola e il costume*. Rimini, 1983.

Sarfatti, Margherita. *The Life of Benito Mussolini*. Rome, 1925.

Sarfatti, Michele. *Mussolini contro gli ebrei*. Milan, 1994.

Sarti, R. *Fascism and the Industrial Leadership in Italy, 1919–1940*. Berkeley, 1971.

Šaš, G. *Der Faschismus in Italien*. Hamburg, 1923.

Sattler, M. *Rechtsextremismus in der Bundesrepublik: Die "Alte," die "Neue" Rechte und der Neonazismus*. Opladen, 1980.

Saz, I. *Mussolini contra la II República*. Valencia, 1986.

Sbacchi, A. *La colonizzazione italiana in Etiopia, 1936–1940*. Bologna, 1980.

Sburlati, C. *Codreanu el capitán*. Barcelona, 1970.

Scalapino, R. A. *Democracy and the Party Movement in Prewar Japan*. Berkeley, 1953.

Scarpellini, E. *Organizzazione teatrale e politica del teatro nell' Italia fascista*. Florence, 1989.

Schäfer, H.-D. *Das gespaltene Bewusstsein: Deutsche Kultur und Lebenswirklichkeit, 1933–1945*. Frankfurt, 1984.

Schechtman, J. B. *The Mufti and the Fuehrer*. New York, 1965.

Schieder, W., and C. Dipper, eds. *Der spanische Bürgerkrieg in der internationalen Politik (1936–1939)*. Munich, 1976.

Schlangen, W. *Die Totalitarismus-Theorie*. Stuttgart, 1976.

Schleunes, K. A. *The Twisted Road to Auschwitz*. Urbana, 1970.

Schmidt, M. *Albert Speer: Das Ende eines Mythos*. Bern, 1982.

Schmitter, P. C. *Corporatism and Public Policy in Authoritarian Portugal*. Beverly Hills, 1975.

Schmitz, D. F. *The United States and Fascist Italy, 1922–1940*. Chapel Hill, 1988.

Schneider, H. W., and S. B. Clough. *Making Fascists*. Chicago, 1929.

Schneider, W., ed. *Vernichtungspolitik*. Hamburg, 1991.

Schnell, R., ed. *Kunst und Kultur im deutschen Faschismus*. Stuttgart, 1978.

Schneller, M. *Zwischen Romantik und Faschismus: Der Beitrag Othmar Spanns zum Konservatismus der Weimarer Republik*. Stuttgart, 1970.

Schoenbaum, D. *Hitler's Social Revolution*. New York, 1966.

Scholder, K. *The Churches and the Third Reich*. 2 vols. London, 1988.

Scholz, W. *Die Lage des spanischen Staates vor der Revolution (under Berucksichtigung ihres Verhältnisses zum italienischen Fascismus)* [sic]. Dresden, 1932.

Schonbach, M. *Native American Fascism during the 1930s and 1940s*. New York, 1987.

Schotthöfer, F. *Il Fascio: Sinn und Wirklichkeit des italienischen Fascismus* [sic]. Frankfurt, 1924.

Schramm, P. E. *Hitler: The Man and the Military Leader*. Chicago, 1971.

Schreiber, G. *Hitler: Interpretationen, 1923–1983*. Darmstadt, 1984.

Schrewe, E. *Faschismus und Nationalsozialismus*. Hamburg, 1934.

Schröder, J. *Italiens Kriegsaustritt, 1943: Die deutschen Gegenmassnahmen*. Göttingen, 1969.

Schüddekopf, O.-E. *Linke Leute von Rechts*. Stuttgart, 1960.

Schüddekopf, O.-E. *Nationalbolschewismus in Deutschland, 1918–1933*. Frankfurt, 1973.

Schüddekopf, O.-E. *Revolutions of Our Time: Fascism*. New York, 1973.

Schulte, T. *The German Army and Nazi Policies in Occupied Russia*. Oxford, 1989.

Schulz, G. *Faschismus-Nationalsozialismus: Versionen und theoretische Kontroversen, 1922–1972*. Frankfurt, 1974.

Schulz, G. *Aufstieg des Nationalsozialismus*. Berlin, 1975.

Schwierskott, H. J. *Arthur Moeller van den Bruck und der revolutionäre Nationalismus in der Weimarer Republik*. Göttingen, 1962.

Scoppola, P. *La Chiesa e il fascismo durante il pontificato di Pio XI*. Bologna, 1966.

Scoppola, P. *La Chiesa e il fascismo*. Bari, 1971.

Scoppola, P., and F. Traniello, eds. *I cattolici tra fascismo e democrazia*. Bologna, 1975.

Scorza, C. *La notte del Gran Consiglio*. Milan, 1968.

Seager, F. H. *The Boulanger Affair*. Ithaca, 1969.

Seaton, A. *The Russo-German War, 1941–45*. London, 1971.

Sechi, M. *Il mito della cultura fascista*. Bari, 1984.

Sechi, S. *Dopoguerra e fascismo in Sardegna*. Turin, 1969.

Segrè, C. G. *Fourth Shore: The Italian Colonization of Libya*. Chicago, 1974.

Segrè, C. G. *Italo Balbo: A Fascist Life*. Berkeley, 1987.

Seidel, B., and S. Jenkner, eds. *Wege der Totalitarismusforschung*. Darmstadt, 1968.

Sérant, P. *Le romantisme fasciste*. Paris, 1959.

Sérant, P. *Les dissidents de l'Action Française*. Paris, 1978.

Serra, M. *Una cultura dell'autorità: La Francia di Vichy*. Bari, 1980.

Setta, S. *L'Uomo Qualunque, 1944–1948*. Bari, 1975.

Setta, S. *Renato Ricci: Dallo squadrismo alla Repubblica Sociale Italiana*. Bologna, 1986.

Settembrini, D. *Il Fascismo controrivoluzione imperfetta*. Florence, 1978.

Shafer, B. C. *Nationalism*. Washington, D.C., 1963.

Shillony, B.-A. *Revolt in Japan: The Young Officers and the February 26, 1936, Incident*. Princeton, 1973.

Shillony, B.-A. *Politics and Culture in Wartime Japan*. Oxford, 1981.

Shorrock, W. I. *From Ally to Enemy: The Enigma of Fascist Italy in French Diplomacy*. Kent, Ohio, 1988.

Silva, J. da. *Legião Portuguesa*. Lisbon, 1975.

Simon, W. B. *Oesterreich, 1918–1938: Ideologien und Politik*. Vienna, 1984.

Simpson, H. *The Social Origins of Afrikaner Fascism and Its Apartheid Policy*. Uppsala, 1980.

Skidelsky, R. *Oswald Mosley*. London, 1935.

Sklar, D. *Gods and Beasts: The Nazis and the Occult*. New York, 1978.

Smelser, R. M. *The Sudeten Problem, 1933–1938*. Middletown, Conn., 1975.

Smelser, R. M. *Robert Ley, Hitler's Labor Front Leader*. Oxford, 1988.

Smith, A. D. *Nationalism in the Twentieth Century*. Oxford, 1979.

Smith, A. D. *Theories of Nationalism*. London, 1983.

Smith, B. *Adolf Hitler: His Family, Childhood and Youth*. Stanford, 1967.

Smith, B. *Heinrich Himmler: A Nazi in the Making, 1900–1926*. Stanford, 1971.

Smith, B. F. *The Road to Nuremberg*. New York, 1981.

Smith, D. M. *Italy: A Modern History*. Ann Arbor, 1959.

Smith, D. M. *Mussolini's Roman Empire*. New York, 1976.

Smith, D. M. *Mussolini*. New York, 1982.

Smith, D. M. *Italy and Its Monarchy*. New Haven, 1989.

Smith, W. D. *The Intellectual Origins of Nazi Imperialism*. New York, 1986.

Smith, W. D. *Politics and the Sciences of Culture in Germany, 1840–1920*. Oxford, 1991.

Snowden, F. *The Fascist Revolution in Tuscany, 1919–22*. Cambridge, 1989.

Snyder, L. L. *The Idea of Racialism*. Princeton, 1962.

Snyder, L. L. *Hitler's Elite*. New York, 1989.

Sominini, A. *Il linguaggio di Mussolini*. Milan, 1978.

Sontheimer, K. *Antidemokratisches Denken in der Weimarer Republik*. Munich, 1962.

Soper, S. P. *Totalitarianism: A Conceptual Approach*. Lanham, Md., 1985.

Soucy, R. *Fascism in France: The Case of Maurice Barrès*. Berkeley, 1972.

Soucy, R. *Fascist Intellectual: Drieu La Rochelle*. Berkeley, 1979.

Soucy, R. *French Fascism: The First Wave, 1924–1933*. New Haven, 1986.

Speer, A. *Infiltration*. New York, 1981.

Spinosa, A. *D'Annunzio*. Milan, 1987.

Spriano, P. *Storia del Partito Comunista Italiano*. Vol. 3. Rome, 1979.

Stachura, P. D. *Nazi Youth in the Weimar Republic*. Santa Barbara, 1975.

Stachura, P. D. *Gregor Strasser and the Rise of Nazism*. London, 1983.

Stachura, P. D., ed. *The Shaping of the Nazi State*. London, 1978.

Stachura, P. D., ed. *The Nazi Machtergreifung*. London, 1983.

Stearns, P. *Revolutionary Syndicalism and French Labor*. New Brunswick, N.J., 1971.

Steenson, G. P. *After Marx, before Lenin: Marxism and Socialist Working-Class Parties in Europe, 1884–1914*. Pittsburgh, 1991.

Stein, G. H. *The Waffen-SS*. Ithaca, 1966.

Steinberg, J. *All or Nothing: The Axis and the Holocaust, 1941–43*. London, 1990.

Steinberg, M. P. *Sabers and Brownshirts: The German Students' Path to National Socialism, 1918–1935*. Chicago, 1977.

Steinert, M. *Hitler's War and the Germans*. Athens, Ohio, 1977.

Steinert, M. *Hitler*. Paris, 1991.

Steinweis, A. E. *Art, Ideology, and Economics in Nazi Germany.* Chapel Hill, 1993.

Stephenson, J. *Women in Nazi Society.* London, 1975.

Stern, F. *The Politics of Cultural Despair.* Berkeley, 1961.

Stern, J. P. *Hitler: The Führer and the People.* Glasgow, 1975.

Sternberg, F. *Der Faschismus an der Macht.* Amsterdam, 1935.

Sternhell, Z. *Maurice Barrès et le nationalisme français.* Paris, 1972.

Sternhell, Z. *La Droite révolutionnaire, 1885–1914: Les origines françaises du fascisme.* Paris, 1978.

Sternhell, Z. *Neither Right nor Left: Fascist Ideology in France.* Berkeley, 1986.

Sternhell, Z., M. Sznajder, and M. Asheri. *The Birth of Fascist Ideology.* Princeton, 1994.

Stinchcombe, A. L. *Constructing Social Theories.* New York, 1968.

St. John, R. *Foreign Correspondent.* New York, 1957.

Stoakes, G. *Hitler and the Quest for World Domination: Nazi Ideology and Foreign Policy in the 1920s.* Leamington Spa, 1987.

Stolper, G. *The German Economy, 1870–1940.* New York, 1940.

Storry, R. *The Double Patriots.* Boston, 1957.

Stöss, R. *Die extreme Rechte in der Bundesrepublik.* Opladen, 1989.

Strasser, O. *Hitler and I.* Boston, 1940.

Streit, C. *Keine Kameraden: Die Wehrmacht und die sowjetische Kriegsgefangenen, 1941–1945.* Stuttgart, 1978.

Stromberg, R. N. *Redemption by War: The Intellectuals and 1914.* Lincoln, 1982.

Sturzo, L. *Italien und der Faschismus.* Cologne, 1926.

Sueiro Seoane, S. *España en el Mediterráneo.* Madrid, 1993.

Sugar, P. F., ed. *Native Fascism in the Successor States, 1918–1945.* Santa Barbara, 1971.

Surcou Macedo, R. *Hacia la revolución integral.* La Paz, 1961.

Surcou Macedo, R. *Conozca Falange Socialista Boliviana.* La Paz, 1972.

Sutton, M. *Nationalism, Positivism, and Catholicism: The Politics of Charles Maurras and French Catholics, 1890–1914.* New York, 1982.

Suvorov, V. *Icebreaker: Who Started the Second World War?* London, 1990.

Swart, K. W. *The Sense of Decadence in Nineteenth-Century France.* The Hague, 1964.

Sweets, J. F. *Choices in Vichy France.* New York, 1986.

Swire, J. *Bulgarian Conspiracy.* London, 1939.

Sydnor, C. W. *Soldiers of Destruction: The SS Death's Head Division, 1933–1945.* Princeton, 1977.

Szöllösi-Janze, M. *Die Pfeilkreuzlerbewegung in Ungarn.* Munich, 1989.

Taeye-Hedren, M. de. *Le nationalisme d'Enrico Corradini et les origines du fascisme dans la revue florentine "Il Regno" (1903–1906).* Paris, 1973.

Tanin, O., and E. Yohan [pseuds.]. *Militarism and Fascism in Japan.* New York, 1934.

Tannebaum, E. R. *Action Française.* New York, 1962.

Tannenbaum, E. R. *The Fascist Experience: Italian Society and Culture, 1922–1945.* New York, 1972.

Tarrow, S. *Democracy and Disorder: Protest and Politics in Italy, 1965–1975.* Oxford, 1989.

Tauber, K. B. *Beyond Eagle and Swastika*. Middletown, Conn., 1967.

Taylor, T. *The March of Conquest: German Victories in Western Europe, 1940*. London, 1959.

Tedeschi, M. *Fascisti dopo Mussolini*. Rome, 1950.

Teich, M., and R. Porter, eds. *Fin de siècle and Its Legacy*. Cambridge, 1993.

Tella, T. di. *El sistema político argentino y la clase obrera*. Buenos Aires, 1964.

Telo, A. J. *O sidonismo e o movimento operario português*. Lisbon, 1977.

Telo, A. J. *Decadencia e queda da I República portuguesa*. 2 vols. Lisbon, 1980–1984.

Thamer, H.-U. *Verführung und Gewalt: Deutschland, 1933–1945*. Berlin, 1986.

Thamer, H.-U., and W. Wippermann. *Faschistische und neofaschistische Bewegungen*. Darmstadt, 1977.

Thayer, J. *Italy and the Great War: Politics and Culture, 1870–1915*. Madison, 1964.

Théolleyre, J.-M. *Les neo-nazis*. Paris, 1982.

Theweleit, K. *Männerphantasien*. 2 vols. Frankfurt, 1977–78. English trans., 1989.

Thies, J. *Architekt der Weltherrschaft: Die "Endziele" Hitlers*. Düsseldorf, 1976.

Thomas, R. H. *Nietzsche in German Politics and Society, 1890–1918*. New York, 1986.

Thomsen, E. *Deutsche Besatzungspolitik in Dänemark, 1940–1945*. Düsseldorf, 1971.

Thurlow, R. *Fascism in Britain: A History,, 1918–1985*. Oxford, 1987.

Tillmann, H. *Deutschlands Araberpolitik im Zweiten Weltkrieg*. Berlin, 1965.

Tilton, T. *Nazism, Neonazism and the Peasantry*. Bloomington, 1975.

Tinghino, J. J. *Edmondo Rossoni*. New York, 1991.

Togliatti, P. *Lezioni sul fascismo*. Rome, 1970.

Toland, J. *Adolf Hitler*. New York, 1976.

Tomasevich, J. *War and Revolution in Yugoslavia, 1941–1945: The Chetniks*. Stanford, 1975.

Tombs, R. *Nationhood and Nationalism in France: From Boulangism to the Great War, 1889–1919*. New York, 1992.

Toniolo, G. *L'economia dell'Italia fascista*. Bari, 1980.

Topitsch, E. *Stalin's War*. New York, 1987.

Toscano, M. *The Origins of the Pact of Steel*. Baltimore, 1967.

Trevor-Roper, H., ed. *The Goebbels Diaries*. London, 1978.

Trindade, H. *Integralismo*. São Paulo, 1974.

Trindade, H. *La tentation fasciste au Bresil dans les années trente*. Paris, 1988.

Trotsky, L. *The Class Nature of the Soviet State*. London, 1937.

Tsipko, A. S. *Is Stalinism Really Dead?* New York, 1990.

Tucker, W. R. *The Fascist Ego: A Political Biography of Robert Brasillach*. Berkeley, 1975.

Tull, C. J. *Father Coughlin and the New Deal*. Syracuse, 1965.

Turi, G. *Il fascismo e il consenso degli intellettuali*. Bologna, 1980.

Turner, H. A., Jr. *German Big Business and the Rise of Hitler*. New York, 1985.

Turner, H. A., Jr., ed. *Nazism and the Third Reich*. New York, 1972.

Turner, H. A., Jr., ed. *Hitler—Memoirs of a Confidant*. New Haven, 1985.

Turner, S., and D. Käsler, eds. *Sociology Responds to Fascism*. London, 1992.

Tusa, A. *The Nuremberg Trial*. New York, 1984.

Tusell, J. *Radiografía de un golpe de Estado: El ascenso al poder del general Primo de Rivera*. Madrid, 1987.

Tusell, J. *Franco en la guerra civil*. Madrid, 1992.

Tusell, J., and G. G. Queipo de Llano. *Franco y Mussolini*. Barcelona, 1985.

Tusell, J., et al., eds. *El régimen de Franco (1936–1975)*. Vol. 1. Madrid, 1993.

Tusell, J., et al., eds. *Estudios sobre la derecha española contemporánea*. Madrid, 1993.

Tweton, D. J. *The Marquis de Morès*. Fargo, N. Dak., 1972.

Tyrell, A. *Vom "Trommler" zum "Führer."* Munich, 1975.

Ungari, P. *Alfredo Rocco e l'ideologia giuridica del fascismo*. Brescia, 1963.

Unger, A. L. *The Totalitarian Party*. London, 1974.

Uthman, J. von. *Le diable est-il Allemand? Deux-cent ans de préjugés franco-allemands*. Paris, 1984.

Uva, B. *La nascita dello Stato corporativo e sindacale fascista*. Assisi, 1974.

Vajda, M. *Fascism as a Mass Movement*. London, 1976.

Valeri, N. *D'Annunzio davanti al fascismo*. Florence, 1963.

Valesio, P. *Gabriele D'Annunzio: The Dark Flame*. New Haven, 1992.

Valiani, L., et al. *L'altra Europa, 1922–1945*. Turin, 1967.

Vallaura, C. *Le radici del corporativismo*. Rome, 1971.

Vasconcelos, G. *Ideologia curupira: Análise do discurso integralista*. São Paulo, 1979.

Vecchini, F. *La pensée politique de Gaetano Mosca et ses différentes adaptations au cours du XXme siècle*. Paris, 1968.

Veen, H.-J., N. Lepszy, and P. Mnich. *The Republikaner Party in Germany*. Washington, D.C., 1993.

Venè, G. F. *Il golpe fascista del 1922*. Milan, 1975.

Veneruso, D. *La vigilia del fascismo: Il primo ministero Facta nella crisi dello stato liberale in Italia*. Bari, 1968.

Vergani, P. *Achille Funi*. Milan, 1949.

Vermeil, E. *Doctrinaires de la révolution allemande*. Paris, 1939.

Vermeil, E. *Germany's Three Reichs*. New York, 1969.

Versari, S. *Una pagina di storia del fascismo fiorentino: Il fascismo autonomo*. Rocca S. Casciano, 1938.

Viereck, P. *Metapolitics: From the Romantics to Hitler*. Boston, 1941.

Vigezzi, B. *L'Italia dalla neutralità all'intervento nella prima guerra mondiale*. Milan, 1965.

Villari, L. *Italian Foreign Policy under Mussolini*. New York, 1956.

Visser, G. C. *OB: Traitors or Patriots?* Johannesburg, 1976.

Vivarelli, R. *Storia delle origini del fascismo: L'Italia dalla grande guerra alla marcia su Roma*. 2 vols. Bologna, 1967, 1991.

Voegelin, E. *Political Religions*. Lewiston, N.Y., 1986.

Vogelsang, T. *Reichswehr, Staat und NSDAP*. Munich, 1962.

Vogelsang, T. *Die nationalsozialistische Zeit: Deutschland 1933 bis 1939*. Frankfurt, 1967.

Volkmann, H.-E. *Die Krise des Parlamentarismus in Ostmitteleuropa zwischen den beiden Weltkriegen*. Marburg, 1967.

Volpe, G. *L'Italia in cammino: L'ultimo cinquantennio*. Milan, 1927.

Volpe, G. *Storia del movimento fascista*. Milan, 1939.

Wagner, W. *Belgien in der deutschen Politik während des Zweiten Weltkrieges*. Boppard, 1974.

Waisman, C. H. *Reversal of Development in Argentina: Postwar Counterrevolutionary Policies and Their Structural Consequences*. Princeton, 1987.

Waite, R. G. L. *Vanguard of Nazism*. Cambridge, Mass., 1954.

Waite, R. G. L. *The Psychopathic God*. New York, 1977.

Waldmann, P. *Der Peronismus, 1943–1955*. Hamburg, 1974.

Walker, L. *Hitler Youth and Catholic Youth, 1933–1936*. Washington, D.C., 1970.

Walker, M. *German National Socialism and the Quest for Nuclear Power, 1939–1949*. New York, 1989.

Walser, H. *Die illegale NSDAP in Tirol und Vorarlberg, 1933–1938*. Vienna, 1983.

Walter, J.-J. *Les machines totalitaires*. Paris, 1982.

Warmbrunn, W. *The Dutch under German Occupation, 1940–1945*. Stanford, 1963.

Webb, J. *The Occult Establishment*. London, 1976.

Weber, E. *The Nationalist Revival in France, 1905–1914*. Berkeley, 1959.

Weber, E. *Action Française*. Stanford, 1962.

Weber, E. *Varieties of Fascism*. New York, 1964.

Weber, R. G. S. *The German Student Corps in the Third Reich*. New York, 1986.

Webster, P. *Pétain's Crime: The Complete Story of French Collaboration in the Holocaust*. Chicago, 1990.

Webster, R. A. *The Cross and the Fasces*. Stanford, 1960.

Webster, R. A. *Industrial Imperialism in Italy, 1908–1915*. Berkeley, 1975.

Wegner, B. *The Waffen-SS*. Oxford, 1990.

Weinberg, G. L. *The Foreign Policy of Hitler's Germany*. 2 vols. Chicago, 1970–80.

Weinberg, G. L. *A World at Arms*. New York, 1993.

Weinberg, L. B. *After Mussolini: Italian Neo-Fascism and the Nature of Fascism*. Washington, D.C., 1979.

Weingart, P., J. Kroll, and K. Bayertz. *Rasse, Blut und Gene: Geschichte der Eugenik und Rassenhygiene in Deutschland*. Frankfurt, 1988.

Weinstein, F. *The Dynamics of Nazism: Leadership, Ideology and the Holocaust*. New York, 1980.

Weiss, J. *The Fascist Tradition*. New York, 1967.

Welch, D. *Propaganda and the German Cinema*. New York, 1985.

Welch, D. *The Third Reich: Politics and Propaganda*. New York, 1993.

Wheeler, D. *A ditadura militar portuguesa (1926–1933)*. Lisbon, 1986.

White, D. S. *Lost Comrades: Socialists of the Front Generation, 1918–1945*. Cambridge, 1992.

Whiteside, A. G. *Austrian National Socialism before 1918*. The Hague, 1962.

Whiteside, A. G. *The Socialism of Fools*. Berkeley, 1975.

Whiting, C. *The Home Front: Germany*. Chicago, 1982.

Wiarda, H. J. *Corporatism and Development: The Portuguese Experience*. Amherst, 1977.

Willequet, J. *La Belgique sous la botte: Résistances et collaborations, 1940–1944*. Brussels, 1986.

Williams, T. H. *Huey Long*. New York, 1969.

Williamson, P. J. *Varieties of Corporatism*. London, 1985.

Williamson, P. J. *Corporatism in Perspective*. London, 1989.
Willmott, H. P. *The Great Crusade*. New York, 1989.
Wilson, G. M. *Radical Nationalist in Japan: Kita Ikki, 1883–1937*. Cambridge, Mass., 1969.
Wilson, M. *Das Institut für Sozialforschung und seine Faschismusanalysen*. New York, 1982.
Wiltschegg, W. *Die Heimwehr*. Munich, 1985.
Winkler, H. A. *Mittelstand, Demokratie und Nationalsozialismus*. Cologne, 1970.
Winkler, H. A. *Revolution, Staat, Faschismus*. Göttingen, 1978.
Winkler, H. A. *Der Weg in die Katastrophe: Arbeiter und Arbeiterbewegung in der Weimarer Republik 1930 bis 1933*. Berlin, 1987.
Winock, M. *Edouard Drumont et Cie*. Paris, 1982.
Winston, C. M. *Workers and the Right in Spain, 1900–1936*. Princeton, 1985.
Wippermann, W. *Zur Analyse des Faschismus: Die sozialistischen und kommunistischen Faschismustheorien, 1921–1945*. Frankfurt, 1981.
Wippermann, W. *Die Bonapartismustheorie von Marx und Engels*. Stuttgart, 1983.
Wippermann, W. *Faschismustheorien*. Darmstadt, 1989.
Wolf, D. *Die Doriot-Bewegung*. Stuttgart, 1967.
Wolf, W. *Faschismus in der Schweiz*. Zurich, 1969.
Wolff, R. J. *Between Pope and Duce: Catholic Students in Fascist Italy*. New York, 1990.
Wortmann, K. *Geschichte der Deutschen Vaterlandspartei, 1917–1918*. Halle, 1926.
Wright, G. *The Ordeal of Total War, 1939–1945*. New York, 1968.
Wynot, E. D., Jr. *Polish Politics in Transition: The Camp of National Unity and the Struggle for Power, 1935–1939*. Athens, Ga., 1974.
Wytwycky, B. *The Other Holocaust*. Washington, D.C., 1980.
Yahil, L. *The Holocaust*. New York, 1990.
Yamaguchi Yasushi. *Fuashizmu*. Tokyo, 1979.
Yanov, A. *The Russian New Right*. Berkeley, 1978.
Yanov, A. *The Russian Challenge and the Year 2000*. New York, 1987.
Zamagni, V. *The Economic History of Italy, 1860–1990*. Oxford, 1993.
Zambroni, G. *Mussolinis Expansionspolitik auf dem Balkan*. Hamburg, 1970.
Zangrandi, R. *Il lungo viaggio attraverso il fascismo*. Milan, 1962.
Zani, L. *Italia Libera: Il primo movimento antifascista clandestino (1923–1925)*. Bari, 1975.
Zani, L. *Fascismo, autarchia, comercio estero: Felice Guarneri, tecnocrata al servizio dello "Stato Nuovo."* Bari, 1988.
Zeldin, T. *The Political System of Napoleon III*. Oxford, 1958.
Zeman, Z. A. B. *Nazi Propaganda*. London, 1972.
Zeppi, S. *Il pensiero politico dell'idealismo italiano e il nazional fascismo*. Florence, 1973.
Zerjavić, V. *Opsesije i megalomanije oko Jasenovca i Bleiburga*. Zagreb, 1992.
Zhelev, Z. *Fashizmut*. Boulder, 1990.
Ziegler, H. F. *Nazi Germany's New Aristocracy: The SS Leadership, 1925–1939*. Princeton, 1989.
Zitelmann, R. *Hitler: Selbstverständnis eines Revolutionärs*. Hamburg, 1987.

564   Bibliography

Zitelmann, R. *Hitler*. Bari, 1992.
Zuccotti, S. *The Italians and the Holocaust*. New York, 1988.
Zunino, P. G. *L'ideologia del fascismo*. Bologna, 1985.
Zunino, P. G. *Interpretazione e memoria del fascismo*. Bari, 1991.

ARTICLES

Abbreviations

JCH   *Journal of Contemporary History*
JMH   *Journal of Modern History*
SC   *Storia Contemporanea*

Acquarone, A. "La milizia volontaria nello stato fascista." In Acquarone and Vernassa, eds., *Il regime fascista* 85–111.
Ahmann, R. "Soviet Foreign Policy and the Molotov-Ribbentrop Pact of 1939: An Enigma Reassessed." *Storia delle Relazioni Internazionali* 5:2 (1989): 349–69.
Albers, J. "Nationalsozialismus und Modernisierung." *Kölner Zeitschrift für Soziologie und Sozialpsychologie* 41 (June 1989): 346–65.
Allardyce, G. "What Fascism Is Not: Thoughts on the Definition of a Concept." *American Historical Review* 84:2 (April 1979): 367–88.
Amann, P. H. "Les fascismes américains des années trentes: Aperçus et reflexions." *Revue d'Histoire de la Deuxième Guerre Mondiale* 126 (1982): 47–75.
Amann, P. H. "Vigilante Fascism: The Black Legion as an American Hybrid." *Comparative Studies on Society and History* 25:3 (July 1983): 490–524.
Armon, T. I. "Fascismo italiano e Guardia di Ferro." *SC* 3 (1972): 505–27.
Armon, T. I. "La Guardia di Ferro." *SC* 7:3 (Sept. 1976): 507–44.
Armon, T. I. "Fra tradizione e rinnovamento: Su alcuni aspetti dell'antisemitismo della Guardia di Ferro." *SC* 11:1 (Feb. 1988): 5–28.
Aschheim, S. E. "Modernity and the Metapolitics of Nazism." University of Wisconsin, 1975. Seminar paper.
Azzi, S. C. "The Historiography of Fascist Foreign Policy." *Historical Journal* 36:1 (1993): 187–203.
Bairoch, P. "Europe's Gross National Product (1800–1975)." *Journal of European Economic History* 5:2 (Fall 1976): 273–340.
Baldwin, P. "Social Interpretations of Nazism: Renewing a Tradition." *JCH* 25:1 (Jan. 1990): 5–37.
Barbu, Z. "Romania." In *European Fascism*, ed. S. J. Woolf (London, 1969), 146–66.
Bassin, M. "Race contra Space: The Conflict between German *Geopolitik* and National Socialism." *Political Geography Quarterly* 6:2 (April 1987): 115–34.
Bauer, O. "Das Gleichgewicht der Klassenkämpfe." *Der Kampf* 17 (1924): 57–67.
Ben Plotkin, M. "Perón y el peronismo: Un ensayo bibliográfico." *Estudios Interdisciplinarios de América Latina y el Caribe* 2:1 (1991): 113–36.
Berezin, M. "The Organization of Political Ideology: Culture, State, and Theater in Fascist Italy." *American Sociological Review* 56:5 (1991): 639–51.
Beyme, K. von, ed. "Right-Wing Extremism in Western Europe." *West European Politics* 11:2 (1988). Special issue.

Bix, H. P. "Rethinking 'Emperor-System Fascism': Ruptures and Continuities in Modern Japanese History." *Bulletin of Concerned Asian Scholars* 14:2 (April–June 1982): 2–14.

Borkenau, F. "Zur Soziologie des Faschismus." In Nolte, ed., *Theorien* 156–81.

Botz, G. "Austro-Marxist Interpretations of Fascism." *JCH* 11:4 (Oct. 1976): 129–56.

Botz, G. "The Changing Patterns of Social Support for Austrian National Socialism (1918–1945)." In Larsen, Hagtvet, and Myklebust, eds., *Who Were the Fascists?* (1980), 202–25.

Botz, G. "Political Violence in the First Austrian Republic." In *Social Protest, Violence and Terror in Nineteenth- and Twentieth-Century Europe*, ed. W. Mommsen and G. Hirschfeld (New York, 1982), 300–29.

Bracher, K. D. "The Role of Hitler: Perspectives of Interpretation." In Laqueur, ed., *Fascism* (1976), 211–25.

Bracher, K. D. "Il nazional-socialismo in Germania: Problemi d'interpretazione." In *Fascismo e nazionalsocialismo*, ed. K. D. Bracher and L. Valiani (Bologna, 1986), 31–54.

Braunthal, J. "Der Putsch der Fascisten" [*sic*]. *Der Kampf* 15 (1922): 320–33.

Brose, E. D. "Il nazismo, il fascismo e la tecnologia." *SC* 18:2 (April 1987): 387–405.

Brustein, W. "The 'Red Menace' and the Rise of Italian Fascism." *American Sociological Review* 56 (Oct. 1991): 652–64.

Buchheim, H. "Die SS in der Verfassung des Dritten Reiches." *Vierteljahrhefte für Zeitgeschichte* 3 (1955): 127–57.

Byrnes, R. F. "Morès, the First National Socialist." *Review of Politics* 12:3 (July 1950): 341–62.

Cammett, J. M. "Communist Theories of Fascism, 1920–1935." *Science and Society* 31:1 (Winter 1967): 149–63.

Caplan, J. "Bureaucracy, Politics and the National Socialist State." In Stachura, ed., *Shaping of the Nazi State* (1978), 234–56.

Caplan, J. "National Socialism and the Theory of the State." In *Reevaluating the Third Reich*, ed. T. Childers and J. Caplan (New York, 1993), 54–69.

Cärtringen, F. H. von. "Die Deutschnationale Volkspartei." In *Das Ende der Parteien: 1933*, ed. E. Mathias and R. Morsey (Düsseldorf, 1960), 543–652.

Cassels, A. "Janus: The Two Faces of Fascism." *Canadian Historical Papers, 1969* 166–84. Reprinted in *Reappraisals of Fascism*, ed. H. A. Turner Jr. (New York, 1975), 69–92.

Chanady, A. "The Disintegration of the German National Peoples' Party, 1924–1930." *JMH* 39:1 (1967): 65–91.

Chiarini, R. "The 'Movimento Sociale Italiano': A Historical Profile." In *Neo-Fascism in Europe*, ed. L. Cheles, R. Ferguson, and M. Vaughan (London, 1991), 19–42.

Ciccarelli, O. "Fascism and Politics in Peru during the Benavides Regime, 1933–1939: The Italian Perspective." *Hispanic American Historical Review* 70:3 (1990): 405–32.

Ciocca, P. "L'economia nel contesto internazionale." In *L'economia italiana nel periodo fascista*, ed. P. Ciocca and G. Toniolo (Bologna, 1976), 27–49.

Cliadakis, H. "Le régime de Metaxas et la Deuxième Guerre Mondiale." *Revue d'Histoire de la Deuxième Guerre Mondiale* 107 (July 1977): 19–38.

Coetzee, F., and M. S. Coetzee. "Rethinking the Radical Right in Germany and Britain before 1914." *JCH* 21:4 (Oct. 1986): 515–38.

Cofrancesco, D. "Appunti per un analisi del mito romano nell'ideologia fascista." *SC* 11:3 (June 1980): 383–411.

Cofrancesco, D. "Il mito europeo del fascismo (1939–1945)." *SC* 14:1 (Feb. 1983): 5–45.

Cofrancesco, D. "Fascismo; destra o sinistra?" In *Fascismo e nazionalsocialismo,* ed. K. D. Bracher and L. Valiani (Bologna, 1986), 107–24.

Conzemius, V. "Eglises chrétiennes et totalitarisme national-socialiste: Un bilan bibliographique." *Revue d'Histoire Eclesiastique* 63 (1968): 437–503.

Cruz, M. Braga da. "Notas para uma caracterizacão política do salazarismo." *Análise Social* 72 (1982): 897–926.

Cullen, S. "The Development of the Ideas and Policy of the British Union of Fascists, 1932–1940." *JCH* 22:1 (Jan. 1987): 115–36.

Cullen, S. "Political Violence: The Case of the British Union of Fascists." *JCH* 28:2 (April 1993): 245–67, 513–29.

Deak, I. "The Peculiarities of Hungarian Fascism." In *The Holocaust in Hungary,* ed. R. L. Braham and B. Vago (New York, 1985), 43–51.

De Grand, A. J. "Cracks in the Façade: The Failure of Fascist Totalitarianism in Italy, 1935–9." *European History Quarterly* 21:4 (Oct. 1991): 515–35.

Del Noce, A. "Per una definizione storica del fascismo." In *Il problema storico del fascismo,* by A. Del Noce (Florence, 1970), 11–46.

Detragiache, D. "Il fascismo femminile da San Sepolcro all'affare Matteotti (1919–1925)." *SC* 14:2 (April 1983): 211–51.

Di Nardo, R. L., and A. Bay. "Horse-Drawn Transport in the German Army." *JCH* 23:1 (Jan. 1988): 129–42.

Djursaa, M. "Who Were the Danish Nazis?" In *Die Nationalsozialisten,* ed. R. Mann (Stuttgart, 1980), 137–54.

Dülffer, J. "Bonapartism, Fascism and National Socialism." *JCH* 11:4 (Oct. 1976): 109–28.

Dülffer, J. "Der Beginn des Krieges, 1939: Hitler, die innere Krise und das Mächtesystem." *Geschichte und Gesellschaft* 2:4 (1976): 443–70.

Duprat, F. "Naissance, développement et echec d'un fascisme roumain." In *Etudes sur le fascisme,* by M. Bardèche et al. (Paris, 1974), 113–64.

Duus, P., and D. Okimoto. "Fascism and the History of Prewar Japan: The Failure of a Concept." *Journal of Asian Studies* 39:1 (Nov. 1979): 65–76.

Eastman, L. E. "Fascists in Kuomintang China: The Blue Shirts." *China Quarterly* 49:1 (Jan. 1972): 1–31.

Eatwell, R. "The Holocaust Denial: A Study in Propaganda Technique." In *Neo-Fascism in Europe,* ed. L. Cheles, R. Ferguson, and M. Vaughan (London, 1991), 120–46.

Eatwell, R. "Towards a New Model of Generic Fascism." *Journal of Theoretical Politics* 4:1 (April 1992): 1–68.

Eatwell, R. "Neo-Fascism and the Right: Conceptual Conundrums?" In *The Radical Right in Western Europe,* ed. J. Munholland (forthcoming).

Eberstadt, F. "Reading Primo Levi." *Commentary* 80:4 (Oct. 1985): 41–47.

Evans, R. J. "Women and the Triumphs of Hitler." *JMH* 48:1 (March 1976): 73–91.

Falter, J. "War die NSDAP die erste deutsche Volkspartei." In Prinz and Zitelmann, eds., *Nationalsozialismus* 21–47.

Falter, J., and D. Hänisch. "Die Anfälligkeit von Arbeitern gegenüber der NSDAP bei den Reichstagswahlen, 1928–1933." *Archiv für Sozialgeschichte* 26 (1986): 179–216.

Falter, J., and R. Zintl. "The Economic Crisis of the 1930s and the Nazi Vote." *Journal of Interdisciplinary History* 19 (1988): 55–85.

Fest, J. "Hitlers Krieg." *Vierteljahrshefte für Zeitgeschichte* 38:3 (1990): 359–73.

Fritzsche, P. "Machine Dreams: Airmindedness and the Reinvention of Germany." *American Historical Review* 98:3 (June 1993): 685–709.

Funk, M. "Das faschistische Italien im Urteil der 'Frankfurter Zeitung' (1920–1933)." *Quellen und Forschungen aus Italienischen Archiven und Bibliotheken* 69 (1989): 255–311.

Furuya, T. "Naissance et développement du fascisme japonais." *Revue d'Histoire de la Deuxième Guerre Mondiale* 86 (April 1972): 1–16.

Gable, G. "The Far Right in Contemporary Britain." In *Neo-Fascism in Europe,* ed. L. Cheles, R. Ferguson, and M. Vaughan (London, 1991), 244–63.

Galkin, A. A. "Capitalist Society and Fascism." *Social Sciences: USSR Academy of Sciences* 2 (1970): 128–38.

Galkin, A. A. "Fashistskii ideinyi sindrom: Genesis germanskogo varianta." *Voprosy Filosofii* 11 (1988): 124–34.

Gentile, E. "Fascism as Political Religion." *JCH* 25:2–3 (May–June 1980): 229–51.

Gentile, E. "Fascism in Italian Historiography: In Search of an Individual Historical Identity." *JCH* 21:2 (April 1986): 179–208.

Gentile, E. "Il futurismo e la politica." In De Felice, ed., *Futurismo* (1988), 105–57.

Gentile, E. "Fascismo." *Enciclopedia Italiana.* 1992.

Gentile, E. "Impending Modernity: Fascism and the Ambivalent Image of the United States." *JCH* 28:1 (Jan. 1993): 7–29.

Gentile, E. "La nazione del fascismo: Alle origini della crisi dello Stato nazionale in Italia." *SC* 24:6 (Dec. 1993): 833–87.

Geyer, M. "The State in National Socialist Germany." In *Statemaking and Social Movements,* ed. C. Bright and S. Harding (Ann Arbor, 1984), 193–232.

Goglia, L. "Note sul razzismo coloniale fascista." *SC* 19:6 (1988): 1223–66.

Gregor, A. J. "African Socialism and Fascism: An Appraisal." *Review of Politics* 29:3 (July 1967): 353–99.

Gregor, A. J. "Fascism and Modernization: Some Addenda." *World Politics* 26:3 (April 1974): 370–84.

Gregor, A. J., and M. H. Chiang. "*Nazionalfascismo* and the Revolutionary National-ism of Sun Yat-Sen." *Journal of Asian Studies* 39:1 (Nov. 1979): 21–37.

Grill, J. H. "Local and Regional Studies of National Socialism: A Review." *JCH* 21:2 (April 1986): 253–94.

Gudmundsson, A. "Nazism in Iceland." In Larsen, Hagtvet, and Myklebust, eds., *Who Were the Fascists?* 743–50.

Hagtvet, B. "On the Fringe: Swedish Fascism, 1920–45." In Larsen, Hagtvet, and Myklebust, eds., *Who Were the Fascists?* 715–42.

568   Bibliography

Hauner, M. "A German Racial Revolution?" *JCH* 19:4 (Oct. 1984): 669–88.

Hayes, P. "Polyocracy and Policy in the Third Reich: The Case of the Economy." In *Reevaluating the Third Reich*, ed. T. Childers and J. Caplan (New York, 1993), 190–210.

Hennessy, A. "Fascism and Populism in Latin America." In Laqueur, ed., *Fascism* 255–62.

Hildebrand, K. "Le forze motrici di politica interna agenti sulla politica estera nazional-socialista." *SC* 5:2 (June 1974): 201–22.

Hildebrand, K. "Monokratie oder Polykratie? Hitlers Herrschaft und das Dritte Reich." In Hirschfeld and Kettenacker, eds., *Der "Führerstaat"* (1986), 242–63.

Hilferding, R. "State Capitalism or Totalitarian State Economy." *Modern Review* 19:2 (June 1947): 266–71. Reprinted in Daniels, ed., *Stalin Revolution* 94–97.

Hillgruber, A. "England's Place in Hitler's Plans for World Dominion." *JCH* 9:1 (Jan. 1974): 6–22.

Hilton, S. "Ação Integralista Brasileira." *Luso-Brazilian Review* 9:2 (Dec. 1972): 3–29.

Hofer, W. "Fifty Years On: Historians and the Third Reich." *JCH* 21:2 (April 1986): 225–51.

Horne, J., and A. Kramer. "German 'Atrocities' and Franco-German Opinion, 1914: The Evidence of German Soldiers' Diaries." *JMH* 66 (March 1994): 1–33.

Horster-Philipps, U. "Grosskapital, Weimarer Republik und Faschismus." In *Die Zerstörung der Weimarer Republik*, ed. G. Hardach and R. Kühnl (Cologne, 1977), 38–141.

Howard, W. "Nietzsche and Fascism." *History of European Ideas* 11 (1989): 893–99.

Hughes, A., and M. Kolinsky. " 'Paradigmatic Fascism' and Modernization: A Critique." *Political Studies* 24:4 (Dec. 1976): 371–96.

Husbands, C. T. "The State's Response to Far-Right Extremism." In *The Radical Right in Western Europe*, ed. J. Munholland (forthcoming).

Hüttenberger, P. "Nationalsozialistische Polykratie." *Geschichte und Gesellschaft* 2:4 (1976): 417–42.

Hutton, P. H. "Popular Boulangism and the Advent of Mass Politics in France, 1886–1890." *JCH* 11:1 (Jan. 1976): 85–106.

Ignazi, P. "La cultura politica del Movimento Sociale Italiano." *Rivista Italiana di Scienza Politica* 19:3 (Dec. 1989): 43–65.

Ignazi, P. "Nuovi e vecchi partiti di estrema destra in Europa." *Rivista Italiana di Scienza Politica* 22:2 (Aug. 1992): 293–333.

Ioanid, R. "Nicolae Iorga and Fascism." *JCH* 27:3 (July 1992): 467–92.

Irvine, W. D. "Fascism in France and the Strange Case of the Croix de Feu." *JMH* 63 (1991): 271–95.

James, H. "Innovation and Conservation in the Economic Recovery: The Alleged 'Nazi Recovery' of the 1930s." In *Reevaluating the Third Reich*, ed. T. Childers and J. Caplan (New York, 1993), 109–31.

Jellinek, Y. "Stormtroopers in Slovakia: The Rodobrana and the Hlinka Guard." *JCH* 6:3 (July 1971): 97–119.

Jellinek, Y. "An Authoritarian Parliament: The Croatian State Sabor of 1942." *Canadian Slavonic Papers* 22:2 (June 1980): 259–73.

Jellinek, Y. "Nationalities and Minorities in the Independent State of Croatia." *Nationalities Papers* 8:2 (1984): 195–210.

Joes, A. J. "Fascism: The Past and the Future." *Comparative Political Studies* 7:1 (April 1974): 107–33.

Joes, A. J. "The Fascist Century." *Worldview* 21:5 (May 1978): 19–23.

Jones, L. E. " 'The Greatest Stupidity of My Life': Alfred Hugenburg and the Formation of the Hitler Cabinet, January 1933." *JCH* 27:1 (Jan. 1992): 63–87.

Kasekamp, A. "The Estonian Veterans' League: A Fascist Movement?" *Journal of Baltic Studies* 24:3 (Fall 1993): 263–68.

Kasza, G. J. "Fascism from Below? A Comparative Perspective on the Japanese Right, 1931–1936." *JCH* 19:4 (Oct. 1984): 607–27.

Kasza, G. J. " 'Fascism from Above'? The Renovationist Right in Wartime Japan." (Forthcoming).

Kenworthy, E. "The Function of the Little Known Case in Theory Formation; or, What Peronism Wasn't." *Comparative Politics* 6 (Oct. 1973): 16–45.

Kitchen, M. "August Thalheimer's Theory of Fascism." *Journal of the History of Ideas* 34:1 (Jan.–March 1973): 67–78.

Klein, H. "David Toro and the Establishment of 'Military Socialism' in Bolivia." *Hispanic American Historical Review* 45:1 (Feb. 1965): 25–52.

Klein, H. "Germán Busch and the Era of 'Military Socialism' in Bolivia." *Hispanic American Historical Review* 47:2 (May 1967): 166–84.

Klingemann, C. "Social-Scientific Experts—No Ideologues: Sociology and Social Research in the Third Reich." In Turner and Käsler, eds., *Sociology Responds to Fascism* 127–54.

Knox, M. "Conquest, Foreign and Domestic, in Fascist Italy and Nazi Germany." *JMH* 56:1 (March 1984): 1–57.

Knox, M. "Il fascismo e la politica estera italiana." In *La politica estera italiana, 1860–1985,* ed. R. Bosworth and S. Romano (Bologna, 1991), 287–330.

Kocka, J. "German History before Hitler: The Debate about the German *Sonderweg.*" *JCH* 23:1 (Jan. 1988): 3–16.

Koehl, R. "Feudal Aspects of National Socialism." *American Political Science Review* 54:4 (Dec. 1960): 921–33.

Kovacs, M. "Luttes professionelles et antisemitisme: Chronique de la montée du fascisme dans le corps medical hongrois, 1920–1944." *Actes de la Recherche en Sciences Sociales* 56 (March 1985): 31–44.

Kovacs, M. "The Ideology of Illiberalism in the Professions: Leftist and Rightist Radicalism among Hungarian Doctors, Lawyers and Engineers, 1918–1945." *European History Quarterly* 21:2 (April 1991): 185–208.

Kozub-Ciembroniewicz, W. "La ricezione ideologica del fascismo italiano in Polonia negli anni 1927–1933." *SC* 24:1 (Feb. 1993): 5–17.

Kren, G. M. "Psychohistorical Interpretations of National Socialism." *German Studies Review* 1:3 (1978): 150–72.

Kuin, S. "O Braço Longo de Mussolini: Os 'Comitati d'Azione per l'Universalità di Roma' em Portugal (1933–1937)." *Penélope* 11 (1993): 7–20.

Lacko, M. "Zur Frage der Besonderheiten des südosteuropaischen Faschismus." In *Fascism and Europe: An International Symposium* (Prague, 1970), 2:1–22.

Lacko, M. "The Social Roots of Hungarian Fascism." In Larsen, Hagtvet, and Myklebust, eds., *Who Were the Fascists?* (1980), 395–400.

Landkammer, J. "Nazionalsocialismo e bolscevismo tra universalismo e particolarismo." *SC* 21:3 (1990): 511–39.

Lasswell, H. D. "The Psychology of Hitlerism." *Political Quarterly* 4 (July–Sept.
1933): 373–84.

Ledeen, M. A. "Renzo De Felice and the Controversy over Italian Fascism." *JCH* 11:4
(Oct. 1976): 269–82.

Lestz, M. E. "Gli intellettuali del Fuxingshe: Fascismo e dittatura del partito in Cina,
1932–1937." *SC* 18:2 (April 1987): 269–86.

Lewis, P. H. "Was Perón a Fascist? An Inquiry into the Nature of Fascism." *Journal of
Politics* 42:1 (Feb. 1980): 242–56.

Linz, J. J. "Totalitarian and Authoritarian Regimes." In *Handbook of Political Science,*
ed. F. Greenstein and N. Polsby (Reading, Mass., 1975), 3:175–411.

Linz, J. J. "La crisis de las democracias." In *Europa en crisis, 1919–1939,* ed. M.
Cabrera et al. (Madrid, 1992), 231–80.

Lipset, S. M. "Fascism—Left, Right and Center." In *Political Man,* by S. M. Lipset
(New York, 1960), chap. 5.

Lyttelton, A. "Fascism and Violence in Post-War Italy." In *Social Protest, Violence
and Terror in Nineteenth- and Twentieth-Century Europe,* ed. W. Mommsen and
G. Hirschfeld (New York, 1982), 257–74.

Mangoni, L. "Per una definizione del Fascismo: I concetti di Bonapartismo e Cesarismo." *Rivista Italiana Contemporanea* 135 (1979): 18–52.

Manzari, F. "Projects for an Italian-led Balkan Bloc of Neutrals, September–December
1939." *Historical Journal* 13:4 (1970): 767–88.

Marston, E. "Fascist Tendencies in Pre-War Arab Politics: A Study of Three Arab
Political Movements." *Middle East Forum* (May 1959): 19–22, 33–35.

Martin, B. "Zur Tauglichkeit eines übergreifenden Faschismus-Begriff." *Vierteljahrshefte für Zeitgeschichte* 1 (1981): 48–73.

Mason, T. W. "The Primacy of Politics." In *European Fascism,* ed. S. J. Woolf (London, 1969), 165–95.

Mason, T. W. "Whatever Happened to Fascism?" *Radical History Review* 49 (1991):
89–98.

Mason, T. W. "The Domestic Dynamics of Nazi Conquests: A Response to Critics."
In *Reevaluating the Third Reich,* ed. T. Childers and J. Caplan (New York, 1993),
161–93.

Masso, M. "The Ideology and Dynamics of Japanese Fascism." In *Thought and Behavior in Modern Japanese Politics,* ed. I. Morris (London, 1963), 25–83.

Matzerath, H., and H. Volkmann. "Modernisierungstheorie und Nationalsozialismus."
In *Theorien in der Praxis des Historikers,* ed. J. Kocka (Göttingen, 1977), 86–116.

Mavrocordatis, H. "Le fascisme en Grèce pendant la guerre (1941–1944)." In *Etudes
sur le fascisme,* by M. Bardèche et al. (Paris, 1974), 98–102.

McCormack, G. "Nineteen-Thirties Japan: Fascism?" *Bulletin of Concerned Asian
Scholars* 14:2 (April–June 1982): 15–34.

McIntyre, J. "Women and the Professions in Germany, 1930–1940." In *German De-*

mocracy and the Triumph of Hitler, ed. A. Nicholls and E. Matthias (London, 1971), 175–213.

McKibbin, R. I. "The Myth of the Unemployed: Who Did Vote for Hitler?" *Australian Journal of Politics and History* 15:2 (Aug. 1969): 25–69.

Meaker, G. "A War of Words: The Ideological Impact of the First World War on Spain, 1914–18." In *Neutral Europe between War and Revolution, 1917–23*, ed. H. Schmitt (Charlottesville, 1988), 1–65.

Meinecke, F. "Nationalsozialismus und Bürgertum." In *Werke*, by F. Meinecke, vol. 2 (Stuttgart, 1969), 441–45.

Melograni, P. "The Cult of the Duce in Mussolini's Italy." *JCH* 11:4 (Oct. 1976): 221–37.

Meneghello-Dinčić, K. "L'état 'Oustacha' de Croatie (1941–1945)." *Revue d'Histoire de la Deuxième Guerre Mondiale* 74 (April 1969): 46–49.

Merkl, P. H. "Comparing Fascist Movements." In Larsen, Hagtvet, and Myklebust, eds., *Who Were the Fascists?* 752–83.

Michaelis, M. "I rapporti tra fascismo e nazismo prima dell' avento di Hitler al potere (1922–1933)." *Rivista Storica Italiana* 85:3 (Sept. 1973): 544–600.

Milward, A. "Fascism and the Economy." In Laqueur, ed., *Fascism* 379–412.

Moeller, R. G. "The Kaiserreich Recast? Continuity and Change in Modern German History." *Journal of Social History* 17 (1984): 442–50.

Mommsen, H. "National Socialism: Continuity and Change." In Laqueur, ed., *Fascism* (1976), 179–210.

Mommsen, H. "Hitlers Stellung im nationalsozialistischen Herrschaftssystem." In Hirschfeld and Kettenacker, eds., *Der "Führerstaat"* (1986), 43–72.

Mommsen, H. "Nationalsozialismus als vorgetäuschte Modernisierung." In *Der historische Ort des Nationalsozialismus*, ed. W. Perle (Frankfurt, 1990), 31–46.

Mommsen, H. "Reflections on the Position of Hitler and Göring in the Third Reich." In *Reevaluating the Third Reich*, ed. T. Childers and J. Caplan (New York, 1993), 86–97.

Mosse, G. L. "The Genesis of Fascism." *JCH* 1:1 (April 1966): 14–26.

Mosse, G. L. "Ernst Nolte's Interpretation of Fascism." *Journal of the History of Ideas* 24:4 (Oct.–Dec. 1966): 621–25.

Mosse, G. L. "The French Right and the Working Classes: Les Jaunes." *JCH* 7:3–4 (July–Oct. 1972): 185–208.

Mosse, G. L. "The Political Culture of Italian Futurism: A General Perspective." *JCH* 25:2–3 (May–June 1990): 229–52.

Mosse, G. L. "Fascist Aesthetics and Society: Some Considerations." 1993. Unpublished.

MSI-DN, Assemblea Congressuale. "Documento base per la commissione 'Valori e Solidarietà.' " Jan. 1994.

Müller, K.-J. "French Fascism and Modernization." *JCH* 11:4 (Oct. 1976): 75–107.

Mussolini, B. "Fascismo." *Enciclopedia Italiana*. 1932.

Nascimbene, M. C., and M. I. Neuman. "El nacionalismo argentino, el fascismo y la immigración en la Argentina (1927–1943): Una aproximación téorica." *Estudios Interdisciplinarios de America Latina y el Caribe* 4:1 (Jan.–June 1993): 115–40.

Nevistic, F., and V. Nikolic. "La Tragedia de Bleiburg." *Studia Croatica* (Buenos Aires) 4:2 (1963): 113–41.

Oberkrome, W. "Reformansätze in der deutschen Geschichtswissenschaft der Zwischenkriegszeit." In Prinz and Zitelmann, eds., *Nationalsozialismus* 216–39.

Organski, A. F. K. "Fascism and Modernization." In *The Nature of Fascism*, ed. S. J. Woolf (London, 1968), 19–41.

Painter, B. W. "Renzo De Felice and the Historiography of Italian Fascism." *American Historical Review* 95:2 (April 1990): 391–405.

Parsons, T. "Some Sociological Aspects of the Fascist Movements" and "Democracy and Social Structure in Pre-Nazi Germany." In *Essays in Sociological Theory,* by T. Parsons (Glencoe, Ill., 1954), 124–41, 104–23.

Pastori, P. "Sergio Panunzio fra cesura rivoluzionaria e riordinamento dei poteri del regime fascista." *Archivio Storico Italiano* 146:2 (1988): 281–309.

Perfetti, F. "Ugo Spirito e la concezione della 'Corporazione Proprietaria' al Convegno di Studi Sindacali e Corporativi di Ferrara del 1932." *Critica Storica* 25:2 (1988): 202–43.

Petersen, J. "Elettorato e base sociali del fascismo italiano negli anni venti." *Studi Storici* 16 (1975): 627–29.

Petersen, J. "Wählerverhalten und sozialer Basis des Faschismus in Italien zwischen 1919 und 1928." In *Faschismus als soziale Bewegung,* ed. W. Schieder (Hamburg, 1976), 119–56.

Petersen, J. "Violence in Italian Fascism, 1919–25." In *Social Protest, Violence and Terror in Nineteenth- and Twentieth-Century Europe,* ed. W. Mommsen and G. Hirschfeld (New York, 1982), 275–99.

Pietrow, B. "Stalins Politik bis 1941." In *Streit um Geschichtsbild,* ed. R. Kühnl (Cologne, 1987), 140–43.

Pike, D. W. "Aide morale et matérielle de l'URSS a l'Allemagne Nazie." *Guerres Mondiales* 160 (1990): 113–22.

Pinto, A. Costa. "Fascist Ideology Revisited: Zeev Sternhell and His Critics." *European History Quarterly* 16 (1986): 465–83.

Pinto, A. Costa. "The Radical Right and the Military Dictatorship in Portugal: The National May 28 League (1928–33)." *Luso-Brazilian Review* 23:1 (Summer 1986): 1–16.

Pollard, J. F. "Conservative Catholics and Italian Fascism: The Clerico-Fascists." In *Fascists and Conservatives,* ed. M. Blinkhorn (London, 1990), 31–49.

Poppetrov, N. "Die bulgarische Wissenschaft über die Probleme des bulgarischen Faschismus." *Bulgarian Historical Review* 14:1 (1986): 78–93.

Poppetrov, N. "Ideino-politicheskite skhvashtaniia na 'Suiuz Natsionalni Legioni' i 'Ratnitsi za Napreduka na Bulgarshtinata' v godinite na Vtorata Svetovna Voina." *Istoricheski Pregled* 47:6 (1991): 53–67.

Poulsen, H., and M. Djursaa. "Social Basis of Nazism in Denmark: The DNSAP." In Larsen, Hagtvet, and Myklebust, eds., *Who Were the Fascists?* 702–14.

Prinz, M. "Die soziale Funktion moderner Elemente in der Gesellschaftspolitik des Nationalsozialismus." In Prinz and Zitelmann, eds., *Nationalsozialismus* 267–96.

Puhle, H. J. "Radikalisierung und Wandel des deutschen Konservatismus vor dem ersten Weltkrieg." In *Deutsche Parteien vor 1918*, ed. G. Ritter (Cologne, 1973), 165–86.

Quinnett, R. L. "The German Army Confronts the NSFO." *JCH* 13:1 (Jan. 1978): 53–64.

Rabinbach, A. G. "The Aesthetics of Production in the Third Reich." *JCH* 11:4 (Oct. 1976): 43–64.

Ranki, G. "The Fascist Vote in Budapest in 1939." In Larsen, Hagtvet, and Myklebust, eds., *Who Were the Fascists?* 401–16.

Rauh, M. "Anti-Modernismus in nationalsozialistischen Staat." *Historisches Jahrbuch* 107 (1987): 94–121.

Rintala, M. "Finland." In Rogger and Weber, eds., *European Right* 408–42.

Ritschl, A. "Die NS-Wirtschaftsideologie—Modernisierungsprogramm oder reaktionäre Utopie?" In Prinz and Zitelmann, eds., *Nationalsozialismus* 48–70.

Rochat, G. "Mussolini e le forze armate." In Acquarone and Vernassa, eds., *Il regime fascista* 112–32.

Rodrigues, L. N. "A Legião Portuguesa no espectro político nacional (1936–1939)." *Penélope* 11 (1993): 21–36.

Rogger, H. "Was There a Russian Fascism? The Union of Russian People." *JMH* 36:4 (Dec. 1964): 398–415.

Rogger, H. "Russia." In Rogger and Weber, eds., *European Right* (1965), 443–500.

Rosen, E. "Italiens Kriegseintritt im jahre 1915 als innen politisches Problem der Giolitti-Ara." *Historische Zeitschrift* 187:2 (April 1959): 289–363.

Rosi, M. "L'interventismo politico-culturale delle reviste tradizionaliste negli anni venti: Atanor (1924) e Ignis (1925)." *SC* 18:3 (June 1987): 457–504.

Sadkovich, J. J. "Il Regime di Alessandro in Iugoslavia, 1929–1934: Un'interpretazione." *SC* 15:1 (Feb. 1984): 5–37.

Sadkovich, J. J. "Terrorism in Croatia, 1929–1934." *East European Quarterly* 22:1 (March 1988): 55–79.

Sadkovich, J. J. "Understanding Defeat: Reappraising Italy's Role in World War II." *JCH* 24:1 (Jan. 1989): 27–61.

Sadkovich, J. J. "The Italo-Greek War in Context: Italian Priorities and Axis Diplomacy." *JCH* 28:3 (July 1993): 439–64.

Santarelli, E. "Uno schema del fascismo italiano." In Santarelli, *Ricerche sul fascismo* 181–91.

Sarti, R. "Fascist Modernization in Italy: Traditional or Revolutionary?" *American Historical Review* 75:4 (April 1970): 1029–45.

Sauer, W. "National Socialism: Totalitarianism or Fascism?" *American Historical Review* 73:2 (Dec. 1967): 404–22.

Schepens, L. "Fascists and Nationalists in Belgium, 1919–1940." In Larsen, Hagtvet, and Myklebust, eds., *Who Were the Fascists?* 501–16.

Schieder, W. "Der Strukturwandel der Faschistischen Partei Italiens in der Phase der Herrschaftsstabilisierung." In *Faschismus als soziale Bewegung*, ed. W. Schieder (Hamburg, 1976), 69–96.

Schmitter, P. C. "Still the Century of Corporatism?" In Pike and Stritch, eds., *New Corporatism* (1974), 85–131.

Schmitter, P. C. "Reflections on Mihail Manoilescu." In *Social Change in Romania, 1860–1940*, ed. K. Jowitt (Berkeley, 1978), 117–39.

Schmuhl, H.-W. "Reformpsychiatrie und Massenmord." In Prinz and Zitelmann, eds., *Nationalsozialismus* 239–68.

Schnapp, J. T. "Epic Demonstrations." In *Fascism, Aesthetics, and Culture*, ed. R. Golsan (Hanover, N.H., 1992), 1–37.

Schreiber, G. "Politik und Kriegführung im zeichen von Nationalsozialismus und Faschismus." *Neue Politische Literatur* 35:2 (1990): 179–94.

Shapiro, P. "Prelude to Dictatorship in Romania: The National Christian Party in Power, December 1937–February 1938." *Canadian American Slavic Studies* 8 (1974): 51–76.

Silverman, D. P. "Fantasy and Reality in Nazi Work-Creation Programs, 1933–1936." *JMH* 65:1 (March 1993): 113–51.

Smith, P. H. "Social Mobilization, Political Participation, and the Rise of Juan Perón." *Political Science Quarterly* 84:1 (March 1969): 30–49.

Smith, P. H. "The Social Base of Peronism." *Hispanic American Historical Review* 52:1 (Feb. 1972): 55–73.

Solliers, R. "Notes sur le fascisme bulgare." In *Etudes sur le fascisme*, by M. Bardèche et al. (Paris, 1974), 166–73.

Sonnenberger, F. "Die vollstreckte Reform—Die Einführung der Gemeinschaftsschule Bayern, 1935–1938." In Prinz and Zitelmann, eds., *Nationalsozialismus* 172–98.

Soucy, R. "French Fascism and the Croix de Feu: A Dissenting Interpretation." *JCH* 26:1 (Jan. 1991): 159–88.

Spektorowski, A. "The Ideological Origins of Right and Left Nationalism in Argentina, 1930–1943." *JCH* 29:1 (Jan. 1994): 155–84.

Spiro, H. "Totalitarianism." *International Encyclopedia of the Social Sciences* (New York, 1968), vol. 16.

Stachura, P. D. " 'Der Fall Strasser.' " In Stachura, *Shaping of the Nazi State* 88–130.

Staderini, A. "Mobilitazione borghese e partecipazione politica a Roma alla vigilia della prima guerra mondiale." *SC* 18:3 (June 1987): 507–48.

Stegmann, D. "Zum Verhältnis von Grossindustrie und Nationalsozialismus, 1930–1933." *Archiv für Sozialgeschichte* 13 (1973): 399–482.

Stegmann, D. "Kapitalismus und Faschismus in Deutschland, 1929–1934." *Beiträge zur Marxschen Theorie* 6 (1976): 19–91.

Stengers, J. "Belgium." In Rogger and Weber, eds., *European Right* 128–67.

Sternhell, Z. "Anatomie d'un mouvement fasciste: Le Faisceau de Georges Valois." *Revue Française de Science Politique* 26:1 (Feb. 1976): 5–40.

Sternhell, Z. "Fascist Ideology." In Laqueur, ed., *Fascism* (1976), 315–76.

Sternhell, Z. "The 'Anti-Materialist' Revision of Marxism as an Aspect of the Rise of Fascist Ideology." *JCH* 22:3 (July 1987): 379–400.

Stone, M. "Staging Fascism: The Exhibition of the Fascist Revolution." *JCH* 28:2 (April 1993): 215–43.

Storry, R. "Japanese Fascism in the Thirties." *Wiener Library Bulletin* 20:4 (Autumn 1966): 1–7.

Sullivan, B. R. "Roosevelt, Mussolini e la guerra d'Etiopia." *SC* 19:1 (Feb. 1988): 85–106.

Sweets, J. F. "Hold That Pendulum! Redefining Fascism, Collaborationism and Resistance in France." *French Historical Studies* 15:4 (1988): 731–58.

Sznajder, M. "Economic Marginalism and Socialism: Italian Revolutionary Syndicalism and the Revision of Marx." *Praxis International* 11:1 (April 1991): 114–27.

Sznajder, M. "I miti del sindacalismo rivoluzionario." *SC* 24:1 (Feb. 1993): 21–57.

Sznajder, M. "A Case of Non-European Fascism: Chilean National Socialists in the 1930s." *JCH* 28:2 (April 1993): 269–96.

Tannenbaum, E. R. "The Goals of Italian Fascism." *American Historical Review* 74:4 (April 1969): 1183–204.

Thalheimer, A. "Ueber den Faschismus." *Gegen den Strom*, nos. 2–4 (Jan. 1930). Reprinted in De Felice, *Il fascismo* 272–95.

Trifiletti Saldi, R. "La Scuola di Francoforte." In Cavalli, ed., *Il fascismo* 85–121.

Trindade, H. "La question du fascisme en Amérique Latine." *Revue Française de Science Politique* 33:2 (April 1983): 281–312.

Tudman, F. "The Independent State of Croatia as an Instrument of the Occupation Powers in Yugoslavia, and the People's Liberation Movement in Croatia from 1941 to 1945." In *Les systèmes d'occupation en Yougoslavie, 1941–1945* (Belgrade, 1963), 135–262.

Turner, H. A., Jr. "Fascism and Modernization." *World Politics* 24:4 (July 1972): 547–64. Reprinted in *Reappraisals of Fascism*, ed. H. A. Turner Jr. (New York, 1975), 117–39.

Turner, H. A., Jr. "Hitlers Einstellung zu Wirtschaft und Gesellschaft vor 1933." *Geschichte und Gesellschaft* 2 (1976): 89–117.

Tusell, J., and I. Saz. "Mussolini y Primo de Rivera: Las relaciones diplomáticas de dos dictaduras mediterráneas." *Boletín de la Real Academia de la Historia* 179:3 (1982): 413–83.

Ucelay da Cal, E. "Vanguardia, fascismo y la interacción entre nacionalismo español y catalán." In *Los nacionalismos en la España de la II República*, ed. J. Beramendi and R. Maíz (Madrid, 1991), 39–95.

Upton, A. K. "Finland." In *European Fascism*, ed. S. J. Woolf (London, 1969), 184–216.

Vajda, M. "Crisis and the Way Out: The Rise of Fascism in Italy and Germany." *Telos* 12 (Summer 1972): 3–26.

Valiani, L. "Il fascismo; controrivoluzione e rivoluzione." In *Fascismo e nazionalsocialismo*, ed. K. D. Bracher and L. Valiani (Bologna, 1986), 125–51.

Visser, R. "Fascist Doctrine and the Cult of the *Romanità*." *JCH* 27:1 (Jan. 1992): 5–22.

Vivarelli, R. "Interpretations of the Origins of Fascism." *JMH* 63:1 (March 1991): 29–43.

Walker, M. "National Socialism and German Physics." *JCH* 24:1 (Jan. 1989): 63–90.

Wandycz, P. S. "Fascism in Poland, 1918–1939." In Sugar, ed., *Native Fascism* 92–97.

Weber, E. "Nationalism, Socialism and National-Socialism in France." *French Historical Studies* 2:3 (Spring 1962): 273–307.

Weber, E. "France." In Rogger and Weber, eds., *European Right* (1965), 71–127.

Weber, E. "Romania." In Rogger and Weber, eds., *European Right* (1965), 501–74.

Weber, E. "The Men of the Archangel." *JCH* 1:1 (April 1966): 101–26.

Weber, E. "Revolution? Counterrevolution? What Revolution?" *JCH* 9:2 (April 1974): 3–47. Reprinted in Laqueur, ed., *Fascism* 435–67.

Wegner, B. "Die garde des 'Führers' und die 'Feuerwehr' der Ostfront: Zur neueren Literatur über die Waffen-SS." *Militärgeschichtliche Mitteilungen* 23 (1978): 210–36.

Weinberg, G. L. "Hitler's Image of the United States." *American Historical Review* 69:4 (July 1964): 1006–21.

Wilson, G. M. "A New Look at the Problem of 'Japanese Fascism.' " In *Reappraisals of Fascism*, ed. H. A. Turner Jr. (New York, 1975), 199–214.

Wippermann, W. "The Post-War German Left and Fascism." *JCH* 11:4 (Oct. 1976): 185–219.

Wippermann, W. "Friedrich Meineckes 'Die deutsche Katastrophe'—Ein Versuch zur deutschen Vergangenheitsbewältigung." In *Friedrich Meinecke heute*, ed. M. Erbe (Berlin, 1982), 101–21.

Wohl, R. "French Fascism, Right and Left: Reflections on the Sternhell Controversy." *JMH* 63:1 (March 1991): 91–98.

Wusten, H. van der, and R. E. Smith. "Dynamics of the Dutch National Socialist Movement (NSB): 1931–1935." In Larsen, Hagtvet, and Myklebust, eds., *Who Were the Fascists?* 524–41.

Yanov, A. "Pamyat." *Nationalities Papers* 19:2 (Fall 1991): 41–69.

Zacek, J. F. "Czechoslovak Fascisms." In Sugar, ed., *Native Fascism* (1971), 56–62.

Zacek, J. F. "The Flaw in Mazaryk's Democracy: Czech Fascism, 1927–1942." Unpublished.

Zapponi, N. "La politica come espedienti e come utopia: Marinetti e il Partito Politico Futurista." In *F. T. Marinetti Futurista* (Naples, 1977), 220–39.

Zibordi, G. "Critica socialista del fascismo." In *Il fascismo e i partiti politici: Studi di scrittori di tutti partiti* (Bologna, 1922), 1–61.

Zorach, J. "The Enigma of the Gajda Affair in Czechoslovak Politics in 1926." *Slavic Review* 35:1 (March 1976): 683–98.

DISSERTATIONS AND THESES

Allardyce, G. "The Political Transition of Jacques Doriot." Ph.D. diss., State University of Iowa, 1966.

Argenteri, L. "Victor Emmanuel III: The Fusion of Monarchy with Fascism. Dyarchy or Deception?" Ph.D. diss., University of California, Los Angeles, 1989.

Brock, J. J., Jr. "The Theory and Practice of the Union of the Russian People, 1905–07." Ph.D. diss., University of Michigan, 1972.

Broxson, E. R. "Plinio Salgado and Brazilian Integralism." Ph.D. diss., Catholic University, 1973.

Burton, R. B. "The Vlassov Movement of World War II: An Appraisal." Ph.D. diss., American University, 1963.

Chertok, R. "Belgian Fascism." Ph.D. diss., Washington University, 1975.

De Caprariis, L. "Fascism and Italian Diplomacy, 1925–1928." Ph.D. diss., University of Wisconsin–Madison, 1995.

Etue, G. E., Jr. "The German Fatherland Party." Ph.D. diss., University of California, Berkeley, 1959.

Gerber, L. K. "Anti-Democratic Movements in the United States since World War I." Ph.D. diss., University of Pennsylvania, 1964.

Haag, J. J. "Othmar Spann and the Politics of Totality." Ph.D. diss., Rice University, 1969.

Kessler, J. A. "Turanism and Pan-Turanism in Hungary, 1890–1945." Ph.D. diss., University of California, Berkeley, 1967.

Melka, R. W. "The Axis and the Arab Middle East, 1930–1945." Ph.D. diss., University of Minnesota, 1966.

Meuser, N. "Nation, Staat und Politik bei José Antonio Primo de Rivera." Ph.D. diss., University of Mainz, 1993.

Myers, W. L. "Revolution and Retribution: The Theory and Practice of Revolutionary Justice in the Italian Fascist Republic of Salò." Ph.D. diss., University of Colorado, 1989.

Nelson, E. J. "To Ethiopia and Beyond: The Primacy of Struggle in Mussolini's Public Discourse." Ph.D. diss., University of Iowa, 1988.

Portzline, D. B. "William Dudley Pelley and the Silver Legion of America." Ed.D. diss., Ball State University, 1965.

Potashnik, M. "Nacismo: National Socialism in Chile, 1932–1938." Ph.D. diss., University of California, Los Angeles, 1974.

Rawson, D. C. "The Union of the Russian People, 1905–07." Ph.D. diss., University of Washington, 1971.

Ribuffo, L. P. "Protestants on the Right." Ph.D. diss., Yale University, 1976.

Uren, S. "Fascism and National Socialism in South Africa." M.A. thesis, University of Wisconsin–Madison, 1975.

Werly, J. M. "The Millenarian Right." Ph.D. diss., Syracuse University, 1972.

Index

579